Developing the
Secondary School Curriculum

Revised Edition

Rinehart Books in Secondary Education

Developing the Secondary School Curriculum

Revised Edition

J. Paul Leonard

President, American University of Beirut
Formerly President, San Francisco State College

Holt, Rinehart and Winston · New York

November, 1960
25211-01A3

Library of Congress Catalog Card Number: 52-14016

To Two Great Teachers

Lewis E. Meador
Thomas H. Briggs

Preface

SECONDARY EDUCATION, once considered a luxury, has become a necessity for all youth. States and industries recognize this by basing many of their laws and regulations on the statement that the youth "must have graduated from high school or attained the age of eighteen years." Selective service recognizes the need for completion of high school; and many states require that a youth complete the secondary school if he is intellectually able to do so.

This emphasis upon the necessity for secondary education is the result of three conditions in the United States. First, society recognizes that, if democracy is to be continued, all youth must become competent to discharge their civic responsibilities, and this cannot be safely accomplished short of a secondary education. Second, our culture is an industrial one requiring skills in machine operation, social organization, professional service, personnel management, financial management, creative designing, and the like. Secondary education provides the basis for later study and experience for success in these enterprises. And, third, to provide a sound economy, men with families must be kept employed. Since the importance of school during the teen-age years exceeds the importance of income, youth should be kept out of the labor market—in large numbers or for permanent employment—until after high school graduation.

These conditions thrust upon the secondary school the responsibility for preparing a program of education in harmony with the social needs of our country. But this program must also be well adapted to *all* youth in school. We cannot force a youth to stay in school to waste his time, nor can we justify using the high school merely as a device to keep youth from working. Yet it has been estimated from different sources that a large percentage of our youth, some say as high as 40 per cent, are consciously wasting their time pursuing the conventional high school curriculum. No one knows the exact percentage of youth failing to profit from the courses they are taking, but figures are available to show how pupils are failing to learn what they study and how deficient they are in basic social competencies. The figures are alarming to those who are working with youth.

For many years there has been very little concern among secondary school teachers about this situation. Pupils who failed to pass the standard courses dropped out or, if they persisted long enough, were graduated, ignorant as they might be. In recent years, however, there has been a growing concern about school failures, individual eliminations, and personal maladjustment; and criticisms have been leveled at the standard curriculum. While much work has been done on the secondary school curriculum by national and local committees and by local teachers, an examination of the field reveals two major deficiencies. (1) There has been very little creative thinking about fundamental change in the curriculum of the secondary school. The dead hand of tradition still guides the selection of the courses. By and large, the heart of the secondary curriculum (content and methods) is essentially the same today as it was forty years ago. (2) What changes have been made in the elementary school, due to studies of growth and development and to a resulting philosophy of learning and experience, have barely influenced the secondary teacher, her principal, or her courses.

There are, therefore, vast unexplored fields of knowledge regarding the program of education which could, with proper methods, produce the kinds of citizens democracy needs.

This book is written to review the development of the secondary curriculum for teachers and administrators in service and for prospective teachers and other workers with youth who are in training in our teacher-education institutions. It attempts to describe the social philosophy in which the modern secondary school operates and the current philosophy of education, the changes that have taken place in secondary education, and recent proposals for improvement. Reports of the important national committees and commissions are discussed; and an abundance of illustrations of programs and practices is provided from local and state course outlines and from local classroom situations. The book also suggests practical ways in which changes may be made from various approaches—all out, a bit at a time, and even gradual modifications. However, to the student in the field it is obvious that there should be an acceleration of change if the profession of education is to serve society and youth adequately in the years ahead.

I am indebted to many people for the ideas explored in these pages, many whose names I could not recall if I tried, for as years go by the ideas we exchange lose their authorship. During eight years at the College of William and Mary in Virginia and another eight years at Stanford University, I learned much from my colleagues and students. Through work on curriculum reorganization with secondary teachers in many states I have kept close to the problems of the secondary curriculum. As the father of two children whose progress I watched through high school, and as an administrator in a college which draws widely from high schools in the San Francisco Bay Area, I have observed the problems and experiences and attitudes and state of accomplishment of youth. From all these experiences I am convinced that the high school needs fundamental improvement.

I am particularly indebted to those whose writings I have quoted freely in this book. Their opinions stand as their own testament to the problems explored. I want also to give special recognition to Dr. Frederic T. Shipp, Professor of Education, San Francisco State College, who searched diligently the literature that has appeared in the field since the first edition was prepared and made available to a busy administrator the research, philosophy, and curriculum practices which constitute the basis of the revision of this book.

J. PAUL LEONARD

San Francisco, California
March, 1953

Contents

Developing the
Secondary School Curriculum

Revised Edition

Chapter One

Education and Political Revolution

I N THE last two and one-half centuries the people in the United States have created a system of public education unlike any other in the world. The development of this system is difficult to describe and even more difficult to make meaningful and comprehensible to those outside the United States. Yet the public school has shared in building the nation into one of the two great world powers and the one great political unit with a deep penetration of democratic theory and practice.

Every shade of opinion and every change in material condition have played upon the public school, for nowhere else in the world has the school been so sensitive to public opinion. Early forces, rooted in Britain and France, and even earlier ones, rooted in Greece and Rome and Palestine, have had their effect. Later, other concepts made their influence felt—Josiah Royce's absolute idealism, individualism, and collectivism; Andrew Carnegie's doctrine of stewardship; Theodore Roosevelt's ideal of the strenuous life; Charles Darwin's and Herbert Spencer's substitution of the principles of science for theological authoritarianism; Auguste Comte's doctrine of determinism; the pessimism of Henry Adams; "old-time religion" versus "the law of love"; William Graham Sumner's idea of the social-service state; the pragmatism of William James, evolving later into the instrumentalism and experimentalism of John Dewey; and finally the economic theories of John Maynard Keynes succeeded by the New Deal theories of Franklin D. Roosevelt. All of these have made their impact upon our society and in turn upon our public schools. The basic question in education is not whether the school deals with the past, but rather the degree to which the environment influences the instructional program and the functions of education. Truly, the history of American education cannot be written without reference to the social forces and the political, religious, and economic theories which have produced the basic system of values dominant at any one time in the United States.[1]

The presence of certain philosophies in our culture has been a vital factor in determining the nature of the educational program. This in turn has had a marked effect upon producing the kind of person generally described as an American, and he in turn, through exercising his rights as a democratic citizen, has had an important influence upon the school. Lee Coleman inquired recently of many citizens and scholars what characteristics an American possessed.[2] General agreement was reached on many traits, chief among them being a belief in individualism with a worship of schooling and public education; a distrust of strong government; a love of size and bigness; an aptitude for organization; a belief in equal opportunity; great optimism. An American is a strong "localist"; a missionary in spirit; a humanitarian with strong pioneer leanings and with national self-confidence; a great believer in freedom, liberty, and independence; a very mobile and restless person; and a political isolationist. He is enthusiastic about making money, practical and ready to glorify the common man, and suspicious of the expert.

Obviously, the school, operating in this environment and being a tool of the state in a society of changing cultural values, will reflect both traditional and current ideals. Those who determine the curriculum will need two pairs of

---

1. A few scholars have interpreted the character of the development of the United States or of an "American" through studies of philosophy, literature, the arts, or economics. The most penetrating analysis by a foreigner is *Democracy in America* by Alexis de Tocqueville. The three best general ones to date are Vernon L. Parrington, *Main Currents of American Thought,* 3 vols.; Ralph H. Gabriel, *The Course of American Democratic Thought: An Intellectual History since 1815;* and Henry Steele Commager, *The American Mind.* More encyclopedic and historical but vital is Merle Curti, *The Growth of American Thought,* and directly economic in character is *The Economic Mind in American Civilization,* 1606–1865, by Joseph Dorfman. All of these will make vital contributions to the development of an understanding of the American mind and character. For a significant treatise of the relation between education and social policies, see Newton Edwards and Herman G. Richey, *The School in the American Social Order.*
2. Lee Coleman, "What is American," *Social Forces,* May, 1941.

eyes, one to interpret the past and one to predict the extent to which current values will continue into the future. The educator will need, then, to understand social change, both evolutionary and revolutionary, and be sensitive to the factors which in permanence and power will most affect the school program. The value of the school and the success of an educator in our democratic society will depend upon the extent to which they are sensitive to but firmly rooted in the dominant forces of our society.

There is not time for an extended picture of the forces and pressures controlling change. But typical periods of practice in the secondary curriculum can be examined, and from them a characterization of the dominant thought of each period can be developed. For this purpose typical schools of the following periods will be discussed:

1. The Latin grammar school curriculum of 1635
2. The academy of Franklin, 1751, and the Massachusetts Academy
3. The typical public high school from 1821 to 1890
4. The typical high school of 1930

The Massachusetts Bay Colony

In 1629 a small group of ships landed on the shores of Massachusetts Bay, and their passengers established a colony. They were outcasts of a kind, representatives of a hundred years of confusion in English thought, a strange mixture of English idealism, papal absolutism, theological disputism, and social transition. English feudal life was being destroyed, individualism was emerging from the conflict, and social classes were disintegrating. There was need for a new force, an ideology to bind together this dissociate group of thoughts and thinkers. America, without traditions and precedents and with an unlimited supply of natural opportunities, offered the chance to work out a new society.

But men cannot dispense with ideas by merely changing their place of residence. They bring with them their thoughts and their conflicts. So did the settlers of Massachusetts. They were not all of one mind. There were those who believed in the absolutist principle of church and state. Some believed in the doctrine of "elective stewardship," and they early sought to tie up the doctrine of natural rights to property, thus laying the foundation for a class of God's stewards who were to acquire the goods of life and hold them in trust. They were the ones who had the "talents"—five, ten, and twenty—and who were to put them to work. Their success was to be crowned with God's benediction and with the right to rule over men. There were also the underdogs, those who believed essentially and sincerely in the right of individual self-government.

Theory of the Church-State

Out of these conflicts emerged certain thoughts which gained controlling force and for a generation determined the basic pattern of personal and institutional life and thought in Massachusetts. To be sure, the ideas were constantly challenged and undermined by such minority groups as the Plymouth Separatists. Struggle and conflict, persecution and dictum, intolerance and stupidity were intermingled, but out of the conflict a prevailing pattern of thought emerged.

This dominant pattern was one of a church-state, with "authority reserved to the aristocracy of Christian talent."[3] The leaders in this church-state were the English middle class who had brought with them their love of class, rank, precedent, patronage, and self-elevation. They endeavored to seize control of the economic life, the religious life, and the state, and through such power to dominate the customs and institutions of the colony. They cast out those who disagreed with them, thus eliminating a large measure of liberalism from the colony. Once in power, they settled down to protect their position—and to intellectual decay.

With the doctrine of divine election they built up their own class. According to this doctrine, man was a worm, a sinner; only the elect would be saved; divine power and will were to be understood and followed; and the elect were the rulers of the world. Thus, they laid the basis for the kind of life reflected in the writings and education of the Massachusetts Bay Colony. Life was cold, harsh; warmth was gone. Living was strictly an either-or proposition— one was either good or bad, a sinner or a saint, an underdog or one of the elect, an enemy or a benefactor of progress.

The state was the servant of the church, and, since power in both institutions was vested in the same people, certain positions came to be written into law. In 1631 franchise was given only to members of the church; in 1635 attendance at church was made compulsory; in 1636 the establishment of a church without the consent of the magistrates became an offense; in 1638 provision was made for state support of the ministry; in 1642 the councilmen were required to see that parents and masters were carrying out their duty in educating children to read and write, thus giving legal recognition to the unity of learning and religion in America. In 1647 laws with penalties for violation were enacted which required every town of fifty householders to establish a school to teach reading and writing and every town of a hundred householders to set up a grammar school to fit youth for the university, thus establishing a basis for the adequate training of community leaders.

---

3. Vernon L. Parrington, *Main Currents of American Thought*, Vol. 1: *The Colonial Mind, 1620–1800* (New York: Harcourt, Brace, and Company, 1927), p. 18. I wish to acknowledge my debt to this author for many of the concepts developed here.

These last two laws are significant for two reasons: (1) they were the first laws in America relating to education; and (2) they gave legal sanction to the direct union of religion and education for the advancement of the state. But neither of them contained the idea of democracy or the development of the individual. Their primary aims were to provide for rudimentary education among the masses and to develop proper leadership among the elect for the church-state development of the colony.

George H. Martin, a scholarly historian of the Massachusetts school system, sums up the fundamental principles of these laws as follows:

1. The universal education of youth is essential to the well-being of the state.
2. The obligation to furnish this education rests primarily upon the parent.
3. The state has a right to enforce this obligation.
4. Public money raised by general tax may be used to provide such education as the state requires. The tax may be general, though the school attendance is not.
5. Education higher than the rudiments may be supplied by the state. Opportunity must be provided at public expense for youth who wish to be fitted for the university.[4]

This emphasis upon the need for learning the rudiments was a direct offshoot of the Protestant Reformation, based upon a belief that men must be made to scoff at ignorance, seek learning to use in criticizing existing conditions, and in turn be receptive to new truth. Reform tends to follow this process, and reformers generally turn to education to perpetuate their doctrines.

The Boston Public Latin School

While this concept was dominant in the Massachusetts Bay Colony the first Latin grammar school was founded in Boston in 1635. Its curriculum was in harmony with the prevailing thought of the elect. There is no record of the curriculum of the Boston Public Latin School from 1635 until 1708. Inferences that can be drawn indicate that in all probability the classics, reading, writing, "cypering," and spelling were all taught at this school, which was a seven-year school until 1789, when it was changed to a four-year course. The first recorded curriculum was in 1708. At that time Cotton Mather says:

"All the eight parts of speech he [Cheever] taught to them" and "We learnt Prosodia." He also mentions the following: Ovid's *De Tristibus* and *Metamorphoses;* Tully's (Cicero's) *De Officiis* and *Orations;* Virgil; Homer; The testament; "Lily" (Lily's Latin Grammar); *Sententiae Pueriles;* Cato; Corderius's *Colloquies;* and the "Making of Themes." Mather testi-

4. George H. Martin, *The Evolution of the Massachusetts Public School System* (New York: Appleton-Century-Crofts, Inc., 1897), pp. 14–18. By permission of the publishers.

fies, in his writings, that when he was young he studied Aesop and Terence. In the elegy, furthermore, Mather calls Cheever "A Christian Terence," which may be taken as indirect evidence that Terence was also read at the Latin school as early as the seventeenth century. The Reverend John Barnard, who entered the Latin school in 1689, under Ezekiel Cheever, has recorded that he studied "the accidence," translated "Aesop's Fables into Latin verse," and was perfectly acquainted with prosody.[5]

The subjects of study recorded in 1712, 1734, and 1776 do not differ extensively from this account. When the organization of the school was changed in 1789, the following four-year curriculum was established:

First class: Cheever's Accidence
                Corderius's Colloquies—Latin and English
                Nomenclator
                Aesop's Fables—Latin and English
                Ward's Latin Grammar, or Eutropius
Second class: Clarke's Introduction—Latin and English
                Ward's Latin Grammar
                Eutropius, continued
                Selectae e Veteri Testamento Historiae, or
                Castalio's Dialogues
                The making of Latin, from Garretson's Exercises
Third class: Caesar's Commentaries
                Tully's Epistles, or Offices
                Ovid's Metamorphoses
                Virgil
                Greek Grammar
                The making of Latin from King's History of the Heathen Gods
Fourth class: Virgil, continued—Tully's Orations
                Greek Testament—Horace
                Homer—Gradus ad Parnassum
                The making of Latin continued[6]

A study of the characteristics of this curriculum warrants the following observations:

1. *The major portion of time was devoted to languages.* The reason for this is amply understood when one remembers that Luther, in speaking to the councilmen of all the towns in Germany in 1524, said:

This is the best and the richest increase, prosperity and strength of a city—that it shall contain a great number of polished, learned, intelligent, honorable, and well-bred citizens; who, when they have become all this, may

---

5. Pauline Holmes, *A Tercentenary History of the Boston Public Latin School, 1635–1935* (Cambridge, Mass.: Harvard University Press, 1935), pp. 256, 258. By permission of the publishers.
6. *Ibid.*, p. 267.

then get wealth and put it to good use. Since, then, a city must have citizens, . . . we are not to wait until they are grown up. . . . We must use the appointed means, and with cost and care rear up and mold our citizens.[7]

Languages were considered essential in producing the refinement and polish necessary for intelligent well-bred citizens. They were the sources of profit and of religious understanding. These schools even took the name of the grammar of the major language taught—Latin grammar schools.

2. *The curriculum was set up so that the school must be selective in character.* It stands to reason that only the most capable could achieve any sizable measure of success with the courses offered and it is clear that the founders of the Massachusetts Bay Colony never meant to make secondary education universal.

3. *The school was designed to meet the needs of a small number of youth.* These needs were clearly twofold: (1) to attend the university, and (2) to prepare to be leaders of church and state. These needs were determined entirely by the elders of the colony, who tolerated no compromise with authority.

4. *While the offerings were not directly religious in character, they were spiritual in purpose.* It has already been pointed out that the language courses and the doctrines of the church were part of the same pattern.

5. *The curriculum was traditional, being based upon European precedent.* In this sense the offerings were not indigenous to the new soil but directly imitative of European education. One can hardly tell the difference between the curriculum of the Boston Public Latin School and the Free Grammar School of Boston, England.

6. *The curriculum was disciplinary in character.* Europeans had been nursed in the doctrine of discipline, and discipline to the Puritans became a religion. The Puritans were hysterically religious and disciplinary. Bruce Barton Perry of Harvard describes their attitude by the term "moral athleticism."

7. *The schools were harsh and monotonous.* Language was taught all day with little variety, and the day usually ran from seven until five, with ample study outside the classroom.

8. *There was no attempt to provide for individuality or for differences among the pupils.* The teaching was all aimed at one purpose—the development of well-bred citizens by pursuance of the same subjects. In fact there was little need for education beyond meeting a man's need for scriptual understanding and for cultural and economic power. Since the pupils were all so nearly alike, one program would suffice for all. As Lewisohn pointedly exaggerates: "By consigning nine-tenths of human life to the devil, they withdrew it from cultivation and control."[8]

---

7. *Barnard's Journal of Education*, 4 (1857–1858), 429.
8. Ludwig Lewisohn, *Story of American Literature* (New York: Random House, Inc., 1939), p. 1.

Forerunners of Change

New Ideas

It is very difficult to keep an idea dominant over a long period of time. The human race has been fortunately blessed throughout the ages with those who see things differently. So in the Massachusetts Colony all men were not of one mind. A firebrand, intelligent and well educated in England, entered the colony in 1631 and plagued the elders until they exiled him. Roger Williams, who left England to get away from the union of church and state, found in America not an alliance between the two but an amalgamation. He went about the colony accusing the elders of dishonesty in their dealings, citing injustices perpetrated by the churchmen who were also the magistrates, and crying out against the union of church and state. Man's soul is the job of the church, he maintained, and his civil duties the job of the court. This was plain heresy in the Massachusetts Colony, where theocracy was the established rule.

The Separatists in the Plymouth Colony were a discordant force. Their covenant of civil rights drawn up on board ship, their democratic church order, and their background of radicalism made the strict Puritans uncomfortable. Slowly and by degrees their doctrines began to make inroads into the Bay Colony, which accepted the Plymouth covenant's principle of church organization even though it rejected the plantation covenant. Oppression and dearth of creative ideas worked together to win converts to the dissenting faith. It was a struggle between the "eye for an eye" doctrine of the Old Testament and the "love thy neighbor" doctrine of the New Testament. It was a struggle of Calvinism versus Lutherism, and the latter was more suited to creative and magnanimous souls. Finally, Calvinism was discovered to be out of harmony with the doctrines of revolution and to serve ill a group who could write the Declaration of Independence.

New Blood

New blood came into the New World—French Huguenots, German peasants, English bond servants, Scotch-Irish individualists. Many of these had nothing to lose by leaving Europe and everything to gain by relocating themselves. This group came largely for economic reasons. Many of them formed the vanguards of the frontier, and any frontier tends to sweep away precedent and intolerance.

New Economic Groups

Another factor of importance which weakened the power of the Massachusetts Bay theocrats was the granting of land in fee simple to freemen. This policy led to the decentralization of the land; it also contributed to the development of the individual whose stake in the land gave him power and later prevented him from being "controlled." As a result, the democratization of political institutions in America was possible, for if property ownership rather than church membership becomes the qualification for suffrage, the basis of political power has been changed.

A third factor of note was the rising importance of commercialism. Trade and agricultural production had become more and more profitable in the New World from Massachusetts to Virginia. European countries offered a good market, and recent immigrants had come chiefly for economic profit. There arose rapidly a group of capable and successful merchants—colonial gentry— who were very frequently in conflict in their ideology with both the aristocratic plantation owners in the South and the frontiersmen on the Allegheny ridge.

The Revolution

Conflicting opinions demanded expression and eventually a showdown. Expression broke out from North to South. There were debates on the powers of Parliament, the rights of dependencies, the rights of individuals and the source of such rights, the source, place, and function of government, and the character of human nature. Calm reason was mixed with emotional outbursts. Men talked and argued and shouted by tongue and pen. Change was on its way. Revolution was in the air. As George Soule has pointed out, the Revolution was the process of changing the control of the people and was not the psychological explosion of 1776.[9] This was also in harmony with the opinion expressed by John Adams in his letter to a Mr. Niles on January 14, 1818, in which he said: ". . . the revolution was effected before the war commenced. The revolution was in the minds and hearts of the people."[10]

Benjamin Franklin

Education in 1750

By 1750 there were established in America three distinct types of educational theory and practice. Cubberley sums these up as follows:

  1. The strong Calvinistic conception of a religious State, supporting a
     system of common vernacular schools, higher Latin schools, and a col-

9. George Soule, *The Coming American Revolution* (New York: The Macmillan Company, 1934).
10. Quoted in Parrington, *The Colonial Mind,* p. 179.

lege, for both religious and civic ends. This type dominated New England and was best represented by Massachusetts.

2. The parochial-school conception of the Dutch, Moravians, Mennonites, German Lutherans, German Reformed Church, Quakers, Presbyterians, Baptists, and Catholics. This type was best represented by Protestant Pennsylvania and Catholic Maryland.

3. The third type, into which the second type tended to fuse, conceived of public education, aside from collegiate education, as intended chiefly for orphans and the children of the poor, and as a charity which the state was under little or no obligation to assist in supporting. This type was best represented by Anglican Virginia, which typified well the *laissez-faire* policy which dominated England from the time of the Protestant Reformation until the latter half of the nineteenth century.[11]

Franklin's Philosophy

In the midst of Revolutionary ferment there appeared an interesting spokesman for the new order, a wise, learned, witty, charming commoner—Benjamin Franklin. His keen interest in economics early led him him into politics, and his strong belief in the value of an abundance of free land got him into numerous difficulties. A social philosopher, he wanted to make the world a better place in which to live, and he cried out against the depressions created by industrialism.

Franklin had been doing a good deal of thinking about the problem of education and in 1751 was successful in establishing an academy in Philadelphia. Franklin's writings reflected his wide interests and also influenced educational developments. For example, his scientific interest led him to lay the beginnings of an American Philosophical Society directly connected with the Royal Society in London.[12] A second type of writing was a series of admonitions to adults on frugality and sincerity in their work.[13] In a third type, which dealt with the education of the young in school, were expressed the ideas which influenced the establishment of the Philadelphia academy.

Franklin was a practical man. He wanted people to learn everything useful, to be moral, to be honest, to be successful occupationally, to be competent in marital relations, to care for their bodies, and to learn the major trades of the time. In other words, knowledge was for use, and useful knowledge came from

---

11. Ellwood P. Cubberley, *History of Education* (Boston: Houghton Mifflin Company, 1920), pp. 373–374. By permission of the publishers.

12. See his "Proposal for Promoting Useful Knowledge among the British Plantations in America," Thomas Woody (ed.), *Educational Views of Benjamin Franklin* (New York: McGraw-Hill, 1931), pp. 58–62; or in John Bigelow, *Complete Works of Benjamin Franklin*, 10 vols. (New York: 1887), II, 67–71.

13. See Franklin's "Advice to a Young Tradesman." "The Way to Wealth." (In Bigelow, cited above.)

understanding one's environment and the advances of science then being made. To Franklin, the existing schools, particularly the colleges, were simply storehouses of impractical learning. His criticism of Harvard College, which he described as a "Temple of Learning" where people "learn little more than how to carry themselves handsomely and enter a room genteelly, and from whence they return, after abundance of trouble and charge, as great blockheads as ever, only more proud and self conceited,"[14] is an excellent illustration of his opinion of the classical learning offered in the schools of his time.

Franklin's Plan for a School

In drawing up his plan for the academy, Franklin gave chief emphasis to the teaching of the English language. In this category he included spelling and vocabulary building, as well as rhetoric and grammar, for he stressed the importance of speaking the English language, and thought that rhetoric and grammar offered excellent training for speaking and reading English. Merchants could profit by reading history, by learning to write business letters, and they could become better civil servants if they were thoroughly acquainted with what had been written in English. Foreign languages, he felt, had less value for the practical man of business.[15]

In 1749 he drew up his "Proposals Relating to the Education of Youth in Pennsylvania" in which he suggested the following curriculum:

I. Basic courses for all students for "utility" and citizenship
   A. Penmanship
   B. Drawing
   C. Arithmetic and some of the elementary principles of geometry and astronomy
   D. English grammar, rhetoric and logic
   E. English classics such as those by Tillotson, Addison, Pope, Algernon Sidney
   F. Reading (English language)
   G. Writing stories and letters
   H. Making speeches and orations
   I. History, such as the translations of the Roman and Greek historians, chronology, by the help of Helvetius, morality; geography by reading with maps; history of trade, art, commerce, manufacturing and the use of machines; natural and mechanic philosophy

II. For "ornament" and professional preparation
   A. For the divinity, Latin and Greek
   B. For the doctor, Latin, Greek, French

---

14. See Franklin's "A Letter on the Temple of Learning." (In Bigelow, cited above.)
15. See Franklin's "Idea of the English School," written in 1750. (In Bigelow, cited above.)

    C. For the lawyer, Latin and French
    D. For the merchant, German, Spanish, French

III. For utility, variety, and joy of living
    A. Gardening, planting, grafting, agriculture
    B. Excursions to well-run plantations

This curriculum proposal was a far cry from the subjects studied in the Boston Latin School. It reflected the following beliefs:

1. That education is essential for youth in many vocations
2. That education should be useful and purposeful—for citizenship, for vocations, and for the joy of living
3. That the curriculum should be differentiated for the professions but that basic social education should be common for everybody in school
4. That English should be the basic medium of study and communication
5. That certain subjects, such as logic and mathematics, had disciplinary as well as utilitarian values
6. That the school should be interesting in and of itself, where the development of the individual and the improvement of the citizenry are objectives

This curriculum was truly a radical proposal, too different from the thought of the time to win acceptance. Franklin's difficulty in getting the idea adopted and the struggle among the trustees of the Academy for the Education of Youth, some of whom believed in the basic proposal while others were "Latinists" at heart, indicate clearly that this academy was not typical of the academy movement in America. This was a "progressive school proposal" by a man who differed with his times. Other forces must be analyzed before the academy movement can be understood.

Ideas in Conflict

The last quarter of the eighteenth century was a period of argument. The intellectual crucible contained a curious mixture of ideas: "The true source of political power is economic power." "The chief end of government is the preservation of property." "Property rights are inviolable." "Trade must be uncontrolled." "The powers of the state must be limited for commercial freedom." "Production is for profit." "The chief goal of life is material prosperity." "God loves labor, and the acquisition of wealth is man's sacred right." "Only the landholder has a stake in society and has a right to cast a vote." Opposed to these were: "Man's inherent right to share in government depends upon his existence as an individual, not upon his ability to accumulate property." "Society can be improved by appeal to reason." "Centralization is destructive of human values." "Liberty is for all." Each man has the "right of life, liberty, and the pursuit of happiness." The arguments had a common ground in the hatred of centralization and in the struggle to obtain liberty. Liberty to do as one pleased, to exploit anything for one's own advantage, served alike the frontiersman and the merchant. Such a philosophy of *laissez faire* left America free to be exploited by the "new Americans." It was a curious struggle resulting in a paradox—the Constitution and the Declaration of Independence, Rhode Island "anarchy," Shays' rebellion, French humanitarianism, English liberalism, *laissez faire;* the large landholders, the powerful money group, the older gentry, professional groups, military men, frontiersmen, and the "disappointeds"; property rights, human rights; jealousy, distrust, radicalism, conservatism, vehemence—a strange world of conflict. As Emerson put it, "Things are in the saddle and rule mankind."

During this period one might reasonably expect education to be undergoing tremendous changes, changes representative of the confusion in thought or the desire for new practice. But more was going on in men's minds than in their institutions. "Polite culture" was still in control of social customs and the schools. Men who had not been to school were succeeding in business and politics. People were too poor to tax themselves for general education; after all, if success is not dependent upon education beyond the rudiments, then secondary education and collegiate education are a luxury. No dominant educational leaders arose. Political leaders, however, began to sense the "twilight zone" of Old World culture and the need for education to guide the nation safely through its emerging adventure into republicanism. The constitution had given to all the right to vote for national officials, and the older states began to eliminate their property qualifications for voting. A new need for education arose. In 1796 Washington, in his Farewell Address, called attention to the need for public education if the state was to be safe. Thomas Jefferson, John Jay, James Madison, John Adams, and other statesmen echoed his words.

The Academy

Public-spirited men of wealth, patriotic in their faith in the service of education to the state, made grants of their wealth and their homesteads for the purpose of starting "higher schools." Had the spread of free town grammar schools not been so long delayed, the academies might not have started or at least might not have attained much power and position. The Phillips families were representatives of this group of public-minded citizens who wished to aid education. Two branches of the family started rival schools—the Phillips Academy at Exeter (1783) and the Phillips Academy at Andover (1778). These schools were more typical of the academy than was the one established earlier by Franklin.

Phillips Exeter Academy

The curriculum of Phillips Exeter Academy from 1788 to 1838 shows the tremendous influence of the Boston Latin School, its classical department being almost identical with that of the Boston school. During this period the subjects of study in the preparatory department were as follows:

First Year: Adam's Latin Grammar
              Liber Primus or similar work
              Viri Romani or Caesar's Commentaries
              Latin Prosody
              Exercises in reading and making Latin
              Virgil
              Arithmetic
              Ancient and modern geography
Second Year: Virgil
              Arithmetic
              Exercises in reading and making Latin
              Volpy's Greek Grammar Delectus
              Roman History
              Cicero's select orations
              Greek Testament
              Dalzel's Collectania Graeca-Minora
              English Grammar
              Declamation
Third Year: The same Latin and Greek authors in revision
              English Grammar
              Declamation
              Sallust
              Algebra
              Exercises in Latin and English translations
              Composition
Fourth Year: Horatius Flaccus
              Titus Livius
              Excerpha Latina
              Parts of Terence's Comedies
              Collectania Graeca-Majora
              Homer's Iliad, or such Latin and Greek authors as may best
                comport with the student's future destination
              Algebra
              Geometry
              Adam's Roman Antiquities
              Elements of Ancient History[16]

---

16. Quoted in Thomas H. Briggs, J. Paul Leonard, Joseph Justman, *Secondary Education* (rev. ed.; New York: The Macmillan Company, 1950), pp. 21–22, after F. H. Cunningham, *Familiar Sketches of Phillips Exeter Academy and Surroundings*. By permission of the publishers.

Harassing pupils with materials and studies unsuited to their interests and stage of development, such a curriculum had no consideration for childhood. It was disciplinary in character and taught the "polite culture" of the Old World.

Spread of the Academy

The academies grew rapidly, having their greatest period of development from 1825 to 1840, and enjoying their greatest prosperity in New York State. There their curriculum was enlarged greatly, and by 1837 the following list of courses offered was reported to the Board of Regents of New York State:

Arithmetic, algebra, conic sections, analytic geometry, plane geometry, leveling, logarithms, mensuration, perspective, statistics, trigonometry

Astronomy, botany, chemistry, geology, mineralogy, physiology, technology

Architecture, drawing, civil engineering, mapping, navigation, nautical astronomy, surveying, topography

Bookkeeping, orthography, penmanship, stenography

Biblical antiquities, evidences of Christianity, natural theology, philosophy (natural and moral), intellectual philosophy

Biography, Constitution of the United States, Constitution of New York, geography, physical geography, Grecian antiquities, general history, history of the United States, Latin law (constitutional, select revised statutes, criminal, mercantile, Blackstone's *Commentaries*)

Natural history, political economy, Roman antiquities

Composition, declamation, elements of criticism, English grammar, extemporaneous speaking, logic, mythology, English pronunciation, reading, rhetoric

French, Greek, German, Italian, Hebrew, Spanish

Embroidery, music (vocal and instrumental), painting

Principles of teaching[17]

But all academies did not develop in this way. Many of those in Massachusetts became college preparatory schools and have so continued to this day. Some of the schools for girls became girls' "finishing schools" for "polite culture." Franklin's academy early became the University of Pennsylvania, and in 1787 the academies in New York were made a part of the University of the State of New York. Others sprang up as investments on the part of their owners, but many of these schools closed their doors when they presently had to compete with the public high schools.

Evaluation

Inglis sums up the influence of the academy as follows:

---

17. Paul Monroe (ed.), *Principles of Secondary Education* (New York: The Macmillan Company, 1914), p. 58. By permission of the publishers.

Good effects:

1. It introduced, or at least met, the conception that secondary education should be provided for the large number of boys and girls not preparing to enter college.
2. It enriched and extended the course of study.
3. It introduced and developed secondary education for girls.
4. It popularized if not democratized secondary education in America and prepared the public mind for universal secondary education which was to be attempted later through the public high school.

Bad effects:

1. The academy was essentially a private, sometimes a denominational, or at least a religious institution.
2. With the possible exception of New York State, the academies were not organized into a state system and standards were not established.
3. While academies did popularize secondary education in the United States, they did not democratize it in the sense that they equalized secondary education for all.
4. While the academy did much to pave the way for the later public high school, both by establishing a form of organization, curriculum, etc., and by preparing the mind of the public for extensive secondary education, it also constituted the greatest impediment to the early development of a really public secondary school.[18]

Conflicting Philosophies

Again new forces were forming in America. The American Revolution started a period of idealism which captured men's minds, brought hope, and fed aspirations. Caution was swept aside, and the vision of the possible good life guided men forward. Spurred by the thrill of conquering vast stretches of land and drunk with the spoils of economic exploitation, nineteenth-century America heaped wealth and power upon a rising middle class, which built for itself what it wanted. The thirst for conquest brushed away tradition, precedent, formalism, "polite culture," theological debate, and the status quo. "Progress" was the order of the day, and whatever was new was progress. Fac-

---

18. Alexander Inglis, *Principles of Secondary Education* (Boston: Houghton Mifflin Company, 1918), pp. 182–183. By permission of the publishers.

This impediment was probably a psychological one, for it established a private-school concept of secondary education. On this subject Chapter III of George Martin, *The Evolution of the Massachusetts Public School System,* is interesting. He maintains that the more the academies flourished the worse became the town schools. He makes this significant statement, as applicable today as when it was written: "People will never willingly and cheerfully support two systems of schools. Whenever the private-school system in any community gets on its side the social and political leaders, it will grind the public schools to the wall, and do it under legal and constitutional sanctions."

tories and cities were growing in New England, fed by cotton from the South and immigrants from the Old World. The South "used" the Negro, the North "used" the immigrant, and the growing Midwest "used" the abundant natural resources. Each used what it could to acquire what it wanted. But in using what was available or could be acquired, people developed different philosophies, philosophies which later must be subjected to review and changed through conflict, if national unity was to become a principle and a reality.

The conflicting philosophies at work, which in turn determined the characteristics of the political, economic, and educational struggles that were to follow, are ably described by Parrington in an analysis worth careful study:

> The first stage in the romantization of American thought resulted from the naturalization of French revolutionary theory. Its devious progress through the country can be traced fairly accurately. Landing first in Virginia in the early seventeen-seventies, it met with a hospitable reception from the generous planter society and spread widely there the fashion of Physiocratic agrarianism. Traveling thence westward into the Inland Empire it domesticated itself in frontier log cabins under the guise of an assertive individualism, to issue later as the coon-skin democracy of the Jacksonian revolution. Eventually reaching New England, the last haven and refuge of eighteenth-century realism, it disarmed Yankee antagonism by assuming the dress of Unitarianism and preached the doctrine of human perfectability with such conviction as to arouse the conscience of New England to an extraordinary enthusiasm for reforming man and society. And coming finally to New York it inoculated the mind of the emerging proletariat with its doctrine of the rights of man, with Fourieristic and other Utopias, and turmoiled contemporary politics with equalitarian Locofoco programs. No other philosophy assumed so many and such attractive disguises, or wrought such changes in American Ideals, as this French romanticism with its generous humanitarian impulses. . . .
>
> The rival philosophy, which came to view with increasing dislike the doctrines of French romanticism, was of English middle class origin and sprang from the long struggle of that class to loose the hands of the landed gentry from control of the state. Phrased persuasively by Adam Smith, it embodied the principle of liberalism as that principle was understood by men of affairs. It conceived of a social Utopia that must result if economic forces were given free play; if governmental restrictions on trade were done away with and individual enterprise were free to buy and sell in the open market. Springing from the same root of individualism that brought forth French romanticism, it flowered in an economics that denied the aspirations of the French school. . . .
>
> Meanwhile in the imperialistic South was arising a distinctive philosophy, native to the special conditions imposed by slavery, that was to set it apart from both eastern and western economics and draw it inevitably into a narrowing isolation. Frankly defensive in purpose, rejecting alike French equalitarianism and English individualism, it sought to justify the institu-

tion of slavery by an appeal to reason and square it to the theory of democracy by analogy with northern industrialism. The conception of a Greek democracy, which was the last citadel of the southern mind, was a skillful compromise between the antagonistic principles of aristocracy and democracy, the most romantic ideal brought forth by our golden age of romance. Assuming the middle class principle of exploitation as the creative source of every civilization, it proposed to erect a free state on the basis of a slave proletariat after the model of ancient Athens. A democracy, it argued, is possible only among equals. In every society hitherto the inevitable inequality between economic class has nullified every democratic program. Master and man, exploiter and exploited, are necessarily opposed in economic interests; and this potential clash, this fundamental antagonism of classes, has been intensified by the rise of industrialism. Exploitation has been brutalized by the impersonal wage system and the proletariat has been reduced to sodden and embittered beasts. If now as honest realists we recognize frankly that equality cannot exist between superior and inferior races, if we accept the inevitable proletarian status of the negro, if finally we concede the truism that the life long relations between master and slave are more humane than the temporary relations between wage-giver and wage-earner, we shall concern ourselves less with a romantic equalitarianism and more with a rational conception of a democracy of equals that may conceivably erect a civilization worthy of the name. . . .

It was an ingenious theory, but unfortunately it left out of account the ambitions of the middle class, and it was this class that in the end destroyed it. Whether they will it or not, imperialisms have a way of clashing with rival imperialisms. Reality persists though reality may deny it, and in their several programs the three diverse sections of America were driving blindly to a collision. In that bitter collision the dream of the South was destroyed. With the overthrow of the aristocratic principle in its final refuge the ground was cleared of the last vestiges of the eighteenth century. Thenceforth America was to become wholly middle class, and such romance as it might bring forth was to be of another sort.[19]

The period from approximately 1800 to 1860 in America was a period of intellectual debate over the relations of men living together in a new world. It was a period of experimenting with social institutions and of opening settlements in different geographical areas. But these settlements were more interdependent than some of their leaders realized, and if they were to work together some common basis of thought had to prevail. It was also a period of expansion—geographically, commercially, institutionally, conceptually—as well as a period of growth of cities, of population, of poverty, and of the middle class. A day of settlement was inevitable, during which the fire would test which doctrines should endure. It took a war which Lincoln aptly characterized as "a great civil war testing whether that nation or any nation so conceived

19. Vernon L. Parrington, *The Romantic Revolution in America, 1800–1860* (New York: Harcourt, Brace and Company, 1927), pp. vi–ix. By permission of the publishers.

[based upon liberty and equality] and so dedicated can long endure" to determine the ultimate principles which would dominate during the next generation.

The Public High School Movement

In trying to discover from these diverse social and political forces those which were most influential in determining the pattern of educational development, Faulkner attributes to the following the greatest influence:

> Many important influences were at work to promote public education: the development of urban life, which necessitated a new system; the increase of crime and pauperism in the rapidly growing cities, which, it was believed, might be prevented by education; the extension of the franchise, which gave the voters the opportunity of achieving their demands; the possibility in the new states of endowing education from the public lands; and, finally, the belief that democracy could survive only if the masses were educated.[20]

The wishes and demands of the middle class were probably among the most powerful influences determining the type of education that was to follow the Latin grammar school or the academy. The public high school did not follow the academy in the sense that one died and the other sprang up immediately afterward. The first high school, which was a protest institution, began even before the academies had reached their most flourishing period. The idea of an education beyond the elementary school for youth not intending to enter college had made an appeal, but the idea of each parent paying for it individually had not received such wide support. Quite naturally there appeared, then, a movement to secure such a school free to all children.

The English High School of Boston

The first result was the establishment of the English High School of Boston in 1821. The first curriculum of this school looks more like Franklin's original idea than did any of the New England academies.

First class: Composition; reading from the most approved authors; exercises in criticism, comprising critical analyses of the language, grammar, and style of the best English authors, their errors and beauties; declamation; geography; arithmetic continued
Second class: Composition, reading, exercises in criticism, declamation; algebra; ancient and modern history and chronology; logic, geometry;

---

20. Harold U. Faulkner, *American Political and Social History* (New York: Appleton-Century-Crofts, Inc., 1937), p. 271. By permission of the publishers.

plane trigonometry and its applications to measurements of heights and distances; navigation; surveying; mensuration of surfaces and solids; forensic discussions

Third class: Composition; exercises in criticism; declamation; mathematics, logic; history, particularly that of the United States; natural philosophy, including astronomy; moral and political philosophy[21]

The curriculum of the English Classical School is of no significance in the public-school curriculum movement. As would be expected, the curriculum represented a cross between the Latin school and the academy in New England, a fusion of the English program of the academy and the classical department of the Latin school.

Public Pressure

It was not the wealthy or cultured class of New England which pushed the public high school forward. The rich everywhere could educate their own children, and they in general opposed the public high school on account of taxes. To push into being the American public high school, the efforts of the masses were needed—the farmers, the laborers in the factories, the struggling middle class from many occupational fields.

In 1830 in Philadelphia a workingmen's meeting resolved that "there can be no real liberty without a wide diffusion of real intelligence—that until means of equal instruction shall be equally secured to all, liberty is but an unmeaning word, and equality an empty shadow."[22] For the poor middle class and the laborers the only school that was self-respecting for their children was one supported by the state and open and free to everybody alike. There must be no class distinction, sectarianism, or charity. The first public-school law was passed in Massachusetts in 1827, but it was in the frontier states that the high school made its greatest strides, and it was certainly in these states that the curriculum was liberalized. Its purposes were not realized satisfactorily, however, until 1850, when the modern public high school evolved.

---

21. Quoted in Inglis, *Secondary Education,* pp. 186–187, originally taken from the catalogue of the English High School, Boston, 1890.

22. Quoted in James T. Adams, *The Epic of America* (Boston: Little, Brown & Company, 1934), p. 197.

For a detailed recording of the resolutions of organized labor regarding education from 1881 to 1938, see *Labor and Education* (Washington: American Federation of Labor, 1939).

Chapter Two

The School in an Industrial
and Agrarian Revolution

RAMPANT OPTIMISM characterized America from 1830 until 1861. Immigrants had fared better in America than in their own country, even though many of them were living here in dire poverty. Class distinctions were on the way out; secularism had championed over sectarianism in politics and education; the American was coming to believe that he was master of his own fate and that being born in a log cabin was a peculiar badge of merit. There was no limit to the possibilities of wealth; chance played a tremendous part in the game of raising oneself in social rank; haste was just as important a factor; and the man who did not work was frowned upon. Everybody must have either a profession, a piece of land, or a business. People were in a state of mind which James Truslow Adams characterized by the term "nervous haste." The West mistrusted the East and the East thought the West vulgar. The pursuit of the cultural arts was for women and useful only for parlor conversation in which vigorous men had no time to engage. In fact, time could not be wasted on anything which did not make money. The duties of American citizenship were not discussed. Rights were the the sole topic of political polemics. It was an age of mass movements.[1]

Civil War and Reconstruction

Then came the struggle which tried out the conflicting theories that had been cultivated in the past generation, frequently called the "Second American Revolution." It was bitter and it left bitterness and devastation for a period to follow. To achieve reconstruction the American people had to rebuild their thinking and habits of living upon the basis of a unified nation. The romance of slavery was gone, and there were left only the possible conflicts between Eastern capitalism and Western agrarianism. Discussion of the philosophy of government was swept aside, not to be revived until the days of the "New Deal," when again the conflicting interests left standing at the close of the War between the States became sharper. Men must make money now. There was need for a flood of capital to industrialize the East, to lay rails to the newly founded West, and to push farther into the Western wilderness. There was gold in California, fertile soil in Oregon, and the chance to live as one pleased west of the Mississippi. Everything was expansion, building—fortunes and structures alike. In the hurry to acquire things, control slipped from the farmer to the industrialist, and men had no time to consider what it meant. The evaluation of this shift had to wait until interests clashed more sharply. But control is like an accumulating snowball, and the early part of the twentieth century saw an emerging criticism which took the form chiefly of evaluation. Such criticism, as will be shown later, resulted in the first attempt in a hundred years to evaluate the existing secondary-school curriculum.

A Wave of Criticism

As the student of social affairs runs through the history of the fifty years following the Civil War, he finds enumerated many factors which were to influence later education. The struggle for political control of the South, the triumph of industrialism, a 250 per cent increase in the population of America between 1859 and 1899, a 600 per cent increase in the value of manufactured products, political control by barons of finance, the uniting of the West and the East by rail, the consolidation of the frontiers of ranching, farming, and mining—these were characteristic features of a period that the Farmers' Alliance characterized in 1890 as follows:

---

1. Charles and Mary Beard give an excellent picture of this period in Chapter 16 of their *Rise of American Civilization* (New York: The Macmillan Company, 1930).

There are three great crops raised in Nebraska. One is a crop of corn, one a crop of freight rates, and one a crop of interest. One is produced by farmers who by sweat farm the land. The other two are produced by men who sit in their offices and behind their bank counters and farm the farmers.[2]

This was a symptom of the rising tide of criticism and evaluation of the practices which had resulted when men transferred control to those who supplied the capital. This was the Gilded Age. Everybody gilded himself, his person, and his home with whatever glittered. And if he had no time for gilding his mind the slow way, by hard study and creative expression, he did it the fast way, by purchasing and displaying the works of others.

The farmers were not alone in criticizing the state of affairs; the factory workers, in an effort to improve their position, consolidated their various labor groups in 1886 into the American Federation of Labor. Abuses of industry forced federal regulation, reflecting again the evaluation of existing conditions by the suppressed group. The conflicts reached a climax in the devastating panic of 1893. The struggle for control was fought hard and bitterly, ending in 1900 with the defeat of William Jennings Bryan and the election of William McKinley. Conservative capitalism had won over agrarian democracy, and America was again to turn toward a new period of business prosperity. Vachel Lindsay described this period clearly in his poem "Bryan, Bryan, Bryan, Bryan":

> Boy Bryan's defeat
> Defeat of western silver
> Defeat of the wheat
> Victory of letterfiles
> And plutocrats in miles
> With dollar signs upon their coats,
> Diamond watch chains upon their vests
> And spats on their feet
> Victory of custodians,
> Plymouth Rock,
> And all that inbred landlord stock,
> Victory of the neat[3]

Expansion and Consolidation

The overthrow of agrarian democracy in 1896 was accompanied by imperialistic expansion. The United States dominated Central America; annexed

---

2. Quoted in Harold U. Faulkner, *American Political and Social History* (New York: Appleton-Century-Crofts, Inc., 1937), p. 433. By permission of the publishers.
3. Vachel Lindsay, *Collected Poems* (New York: The Macmillan Company, 1923), p. 103. By permission of the publishers.

Puerto Rico, the Philippines, Hawaii, and Guam; established protection over Panama, Haiti, Santo Domingo, Cuba, and Nicaragua; and purchased the Virgin Islands. Our industrial expansion required new raw materials and new markets. New coaling stations and new naval bases were needed for protection.

Before 1895 there was no significant trend toward the consolidation of large industries. But in the few years following, consolidation grew fast. Supported by a continuous period of industrial success, a series of successful political campaigns based on economic conservatism, and the ever-increasing markets, about "300 greater or lesser industrial trusts representing mergers of nearly 5300 distinct plants with a capitalization of over $7,000,000,000" were created between 1896 and 1904.[4] In speaking to Congress in 1901, Theodore Roosevelt expressed a widespread conviction that such consolidation was harmful to the public welfare, and in 1903 Congress passed three acts aimed at regulating big business.[5] Then followed the Pure Food and Drug Act and the Hepburn Act in 1906, the Federal Reserve Act, the Erdman Act of 1913, the Adamson Eight-Hour Act of 1916, and so on. Growing out of all this capitalistic expansion was a type of organization and control which was to be one of the most significant and far-reaching contributions to world finance—absentee ownership, which affected not only the financial world, but legislation, social justice, and institutional administration.

Other social changes were taking place. Overcrowding in rapidly growing cities, lack of recreation, improper sanitary conditions, the influx of immigrants from Eastern Europe, low wages for industrial work, uneven distribution of wealth, economic injustice, domination by big business, exploitation of human labor—all contributed to a wave of reform in politics, economics, religion, and the schools.

Review and Reform of the Schools

Practically no important changes were made in the American high-school curriculum from 1820 until 1890. The standardization of the secondary-school program was completed in 1893 with the report of the Committee of Ten of the National Council of Education. The committee, better than it knew, not only summed up the seventy-five years of American struggle for wealth but sanctioned the static institutional life of its young. The eyes of the secondary school were still turned to the selected few who would be able to go to college, and the curriculum betrayed its real major purpose and belied its stated one of preparing youth to participate in activities other than those of a college

---

4. Faulkner, *Political and Social History*, p. 553.
5. The Expediting Act, the Elkins Antirebate Act, and the establishment of a Department of Commerce and Labor.

type. The committee summed up, it did not build; rather, it took a backward step in secondary education. It really endeavored to push the work of the secondary school down into the last two years—the seventh and eighth—of the elementary school. This committee not only did not sense the need for a changed curriculum to meet the needs of a growing nation; it provided a sad commentary on the vision of American educators. It concerned itself with recommending that "the study of Latin begin one year earlier than customary," that "the study of French or German begin at about the age of ten," that "school readers be superseded by whole classics," that "Greek and Roman history be taught in the eighth grade," and that instruction in concrete or experimental geometry begin at the age of about ten and occupy one school hour per week for at least three years. This committee also recommended that secondary education include the seventh and eighth grades.

Two years later the Committee on College Entrance Requirements of the Department of Secondary Education of the National Education Association came to the same conclusion about the seventh and eighth grades. John Dewey supported this idea at an educational conference at the University of Chicago in 1901. In 1902 President Harper proposed a plan for educational reorganization which would group the eighth grade, the four years of high school, and the first two years of college together into seven years of secondary education. Such proposals as these were followed by the establishment of a junior-college department in the high school at Joliet, Illinois, in 1902; the organization of the elementary school of the University of Chicago on a seven-year basis; the Kansas City experiment in which pupils in seven-year elementary schools were found to be "better educated" than those in eight-year schools elsewhere; and a change in the organization of other secondary schools. The establishment of the junior-college movement; the three reports of the Committee on Six-Year Courses (1907–1909) of the National Education Association, which advocated strongly a six-year elementary school; the Committee on the Economy of Time of the National Education Association, which submitted its final report in 1913 and advocated a six-year elementary school and a six-year secondary school; the Committee on Economy of Time in Public School Education, appointed by the Department of Superintendence in 1911, which made research studies that led to the purging of many useless and unsuitable materials from the elementary school; the National Commission on Vocational Education of 1913 followed by the Smith-Hughes Act of 1917; and finally the Commission on the Reorganization of Secondary Education, which made various reports over a ten-year period, culminating in the report of 1922—all these indicate clearly the widespread dissatisfaction with the static organization and offerings of the public-school program, both elementary and secondary. They also reflect the criticism directed against other social institutions and conditions during this period from 1895 to 1920. These reforms constituted the first significant attempt in a hundred years of American life to readjust the offerings of the secondary school to the pupils attending it. The junior high school came into being about 1909 and spread rapidly, dividing the six-year secondary period into two halves equal in time. Then came the two-year public junior college, and the present form of secondary education was developed—a three-year junior high school, a three-year senior high school, and a two-year junior college—eight years of secondary education. Although this time period is standard today, local communities vary greatly in the extent to which they unify these various divisions into administrative units.

Specific Criticisms

From 1910 to America's entry into World War I, educators and public alike criticized the schools continually. In 1912 Calvin O. Davis summed up these criticisms as follows:

1. The curriculum is overcrowded.
2. There is little correlation of subject matter.
3. Exaggerated attention is given to unessential and impractical topics.
4. Many topics presented have no legitimate place in any curriculum.
5. The study of many secondary subjects is postponed beyond the proper time for their best presentation.
6. There is no close articulation of the elementary school and the secondary school.
7. Individual tastes and capacities are not rightly considered.
8. Insufficient attention is paid to the retarded pupils and to those of superior ability.
9. There is not sufficient hand work.
10. Vocational work is not effectively vocational.
11. Promotions are based on an unsound principle.
12. The whole system is overmechanized.[6]

Two years later, in 1914, W. D. Lewis summarized the complaints then current:

1. The course of study is almost exclusively academic.
2. Many of the pupils, particularly boys, are sent from the school as failures "who either could not or would not apply themselves to a curriculum consisting mainly of memorizing textbooks."
3. The curriculum has failed to enlist the interest of motor minded pupils because its relation to their lives is at best uncertain and remote.

---

6. Calvin O. Davis, *Our Evolving High School Curriculum* (New York: World Book Company, 1927), p. 49. Printed originally in C. H. Johnston (ed.), *High School Education* (New York: Charles Scribner's Sons, 1912), pp. 73–74. Reprinted here by permission of the author.

4. Stress is laid on individualistic development, not on training for social betterment.[7]

5. Student mortality is excessive and inexcusable.

6. Students who spend but a year or two in the school often carry into the practical affairs of life no superiority in efficiency over the grammar school graduate.

7. The boy who enters practical life after completing the high school course finds that his four years have given him little that is useful.

8. The culture acquired in high school is too often a haze which evaporates in thin air.

9. About all the high school graduate really has is a residuum of mental discipline which at its best functions in a habitual persistence.

10. Often, habits detrimental to both culture and discipline are formed.

11. The boy who goes to college seems to be the only one that the course of study really fits and it is a question whether either he or the community profits by the expensive gift bestowed upon him.

12. If the service of the school to the boys is vague and uncertain, its practical value to the great mass of girls approaches absolute zero.

13. Ideals of "getting by" dominate in altogether too many schools.

14. Snobbery in the schools has become a common trait.[8]

But why all this criticism? Two things are significant. From 1890 to 1915 the total high-school population had increased from 211,596 pupils in 2,771 high schools to 1,328,984 pupils in 11,674 high schools.[9] Here was an increase of over 500 per cent in high-school enrollment in twenty-five years. This figure is significant because it is a commonly recognized statistical principle that the greater the increase in number, the greater the heterogeneity. Nevertheless, the core of the curriculum was not changing. In 1915 the major part of the pupil's time was still taken up with studying Latin, French, German, algebra, geometry, physics, chemistry, rhetoric, and history.[10]

Curriculum Changes

There were emerging experiments, however, at liberalizing the high-school curriculum. These took three interesting forms: the division of the high-school

---

7. Lewis seems to be the only one who thought this was true.

8. Davis, *High School Curriculum*, pp. 49–50. Printed originally in W. D. Lewis, *Democracy's High School* (Boston: Houghton Mifflin Company, 1914), Chap. 1.

9. *Report of the United States Commissioner of Education*, 1916, II, 449. The accuracy of these early figures is affected by the incompleteness of returns.

10. See Carl A. Jessen and Lester B. Herlihy, *Offerings and Registrations in High School Subjects* (U.S. Office of Education, *Bulletin* No. 6; Washington: Government Printing Office, 1938). See also Table I, page 50, for figures on the gains and losses in enrollment in forty-seven subjects.

subjects into different types of "courses"; the wider introduction of vocational and industrial work; and the gradual introduction of a greater number of elective subjects. These may well be illustrated by the subject offerings in 1914 in the Abilene (Kansas) High School[11] and the Twin Falls (Idaho) High School.[12]

THE ABILENE HIGH SCHOOL

College Preparatory Course	General Course

Freshman

Required:	Required:
English	English
Algebra	Algebra
Latin	
Elective:	Elective:
General science	General science
Physiography	Physiography
Bookkeeping	Bookkeeping
Commercial geography	Commercial geography
Word study	Word study

Sophomore

Required:	Required:
English	English
Geometry	Geometry
Latin	
Elective:	Elective:
Ancient history	Ancient history
Botany	Botany
Agriculture	Agriculture
Manual training	Manual training
Domestic science	Domestic science
German	German

---

11. This school also offered a normal training course which differed from the one cited here chiefly in that agriculture was required in the sophomore year; civics, psychology, and physiology were required in the junior year; and American history, teaching methods, arithmetic, physics, and methods in the senior year.

12. The curricula for these two cities were taken from J. E. Stout, *The High School: Its Function, Organization, and Administration* (Boston: D. C. Heath and Company, 1914), pp. 305–311. By permission of the publishers.

THE ABILENE HIGH SCHOOL, *Continued*

College Preparatory Course	General Course
Junior	
Required:	Required:
English	English
Algebra	
Latin	
Elective:	Elective:
Psychology	Psychology
Civics	Civics
English history	English history
Chemistry	Chemistry
German	German
Geometry	Geometry
Senior	
Required:	Required:
None	None
Elective:	Elective:
Latin	American history
American history	Economics
Economics	English
English	Physics
Physics	German
German	

THE TWIN FALLS HIGH SCHOOL.   In Twin Falls two general types of courses were offered—the Preparatory and the Vocational courses. The first was divided into the Classical and the Scientific, and the Vocational was divided into the Home Economics, the Manual Arts, the Agriculture, and the Commercial.

THE TWIN FALLS HIGH SCHOOL PREPARATORY COURSES

Classical Course	Scientific Course	Vocational Home Economics
First Year		
Required:	Required:	Required:
English	English	English
Algebra	Algebra	Elementary cooking $\frac{3}{5}$
Latin	Physical geography $\frac{1}{2}$	Cleaning $\frac{2}{5}$
	Commercial geography $\frac{1}{2}$	Handwork $\frac{3}{5}$
		Physiology and hygiene $\frac{2}{5}$

THE TWIN FALLS HIGH SCHOOL, *Continued*

Classical Course	*Scientific Course*	*Vocational Home Economics*
Elective:	Elective:	Elective:
Ancient history	Latin	Algebra
Physical geography	German	Physical geography
Commercial	Ancient history	Commercial geography
geography	Manual training	Ancient history
	Domestic science	German

Second Year

Required:	Required:	Required:
English	English	English
Plane geometry	Plane geometry	Plain sewing $\frac{3}{5}$
Caesar and composi-	Botany	Designing $\frac{2}{5}$
tion		Bookkeeping $\frac{2}{5}$
		Manual training $\frac{3}{10}$
		Poultry $\frac{1}{5}$
		Gardening $\frac{1}{10}$
Elective:	Elective:	Elective:
Medieval and modern	Latin	Plane geometry
history	German	Botany
Botany	Medieval and modern	Medieval and modern
	history	history
	Manual training	German
	Domestic science	

Third Year

Required:	Required:	Required:
English	English	English
Advanced algebra $\frac{1}{2}$	Advanced algebra $\frac{1}{2}$	Advanced cookery $\frac{2}{5}$
Solid geometry $\frac{1}{2}$	Solid geometry $\frac{1}{2}$	Dietetics $\frac{2}{5}$
Cicero and composi-	Chemistry	Chemistry
tion		
Elective:	Elective:	Elective:
German	German	Commercial law $\frac{1}{2}$
French	French	Political economy $\frac{1}{2}$
Argumentation and	Argumentation and	Argumentation and
debate $\frac{1}{2}$	debate $\frac{1}{2}$	debate $\frac{1}{2}$
Public speaking $\frac{1}{2}$	Public speaking $\frac{1}{2}$	Public speaking $\frac{1}{2}$
English history	English history	English history
		German or French

THE TWIN FALLS HIGH SCHOOL, *Continued*

Classical Course	Scientific Course	Vocational Home Economics
	Fourth Year	
Required:	Required:	Required:
English ⅗	English ⅗	English ⅗
American history and civics	American history and civics	American history and civics
Vocational direction ⅖	Vocational direction ⅖	Vocational direction ⅖
Virgil and mythology	Physics	Dressmaking ⅗
		Millinery ⅖
Elective:	Elective:	Elective:
German	French	Physics
French	Trigonometry ½	Psychology
Trigonometry ½	Political economy ½	Home sanitation 3/10
Political economy ½	Psychology ½	House planning 2/10
Psychology ½	Principles of teaching ½	French
Principles of teaching ½		
Physics		

VOCATIONAL COURSES

Manual Arts	Agriculture	Commercial
	First Year	
Required:	Required:	Required:
English	English	English
Commercial arithmetic	Physical geography ½	Physical geography ½
Mechanical drawing ⅖	Commercial geography ½	Commercial geography ½
Manual training ⅗	Agriculture 3/10	Spelling and word analysis ½
	Soils 3/10	Spelling and penmanship ½
	Breeds of Livestock ⅖	
Elective:	Elective:	Elective:
Algebra	Algebra	Algebra
Physical geography ½	Commercial arithmetic	Ancient history
Commercial geography ½	Manual training	German
Ancient history	Domestic science	
German		

THE TWIN FALLS HIGH SCHOOL, *Continued*

Manual Arts	*Agriculture*	*Commercial*

Second Year

Required:
English
Mechanical drawing $\frac{2}{5}$
Manual training $\frac{3}{5}$

Required:
English
Botany
Stock judging $\frac{2}{5}$
Fertilizers $\frac{2}{10}$
Grain judging $\frac{1}{10}$
Poultry $\frac{2}{10}$
Gardening $\frac{1}{10}$

Required:
English
Bookkeeping and business practice
Commercial arithmetic

Elective:
Plane geometry
Botany
Bookkeeping
German
Medieval and modern history

Elective:
Plane geometry
Bookkeeping
Manual training
Domestic science

Elective:
Plane geometry
Medieval and modern history
German

Third Year

Required:
English
Designing and drafting $\frac{2}{5}$
Manual training $\frac{3}{5}$

Required:
English
Farm dairying $\frac{4}{5}$
Farm crops $\frac{2}{5}$
Irrigation $\frac{1}{5}$
Horticulture $\frac{2}{5}$
Farm machinery $\frac{1}{5}$

Required:
English
Bookkeeping and banking

Elective:
Advanced algebra $\frac{1}{2}$
Solid geometry $\frac{1}{2}$
Chemistry
Commercial law $\frac{1}{2}$
Political economy $\frac{1}{2}$
Argumentation and debate $\frac{1}{2}$
Public speaking $\frac{1}{2}$
German or French

Elective:
Chemistry
Commercial law $\frac{1}{2}$
Political economy $\frac{1}{2}$
Argumentation and debate $\frac{1}{2}$
Public speaking $\frac{1}{2}$
Domestic science
Manual training

Elective:
Argumentation and debate $\frac{1}{2}$
Public speaking $\frac{1}{2}$
Commercial law $\frac{1}{2}$
Political economy $\frac{1}{2}$
Stenography
Typewriting
German or French

Fourth Year

Required:
English $\frac{3}{5}$

Required:
English $\frac{3}{5}$

Required:
English $\frac{3}{5}$

Manual Arts	Agriculture	Commercial
Fourth Year—Continued		
American history and civics	American history and civics	American history and civics
Vocational direc- tion $\frac{2}{5}$	Vocational direc- tion $\frac{2}{5}$	Vocational direc- tion $\frac{2}{5}$
Architectural draft- ing $\frac{3}{5}$	Feeds and feeding $\frac{3}{10}$	
	Farm manage- ment $\frac{2}{10}$	
	Insect pests $\frac{2}{10}$	
	Fungous diseases $\frac{2}{10}$	
	Farm law $\frac{1}{10}$	
Elective:	Elective:	Elective:
Trigonometry $\frac{1}{2}$	Physics	Physics or chemistry
Agriculture $\frac{1}{2}$	Breeding $\frac{3}{10}$	History of com- merce $\frac{1}{2}$
Physics	Farm surveying $\frac{2}{10}$	Advertising and salesmanship $\frac{1}{2}$
French	Marketing farm prod- ucts $\frac{1}{10}$	Stenography
	Manual training	Typewriting
	Domestic science	French

This curriculum program from Twin Falls is remarkably liberal in comparison with the other programs of its time. One may hazard the guess, objective evidence lacking, that it represented one of the unusual programs of that date, being especially suited to the needs of the pupils living in the vast irrigated agricultural section around Twin Falls.

War and Depression

At the beginning of World War I we were neutral; then we sympathized, sold goods, loaned money; and in 1917 we sent men to bolster the efforts of the Allies. Near the end of 1918 the struggle ceased, and most of the world concentrated on returning to "normalcy," to salvaging everything possible from the holocaust, and to getting what it could from the defeated nations.

In America forces again came into conflict. Science, thought some, might again lead the way to realism; government might be effectively decentralized; economic law is not the final and all-in-all force of control; industrialism might still be humanized; environment is an effective force for molding the organism, and therefore there is still room for social readjustment and a better life for individuals. But alongside of this was also emerging a skepticism, itself a by-product of industrialism, which began to question the ideal of democracy. Many of our literary intellectuals pessimistically cried out against the mechanistic character of society. Revolt was in the air. The farmer cried out against the banker and the market; the laborer was engaged in bitter strife with the industrialist; the common man demanded that his government curb the vices of the factory and credit systems and permit all men to share in the nation's abundant physical resources; the intellectual was in revolt against the impersonalized system of labor and production and urged that the social institutions take a firm hand in making it possible for each individual to achieve adequate recognition and prosperity. Law and corporate structure had conspired to confiscate and hold the materials of rich living. After the collapse of Wall Street in 1929, the mass of American people assumed control by putting in the White House a leader who was a social idealist. Under him they were able to secure social benefits that others had considered were out of reach.

Franklin Delano Roosevelt voiced the attitude of the people when he said:

> I believe the individual should have full liberty of action to make the most of himself; but I do not believe that in the name of the sacred word "individualism," a few powerful interests should be permitted to make industrial cannon fodder of the lives of half of the population of the United States. . . .
>
> I believe that our industrial and economic system is made for individual men and women,—and not individual men and women for the benefit of the system.[13]

This was not a revolt against the form of government; it was a revolt against an economic and industrial system which had raised the middle class to power and dominance at the expense of the masses of men.

In the maelstrom of depression, America was puzzled. What was "our way"?[14] Whatever industrial leaders supported, labor leaders condemned. Whatever youth thought was hopeful, age thought was destructive of "American principles." Whatever frontier school men considered appropriate, parents feared as frills. Whatever departed from tradition was considered "revolutionary." Each man suspected the other's motives.

The years from 1933 saw a quick succession of Congressional measures designed to pull America out of the economic and psychological depression into which it had fallen. Many legislative enactments passed to control in-

---

13. Quoted in Harold O. Rugg, *American Life and the School Curriculum* (Boston: Ginn and Company, 1936), p. 84.
14. For interesting analyses see Sherwood Anderson, *Puzzled America;* John Spivak, *America Faces the Barricades;* Alfred M. Bingham, *Insurgent America;* Edmund Wilson, *The American Jitters;* Herbert Agar, *Land of the Free;* and Franklin D. Roosevelt, *On Our Way.*

dustry, to prevent exploitation of the laborer and the sale of useless stocks, to control the credit structure, to curb the power of large corporations, and to put people back to work were evidence that America could be made to serve the needs of its people. Hope revived and a new relationship between the federal government and its people appeared. Probably not since the first part of the nineteenth century had the mass of people so closely and genuinely followed the activities of the government or discussed the fundamental concepts of democracy as they did from 1933 to 1940.

Further Educational Reform

To education in general [wrote Charles and Mary Beard] as well as to the social studies in particular, the noise produced by the grinding of the Ship of State on the rocks of depression gave tremors and qualms. While prosperity lasted, the huge system from the primary school to the university could turn endlessly, pouring out lawyers, doctors, engineers, bond salesmen, craftsmen, stenographers, and mistresses of domestic science and bonnet-making without making any fundamental queries respecting the course of things. But when starvation threatened its graduates and defaults menaced its endowments, disconcerting questions arose about the purpose of education and its relation to a society periodically sick from a mysterious economic malady.[15]

This depression period of which they speak, which had been preceded by a decade of criticism and pessimism, led educators all over America to make a wholesale attack on the materials of study prescribed for the children of the schools. Such a reaction, long overdue, was materially facilitated by the construction of instruments for evaluating learning. In city after city surveys were made, and these instruments were used as a basis of evaluation and later of criticism of the program of the school.

Gradual Curriculum Changes

A summary of the changes that took place may be drawn from three studies, one made by Stout on the development of the high-school curriculum from 1860 to 1918;[16] the second made by Van Dycke, a follow-up in 1930 of the

15. Charles and Mary Beard, *Rise of American Civilization*, p. 835 of Book II of the one-volume edition. Chapter 31 on the machine age is an excellent review of the chief features of American life in the last fifty years and should be read by people interested in the curriculum.

16. John E. Stout, *The Development of High School Curricula in the North Central States from 1860–1918* (University of Chicago; Supplementary Educational Monographs, No. 15, 1921).

thirty-five schools Stout used in his investigation;[17] and the third, that of the National Survey of Secondary Education dealing with programs of study, made by Loomis, Lide, and Johnson.[18] The following situations were revealed by these studies:

1. In the Midwest 80 per cent of the high schools organized their offerings with the purpose of preparing "for college and for life."

2. Starting with a single list of offerings, like that of the Boston Latin School, the subjects were grouped into departments and were later organized under courses, such as classical, general, scientific, vocational, English, college preparatory. Thus several types of education were to be provided.

3. Many of the older subjects, such as moral philosophy, higher mathematics except trigonometry, astronomy, geology, and logic ceased to have any important place in the curriculum after 1885. But the new subjects did not exactly take the place of these older ones; that is, "less time was not given to mathematics but more time was given to the subjects remaining."

4. From 1860 to 1900 there was practically no change in the number of years devoted to the subject fields of mathematics, science, and classical languages. About one year's gain in time was shown in the subjects of English, social studies, and modern languages, and about one and one-half years' gain in commercial subjects.

5. Until about 1890 only one commercial subject was offered in the high schools—bookkeeping. This, with other commercial subjects, gained from 1895 and, with industrial arts, spread into both the general high school and the special vocational high schools.

6. When differentiation of subjects is made for classical, general, college preparatory, and other types of "courses," there is a more or less common base of academic subjects running through all of them with a few special subjects which lend their names to the type of course division, such as commercial or science.

7. Considerable similarity prevailed among the subjects offered in the small high schools, while in the large high schools there was great variation.

8. In 1906 the thirty-five schools studied by both Van Dycke and Stout offered an average of 23.7 subjects or a total of 53 different subjects. By 1930 this average number had increased to 48.1 and the total increased to 306. In English, subjects had increased in number from 6 to 15; in science from 8 to 38; in commercial from 8 to 44; in industrial arts from 2 to 43; in music from 0 to 15; and in art from 1 to 13. Very little increase was noted in languages, science, and mathematics. In 152 schools studied in 1930–1931 there were 419 different subject courses offered.

---

17. George E. Van Dycke, "Trends in the Development of the High School Offering, I and II," *School Review*, 39:657–664, 1931; 737–747, 1931.

18. A. K. Loomis, Edwin S. Lide, and B. Lamar Johnson, *The Program of Studies* (U.S. Office of Education, National Survey of Secondary Education, Monograph No. 19; Washington: Government Printing Office, 1932).

9. In 1906 English, social science, science, mathematics, and foreign languages made up 76 per cent of the total subject offerings of the high schools, while in 1930 this percentage had dropped to 50. The practical-arts subjects gained from 23 per cent to 43 per cent during that time and the fine arts from practically nothing to about 10 per cent of the total subject offerings.

10. From 1925 to 1930 there was a decrease in the number of types of courses offered (classical, college preparatory) and an increase in interest in the organization of the curriculum into constants with variables, that is, a few required subjects constant for all youth with electives varying with pupils.

11. In 152 schools studed in 1930–1931, nine-sixteenths of the work of the average high school was required, ranging from an average of 2 elective units in the college preparatory course to 3 in the commercial. The average subjects required in these schools at this date were: English, 4 units; history, 1.8; social studies, 0.7; mathematics, 1.5; and 0.9 in science. In 1930–1931, 100 per cent of the schools required English for graduation, 85.7 per cent required American history, 60 per cent required physical education, 45.7 per cent required algebra, 34.3 per cent required geometry, 8.6 per cent required biology.

12. Los Angeles affords a good illustration of the large number of separate subject courses which were offered in all the high schools of that city in 1930–1931. They are as follows:

SUBJECT COURSES IN LOS ANGELES

Subject	Courses
English	29
Social studies	16
Mathematics	14
Science	41
Health and physical education	17
Music	24
Fine arts	46
Industrial arts	132
Home economics	47
Classical languages	14
Modern languages	30
Agriculture	17
Commerce	42
TOTAL	469

Changes in Subjects and Textbooks

An examination of the textbooks may reveal the nature of the changes in the subjects actually offered. It is not possible to tell the changes which took place in the curriculum by noting the number of pupils who took the subjects offered. Frequently there have been very significant changes made in content while the old title of a subject course remained unchanged. Since this was an era in which the textbook was used as the basis of study, an examination of textbooks is probably a very good method of determining the actual changes in the curriculum. The textbook method was the dominant method of determining curriculum materials in the United States until 1920, as attested by a number of surveys. Since then its emphasis has been lessened, but as late as 1930 it was still the major determinant in about 30 per cent of the schools.[19]

Stout undertook to analyze the changes in the subject matter by studying the various textbooks used in the several subject courses from 1860 to 1918. A summary of Stout's findings adds significance to the observations already made of changes in the time element, in the total subject offerings, and in the percentages of pupils taking each subject course.[20] For the years following 1918 the National Survey of Secondary Education has been used.[21]

MATHEMATICS. In mathematics trigonometry declined in importance, and calculus, analytics, surveying, and navigation disappeared from the high-school curriculum. In arithmetic common daily problems were substituted for the puzzle type. In algebra and geometry there have been no significant innovations since the seventeenth century. The influence of commercial groups is reflected in the increase in commercial arithmetic and in common business problems in general mathematics courses. The most significant improvements in mathematics have been the organization of courses combining materials from algebra, geometry, and arithmetic into a mixed course, frequently called general mathematics.

ENGLISH. Innovations in grammar between 1860 and 1918 are unimportant.

> A knowledge of grammar as an end in itself and mental discipline, in spite of all statements to the contrary, continued to constitute the chief aims in the teaching of grammar, so far as the texts themselves were concerned, to the end of the century. These ideas had become so fixed that composition and later literature were drafted more or less into service to accomplish these ends.[22]

Composition started in relation to grammar and declamation. Attention was then shifted to rhetoric, then to figures of speech and literary forms, and finally to the themes of models of style provided by literature.

---

19. National Society for the Study of Education, *The Textbook in American Education* (Thirtieth Yearbook; Bloomington, Ill.; Public School Publishing Company, 1931), Part II, Chap. 2.
20. Stout, *High School Curricula*, pp. 117–196, 228–259.
21. National Survey of Secondary Education, *Summary* (U.S. Office of Education, Monograph No. 1; Washington: Government Printing Office, 1932). For greater details see the separate volumes for each subject field.
22. Stout, *High School Curricula*, p. 126.

In 1930 the analysis of 156 courses showed that composition teaching emphasized the fundamentals of expression and functional grammar, at the same time stimulating interest in successful oral expression through such means as conversation, storytelling, and announcements. Much drill, considerable emphasis upon the mechanics of expression, and relatively little emphasis upon having something to say continued to be characteristic. More time was spent on writing than upon speaking and an undue proportion of time was given to grammar. A wave of setting up "minimum essentials" was accompanied by a series of classes on remedial language, an indication that the content of the English language work was so difficult for students to learn in normal situations that 50 per cent had to be given added drill on the principles of grammar and composition that were thought to be essential.

The term "literature" usually refers to English literature, for relatively little attention was given to American literature. The teaching of literature passed through three stages. The first stage emphasized "select readings," short selections from a large number of authors. These were to train the pupil in oral reading and declamation and to familiarize him with good literature. Literature then shifted from a study of writings to a history of literature, consisting chiefly of the biography of authors and lists of their writings. The third stage stressed the "classics" with the emphasis either upon wide extensive reading of many selections or upon the intensive study of a few masterpieces.

> Recently, current literature is coming to be used much more than formerly. The whole tendency in the recent movement in teaching English is away from the formal. Old divisions of subject matter are being ignored, the interests of students are more fully taken into account, and social demands of various kinds are beginning to function in the selection of material. Theoretically the correlation of English with other school subjects is receiving emphasis, but not much, apparently, in practice has been accomplished.[23]

In 1930 the two chief aims of teaching literature seemed to be to acquaint the pupil with good reading material to broaden his interests and to develop tastes and standards of evaluation for his continued reading. There was a great swing toward extensive free reading programs, but the traditional requirements that each pupil read critically four classics a year still hung over the literature program. The type treatment of literature was a common approach, but in the junior high school the emphasis was upon themes treated in literature.

SCIENCE. Stout indicates that three purposes determined the nature of the content of the courses in science: (1) the religious aim; (2) the knowledge aim, consisting of two points of view: the idea of truth for truth's sake, and

---

23. *Ibid.,* p. 235.

the value of science from a practical point of view; and (3) the mental-discipline aim.

The study of biology early centered upon natural history and religious explanations of the sources and variations in living things and was heavily burdened with comparative anatomy and technical terminology. Later the emphasis shifted to anatomical structure and thus to morphology. Then came the laboratory method emphasizing the lesser importance of the knowledge and the greater importance of the method (disciplinary point of view). At the last of the period studied, biology texts were combining the earlier natural-history information with the formal anatomical structure, supplemented with laboratory exercises and field trips. The same general trend is found in the courses in botany and physiology.

About 1905 a movement to eliminate so much specialization in the science courses resulted in the offering of general science. The course was not to supplant the separate science courses, but to offer an overview of science materials in the form of an orientation or beginning course. Each of the general science texts, however, stressed the author's special field of interest in science. Snyder's 1914 text was chiefly a physical geography; and Clark's was a physical science with considerable chemistry. Opinion differed regarding the purpose of general science courses. Some contended they were to help pupils find what they wanted to study further in science, some that they were an overview of all sciences, some that they were to be of intrinsic worth within themselves, and others that they were to deal with everyday household and industrial problems.

In 1930 the special courses in science—biology, chemistry, physics—still stressed knowledge; "to learn atomic weights," "to learn that metals increase their weight when heated" were typical expressions of purposes. But the emphasis had shifted somewhat to the use of knowledge in acquiring principles and making scientific generalizations. There was greater emphasis upon the study of the environment, although pupils were still required to keep notebooks of data observed as well as records of experiments. Progress toward less rigidity was probably greater in biology than in the other sciences.

SOCIAL STUDIES.   In the early part of the period under discussion, history as taught in the secondary school was largely a study of the political development and military conquests of European countries and the ancient world. This approach remained practically unchanged until the twentieth century, when there was a gradual shift in emphasis from the military and political to the economic and social life of the people. The American history course in 1930 was still largely concerned with the political character of the country's development. This same criticism is applicable to other history courses, in spite of the emphasis lately given by national committees to social and economic history. History is still an orientation course or background study for pupils.

The study of modern problems, a recent development in some schools, had not made any headway in the conventional high-school curriculum of 1930.

In civics the work at first dealt wtih interpretations of constitutions, federal and state. Nothing was done to give pupils a knowledge of the practical working of government or to help them with their own problems of citizenship. However, as the course developed it shifted its attention to a study of the local government and later to the problems of city and state government. The teaching of economics and sociology did not move much beyond the stage of presenting the factual knowledge about the structural organization of society and the economic system.

FOREIGN LANGUAGES. Evidence suggests that from 1860 to 1918 no important changes occurred in the teaching of languages, either modern or classical. Reading and writing the language were the principal objectives, achieved through a close study of syntax and through numerous exercises in turning English into the foreign language.

The National Survey indicates that courses of study in 1930 emphasized the importance of reading and interpreting the foreign language and subordinated writing and speaking the language. The observation of classes, however, showed that little change had been made in teaching the subject and that grammar and exercises were still the chief materials of instruction. Some attention was given to the social life of the people speaking the language.

In Latin the courses of study reduced the amount of grammar, provided greater variety in reading matter, stressed the relation of Latin to the English language, and considered something of the life of the Roman people. Here, too, classroom observation did not indicate that these objectives had been carried out to any appreciable extent. Emphasis was still upon word-by-word translation, vocabulary building, forms, and syntax. Since reading was set up as the chief objective, the continued teaching of grammatical forms and word understanding seemed to be essential. Similar justification was also offered for the stress upon the writing of Latin.

MUSIC AND ART. A two-year course in general music (involving singing, music reading, theory, and appreciation) was required in 1930 by most of the junior high schools covered by the National Survey. To this were added elective areas in instrumental music, glee clubs, and choruses. Many of the music selections taught were of the classical type and were frequently unsuited to the interests and abilities of the pupils studying them. Courses have changed, however, from limited training in voice, offered in the first part of the nineteenth century, to a wide range of musical opportunities.

General trends in the study of art, as shown from an examination of courses of study, indicate (1) appreciation and (2) creative self-expression. Although this is a reversal of the principal objectives at the time when art was introduced, there is still a strong tendency in spite of the stated aims to develop skills and techniques for drawing and painting. The courses are organized in logical sequence. There is also a tendency to adapt the art work of the school to the community needs, to integrate it with other subjects, and, in the large cities, to require a course in art appreciation. Art teaching has been enriched by museums, exhibits, and the radio.

Direction of Change

During these years, when America was primarily concerned with the development of the West, the expansion of industry, and the political balance between farming and commercial interests, the school was gradually changing from a narrow institution designed to educate college-bound youth to a broadly centered institution designed to develop citizens and workers as well. Still the heavy hand of tradition kept the conventional subjects in a place of pre-eminence. However, strong social forces were at work to change the curriculum to match the changes in pupil population and the newer purposes of education.

Chapter Three

The Determinants of the Curriculum

CITIZENS from abroad have difficulty in understanding the character and purposes of secondary education in the United States. Living as they have in countries where education is less valued, and thus less supported, they bring to their interpretation of American schools a concept of education which the citizens of our states have renounced. Those from abroad look at our large educational budgets, our statistical reports on school attendance, our curriculum, covering everything from Greek to fly fishing, and our many beautiful, functional school buildings. From an examination of our school system, some conclude that we may be "overdoing education." They fail to connect the prosperity and freedom in our society with the nature of our educational program. Secondary education in the United States is determined by our belief in the value of education for an industrial and democratic society, by our concepts of human growth and development, and by the organization and support of the schools. Against these backgrounds we will need to study the changes in our curriculum.

The Industrial Character of Our Society

The United States is an industrial society, highly technical in the production of goods and largely urban in its basic cultural pattern. The abundance of natural resources and the ready market created by the desires of the American citizen prompted us early to develop the machinery to fabricate raw materials into finished consumer goods. As the needs increased, inventions multiplied. Between 1880 and 1890 there were 218,000 patents issued in the United States. From 1921 to 1930 there were 442,000 issued, and a total of 1,330,000 patents were issued in the first third of the twentieth century.[1] During this period six inventions revolutionized our society—the telephone, the automobile, the airplane, the motion picture, rayon, and the radio. They not only solved problems for us, but they created many more. Probably of equal significance are those inventions which have been stimulated by war, particularly the use of radar, rockets, and atomic energy. Of equal social significance is the great progress in medicine, surgery, and public health, which has prolonged the life of man to where today the expected average life span is sixty-eight years. All of these inventions have kept society in a stage of evolution, and one does not need much vision to foresee great impacts upon our culture as we go further with such instruments as the X ray, television, photoelectric cells, and in such fields as chemical agriculture and nuclear physics.

The Factory System

With this great wave of inventions came our factory system of production, bringing with it great concentrations of population in cities, multiple-housing units, large traffic arteries, suburban living, and the borough system of government. The assembly line with its high concentration on specialization of processes changed the worker's relation to the finished product and practically destroyed the artisan. It did, however, result in much greater output of goods, in standardization, and in decreased cost of finished products. These results, together with increased wages, raised our standards of living and shortened the hours of work; and as long as goods could be distributed, prosperity and employment were increased. Assembly production did, however, greatly decrease the need for skilled workers, for machine operators can be trained quickly.

For many of the jobs in modern industry, little education or experience is required. It is estimated that in the automobile industry approximately 50 per cent of the jobs can be learned in from one to three days, and less than 5 per cent require longer than a month. About two-thirds of the jobs have no

---

1. National Resources Committee, "Technological Trends and National Policy," *House Document* No. 360, 75 Cong., 1 Sess., p. 5.

educational requirements beyond a grammar-school education.[2] With requirements such as these, there is not much the school can do for a large percentage of workers in modern industry beyond teaching them good citizenship, character, home and family living, and the nature of productive work in a technological society. Social skills become more important than direct vocational skills. Such low degree of training and experience for these jobs also create the conditions which could lead to high turnover and exploitation. The progress of labor unions in protecting the jobs of their members, however, has tended largely to offset the factor of uncertainty in unskilled employment.

Distribution of the Labor Force

In 1850 there were 7.5 million workers, in 1950 there were 57.5, and by 1960 it is estimated that there will be 60 million. Chart I shows the distribution of the labor force.

In 1870, 51 per cent of the workers were employed in agriculture and forestry, 24 per cent in mining and manufacturing, 10 per cent in trade and transportation, and 15 per cent in clerical and other services. In 1940 these figures had become 19, 31, 25, and 25 per cent, respectively.

In 1900 there were 6 million farm dwelling units; in 1940, there were 7.5 million. In 1900 there were 4 million rural nonfarm units; in 1940 there were 8 million. In 1900 there were 8 million urban dwelling units, in 1940 there were 22 million.

Increased Productivity

Marked shifts have been made in the source of productive power. In 1850 the sources of productive power were as follows: 15 per cent men, 79 per cent animals, 6 per cent machines. In 1930 it was 4 per cent men, 12 per cent animals, and 84 per cent machines. By 1960 it is predicted it will be 3 per cent men, 1 per cent animals, and 96 per cent machines. This productive power in 1850 produced $0.27 per man-hour of goods, in 1930, $0.82 and in 1960 the estimate is $1.61. With this great increase the total national income in 1850 was 7.3 billion dollars, in 1950, it was 165.4 billion dollars, and it is estimated at 190.3 billions in 1960 (these figures are all in terms of 1947 dollars). Our wartime production in 1944 was 198.7 billion dollars.[3]

---

2. For a complete treatise on the topics discussed in this section together with their educational implications, see Newton Edwards and Herman G. Richey, *The School in the American Social Order* (Boston: Houghton Mifflin Company, 1947), Chaps. 11–15.

3. Figures quoted above on the labor force and productivity are taken from Thomas R. Carskadon and Rudolf Modley. *U.S.A. Measure of a Nation; A Graphic Presentation of America's Needs and Resources* (Twentieth Century Fund; New York: The Macmillan Company, 1949), which is a summary of a very extensive analysis by J. Frederic Dewhurst and Associates, *America's Needs and Resources* (Twentieth Century Fund; New York: The Macmillan Company, 1947).

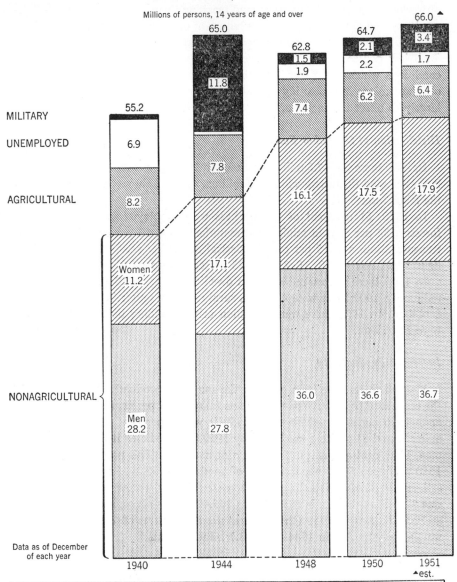

THE LABOR FORCE
UNITED STATES, 1940 - 1951*

Millions of persons, 14 years of age and over

MILITARY

UNEMPLOYED

AGRICULTURAL

NONAGRICULTURAL

Data as of December
of each year

1940   1944   1948   1950   1951
                                 ▴est.

| With defense expenditures currently estimated at a rate of 45 billion dollars per year, employment stands at record levels. There were some 54.6 million working in nonagricultural jobs in December, 1951, compared with 45 million in | 1944. Government experts estimate that non-agricultural employment at the end of 1952 will be just under 56 million. SOURCES: Bureau of the Census; Bureau of Labor Statistics. |

The Conference Board, 247 Park Avenue, New York 17, N. Y.

The per cent of change in hourly earnings, output per man-hour, and unit labor cost in manufacturing industries is significant. From 1923 to 1935 the average hourly earnings in iron and steel increased 9.9 per cent, the output per man-hour rose 48.2 per cent and the unit labor cost decreased 20.0 per cent. During the same years in the rubber products industry the average hourly earnings increased 28.0 per cent, the output per man-hour increased 79.6 per cent, and the unit labor cost decreased 32.2 per cent.[4] Thus the production per man-hour in American industries has increased greatly, wages have increased less, and the unit cost has fallen markedly. This has provided more goods at less cost.

These improved methods of production have provided both more leisure time and more goods for workers. Between 1890 and 1950 the average work week of factory workers decreased from 60 to 40 hours, in railroads from 60 to 44, in anthracite and bituminous coal mining from 60 to 35.[5]

In 1940 the equipment in American homes was as follows:

HOUSEHOLD EQUIPMENT, 1940*

Item of Equipment	Percentage with it	Percentage without it
Electric lights	78	22
Mechanical refrigeration	45	55
Gas or electric cooking	55	45
Running water	70	30
Private bath	55	45
Private flush toilet	60	40
Central heating	42	58
Radio	82	18

* Thomas R. Carskadon and Rudolf Modley. *U.S.A. Measure of a Nation* (Twentieth Century Fund; New York: The Macmillan Company, 1949), adapted from diagram on p. 35.

Dependency in Employment

Another result of technology is the great increase in the number of people who are dependent upon some employer for a livelihood. Government, business, and industry employ the majority of wage earners. The family income and stability are dependent largely upon social and economic factors beyond the control of the worker. They depend upon domestic and foreign relationships, war and peace, continued purchasing power and free flow of markets, govern-

4. Temporary National Economic Committee, *Technology in Our Economy* (Investigation of Concentration of Economic Power, Monograph No. 22; Washington: Government Printing Office, 1941).
5. *Ibid.*, p. 167.

ment controls, and a number of major economic conditions. Such dependence has produced feelings of insecurity in the worker and has led to the strong labor unions, a government security system, unemployment insurance, and other protective measures for the worker. During the depression following World War I, the government provided public employment and relief for vast numbers of workers. Stability of income is essential if the country is to remain prosperous and the worker remain solvent. Private industry provides the bulk of positions during stable economic periods, supplemented by government employment for the normal activities of state; but during periods of considerable private unemployment, the government has increased its assistance by providing work above that required normally.

Industrial Management

A characteristic of American industry is absentee ownership. Factories managed by employed directors working under boards elected by a small number of investors are typical of American industrial organization. Management has thus become a profession, and large numbers of positions of various levels of power and responsibility have been created. Some of these are highly technical, requiring an extended amount of education; while others require administrative or personnel skills gained largely through judgment and experience. The increasing number of these positions, together with the greater amount of training required for success in them, have added materially to the amount of education pursued by youth ambitious in these fields. The content of educational courses has also been materially altered.

During the past fifty years, organized labor has exerted increasing pressure upon management to improve working conditions, increase wages, and provide pensions and insurance against accidents and illness. Labor has also asked for a share in the formation of managerial policies. Many of their demands have resulted in direct gains from the industries themselves, but labor has also sought to influence industrial policies through government control and through direct legislation of benefits. Organized labor has gone into politics to secure gains which cannot be secured directly from industry or which are the natural prerogative of government. As a result of greater income and stability, workers are therefore able to place their youth in school in large numbers, holding them there until they have graduated from high school, and many of them have pursued higher education.

The Problem of Natural Resources

In recent years the problem of the wise use of natural resources has received increasing recognition. During the nineteenth century the policy of "grab it first" was the characteristic method of developing resources. Naturally, it led to the rapid depletion of resources and to enormous waste in production methods. When there is plenty, people are careless. But when we reach the point where timber is being removed faster than it is being restored, where streams are polluted to save cost in discharging wastes, and where enormous quantities of soil are being lost through erosion and floods, it then becomes necessary to pay more attention to conserving our natural resources. War has also caused us to take a greater interest in the intelligent use of our resources.

The work of the agricultural and forestry agencies, both federal and state, and that of many voluntary organizations, in addition to legal restrictions and war demands, have made us conscious of the need for conservation. As a people we are beginning to realize that with proper use and intelligent planning the resources of the land can be made available to all. There are issues of ownership, regulation, and control, as well as issues of education, involved in these problems.

American schools have become greatly interested in teaching about the wise utilization of our natural resources. From the elementary schools through college, the ways and means of conservation are taught. The federal government has also aided conservation by reclaiming wasteland, requiring the application of selective cutting of timber to sustain yields, draining swamps, constructing dams and irrigation systems, and creating large-scale plans for such areas as the Tennessee Valley, the Central Valley in California, and the Columbia River Basin. Important needs still are unmet, and education has a major service to render in the conservation of our basic resources.

The Political Character of Our Society

The American theory of democratic government rests upon certain fundamental beliefs. Chief among them are

1. The value of each individual human is of supreme importance and that each must respect the worth and dignity of each other person.
2. Individual development—moral and intellectual—proceeds best in a favorable environment, and that certain freedoms are guaranteed men to insure the maximum of individual achievement.
3. Individuals differ in abilities and beliefs; that there is a place for each person; and that respect for differences must be encouraged.
4. Man is capable of self-government, and government is created by men to serve them.
5. Education is basic to free popular government.

Emphasis on the Individual

Much has been written on the worth and dignity of the individual. Even though the meanings and implications of it for social behavior have been but vaguely understood, all people consider it a fundamental of our way of life. The concept is deeply rooted in Hebraic-Christian ethics, and the church has sought to teach and explain it, while the state has acted to protect it in civil affairs. The principle has been applied to prevent industrial exploitation, to permit freedom of expression, to ensure fair trial and punishment for offenses, and to further social justice and educational opportunities for all races and abilities. It has even been at the base of regulations and laws relating to the conduct of warfare.

Throughout our history, the people of the United States have placed great confidence in individual development. Some have contended that if all men were honest and well meaning we would have no worries about group behavior. At one period so much emphasis was placed upon individual interest and needs in education that we tended to lose sight of the social function of education. We have feared uniformity because it would neglect individual differences and expressions. However, today we tend to equalize the emphasis upon personal and group development, especially since sociologists and psychiatrists have pointed clearly to the fact that individual behavior is largely conditioned by the structure, mores, and approval of social groups. Men tend to do what is expected of them.

Community Contacts and Behavior

Human behavior is influenced by the environment. Students of adolescent behavior have sought to determine the forces that play upon youth and the effect of these forces in the building of behavioral characteristics. Typical of studies made on this subject is the one by Hollingshead of a Midwestern community. After carefully analyzing the social behavior of 735 high-school-aged adolescents, he concluded:

> Adolescent behavior is a complex response to a series of definitions the child has learned in the family, the play group, and the school which have varying degrees of relevancy in recurrent and new social situations to which he has to adjust. Situations which children face daily are defined in a general way by the communal, the class, and the family cultures, but they are defined explicity by the clique in which a child plays. Within the clique, definitions are placed on situations which influence the child's behavior in that situation. The adjustments he makes to these definitions appear to be determined by the meaning each has for him, in relation to the others, as it applies in the situation of the moment. The effective definition that he follows appears to be more closely related to the definitions other children place upon the situation, at least which he thinks the others think, than it is to definitions his parents, teachers, ministers, police, and other adults place upon it. Therefore, the specific behavior traits exhibited by adolescents tend to be along lines approved by their clique mates, who also tend to be members of the same class.

The definition the child thinks his associates place upon the behavior demanded of him cannot be ignored, nor should it be separated from the complex, for the social situation the child participates in is a shared experience, and the definition placed upon it is shared generally by the participants. Moreover, the form it takes is often a response to what the group has learned previously, in similar situations. Thus, past learning is redefined, when necessary, to fit the present. This process results in the constant projection of past learning into the present, the adolescent's present behavior being an adjustment to past learning interpreted in terms of the demands of the moment.[6]

These conclusions were confirmed in a more specific study, in a similar community, of adolescent character and personality. Havighurst and Taba found the high school to be the major social influence on sixteen-year-old youth:

> The adolescent who has a good relationship to the social environment, as constituted by the high school, is the one who enjoys good character reputation. The majority of young people in Prairie City try to live up to the standards and expectations of the school. For this, they are rewarded by the approval of most of their age mates, their teachers, and most of the adults of the community. Their behavior in the school environment tends to be honest, responsible, morally courageous, loyal, and friendly, because they are rewarded for this behavior. . . .
>
> Those boys and girls with low reputations came largely from certain lower-class homes which have not supported the values of the school. Where the home is at odds with the school, the child's behavior and reputation are usually unsatisfactory. This is true of two groups . . . the out-of-school group and the unadjusted group in school. The actions of members of these groups will in general be irresponsible, unfriendly, disloyal, and even dishonest in relation to the school's values . . .
>
> All the evidence from both group studies and the studies of individuals points to the strategic importance of the school in the lives of the adolescents of Prairie City. The school, for certain individuals at least, makes up for shortcomings in other areas of the social environment.[7]

It is clear that much of the development of an individual is dependent upon the social conditions and pressures under which he lives.

His health depends largely upon the care the community uses to protect him from disease, as well as upon the availability of skillful medical care and upon an income that enables him to live and eat well.

His morality develops with the contacts he has with spiritual ideals, with the prestige value a community places upon honesty or integrity or conformity

---

6. August B. Hollingshead, *Elmtown's Youth* (New York: John Wiley & Sons, Inc., 1949), pp. 445–446.

7. Robert J. Havighurst and Hilda Taba, *Adolescent Character and Personality* (New York: John Wiley & Sons, Inc., 1949), p. 181.

to the moral code, and with the beliefs and actions of his closest associates. If society accepts graft, he soon learns it is to his advantage to engage in it. If his friends approve his sharp practices and acclaim his success for being a slightly dishonest trader, he continues those practices. If ownership of an automobile is essential for status in high school, the youth will press for it and if necessary steal to get it. Thus acceptance of behavioral patterns in a community is an important factor in the determination of conduct.[8]

Individuals also thrive or rebel in those environments which enable them to be treated according to their abilities and ambitions without prejudicial restrictions imposed because of race or color or creed or belief. Where a group depresses an individual by singling him out for special treatment because he is a Negro or a Jew, or a Pole or a Protestant, he builds quickly those defenses he needs for security. Some will fight, some will move to new territories, some will retaliate with violence, some will work through established channels for justice, and some will deteriorate mentally and spiritually. One of the tenets of democracy, therefore, which ensures social stability is equal treatment of all people in accordance with their abilities and accomplishments.

Finally, growth and development are enriched when men live in an environment of freedom—freedoms which release men's minds to search for truth, to experiment, to differ in theory and practice. Many times in our history men have given their "last full measure of devotion" to protect these freedoms. Whenever the organized and disciplined party replaces the free and voluntary organization of people of kindred minds, freedom has been lost. Whenever men fear or experience reprisal for their expression, freedom is gone. When men become impatient with differences, suspicious of those who disagree with them, or judge people on the basis of unfounded or unproved evidence, then the nation has moved from the pole of freedom toward the pole of dictatorship. This is especially significant for education, for from time immemorial it has been the youth who have provided dictators with the force to overthrow governments and established regimes. The school has no higher obligation than to give to the young the knowledge and attitudes necessary for free men.

In early American education only those individuals who clearly showed

---

8. A number of studies substantiate this general idea of the relation of social class to behavior. Among them are Robert S. and Helen Merrill Lynd, *Middletown* (New York: Harcourt, Brace and Company, 1929) and *Middletown in Transition* (New York: Harcourt, Brace and Company, 1937); W. Lloyd Warner and Paul S. Lunt, *The Social Life of a Modern Community* (New Haven: Yale University Press, 1941) and subsequent volumes in the Yankee City Series; Allison Davis, Burleigh B. Gardner, and Mary S. Gardner, *Deep South* (Chicago: University of Chicago, Press, 1941); Allison Davis and John Dollard, *Children of Bondage* (Washington: American Council on Education, 1940); James West, *Plainville, U.S.A.* (New York: Columbia University Press, 1945); W. Lloyd Warner, *Democracy in Jonesville* (New York: Harper & Brothers, 1949); W. Lloyd Warner, Robert J. Havighurst, and Martin B. Loeb, *Who Shall Be Educated?* (New York: Harper & Brothers, 1944).

ability to enter professional life were educated beyond the elementary school. With the expansion of educational facilities and with the general acceptance of all youth into high school, youth of great differences in purpose, energy, abilities, and desires entered school. Obviously, the curriculum and processes of instruction had to change, but for many years teachers expected all pupils to pursue the same content, differing chiefly in the amount they were able to cover in a period of time. Psychological studies have demonstrated that youth differ in quality and insight, in speed and degree of comprehension, and in depth of perception. Educational practices, therefore, have tended to recognize these differences and to provide appropriate opportunities for all youth to achieve success in those things which are in harmony with their abilities and interests. Nothing is gained by trying to make uniform the programs of education or by trying to standardize the speed of acquiring learning; quite to the contrary, psychologists have demonstrated that definite harm is done to individuals when these differences are ignored.

Education for Self-Government

One of the great skepticisms advanced by those opposed to democracy is that men are incapable of governing themselves. Friends of Thomas Jefferson often gave him examples of men's mistakes and reasoned that these argued against their ability to govern themselves. Fortunately for democracy, Jefferson argued that these illustrations only proved men's inexperience and need for more education. Truly, self-government depends upon education just as much as it does upon a constitution and sets of laws, for no laws are stronger than the will of the people to obey and support them. One of the striking contrasts between America and other countries in the world is the great lack of interest in government among the masses of people in those countries where few people are educated. Popular government rests first upon knowledge. Without it people have no basis for choice, and democracy means that choice is in the hands of the people. It rests second upon the will to participate, and unless men exercise their right of choice the effects of democracy are vitiated. It rests in the third place upon maintenance of the power to change. A dictatorship cannot be changed by the people except through revolution, but a vital democracy will sustain those who serve it faithfully and remove from office quickly those who are incompetent or unjust.

Education is an investment by the state and it attains its greatest stature when it educates boys and girls to be competent and willing to discharge the responsibilities of popular government. Our youth must be taught at all times to guard against men becoming subservient to government; government is the work of men who by popular consent codify the opinions of the governed, and enforce them upon the willfully negligent. In a free country men do not resist crimes because it is against the law, but because it is contrary to the general welfare. Democratic government also seeks to guarantee to all equal justice and equality of opportunity.

A significant and provocative statement on the relation of education to American democracy was made recently by Robert M. Hutchins. He said:

> The foundation of democracy is universal suffrage. Universal suffrage makes every man a ruler. If every man is a ruler, every man needs the education that rulers ought to have. If liberal education is the education of rulers, then every man needs a liberal education. . . .
>
> Where we get into trouble is that the kind of education we accept now when everybody is destined to rule is fundamentally an extension of the kind that in Jefferson's time was thought suitable for those destined to labor but not to rule. When we talk of our political goals, we admit the right of every man to be a ruler. When we talk of our educational program, we see no inconsistency in saying that only a few have the capacity to get the education that rulers ought to have. The popular syllogism—and it is popular in the highest educational circles—runs like this: everybody has the right to education. But only a few are qualified for a good education. Those who are not qualified for a good education must be given a bad education, because everybody has the right to education. Anybody who favors a good education must, therefore, be antidemocratic, because only a few are qualified for a good education.
>
> If the main purpose of a democratic educational system is the education of rulers, then everything that does not contribute to the achievement of that purpose must be excluded, or at least postponed until that purpose has been achieved.
>
> I embrace the radical and democratic idea of liberal education for all. I reject the notion that some of our rulers are incapable of being educated for their task of ruling. I insist that, if some of them act as though they were incapable, it is because we have not found out how to teach them, not because they cannot learn.
>
> Liberal education in a society built on slavery was the education of free men. In a society divided into a class that ruled and a class that was ruled it was education of the ruling class. Liberal education was an aristocratic education. It was so because the society in which it was developed was aristocratic. When society becomes democratic, should the citizens have the education of free men or the education of slaves? Should they have the education of the ruling class or of the class that was to be ruled?
>
> The way to determine who is to have a liberal education is to ask who are to be the rulers of your society. If the answer is everybody, then the conclusion follows that everybody is to have a liberal education. If you do not like this conclusion, you do not like democracy; you do not like universal suffrage. The one thing you cannot do is to say that at one and the same time everybody has the right to vote and only the few have the right to a liberal education.
>
> The slogan "Education for All" cannot mean merely that all young people must go to school. It cannot mean that the educational system has

done its duty if everybody is in school up to the age of twenty, regardless of what he is doing there. Education for all, if it means anything, must mean that everybody is to be educated.[9]

If education is to prepare our youth for self-government, it must deal with the factors involved in our society, as well as make clear the nature and function of the social institutions which serve men. Social groups and group processes, institutions for the protection of citizens—their person, their health, their rights, their freedom; institutions which educate them—the home, the church, and all others which contribute to their welfare must all be understood. Modern social life is a fabric of many patterns, and the thread of government runs through every pattern.[10]

From Isolationism to Internationalism

Early in our national history America decided to stay out of "entangling alliances" with foreign countries. We reasoned that we could run our own domestic affairs without becoming embroiled in the constant quarrels and wars characteristic of other countries. Upon this logic we developed a theory of isolationism and of America for Americans. We abused the theory when it came to foreign trade but held to it rather strictly when it came to helping another country drive out a tyrant. This philosophy largely characterized our foreign policy until World War I, when we started by remaining neutral, then sold implements of war, then sympathized, later took sides, and finally entered the war as an active belligerent. Even then we had little intention of participating in European affairs. We thought more of making the world "safe for democracy" and keeping invasion from our shores.

After the war we again left Europe largely to her own ways and returned home to enjoy our own democracy and to revive our campaign for greater prosperity, temporarily delayed by the war. But European affairs worsened and Hitler came to power. On our right flank, as it were, a threatening fire broke out, and we had the choice of joining to put it out on our neighbors lot or wait until it had engaged our own house. On our left flank another fire broke out by actually striking our own land. We became engaged in another world war, which some believed might have been avoided had we been more active in reorganizing Europe after World War I. Nevertheless, we fought by the side

---

9. Robert M. Hutchins, "Education and Democracy," *School and Society,* 69:425–428, 1949. For a critical analysis of Hutchin's position, see John A. Childs, *Education and Morals,* especially Chap. 5, "The Alternatives of Classical Humanism" (New York: Appleton-Century-Crofts, 1950).

10. For an interesting and valuable treatment of freedom and education, see Educational Policies Commission, *The Education of Free Men in American Democracy* (Washington: National Education Association, 1941).

of our Allies and sent our American boys throughout the world to recapture countries taken by our enemies, countries which were not ours.

Following World War II we changed our foreign policy to where we decided definitely to participate in the affairs of other countries. We came to this conclusion largely for two reasons: (1) We concluded that our own future interests lay in keeping other countries prosperous and able to resist aggression. (2) We concluded that Russian communism must be confined to Soviet Russia.

Toward World Leadership

At the close of the war Europe was in an exhausted economic condition. During this period of conflict the United States changed again from a debtor to a creditor nation, and nearly every country in the world owed more money than it could repay within several generations. Greece was starving, so were Italy and France, and England had lost most of her former resources which made her prosperous. The Allied nations and Russia divided Germany into four zones, each controlled by a nation, and in different ways and degrees were forced to rehabilitate their territory. The United States realized that if these European countries were economically destitute they would soon become political liabilities, would likely be taken over by the Communists, and would become our enemies. If the free world was to be saved, Europe must be made strong. As a result the United States engaged in technical assistance programs, the Marshall Plan, the Economic Cooperation Administration (ECA), and later on mutual-defense pacts, such as the North Atlantic Pact, for the defense of Europe against communism.

The same conditions existed in the Far East. There we occupied Japan and completely controlled her economic, educational, and political life until the signing of the peace treaty in the summer of 1951. We vacillated in our policy on China, finally losing her to the Communists; we freed the Philippines, encouraged the Indonesians against aggression, and supported Formosa.

In addition to aiding foreign countries we began to strengthen our own military defenses and work actively for peace and international understanding through the United Nations. We also contributed the major financing to United Nations Educational, Scientific, and Cultural Organization (UNESCO).

All these activities drew us into a position of world leadership and into alliances, loans, gifts, and negotiations with every major country in the world.

Internationalism and Education

Education has been greatly affected by this sudden shift in the foreign policy of the United States. It has led to placing much material into the secondary school on activities in other countries, on the United Nations, and on UNESCO. For the first time in our history, some colleges have begun to require courses in world affairs. Adult groups under the public schools and under many organizations set up to promote the study of world affairs have enlisted large numbers of adults to discuss international problems.[11] Never before have magazines, newspapers, and the radio given as much time and space to world affairs, and the people in the United States even though still uninformed to a considerable extent have a better knowledge of the world and its people today than ever before. The schools have a great responsibility in helping youth and adults to understand other people and their problems and in helping the American people to become able to make foreign policy more intelligently. This policy will inevitably be broad enough to cover technical advice, political leadership, and economic assistance. Attention will also have to be given to solving the problem of the intelligent use of atomic energy.[12]

Organization and Control of the School

The organization and control of the American secondary school, as well as the social character of our society, affects the nature of the curriculum.

Cosmopolitan High Schools

The American people desire to maintain large cosmopolitan high schools. Not much support has been given to a dual system of mass public education. The very idea of the separation of one group of youth into a trade school and another into academic high schools has received little support, tending, most parents believe, to represent undemocratic segregation.

Public sentiment in this regard, together with the increasing numbers attending school, makes the curriculum problem a difficult one, just as the aim of preparation for life complicates the selection of desirable learning experiences. Everybody needs to have experience with a common core of basic problems designed to enable him to participate successfully in a democratic society. This residuum is for all pupils alike regardless of the economic class

11. Notably among these are the Foreign Policy Association and the World Affairs Councils of Northern California and of Cleveland.
12. For further development of this problem, see Educational Policies Commission, *American Education and International Tensions* (Washington: National Education Association, 1949) ; studies by the Commission on International Relations, National Education Association; studies by the Association of Supervision and Curriculum Development, National Education Association; and National Council for the Social Studies, *Education for International Understanding in American Schools* (Washington: National Education Association, 1948).

from which they come. Paralleling this there needs to be developed the special interests of each for all sorts of purposes—individual development, vocational purposes (whether college or immediate), and leisure pursuits. What shall be this common core? What shall determine the special offerings? Shall differentiations in either or both be made on the basis of differences in backgrounds, interests, and abilities? The intelligence-test movement and its corollary—ability grouping—ran headlong into these social and pedagogical issues.

This desire for a large unified high school is also being recognized in the rural areas of America, where provisions are being made for consolidated or union high-school districts. In these districts a single high school will serve a large territory, will be cosmopolitan in character, and will be large enough to offer a variety of subjects, provide some vocational preparation, and, in many instances, serve the adults in the area. It is very difficult, indeed, to offer in a small rural high school the breadth of curriculum program that should be given to the boys and girls. Our large, rural, union or consolidated high schools are very similar in many respects to the cosmopolitan high school in the cities. They offer the basic core of experiences common to all and usually offer a carefully selected list of electives suited more or less to the needs of the pupils in the surrounding area. There is a marked contrast between these schools and the vast number of small high schools running from 75 to 150 in enrollment. In these smaller schools, the basic core of experiences usually becomes the college entrance requirements, since it is impossible to offer college requirements and at the same time enrich the offerings with very many electives, or to offer two-track plans, one for those going to college and one for those who plan to leave formal schooling at the end of high school. The problem of differentiation becomes more crucial as the size of the school decreases.

Coeducational High Schools

Another aspect of this problem is the coeducation movement to which America is committed. Traditionally, the curriculum in the high school has been essentially a boys' curriculum, being in the main only a diluted version of the subjects offered in boys' universities, plus some training for business and industry. With the large influx of girls into high school, little change was made in the curriculum beyond the addition of a few courses for them. Both boys and girls were thrown into the same courses on the assumption that the material was equally appropriate for both. The problem now becomes one of supplying educative experiences in recognition of the function each of the sexes is to serve in a society such as ours. This applies equally to basic and elective areas, for even our elective areas today, in the main, operate on the assumption that both boys and girls can elect with equal profit from the fields of mathematics, languages, science, and history. Sex differences are not great enough to require separate and distinct curricula. Similarities are far greater than differences between the sexes, but more careful thought needs to be given to selecting material common to the sexes and special material of relatively different worth to boys and girls.

Compulsory Attendance

Another movement of importance is the demand for compulsory attendance of pupils through the secondary school. Writing into the statutes the idea that the welfare of the state depends upon an educated citizenry, we have forced every parent to send his child to school until the child is fourteen, sixteen, or eighteen, depending upon the state in which he lives. The very tone of this law carries with it two implications: (1) that the school will provide experiences which will fit all youth for effective citizenship, experiences which they could not secure outside of school; and (2) that they would not choose these experiences voluntarily. The result of the legislation has been to enlarge the high-school population tremendously. This has meant added expenditure for staff, buildings, and equipment, but the most significant aspect of the law is its pressure upon the curriculum.

On reflection it seems obvious that one cannot do the same thing for a large heterogenous mass of pupils that one can for a small homogeneous group of capable, college-bound boys. The change in the character of the school population should have precipitated an immediate and long-term study of the thorough reorganization needed in the curriculum content of the secondary school. But this reorganization should have stemmed from the determination of a basic social theory of the society from which these youth come and into which they are going and of the differences in content and method which should prevail in a changed school population. But, like the report of the Commission on the Reorganization of Secondary Education and those of a number of special-subject commissions, the proposals were either in terms of subject shifts or in terms of vague generalizations.

We have no right to force youth to spend time in an institution unsuited to their interests, needs, or capacities, doing things which cause them failure and frustration. Many studies have shown the tremendous load of failures and the high rate of elimination from the high school,[13] and their criticisms have again

---

13. See especially L. V. Koos, *The American Schools* (Boston: Ginn and Company, 1927), pp. 114–146; L. V. Koos, J. M. Hughes, P. W. Hutson, and W. C. Reavis, *Administering the Secondary School* (New York: American Book Company, 1940), Chap. 6; G. N. Kefauver, V. C. Noll, and C. E. Drake, *Secondary School Population* (U.S. Office of Education, National Survey of Secondary Education, Monograph No. 4; Washington: Government Printing Office, 1932).

For recent studies of this problem see Harold J. Dillon, *Early School Leavers* (New York: National Child Labor Committee, 1949); Walter H. Gaumnitz and Ellsworth Tompkins, *Holding Power and Size of High Schools* (U.S. Office of Education, Circular

been met largely by a little less of the same subject matter or a little more time to do what others do in less time, or passing with less proficiency, all of which have been accompanied by the cry of lowering standards. When youth are forced to do what fails to improve them, neither democracy nor its future citizens are served. The influx into our high school of masses of youth should give us grave concern and should launch us into a basic program of curriculum reorganization.

Teachers and Administrators

Secondary education has reflected the motives and ideals of the dominant social class in our society. The American secondary school was established, maintained, and controlled under the watchful eye of the clergy and their most faithful communicants. Under the Jeffersonian and Jacksonian democracy of agrarianism it slipped into the hands of the farmers, who in turn had it seized from them by the rising industrial, commercial, and professional middle class, which became the dominant political and economic class of wealth and power, running the factories and banks and fashioning everything in society to its liking. In spite of the struggle for control since this seizure during the latter half of the nineteenth century—a struggle between business and labor and rural interests—the school is still under the dominance of this economically powerful group.

The teachers and administrators, of course, have exercised a large measure of control over the school program and they, as a general rule, come from the middle class and tend to be conservative. Martin makes a significant characterization of the profession when he says:

> The profession of teaching tends to make men conservative. The necessities of instruction compel the teacher to reverence what is known, what is fixed, and to be suspicious of the untried. Occupied in restraining the eccentricities and vagaries of childhood, his first instinct is to oppose the new as visionary and fantastic.[14]

In spite of the fact that the statement, by its very nature, is dated in some respects, by and large the characterization seems to be as true today as when it was written. We are in a cycle in this matter. We select capable people to go to college to learn the story of civilization to become fit to teach and then

No. 322; Washington: Government Printing Office, 1950); James E. Nancarrow, "Reducing Drop-Outs," *Bulletin,* National Association Secondary School Principals, 34:183–188, 1950; Working Conference on Life Adjustment Education, *Why Do Boys and Girls Drop Out of School and What Can We Do about It?* (U.S. Office of Education, Circular No. 269; Washington: Government Printing Office, 1950).

14. George H. Martin. *The Evolution of the Massachusetts Public School System* (New York: Appleton-Century-Crofts, Inc., 1897), pp. 83–84. By permission of the publishers.

send them into the school to teach what they have learned. Conservatism lays a heavy hand upon the high school through this technique.

Power of the School Board

But more significant than teachers and administrators in the control of education is the school board, for it largely reflects the major interests of the community in the program of the local school. Who composes the school board? Counts made a study of 1,654 county, city, district, state, and university boards of education in 1920 and in 1926.[15] In age, the members of the public school boards average 48.3 years. Seventy-six per cent of the city board memberships were drawn from the upper economic classes—managerial, professional, and commercial people—and 8 per cent from laboring groups. State boards of education drew 73 per cent of their membership from these upper groups, 2 per cent from agriculture, and none from labor. Only in the rural areas was there a heavy representation from agricultural groups, and nowhere was labor represented above 8 per cent. In cities where 60 per cent of the people were of the laboring class, only 8 per cent of the board represented this group.

In 1946 the Research Division of the National Education Association studied the composition and work of school boards in 3,068 school districts.[16] They found that 90 per cent of the board members were men and 10 per cent women; that the median age was 48.5 years; that the median personal income was $3,978 (in 1946), ranging from $2,067 in small rural boards to $7,516 in cities over 100,000. The educational history of these board members showed that 30 per cent were college graduates, 42 per cent high-school graduates, and 28 per cent had not finished high school. Board members still come from the upper-middle-class social levels.[17]

Regardless of the argument that a board of business and professional men is supposed to supply familiarity and efficiency, there is little support for the idea that any one group can completely represent a cross section of the interests of a community. Nevertheless, urban, commercial, and professional groups are dominating the policy-forming bodies of public education. Counts

---

15. George S. Counts, *The Social Composition of Boards of Education* (University of Chicago, Supplementary Education Monographs, No. 33; Chicago: University of Chicago Press, 1927).

16. *Status and Practices of Boards of Education* (National Education Association, *Research Bulletin,* Vol. 24, No. 2, April 1946).

17. For additional information of schools boards, see *School Boards in Action* (Twenty-fourth Yearbook of American Association of School Administrators; Washington: National Education Association, 1946). See also Daniel R. Davies and Fred W. Hosler, *The Challenge of School Board Membership* (New York: Chartwell House, Inc., 1949); Florence Campbell Porter, *Manual for School Board Members* (Bakersfield, Calif.: California School Trustees Associations. 1950), Book II.

considers this significant because of the difficulty we have in transcending the limits of our own experience, but he states further that

> a dominant class is a privileged class, a class that is favored by the existing social arrangement. It therefore tends to be conservative, to exaggerate the merits of the prevailing order, and to fear any agitation favoring fundamental changes in the social structure. It represents the past rather than the future; its creative period lies in a preceding age; its genius has already found expression.[18]

The matter of the control of education, a matter of change from clergy to farmer to professional man to industrialist and banker and then to the middle class in America, is coincident with the struggle for power over the social forces of our civilization. It is significant for the curriculum because the controlling group holds in its hands the power to sanction or disapprove the fundamental reorganization of the content of the secondary curriculum. It is not likely to approve the introduction of materials fundamentally criticizing or even analyzing carefully the difficulties of the existing social order. Neither is it likely to permit the school to assume leadership in any area of public importance which has not at least been approved by a majority of the people in power. This group will tend to be more hospitable to the innocuous reorganization of existing subjects than to any basic study of the needs of education for an industrial society. It will work to retain the academic subjects and to stress the teaching of skills and conventional ideas.

Public Tax Support

Another factor in determining the curriculum is public tax support. After the policy of public support for education had been established, people began to require free education for their children and expected to pay for it through increased taxes. In recent years school costs have increased greatly due to four factors: (1) the increased number attending schools; (2) the extension upward of free public education beyond high school; (3) the increased facilities offered youth in school; and (4) the increase in costs due to inflation and better salaries for teachers. As these costs have increased, greater attention has been paid to taxes for schools by legislators, supervisors, tax leagues, various business groups, and the average citizen. The schools have come in for criticism and in some places have been forced to curtail their services.

Those supporting education have in certain communities sought to curtail the range of curricular offerings, dictate the nature of the content, and prescribe the methods of teaching. Pressure groups and influential citizens exercise controls over the curriculum of the high school, and it is not likely that they

---

18. George S. Counts, *op. cit.*, pp. 91–92.

will support any curriculum which challenges the conventional economic pattern.

Textbooks

A final factor in the organization and control of the school is the effect of the textbooks on the curriculum. In the early secondary school the textbooks were practically the sole source of curriculum content, since teachers confined themselves almost exclusively to them. Then teachers became better educated and began to depart from their former adherence to textbooks. Courses of study were written which called for several sources, but still today pupils in our secondary schools rely largely upon textbooks, basic and supplementary, for most of the content discussed in school courses.

Textbooks are printed by companies that seek to earn profits by their sale. Therefore, they of necessity must be approved by the majority of teachers, and this majority tends to be conservative. Those companies that have pioneered have had difficulty in selling their books, by and large. Furthermore, many of the high-school texts are written by college professors seeking to supplement their meager incomes. In general, therefore, textbooks by the very nature of their preparation and sale have to be reasonably conservative, and in many instances tend to retard curricular innovations. Furthermore, the dearth of printed materials dealing with modern curriculum concepts has tended to discourage curriculum workers from including them in curriculum studies. However, it is obvious that when teachers develop their thinking to where they will select improved textbooks, such books will be printed.

Public Opinion

Education is a social process and is affected by the primary forces which control our society. If changes are to be made, they must be made within the framework of a democratic society, and such changes will inevitably be slow and will be made with public approval.

Chapter Four

Conflicting Educational Theories

S CHOOLS, like people, differ. They tend to take on the individuality of the people who design and administer them, and each one doubtless has some distinctive feature of its own. Some tend to be more rigid than others; some lean toward large amounts of freedom. Many have quite rigid requirements; a few depend upon pupils for assistance in developing the curriculum. And so it goes. It is obvious, however, that in spite of the individuality that local schools may possess, they are all drawing upon a more or less common storehouse of conflicting points of view regarding the purpose and nature of education. This common storehouse comes from philosophers and psychologists, curriculum workers, teachers and administrators, scientists, businessmen, politicians, and parents.

Differences in Classroom Practices

Teachers differ widely in the way they teach. Some teachers feel that the pupil should have no part in planning or organizing learning experiences;

others feel there may be occasional opportunities where the pupil should take an active part in planning some aspect of the lesson; still others feel the need for pupil participation strongly enough to make more than accidental provision for it. There are some who want to separate drill from social learnings and are willing to have pupils become active participants in the latter if they will be obedient learners in the former. There are those who are willing to discard all these notions and support the contention that all learning comes about through active experience in planning and executing activities. Some prefer to have a reasonable amount of adult guidance, while others hold to the idea that the learner develops only through his own initiated activity. In general, teachers may be divided into three groups:

1. Those who demand the mastery of previously planned subject matter and are willing to permit more or less pupil activity for the sake of facilitating this learning
2. Those who want to divide the work of the school into two groups—drill and social learning—and want to formalize one and liberalize the other
3. Those who demand that there be a unity in all learning and that it grow out of active experience

These basic differences in belief produce differences in practice, organization, curriculum, and administration. A look at administrative aspects of different schools will point up the implications of different philosophies.

Differences in Administrative Practices

The Educational Policies Commission appointed a committee to make a first-hand study of the teaching of democratic citizenship in the secondary schools of the United States. The report describes six types of schools. For each type a teacher, an administrator, and a pupil speaks, but except in one case we will quote only the comments of the administrators. For the complete description, the reader will want to consult the report.[1]

First School

I selected most of the teachers who are now on this high-school staff. They are competent people, thoroughly in sympathy with the principles under which the school is operated. If they were not in sympathy with those principles, I would soon get rid of them. It is hard enough to teach democracy under the best of conditions, without being troubled with disloyal or insubordinate teachers. Certainly, I believe in democracy, and I believe in democratic schools, too. I want every pupil in this school to have a fair chance for an education that will help him to be a self-respecting, self-supporting citizen.

---

1. Educational Policies Commission, *Learning the Ways of Democracy* (Washington: National Education Association, 1940), pp. 2–14.

Second School

Of our six hundred students, four hundred are actively taking part in student activities. We have almost everything in the way of clubs, programs, and organizations. We try to get all our students into something. When I first came here there were no hobby clubs at all. Now we have more than twenty. There were then only thirty boys who turned out for football. Now we have two full squads for our varsity teams, as well as a twelve team intramural league. We have the biggest band in the state. We believe you can't have successful democracy on a large scale unless everybody has a lot of experience in democratic activities in small groups.

Third School

We have developed in this high school a democratic system of student-teacher cooperation in planning units of work. At the beginning of each unit in each course, the whole group, teachers and students working together, sets up the goals, determines the ways in which those goals may be achieved, and selects the needed materials. We do not think you can have democracy when a state department of education, a city school superintendent, or any other higher-up hands down ready-made programs of work for us to follow. Of course we welcome suggestions from the top offices, but we use them or not as we see fit or find convenient.

Fourth School

We believe in freedom here. Our greatest concern in administration is to see that the individual liberties of students and teachers are protected at all times. We avoid uniformity of any kind. We do not try to impose our notions upon the teachers. We give them academic freedom to the fullest extent. This practice seems to us to be the essence of democracy. It protects the individual and allows him the greatest possible opportunity for self-development. Isn't that what democracy is for?

Fifth School

We are concerned above all in this school with the possibilities of school and community service, with initiating and helping to carry through projects for the public welfare. Whenever any of us conceives a plan of action for the school, he begins at once to share it with the rest of the group. He invites criticism and revision of his proposal. Students, teachers, and parents are encouraged to make the plan their own before we try to put it into operation. The process of starting the project is slowed up, therefore, while committees scrutinize it, reshape it, study ways of making it work, and suggest means of evaluating its success after it is once under way.

A teacher continues:

We don't bother much about the forms and machinery of school government. Organization charts? We hardly know what they are. We are so busy planning big jobs that need to be done in this school and community and performing the day-by-day labor which they entail that we have no time to fool around with useless organization. The only organization we have is just what is needed to do the things we want done. Do we teach democracy? We certainly do. Our entire community service program is a demonstration of democracy. We may not talk much about democracy in our classes, but we think it is more important that boys and girls catch the spirit of democracy through first-hand experience than that they learn the right definitions.

Sixth School

We have to consider the level of maturity of our students and the abilities of our teachers before we can say what we can do in democratic education. The ways of democracy are not part of our native equipment. They must be *learned* just as surely as the ways of language and numbers must be learned, and they should be learned under the guidance of teachers who know how to teach them. Furthermore, state laws lay certain binding obligations upon the school board and upon me which we cannot delegate to anybody. Public opinion also puts responsibilities of almost equal weight upon us and upon the teachers, too. We cannot share these responsibilities with students without changes in the law or other definite consent of the community. To pretend that we are doing so is not good education but merely dishonesty. We publish a list of requirements for which the administrative and teaching staff are directly responsible to the school board and the public. It is understood that students and teachers may recommend changes in these requirements, but they have only the voices of citizens in changing them.

It is obvious from these statements that administrators differ as much as teachers in their points of view regarding the school. The types of leadership differ. The commission calls the first type that of the "master mind," the second type that of "busy work," the third "freedom by formula," the fourth "do-as-you-please," the fifth "get-jobs-done," and the sixth the "liberty-within-limits" type. In the first type the principal is a sympathetic, domineering, benevolent boss; in the second, everybody does everything and there is no evident purpose or unity in the organization. In the third school there is a pseudo motivation. In the fourth school there is really no leadership; it is an individual-centered affair. In the fifth school there is little evident purpose or unity but ample notion of the "big-job-to-be-done" idea. Some would call the sixth school leader a realist; others would call him honest or reasonable, or dub him full of common sense; while still others would think him entirely too cautious.

The Bases of Differences

Here are differences in school practices in both the administrative offices and in the classrooms. But behind these differences are ideas more fundamental than the surface evidence of lack of uniformity. The very existence of the variations themselves is a characteristic of localized education in America, but their nature indicates that various leaders of educational thought have been followed. These differences are to be found in the psychological theories, the democratic philosophy, and the conceptions of the function of education.

No argument is probably more basic to the discrepancies in school practice than is the one over how people learn. Psychological study has been fundamental to the organization of the curriculum, to the determination of subject matter, and to the classroom methods used by the teacher. Explanations of learning range all the way from the most mechanistic or atomistic to the most general and unified conceptions. Let us first consider the matters of inheritance and environment.

Nature versus Nurture

For generations man has discussed the relative importance of his inheritance and his environment in making him what he is. Here, as in many other fields, a dichotomy has tended to be developed, even though it is impossible to tell which factor caused a certain behavior pattern. Man is born with certain capacities which he inherits directly from his parents. Some believe these capacities set rather narrow limits to his potential development, and the school is effective only to the extent that it can develop these powers within the limits set by heredity.

More recently, biological studies have weakened considerably the position that the limits of mental and personal development are fixed by heredity. In 1925 Jennings, the biologist, made this contention:

> It is not true that what an organism shall become is determined, foreordained, when he gets his supply of chemicals or genes in the germ cells, as the popular writers on eugenics would have us believe. The same set of genes may produce many different results, depending upon the condition under which it operates. True it is that there are limits to this; that from one set of genes under a given environment may come a result that no environment can produce from another set. But this is a matter of limitation, not of fixed and final determination; it leaves open many alternative paths.[2]

A few years after this attack on hereditary rigidity, Jennings again wrote:

> When however we recognize that the genes are but chemicals, whose interaction with each other and with other things produces the organism —the adult characteristics being but the ultimate outcome of it all—then

---

2. H. S. Jennings, *Prometheus, or Biology and the Advancement of Man* (New York: E. P. Dutton & Company, 1925), p. 40. By permission of the publishers.

there is no *a priori* reason why those chemicals may not be added to, or subtracted from or chemically altered; nor why their interaction should not be controlled by the conditions, so as to yield other characteristics. These possibilities are not closed off at the start, as by the other notion; they are opened up, as questions of fact, to be determined by experimentation. And experimentation has indeed showed that these possibilities represent realities, as we have attempted to show in detail in other chapters. The genes supply one set of materials and conditions for development, nutrition and environment another. How a given substance or condition affects development and its outcome depends, not on its source, not on whether it belongs to one set or the other, but upon its nature, and upon where and when it comes into action. To recognize these things displaces the entire subject from a basis of general principle and *a priori* argumentation to one of particular fact, of actual investigation of each case for itself.³

Jennings has thus opened the way for a new study of the growth and development of the organism and has dealt a heavy blow to the general argument for fixed heredity.

CURRICULUM IMPLICATIONS. Fundamentally, there are three basic theories of the nature of man in relation to his environment. The first and most traditional is the *free soul* concept, where the soul, independent of the body, acts as a free moral agent. The second is the theory of man as a *natural animal* acting in conformity to the laws of nature. The third, and most recent, is the concept of man as a *field of energy* acting as a dynamic force within an environment.

If the teacher believes in the *free soul* concept he will plan his curriculum to include those subjects which will discipline the mind and cause the student to pursue diligently knowledge for its own end.

If the teacher believes in the *natural animal* concept, he will select those stimuli from the environment of the student which will produce in the learner the responses the teacher desires. The curriculum will be simple and quantitative.

If the teacher holds the *field of energy* theory, he will look upon the student as a purposeful, goal-seeking creature, constantly trying to balance his desires and successes and forever choosing from his environment those things which produce behavior consistent with his purposes. The teacher following this theory will use a varied set of activities, stress processes over products, make use of problems, stress differences of perception, and provide a wealth of experiences for personal growth and development.

Anderson considered these three points of view in terms of their implications for the curriculum and said the following:

---

3. H. S. Jennings, *The Biological Basis of Human Nature* (New York: W. W. Norton & Company, 1930), pp. 201–202. By permission of the publishers.

A curriculum which develops man as a free soul is limited and narrow in its objectives. It is unitary in its scope. Sequence is not highly significant, although logically derived. The curriculum is also characterized as having a logical organization. Association theories are consistent with a curriculum for which the objectives are multiple and varied. The scope of the curriculum is broad, diversified, but often fragmented. Sequence is logically determined and organization is frequently logical although it may be in terms of functional relations. Field theories are consistent with a curriculum for which the objectives are generalized rather than specific, although these objectives are not essentially unitary. The scope of the curriculum is determined by a study of the organism rather than by an analysis of the environment. Sequence which is not always predictable rather than having a sequence determining the activities. An organization which is often characterized as psychological rather than logical seems to characterize this curriculum.[4]

The argument over nature and environment is of significance to the curriculum movement for several reasons. In the first place, if there is one very definite, general set of inherited characteristics and another set which is determined only by the environment, then education must seek to discover which is which. The first group is, of course, outside the influence of the school and is within the sphere of the eugenists. Such a concept leads to a fatalism about certain types of individual behavior. In the second place, much is said by curriculum workers about adjusting the individual to his environment. If the environment is something "without" the individual which his inherited characteristics act upon, then adjustment is the major job of education. If, on the other hand, the environment is an integral part of the functioning organism, something which it is using in its own growth and development, the idea of simple adjustment to an environment loses its meaning. Such an idea opens up to education a vast area of potentialities for development by the skillful rearrangement of forces which act upon each other. The environment becomes tremendously important. The argument also has a bearing upon the concept of intelligence.

The Theory of Innate Intelligence

If intelligence is localized, specific, and determined at conception, the limits of educability for each person are set by the time he enters life. Some psychologists have contended for years that intelligence is an aggregation of structural parts, a theory which has led to arguments over the nature of mind and body, again a dichotomy. Lashley states it pointedly:

---

4. G. Lester Anderson, "Theories of Behavior and Some Curriculum Issues," *Journal of Educational Psychology*, 39:133–140, 1948.

The most fundamental difference among the theories is with respect to the unity of intelligence. By one group it is regarded as an aggregate of the separate efficiencies of specialized faculties; by the other, as a unitary function which transcends the special capacities and adds to or subtracts from their several efficiencies.[5]

E. L. Thorndike's theory of S-R bonds, where each bond leads from a specific stimulus to a specific response, is an illustration of the "aggregate" theory.

Early attempts to measure intelligence revealed that psychologists considered intelligence an innate or inborn quality. Cattell, one of the profound psychologists of his generation, expressed the idea thus: "The psychologist is likely to consider intelligence as the quality enabling an individual to learn readily or to meet new situations successfully, in so far as this depends on his congenital equipment."[6] Terman has held essentially the same position, as evidenced by this statement: "Facts have been presented which show that the limits of a child's educability can be fairly accurately predicated by means of mental tests given in the first school year."[7] His more recent position, which is essentially unchanged from this earlier statement, is evident from his participation in the arguments over the improvability of the I.Q., arguments in which he has taken the negative position.

The humanistic point of view regarding intelligence, which N. M. Butler, I. L. Kandel, Norman Foerster, W. S. Learned, and Robert M. Hutchins advocate, is essentially that intelligence is

the capacity that determines to what extent intellectual power may be achieved. It is the capacity for dealing with concepts, with abstractions from the concrete; for reducing the world of sense-objects to a system of abstractions. The higher the capacity of the individual for dealing with abstractions and for dealing with the world through abstractions, the greater his intelligence.[8]

Those who class themselves as realists in terms of modern social life hold rather closely to the Thorndike position regarding intelligence. They refer to themselves as pragmatists and contend that

the total intelligence of the individual must be regarded as a complex of

---

5. K. S. Lashley, *Brain Mechanisms and Intelligence* (Chicago: University of Chicago Press, 1929), p. 10.
6. J. M. Cattell, "The Interpretation of Intelligence Tests," *The Scientific Monthly*, 18: 511, 1924.
7. L. M. Terman, *The Intelligence of School Children* (Boston: Houghton Mifflin Company, 1919), p. 268.
8. Joseph Justman, *Theories of Secondary Education in the United States* (Teachers College Contributions to Education, No. 814; New York: Columbia University, Teachers College, Bureau of Publications, 1940), p. 134.

specific capacities implanted by heredity. Another way of saying this is that, for practical purposes, a person may be regarded as possessing *intelligences* or different *types of intelligence*. How specific these capacities or intelligences are we do not as yet know; we can, however, easily recognize such different capacities as the capacity for abstract thinking, the capacity for carrying on social relationships, and the capacity for motor activity. . . . A person may possess one kind of intelligence to such a degree that it expresses itself in certain marked special aptitudes, and at the same time be singularly lacking in another type of intelligence.[9]

The Theory of Developmental Intelligence

So much then for this point of view regarding intelligence. What is a contrary theory of intelligence? We have indicated that recent biological studies contend that man is an organism interacting with his environment, that he is unique both as a species and as an individual in the species. Man has the capacity to develop meanings out of his experiences, the situations he faces. As he analyzes these experiences, he improves his living; his behavior becomes more intelligent. He expresses his intelligence in his adjustment to problems he faces. Intelligence is not an abstract quality existing in isolation from the experience process.

The environment requires the individual to behave in new ways. Man cannot rely simply upon old learnings or meanings to fit these new situations. He must devise new solutions for them, and his intelligent behavior depends upon the extent to which he can do this. Life is thus experimental, and intelligence is constantly active and on the alert. Man possesses an initial capacity to direct his experience, but the extent to which he develops depends upon the manner in which he derives and applies meanings successfully. Intelligence and personality are developed in the course of human experience. Education cannot develop these attributes by requiring passive assimilation of abstract or cut-and-dried subject matter. Intelligence, from this point of view, is acquired through behavior.

This concept grows out of the recent emphasis upon the unity of the organism, acting purposefully to resolve tensions or disturbances in the individual. It has much to do with understanding the place of experience, purpose, activity, interests, and needs. The emphasis in this concept of intelligence is upon human experience. A person acts intelligently when he fits his behavior to purposes, when he attaches meaning to knowledge and events, and when he sees relationships among things. Inability to do this is a mark of dullness.

Many of the recent discoveries made in the field of child growth and development have strengthened the faith in the unity of the human organism. All psychologists are agreed that people differ, but the belief that the thing that

9. *Ibid.,* p. 179.

causes these differences is intelligence is fast being undermined. There seems no more reason to believe that intelligence is the cause of differences than to assume that health is a single factor which causes differences. Both health and intelligence are complex components which are factors in the actions and thoughts of people. Both are affected by such things as age, sex, environmental opportunities, experience, motivation, and heredity.

Modern psychologists in child-growth and development research have collected many types of data on individuals and have developed longitudinal and individual perspectives on children. They have gained evidence to support their fundamental contention that intellectual capacity must be nurtured if particular performances are to be taken as an index of it. The concept of general standards has given way to the theory of individual standards, these being produced by individual action within a field of potentials and conditions. Studies in this field have called for the collaboration of many specialists in describing the physical, mental, and social changes in individuals as well as the relation of these to the potentials of individuals and the character of their environment.[10]

The Question of I.Q. Constancy

Ever since psychologists have endeavored to measure intelligence they have debated the constancy of the intelligence quotient. Even before that, of course, appeared the controversies which have been discussed previously regarding the nature of intelligence and its relation to heredity and environment. These arguments all belong together, as they revolve around the same general basic assumptions.

In 1928 the National Society for the Study of Education invited a committee of its members to report on the status of the controversy;[11] a second report was issued in 1940.[12] A study of the reports of these two committees suggests that psychologists simply do not agree on what intelligence is, and

---

10. For some of the most significant documents in these fields, see Willard C. Olson, *Child Development* (Boston: D. C. Health and Company, 1949). Arthur T. Jersild, and others, *Child Development and the Curriculum* (New York: Columbia University. Teachers College, Bureau of Publications, 1946). Association for Supervision and Curriculum Development, *Fostering Mental Health in Our Schools* (1950 Yearbook; Washington, National Education Association, 1950), especially Chap. 6 by Caroline Tryon and Jesse W. Lilienthal III; Robert J. Havighurst and Hilda Haba, *Adolescent Character and Personality* (New York: John Wiley & Sons, 1949) ; Luella Cole, *Psychology of Adolescence* (New York: Rinehart & Company, 1948).
11. National Society for the Study of Education, *Nature and Nurture: Their Influence upon Intelligence,* Part I, and *Their Influence upon Achievement,* Part II (Bloomington, Illinois; Public School Publishing Co., 1928).
12. National Society for the Study of Education, *Intelligence, Its Nature and Nurture,* Parts I and II (Bloomington, Illinois; Public School Publishing Co., 1940).

that there is tremendous confusion over nature and nurture and over the constancy of the I.Q. Studies of the problem are so conflicting that only tentative conclusions are possible. During the last twelve years the hereditarians have tended to be more and more on the defensive as the importance of the environment is being increasingly stressed.

The theory of the fluctuating I.Q., however, had drawn converts long before the recent controversy between the Terman group of "constants" and the Iowa group of "fluctuants." In 1909 one of the most brilliant minds in the intelligence-test movement made a significant statement which has recently been resurrected.

> Some recent philosophers appear to have given their moral support to the deplorable verdict that the intelligence of an individual is a fixed quantity, a quantity which cannot be augmented. We must protest and act against this brutal pessimism. . . . We shall endeavor to show that it has no foundation whatsoever. . . .
>
> A child's mind is like a field for which an expert farmer has advised a change in the method of cultivating, with the result that in place of desert land, we now have a harvest. It is in this particular sense, the only one which is significant, that we say that the intelligence of children may be increased. One increases that which constitutes the intelligence of a school child; namely, the capacity to learn, to improve with instruction.[13]

For several years Bagley fought against what he termed determinism in education, against the constant, congenital-intelligence concept. He wrote:

> The term general intelligence should provisionally be accepted as connoting the most important function of mind, namely, the ability to control behavior in the light of experience . . . General intelligence is determined in part by physical heredity and in part by environment. Probably the most important environmental pressures are those represented by systematic schooling. The contribution of systematic schooling to general intelligence is probably equal to the combined contributions of native endowment and informal pressures of the average social environment.[14]

Along with this conception, however, Bagley, in common with Charles H. Judd and Henry C. Morrison, held to a concept of discipline as the method of improving intelligence.

Most of the recent studies on the changing I.Q. indicate that some changes can be expected under certain conditions. The studies have progressed only far enough to offer a challenge and a ray of hope to those who wish it. These

---

13. The statement originally comes from Binet's *Les Idées modernes sur les Enfants* (Paris: Flammarion, 1909), pp. 141, 146. George Stoddard translated it and quoted it in the *Educational Record,* 20:44–57 (January supplement, 1939), in his article on "The I.Q.: Its Ups and Downs."

14. W. C. Bagley, *Determinism in Education* (Baltimore, Maryland; Warwick and York, 1925), pp. 157–58.

studies seem to indicate that the I.Q. is determined by four things: (1) hereditary factors (the genes), (2) constitutional factors (organic but not traceable
to the genes or social pressures), (3) motivation (frustration, and the like),
and (4) environmental factors (nutrition, stimulation, education, type of
social system). Some of these can be influenced by prenatal care, some by
the home and school, some by the character of the social structure, and some
by the individual himself.

In a recent analysis of the use and meaning of intelligence tests, Courtis
contends that psychologists have never analyzed behavior experimentally to
find an elemental factor called intelligence, as scientists have found copper
or silver. He says:

> The concept of "mental age" or developmental level was, and is, a
> great contribution to educational thinking. Intelligence tests are valuable
> instruments for determining quickly the developmental status of a child.
> . . . But neither mental age nor I.Q. determines capacity. . . . Essentially
> the I.Q. is merely a measure of relative rates of development (mental
> development compared with chronological development). On the same
> basis one can obtain quotients for height, reading, social development,
> and so on, and by averaging all a child's developmental ages can obtain
> what Olson calls his organismic age.
>
> Behind these developments is some major factor in the maturation
> process, perhaps the energy of the process itself. But individuals differ
> in this factor, whatever it is, and such differences account for approximately
> 90 per cent of all test scores, whether of intelligence, academic abilities,
> or social graces. A child's score in a test increases from year to year whether
> he learns anything or not, just because he is larger, stronger, more mature.[15]

The research studies of Eells and Murray have shown that present-day
intelligence tests differentiate between middle-class and lower-class children.
Not only do social-class environments differ but a similar distinction exists
among different class groups in the nature and extent of vocabulary pupils
will have. Ten-year-old children of high status groups were found to have
better vocabularies and greater facility with words than fourteen-year-olds in
low status groups. Intelligence tests generally use words that favor the middle
class, even the urban middle class. In other words, the content of the tests
and the experiences of the upper and middle class correlate so closely that
the tests favor these groups of children.[16]

---

15. S. A. Courtis, "Debunking the I.Q.," *The Nation's Schools*, 45:57–59, 1950.
16. Four of the most significant studies in this area are: Kenneth W. Eells, "Social
Status and Factors in Intelligence Test Items"; Walter Isaiah Murray, "The Intelligence
Test Performance of Negro Children of Different Social Classes"; David R. Stone,
"Certain Verbal Factors in the Intelligence Test Performance of High and Low Social
Status Groups." These three studies are unpublished doctoral dissertations, University of
Chicago, Department of Education, 1947. The fourth study is Kenneth W. Eells and
others, *Intelligence and Cultural Differences* (Chicago: University of Chicago Press, 1951).

CURRICULUM IMPLICATIONS.   The arguments over the nature and constancy of intelligence are important for the educational process and for the curriculum. If intelligence is a congenital capacity formed permanently and rigidly at birth and is a series of aggregate parts which must be disciplined, then the educational program must focus upon the acquisition of knowledge and upon a series of specific exercises aimed at developing native capacities. If intelligence is an inherited general capacity functioning more as a unit than as a series of aggregate parts, not amenable to improvement but capable only of fruition, then education must design more unified exercises of a disciplinary type which will develop general powers so that they may be applied specifically. However, if intelligence is part of a unified series of potentialities, then the learning program should be one of experiences carefully selected to suit the potentials of each individual organism. Without doubt much of the great confusion in education today is due to the even greater confusion in psychology. We need a more acceptable and convincing explanation of human learning and behavior.

The Process of Learning

Coming a little closer to educational practice with the argument, we get into the area of learning. Learning is nothing more than man's attempt to secure what he needs to live intelligently, and the process and content are related to his basic concept of himself. Let us look, then, at the different points of view regarding learning.[17]

There are a number of individual interpretations of the meaning and nature of learning. Although each man is prone to add his own particular twist to a basic generalization of the psychological theory which he accepts, these various interpretations may be classified under three general views of how learning takes place.

Learning by Specific Reactions

First, learning may be conceived as the establishment of a series of specific reactions to specific stimuli. This theory holds that there is no such thing as generalized intellectual power to be developed, but rather that there are specific knowledge, habits, skills, and attitudes to be acquired. Learning is dependent upon the readiness of the learner, his attitude toward the thing to be learned,

---

17. For a good summary and critique of several theories of learning, see E. R. Hilgard, *Theories of Learning* (New York: Appleton-Century-Crofts, Inc., 1948). See also National Society for the Study of Education, *Learning and Instruction* (Forty-ninth Yearbook, University of Chicago Press, Chicago, Illinois; 1950), Part I.

the application of his ability and attention to the learning (his exercise), and the satisfaction which he derives from the effort. When these conditions are met, learning proceeds both economically and satisfactorily. Change the conditions and we have trouble. Such a theory allows for the development of habits and emotionalized attitudes, as well as for the acquisition of factual information. Individuals have many capacities which must be discovered. And the ability of individuals to live in modern society must be analyzed, isolated for training, and cultivated with adequate and appropriate instruction. Experience cannot be handled in broad areas but must be broken down into ideals, attitudes, habits, character traits, skills, behavior traits, and information. Such a technique will develop a host of specific areas of social competence in each individual, but it must be supplemented by specific and specialized training of the individual along the lines of the capacities in which he has demonstrated peculiar fitness. The selection of appropriate subject matter for this training program is important and must be done by competent people. If they are trained in this way, individuals will leave school with the necessary social habits and skills, the proper information, the right emotionalized attitudes, and properly developed interests.[18] The theory of identical elements, designed to explain transfer of learning from these specific situations to new and novel ones not learned specifically, is a part of the general theory of this point of view. The theory of learning by specific reactions represents a reconstruction of a more plausible explanation by those who have rejected the formal discipline theory. It may be a reasonably plausible theory of how disciplining may actually take place, if there is any such thing, but it still clings tenaciously to the use of the same materials which the formal disciplinarians used—the formal subjects—even though its proponents have rejected the theory.

CURRICULUM IMPLICATIONS.   Such a point of view applied to the curriculum would enthrone the subject matter of traditional education, even though it would be organized in a new way. The base would be the same as it has been for generations in America. The application of this theory would also mean the teaching of specifics through drill and recitation. It would center upon the selection of specifics of learning, upon the determination of "appropriate subject matter" for the bright and the dull, for those with normal and those with "special capacities." The subject matter would be selected by experts in

18. For further elaboration of this point of view, see Thomas H. Briggs, "Jeremiah Was Right," *Teachers College Record*, 32:679–695, 1931; see A Program for Secondary Education, *Bulletin*, No. 40 (Washington: National Association Secondary School Principals, 1932), pp. 1–12; Thomas H. Briggs, *Secondary Education* (New York: The Macmillan Company, 1933). See also Committee on Orientation of Secondary Education, *Functions of Secondary Education Bulletin*, No. 64 (Washington: National Association Secondary School Principals, 1937); Francis T. Spaulding, *Interest in Learning Bulletin*, No. 74 (Washington: National Association Secondary School Principals, 1938), pp. 52–54; E. L. Thorndike, *Human Learning* (New York: Appleton-Century-Crofts, Inc., 1931).

advance and applied individually to pupils for whom it is appropriate. It would mean that the learning is "without" the individual and not drawn from his own immediate experience so that he himself participates in the drawing, the planning, and the purposing. Learning would have a purpose, certainly, but it would be one which the teacher sets up and which the pupil is asked to accept. Subject matter would be drawn from both past and present and it would be carefully planned, organized for horizontal and vertical sequence, and scientifically allocated according to individual need and capacity. There would be considerable repetition and little emphasis upon "catching on," upon the seeing of relationships. Insight, creating, meaning, and inner purpose would not be stressed.

Learning by Developing General Ability

A second conception of learning is that it is the disciplining or developing of general intellectual ability. Stress is laid here upon the development of the ability to deal with the meaning of things. There is a good life to be lived and it is lived individually. Man comes into this manner of living by the application of intelligence, a disciplined intellect, through a mind which sees relationships and meanings. Ideas are the things which give the individual control, and the mastery of these requires intelligence; the higher the ideas, the higher is the intelligence required to deal with them.

Everybody is born with some intelligence, but individuals vary in this original capacity. Intelligence is a unitary capacity and is susceptible to development as a whole, but this development depends upon the right materials and the right methods. Education should seek to establish meanings, the more the better, which must be organized into broad patterns. The more of these the individual possesses, the more he will be able to apply them directly to life activities. He does not need practice in the specifics of these activities to make this application.

> The man who has learned to think and to reason and to compare and to discriminate and to analyze, who has refined his taste and formed his judgment and sharpened his mental vision will be placed in that state of intellect in which he can take up any one of the sciences or callings I have referred to (law, medicine, business), or any other for which he has a taste or special talent, with an ease, a grace, a versatility, and a success to which another is a stranger.[19]

This concept of learning rings with a faith in mental discipline or at least in general transfer, even though the advocates of this theory reject the theory of formal discipline. Learning is the process of disciplining the mind with

19. Norman Foerster, *The American State University* (Chapel Hill, N.C.: University of North Carolina Press, 1937), p. 203. By permission of the publisher.

ideas and meanings of an abstract nature, so that a condition may result which will enable the individual to live the good life, whatever the social definition of it may be at the time. The particular social and political nature of the existing society is relatively unimportant, just as long as ample opportunities for freedom of study of expression and meaning are possible. The human mind takes in ideas; it does not create them as much as it receives them.

CURRICULUM IMPLICATIONS.   Those who support this theory disagree over whether the ideas shall all be intellectual or abstract. Some hold that spiritual, moral, and esthetic training shall be given specifically, while others feel that if youth are given big enough ideas, they can handle the emotional and moral phases of life. There is a difference also over the method of teaching. Some hold that all people to their own degree can profit by thinking "big ideas," which is the cloak under which they maintain self-respect in a democracy,[20] while others maintain that the educational process should seek

> to help each individual to acquire to the limit of his capacity important general meanings and the ability to use them. The method through which these meanings and this ability are imparted will in various degrees be characterized by abstractness or concreteness, according to the intelligence of the person who is being educated . . . The result is that individuals of inferior intelligence are thought to be trained through more concrete educative instruments, individuals of superior intelligence with more abstract instruments.[21]

Such an idea applies particularly to moral or character training given to those of inferior ability. The intellect is to be developed, therefore, through the use of certain educational materials, some of which are far better for establishing these habits and ideals and meanings than are others.

This school of thought holds that some learnings require experience and others do not. Those which do not should be taught first. This is in direct contrast, interestingly enough, to the practice in activity schools, where the earlier years contain more experimental activities than the later years. Hutchins maintains that the curriculum of the school should be the cultural heritage of America, which in turn is the civilization of Western Europe. This he would teach, and

---

20. See the writings of Robert M. Hutchins. His article in *Harper's Magazine* for October, 1941, pp. 512–526, entitled "Education for Freedom," is a good illustration of this point of view. See also Robert M. Hutchins, "Toward a Durable Society," *Fortune,* 27:159, 1943; and John Dewey, "Challenge to Liberal Thought," *Fortune,* 30:155, 1944, an answer to Hutchins. The Curriculum of St. John's College is an illustration of a program in the later years of secondary education based in this general concept. Kandel's suggestions in the main follow this line of reasoning, as well as those of Learned.
21. Justman, *Theories of Secondary Education,* pp. 136–137.

the means of understanding it is the liberal arts, the arts of reading, writing, speaking and calculating. Education for freedom consists in transmitting to the rising generation the civilization they have inherited, together with the techniques by which it may be understood. No man or woman is equipped to be a ruler in America without this education.[22]

He contends further that such an education will give a common basis of communication; freedom through trained free intellect, and adjustment to the environment. He boldly claims that it "gives us adjustment to the environment of 1951, because the liberally educated man is prepared for any world that comes." It shows us "the aim of life and the path to happiness." Such statements sound more inspirational than scientific. Hutchins would have youth study the principles of science to find out what science can and cannot do; the social sciences would be taught as moral and political philosophy; a foreign language would be learned in order to understand one's own language; and youth would be required to read widely.

Transmission of the cultural heritage is the basic characteristic of this curriculum. Organization, logical sequence, mastery, adaptability, acquisition of subject matter are all of great significance in this concept. Those who organize and select learning materials would differ over the design of the learning program to carry out these ideas. Little change would be made in the content of the school studies as we have known them traditionally. They should, however, be kept up to date, be psychologically adapted to the individuals learning them. Here method of organization comes in, and such men as Morrison have been instrumental in grouping the subjects around topics and arranging them in serial fashion, more commonly called the Morrison units.[23] Mastery of the material in these units is to affect the personality of the individual, and little by little he should become more adaptive to his environment. Judd varies this concept of learning by holding that learning on lower levels is more automatic and specific, while that of the higher mental processes is of a different nature.[24] Man must be motivated to release these processes, as they are not automatic. The higher processes determine man's adaptability. As Judd puts it:

> The psychology of the higher mental processes teaches that the end and goal of all education is the development of systems of ideas which can be carried over from the situations in which they were acquired to other

22. Hutchins, "Education for Freedom," *Harper's Magazine,* October, 1941, p. 521. For a more complete and later statement on this position see Robert M. Hutchins, "Education and Democracy," *School and Society,* 69:425–428, 1949. Significant statements from this article are given in Chap. 3.
23. See Henry C. Morrison, *The Practice of Teaching in the Secondary School* (Chicago: University of Chicago Press, 1931).
24. See Charles H. Judd, *Education as Cultivation of the Higher Mental Processes* (New York: The Macmillan Company, 1936).

situations. Systems of general ideas illuminate and clarify human experiences by raising them to the level of abstract, generalized, conceptual understanding.[25]

This theory of Judd renounces the explanations of the mental life of man on the higher levels by the simple formulas of animal behavior. Man possesses the power of generalization, and Judd would develop this in youth through word symbols meaningful to them. He would use scientific findings to select and organize appropriate learning experiences. The teaching of mathematics, for instance, would enable man to acquire generalizations about a number system, rather than specific arithmetical facts; the study of language would show him not specific facts and rules about a language, but the means of communication which can be used in any communicating situation.

Learning by Changing Behavior

A third concept of learning is that it is the process of changing the behavior of the individual as he adjusts himself to basic organic disturbances. Behavior is characteristic of all living things, and as the organism tends to be a balanced affair, disturbances upset its equilibrium. Thus it is constantly in motion trying to restore balance. In the process, it uses the physiological, mental, and social conditions which can be brought to bear upon the tensions. Learning emerges from the reactions of individuals to the total situation. It involves purpose, identification with the situation, goals, insight, activities, ideas and information, skills, attitudes, experience, all of which are inseparable in their functioning relationship.

Since man is a unique species in nature and is an organism constantly interacting with his environment, he can determine to a large degree the kind of life he wants to live. The particular forces operating within and around a person determine his individuality, and if he understands the life in which he lives and its processes, he, with others like him, can through insight and purposeful action design and establish a satisfactory and intelligent social order. This process of the interaction of man and his environment is known as experience, and out of it man gains knowledge for the redirection of continued experience. Experience is constantly new, for with each experience a new pattern of action is created. If man continues this practice, he will gain intellectual command of the forces which make and condition him. He develops a personality. The important thing is the kind of experiences an individual faces.

Living is improved when individuals share experiences and communicate meanings. The character of society is important in determining the nature of the individual. While much of man's behavior is in response to basic biological

---

25. *Ibid.*, p. 201.

and socal needs, he meets these needs by deriving meanings from his own experience with the social conditions and mores with which he is surrounded.

The most recent and important developments in psychology have been concerned with explaining this concept of learning. Efforts have been made to discover the significance of cognition, of meaningfulness, of concept formation and of perception. Environmental stimulation, incentives, the utilization of past experience, the differences in perception of individuals are factors which have received much attention. That the quality of experience an individual has determines the quality of learning which takes place is receiving more general acceptance.

The old trial-and-error method of learning has been given a different interpretation by Hilgard:

> Many learning situations require the selection of one or another possible modes of action in order to reach a goal. Because alternatives are selected one after another until the correct one is stumbled upon, this learning is commonly described as trial and error. . . .
>
> The alternative [to a trial-and-error description] is that the original behavior is not the running-off of earlier habits in the new situation but a *genuine attempt at discovering* the route to the goal. Past experience is used, but in a manner appropriate to the present. Such an interpretation makes the original adjustment a *provisional* try, to be confirmed or denied by its success or failure.[26]

The importance of experience in the instructional process has been stressed by the National Society for the Study of Education:

> We can direct learning by determining the kind of experiences which children are to have. Not all experiences are equivalent. What experiences teachers should provide for pupils cannot be determined without consideration of the pupil and of the end products—the nature of the child at the time as well as the educational objectives to be attained. But the only control we have over product is through experience. The teacher can never impose the product directly. It is the pupil, not the teacher, who is the active learner. The major control which the teacher has, then, is to make sure that the pupils have certain experiences and also to make sure that they do not have certain others.[27]

If the quality of experience is the most important factor in learning, then the selection of experiences and the guidance of them become very important in education. It then makes a great difference what is taught and who teaches.

To the "gestaltists" who have concentrated on learning, the center of learning is in problematical situations. These give rise to tensions and disturb-

---

26. Hilgard, *Theories of Learning*, p. 343.
27. National Society for the Study of Education, *Learning and Instruction* (Forty-ninth Yearbook; Chicago: University of Chicago Press, 1950), Part I, pp. 29–30.

ances, and behavior is toward the completion of the actions which resolve problems. A most important factor in human learning is insight, which depends upon (1) capacity, (2) experience, and (3) identification and observation of all factors in the problem. The practice follows closely that of the experimental scientist.

The significant thing about these concepts for education is the emphasis upon goal seeking, the effect of environment upon capacity, and the importance of establishing meaningful experiences. The school must, then, seek to create experiences which make sense to the learner and carefully assist him to weave his way through his confusions toward a goal he deems worthy of achievement.

Another important consideration is that growth and development must be guided carefully from the very earliest years until the individual is released from the guidance of the teacher and made entirely self dependent. The developing individual reveals certain characteristics of growth. For instance, he gradually develops from sole dependence upon primary incentives to where secondary ones are of significance to him. His attention is lengthened and he can pursue long-term instead of only short-term goals. He organizes his behavioral patterns around principles and generalizations and value systems. He becomes less concerned with fleeting interests and dramatic stimuli, and he acquires a persistence characteristic of maturity. He gradually develops to where he relates himself to those in the world about him, carefully analyzes the factors in his perspective, and evaluates the possible outcomes of actions.[28]

Another valuable contribution to the concept of child growth and development is found in the exploration of the idea of developmental tasks.[29] These tasks are defined as guideposts which are helpful in gaining an over-all picture of growth and development. They are those common tasks that face all individuals within a society, tasks which need to be accomplished if individuals are to make normal progress. The two major areas of force which interact to set these tasks are the expectancies and pressures of society and the changes that take place in the maturing physical organism.

Tryon and Lilienthal maintain that children must be ready for the tasks, that they pose problems which have deep personal significance for the child, that none are mastered in a day, and that they all are interrelated in a complex fashion. These authors deal with five stages of growth: (1)infancy, (2) early childhood, (3) late childhood, (4) early adolescence, and (5) late adolescence. They deal with these tasks under the following ten categories of behavior:

28. A very interesting treatise on perspective and its meaning is to be found in Earl C. Kelley, *Education for What Is Real* (New York: Harper & Brothers, 1947). A good review of the relation between modern psychology and the curriculum is found in the *Journal of Educational Psychology,* Vol. 39, March, 1948.
29. See Chap. 6, entitled "Developmental Tasks: The Concept and Its Importance," by Tryon and Lilienthal, in *Fostering Mental Health.*

1. Achieving an appropriate dependence-independence pattern
2. Achieving an appropriate giving-receiving pattern of affection
3. Relating to changing social groups
4. Developing a conscience
5. Learning one's psycho-socio-biological sex role
6. Accepting and adjusting to a changing body
7. Managing a changing body and learning new motor patterns
8. Learning to understand and control the physical world
9. Developing appropriate symbol and conceptual abilities
10. Relating one's self to the cosmos

CURRICULUM IMPLICATIONS.   This point of view regarding learning requires a different school program—a program originating in the basic needs of the individual. Some who hold the general tenets of this theory believe that basic needs originate entirely within the individual and argue that his personal and immediate "needs" and "interests" should determine the nature of the program of education. On the other hand, those who emphasize the effect of the social order on the individual contend that these personalized needs are only one side of the program and that no curriculum is complete that does not at one and the same time deal with both the individual and group forces which play upon him.

In the planning of a curriculum in harmony with this theory, at least three practices are evident. The first provides that curriculum content not be planned in advance, but that reliance be placed upon the spontaneous interests of the children of the class. This procedure is practically nonexistent although some parents believe that it exists in a number of elementary schools. Those who believe in the second practice rely upon the organized fields of subject matter, but endeavor to rearrange the materials within each field so that they become functionally related to the behavior of youth. A good illustration of this is the work of the Commission on Secondary School Curriculum of the Progressive Education Association, which did not break away from the organized subjects. Those following the third procedure select materials from personal and social life and organize them around certain major problems vital to youth.

Before we examine curriculum programs, we need to understand the meaning of certain other terms used by curriculum workers, such as *needs, interest, purpose, experience,* and *activity.*

The Nature of Needs

There have been several uses of the term "needs" in educational literature and practice. In the first place, needs have been thought of as facts, behavior, or skills that the young person does not possess, but which the adult thinks he ought to have. The adult says that the youth needs to learn social customs and manners; he needs to have certain interests; he needs to learn to be a good citizen or he needs Latin, mathematics, or English grammar. These are needs defined by the adult for the young.

A second use of the term "need" is in relation to some inner demand which the child makes upon his environment. He needs food or clothing or shelter or medical attention. The term has sometimes been used more specifically to apply to detailed needs, such as a red dress, a new baseball, membership in a certain club, or a certain breakfast food.

A third use of the term "need" is a psychological one, gained from a study of the behavior of youth in social situations. We say that the youth needs to feel that he is wanted in the community; he needs to become a participating member of society; he needs economic stability; he needs security. When these needs are unfulfilled in an individual, there is a basic disturbance which drives him to action. These needs arise in different areas of experience. The Progressive Education Association's Commission on Secondary School Curriculum stipulated four basic areas of needs of this type—immediate social relationships, wider social relationships, economic relationships, and personal living.[30]

Kinds of Needs

The first use of the term "need" is based on a concept of shortage. We say that young people do not possess certain characteristics which we as adults deem to be desirable, either because we possess them or wish we did. We then conclude that youth need these things. A program built on this concept is bound to be adult-centered and will be applied as a coercive standard. There is, of course, a place for adult judgment regarding the shortcomings of youth, but this point of view cannot be the determinant of the curriculum, for it leaves the learner out of consideration and may require of him accomplishments totally unsuitable to his interests and abilities.

The second type of need is that which comes from the physiological nature of the individual—any condition of the body tissues which demands activity to satisfy it. These have largely to do with the functioning of the organs of the body, but they of course flow over into social considerations. We say the body needs food, heat, sexual expression, but the satisfaction of these depends not alone upon the individual but upon the availability of those material things, human beings, and ideas which are needed to satisfy them. These needs expand into the social realm, and their acquisition almost becomes a goal for

30. See Reports of the Commission on Secondary School Curriculum, particularly V. T. Thayer, Caroline B. Zachry, and Ruth Kotinsky, *Reorganizing Secondary Education* (New York: Appleton-Century-Crofts, Inc., 1939); also *Science in General Education; A Report of the Committee on the Function of Science in General Education* (New York: Appleton-Century-Crofts, Inc., 1938).

living. The set of needs which Hopkins gives is typical of this type and use of needs:

> The needs which the American people must satisfy in order to feel the goodness in life are reasonably clear. They need (1) adequate food, clothing, and shelter to keep the body functioning effectively; (2) reasonable freedom of movement, speech, and thought; (3) some personal distinction before others; (4) acceptance by others into the activities of group life; (5) opportunity to build an unique self and personality; (6) favorable conditions for earning a livelihood; (7) economic security for old age; (8) opportunity to marry and rear children in a wholesome family life; and (9) faith in their ability to make life continually better or faith that the best efforts of the group will bring the better life in the present and reveal new needs to raise their level of living in the future.[31]

Some of the "progressives" maintain that needs arise from within the learner. If this assumption is held, the curriculum program is likely to be based upon the schools' attempt to discover the spontaneous needs of children and to provide experiences immediately that will satisfy them. If the position is taken that needs arise both from "within" and "without" the individual, that they change with experience and with age, the curriculum will become unified around social goals, group purposes, and problems rather than around individual whims or interests. The typical child-centered school held largely to the first position.[32]

The third category of needs is merely a convenient method of classifying needs into areas for organization purposes. The Progressive Education Association used these to point up the different areas in which adolescents function. Others have classified needs into two big areas—personal and social. Any of these classifications is a thought process or a working technique; it is not necessarily a functional classification as far as individuals are concerned.

Needs, then, arise from a growing, acting personality and are the result of adolescents undergoing tensions and conflicts. Justman contends that they

> emerge also as intellectual needs: the adolescent seeks to understand his world, to create his own values, to form his own judgments and regulate his own behavior, to function in healthy independence of his parents and

---

31. L. Thomas Hopkins, *Interaction: The Democratic Process* (Boston: D. C. Heath and Company, 1941), pp. 4–5.

32. For a description of this position see Harold O. Rugg and Ann Shumaker, *The Child Centered School* (New York: World Book Co., 1928). For a pointed criticism of this position see Boyd H. Bode, *Progressive Education at the Crossroads* (New York: Newson, 1938), pp. 62ff. See also John Dewey, *Experience and Education* (New York: The Macmillan Company, 1938). Rugg also criticizes the overemphasis upon child nature as an end, in the Twenty-sixth Yearbook of the National Society for the Study of Education, Part I, *Curriculum Making: Past and Present* (Bloomington, Ill.: Public School Publishing Co.), pp. 436–437.

of others. They are the normal characteristics of healthy developing young people; they touch upon every aspect of living.[33]

If needs are of this nature, then the term "felt need" may be said to apply to a need of which a person is thoroughly conscious. Needs change, and the job of the school is not only to meet them as they emerge but to create desires by building upon established ones.

How Needs Are Determined

One way to discover needs is to study adolescent growth and development to determine the factors and forces involved in the process.[34] A second method is to analyze the culture. This consists largely of empirical reasoning or subjective analyses of social conditions with suggestions for their improvement.[35] A third method of determining youth needs is to interview youth in school regarding what they consider to be their interests, needs, desires, or problems. Many studies of this character have been made in local situations.[36] Out-of-school youth have also been interviewed to determine their opinions of the school, of their own problems, of the relation of the school to them, and their interpretation of the society in which they are trying to find themselves.[37]

---

33. Justman, *Theories of Secondary Education,* p. 369.

34. Typical of these studies are: H. S. Dimock, *Rediscovering the Adolescent: A Study of Personality in Adolescent Boys* (New York: Association Press, 1937); Allison Davis and John Dollard, *Children of Bondage* (American Youth Commission; Washington: American Council on Education, 1940); E. Franklin Frazier, *Negro Youth at the Crossways: Their Personality Development in the Middle States* (American Youth Commission; Washington: American Council on Education, 1940); Charles S. Johnson, *Growing Up in the Black Belt: Negro Youth in the Rural South* (American Youth Commission; Washington: American Council on Education, 1940); A. B. Hollingshead, *Elmtown's Youth: The Impact of Social Classes on Adolescents* (New York: John Wiley & Sons, 1949); Robert J. Havighurst and Hilda Taba, *Adolescent Character and Personality* (New York: John Wiley & Sons, 1949).

35. Such studies as the following are typical: Educational Policies Commission, *The Education of Free Men in American Democracy* (Washington: National Education Association, 1941); Thomas R. Carskadon and Rudolf Modley, *U.S.A.: A Measure of a Nation; A Graphic Presentation of America's Needs and Resources* (Twentieth Century Fund; New York: The Macmillan Company, 1949); Goodwin Watson, *Youth after Conflict* (New York: Association Press, 1947); George S. Counts, *The Prospects of American Democracy* (New York: John Day Company, 1938); President's Research Committee, *Recent Social Trends* (New York: McGraw-Hill Book Company, Inc., 1934).

36. For a good illustration of this type of study and for others dealing with this kind of investigational technique, see a doctoral dissertation at Stanford University by Ralph R. Fields, entitled *The Identification of the Interests and Problems of High School Students and Their Implications for Curriculum Development,* 1940. See also Donald C. Doane, *The Needs of Youth: An Evaluation for Curriculum Purposes* (Teachers College Contributions to Education, No. 848; New York: Columbia University, Teachers College, Bureau of Publications, 1942).

37. A large number of these have been made recently. See the list of those made by the American Youth Commission and consult particularly the annoted bibliography of youth

The Use of Interests

The term "interests" has been used in educational literature and practice with at least three distinct connotations. In one connotation it has been used to refer to a means of motivation. One is said to learn more easily if he is interested in learning or has a desire to learn. In another, interests are stressed as ends of education; that is, one of the functions of education has been to establish, nourish, sustain, enrich, and extend interests. In a third, interests of children have been used as the source of curriculum content. The curriculum should start, so this theory goes, with the existing attitudes, favoritisms, or attachments which youth bear to certain materials, objects, or conditions.

A further analysis of thinking, together with some illustrations, will probably clarify the uses of these terms. The adult use of the term "interest" as a stake in something need not be considered here. This use is frequently applied to situations in education, such as the interest which a pressure group might have in forcing the school to teach a certain point of view, but in general it has less significance for the curriculum movement than have the other three usages.

Interests as Motivation

There is little disagreement anywhere that youth learn better those things for which they have a voluntary desire or drive. Practically all psychologists have had to make place for some kind of satisfactions, drives, or motives for learning. The drive may be an inner one or an outer one. It may be physiological, sociological, or self-imposed as a result of intelligent calculations. All these forces exert pressures for certain types of behavior, and if the desire to acquire a new way of behaving, to acquire new information or a new skill, or to engage in a certain activity is self-imposed, there is gain in the speed and effectiveness of learning. If, on the other hand, the desire is absent, and it is necessary to resort to coercion to secure activity, then learning is slowed, greater effort is required, or concomitant learnings are lost.

This notion of interest is psychological and is variously defined as "the attitude developed through a pleasant or satisfying experience,"[38] the desire to

---

studies entitled *American Youth,* by L. A. Menefee and M. M. Chambers (American Youth Commission; Washington: American Council on Education, 1938). This volume reviews about 2,500 youth studies. A helpful review of a large number of youth studies may be found in Robert N. Bush, *The Needs Concept in Curriculum Development* (Stanford Social Studies Investigation, *Bulletin* No. 12; Stanford University, Calif., 1940). Mimeographed. See also the supplement to the 1938 bibliography of the American Youth Commission bibliography entitled *Youth: Key to America's Future* (Washington: American Council on Education, 1949).

38. H. L. Caswell and Doak Campbell, *Curriculum Development* (New York: American Book Company, 1935), p. 209.

satisfy a need, an identity with something,[39] "acting with a purpose and an appreciation of the activity."[40] Briggs points out that an "intrinsic interest causes activity that is abundant in proportion to the strength of the desire for the objective, that is intelligent because directed toward the satisfaction of a felt need, and that is economical because, not divided, it is always contributory to a carefully made plan."[41]

This concept of interest is tied up with psychological needs and with satisfactions from the resolution of disturbances. Interests are directional forces gained from satisfying experiences. As drives they are not mystical forces, but are established attitudes gained from experience and from biological urges. They arise from the organism and from the nature of the social group. Personal development is frequently defined as the accumulation of those interests which beguile the individual into continued activity. Kilpatrick has developed a theory of continuous growth based upon this general pattern of thought.

Some contend that interests are very narrow, limited things, applying to only a few areas of learning, and that while some things are naturally interesting, others are neutral or uninteresting. Therefore, the teacher is advised to stimulate as much interest as he can in teaching and to resort to coercion only in those other areas where interest wanes. Some feel that the individual has no interests until he has knowledge and that if he just studies things long enough he will develop an interest in them. This has led to the practice of making things interesting to the pupil through various kinds of educational bribes or threats. John Dewey has charged that this cannot be done, that it is impossible to make things interesting. He contends that interest is the result of a feeling of significance or meaning attached to the learnings. One develops it by experience, not by acquiring simple knowledge or skill.

Interests as Ends of Education

Interests have also been considered to be educational ends. Briggs has been one of the chief exponents of this idea, which he expressed as one of the functions of secondary education. In speaking of this use of interests, Briggs says, "As an end, to be sought that one may have intellectual life more abundantly, they [interests] have as yet failed to be accepted as the most important objective that liberal education has to seek."[42] In discussing the

---

39. See Joseph K. Hart, *A Social Interpretation of Education* (New York: Henry Holt and Company, 1929), Parts III and IV.
40. W. A. Saucier, *Introduction to Modern Views of Education* (Boston: Ginn and Company, 1937), p. 236.
41. Thomas H. Briggs, J. Paul Leonard, and Joseph Justman, *Secondary Education* (rev. ed.; New York: The Macmillan Company, 1950), p. 369. There are three excellent chapters on interests, Chaps. 15, 16, 17.
42. *Ibid.,* p. 370.

sources of such interests he points out that they " 'spring up' from unsuspected and unknown causes; they are invited by environment; they are induced, fortuitously or with intent, by parents, teachers, and friends; they are evoked by readings; and most of all they are 'caught' from others who have them."[43] Seldom, it seems, does one acquire an interest by deliberately deciding that he will get it, though there is no apparent reason why he should not do so. Briggs takes one more step and contends that "if the subject-matter of the curriculum cannot be revealed as interesting to a student, there is something wrong either with the time when it is presented or in the presentation."[44] He thinks this is true of everything, since he preceded this statement with the announcement that "there is not an atom of this universe that is not interesting."

This same point of view is echoed in the report of the Commission on Secondary School Curriculum of the Progressive Education Association. In speaking of personal needs the commission states that

> cherishing the personal life of the student implies giving play to those of his personal interests and activities which entice him for no reason at all except that they promise to increase his sense of personal worth throughout life. It demands a school program in which interests are encouraged because of what they mean to the individual student, what they promise by way of genuine success for him in the course of the years—irrespective of either their practical import or the traditional academic idols.[45]

In the curriculum movement, attempts have been made to establish such interests by trying to discover the special talents which boys and girls have and by developing them "creatively" or by giving attention to them through specially designed courses. Another way has been to organize clubs and other groups for the purpose of stimulating and sponsoring hobbies. Still another method has been by attaching adult values and social approval to the possession of certain bits of information or identification with certain activities. This theory of interest is a theory of "outsideness," as far as interests are concerned, as they are set up as objects of personal identification to be acquired from the outside world. It is maintained in general that they come from the outside, that they exist in society or in the environment as a whole, that they have within themselves an attractiveness, and that the problem of getting them identified with the learner is one of instruction or contagion. Spaulding elaborates upon this idea of interests when he says of teachers:

> They ought *not* to assume that the way to get interest is to wait until their pupils show some "spontaneous interest" and then to teach whatever that interest suggests. There is no such thing as a truly spontaneous inter-

43. *Ibid.*, pp. 379–380.
44. *Ibid.*, p. 388.
45. Thayer, Zachry, and Kotinsky, *Reorganizing Secondary Education*, p. 312.

est. Every interest that a boy or girl has comes to him originally from out-side—if not from the school, then from the movies, the radio, the funnies, the gang swapping yarns on the corner, and the stories that fathers tell of what they used to do when they were boys. It is a poor teacher who will let what he teaches be dictated by the notions that his pupils get from everyone except himself. The teacher who is worth his salt starts interests; he does not wait for them to be started by some chance incident over which he has no control.

He starts interests most often by making no secret of his own interests. There is no getting around the need of his having interests of his own if he is to awaken interests in others. Granting that he does have such inter-ests, he sets out to make his pupils feel them as he does. He recalls how he himself first became interested, and he provides for his pupils the same experiences, or experiences like them, that gave him his original thrill.[46]

George Counts, however, has a different idea in mind when he says, "All interests are 'spontaneous' in the sense that they spring from the individual's own nature; . . . interests are always products of the union of the organism with circumstance."[47]

Interests as the Source of Curriculum Content

The third position is one that has been supported by a small group of leaders in "progressive schools" where the spontaneous interests of children have been used as the source of curriculum content. It is argued that individual pupil interests should become the basis of learning, if the true nature of the pupil is to be discovered and fostered, and if individuality is to be "unfolded from within." This theory springs from some of the ideas of Rousseau. It was characterized by such expressions as "take off the lid."

Belief in such a doctrine is quite limited, and it has received some stunning blows from educational leaders. John Dewey, who many thought sponsored the idea, cried out against such practice:

> There is a present tendency in so-called advanced schools of educational thought (by no means confined to art classes like those of Cizek) to say, in effect, let us surround pupils with certain materials, tools, appliances, etc., and then let pupils respond to these things according to their own desires. Above all let us not suggest any end or plan to the students; let us not suggest to them what they shall do, for that is an unwarranted trespass upon their sacred intellectual individuality since the essence of such individuality is to set up ends and aims.

---

46. Spaulding, *Interest in Learning,* pp. 52–54.
47. See George Counts' statement on interest in National Society for the Study of Educa-tion, *The Foundations of Curriculum Making* (Twenty-sixth Yearbook; Bloomington, Illinois: Public School Publishing Co., 1927), Part II, pp. 77–80.

Now such a method is really stupid. For it attempts the impossible, which is always stupid; and it misconceives the conditions of independent thinking.[48]

Counts expressed himself also about this point of view:

Much is said concerning the need of organizing the curriculum about the child's interests. That curriculum making must have regard for these interests is obvious; but that this means an uncritical incorporation into the school program of any activity in which under any conditions the child may display an interest is clearly an indefensible article of faith. Yet the principle that the child's interest should be recognized is often given this interpretation. Any interest that the child may manifest is then regarded as a safe, and an almost sacred, pedagogical guide. The logical implication of such a doctrine is that the curriculum-maker has no function and should abdicate his office in favor of the interests of the child. The learner is made the artisan of his own educational program.[49]

It seems reasonably clear that the curriculum maker must use these various connotations of interest. There must be an inner motive based upon an identification of the self with the activity or experience if learning is to proceed satisfactorily; individuals need to have life-long sustaining interests which give them pleasure and foster their growth and development; and the curriculum must use the interests which the learner has developed. These interests, however, at any particular time are specifics which are the result of maturation. It is not enough for people to have interests, nor enough for the curriculum to be built solely on the interests of individual learners. To what extent, then, should the interests of individual learners be utilized? To what extent should the larger interests of the group be used? Who should determine what these larger interests are? In a democratic society these are important questions, for one of the needs of society today is the multiplication of mutual interests and the enlargement of individual interests to national and international ones.

The Meaning of Purpose

In the discussions regarding both interests and needs the term "purpose" has frequently arisen. Probably no idea has been more difficult for the psychologist to explain than the one of purpose in the human organism. Let us therefore look at some of the meanings implied in the use of the term.

All behavior moves toward certain goals. The disturbed organism, seeking to regain balance, moves in certain directions, and whatever it does is pur-

---

48. John Dewey and others, *Art and Education* (New York: Barnes Foundation Press, 1929), p. 180. By permission of the publishers.
49. Counts, in *Foundations of Curriculum Making*, p. 77.

posive in the direction of the balance it wishes to restore. Behavior or activity is intentional, planned, directional; it is selective, unified, and consciously discharged. This restored balance may be temporarily satisfying, and thus a minor purpose may be achieved; but it may be for a period of time only partially satisfying, but later quite satisfying, and thus a larger purpose is set up. This larger purpose rests upon major social drives and derives from the nature of the culture. These purposes lead to a system of values which offer directional force to the character of the moves we make. When minor purposes are followed, they tend to cause an individual to persist in his endeavors to achieve larger purposes and really become disciplined, which, Allport points out,[50] is a quality of persistence under internal pressure. He contends that this internal pressure is purpose. One of the interesting things in social life is that we have different terms for this persistence, depending upon whether or not it meets our own criterion of goodness. If this persistence is consistently toward a goal we deem good, we call it loyalty; if it is toward one we disdain, we call it stubbornness or even foolhardiness.

Dewey defines purpose as "an end view. That is, it involves foresight of the consequences which will result from acting upon impulse."[51] Childs thinks it is an activity "freely initiated" by the individual when he faces a situation with difficulties which challenge him.[52] Caswell characterizes purpose thus:

> Purpose is looked upon as that characteristic of experience which serves the general function of organizing, vitalizing, and relating the activities in which people engage and the objects with which they deal. It is the operation of purpose through activities which makes the difference between a mere series or sequence of acts and a "progressive co-ordination" of acts as means to an end. Activities and objects take on unity and meaning as they are related to particular ends or purposes an individual is endeavoring to realize.[53]

Purpose and Growth

Purpose seems to be central to the development of the individual. It is both the starting point of human activity and the end toward which it is moving. Growth is a continuous reformulation of ever-higher purposes. Thus the whole organism is engaged. When a purpose is satisfied, the organism develops into

---

50. See G. W. Allport, *Personality: A Psychological Interpretation* (New York: Henry Holt and Company, 1937).

51. John Dewey, *Experience and Education* (New York: The Macmillan Company, 1938), p. 78.

52. See John L. Childs, *Education and the Philosophy of Experimentalism* (New York: Appleton-Century-Crofts, Inc., 1931).

53. Caswell and Campbell, *Curriculum Development*, p. 191. By permission of the publishers.

an integrated personality; but when the purpose is thwarted, disintegration begins and continues until a reconciliation has taken place. Purpose is, then, explained as a unified affair involving the organism and the environment and cannot be explained as a series of separate parts or reactions.

CURRICULUM IMPLICATIONS.　The formulation of purposes is a rather difficult task because it involves not only the knowledge of both past and present conditions but also the making of judgments about what is the desirable thing to do in the situation. Obviously, much attention must be given in school to practice in stating purposes. This means pupils must set their own purposes in so far as is possible, but where they may not voluntarily choose to act in acceptable ways, they must be led to accept willingly those purposes which the teacher deems desirable. Society through the social mores sets many of the patterns of behavior and these need to be accepted willingly until they can be improved by the individual. On the other hand, care must be exercised that choosing another's purposes does not become a habit, for if adults tend continuously to set learning purposes, youth will fail to learn to formulate their own. They will learn to live by authority rather than by their own judgment.

If purposes direct behavior, the teacher cannot be neutral about their formulation. Purposes must be in harmony with the nature of the democratic society we desire, in harmony with the most desirable goals of the particular individual, and must be developed in such a way as to provide for a continuity in the process.

The Meaning of Experience

A major philosophical-psychological argument ensues when the term "experience" is used. If growth and development proceed normally by accretion through the use of congenital capacities, the educational program will be of one type. If, on the other hand, the individual develops his personality through experience, then education will be something quite different. Dewey formulated the theory of experience as an organic adjustment process of growth and development. He has been criticized for this explanation of human behavior, but he has ridden out these vigorous attacks and has tremendously affected educational practice.[54] It is necessary, then, to understand the meaning and implications of his theory.

---

54. For vigorous criticisms of Dewey's idea of experience see Frederick S. Breed, *Education and the New Realism* (New York: The Macmillan Company, 1939); H. H. Horn, *The Democratic Philosophy of Education* (New York: The Macmillan Company, 1932). See also the attack by Robert M. Hutchins in *Fortune,* June, 1943, p. 159. For arguments on these positions, see the report of the Second Conference on the Scientific Spirit and Democratic Faith, entitled *The Authoritarian Attempt to Capture Education* (New York: The King's Crown Press, 1945), Chaps. 1–3.

John Dewey's Theory

For years the theory of "development from without" has dominated education, thus leading to a knowledge-to-be-learned type of curriculum. Such a theory is in harmony with the authoritarian concepts which have prevailed in all areas of life, but when the sacred authoritarian idols have been swept away, there must come in their place some theory to explain the nature of development. Such a theory is the one proposed by Dewey—the explanation of development through experience.

Dewey defines experience as having an active and a passive phase. It involves both the individual and some aspect of the environment; as they interact, each modifies the other, and a relationship is detected between the two. The result is experience. But he hastens to say that there is a difference between "experience" and "an experience." He distinguishes them in this fashion:

> Experience occurs continuously. . . . Oftentimes, however, the experience had is inchoate. Things are experienced but not in such a way that they are composed into *an* experience. There is distraction and dispersion; what we observe and what we think, what we desire and what we get, are at odds with each other. We put our hands to the plow and turn back; we start and then we stop, not because the experience has reached the end for the sake of which it was initiated but because of extraneous interruptions or of inner lethargy.
>
> In contrast with such experience, we have *an* experience when the material experienced runs its course to fulfillment. Then and then only is it integrated within and demarcated in the general stream of experience from other experiences. A piece of work is finished in a way that is satisfactory; a problem receives its solution; a game is played through; a situation, whether that of eating a meal, playing a game of chess, carrying on a conversation, writing a book, or taking part in a political campaign, is so rounded out that its close is a consummation and not a cessation. Such an experience is a whole and carries with it is own individualizing quality and self-sufficiency. It is *an* experience.[55]

This contrast between doing something just for the sake of activity and doing something with a purpose, carrying it out to its ultimate satisfactory completion, is exceedingly valuable. One of the boasts of the traditional school was that it required hard work and a completed task, thus providing discipline. Likewise, one of the criticisms of modern education, and very just criticism of some practices, has been that pupils engaged in random activities which were supposed to have educative values because they were chosen by the boys and girls themselves. The idea that things must have meaning in the individual's

---

55. John Dewey, *Art as Experience* (New York: G. P. Putnam's Sons, 1934), p. 35. By permission of the publishers.

own development and that the activities in which he engages must have relationship is important. But just as important, if not more so, is the emphasis upon *completing* the task, so that proper growth and development take place. Thus, under this concept of inner development through meaningful experience, more "discipline" is acquired than under the traditional program, and it is a kind of discipline which engages the total self or personality.

Such an experience also builds knowledge and is an essential part of the total resolution of a disturbance. Wisdom, then, is not just for the competent few, and knowledge is not a series of facts to be classified on the basis of abstract difficulty; rather it is the stuff of which individuality and personal competence are built, for it is used in each individual experience. Each person builds his own logic of life and wisdom. Information and solutions will vary with time, conditions, and individuals; and the selection of the necessary knowledge is a function of whatever is involved in the particular situation. The worth of subjects varies for individual minds and experience. Even a book is suited to an individual with a particular problem.

Experiences tend to flow from one into another. A "Flow Chart" will help to show how they affect one another.

"FLOW CHART" OF A COMPLETE LIVING EXPERIENCE*

Individual with past experiences →	faces a new situation, novel to him, resulting in →	a disturbance, disequilibrium →
out of which emerges a *purpose* →	*to do something*)→	i.e., to share a thought or feeling, acquire an object or information, express a mood, etc. →
Each type of behavior suggested has its own medium of expression— →	constructing, dramatizing, reading, asking questions, writing, speaking, figuring, drawing, etc.— →	and each medium has its own appropriate skills, techniques, facts, attitudes, appreciations, etc., ←
which have to be acquired in the normal process of achieving the purpose set; →	when these skills, facts, attitudes are thus built into the learner in normal goal-seeking, →	they give satisfaction in restoring the equilibrium of the personality and leave him ready to face the next novel situation with increased power to live and learn.

* Prepared by Paul R. Hanna for use in curriculum classes at Stanford University.

CURRICULUM IMPLICATIONS.   The acceptance of this idea of experience casts heavy burdens upon the educator. In the first place, the teacher must see the direction in which the experience is moving, Aimlessness is not a virtue, nor is it an adequate substitute for formalism. Experience so affects the individual that he acquires a direction through having had it. He is then more likely to make second choices in the direction of the experiences just undergone. Adults, because of their greater maturity and insight, need to give direction to the experience of children. Dewey makes this point:

> Failure [of the adult] to take the moving force of an experience into account so as to judge and direct it on the ground of what it is moving into means disloyalty to the principle of experience itself. The disloyalty operates in two directions. The educator is false to the understanding that he should have obtained from his own past experience. He is also unfaithful to the fact that all human experience is ultimately social; that it involves contact and communication. The mature person, to put it in moral terms, has no right to withhold from the young on given occasions whatever capacity for sympathetic understanding his own experience has given him.[56]

The teacher, then, must help guide the direction of the experiences of his pupils. This is a difficult task and is the chief reason why teaching in this fashion is a more difficult responsibility than teaching in a more traditional setup.

In the second place, acceptance of this theory places responsibility upon the teacher for selecting and evaluating each experience most suited to each individual. An environment good for one person may be disorganizing to another; an experience may stimulate one while it discourages another; an activity may develop one while it injures another. Thus is laid upon the teacher the responsibility for selecting particular experiences to suit individuals. Activities require the same careful attention. The mere performance of an act of an overt nature is not of itself valuable nor is multiplicity of activities necessarily educative, even though they may be informal. They must be related to the goals established and to the abilities of the individual.

In the third place, the subject matter of experience must be carefully organized. Some have maintained that there can be no advance organization of subject matter without injuring the "delicate growth mechanisms" of the child. Organization is a form of maturation, is the function of each orderly mind; but as a necessary part of learning, it is to be carefully distinguished from a ready-made organization of materials prepared by one mind to be assimilated by another. But organization implies continuity of experience as well. Simply to have breadth of experience is not enough. Experiences must be in sequence toward a given purpose. This involves a relation to the past as well as to the ongoing present and future. A clear line of continuity of experiences

---

56. John Dewey, *Experience and Education* (New York: The Macmillan Company, 1938), p. 32. By permission of Kappa Delta Pi. This entire book is one of the best treatises available on the subject.

should guide the selection of particular activities. Organization, pattern, and plans are necessary if there is to be continuity in the content of experiences. The acceptance of this position commits the individual to believe in the necessity for orderly planning on the part of the teacher.

Relation of Activities to Experience

The word "activity" has been one of the most confusing in educational literature, largely because of the different practices to which it has been applied. In 1934 a committee of the National Society for the Study of Education tried to clarify the meaning of the term, particularly as it applied to the elementary school and to the activity movement.[57] The committee examined forty-two definitions from educational leaders, twenty-five curricula, and fifteen books on the subject and found great diversity of opinion. In general, as applied to curriculum matters, the term has two basic usages. One of these is in relation to a type of curriculum movement, largely in the elementary school; the other is in relation to a kind of action in connection with all learning.

Since the first use of the term is confined largely to the elementary school, we shall examine it only slightly. About the turn of the century there grew up a movement in this country against the passive type of education offered to elementary school children.[58] The old-fashioned "sitting school" was thought to be injurious to children and to use unnatural means of teaching them to improve their behavior. Stimulated by the ideas of Rousseau, Froebel, Pestalozzi, and others, schools adopted the practice of having children engage in many activities other than reading or passive seatwork. This, like most movements, went to extreme, and many people came to associate the word "activity" with overt bodily movement. A child reading a book, listening to music, doing arithmetic problems was not engaging in activities, but he was if he was running, cutting out pictures, building a cabin, or drawing a donkey. The movement gained momentum, and children overindulged in physical activities of all types.

Quite naturally a reaction set in and questions arose. Was this the right emphasis? Who should select the activities—teachers or pupils, or both? Did it make any difference in what activities children engaged? Was the teacher to make any attempt to relate, suggest, control, or unify these activities? Educational discussions on the elementary school devoted much time to these questions. The movement did not affect the secondary school, beyond probably helping to liberalize the number and variety of things which pupils did in and out of schools.

The second use of the term arose out of a conflict over whether an activity

---

57. National Society for the Study of Education, *The Activity Movement* (Thirty-third Yearbook; Bloomington, Illinois: Public School Publishing Co., 1934). Part I.
58. See *Ibid.*, Chap. 2 for the history of the entire movement in this country and in Europe.

was a method of learning or a worth-while thing in itself. Some felt that pupils could be induced to learn better if they used means other than reading. To learn the geography of Europe they could build a map, instead of simply studying one from a book. To become familiar with the structure of a house, children could build one instead of watching it being built by others or studying a constructed house. The use of the term in this fashion implies a technique of teaching. Difficulties arose here because of the feeling that such activity was purely physical and that it was a procedure to elevate "handwork" to a place of equal importance with "intellectual work." Some thought handwork did not involve thought; it was not intellectual. Hence, a dichotomy was debated, one between handwork and headwork; and subjects in school tended to be respected in proportion to the amount of physical activities involved in their learning.

Contrary to this position is the idea that activities are not higher or lower in importance according to the amount of headwork or handwork involved. Both kinds are an integral part of the total life process, and each is to be equally respected for the service it renders to personality development. If a purpose is set up and a need established, any activity which is necessary to secure the proper personality or behavioral adjustment is educationally valuable. Each is to be judged by the extent to which it contributes to the desired pattern of development, rather than by the nature of the process involved in carrying it out.

Activities are not ends in themselves; they are means by which goals are reached. Direction should not be derived from an action, and pupils should not be stimulated simply to get busy and act, so that out of such actions the teacher may draw something significant. Purposes, goals, needs should come first, and activities should be selected to satisfy them. There must be in any normal learning situation a large variety of activities—planning, reading, appreciating, creating, constructing—because ends are achieved differently by different people. An activity is not a method of teaching, or even a method of organizing instruction; it is a way the organism has of responding to needs. An intellectual act of reading is just as much an activity as nailing boards together. Activities also need to be related to one another in their contribution to total development. Any desirable school program, then, should contain a variety of activities, selected so that they accomplish the purpose of the learner, further the process of personality development, and achieve the goals of education. They are a total and an integral part of the learning process.

Theory and Practice

Educational theory furnishes the basis for improved educational practice. Each generation of teachers has fashioned the curriculum upon the goals of society and their prevailing belief in the nature of learning. What one believes is important, for it determines the kind of school program that will prevail. Unless teachers and other curriculum workers understand conflicting theories and accept certain basic beliefs, they will have nothing upon which they can build soundly. Let us, then, turn our attention to the curriculum practices which have evolved from these opposing theories.

Chapter Five

Basic Conflicts in

Curriculum Practices

FROM ARISTOTLE'S TIME to the present, many men have held that the cultivation of reason or of thinking power is the highest aim of education. Plato even went so far as to contend that the mechanic arts debased men's bodies and souls. The lack of confidence in democracy and the consistent aristocratic ideas of Plato and Aristotle make them poor guides to follow in the determination of the subject matter of democratic education; yet through tradition they have kept a phenomenal influence upon the curriculum of the secondary school.

The curriculum, then, will be partially determined by the way we conceive of thinking. Thorndike sees it as a series of connections, a theory which means that we should choose the subject matter which enables the pupils to make the proper connections. Dewey sees it as a problem-solving process involving a difficulty, observation, suggested solutions, testing, and the drawing of conclusions. If we follow Dewey's analysis, we will select subject matter which is problematical in nature and based upon the ever-present experience of the learner in his own life situations. Until psychology helps us more adequately to analyze the thinking act and to determine just what kinds of exercise produce different types of thinking, we shall still be in the area of argument without proof. If we want a democracy where each person is to think his way through life situations and where his solution is to have the respect of other men, then we will choose a type of education suited to the social pattern we desire. On the other hand, if we want a society of aristocrats who are supposed to do the thinking for men and who are to be supported by contented followers only partially informed, we will need a different type of education and thinking. If we want a dictatorship where individual thinking leads to the firing squad, our education will be of still another order. But all education will be influenced by the type of social order we desire. While it is therefore necessary that we know how people think and how to secure competence in thinking, the nature of the social order must influence our decision on subject matter and on the types of thinking we desire. Education is truly a social process related closely to the political character of our society.

Another argument in this area is over whether the materials of instruction shall be taken from the life of the adult or of the child. Again this has been thought to be a dichotomy. To build a curriculum upon the immediate interests or whims of the young child or youth is to be on unsafe ground. Too much concern is given to immediate experience or knowledge of the individual, and the necessity for adult guidance in the development of youth is ignored. On the other hand, to take all the materials from the world of the adult is to disregard the maturation level of the youth and to present him with materials and problems which are not his own and have no meaning or significance to him. To confront him only with experiences that have been undergone by men in the past makes it impossible for him to relive them in his own areas of activity. We must teach him the "pregnant realities of life."

Criteria for Selecting Subject Matter

The selection of materials, then, must proceed on the basis of the level of growth of the individual, his own purposes, the needs he sees or can be brought to feel, and the pressures of the social mores around him at his own level of growth. He builds and grows with what he can incorporate into his own experience. All other materials will be superfluous or unused. Subject matter is a function of the individual, of time, and of social customs. What may be suitable for one individual is worthless for another. Louise Rosenblatt had this in mind when she argued that the pupil was as important as the book.[1] Also, what may be subject matter at one time may not be at another.

---

1. See Louise Rosenblatt, *Literature as Exploration* (New York: Appleton-Century-Crofts, Inc., 1938).

The selection must suit the purpose, the time, the problem at hand. For the curriculum worker this means that subject matter should be selected in terms of potential values and that teachers should cooperate in selecting these potentials. A course outline is properly conceived as a body of potentials. The eventual selection of actual subject matter will rest with the teacher and the pupils at the time of learning.

The one remaining criterion for selecting subject matter is the behavior desired of the individual—the aims of education in a democratic society. If we want individuals to have certain attitudes, knowledge, skill for social participation, it is necessary that we plan our materials of instruction so that the desired behavior patterns will have opportunity to develop. Careful study needs to be made of individual and social needs and of the multiplicity of activities necessary to secure adequate practice in satisfying these needs. If we wish merely to acquire information, we need to allow plenty of opportunity for youth to read. If we wish to establish attitudes and social behavior compatible with our form of life, we will provide experiences in carrying on life activities.

Wingo points out that the most significant principle contributed by the philosophy of experimentalism for teachers is that

> thinking occurs only in response to a problematic situation; and the point of greatest importance is that the situation must be *problematic to the learner, not merely to the teacher*. The greatest enemies of reflective thought are those things which destroy the necessity for thinking—routine, arbitrary prescription of activities, insistence on passive absorption of predetermined content. While habit gives experience pattern and continuity, and thus makes thought possible, habit is insufficient to meet the needs of a constantly changing natural and social environment.[2]

One state committee recently sought to identify its educational landmarks for curriculum planning in terms of the type of citizen to be educated. After stating the role of the modern school as an institution of all the people, it goes on to say:

> The major function of public education is to make it possible for each learner to become more and more effective as a citizen in a democracy that is continuously changing, improving, and playing a significant role in the world scene. Education must develop the basic principles and fundamental ideals of American democracy within the minds and hearts of American youth. Hence it is important to instill a love and an appreciation for the developing American way of life.

---

2. G. Max Wingo, "A Theoretical Basis for the Activity Program," Chap. 9 of *Toward Improved Educational Theory* (Supplementary Educational Monographs, No. 71; Chicago: University of Chicago Press, 1950), p. 94.

The educational point of view of the California public schools is rooted in a deep, abiding faith in American democracy. Education in a democracy must aim toward building citizens who are enthusiastic about the values of democracy for all peoples; who accept the responsibilities as well as the privileges of citizenship; and who are capable of grappling creatively with problems that arise.

Education in a democracy is concerned with the education of free men— loyal to the values and process of democracy, with knowledge to guard their freedom, and possessing the discipline and vision to enable them to sacrifice personal and immediate gain to the general welfare. This is the kind of education that faith in American democracy demands and this is the keynote of public education in California. Belief in the welfare of society and belief in the welfare of the individual are both basic to the democratic ideal.

We are more and more concerned with the facility in living democratically. This involves the processes of group planning, deliberating, deciding, and acting. We are equally insistent that participants in the democratic process have common understandings essential to reach sound solutions and a deeper understanding of the nature of the world community. The skills that are necessary for the individual and the group to arrive at appropriate democratic behavior in specific situations are basic to the purposes of public education in California.[3]

No *single* source of subject matter can be used—cultural heritage, child interest, or adult interest. The curriculum worker will draw upon all of them, but he must draw upon them with a new central focus in mind, the focus of the emerging democratic citizen.

Values to Be Sought

Any program of education is governed by the values it seeks to establish. These values grow out of the collective opinion of the group and are reflected in the content and method of the school program. In determining values and in speaking of them in curriculum literature, educators have used a series of opposed terms, or have used dual terms in opposed fashion. This again is another case of dualism and is not likely to lead to clear thinking. The most commonly used terms in this connection are (1) instrumental or consummatory values, (2) immediate or deferred values, (3) personal or social values, (4) cultural or vocational values, (5) child or adult values. A word about each may be helpful.

---

3. California State Curriculum Commission, *A Framework for Public Education in California* (Sacramento, Calif.: California State Department of Education, 1950), pp. 4–5.

Instrumental versus Consummatory

Many subjects in the curriculum have been considered to have instrumental values, and apparently there was little other need for teaching them. This was especially true in the days when the theory of formal discipline was accepted. Latin or geometry, for instance, was taught because of the mind-training value each possessed. These subjects were thought to possess transferable disciplines and were instrumental because they helped the learner do something else. Later, Latin acquired another instrumental value—helping the child with his English grammar or with word study. Music sometimes suffered under the instrumental value of keeping boys out of mischief.

On the other hand, we have what we may call consummatory values which are those worthy in themselves. Thomas H. Briggs, by his doctrine of interests, did much to give place and purpose to anything which seemed significant for the pupil to cherish. In claiming that everybody should have interests, that these were individual, that any interest was better than none, that each should respect the interest of others, and that interests were worth while in themselves, he gave many things a new reason for being. Doubtless this is the greatest place for Latin today, as its claims to instrumental values have been difficult to support. In short, then, any value which leads to a purpose outside itself or contributory to itself is instrumental; those which have their own reason for being are consummatory.

Immediate versus Deferred

Immediate values are those which an individual can cash immediately; a deferred one accumulates in value to be utilized at a later time. We often speak of teaching a child how to dress himself, to eat with a fork, to play a musical instrument, to make a dress, and to learn to run a lathe because these give him an opportunity to do something immediately. There is an immediate use for some skills and for certain types of information. One of the best illustrations of this is the war-training program during World War II. Goals were immediate and tangible, and the learning could be easily identified with the values to be gained from the training.

On the other hand, there are said to be values which are realized later. Some teachers claim that a knowledge of certain terms used in chemistry will later be useful in reading books and magazines where science terms are used, that learning the facts of the development of Western civilization will help one to understand throughout life the daily happenings abroad, that learning algebra will help one to teach his own children later. These learnings must look to the future for their utility. Frequently, modern languages are similarly represented: they may later aid pupils in finding employment in foreign countries. The same type of justification is made for most college entrance requirements.

Personal versus Social

Another dualistic classification is sometimes called personal and social values. We speak of values accruing to an individual from the study of a subject. Certain learnings may make him a more interesting conversationalist, or may develop his personality in a certain way, or may give him abilities to engage successfully in certain social affairs and thus bring credit and attention to himself. Any values which are primarily lodged in the enhancement of the individual are, then, of this category.

On the other hand, we often speak of values as being chiefly social. That is, the things learned contribute to the enhancement of the group or the general welfare. One may develop certain attitudes in studying history and economics which will cause him to give his time to reforming the social system to bring about more equitable living conditions, or he may develop a social-mindedness which causes him to participate in every good social cause, or he may develop skills which result in inventions of value and importance to society.

Cultural versus Vocational

Many educational arguments have developed over the difference between cultural and vocational values. Some have maintained that anything which produced a salable skill was vocational in nature and should come under that category; others have maintained that such a classification is individual in nature rather than general, because what might be a vocational skill for one person would be an entirely different skill for another. One man might build houses for a living with his skill in carpentry, while another might make model ships for a hobby. One woman might use superior knowledge of English to teach others, while another might use it for her own interest in reading literature for leisure. Those who support this division between cultural and vocational have claimed that those skills and facts which were general in nature or which led to an understanding of the factors of life common to all of us were cultural and not vocational. According to this theory, knowledge of history, of art forms, of musicology, and of languages was cultural.[4]

Child versus Adult

The matter of child or adult values has also dogged education. It is probably

---

4. For a discussion of this conflict see Chap. I in National Society for the Study of Education, *Vocational Education* (Forty-second Yearbook; Chicago: University of Chicago Press, 1943), Part I.

as old as civilization, this gulf between youth and age, but it is most apparent in an educational system operated by adults for children, especially when older adults are so numerous in the classrooms of the nation. If a value is one which a child can recognize, which he accepts, and which motivates his effort in learning, it is said to be a child value. Frequently, these have been said to come only from the child himself; he must propose them. On the other hand, this position has been modified so that it matters not who discovers or proposes these values as long as the child accepts or recognizes them. Those values which are determined by adults and are more characteristic of adult than of child experience are said to be adult values, such as good citizenship or a knowledge of what to do about certain social problems.

When one analyzes these classifications, it appears that they, too, are academic terms selected by people to point out differences in their thinking. They serve best those who formulate them and are more valuable as ideas for discussion than for their functional use in selecting curriculum content. It stands to reason that none of these is exclusively "either . . . or." By their very nature, they cannot be. In the first place, value differences are a matter of degree, not of kind. Every value has some of both qualities in each of the supposed opposites. In the second place, values are individual rather than general in their actual use. The old saying that "one man's meat is another man's poison" is true here. What one uses immediately, the other postpones. In the third place, this classification of extremes is out of harmony with modern psychological interpretation of experience and more in line with a mechanistic or formalistic conception of mind and intelligence.

Values, then, are not abstract goods or ideas which can be isolated from experience and classified. As Thorndike put it a number of years ago, "Value or worth or the good means *power* to *satisfy wants*,"[5] and as Dewey points out, we are aware of them as "qualities in qualitative relations." Values are tendencies in experience and are too complicated to be defined in a dualistic fashion. The direction they take, from a degree standpoint, may be more toward one than toward another, but in traveling in that direction they do not slough off attendant relationships.

> Tendencies of experience do not have limits that are exactly fixed or that are mathematical lines without breadth and thickness. Experience is too rich and complex to permit such precise limitation. The termini of tendencies are bands, not lines, and the qualities that characterize them form a spectrum instead of being capable of distribution in separate pigeon-holes.[6]

5. E. L. Thorndike, *Education* (New York: The Macmillan Company, 1912), p. 10.
6. John Dewey, *Art as Experience* (New York: G. P. Putnam's Sons, 1934), p. 224. By permission of the publishers.

Formation of Value Patterns

What distinguishes people is not only what they know and can do but the things they place value upon. What people believe is important, for it is a force in determining behavior. Beliefs have directional power. Experience causes people to generalize upon what activities produce satisfying adjustments, and these they hold to be good. From experience criteria are evolved which are used to judge new experiences. Relationships are then established among experiences. As these relationships change, values change. Criticism and the use of the critical method in evaluating experience are tools in the formation of values. Understanding is important, facts are essential, and skills are necessary in the formation of values, but attitudes also play a most prominent part. These attitudes in turn serve to guide the use to which understandings and skills may be put. They are important in helping man to choose what he wants from life. They cause him to assess some things high and other things low. He assigns worth, importance, value; and he fights to sustain those things which he has assessed highly.

Prescott points out that these attitudes may range all the way from simple bodily self-interest up to a complex mental organization of abstract values.[7] These attitudes may fall into four groups: (1) self-preservation drives, (2) generalized concepts growing out of satisfying experience (particular and a series of experiences), (3) attitudes arising from abstract value concepts, and (4) purposive attitudes, the highest form. This analysis of values is interesting for several reasons, but we need to see the implications in building the attitudes.

Educationally, there are three types of attitudes: (1) those which are primarily bodily, (2) those which are affected primarily by experience, individual and group, and are determined much by the nature of the mores, customs, demands of the social group; and (3) those which grow out of a mental process of rationalization, organization, and generalization. Again, the abilities of individuals to form these attitudes are matters of individual differences, and, like intelligence, the difference is one of degree, a difference in the power to utilize experience and to deal with it. Behavior is a matter of maturity and of the relationships of drives. Prescott summarizes the position helpfully thus:

> The process of maturing involves the building up of the capacity for the realistic differentiation of patterns of affective behavior appropriate to the different situations in which the individual finds himself. This process is highly individual, for behavior always is a function of the

---

7. Daniel A. Prescott, *Emotion and the Educative Process* (Washington: American Council on Education, 1938), pp. 59–61.

dynamic relationships between the attitudes (quasi-needs) of the individual and the immediate situations in which he finds himself. The patterns of affective behavior which he shows are, then, the results of the attitudes ingrained by experience and self-interest. Naturally, innate structural factors are more influential in determining some behavior patterns, and experimental factors are relatively more important in others. In sexual behavior, for example, structural factors are more important, while experiential factors are more important in shaping behavior in response to fear of unemployment or of poverty in old age. The important point is that the emerging behavior must be appropriate to satisfy the individual's needs in the culture in which he finds himself and that the culture sets certain limits upon the behavior which it will accept. There is the further point that the behavior, to be appropriate, must take into consideration the realities of the physical world and of other people's needs. To gain insight into what constitutes affective maturity, then, is to learn what behavior will satisfy needs in the culture in which the individual lives, while it takes all aspects of reality into consideration. The problem which educators face, once they know this, is to find out what experiences will give developing young people the attitudes and ruling value concepts that can be the basis for valid choices of behavior patterns in the situations which they will meet.[8]

Values, then, are partially determined by the communities—social and physical—in which one lives, and one basic criterion of successful education is the extent to which the schools are able to cause the individual to reconcile his behavior, in a world of conflicting values, through insight into environmental experience. Kelley forcefully makes the point:

> The capacity to become educated depends on the capacity of the individual to relinquish what he has held and to build new habit patterns in keeping with new environmental demands. The most important factor in education then becomes the arrangements that the one to be educated makes with his environment through his senses, of which vision is the most important.[9]

Jersild's studies show that any sound educational program must take into full account the individual's powers and capacities as well as the most prominent developmental tendencies at a particular period of growth if the student is to reach his potential level of maturity. Every child has not only the capacity to learn, but has an "appetite for learning." Recognizing these "appetites" at the appropriate point of development is a challenge to the school to capitalize on this principle of spontaneous use. He says:

> While education should count upon the child's impulse to use growing capacities as an integral feature of his development, it is the responsibility

---

8. *Ibid.*, pp. 94–95. By permission of the publishers. See Thomas Briggs, J. Paul Leonard, and Joseph Justman, *Secondary Education,* Chaps. 11 and 15 on "Emotionalized Attitudes" (New York: The Macmillan Company, 1950), pp. 261–309.

9. Earl C. Kelley, *Education for What Is Real* (New York: Harper & Brothers, 1947), p. 52.

of education, increasingly as the child grows older, to find the best channels through which such impulses can be expressed. In exercising this responsibility, educators must weigh particular interests against larger aspects of the child's present and future welfare. In so doing, they can also properly capitalize on the fact that where there is potential ability there is also potential interest, that a child can learn to like to do anything that he is able to do and that offers a continuing challenge to his energies.[10]

Nature of Curriculum Aims

There have been many ways of stating aims or objectives of education. Usually they have been formulated by committees engaged in curriculum revision and have varied tremendously in their relationship to the subsequent program. Four methods of stating aims are most common: (1) in terms of specific achievement, (2) in terms of desired social goals, (3) in terms of individual behavior traits, and (4) in terms of problems. Illustrations of each of these will further clarify the differences.

Illustrations of Specific Achievement Aims

Aims looking toward specific achievement are directed toward the acquisition of certain information, facts, skills, and principles. These are usually in connection with a subject, although they may be more generalized in that they may be acquired through many subjects.

Some illustrations of these types of objectives operating in actual curriculum programs will demonstrate the meaning of these types of aims.

ALGEBRA, OAKLAND

ALGEBRA I

(Secondary Schools)

1. An understanding of the language of algebra and the ability to use its basic concepts and ideas intelligently
2. An appreciation of the significance of the formula, and the ability to construct, evaluate, and transform simple formulas
3. The ability to analyze a simple verbal problem and to express the relationships involved in equation form
4. An appreciation of the importance of graphic representation in everyday life, and the ability to use the graphical method as a valuable mathematical tool
5. An appreciation of the fundamental laws and operations of algebra as

---

10. Arthur T. Jersild and others, *Child Development and the Curriculum* (New York: Columbia University, Teachers College, Bureau of Publications, 1946), pp. 16–17.

applied to signed numbers, and the ability to perform the essential algebraic operations with reasonable skill and accuracy

6. An appreciation of the importance of the equation, and the ability to apply the equation method in the solution of verbal problems[11]

LATIN, HARRISBURG

LATIN I

(Secondary Schools)

1. Growth in the ability to read Latin with understanding and enjoyment
2. Development of the ability to correlate the basic principles of Latin and English
3. Recognition of the precise meaning of many English words through understanding the dynamic significance of their Latin roots, prefixes, and suffixes
4. Acquisition of a body of Latin roots and linguistic concepts that will aid the student in the study of French, Italian, Spanish, German, Greek, Russian, and other foreign languages
5. Practice in linguistic processes that stimulate the development of accuracy, thoroughness, and perseverance
6. Development of an appreciation of literary excellence through the study of the logical structure, selective use of words, figures of speech, and the euphony that characterize classic Latin expression[12]

CHEMISTRY, SAN FRANCISCO

CHEMISTRY

(Grade 11)

1. To know the contributions to chemistry of ancient people
2. To see and understand cause-and-effect relationships
3. To understand thoroughly and be able to apply to life's problems the scientific method of problem solving
4. To know and understand the metric system of measurements as a useful tool in life's work
5. To see the value of scientific research to mankind
6. To know and understand the law of conservation of matter
7. To know and understand the law of conservation of energy
8. To know and understand the difference between physical and chemical changes[13]

---

11. Oakland Public Schools, *Tentative Course Outline, Algebra I and Algebra II* (Oakland, Calif., 1940), p. 2.
12. Department of Public Instruction, Commonwealth of Pennsylvania *Course of Study in Latin* (*Bulletin* No. 244; Harrisburg, Pa., 1950), p. viii.
13. Robert Bolt and Others, *A Guide in the Teaching of First Semester High School Chemistry* (San Francisco, Calif., 1949). Mimeographed.

BUSINESS EDUCATION, ST. PAUL

BUSINESS EDUCATION

Transcription

(Secondary Schools)

Provide experiences for the student which will enable him to:

1. Transcribe business letters neatly and accurately in various styles
2. Use stationery of various sizes
3. Adjust the position on the page to the various lengths of letters
4. Type the simplified style of letter (the NOMA letter)
5. Use correctly the . . . related parts of the letter
6. Make neat erasures
7. Make several carbon copies of a letter
8. Keep the typewriter, typewriter cover, desk and chair clean and orderly
9. Change ribbons on the various typewriters[14]

Illustrations of Social Aims

Aims have also been stated in terms of social goals. That is, there are certain social goals which are important, and individuals are trained to be able to accept responsibilities for carrying them forward. These aims, purposes, or objectives of education derive primarily from the nature of the culture in which we live. They represent general abilities, attitudes, appreciations, skills which are to function in social practice. They serve to give a point of view to the total school program and to keep it focused beyond the immediate learning in specific subjects. However, this long view is also a pitfall for the teacher who is not able to identify his materials of instruction with such major objectives. Frequently, teachers assent to such aims and then proceed to teach the same thing they were teaching, claiming that the subject matter achieves the aims agreed upon.

NATIONAL EDUCATION ASSOCIATION.　One illustration of these is found in the Seven Cardinal Principles:

1. Health
2. Command of fundamental proccsses
3. Worthy home membership
4. Vocation
5. Citizenship
6. Worthy use of leisure
7. Ethical character[15]

---

14. Lucy R. Foster (ed.), *Vocational Business Education* (St. Paul, Minn.: State Department of Education, 1950), Chap. 5, pp. 197–198.
15. Commission on Reorganization of Secondary Education, *Cardinal Principles of Secondary Education* (Bureau of Education, *Bulletin* No. 35; Washington: Government Printing Office, 1918).

AMERICAN HISTORICAL ASSOCIATION. Another set of educational objectives stated in terms of social aims was set up by the American Historical Association's Commission on the Social Studies, which suggested the following:

1. To use efficiently the material endowment, technical arts, and productive skills in raising the standard of living of all
2. To create a civilization in the United States which combines utility and esthetics in a grand conception of the potentialities in American life
3. To direct the cooperative and moral powers of the American people into channels of utility and beauty
4. To free the American people from absorption in material things and enable them to devote greater attention to ideals of spiritual, scientific, and cultural development[16]

SOCIAL STUDIES, SAN DIEGO

SOCIAL STUDIES
(Grade 11)

Understandings by the student that

1. America has been the symbol of equal opportunity to many people in foreign lands
2. Americans have made progress in and are continuing to expand equality of opportunity for all Americans
3. America's contribution to world culture has been the work of all the individuals and groups which comprise American society[17]

CONSERVATION STUDIES, ARLINGTON. The conservation studies program of the Barcroft School in Arlington, Virginia, dealing with soil, forests, and animals, and the interrelationships between them, lists the following student goals as having been achieved:

1. Developed an appreciation of the services society provides for the conservation and development of natural resources in the form of government and private agencies
2. Helped students to recognize and know some of the characteristics of a greater number of trees, plants, and animals
3. Led to a more authentic understanding of the origin and growth process
4. Made clear the theories about "balances in nature" and "survival of the fittest"
5. Led to a realization of our dependence on the natural resources for the necessities and luxuries of life

---

16. Commission on the Social Studies of the American Historical Association, *Conclusions and Recommendations* (New York: Charles Scribner's Sons, 1934). Reworded from material on pp. 19–23. By permission of the publishers. See pp. 19–27 for complete listing.
17. Thomas E. Walt, *How the American People Are Progressing toward Equality of Opportunity for All* (Unit VIII, Grade 11; San Diego, Calif.: San Diego City Schools, 1950), p. 3. Mimeographed.

6. Gave students a feeling of "partnership" in this big business of wise resource-use[18]

LANGUAGE ARTS, LONG BEACH. The social values to be secured from an eleventh-grade unit in reading and literature are found in the *Teacher's Guide to Language Arts* in the Long Beach Public Schools, California:

I. People of the United States (5 weeks' time allotment)
   A. Recognize the individual worth of each person regardless of racial background.
   B. Appreciate the contributions which minority groups have made to the American culture.
   C. Recognize the problems of minority groups within our gates.
   D. Understand the responsibilities as well as the privileges of one who is an American.
   E. Recognize the heterogeneous composition of the American people, and
   F. Strive toward the resolution of social conflicts within America as the first step toward a united and peaceful world.

II. Democratic ideas and ideals (8 weeks)

III. The American economic scene (5 weeks)

IV. The frontier and world power (8 weeks)

V. The American way of life (2 weeks)

VI. The American government (8 weeks)
   A. Realize and appreciate what services the government provides for him as an individual and as a member of a family group.
   B. Understand the problems that arise in the lives of men and women engaged in government. . . .
   C. Realize that with service received he has certain duties and responsibilities to his government. . . .
   D. Be able to vote intelligently. . . .
   E. Appreciate democracy's rights of the individual—rights that must be limited for the common good, and
   F. Realize his responsibility as a future citizen to assist in solving democracy's problems.[19]

Illustrations of Individual Behavior Aims

Another way of bringing the aims of education down to identifiable practices for the teacher, while keeping them in the scope of social aims, is to specify

18. Described in 1948 Yearbook, Association for Supervision and Curriculum Development, *Large Was Our Bounty: Natural Resources and the Schools* (Washington: National Education Association, 1948), pp. 71–72.

19. Long Beach Public Schools, *Language Arts in the Eleventh Grade: A Teacher's Guide* (tentative edition; Long Beach, Calif., 1951), pp. 1–34.

aims in terms of the individual's behavior. Behind this is a notion of the characteristics of a democratic society and of the kind of individual needed for successful participation in it. This kind of individual is then defined in terms of the behavior he exhibits in situations. An illustration of a few of these in practice will give an idea of the nature of such aims.

SANTA BARBARA. Santa Barbara City and County each developed its statement of the general aims of education in terms of the desired behavior of children and youth, following it up with the statement that the major purpose of the total school program was to "guide children in their behavioral environment." The aims suggested were

1. Self-respect
2. Creativeness
3. Scientific attitude
4. Cooperation
5. Responsibility
6. Social effectiveness[20]

Under each one of these were questions which indicated the behavior deemed desirable. One example will suffice for the type. Under the scientific attitudes such questions as the following are listed:

1. Is the pupil willing to entertain new ideas and points of view?
2. Is he inclined to welcome suggestions?
3. Is he accurate and impartial?
4. Does he base his judgments on all the available pertinent facts?
5. Does he hold conclusions tentatively?
6. Does he endeavor to test the validity of his conclusions?
7. Does he seek and accept improved ways of doing things?

PASADENA. Another statement of aims of this general type comes from the Pasadena Junior High Schools. These schools have as their general purpose the development in youth of the characteristics which the staff believes they must possess in order to be effective citizens in a democracy. Some of the characteristics which they list as more easily observed are

I. Responsibility and self-direction: A responsive and self-directing student is one who increasingly

A. Plans and carries out his activities
B. Knows when and how to seek help
C. Does what he agrees to do
D. Follows directions
E. Works independently
F. Takes care of property

---

20. Santa Barbara County, *Curriculum Guide for Teachers in Secondary Schools* (Santa Barbara, Calif.: Schauer Printing Studio, 1941), IV, 10–16.

II. Relationships with others: A student who has good relationships with others increasingly
   A. Works and plays well with others
   B. Respects the rights of others
   C. Leads or follows as needed
   D. Serves unselfishly

III. Skills, understandings, and appreciations: A student who shows skills, understandings and appreciations is one who increasingly
   A. Acquires a fund of reliable information
   B. Uses this information in new situations
   C. Expresses himself clearly and correctly
   D. Develops the skills necessary to accomplish the above[21]

NATIONAL EDUCATION ASSOCIATION. The Educational Policies Commission set up the objectives of education in terms of the characteristics of a well-educated person, the educated member of the family and community group, the educated producer or consumer, and the educated citizen. Education is concerned, they said, with these four areas: the objectives of (1) self-realization, (2) human relationships, (3) economic efficiency, and (4) civic responsibility. For each of these four areas, detailed descriptions were given of what the educated person *does*. An analysis of the one under self-realization will illustrate the pattern of the statements:

THE OBJECTIVES OF SELF-REALIZATION

1. *The inquiring mind.* The educated person has an appetite for learning.
2. *Speech.* The educated person can speak the mother tongue clearly.
3. *Reading.* The educated person can read the mother tongue efficiently.
4. *Writing.* The educated person writes the mother tongue effectively.
5. *Number.* The educated person solves his problems of counting and calculating.
6. *Sight and hearing.* The educated person is skilled in listening and observing.
7. *Health knowledge.* The educated person understands the basic facts concerning health and disease.
8. *Health habits.* The educated person protects his own health and that of his dependents.
9. *Public health.* The educated person works to improve the health of the community.
10. *Recreation.* The educated person is participant and spectator in many sports and other pastimes.
11. *Intellectual interests.* The educated person has mental resources for the use of leisure.

---

21. Pasadena Junior High School Report Card, Pasadena, California, 1941–1942. Quoted in I. James Quillen and Lavone A. Hanna, *Education for Social Competence* (Chicago: Scott, Foresman and Company, 1948), p. 57.

12. *Esthetic interests.* The educated person appreciates beauty.

13. *Character.* The educated person gives responsible direction to his own life.[22]

CALIFORNIA STATE CURRICULUM COMMISSION.   The California State Curriculum Commission recently stated the purposes of education in California as follows:

I. *The objectives of civic responsibility:* Effective citizenship requires that the individual and the group

A. Act upon an understanding of and loyalty to our democratic ideals

B. Understand and appreciate the positive advantages of American institutions

C. Be sensitive to the disparities of human circumstances

D. Act with others to correct unsatisfactory conditions

E. Understand local, state, national, and international social structures and social processes

F. Achieve skill with processes of group action; in student self-governing groups develop criteria for making wise choices of action

G. Know the achievements of the people who have made the United States a great nation

H. Develop defenses against destructive propaganda

I. Accept honest differences of opinion

J. Realize the importance of wise use of human and natural resources

K. Measure scientific advances by contributions to the general welfare

L. Be active, co-operating members of the world community

M. Work to achieve and maintain peace in the world

N. Respect the law

O. Meet their civic obligations

II. *The objectives of full realization of individual capacities:* The full realization of individual capacities requires that the individual, in accordance with his ability and experience,

A. Desire to learn, to grow

B. Speak English clearly

C. Read English efficiently

D. Write English effectively

E. Use the skills of counting and calculating

F. Listen and observe accurately

G. Understand the essential facts concerning health and disease

H. Protect his health and that of others

I. Work to improve the health of the community

J. Work to achieve poise and co-ordination in bodily movement

K. Participate in a range of leisure time activities—physical, intellectual, and creative

22. Educational Policies Commission, *The Purposes of Education in American Democracy* (Washington: National Education Association, 1938), pp. 39–124.

    L. Develop a sense of humor

    M. Seek and enjoy beauty

    N. Understand and value the contributions of art, literature, music, and the dance

    O. Give responsible direction to his own life

    P. Develop a set of sound moral and spiritual values

    Q. Utilize values as determiners of choices

    R. Arrive at appropriate decisions in specific situations as a result of critical thinking

    S. Formulate his purposes

III. *The objectives of human relationships:* The achievement of increasingly effective human relationships requires that the individual and the group

    A. Place human relations first

    B. Enjoy a rich, sincere, and varied social life

    C. Work and play with others effectively

    D. Observe the amenities of social behavior

    E. Recognize the family as a basic social institution

    F. Conserve family ideals

    G. Exercise skill in homemaking

    H. Maintain democratic relationships in the family and in all other group situations

    I. Work to improve intergroup relationships

IV. *The objectives of economic efficiency:* The attainment of economic efficiency requires that the individual

    A. Understand the interdependency of economic structures and procedures

    B. Understand the satisfactions of good workmanship

    C. Recognize the obligation to perform an honest day's work

    D. Understand the requirements and opportunities for various jobs

    E. Select his occupation and prepare for it

    F. Maintain and improve his efficiency

    G. Realize the social value of his work

    H. Plan the economics of his own life

    I. Develop standards for guiding his expenditures

    J. Become an informed and skillful buyer

    K. Take ethical measures to safeguard his interests[23]

Illustrations of Aims in Terms of Problems

    A modification of the last two categories of aims, social goals and behavioral traits is being given increased emphasis among certain forward-looking groups concerned with curriculum development. Aims in this area draw upon the needs of youth, the requirements of society, and the role of the school in achieving a satisfactory compromise. Cummings points out that the responsi-

---

23. California State Curriculum Commission, *Framework for Public Education*, pp. 5–7.

bility of the school in developing a program which reconciles these two bases is twofold: "that of a mediator between the two groups in the preliminary work of formulating statements; and that of an implement agent which has an understanding of the national and international aspects of problems and which acts to keep the local program from becoming too parochial in character."[24]

ADJUSTMENT AIMS. A brief illustration of this point of view is found in the following table which seeks to provide a basis for valid objectives in terms of adjustment:

Demands of Youth	*Demands of Society*	*Adjustments*
1. A job which will pay good wages with favorable working conditions	1. That the young worker remain on a job long enough to pay for the cost of training	1. Help youth in self-evaluation of skills and capacities and in making a just estimate of job situations
. . .	. . .	. . .
6. An opportunity to learn the facts of life about sex, economic relationships and political activity	6. That facts in areas where the institutions which make up American society are not in agreement shall be taught by the institutions using their own frames of reference	6. Objective handling of controversial issues. Liaison with institutional representative in the local community to secure a better preparation of youth for life

WISCONSIN COOPERATIVE EDUCATIONAL PLANNING PROGRAM. One of the forward-looking state movements in curriculum development is that found in the Wisconsin Cooperative Educational Planning Program.[25] This group state their objectives in terms of problems to be solved in an effort to resolve any conflict between the demands of youth and those of society. The committee working on junior-high-school curriculum has suggested allocating specific problems to certain grades:

Grade 7: Problems related primarily to school and home living
Grade 8: Problems related primarily to understanding and improving life in the community
Grade 9: Problems related primarily to establishing good human relations

An illustration of the approach is found in a suggested resource unit on How Can Members of the Family Learn to Live Together? The objectives are then stated in problem terms as follows:

---

24. Howard Cummings, "Youth in a Changing Culture," *Educational Leadership,* 6: 349–353, 1949.
25. Curriculum Guiding Committee of the Wisconsin Cooperative Educational Planning Program, *Guides to Curriculum Building: Junior High School Level* (Problems Approach Bulletin No. 2; Madison, Wis.: State Department of Education, 1950), pp. 139–141.

1. How can we help keep the family healthy?
2. How can we make the home a safe place in which to live?
3. Can we share in caring for home property?
4. What responsibilities should we accept for taking care of our personal belongings?
5. How can we help solve family money problems?
6. In what ways can members of the family show they are thoughtful and considerate of one another?
7. How can we have fun in the home during leisure hours?

This plan for curriculum organization contemplates involving the entire junior-high-school curriculum, drawing on all areas and subject fields.

This kind of listing of aims or objectives sets up directly the fixing of certain behavior practices. Such a statement of aims has the double value of being social in nature and behavioral in character. Thus the teacher is left free to choose whatever materials of instruction will serve to develop the desired behavior traits. She is also able to see the immediate relationship between what she teaches and the purposes of the school. Such objectives are superior to specific aims in terms of subjects or skills, and are better than general social aims for practical use by the teacher. These aims stated in terms of experience are in harmony with the general theory of the relations between experience and development and thus enable the teacher to form continuously and immediately both a program of the selection of curriculum materials and one of evaluation.

Preplanning the Curriculum

Some of the features of controversy in this area will be treated more fully in the following chapters, but we will pause here long enough to call attention to a few of the most noticeable differences in the problem of designing the curriculum. One of the issues is over the nature of the preplanning of the curriculum materials.

The earliest curricula were preplanned very definitely; in fact, everything was laid out so long in advance that it was almost like being able to obtain the educational assignments for a four-year high-school course. From this extreme, one goes to the other where no preplanning is done at all, save what the teacher slips in on the side. Probably the claim here is far greater than the practice.

Detailed Planning

There are several ways in which preplanning can take place. In the first place, lessons or assignments or units can be laid out carefully in every detail and handed to pupils. This may be done either by faithfully following a course of study or a textbook or by designing curriculum units which may be mimeographed and given to pupils. All these plans have the same qualities: they are planned in advance by the teacher or some outsider without working with the pupils on the planning. They are only slightly subject to change in contact with pupils and have the qualities of definiteness, order, and finality. Certainly modern education has in its theory moved far beyond this type of practice, even though this is still the prevailing form of preparing curriculum materials for youth in the secondary school.

Resource Units

A second type of preplanning in relation to curriculum materials provides what are known as resource units. These resource units are organized ideas—principles, understandings, references, activities, suggestions for methods and evaluation—on certain social or personal problems which have arisen in connection with a careful study of the pupil and the environment in which he lives. They are built by a single teacher or by a group of teachers cooperatively. They are usually mimeographed for use by the teachers. They *are not* a document for pupils, as are the Morrison units, but are for the counsel of the teacher in planning the selection of subject matter with the class. They are in reality *potential* subject matter. What use is made of them, of course, depends upon the teacher, but if she is using them intelligently, they will serve her as a series of books or as a teacher conference might serve—they will give her ideas she might otherwise not have known or recalled. By the process of teacher-pupil planning, the definite program of work in the classroom is selected from both the resource unit and the ideas of the pupils. If the resource unit and the outline of work actually done in the class agree highly, the teacher has "overused" the resource unit.[26]

Group Planning

A third type of preplanning is that done by a group of teachers. Since several heads are usually better than one, some of the best planning today is being done by groups of teachers with common problems, sitting together for an hour or so daily or weekly to plan their work. The effectiveness of this group planning is enhanced if there are differences in the experiences, training, and interests of the several members of the group. They should not all have majored in English and history and have had the same courses in education. A conference of this kind may help the individual teacher to organize and

26. For more extensive treatments of pupil-teacher planning, see H. H. Giles, *Teacher-Pupil Planning* (New York: Harper & Brothers, 1941), and Bernice Baxter, *Pupil-Teacher Relationships* (New York: The Macmillan Company, 1942).

handle class materials and deal with ideas and with pupils, but one of the greatest contributions it can make is the pooling of ideas and activities which can again become *potential* subject matter for each of the teachers in the group. By sharing ideas upon situations arising daily in their classrooms, the teachers can plan more carefully, effectively, and appropriately.

Education of the Teacher

The fourth type of planning is obvious to the reader—the education of the teacher. This, of course, is a method of preplanning. Any type of educational experience will or should produce the improvement of classroom teaching. Teachers who deal with the problems of modern industry in social studies or with radio, art, music, motion pictures, or community institutions will all profit greatly from experience with them. Any planning should take into account excursions, travel, study, pooling of experience, the cooperative development of resource units, and ample reference material so that youth may have all the necessary opportunities to develop according to their abilities and interests.

Curriculum Builders

One of the arguments which has not yet been settled in academic circles is the question of who shall build the curriculum. Some answer "the pupils"; others cry "the teachers." Some contend that only "experts" shall have the responsibility; some want "supervisors and curriculum directors." There are those who would still like to have "the textbook writers" responsible for selecting the subject matter of the school. Some say everybody that has anything to do with the child, even the parents. Obviously, this is giving a wide range of people definite responsibility for selecting subject matter.

Another issue in this area has to do with the level at which good curriculum designing can be accomplished. Much of the balance of this volume will deal with specific details and illustrations of various approaches to this important problem in curriculum development. Here let us examine briefly the different organizational levels at which curriculum planning has been attempted. The decision as to where this planning takes place will have a far reaching effect upon the ways in which the results are accepted and used. The levels range from national studies and commissions down through the individual classroom and teacher in a particular local school.

National Organizations

In other portions of this book, the work of national study groups on curriculum problems is described in detail. For the past half century these groups have played a prominent role in our educational picture. Growing out of the concerns over the limitations of the narrow subject fields, scores of organizations and commissions have studied and reported upon various aspects of curriculum improvement. Although the period between 1920 and 1940 saw the greatest emphasis upon this type of curriculum study, we continue to have prominent educators advocating curriculum design on the national level. Only a short time ago Briggs called for the development of a hierarchy of committees, headed by a national curriculum committee "of the highest ability, devotion, and reputation" to produce the "new curriculum that every informed person recognizes as desirable and necessary."[27]

These national bodies dealt with a variety of types of curriculum problems, general objectives for entire educational program in broad subject areas, and improvement in specific subject fields. Other groups, involving representative national organizations, have given attention to allied areas which have strong bearing on curriculum improvement. For example, the Educational Policies Commission produced *Education For All American Youth.*

Still another type of national organization is that concerned with supervision and with a wide range of instructional problems. These are general in states throughout the United States and stem from the leadership afforded by the Association for Supervision and Curriculum Development. These associations have through publications, reports, study committees, research, and state and national discussions added much to the curriculum literature.

Differences arise concerning the effectiveness of these national organizations, and the help they provide the local school systems and individual schools. Proponents of these organizations stress their value in (1) providing certain basic materials pertinent to curriculum development, such as a study of youth needs; (2) clarifying the objectives of education, particularly in behavioral terms; (3) bringing together the best thinking from state and local areas to secure greater unity in wide-scale curriculum development. Opponents of the national organizations question the value of devoting time, money, and effort to problems local in character. They claim that much of the national product is general, vague, and highly theoretical, inappropriate for local situations, and consequently of little value at the grass roots level.

State Organizations

The second basic type of organization is that which is state wide. These fall into three categories:

1. State departments of education with their staff specialists and commit-

---

27. Thomas H. Briggs, "The Administrator's Role in Secondary Education," *Bulletin,* National Association of Secondary School Principals, 34:8, 1950. See also Briggs "Proposal for a Curriculum Commission," *Bulletin,* National Association of Secondary School Principals, 29:79–90, 1945.

tees which deal with many phases of curriculum development. Generally, they serve in an advisory capacity and are usually consultative rather than dominant. They publish curriculum guides, aid local systems in solving specific problems, and occasionally form state committees to prepare resource materials.

2. Colleges and universities collectively in cooperation with state departments or singly provide consultation service, in-service training programs, and leadership through individual staff members.

3. The state associations of administrators, curriculum workers, and program specialists have aided materially the growth of the curriculum movement through the stimulation in using audio-visual materials; developing an understanding of general education, vocational education, evaluation; and working as a group to give emphasis to producing among the leadership of the state a more common understanding of the improvements in the curriculum field.

Local Organizations

The third basic type of organization for curriculum is the local school system. This unit is in a position to know definitely the needs of the boys and girls in the area and to set up definite goals, objectives, materials, and procedures to meet them. This is the area which cannot generalize and pass the ideas on to someone else. Here is the last unit. Here the work must be done, the curriculum built. The grass-roots basis for curriculum design rests here in the local system.

Even within such a restricted area as the local system there is a question about who should develop the details of the curriculum. In some instances it is considered a specialist's job, with the central office staff and the administration determining the entire program. In other communities the representatives from the individual schools are actively involved in the total program of curriculum development. In a few instances pupils, the end for which all education exists, not only are consulted but definitely are brought into the process of curriculum planning within their school and even the school system. In equally few instances, the lay public, and especially the parents, are consulted or invited to share in the designing of the local curriculum. This last trend is only in its formative stage, with some very hopeful prospects of intelligent cooperative effort between lay and professional groups working together toward a common goal—a more dynamic curriculum design for the local community.

The extent to which the individual schools and their teachers are included in community curriculum planning is a problem which concerns many educational leaders. Some see great promise in the cooperative endeavor where administrators, supervisors, teachers, pupils and parents wisely join in planning to meet effectively the educational needs of their community.

The answer to this question "Who shall build the curriculum?" cannot be settled in terms of the level of operation. It is unwise to talk about the national committees or the local teacher doing everything. Basic research on child growth and development and on great social trends cannot be done by local teachers, nor can university professors plan materials for daily work in elementary classrooms. Good curriculum planning is therefore a pattern of the cooperation of many people, each contributing what he can to the total task of developing a modern curriculum for an alert child in a modern world.

Curriculum Planning by Teachers

Before we can do any clear thinking on this question, we must relate the issue to the nature of subject matter, for only with this in mind do we stay in the realm of common sense. It seems obvious that if we desire to use as subject matter for youth the carefully organized heritage of the past in its most accurate form, it is foolish to believe that parents or pupils or every teacher should select it. These people do not know this material as the scholar knows it. They cannot do as good a job as the expert, and since, under this concept, there is no need to give children anything short of the best and no need to burden teachers and parents with the job of doing something which they are not prepared to do, it stands to reason that experts should build the curriculum.

On the other hand, if it makes no difference what we study, if there is no need for organization and sequence, if the important thing about subject matter is that it be current and that it be positively identified with each individual even to the point that he proposes it, then it is foolish to have anybody but pupils build the curriculum.

There is another position here which seems more reasonable to most people than either of these two extremes. Let us look first at the rationale behind it. The learning experience is a matter of direct interaction between the environment and the individual organism. The teacher facilitates the learning by teaching methods and by the selection of subject matter. There are an individuality and a spontaneity about the learning act. Consequently, the strict planning and assignment of materials in advance of the learning experience do not characterize the most desirable situation. However, the immediacy is not so important that no previous thought should affect it or be related to it, and the individuality of the experience is not so great that it has never occurred before or is not likely to occur similarly again. The fact that there are observable patterns while there are individual deviations gives a place for the skillful teacher, just as the same case can be made for the skillful diagnostician and for the practicing physician which follows him.

Curriculum planning is teacher education at its best. It is not blocking out materials to use with children the teacher has never seen. It is increasing one's knowledge of things which can be done and achieving a high degree of skill in knowing when and how to use them. In this process the expert assists, for he suggests knowledge and facts and interpretations which may be considered by the teacher. But the expert does not *build the curriculum*.[28] He serves as a consultant with other types of experts. There is no more reason to have the subject-matter specialists lead our curriculum circles than there is to have the sociologist or psychologist in the "head seat." The psychologist, the sociologist, and the subject specialist are as important as the teacher when it comes to constructing and selecting curriculum materials. If we consider that education is a process of carefully guiding the experience of the learner, we need to rid our minds of the notion that the most important thing for the teacher is a mass of subject knowledge or that the most important characteristic of a curriculum is an accurate and complete portrayal of subject knowledge.

In summary, the point is that the final selection of appropriate subject matter must rest with the teacher, if we conceive education to be the interacting process just described. It is to be understood, of course, that the teacher will make use of the interests and suggestions of the pupils and in her selection of curriculum materials will be sensitive to the needs of the community. In that event the teacher draws upon all the resources available to him, using them to give him greater power and knowledge to deal with the situation. He can be aided in this by the types of preplanning suggested, but if he is a superior teacher he cannot take the organizations, outlines, ideas, or interpretations of another and transfer them to his mind. The transference of knowledge is only the first step in the process of thinking and is about the only service the expert can render to the situation. If we believe this transference is the most important thing a teacher can do for the child, then the expert can assume a prominent place. If the acquisition of knowledge is the primary aim, the curriculum may be changed slowly, periodically. But if the direction of experiences is the function of education, the curriculum needs changing rapidly; it should constantly be remade.

There are some who believe that the curriculum should be made by pressure groups and by legislation, as this is "the democratic way." It is true that this is the democratic way of arriving at the formation of adult policies. But the reasoning offered for ruling out the expert is even more applicable to this "democratic" method. Legislators and pressure groups are not only removed from the child and his experience; they are more controlled by immediate

---

28. In this connection it is interesting to compare the ideas of Caswell with those of Briggs. Briggs has repeatedly contended that experts should build the curriculum; Caswell has maintained that it is the job of the teacher, essentially the position taken here (part of the differences are, however, bound up in a complete definition of terms). See Thomas H. Briggs, "Propaganda and the Curriculum," *Teachers College Record*, 34:470–480, 1933. See also Hollis L. Caswell, "Sources of Confusion in Curriculum Theory," in *Toward Improved Curriculum Theory* (Supplementary Educational Monographs, No. 71; Chicago: University of Chicago Press, 1950), pp. 110–117; Hollis L. Caswell and Others, *Curriculum Improvement in Public School Systems* (New York: Columbia University, Teachers College, Bureau of Publications, 1950).

adult "interests" than is the person connected with the guidance of youth. To set up the curriculum by legislation is also to make it exceedingly static, thus causing it to cease to serve the situation or the learner. The public must express its desires for children in other ways than through legislation on the school curriculum. Determining what experiences children and youth shall have is a professional responsibility. It can be decided only by the competent and highly experienced teacher; it cannot be decided intelligently by a legislative committee in conference any more than standard treatments for pneumonia can be written into law.

There is also the contention that the curriculum should be the outcome of research; in fact, we are emerging from a period in which this method of curriculum making was prominent. But the curriculum is partially a series of values, and these cannot be decided by science. The use of values is essential to the best guidance of learning. But research in curriculum materials serves us in the same way that psychological research clarifies the nature of growth and development. The materials used in experiments are suggestive only. Arriving at lists of subject matter in terms of current usage, or determining a course of study by finding out what people do not know, as has been done so much in English grammar and the languages, will never reveal a body of subject matter for learning. Science cannot be serviceable in this fashion. It can give us only the results of applications of certain methods and experiences, and the currency of contemporary ideas. It can also give us directions, but not a complete curriculum.

Place of the Course of Study

The course of study, made up of carefully organized and graded materials for mastery, belongs with the "knowledge-mastery" theory of education. It is an "expert job," prepared by "outsiders." By "outsiders" is meant central office staff, educational experts outside the community, or even a group of local teachers who may retire from their teaching for a period of time to write a course of study.

More important, even, than the authors is the use to be made of the completed document. No guide can be built which can fit the experience of all people. At best, it can represent only the judgments of competent people about what they consider most important. A document of this character is an invaluable asset to a competent teacher who uses it as the principal source of suggestions for the selection of teaching material. The more competent the teacher the less he will be restricted by the suggestions of the course of study. The course should be a liberating force to the teacher in that it saves him much time in searching for instructional materials; it should not chain him to a prescribed program.

As we would conceive a course of study, it would contain the thoughts and ideas of the experts in subject matter, in environmental conditions, and in growth and development. It would be of assistance in formulating objectives, in organizing learning, in determining successful methods, in teaching skills, and in evaluating the success of instruction. It would in every sense be a guide; it would in no sense be a traveler's map. In this way the course of study would be an indispensable aid to the teacher; it would be as necessary as any other equipment or materials; it would be a source of stimulation and guidance. It would be written for and by teachers. It would not be a document for children to follow. It would be for the development and guidance of the teacher.

Continuity of Learning

There have always been both breadth and continuity to the curriculum program. Each successive subject has at least theoretically been built upon the idea of continued progression in the subject field. The whole practice of prerequisites, so well established in college and used in many high schools for certain subjects, is a recognition of this principle of continuity and is one which grows out of the nature of the relationships existing among the various aspects of the subject itself. The acceptance of this concept has caused us to build up an order of learning—first, second, third—which has rested its case upon relationships and upon difficulty. Sequence was thought to be the orderly development of parts within a special field of knowledge.

Some educators contend that there needs to be no planning whatsoever for continuity or sequence of learning, that if let alone the child will develop his own plan of organization. They say that there is within him a natural thread of continuity and if he is permitted to browse in enough experiences which have certain qualities of depth and breadth and extent, he will do the rest. This position would allow for no advance planning for continuity, nor would it allow for any system of continuous guidance between teachers from grade to grade. It would not permit any organization of subject materials from day to day or from grade to grade planned in advance. Each teacher would meet the situation at the time as his best judgment dictated. Such a theory is more interesting than workable. It places too much faith in an inner thread of continuity and in the immature learner. The result may be that teaching degenerates into incoherent learning and even into confusion on the part of the learner.

A third point of view regarding continuity is that sequential learning should be planned cooperatively by teachers in a series of grades.[29] This position

---

29. For a more extended treatment see the article by J. Paul Leonard, "Some Reflections on the Meaning of Sequence" in *Toward Improved Curriculum Theory* (Supplementary Educational Monographs, No. 71; Chicago: University of Chicago Press, 1950), pp. 70–79.

implies that such an important factor as the orderly development of basic understandings and skills should not be left merely to chance. It implies that each teacher in each grade should be conscious of what has happened to children before he gets them and what areas are likely to be discussed after the child leaves him. It implies that teachers mutually understand and agree on the important basic concepts that are to be discussed in the total school program and that each teacher has a distinctive part to play in this total scheme.

The reader should not confuse this idea of sequence of basic concepts with conventional ideas of a sequence in history, based upon chronological development of events, or of a sequence of abstract difficulty, as in mathematics, which were indicated in the first point of view regarding sequence. A sequence of basic concepts requires an advance agreement among teachers in a given school or community that certain ideas of major importance will be discussed during the time the child spends in school and that these will be discussed at times most appropriate to the maturation of the learner. Such a sequence is a guide in the selection and grouping of subject matter. The arrangement of basic concepts is general in its definition, to prevent restricting the individual teacher, yet clear enough to be definitive and to provide some limitations. It is designed to help prevent overlapping and to provide for the introduction of new material as progression in learning takes place.

Whatever the argument over details may be, there are three things to remember. First, *learning follows some sequence and needs to be organized.* The seeming lack of concern of educational workers and teachers over continuity has injured the cause of modern education. As Dewey points out, "The greatest danger that attends its [modern education] future is, I believe, that it is an easy way to follow, so easy that its course may be improvised, if not in an impromptu fashion, at least almost from day to day or from week to week."[30] Dewey contends that the organization of experience is of tremendous importance and that we cannot neglect it and produce intellectual competence. It ought to be clear that learning should be organized and that to organize it there must be advance planning. It cannot be haphazardly acquired, and teachers should not plunge into a modern program of education without adequate planning among themselves and with every expert available.

In the second place, *learning should be carefully planned so that it takes its organizing principle from a combination of group experience and the individual experience of the learner.* In every situation both the learner and the social group must be taken into account in the development of principles of organization and in the selection and arrangement of content. Sequential patterns may be suggestive; they should not be dictatorial.

In the third place, *sequences should be planned so as to provide for the assumption of individual responsibility on the part of the learner in organizing*

---

30. John Dewey, *Experience and Education* (New York: The Macmillan Company, 1938), p. 115. By permission of Kappa Delta Pi.

his own experiences. Experiences are cumulative and each serves to improve the next one, but

> it is a mistake to suppose that the mere acquisition of a certain amount of arithmetic, geography, history, etc., which is taught and studied because it may be useful at some time in the future, has this effect, and it is a mistake to suppose that acquisition of skills in reading and figuring will automatically constitute preparation for their right and effective use under conditions very unlike those in which they were acquired.[31]

If facts, ideas, and skills which are acquired do not then *naturally* lead to continuous development, there must be some guidance in the process. Continuity is not acquired simply by learning things in serial order or by simply engaging in a haphazard set of continuous experiences. There is a quality of inherent relationships in the continuity of experience which is educative, relationships between the individual and the environment with which he comes in contact. Dewey makes the point when he says:

> It is a mistake to suppose that the principle of the leading on of experience to something different is adequately satisfied simply by giving pupils some new experience any more than it is by seeing to it that they have greater skill and ease in dealing with things with which they are already familiar. It is also essential that the new objects and events be related intellectually to those of earlier experiences, and this means that there be some advance made in conscious articulation of facts and ideas.[32]

Dewey thus effectively disposes of the idea that continuity in learning will result either from discrete subject sequences or from unguided new experiences. He places in the center of consideration the need for careful planning to secure continuity in learning.

---

31. *Ibid.,* pp. 47–48.
32. *Ibid.,* pp. 89–90.

Chapter Six

Early Attempts at

Curriculum Improvement

A MERICA is young and has not had time to experiment widely with many social theories. Democracy has passed out of its infancy and is in the present stage of gawky adolescence. The school, too, somewhat fits this pattern. It is an adolescent, and during its relatively short existence in this country it has been nurtured by only two basic educational theories—the theory of adjustment and the theory of experimentalism. Fads have come and gone in administration and curriculum materials, but not until the last two decades have any of them departed basically from the orientation of education as adjustment through acquaintance with the social heritage. Opposed to this philosophy of adjustment through intellectual orientation to social customs and history is the theory that the human organism and its environment are really a whole. There is a oneness about the organism and its environment, and in this process the individual experiments through experience until he forges for himself a satisfying way of life. The basic differences in these two points of view can be clarified by the story of changes in the traditional curriculum as they operate within the usual subject framework.

Administrative Changes

There have been several kinds of changes in the traditional subject curriculum. Probably the first of these was the addition to the existing subject offerings of those which seemed to be more appropriate to the changes in purposes of the pupils who went to school. Franklin proposed the sciences and commercial subjects to meet the needs of sailors and merchants. Civics and government were added to meet the need for acquiring the fundamentals of citizenship. The vocational subjects were introduced to meet the demands of laboring men for a utilitarian school and those of industry for trained workers. Home economics came in with the opening of schools to girls and with the utilitarian concept of education. Subject after subject has been added, but with each new addition there was not an accompanying reorientation of the total offerings or a basic consideration of the unity of the total pattern.

When only a few subjects were offered to a selected student body, all pupils were required to pursue the same subjects. There were no electives. But as the range of subjects increased and as the interests and needs of the enlarged school population became more heterogeneous, there grew up a need for selection in terms of groups of pupils. This led to the division of the secondary curriculum into classifications based upon the purposes which the subjects might serve: (1) general curriculum, (2) academic curriculum, (3) commercial curriculum, (4) scientific curriculum, (5) vocational curriculum. In different communities different names were used to indicate these divisions, but these five represent essentially the manner and extent of organization. All these led to high-school graduation, and as a general rule all had a few subject requirements in common, such as English, mathematics, and some history. College-bound people usually pursued either the academic or the scientific curricula; pupils entering the trades followed the vocational, and youth going into business took the commercial; those who wanted a liberal education, and did not make vocational decisions early, followed the general curriculum.

Closely allied to this type of division was one intended to divide the curriculum into subjects of importance to all and subjects of importance to certain individuals. The curriculum of the Latin grammar school was a single curriculum with common requirements for all and no electives. Then came the constant-variable curriculum, where a set of requirements was established, and electives were permitted beyond this common core. Paralleling this was the one previously described as the multiple curriculum where the divisions were on the basis of purpose and where there were certain constants common to each of the multiples.

These three types of curriculum changes were all chiefly administrative in character. Little if anything was happening within the subjects themselves. Another type of administrative change which did little to alter the content of the subjects was the result of a movement to individualize education and adapt it more closely to the needs and abilities of the large mass of secondary school pupils. Many plans came in for review. One plan tried was the parallel-track plan in which there were two types of pupils dealing with the same materials. The bright or fast pupils were permitted to finish the course in shorter time than were the dull or slower pupils. The course for both was not essentially altered. In some places, however, this took the form of a three-track curriculum—*A* Bright, *B* Average, and *C* Dull. Attempts were made to vary somewhat in terms of quantity and difficulty the material pursued by these three groups. There were also plans whereby extra credit could be earned for doing more than the required minimum for graduation. Each of these plans was accompanied by a promotion system and by systems of grading and awards. In many schools marked changes were made in the schedules of teachers and pupils, and frequent reclassification of pupils was made necessary.

Then came various plans for making the work still more individualized. The Dalton plan made it possible for the individual teacher and pupil to agree that a certain amount of work would be done by the pupil within a given period of time. The Morrison plan provided for a careful outline of the work and made each pupil a matter of individual attention for the teacher. The supervised study plan made possible group recitation but individual attention was also given to the problems of preparing the recitations. A third method arose to make instruction more suited to the interests and abilities of the masses of youth and to make instruction easier for the teacher. Pupils were divided into groups depending upon what score they made on an intelligence test or a battery of tests. This was supposed to put together those who could learn at about equal speeds. But later investigation revealed that these pupils were homogeneous only in the abilities which had been used to classify them. Accompanying such grouping were improved tests, better methods, and more understandable textbooks, but the basic content of the school program did not change. The changes were chiefly administrative in character.

Looking back over these administrative changes we find certain things common to all of them:

1. They were aimed at improving learning and facilitating teaching.

2. They were based upon the belief that the great influx of numbers and variety into the secondary school called for a change in the methods of grouping and teaching youth; they did not take into account the fact that the materials of instruction themselves needed to be changed.

3. They were an honest attempt to meet the individual differences as these differences were conceived, even though the significance of extreme individual differences was not understood.

4. There was no fundamental social or personal orientation at the base of the changes.

5. The same materials of instruction were considered good for all.

6. Electives, where allowed, were considered to be based upon the vocational or future educational plans of the pupil.

7. The problem appeared to be one of adjusting the pupil to the fixed materials of the curriculum.

Three National Committees

Another kind of attack upon the curriculum grew out of an attempt to examine the nature of the subjects themselves. This examination started with the movement to rebuild the curriculum through the work of national committees. In 1893 the Committee of Ten, appointed in 1891 by the National Council of Education, made its report. This was the beginning of the committee approach to curriculum change and, except as the beginning of a movement to make more flexible and effective the school curriculum, can hardly be called more than another example of administrative reorganization. The Committee of Ten and those following it for the next twenty years were devoted chiefly to the task of standardizing and making uniform the existing traditional subject program. The Committee of Fifteen in elementary education (1895), the Committee on Economy of Time (1908, 1914, 1919), the National Committee on Mathematical Requirements (1920–1923), and the Classical Investigation (1921–1925) were all of the same character. They were staffed by college professors and subject teachers who had faith in mental discipline. They were afraid of the loss of the prestige of their subjects and were loath to suggest anything which would leave to individual teachers or administrators the choice of changing or eliminating materials or subjects.

Time is not always a factor in changing people's minds. About 1915 a national Committee on the Reorganization of Secondary Education was organized and made a far-reaching report, one which in tone was quite different from the report of the Committee of Ten. Approximately ten years later two other national committees reported—the National Committee on Mathematical Requirements (1920–1923) and the Classical Investigation (1921–1925). These last two committees were similar in point of view and were close to the philosophy of the Committee of Ten, in spite of the intervening report of the Committee on the Reorganization of Secondary Education.

The Committee of Ten

The report of the Committee of Ten can best be illustrated by showing how the committee operated and by citing some suggestions it made. The Committee divided itself into nine conferences, one each for Latin; Greek; English; other modern languages; mathematics; physics, astronomy, and chemistry; natural history; history, civil government, and political economy; and geography. Each conference set out to study the same set of questions:

1. In the school course of study extending approximately from the age of six years to eighteen years—a course including the periods of both elementary and secondary instruction—at what age should the subject which is the study of the Conference be first introduced?

2. After it has been introduced, how many hours a week for how many years should be devoted to it?

3. How many hours a week for how many years should be devoted to it during the last four years of the complete course; that is, during the ordinary high school period?

4. What topics, or parts, of the subject may reasonably be covered during the whole course?

5. What topics or parts of the subject may best be reserved for the last four years?

6. Into what form and to what extent should the subject enter into requirements for admission? Such questions as the sufficiency of translation at sight as a test of knowledge of a language, or the superiority of a laboratory examination in a scientific subject to a written examination on a textbook, are intended to be suggested under this head by the phrase "in what form."

7. Should the subject be treated differently for pupils who are going to college, for those who are going to a scientific school, and for those who, presumably, are going to neither?

8. At what stage would this differentiation begin, if any be recommended?

9. Can any description be given of the best method of teaching this subject throughout the school course?

10. Can any description be given of the best mode of testing attainments in this subject at college admission examinations?

11. For those cases in which colleges and universities permit a division of the admission examination into a preliminary and a final examination, separated by at least a year, can the best limit between the preliminary and final examinations be appropriately defined?[1]

With this set of questions being stated by the central committee, composed of five college and university presidents, the United States Commissioner of Education, two headmasters, a high school principal, and one college professor, the task of the nine conferences was set. Ninety members were then selected to the nine conferences, eighty-five of whom were administrators.

In general the conferences in the physical and the social sciences were concerned with pleading for equal prestige and weight with Latin, Greek, and mathematics. The English and modern language conferences were concerned somewhat about prestige, but the conferences in mathematics, Latin, and

---

1. National Education Association, *Report of the Committee of Ten on Secondary School Studies. With the report of the conferences arranged by the committee* (New York: American Book Company, 1894), pp. 6–7.

Greek felt themselves secure on this score. The Greek and Latin conferences asked for no more preparation in these subjects, while the geography conference said either less time should be given to attain the present accomplishments or more should be accomplished in the same time.

All conferences agreed that their subjects should be taught earlier, and all except languages wanted broad surveys of the courses given in their elementary schools. The Latin, Greek, and modern-language groups wanted their subjects begun in the elementary school, the modern-language people suggesting the fifth grade and the Latin people suggesting "three to five years earlier." The mathematics group wanted the elements of algebra and some concrete geometry taught in the elementary school; the natural history group desired the elements of botany and zoology taught in the primary school; and the natural science people urged the teaching of nature study as an important part of the elementary course in all grades. The history people wished "a systematic study of history" to begin at the tenth year of age, with courses in mythology and biography in grades five and six; while the geography conference recommended an earlier course in geography in the elementary school treating "broadly of the earth, its environment and inhabitants." The dominant thought of the members of the conference can well be summarized (their curriculum theory and learning theory) in the following statement of the major committee:

> It is inevitable that specialists in any one of the subjects which are pursued in the high schools should earnestly desire that the minds of young children be stored with some of the elementary facts and principles of their subject; and that all the mental habits which the adult student will surely need begin to be formed in the child's mind before the age of fourteen.[2]

On the other hand it is interesting to note that the conference was concerned over the large number of subjects which would confront the elementary school child and recommended:

> If the nine Conferences had sat altogether as a single body instead of sitting as detached and even isolated bodies, they could not have more forcibly expressed their conviction that every subject recommended for introduction into elementary and secondary schools should help every other; and that the teacher of each single subject should feel responsible for the advancement of the pupils in all subjects, and should distinctly contribute to their advancement.[3]

This report is an interesting attempt to improve the curriculum by having a group of subject specialists from colleges tell teachers in the elementary and secondary schools what they ought to teach in order to have the pupil familiar with terms, facts, and principles in the various subjects when he enters college. No one on the committee was either a psychologist or a sociologist or had close

---

2. *Ibid.*, p. 16.
3. *Ibid.*

contact with children and youth. The curriculum aimed at mastery of subject skills, and this committee wanted to improve that mastery.

One other interesting observation may be made on the attitude of the conferences on the question whether the materials in courses should be differentiated for pupils with different vocational interests and purposes or for those who are or are not going to college. The conferences were unanimous in declaring that "every subject which is taught at all in a secondary school should be taught in the same way and to the same extent to every pupil so long as he pursues it." This certainly eases the mind of the teacher who is worried over individual difficulties and justifies standardization, uniform standards, and even the failure of the ones to whom the subject is not adapted. The Committee of Ten left an interesting 250-page portrayal of the mind of the dominating group in secondary education at the close of the century.

The National Committee on Mathematical Requirements

The National Committee on Mathematical Requirements was first organized in 1916 under the auspices of the Mathematical Association of America for for the purpose of "giving national expression to the movement for reform in the teaching of mathematics, which had gained considerable headway in various parts of the country, but which had lacked the power that coordination and united effort alone could give."[4] The original membership was made up of six college and university professors, one each from Chicago, Dartmouth, Illinois, Columbia, Princeton, and the Massachusetts Institute of Technology. To this committee was to be added a representative from each of the three large associations of teachers of mathematics in the secondary school. The committee finally consisted of fifteen members, seven from universities and colleges, three from two state departments of education, and five classroom teachers of mathematics. The committee had difficulty in securing financial support and was hindered by World War I; therefore, it did not really get under way until about 1919 and 1920, when it secured financial support.

Two men devoted their full time to the investigation, and an adequate office and secretarial force were provided. After the committee had drafted its preliminary report, it was submitted to about one hundred organizations of mathematics teachers throughout the United States for their reactions, and the final report boasts of the fact that the committee believes it is safe to say "that the recommendations of this final report have the approval of the great majority of progressive teachers throughout the country."[5] What, then, do these "progressive teachers" think about the teaching of their subject?

---

4. *The Reorganization of Mathematics in Secondary Education.* A summary of the report by the National Committee on Mathematical Requirements. (Bureau of Education, *Bulletin* No. 32; Washington: Government Printing Office, 1921), p. v.
5. *Ibid.,* p. vi,

In the first place the mathematics teachers were impressed by the need and the opportunity to place a reorganized series of courses in mathematics firmly in the junior high school and thus recommended:

> To the end that *all pupils* in the period of secondary education *shall gain early a broad view of the whole field of elementary mathematics,* and, in particular, in order to *insure contact with this important element* in secondary education on the part of the very large number of pupils who, for one reason or another, drop out of school by the end of the ninth year, the national committee *recommends emphatically* that the course of study in mathematics during the seventh, eighth, and ninth years contain the fundamental notions of arithmetic, of algebra, of intuitive geometry, of numerical trigonometry and at least an introduction to demonstrative geometry, and that *this body of material be required of all secondary school pupils.*[6]

In the senior high school, the committee did not wish to require additional mathematics of all pupils, but urged the teachers and principals *to encourage* in every way all pupils to take as much mathematics as possible. They even strengthened their case by declaring that "there is no conflict between the needs of those pupils who ultimately go to college and those who do not."[7] The following courses were recommended for the tenth, eleventh, and twelfth grades,[8] and the report listed the major topics to be developed in each course:

1. Plane demonstrative geometry
2. Algebra (including equations up to three unknowns; exponents, radicals and logarithms; geometric progressions; binomial theorem)
3. Solid geometry
4. Trigonometry
5. Elementary statistics
6. Elementary calculus
7. Mathematics of investment
8. Shop mathematics
9. Surveying and navigation
10. Descriptive or projective geometry

Here again the mathematicians thought well of their field and wanted to insure it an adequate place in the life of the adolescent.

It is interesting to note the purposes which this committee accepted for the teaching of mathematics. Shortly before the committee went to work, E. L. Thorndike and other psychologists had challenged the faith in transfer. Such a movement was devastating to the supporters of the entrenched subjects, who had for a long time been claiming without successful challenge that their fields

6. *Ibid.,* p. 1. Italics mine.
7. *Ibid.,* p. 2.
8. *Ibid.,* pp. 29–33.

of study had disciplinary values. Their claims were limited more by imagination than by modesty or by scientific findings. In the face, therefore, of a new rising conviction that the confidence in mental discipline should be overthrown, this committee had Vevia Blair prepare a report bringing together the present evidence on the status of disciplinary values in education. The young science of experimental psychology was too much of an adolescent to face the older subject of mathematics, but the committee reported cautiously, "Training in connection with certain attitudes, ideals, and ideas is almost universally admitted by psychologists to have general value. It may, therefore, be said that with proper restrictions, general mental discipline is a valid aim in education."[9] The committee saw these mental discipline values as the development of quantitative thinking, the analysis of complex situations, the recognition of logical relations, ability to generalize, the appreciation of form and beauty in nature, the development of ideals of perfection in logical structure, and the appreciation of the power of mathematics.[10]

It should be said, however, that in addition to the mental-discipline functions of mathematics, the committee listed as having more importance the practical aim of the utility of the processes of arithmetic in the life of every individual and "of almost equal importance to every educated person is an understanding of the language of algebra and the ability to use this language intelligently and readily in the expression of such simple quantitative relations as occur in everyday life."[11]

The Classical Investigation

In the preface to the general report of the American Classical League the committee states that the purpose of making the report was to improve the teaching of the classics, thus setting the extent and function of the study. The study, beginning in 1921, had three stages: (1) an inquiry into the facts of the present situation regarding the teaching of the classics, (2) an analysis and impartial criticism of these facts, and (3) the preparation of a plan for the teaching of the classics in the secondary schools of the country. The aspects under consideration had to do with Latin particularly, but the report also dealt with the existing administration, enrollment, curriculum, and methods, as well as with college entrance requirements, the training of classics teachers, the teaching of the classics abroad, and the relation of Latin to the new trends in education at the time—the economy-of-time movement and the junior-high-school movement.

The investigation was to be carried out by experts and by regional com-

---

9. *Ibid.*, p. 5.
10. *Ibid.*, pp. 7–8.
11. *Ibid.*, p. 5.

mittees furnishing the data, which in turn were to be interpreted by the main advisory committee together with the aid of various consultants. The personnel of the committee indicates somewhat the major emphasis expected from the report. Ten of the fifteen members of the advisory committee were from colleges and universities and five were from high schools. The special investigating committee was made up of two college and two high school people. Fifty-five additional people worked on the investigation, representing private academies, high schools, and colleges and universities in fairly even distribution. The collaboration and criticism of forty-eight professors of education and psychology were also drawn upon during the study, thus freeing the investigation from the accusation that it was made solely by teachers of the classics. The report also boasts of having drawn directly upon the services of 8,595 teachers, mostly teachers of classics in the United States, as well as upon the United States Office of Education, the State Department of Education of New York, and the College Entrance Board. This was truly an investigation in which a large number of people with different interests were concerned for over a period of two years from 1921 to 1923. Approximately 150,000 pupils were tested in 1,313 schools.[12]

The report accepts and endeavors to support the following objectives for the teaching of Latin, the main concern of the study:

Instrumental and Application Objectives

1. Ability to read new Latin after the study of the language in school or college has ceased

2. Increased ability to understand Latin words, phrases, abbreviations and quotations occurring in English

3. Increased ability to understand the exact meaning of English words derived directly or indirectly from Latin, and increased accuracy in their use

4. Increased ability to read English with correct understanding

5. Increased ability to speak and write correct and effective English through training in adequate translation

6. Increased ability to spell English words of Latin derivation

7. Increased knowledge of the principles of English grammar, and a consequently increased ability to speak and write grammatically correct English.

8. Increased ability to learn the technical and semitechnical terms of Latin origin employed in other school studies and in professions and vocations

Disciplinary Objectives

1. The development of certain desirable habits and ideals which are subject to spread, such as habits of sustained attention, orderly procedure,

---

12. *The Classical Investigation,* Part I. *General Report* (Princeton: Princeton University Press, 1924), Chap. 1.

overcoming obstacles, perseverance; ideals of achivement, accuracy, and thoroughness; and the cultivation of certain general attitudes, such as dissatisfaction with failure or with partial success

2. The development of the habit of discovering identical elements in different situations and experiences, and of making true generalizations

3. The development of correct habits of reflective thinking applicable to the mastery of other subjects of study and to the solution of analogous problems in daily life

Cultural Objectives

1. The development of an historical perspective and of a general cultural background through an increased knowledge of facts relating to the life, history, institutions, mythology and religion of the Romans; an increased appreciation of the influence of their civilization on the course of Western civilization; and a broader understanding of the social and political problems of today

2. Increased ability to understand and appreciate references and allusions to the mythology, traditions, and history of the Greeks and Romans

3. The development of right attitudes toward social situations

4. A better acquaintance through the study of their writings with some of the chief personal characteristics of authors read

5. Development of the appreciation of the literary qualities of Latin authors read, and development of the capacity for such appreciation in the literatures of other languages

6. A greater appreciation of the elements of literary techniques employed in prose and verse

7. Improvement of the literary quality of the pupil's written English

8. An elementary knowledge of the general principles of language structure.[13]

In order to attain these objectives the investigators thought there must be some improvement in the course materials and organization, but laid strong emphasis upon improved methods and better-trained teachers. They recommended the teaching of less materials in the course and the extension of it over more years of study, and again affirmed their belief that a large part of the superiority of the Latin-prepared pupils in the college entrance examinations was "presumably due to something derived from the study of Latin." They commended the French plan of having the same teacher teach Latin, French, and Greek and indicated that such a plan should be followed in the United States, intimating that such a combination with English would be a good teaching assignment. They advocated a continuous six-year course in Latin, beginning in the junior high school.

Clearly this Classical Investigation report is one to give heart to the teacher of the classics who firmly believes in the objectives accepted by the advisory

---

13. *Ibid.*, pp. 33–35. Reprinted here by permission of the publishers.

committee. It was a report which took a different attack from that of the two preceding ones in that it went directly to statistical reports and gathered original data to discover opinions and facts regarding the status of thought and practice on the teaching of Latin. It was not empirically assumed that certain conditions existed. It was also different in that a large number of educators and psychologists were consulted regarding their opinion about the teaching of Latin. Growing out of a restlessness among the teachers of a subject which was on the decline, in a scholarly fashion it sought to repair the losses in terms of the thought of the working group. However, it was an apologia for Latin and never raised the question whether Latin should be taught at all. The committee assumed it was good and dictated the cultural and disciplinary and academic gains to be sought from it. The members had a strong faith in discipline and in the belief that Latin was quite helpful in improving ability in English. They assumed also that the large masses of pupils could learn Latin well enough to achieve these proposed goals and that Latin would come nearer achieving these ends than other subjects taught for the same period of time.

Summary and Evaluation

In looking back over the studies of the Committee of Ten, the National Committee on Mathematical Requirements, and the Classical Investigation, we may draw certain obvious conclusions for the curriculum:

1. The members of the committees thought the curriculum should be made by a group of experts in the subjects taught and should be introduced by these experts into the local schools.

2. Each subject group was to protect, organize, and further the teaching of its subject.

3. The major purposes of the subjects were still essentially what they had been for several decades before—disciplinary and cultural—with a very small insight into their utilitarian use or their application to life situations.

4. A subject was to be learned through mastery of facts and through drill on the several abilities which were to transfer widely.

5. The committees were made up of subject specialists, chiefly college dominated, with sufficient psychologists and educators on the last two studies to make the commission safe from too much criticism for having ignored the fields altogether.

6. Questions of the relation of the subject to social conditions, to the growth and development of the individual, to other subject fields or life activities, or questions of whether the subject should be taught at all to the increasing mass of youth with differing purposes were neglected or pushed aside.

7. Whatever difficulties inhered in the subject or its status they were to be remedied through administrative organization, through better-trained teachers, or through improved methodology.

8. The reports of these studies are doubly interesting in the light of the

protests arising after the Spanish-American War that the high-school curriculum was a part of the college curriculum and that the secondary school
should become a people's university.

These efforts at reforming the curriculum of the secondary school were being
watched by another group of subject teachers—those of the modern languages.
World War I brought a widespread decline in the study of German and caused
the introduction of Spanish into the secondary school as another modern
language.

The Modern Language Study

In Atlantic City in December, 1923, a group of twenty-four teachers of modern
languages met and drafted a report calling for a study of the teaching of
modern languages in the United States. The Carnegie Corporation agreed to
provide funds for the study, as the General Education Board had financed the
Mathematical and the Classical investigations. The organization for the study
included a special Committee on Direction and Control made up of twenty-five
people, six from high schools, eighteen from colleges, and one from a state
department of education. Three investigators were selected, one from each of
the modern languages, and the country was divided into eight regions, as was
true of the Classical Investigation. The organizational meeting was held in
April, 1924, and the study really got under way in October, 1924, in offices at
Columbia University. One of the representatives on the directing committee
was from Canada, which was included in the study. A psychologist, as advisor,
was added to the study group.

For two years through the use of questionnaires and visits the committee
gathered the data on the status of modern foreign languages. Thirty-five
thousand questionnaires were sent to teachers in high schools and colleges, to
administrators, to registrars, and to graduates of schools. Tests were built and
administered to pupils taking modern languages, and a series of careful re-
searches under the direction of university professors in graduate schools was
planned, dealing with problems in the areas of curriculum and method, such
as the acceleration of the process of learning to read, the effect of age upon
learning a language, the creation of prognosis tests, frequency studies in the
basic materials of vocabulary and idiom, and a bibliography of works on the
teaching of modern languages. The work of the committee resulted in a report
covering eighteen volumes, the last of which is a summary of the other
reports.[14]

---

14. Robert H. Fife (compiler), *A Summary of the Reports on the Modern Foreign
Languages* (Issued by the Modern Foreign Language Study and the Canadian Committee on Modern Languages; New York: The Macmillan Company, 1931). See pp. 1–16
for the outline of the study.

New Basis for Objectives

In setting up the objectives for the study of modern languages, this study departed radically from the three previous ones by inquiring into the social basis for determining the objectives of the teaching of the modern languages in the light of the activities of American men and women. Commercial firms, high-school and college graduates, engineers, journalists, and others were asked what relation the languages had to their life experiences and needs. Thus an attempt was made to discover the demand in American life for the teaching of the languages. The committee then set up a tentative list of objectives and sought the opinion of teachers upon it. As a result of these studies the following objectives were accepted:

> For a two-year course, the immediate objectives call for a progressive development of the ability in reading, in grammar so far as it is necessary for reading purposes, in pronunciation and in oral and aural use, . . . a progressive development of the knowledge of foreign peoples and of an interest in their life and characteristics, as well as a knowledge of English vocabulary and grammar and of the relationship between foreign language and English.
>
> The ultimate objectives include the ability to read the language and use it orally within limits which are clearly defined. They include an interest in the history and ideals and institutions of the foreign country, an increased curiosity about its literature and art, a greater interest in language and an increased understanding of the development and structure of English and other languages.[15]

The report claims that insufficient work had been done to prove the theory of discipline and that therefore any discussion of indirect values to be gained must be eliminated from any practical consideration. This is a far cry from the confidence held by the three previous committees in the disciplinary values of their subjects. Obviously, the investigations of the present abilities of pupils who had studied foreign languages humbled the committee, and discouraged it from placing a halo around the subject, as the other committees sought to do. The committee defended vigorously the use of textbooks containing material on the history and culture of the people speaking the language. It also defended the general principle of using word counts as the basis for selecting reading materials.

Evaluation

This report of the language committee is a distinct step in advance of the rest of the reports. It was a straightforward, honest attempt to appraise exist-

---

15. *Ibid.*, p. 38. Reprinted here by permission of the publishers.

ing conditions in the field and to recommend desirable changes by drawing upon the combined opinion of the language teachers and other educational workers and using whatever experimental evidence could be secured. It did not go beyond the teaching of the modern languages and made only a small beginning in the area of seeking the social justification for the teaching of languages. The study was made at the beginning of the scientific movement in education; it resorted to the best techniques and drew the cautious conclusions typical of the careful use of statistical findings. It did not list pages of specifics to be taught by grades, as the other reports had done. Its reports were marked contrasts in curriculum construction to the other three studies. However, it was still subject-matter work in national committee curriculum building and did not transcend the area of its own investigation. The study did make far more use of scientific means and wider educational experiences than the other studies did. While this committee was interested in the development of definite language abilities and felt there was some transfer to other fields, the members were cautious about these claims. They were seeking the development of a wider range of understandings and some familiarity with cultural movements of civilization.

Before these last two reports were completed, another extensive and influential national committee was formed and it proposed other ways of determining the pattern of secondary education.

The Commission on the Reorganization of Secondary Education

From a report of a committee of the National Education Association in 1911 on the articulation of high school and college came the Commission on the Reorganization of Secondary Education. This committee took the position that the secondary school should adapt its program to meet the needs of its youth population without closing the doors of higher education to them and that, therefore, the college should revise its entrance requirements. It proposed that any well-planned curriculum should meet the requirements for entrance to the college. This recommendation focused attention upon the reorganization of secondary education for the needs of a democracy and an increased school population. For this task the commission was established and was divided into sixteen committees headed by a reviewing committee which later decided to formulate and issue a statement of fundamental principles which would help in reorganizing secondary education. This report, known as the *Cardinal Principles of Secondary Education*,[16] was issued subsequent to the

16. Commission on the Reorganization of Secondary Education, *Cardinal Principles of Secondary Education* (Bureau of Education, *Bulletin* No. 35; Washington: Government Printing Office, 1918).

publication of reports by the committees on community civics (1915), social studies (1916), English (1917), music (1917), physical education 1917), moral values (1917), and vocational guidance (1918). Other reports were issued after the report of the reviewing committee.

The reviewing committee consisted of twenty-six members, headed by the Massachusetts State High School Supervisor (Clarence D. Kingsley). One member was the United States Commissioner of Education, three were professors of secondary education, one was a high-school principal, one a state supervisor of secondary education, one a Y.M.C.A. worker, one a college president, one a normal-school president, and one a leader in the Ethical Culture Society. The remaining sixteen members, who were chairmen of the sixteen committees, were divided about as were the members of the reviewing committee. The opening statement of the reviewing committee was revolutionary for its time and is entirely out of harmony with the character of the other reports just described which emerged even after this report:

> Secondary education should be determined by the needs of the society to be served, the character of the individuals to be educated, and the knowledge of educational theory and practice available. These factors are by no means static. Society is always in process of development; the character of the secondary school population undergoes modification; and the sciences upon which educational theory and practices depend constantly furnish new information. Secondary education, however, like any other established agency of society, is conservative and tends to resist modification. Failure to make adjustments when the need arises leads to the necessity for extensive reorganization at irregular intervals. The evidence is strong that such a comprehensive reorganization is imperative at the present time.[17]

The Seven Cardinal Principles

Following this opening paragraph the report suggests three kinds of changes that the school must recognize in building its program: (1) changes in society; (2) changes in secondary school population; and (3) changes in educational theory, under which they mention individual differences, formal discipline, application of knowledge, and continuity in pupil development. None of these had been treated in the three previous reports except the one on formal discipline, but this commission was convinced that evidence was sufficient to justify thorough reorganization. Then came statements on democracy, on education, and on the main objectives of secondary education. These objectives are famous by now and are known as the Seven Cardinal Principles— health, command of the fundamental processes, worthy home membership, vocation, civic education, worthy use of leisure, and ethical character.

17. *Ibid.*, p. 7.

These aims of education were the first ones to be stated by a national committee organized to study the secondary curriculum in terms of the activities of individuals in a democratic society rather than in terms of subject achievement. According to this concept of curriculum organization, the subjects and skills were to be used as instrumental means of achieving that power within each individual which would enable him to perform successfully his obligations in society, shaping both himself and society to ever nobler ends. With regard to the place of the subjects, the committee summed up its attitude very well in the following statement:

> Each subject now taught in high schools is in need of extensive reorganization in order that it may contribute more effectively to the objectives outlined herein, and the place of that subject in secondary education should depend upon the value of such contribution.[18]

Evaluation

This report was ahead of the current thinking of the time; for the first time in the curriculum movement, it suggests that the traditionally honored structure, in which the acquisition of facts and skills was a primary educational objective, be replaced by a curriculum in which the content of each field was rebuilt in terms of its ability to meet the objectives of education as set up. All subjects were to be reorganized in terms of these objectives. Health as a field of study, for instance, was to be introduced, and physical education and science were specifically asked to focus their attention upon problems of sanitation and personal and community hygiene. To secure worthy home membership, the subjects of art, literature, household arts, and the social studies were specifically mentioned. This type of reorganization gives purpose to the selection of subject materials, and, while the committee had no idea of abolishing subject matter lines, it did insist that a new purpose or central point of organization dominate the selection of subject materials and the purposes for which they were taught. Education was a process of growth, enabling an individual to serve society and improve himself, and this job was to be accomplished directly, not through some mystical faith or confidence in the power of a subject to equip a youth to function in totally different areas of experience.

The National Joint Committee on English

Following the lead of the general report of the Commission on Reorganization of Secondary Education, the various subject committees rendered individual reports. Some of them had slight effects upon the various subjects, some of

---

18. *Ibid.*, p. 16.

them followed the trend of thinking of the central committee, but no one made a more significant report than the committee dealing with English. Since this is probably the field most frequently required in the secondary school, the changes proposed in its organization and teaching are especially significant. The National Council of Teachers of English cooperated with the National Education Association to form a national joint committee on English, headed by James Fleming Hosic.

This committee immediately placed itself on record regarding the theory of taking courses in high school which led to more courses in the same subject and finally to college. In the preface it hastened to say: "The entire doctrine of 'preparation' for higher institutions is fallacious. The best preparation for anything is real effort and experience in the present."[19]

Membership of the Committee

This committee was composed of thirty members selected from the following fields of work: four teachers of English in college, normal school, university or teachers' college; eleven high-school teachers of English; three school superintendents; one state supervisor of English in a state department of education; one dean of a liberal arts college; two city supervisors of English; three school librarians; two high-school principals; one college editor of an agricultural college; and two college professors of public speaking. This committee was "loaded" with high-school teachers, contrary to the first national subject committees which were "loaded" with college professors. It also had a fairly good distribution of public-school people with different interests and had some college representation, but it was an English committee, lacking representatives from other fields, from the elementary school, and from students of the culture and of child development. This deficiency, however, was partially balanced by the personnel of the reviewing committee of the Commission on Reorganization which was made up largely of educators with different interests.

Point of View of the Committee

The pronouncements of this committee are commonplace today: "the college preparatory function of the high school is a minor one"; "the chief problem of articulation is not to connect the high school with the college but with the elementary school"; "make the high school a school for the children of all the people"; "it is a mistake to regard English as merely a

---

19. National Joint Committee on English, James Fleming Hosic, chairman, *Reorganization of English in Secondary Schools* (Bureau of Education, *Bulletin* No. 2; Washington: Government Printing Office, 1917), p. 5.

formal subject"; and probably the most quoted of all, "English must be regarded as social in content and social in method of acquirement." These statements were followed by a statement of the two major objectives of English: "(a) To give the pupils command of the art of communication in speech and in writing. (b) To teach them to read thoughtfully and with appreciation, to form in them a taste for good reading, and to teach them how to find books that are worth while."

The point of view of the committee on the organization of the English course was not typical of the times.

> The subject matter of English consists primarily of activities, not of information. It provides a means for the development of ideals, attitudes, skill, and habits, rather than for the acquisition of a knowledge of facts and principles . . . this knowledge [knowledge of grammar, spelling, rhetoric, literary forms, history of literary production] is subsidiary; that it can actually be gained only through and in contact with genuine constructive activities, and that it should not, therefore, be made the chief basis for the organization of the course or for standards of attainment to be set up from semester to semester. The relating of items of knowledge to the pupil's daily experience is more important than the relating of these items to each other in his memory.[20]

Evaluation

This point of view is entirely out of harmony with that of the other committees reporting near the date of the work of this committee. The English committee was convinced that the direct attack upon problems of speech and reading was the only satisfactory one to take, that this attack was to be made in terms of the uses in daily living which the pupil would have for his mother tongue, and that the course should be so organized that its material would be entirely concerned with communication and intelligent appreciation. Composition topics should be drawn from daily life, and grammar and other techniques of expression should be taught at the time the need or the use of them appeared. The suggestions regarding expression are in harmony with this general point of view.

When it came to literature, the committee was reluctant to let itself be as generous in its thinking. It was interested in getting pupils to read as many good books as possible, feeling that through such reading "high ideals of life and conduct" would be developed, the "imaginative and emotional faculties" of the pupils would be stimulated, and the "mental experience" of youth would be broadened. The suggestions for literature were, in the main, the classics, but no demand was made for the universal reading of a selected few.

---

20. *Ibid.*, p. 33.

These national reports focused attention chiefly on the value of achievement in the subject fields. They varied from those which were really briefs for special subjects, with claims far surpassing the evidence upon which they drew, to suggestions for deriving the values of instruction from prevailing human experience. They probably were what we should expect of the times, but they did little to stimulate curriculum reorganization away from rigid subject lines. This movement occurred later.

Chapter Seven

Recent Efforts in Improving the Traditional Curriculum

B EFORE 1925 most of the work on the curriculum which achieved national importance was confined to the reports of large, well-financed commissions. This movement prompted small subject organizations to study the fields in which they were operating. Specific dates for the beginning of such studies are less important than their accomplishments and points of view. A canvass of a few of the studies will reveal the dominant thought of the time at work in these reports. A fairly full report of a few is better for this purpose than a briefer report of all.

Commission on the Social Studies

By 1922 nearly all the national associations had issued some form of pronouncement regarding reorganization in the field of study they represented, but after 1920 the reports had been increasingly less dogmatic in tone and less sure of what ought to be taught. In the last part of the twenties, attention began to be centered upon needed reorganization in the social studies, and in 1926 a committee of nine members of the American Historical Association drew up and reported a plan for investigating the nature and function of the social studies. This plan was used, with modifications, to secure funds from the Carnegie Corporation to sponsor the work of the commission for five years, beginning January, 1929, and ending December, 1933.

Organization of the Commission

The membership of the commission during this period was relatively unchanged, with the exception of a few replacements. It was composed of eighteen men: one school superintendent, nine professors of social science in colleges and universities, the director of the American Geographical Society, one college president, three professors of education, one member of the Rockefeller Foundation, and two professors of the teaching of the social sciences. In order to provide for both integration and differentiation in the work of the committee, five major committees and numerous special investigators were appointed. The commission itself, with a chairman, a research director, an executive committee, and an executive secretary, integrated the work of the group. Many other people connected with high schools and colleges worked on the reports. The work of the commission was divided into the following six major divisions: (1) philosophy, purpose, and objectives; (2) materials of instruction; (3) methods of teaching; (4) tests and testing; (5) the teacher; and (6) public relations.

The first major committee to start its work was the one on objectives, an interesting committee made up of four college professors in the field of social sciences, two in political science, two in history, and four professors of education—one a sociologist, one a curriculum worker in general, one a psychologist, and one a student of economic and cultural life. After its deliberations the committee invited the chairman, Charles A. Beard, to write the report, and the result was *A Charter for the Social Sciences in the Schools*.[1] Five other supplementary volumes discussed the philosophy, purposes, or objectives of the social studies and were written by individuals sponsored by the commission.[2]

A similar series of volumes dealt primarily with materials of instruction

---

1. Charles A. Beard, *A Charter for the Social Sciences in the Schools* (New York: Charles Scribner's Sons, 1932).
2. These reports (all published by Scribner's) were:
   Charles A. Beard, *The Nature of the Social Sciences*, 1934.
   George S. Counts, *The Social Foundations of Education*, 1934.
   Merle E. Curti, *Social Ideas of American Educators*, 1935.
   L. C. Marshall and Rachel Marshall Goetz, *A Social Process Approach to Curriculum-Making in the Social Studies*, 1936.
   Charles E. Merriam, *Civic Education in the United States*, 1934.

and methods of teaching.[3] Other volumes dealt with the subject of testing,[4] and two volumes with the teacher of social studies.[5] Two were specifically concerned with administration and public relations.[6] The series was completed with one additional volume, the report of the commission, entitled *Conclusions and Recommendations*.

Point of View of the Commission

In its approach to the problem of reorganizing the social studies in the public schools, one of the first jobs any commission must attack is the setting up of a point of view. This task the commission undertook and later reported in *A Charter for the Social Sciences in the Schools*. The members first set up the conditioning factors in teaching the social studies. These they conceived to be the spirit and letter of scholarship, the social realities of our times, the kinds of teachers we have, and the pupils in the schools. While these are limiting factors, they are likewise opportunities, thought the commission, but they do condition the framework in which we must operate. The scholars are conditioned "by the vows of their craft, imposed by the very nature of the mind and the materials in which they delve," and are necessarily stunned by the vast amount of literature of fact and opinion in one of the most extensive fields of human activity.

> Of necessity, those who formulate programs are specialists in particular fields—one-sided persons. This cannot be avoided either. Under the stress of modern specialization, itself the result of intense efforts to see things more accurately and vividly, social science tends in practice to break up into disciplines, such as economics, politics, anthropology, psychology, sociology, geography, esthetics, ethics, imaginative literature, and history, each with an emphasis upon a selected aspect of human affairs.[7]

---

3. In addition to the volumes included in note 2, the following (all published by Scribner's) belong in this group:
   Isaiah Bowman, *Geography in Relation to the Social Sciences*, 1934.
   Ernest Horn, *Methods of Instruction in the Social Sciences*, 1937.
   Henry Johnson, *An Introduction to the History of the Social Sciences in Schools*, 1932.
   Rolla M. Tryon, *The Social Sciences as School Subjects*, 1935.
4. In addition to the casual references to testing in *The Nature of the Social Sciences*, and in *Methods of Instruction in the Social Sciences*, the volume entitled *Tests and Measurements in the Social Sciences*, by Truman L. Kelley and A. C. Krey, deals specifically with this subject. (Charles Scribner's Sons, 1934.)
5. William C. Bagley and Thomas Alexander, *The Teacher of the Social Studies*; Howard K. Beale, *Are American Teachers Free?* (Charles Scribner's Sons, 1936, 1937.)
6. In addition to material in the volume *Social Ideas of American Educators*, see: Bessie L. Pierce, *Citizens and the Civic Training of Youth* (1933); Jesse H. Newlon, *Educational Administration as Social Policy*, 1934. (Charles Scribner's Sons, 1933, 1934.)
7. Beard, *A Charter for the Social Sciences*, p. 17.

Some synthesis has always been made of these separate disciplines, as they are interrelated in the course of human affairs. More is being demanded, but, in the opinion of the commission, if a better synthesis could be effected it would be a "skillfully wrought mosaic rather than sublimal coalescence in which the separate disciplines would disappear and completely lose their identity as law, economics, geography, and history."[8]

But it is impossible to draw up a program of social education alone from the scholarship in the field of the social sciences, for life itself in its changing realities must ever be taken into account in building a program for the development of the young. Regardless of whether we are enthusiastic or depressed about this factor, we must face it realistically. The causes and extent of changing social circumstances must be explored. The character and significance of industrialization need to come in for review as well as the nature of the system of government under which pupils are to live as active participants. Nevertheless, the commission felt that not all social problems could be introduced or should be, but that adequate attention should be paid to developing an understanding of the background of existing causes and relationships in the problems being studied.

There is another very important element in instruction in the social studies which the commission emphasized—the element of creative enterprise, which brings to a focus the ideals we have inherited and the contemporary experiences we are undergoing. If the school does not deal with present activities, the commission warned, "creative enterprise will go forward without them [the schools], reducing their significance in the educative process." There must be a selection of the important problems for youth to study, and neutrality in this selection is suicidal. Moreover, to deal with controversial social matters is dangerous, but necessary. If the school is to make its influence felt in contemporary living it must deal with present-day issues. The commission stated the problem thus:

> The teacher of social science can only escape presenting the necessity of choice in social affairs by fleeing from the world of reality to a land of abstraction. If this is the alternative, then civic instruction might as well be taken out of the schools. By its intrinsic nature, social science requires some picture of the process in which we live and work, and when it is realistically conceived it must deal with what is here and now and also with what is emerging from the here and now.[9]

But civic instruction cannot be expected to accomplish the impossible. Pupils and teachers, as well as the other factors just mentioned, condition the effectiveness of instruction in the social sciences. Teachers in a local community are very likely to find themselves "in a conventional climate of ideas

8. *Ibid.,* p. 21.
9. *Ibid.,* p. 56.

that tends to stifle independent research and the exercise of critical judgment," and the profession itself has developed sufficient routine to make the creative life more difficult. Timidity or lack of breadth of experience or education are hazards to an effective social-education program and must be considered realistically. Pupils themselves offer an element of blockage in the program, for we cannot give generalizations and abstractions beyond their range of experience. The whole program of social education must be geared to the experiences and knowledge of details which youth have. If the major purpose of civic education is, as the commission contends, "the creation of rich and many-sided personalities," then the instruction necessarily hangs on the individual pupil and what it does to him. His abilities release the program as his shortcomings inhibit it.

Thus the commission proposed a point of view around which programs of social education can be developed in local schools and communities. The reports dealt more with the first two conditioning factors—the scholarship of the social sciences and the realities of the social order—than with the third conditioning factor, the teachers and the pupils. It is regrettable that the reports paid far more attention to scholarship in the social sciences than to creative enterprise. One feels that the social scientists had a dream but lost it and fell back upon their own information.

Recommendations of the Commission

Specifically the commission makes several suggestions for organizing the social sciences in the school. In speaking of the organization of the materials of instruction it has this to say:

> The program of social science instruction should not be organized as a separate and isolated division of the curriculum but rather should be closely integrated with other activities and subjects so that the entire curriculum of the school may constitute a unified attack upon the complicated problem of life in contemporary society.[10]

This, however, should not be taken to mean that the commission wanted the subjects of the social sciences to be completely fused with other subjects of the school; the commission in other places indicated that it preferred to see no complete fusion of the various social sciences. The reference here is more to the functional attack upon the problems of understanding social living than upon a particular method of curriculum organization.

When it came to suggesting the actual teaching materials of the social sciences for the schools, the commission indicated that these should be drawn from the fields of physical and cultural geography, economics, cultural sociol-

---

10. American Historical Association, *Conclusions and Recommendations*. Report of Commission on the Social Studies (New York: Charles Scribner's Sons, 1934), p. 48.

ogy, political science, and history. In these different areas more definite suggestions are given. Such goals as the following are proposed:

1. Knowledge and understanding concerning the earth as the physical home of man
2. Knowledge and understanding concerning the major social processes through which the life of society has been carried on throughout all ages
3. A broad and comprehensive conception of the evolution of civilization
4. A study of the evolution of Western civilization
5. The history of the American people
6. A realistic study of the life, institutions, and cultures of the major peoples of the contemporary world
7. A realistic study of the life, institutions, and culture of the life in contemporary America
8. A thorough and judicial study of all the great theories, philosophies, and programs, however radical or conservative they may appear, which have been designed to deal with the growing tensions and problems of industrial society
9. An introduction of the younger generation to *sources* for new and current materials and to *methods* of inquiry, scrutiny, criticism, authentication, and verification[11]

Specifically the commission proposed the following program for the teaching of the social sciences; beyond this the details of organization and selection are up to the local community.

In the elementary school major attention would be devoted to a study of the making of the community and the nation, although materials bearing on the developments of world society and culture would by no means be excluded. The program would begin with the neighborhood in which the child lives. Starting from a first-hand study of the life, institutions, and geography of the community, it would proceed to an examination of social changes taking place in the locality, of the history of the place, of the civilization of the Indian in the same area, of the contrasting elements of European and Indian culture and of early and later American culture. Emphasis throughout would be placed upon actual participation in the social activities of school and neighborhood, and every part or phase of the program would begin and end in the contemporary and surrounding community which the child knows directly. Thus the pupil would develop an active interest in the fortunes of society and acquire a stock of ideas which would enable him to go beyond the immediate in time and space. He would then be led by natural connections—genetic and functional—to the study of the making of the region and the nation. Through such an organization of materials the elementary school would acquaint the child as fully as possible with the evolution of American culture—local and

---

11. *Ibid.*, pp. 50–54. By permission of the publishers.

national—and to some extent with the origins of American culture in the Western world.

In the secondary school the central theme would be the development of mankind and the evolution of human culture, with the emphasis suggested elsewhere in this chapter and with constant reference to the present and to American civilization. This program might culminate in the study, through concrete and living materials, of regional geography, of comparative economics, government and cultural sociology, of the major movements in social thought and action in the modern world, of the most recent developments on the international stage—a study in which the experience, the knowledge and the thought of all the preceding years would be brought to bear, by means of comparison and contrast, upon the emerging problems, tensions, and aspirations, the evolving social programs and philosophies of mankind and of the American people in their regional and world setting. Also special attention would be given in the secondary school to the reading of historical and social literature, including newspapers and magazines, great historical documents, classics of social thought, and to the achievement of familiarity with methods and instruments of inquiry in the social sciences with historical criticism, analysis, verification, and authentication. The program should embrace both the junior and senior divisions of the secondary school and reach into the years of the junior college.[12]

Evaluation of the Commission's Program

Such a program, however, sounds like one proposed by a group of wishful thinkers, hoping that such understandings, skills, and methods of work could be developed in the masses of children and youth now attending the secondary and elementary schools. Its very nature suggests that it came from a group of scholars in the social sciences rather than from teachers who knew children's interests and problems. The commission, however, made a valuable contribution in making such an extensive and scholarly analysis of the field of social sciences and in pointing out the problems from this angle, but to show how these fields can so influence youth that they will become part of their experience is not accomplished. The commission made no contribution here.

Curriculum Commission in English

Harassed by letters from English teachers over the country for curriculum material in English, the National Council of Teachers of English, in November, 1929, appointed a Curriculum Commission to build a course of study in English from kindergarten through graduate school.[13] Six other national organizations

---

12. *Ibid.*, pp. 59–62. By permission of the publishers.
13. A Commission of the National Council of Teachers of English, W. Wilbur Hatfield, chairman, *An Experience Curriculum in English* (New York: Appleton-Century-Crofts, Inc., 1935), pp. v–xv.

approved the project and appointed representatives to serve on the commission. The report was financed largely by the meager resources of the National Council, except for a subsidy from the General Education Board to cover the major expense of the college committee.

Organization of the Commission

The membership of the commission included representatives from the six cooperating organizations—National Education Association, American Association of Teachers Colleges, National Association of Teachers of Speech, National Association of Journalism Directors of Secondary Schools, North Central Association of Colleges and Secondary Schools, Southern Association of Colleges and Secondary Schools. There were eight major committees, one each on literature, reading, creative writing, speech, writing, corrective teaching, grammar, and teacher training. Each of these eight committees, except the last two, was divided into two smaller committees, one dealing with the elementary level and the other with the secondary level. All in all, over one hundred people worked upon this commission—high-school teachers, elementary-school teachers, principals and administrators, editors, college and university teachers of English, college and university professors of the teaching of English, teachers of English in normal schools and teachers' colleges, general supervisors, state-department representatives, education professors, a college president, and a psychologist. This committee was supplemented by the work of many teachers in local communities who supplied the representatives of the commission with materials for the report.

Point of View of the Commission

The purpose of the commission was to build "a pattern curriculum," which the commission explained as "an instrument to assist in the cutting" of the local curriculum in English. The commission emphasized the necessity of keeping in mind constantly this purpose and urged teachers to use the materials as illustrations of the principles, not as details to be followed. Only the principles can be universally applied; the materials to illustrate them must be fashioned by each teacher in each locality after thorough acquaintance with the pupils and their needs. By these very statements the commission indicated the changes that have been taking place in curriculum planning. Here was a national committee advocating not the standardization of its field, as many of the preceding committees had done, but suggesting only a broad set of general principles with adequate illustration to make the principles clear. But, more important, it then stated that each community of teachers should construct its own curriculum in terms of local conditions and youth—a departure and a growth in the technique of curriculum construction, in the development of the teacher, in the concept of the place of the subject, and in the recognition of the significance of individual differences among youth.

Throughout the report the commission constantly emphasizes the need for basing the teaching of English upon experience.

> Experience is the best of all schools. . . . School and college curriculums should consist of experiences [meaning real situations]. The school of experience is the only one which will develop the flexibility and power of self-direction requisite for successful living in our age of swift industrial, social, and economic change. To inculcate authoritarian beliefs, fixed rules of conduct, unreasoned and therefore stubborn attitudes, is to set our youth in futile and fatal conflict with the forces of modern life. By meeting situations, modifying conditions and adapting themselves to the unchangeable, our boys and girls will learn to live in a dynamic and evolving world. Today, more than ever, the curriculum should consist of experiences.[14]

Recommendations of the Commission

Having stated its position regarding the place of daily-living experiences in the content and organization of the curriculum, the report proceeds to suggest "strands of experience" as organizing centers about which the curriculum materials may be grouped. For instance, a major phase of oral communication is divided into seven "experience strands"—conversing, telephoning, discussing and planning, telling stories, dramatizing, reporting, speaking to large groups. From elementary through secondary school, these strands gradually increase in range and complexity, but they always serve to remind the teacher of the major types of activity which the pupil will have and which call for English materials. To illustrate the point, these seven strands of oral communication just given are suggested for the first six grades and are followed by the following seven strands for grades 7–12: social conversation, telephone conversation, interviews and conferences, discussion, questions and answers, and speeches for special occasions. These "experience strands" are the social situations which are parallel to the use of expression in normal living. This is a far cry from the organization of material under such headings as grammar, oral composition, written composition, and rhetoric.

When it comes to the organization of literature, strands are also used, but they differ somewhat in statement. The following five are used for grouping the material of the first six grades; enjoying action and suspense, enjoying humor of various kinds, enjoying the world of the senses, exploring the social world, and enjoying fantasy and whimsy. Grades 7–12 use these: enjoying action, exploring the physical world, exploring the social world, studying human nature, sharing lyric emotion, giving fancy rein, solving puzzles, listening to

---

14. *Ibid.*, p. 3. By permission of the publishers.

radio broadcasts, and enjoying photoplays. For each of these strands a major and an enabling objective are indicated, which are followed by suggested lists of readings, activities, materials or skills, and desirable techniques.

> Something had to be done about the English curriculum; youth, society, and educational theory—all were changing faster than school practice. With the enforcement of compulsory attendance laws, all kinds of children were attending school and were staying on to graduate. Scientific measurements were disclosing a wide range of differences among pupils previously considered alike. Educational theory was taking its color from the Dewey philosophy of education as experience. But even so, a one-sided battle was being waged between out-of-school life and in-school English. The recreational facilities of the photoplay and the radio were offering too successful competition with reading as a leisure time activity. "Pulp" literature was providing a short-circuit to the lower emotions of students not adequately trained to read good literature with ease and enjoyment. As a consequence the "pulps" were winning the contest with the classics in the traditional curriculum. As a final complication in the English situation, unemployment was driving back to school more and more restless youths who, though they "experienced" little of what was being taught, enjoyed camaradie during extra-curricular activities—and the steam heat in the improved school buildings. Yes, something had to be done about the English curriculum.[15]

A Curriculum Commission in Language Arts

The National Council of Teachers of English, in the wake of the communications problems revealed by World War II, sought to reexamine the teaching of the language arts in this country. It sought also to propose measures befitting the importance of the subject in the educational program of a democracy.

Organization of the Commission

The national curriculum study of the council was set up under the supervision of a Curriculum Commission of twenty-five experts representing all sections of the country and all levels of the school system, from preschool through the graduate school and adult education. It was headed by a director and two associate directors.

In an effort to obtain careful articulation from one level of the school system to the next and at the same time to provide adequately for the many-sided aspects of the program in the language arts, four vertical committees were appointed, each with representatives from all levels of the school system on these important phases: writing, speech, reading and literature, and listening.

---

15. A Committee of the National Council of Teachers of English, Angela M. Broening, chairman, *Conducting Experiences in English* (New York: Appleton-Century-Crofts, Inc., 1939), p. v. By permission of the publishers.

Each member of a vertical committee had associated with him six resource persons representing his level of the school system from widely separated sections of the country. These groups, called horizontal committees, were engaged in gathering and preparing materials for actual use in the classrooms to fit into the sequential scheme planned by the vertical committees.

Problems and Program

The committees at first asked themselves several questions: What are the desirable outcomes of education to which the language arts should contribute? Many of these were deeply personal in nature, whereas others had social or civic implications. Next, with the aid of members of the appropriate horizontal committees, they studied the characteristics of young people at each stage of their development so that the requirements of the program might not outrun the potentialities of the learners. Then followed the problem: What kinds of experiences should be furnished if the outcomes desired are to be achieved by the boys and girls who make up the population of the average American school? Involved in these experiences were many skills, mastery of which was imperative if young people were to be prepared adequately for the language needs of living.

Among the many problems inherent in the preparation of such a program was that of articulation and how a continuity of learning experiences could be planned for each student:

> Concerning articulation from grade to grade and from one level of the school system to the next, the Council has begun by making two assumptions. One is that if such articulation is attained, vertical committees must be established having equal representation from each level of the school system. The other is that continuity in the program in the Language Arts can be provided only in terms of the natural sequence of the individual's own development. It cannot be arbitrarily imposed from without. . . . The adolescence Yearbook of the National Society for the Study of Education and similar volumes are invaluable in their emphasis upon the relationship of language and reading to the social and emotional development of young people. In specific fields like group discussion, the body of material descriptive of actual performance of pupils of various stages of growth increases every year. By observation of such performance on the part of young people and adults, it is becoming increasingly possible to plot the direction of growth in various social and personal uses of language. It is obviously futile to expect all young people to be at the same stage of development within any single grade, but it is possible to help teachers define where each one is and what are the next steps in his progress up the scale.[16]

As the study progressed, the commission defined two tasks as essential in the development of a functional, continuous program in the language arts:

---

16. Dora V. Smith, "The Curriculum Study by English Teachers," *California Journal of Secondary Education*, 22:343–348, 1947.

1. It sought to look upon the world to see what part communicative arts plays in it, and what language skills are essential for success in it.

2. It sought to study those aspects of the growth of children which affect their needs and competence in the use of English.

In essaying the first task the commission made a preliminary report in its mimeographed bulletin entitled "An Initial Statement of Platform of the Commission on the English Curriculum." In the study of growth each member prepared lists of characteristics of growth, the interests and needs of young people at one level in the school system—elementary, secondary, and college— and then combined these into a sequential pattern in relation to each one of the four major areas originally defined—writing, speech, reading and literature, and listening.

The commission then set down the kinds of experiences in language arts needed for effectiveness in the modern world. These were printed in a brief statement on "An Outline of Desirable Outcomes and Experiences in the Language Arts." Then they prepared descriptions of actual classroom practices to show how successful teachers have carried out the program. A five-volume report is in the course of preparation.[17]

Commission on Secondary School Curriculum

In October, 1930, the Progressive Education Association established a Commission on the Relation of School and College to set up an eight-year study in certain selected secondary schools in the United States, commonly called the "Eight-Year Study." The commission was also to further cooperative relations between the secondary schools and the colleges to which the graduates of the former went. Approximately thirty schools and over two hundred colleges were selected as the study was started. The colleges began accepting pupils for five years, dating from 1936. In order to accompany this experiment with an adequate study of what the curriculum of the secondary school might be without the restraints of college entrance requirements, another commission, the Commission on Secondary School Curriculum, was formed in May, 1932, "to focus attention upon the educational needs of all classes of adolescents in contemporary American society, to suggest methods of studying curriculum problems, and to further well-considered experimentation in fundamental aspects of curriculum revision."[18]

---

17. Dora V. Smith, "Making a Curriculum in the Language Arts," *Elementary English,* 27:421–424, 1950.

18. V. T. Thayer, Caroline B. Zachry, and Ruth Kotinsky, *Reorganizing Secondary Education* (New York: Appleton-Century-Crofts, Inc., 1939), p. v. See also Wilford M. Aiken, *The Story of the Eight-Year Study* (New York: Harper & Brothers, 1942).

Organization of the Commission

There were seven members of the commission, a curriculum consultant in a private school, a psychologist specializing in adolescence, a former superintendent of schools in a community furthering progressive school programs, a contemporary sociologist, a cultural anthropologist, a student of mental hygiene and secondary education, and a specialist in adult education and in editing educational magazines. Two other people served for a short time.

The work of this commission can be divided into two areas, one of which was a study of the young people themselves, their needs, drives, and experiences. A report was prepared on this area by a group of educators, psychologists, psychiatrists, physicians, anthropologists, sociologists, and social workers.[19] The other area of the commission's work was that of the selection and organization of instructional materials for the secondary school. The work of this division was carried on by subject committees in the fields of English, art, mathematics, science, and social studies. In addition, the central staff of the commission delegated to three of its members the publication of a report on the major principles of curriculum study and organization in the secondary school.[20] The work of the subject committees was carried on by experts in the respective fields assisted in some instances by experienced high-school and college teachers, psychologists, students of society and its institutions, school administrators, and community workers.[21]

---

19. Caroline B. Zachry, *Emotion and Conduct in Adolescence* (New York: Appleton-Century-Crofts, Inc., 1940).
20. V. T. Thayer, Caroline B. Zachry, and Ruth Kotinsky, *Reorganizing Secondary Education* (New York: Appleton-Century-Crofts, Inc., 1939).
21. The reports published by Appleton-Century-Crofts were:
    V. T. Thayer, Caroline B. Zachry, and Ruth Kotinsky, *Reorganizing Secondary Education,* 1939.
    Science in General Education, 1938.
    Language in General Education, 1940.
    Mathematics in General Education, 1940.
    The Social Studies in General Education, 1940.
    The Visual Arts in General Education, 1940.
    Peter Blos, *The Adolescent Personality,* 1941.
    Caroline B. Zachry, *Emotion and Conduct in Adolescence,* 1940.
    Louise Rosenblatt, *Literature as Exploration,* 1938.
    Elbert Lenrow, *Reader's Guide to Prose Fiction* (Bibliography of 1,500 Novels), 1940.
    Lawrence H. Conrad, *Teaching Creative Writing,* 1937.
    The five-volume *Adventure in American Education,* published by Harper & Brothers, consisted of:
    Wilford M. Aiken, *The Story of the Eight-Year Study,* 1942.
    H. H. Giles, S. P. McCutchen, and A. N. Zechiel, *Exploring the Curriculum,* 1942.

Point of View of the Commission

What are the basic generalizations, principles, and methods of curriculum organization which apply to all fields in the realization of the purposes of general education? The commission emphasized first the concern of democracy for certain common understandings among its people. The members accepted the frequent definition of the democratic tradition which stresses the worth of the individual, the necessity for individual and group responsibility for promoting common ends and goals, and the recognition of the value of the free play of intelligence in the solution of social problems. The school, they emphasized, must assume as one of its foremost functions the responsibility of teaching with conviction the meaning and desirability of accepting the democratic tradition.

The social world created by the operation of the democratic tradition needs certain types of behavior which the school can foster. It needs tolerance, cooperativeness, skill in reflective thinking, social sensitivity, creativeness, self-direction, and esthetic appreciation. These become in a way the aims of education in a democracy, and teaching materials should be evaluated in terms of their ability to produce desired results in the behavior of individuals. The social world is a welter of situations in which the individual acts and reacts, and in which the physical environment and other people are component parts of the total process of reaction. Each individual develops wants, desires, wishes, but these are to a degree determined by his past and present social experience. He may have a personal desire which may be defined as a need, or he may lack the ability to behave successfullly in a social situation, which may also be a need. Thus "a working concept of an educational need must always be both personal and social in reference; it must always incorporate both the present desires of the individual and what they should desirably become."[22] From an analysis of individuals and of society, educational needs can be determined which are enough in common to form the working basis for the organization of a program of general education for youth of secondary school age.

The commission then set up four areas into which adolescent needs can be grouped: immediate social relationships, wider social relationships, economic relationships, and personal living. Some illustrations of the more detailed meanings of needs in each of these areas will serve to make clearer the point of view of the committee.

Eugene R. Smith and Ralph Tyler, *Appraising and Recording Student Progress,* 1942.
Dean Chamberlin, Enid Straw Chamberlin, Neal E. Drought, and William E. Scott, *Did They Succeed in College?* 1942.
Thirty Schools Tell Their Story, 1943.
22. Thayer, Zachry, and Kotinsky, *Reorganizing Secondary Education,* p. 38,

I. Area of immediate social relationships
   A. The need for "emancipation from the ties, proper to childhood, which formerly kept their perspective, loyalties, and affections bound within the family circle" (p. 152)
   B. The need for building "increasingly meaningful and satisfying relationships with new persons and groups" (p. 151)

II. Area of wider social relationships
   A. "An increasing awareness of the social bearings and import of their interests, abilities, and activities" (p. 205)
   B. "A coordinately increasing sense of social responsibility" (p. 205)

III. Area of economic relationships
   A. "An increasing awareness on his part of the social bearings and import of his economic activities and vocational interests" (p. 241)
   B. "An always keener appreciation of the ways his own economic welfare relates to that of far wider groups" (p. 241)

IV. Area of personal living
   A. "An ability to guide their own personal conduct and judge that of others intelligently on the basis of predictable consequences, rather than blindly by the rule prevailing among the Joneses, the members of the senior class, or the younger set at the country club" (p. 286)
   B. The need to develop "insight into the full meaning of his interests and activities—vocational and non-vocational—in both their wider social and more narrowly personal bearings" (p. 290)
   C. The need to develop the "ability to use solitude for formulating his philosophy and integrating his life" (p. 296)
   D. The need to secure "a working philosophy of values which facilitates full advantage of those cultural expectations and social possibilities which are favorable to the good life" (p. 297)[23]

Proposals of the Committees

The fact the commission did not go beyond the subject boundaries in its approach to the curriculum problem may be further illustrated by its statement regarding the way in which various subjects might contribute to the concept of the worth of the individual.

Each of the fields studied by various committees recommended the use of its subject in the achievement of the general goals proposed.

THE SCIENCE COMMITTEE. The science committee set up a sizable group of generalizations for the science teacher to use in formulating his own teaching materials. The following suggest the types of generalizations proposed:

The study of the chemical elements, and of their compounds, has given

---

23. *Ibid.*, pages as cited in text.

the chemist power to produce substances with a wide range of useful combinations of properties.

Our material culture has already been greatly enriched and modified by chemical creation and discovery (new foods, flavors, textiles, dyes, alloys, plastics, explosives, fuels, drugs, disinfectants).

Chemistry is becoming a unitary science, with only a few general laws in which larger and larger bodies of facts are summarized in convenient forms (periodic table, free energy tables, combining proportions, atomicity)[24]

These generalizations are not science content to be memorized, but are defined by the committee as potential understandings which are to be developed by student activities.

THE COMMITTEE ON LANGUAGE. The Committee on Language in General Education took the position that language was a part of every individual's development in participating in the world about him. It is a means of personal growth and self-realization. In helping each pupil to use language the committee was not concerned about the particular method of organizing the curriculum, but only with the acceptance of the point of view that functionally language is basic to general education. The committee contended that "teaching language is teaching the technique of classifying, sorting, ordering, clarifying experiences—the technique of thinking straight."[25] To achieve this, however, one uses the content of social experiences. The committee pointed out, with interesting illustrations, the difference between the Latin and the English language in the use of grammar and thus indicated that in English "the meaning must be understood before grammatical constructions can be assigned to words." The committee's position, which is contrary to the method of teaching grammar in the traditional school, emphasized the formulation of thought patterns in expression and not the grammatical construction of a sentence.

The committee stressed the meaning of words, relying for much of its material upon Richards' point of view—the context theory of meaning, which explains how a word can have many meanings.[26] Meanings are not confined to a few authoritarian usages or even to acceptable good usage; they vary according to the context of the word, the situation, and the experience of the author and the reader. The emphasis, however, is more upon words than upon social experience.

---

24. *Science in General Education*, p. 124. By permission of Appleton-Century-Crofts, Inc.

25. *Language in General Education*, p. 341. By permission of Appleton-Century-Crofts, Inc.

26. See I. A. Richards, *Practical Criticism* (New York: Harcourt, Brace and Company, 1929), and his *Interpretation in Teaching* (New York: Harcourt, Brace and Company, 1939). See also C. K. Ogden and I. A. Richards, *The Meaning of Meaning* (4th ed.; New York: Harcourt, Brace and Company, 1936).

THE REPORT ON LITERATURE. A member of the Committee on Human Relations of the Progressive Education Association prepared a statement on literature which was the only report of the association in this field.[27] The report contended that literature can have a real and central relation to growth in the social and cultural life of democracy, but that literature is first of all a form of art. In her report, Miss Rosenblatt took the position that literature is of no more importance than the reader who responds to it, and she attempted to show how it may be treated both from the social and personal documentation point of view and from the esthetic point of view.

In speaking of teachers of literature, the report said: "We, too, play a social role, since the literary materials with which we deal are a potent means of forming the student's images of the world in which he lives, a potent means of giving sharpened insight into human nature and conduct."[28] The study of literature should assist in producing an understanding of human nature and in indoctrinating ethical standards; it should help pupils to make sound social and ethical judgments; and it should help the student to derive pleasure and satisfaction from the reading of literature.

The report suggested that no list of readings can be made for pupils who are not known, that the book must fit the person. It also emphasized the fact that there is no single reaction to writings—the one the teacher has— but that reactions are personal and should be drawn out from the pupils. Since pupils bring different things to their reading of literature and what the pupil brings to any specific literary work is as important as the work itself, the pupil's experience should be built on as broad a base as possible, a base which the teacher can help to extend. Literature teachers need to have and to embody certain social concepts, chief among them being "an understanding of the spirit of the scientific method and its application to human affairs." The study of literature should link intellectual perception and emotional drive and should enable one "to think rationally within the context of an emotionally colored situation." The report offered such general ideas as these to guide the selection of materials in the field of literature.

THE COMMITTEE ON SOCIAL STUDIES. The Committee on Social Studies felt that its field should make very definite contributions to the maintenance of the democratic way of life. The report listed certain principles and social conditions and classified individual needs. Some of these needs to which the social science teacher can contribute are "the need for increasingly mature relationships with age mates of both sexes"; "for satisfying relationships with adults outside the home"; "the need to develop social-civic loyalties"; the need to understand propaganda, symbolism, and mass organization; the need to select and evaluate leaders; the need to have emotional assurance of ade-

---

27. Rosenblatt, *Literature as Exploration.*
28. *Ibid.,* p. 9.

quacy in economic achievement; and the need for guidance and preparation for an occupation, for wise selection of goods and services, for effective economic citizenship, for personal health, for interests adequate enough to enrich life, for an understanding of self and the universe and the nature of our culture, and for developing a personal philosophy. To contribute toward the realization of these needs the teacher must organize the materials in the manner of problems. The use of all community resources is recommended.[29]

THE COMMITTEE ON MATHEMATICS. The Committee on Mathematics expressed its concern about the drop in the number of pupils taking mathematics in the United States and then countered with this defense of their subject:

> Yet mathematicians and teachers of mathematics are convinced of the value of their field in the education of youth. The committee shares the conviction that, divested of much of its conventional content and formal organization, mathematics as a mode of thought and instrument of analysis has an indispensable function in general education. It has much to contribute in meeting the needs of students—both as these are felt by students themselves and as they are defined by educators.[30]

The committee then suggested various reasons, purposes, means, and materials to prove that mathematics was valuable in meeting the needs of youth as determined by the commission. It stated, first, that mathematics should help pupils in any and all conditions whenever quantitative data and relationships or the facts and relationships of space and form are encountered, should help solve life problems involving mathematics, and should throw some light on the process of problem solving. It contended also that mathematics should emphasize where necessary the vocational aspect of the field and that the mathematics teacher should be the representative of "a special field of human activity of inestimable social significance to all." In the third place, the committee saw the fields of economic and business life increasingly permeated with mathematics and prophesied that mathematicians would be responsible for this change. In the fourth place, it felt mathematics was needed to make people fully sensitive to dynamic social factors. The committee argued that the mathematics teacher might help develop sensitivity to esthetic experience and appreciation of geometric forms in nature, art, and business. There are, it said, "esthetic overtones" in mathematical expositions and symbols. Mathematics can help develop tolerance by acquainting the student with its development as a science and can "encourage young people to reach out beyond present experience into uncharted seas." The members also claimed that

---

29. See *The Social Studies in General Education.*
30. *Mathematics in General Education*, pp. 11–12.

creativeness can be developed by originality in proof and by presenting conclusions in expositional forms. This is a remarkable series of claims for one subject.

This committee suggested that mathematics can probably make its greatest contribution in the field of reflective thinking and organized its report on the basis of the major factors involved in problem solving. The committee contended that the need to do reflective thinking is fundamental to successful living as well as to the development of democracy. Reflective thinking involves formulating a problem, collecting data, and analyzing data, which in turn involves approximation in problems of measurement, function, actual experimentation (in mathematics called "operation"), proof, and symbolism. The committee claimed that problem-solving ability "fosters the ideas of democracy" and that thinking applied to the real problems in the basic relationships of living provides a valuable tool for the preservation of the democratic way of life.

Evaluation

When one goes through these various reports of the commission, he is struck both by the fact that the spokesmen for each subject are attempting to prove its worth in developing the basic purposes of education—personal and social needs—and by the common fundamental generalizations, attitudes, and skills which the committees think should be taught to youth. Yet each committee tries to contend that its subject, by remaining intact and by seeking to get some cooperation among the teachers of the other subjects, is best equipped to serve youth.

Another difficulty comes from the serial examination of fields by experts alone. From such an analysis it is very difficult to secure a synthesis, even though the groups started with the same four areas of needs before them. It is obvious from a study of all the reports at the same time that there was a needless attempt to keep segregated the special fields; instead, an effort should have been made to broaden the opportunities and experiences of youth and teachers.

There was also an attempt to use these four areas of basic needs to motivate the learning of the special subject; certainly these areas inspired the members of the committee to see to what extent they could produce materials from their own field. The traditional teacher has long been able to derive considerable satisfaction from the fact that, after all, the subjects have existed for generations of youth in our American high schools and that each few years new bases for justifying them are produced. A little dilution, a different flavor perhaps, a change in the proportion of the ingredients, but the new wine will be found in the same old familiar bottle.

In the fourth place, there were several indications of a need and a desire for the unity of related materials without any provision for the curriculum and administrative organization needed to further this unity. The science report recommends that the science teacher be associated with the social-studies teacher, adding that many of the problems and activities "would probably best be carried out by a group of teachers representing various interests rather than by the science teacher alone." The mathematics report urges as much teamwork as possible between teachers of different subjects.

The very nature of many of these problems indicates that they cannot be treated even intelligently by any one teacher of any one field, but the social-studies report suggests that because the high schools are organized in subject-matter divisions the problems will have to be handled by separate teachers. One wonders again just what is the most valid criterion for realism—the realism of a static institutional condition or the realism of the needs of youth who cry out for a comprehensive understanding of the personal and social problems surrounding them. One is forced to conclude that if his interest is primarily in the growth and development of youth, the realism of traditional school organization should be secondary rather than primary in setting the way for improved school practice. The reports of the Commission on Secondary School Curriculum are fundamentally closer to the nineteenth than to the present twentieth century.

The major achievements of the Progressive Education Association's study of secondary education were not the reports of its Commission on Secondary Education. They were to be found in the work of the experimental schools, to which the work of the commission was to give basic guidance. The schools, however, did not depend heavily upon the reports of the commission; each one forged ahead on revisions planned by its faculties. Each of the thirty schools made some changes; a few made major reorganizations, but others changed their programs only slightly. Some schools made distinct innovations in their curriculum practices, such as setting up a core curriculum or designing their sequential patterns in terms of "centers of interest." Details of the changes cannot be given here. Some of these are described in later chapters.[31]

One phase of the program of the experiment with the thirty schools had to do with determining the success in college of the graduates of these schools. About three hundred colleges agreed to cooperate with the experimental staff in studying the entrants from the thirty schools and evaluating their success at the higher level. This was doubtless the most significant accomplishment of the three phases of this larger study, as it brought evidence to prove that

31. For a complete description of the programs carried out in each school, see *Thirty Schools Tell Their Story*. For the plan of the entire study, consult *The Story of the Eight-Year Study*.

youth could be successful in college without meeting a specific subject pattern of entrance requirements.[32]

Other National Committees

Many other curriculum committees and study groups have prepared reports since 1930 to influence curriculum organization. Among them are the science committee of the National Society for the Study of Education,[33] the committee of the American Council of Science Teachers,[34] the committee of the National Council of the Teachers of Mathematics,[35] the study sponsored by the Southern Association,[36] the committee of the North Central Association,[37] the Civic Education Study of the Educational Policies Commission,[38] and the committee on American History in Schools and Colleges, a committee of the American Historical Association, the Mississippi Valley Historical Association, and the National Council for the Social Studies.[39] The American Youth Commission of the American Council on Education also suggested a curriculum program for the secondary schools.[40] Space does not permit a review of all these studies here. In general they continue the subject approach to the problem and so provide no techniques of curriculum organization different in character from those reports previously reviewed.

---

32. For a more complete description of the results of this study, see Chap. 8. For the complete report, see *Did They Succeed in College?*

33. National Society for the Study of Education, *A Program for Teaching Science* (Thirty-first Yearbook, Part I; Bloomington, Illinois: Public School Publishing Co., 1932).

34. National Committee on Science Teaching, 3 reports: *The Education of the Science Teacher, Science Teaching for Better Living, Redirecting Science Teaching in the Light of Personal-Social Needs* (Washington: National Education Association, 1942).

35. National Council of Teachers of Mathematics, *The Place of Mathematics in Secondary Education* (Fifteenth Yearbook; New York: Columbia University, Teachers College, Bureau of Publications, 1940).

36. Commission on Curricular Problems and Research, Southern Association of Colleges and Secondary Schools, "Report," *Southern Association Quarterly,* 6:194–216, 1942; 7:188–206, 1943; 8:131–133, 1944.

37. North Central Association of Colleges and Secondary Schools, *General Education in the American High School* (Chicago: Scott, Foresman, and Company, 1942).

38. Educational Policies Commission, *Learning the Ways of Democracy* (Washington: National Education Association, 1940).

39. The Committee on American History in Schools and Colleges, Edgar B. Wesley, director, *American History in Schools and Colleges* (New York: The Macmillan Company, 1944).

40. American Youth Commission, Ben G. Graham, chairman, *What the High Schools Ought to Teach* (Washington: American Council on Education, 1940), and Harl R. Douglass, *Secondary Education for Youth in Modern America* (American Council on Education, 1937).

Other studies which cover various fields have contributed also to curriculum principles and content. Among them are the studies of the Institute for Consumer Education at Stephens College, the Sloan Foundation studies on the improvement of community living in the states of Kentucky and Florida, the Cooperative Study of Eighteen Pennsylvania Secondary Schools, the California Cooperating Secondary Schools Study, the Michigan Study of the Secondary School Curriculum, and the Cooperative Study in General Education at the Junior College Level of the American Council on Education.[41]

In addition, two studies carried out in the high schools of the West were significant in stimulating teachers in particular schools and in discovering improved curriculum methods and practices in language arts and social studies. These were known as the Stanford Language Arts Investigation[42] and the Stanford Social Studies Investigation.[43]

The following methods were used in these studies: (1) summer workshops, (2) staff visits to teachers on the job, (3) special helps to teachers, such as bibliographies, outlines, units, (4) a monthly *News Letter,* and (5) bulletins prepared by various staff members on topics in education related to the work of the investigation, such as resource units, needs of youth, evaluation of pupil development, the problems approach, visual aids, and individual differences.

Three significant studies growing out of the work of the investigation are of interest to curriculum workers. One study dealt intensively with the identification of the characteristics of effective student-teacher relationships in social studies classrooms;[44] another dealt with the growth of the teachers in the cooperating schools;[45] and the third dealt with the growth of pupils in the problem approach.[46] This investigation, a superior one in its field, illustrates clearly how teachers and teaching in a given subject field can be

---

41. For a brief description of the purposes and nature of all these studies see *Educational Method,* Vol. 20 (March, 1941).

42. Three reports have been issued covering the work of this investigation: Walter V. Kaulfers, Grayson N. Kefauver, and Holland D. Roberts, *Foreign Languages and Cultures in American Education,* and *English for Social Living;* and Walter V. Kaulfers, *Modern Languages for Modern Schools.* All published in 1942 by McGraw-Hill Book Company in New York.

43. See I. James Quillen and Lavone A. Hanna, *Education for Social Competence,* (1948), and Grayson N. Kefauver and Edwin A. Krug, *Leadership in Social Education: A Guide to In-Service Education of Social Studies Teachers,* (in preparation). Reports of Stanford University Social Studies Investigation, I. James Quillen and Grayson N. Kefauver, Co-Directors (Chicago: Scott, Foresman and Company).

44. Robert B. Bush, "A Study of Student-Teacher Relationships," D. Ed. Dissertation, Stanford University, 1941.

45. Edward A. Krug, "A Study of Teacher Development in an In-Service Education Program," D. Ed. Dissertation, Stanford University, 1941.

46. Lavone A. Hanna, "The Problem Solving Approach in Social Education," D. Ed. Dissertation, Stanford University, 1943.

improved by careful and consistent work on a curriculum development program.

Summary and Evaluation of National Commissions

In looking at the changes in the points of view of national committees organized during the last forty years in America, one is impressed by the fact that the committees up to 1930, with the possible exception of the National Committee on the Reorganization of Secondary Education, have been primarily concerned about growth in subject skills and understandings. They have given little consideration to the changing character of psychological thought and social conditions, or to the relation of these to the teaching of youth. They have overemphasized the place of subject specialists, many of whom have had little or no experience with high-school youth. They have neglected the changing personnel of the secondary school and have ignored an adequate study of the child himself. They have not considered the purposes of education in terms of behavior changes consistent with democratic living, but have placed their faith in the transfer of knowledge into action patterns. The knowing man, they feel, is the man who behaves properly. Human experience fails to indicate that the transfer is an automatic one. The curriculum has been a superimposed one designed by experts and as such has been more concerned with the records of human experience than with the flow of daily living.

The Commission on the Reorganization of Secondary Education definitely placed its point of view in the social setting and suggested a new base for the selection and organization of instructional materials, even though many of the individual committee reports did not catch the significance of the changed foundation. By suggesting that basically the selection of materials should hinge around human activities rather than around the subjects themselves, a modified idea was introduced. The Commission on the Social Studies gave its report a social orientation in terms of modern life, in spite of the fact that heavy emphasis was placed upon the scholarship in the fields of the social sciences themselves. It erred badly in not knowing the pupils for whom the materials were being suggested, and it turned its attention to documenting the source material of the social sciences rather than contributing otherwise to curriculum construction. The Commission of the Progressive Education Association went more directly to another source which the other committees neglected—youth themselves.

The studies of the needs of youth today in terms of their attempt to build a unified personality within the framework of existing and inherited culture will give a new type of approach to curriculum work. This, however, is one of the most mooted areas or approaches in curriculum organization, partially because of its newness, but also because of the looseness of thought connected with it. Schools have always claimed they met the needs of youth, but most teachers and curriculum workers in the past have guessed at the needs of youth from the standpoint of an adult's evaluation of their shortcomings. This commission approached the problem from the standpoint of the growth of the child in behavior patterns. It made other contributions in extending the range of activities and materials useful for instructional purposes—the school, the newspaper, the community, modern machinery, industry. Especially significant is its emphasis upon the problem method, the method associated more closely with democratic living than other methods, the method of scientific or objective discovery.

State Curriculum Programs

State departments of education are charged with providing, supervising, approving, or directing the preparation of curricula for the schools of the respective states. Some prepare guides or basic outlines; others approve curricula prepared by local school systems; while still others assume fundamental responsibility for state-wide curriculum programs. In the 1930's a large number of states engaged in curricular programs—Virginia, Alabama, North Carolina, Georgia, Florida, Texas, and Arkansas being a few of them. Pennsylvania has long prepared special course outlines. Later Michigan engaged in a comprehensive state curriculum program and still later came Wisconsin, California, and Illinois.

These programs differed in each state, although many of them were fundamentally similar. A brief examination of four will show principally the different patterns used.

State of Illinois

One of the most vigorous present state curriculum programs is to be found in the State of Illinois. Now in its sixth year, it is having an influence within the borders of the state itself and is being studied throughout the nation. The State Superintendent of Public Instruction initiated the program, but the development of it is in the hands of a steering committee which includes representatives of institutions of higher education, the office of the state superintendent, the Illinois Secondary School Principals Association, and thirty-two other lay and professional organizations. This committee must approve all policies before they are adopted. It also reads and passes upon all publications. Furthermore, it receives and develops suggestions for changes and improvement in plans, as well as examining proposals for basic studies before they are undertaken. The major functions of this committee are to make available and to direct services to local schools and to establish a coordinated curriculum program in which state-wide organizations will work together.

Each representative on the steering committee serves as a liaison officer between the committee and the organization or agency which he represents. Through him ideas are brought into the deliberations of each organization. By this plan organization members are kept aware of the developments in planning. The people learn what is being proposed in time to have some influence on the proposal.

According to two leaders, the success of the program is due to the fact that (1) the policy-making process is open to the eyes of everyone; (2) there has been cooperation of institutions of higher education and of the staff of the state superintendent; (3) participation is voluntary, and the schools which wish to take part in it must make some effort; (4) it has a strong research base; and (5) communication of research findings and of program improvements is thorough.[47]

The six major purposes of the Illinois Secondary Curriculum Program are

1. *To coordinate on a state-wide level and on a local school level all of the persons or groups who are or who should be interested in the high-school curriculum.* At the local level there are committees comparable to the state steering committee previously described.

2. *To sponsor studies basic to curriculum revision.* Six studies have been completed so far: Holding power, hidden tuition costs, pupil participation in extraclass activities, available guidance services, follow-up of graduates, and national security.

3. *To encourage developmental (experimental) programs.* With the help of consultants from the colleges, universities, and the state department, numerous local developmental projects have been undertaken in the improvement of existing subjects, enrichment of broad fields, and cutting across subject lines.

4. *To conduct workshops for principals and teachers.* Extensive workshops of from one- to three-day sessions have been held for several thousand administrators and teachers in local, county, and state groups.

5. *To prepare and distribute publications.* Nearly thirty publications have been issued to date and more are in process, all aimed at improving local curriculum programs.

6. *To establish relations with higher institutions.* This purpose deals with the bases for admission to higher institutions and still is in the formative stage.

---

47. Charles W. Sanford and Willard B. Spalding, "Illinois Secondary School Curriculum Program," *California Journal of Secondary Education,* 27:28–35, 1952. See also Charles W. Sanford, *The Illinois Secondary School Curriculum Program: The Illinois Life Adjustment Education Program* (Springfield, Ill.: State Department of Education, 1950.) Mimeographed. See also above, Chapter 13.

State of Michigan

For several years the State of Michigan has given particular attention to the community school movement and to a functional community-centered curriculum. Known as the Michigan Curriculum Program, the State Department of Education facilities and personnel were conceived as services to the local schools, as the following quotations from one of the earlier basic reports will indicate:

1. The relationships of the Department with local schools are based upon the service concept of educational leadership.

2. It is appropriate that the Department deal at all times with the total educational needs of a given school system.

3. The local community is responsible for planning, executing, and appraising its educational organization and curriculum. The Department functions by supplementing local guidance and leadership in the planning and appraising activities.

4. Criteria for planning, improving, and appraising of educational programs should be derived from the community.

5. The Department is primarily concerned with constant improvement in the use of facilities and personnel rather than in meeting relatively static standards.

6. Evaluation of local programs shall be made in terms of local objectives.

7. The program of consultation of the Department comprehends practically the entire professional membership of the Department and operates as a unit so far as the local school is concerned.[48]

The early single curriculum steering committee was soon expanded to include more persons, and later several committees were established to carry on the rapidly growing program. Out of this evolving program came a statement of basic policy which has served as a guide to the Michigan Curriculum Program ever since. Drawing on the work of the Educational Policies Commission, the *Basic Instructional Policy for the Michigan Curriculum Program* was phrased in terms of questions and answers:

What is education for?

How shall the decisions be made as to what experiences should be provided for the learner?

What types of experiences and what organization of these experiences bring about the most effective learning?

What is the role of the teacher in the instructional program?

How can individual parents help to improve instruction?

How can community agencies help improve instruction?[49]

48. The Michigan Curriculum Program, *Third Report of Progress* (Lansing, Mich.: Department of Public Instruction, 1939), pp. 4–5.
49. Department of Public Instruction, *Basic Instructional Policy for the Michigan Curriculum Program* (Lansing, Mich., 1941), pp. 3–6.

As can be seen from the nature of the questions, the emphasis in this basic policy was upon the local school, the individual teacher, the parents and agencies making up a specific community. The program on the state level did not attempt to develop specific statements of scope and sequence, or specific courses of study outlines. These were the responsibilities of the local educational units.

During the past decade the "over-arching objective" of the Michigan Curriculum Program was its belief in citizenship, and this conviction is reflected in most of the statements of purpose as well as the projects developed. A number of publications have been released on this important subject, such as "Michigan's Future Citizens," "Michigan Today," "Democracy in Action," "Building Better Citizens," and "The Constitution and Social Life in Michigan." In addition to this primary emphasis on citizenship, extensive demonstration research has been carried on in such areas as character education, teacher education, health services, recreation, camping and outdoor education, home and family-life education.

From the standpoint of the secondary schools, one of the most significant parts of the program came through the work of the professional persons connected with the Michigan Study of the Secondary School Curriculum. Over a period of five years, this group has given particular attention to the relationships of the secondary schools to higher education. Based upon the principle of mutual confidence, a college agreement was effected which constituted an informal contract between the member secondary schools and the member institutions of higher education in Michigan. In this "contract," the colleges have agreed to accept high-school graduates upon the recommendations of the local high-school authorities without the limitation of a fixed subject pattern. In return the high schools agreed to stress guidance and curriculum development processes according to the best theory and practice. A large number of the secondary schools and practically all Michigan colleges have joined in this college agreement.

According to Koopman, the developmental concept of curriculum improvement is the outstanding characteristic of the Michigan Curriculum Program. The multiple-approach method which describes this program at present is found in

> *Research.* Research in the sense of a thoughtful objective testing of hypotheses will probably be stressed more at the local level.
> *Curriculum planning.* Democratic curriculum planning will undoubtedly continue to grow in importance. A steadily increasing number of new superintendents are adopting cooperative curriculum development policies.
> *The college agreement.* The secondary schools freed from external controls will without question develop a much more functional program.
> *General community development.* Curriculum planning need not be done separately. All-round community development programs as contrasted with

school-centered curriculum development programs will doubtless increase as confidence in this complicated but fundamental method grows.

Lay participation. Lay participation, whether in connection with an isolated improvement activity such as the installation of a course in stenography or in a community planning council, will spread. It will gradually become recognized as a phase of adult education.

State servicing. To date, the quantity and quality of state servicing have been unsatisfactory. As more lawmakers and policymakers mix with voters in improving instruction, support should strengthen.

Means of communication. The communicatory system of the program is still admittedly weak. Not only do many rural areas suffer from lack of communication; many cities do also. . . . The Metropolitan Detroit Bureau of Cooperative School Studies, which embraces most of the school systems in the Detroit area, is an excellent example of cooperation and communication.[50]

In brief, the Michigan Curriculum Program, starting with a single committee, now has an extensive organization serving local school systems. Under the leadership of the State Superintendent of Public Instruction, the Curriculum Planning Committee directs a number of subcommittees, each with extensive memberships representing all levels and types of interested persons. These committees are organized under the following headings: Adult Education, Citizenship Education, Conservation and Education, Elementary Education, Guidance, Health Education, Home and Family Life Education, Industrial Arts Education, Education for Occupational Competence, Education in Rural Areas, Safety Education, Secondary Education, School Library, Special Education, Audio-Visual Aids, and Thrift Education.

State of California

The State of California has undertaken to lay a foundation for educational planning and curriculum improvement at the local level through a more indirect approach than that of Illinois. No other state has experienced such a rapid growth in population during the past decade. This pressure of growth has created a most difficult problem for the educational leaders, and the rising cost of housing has compounded the difficulties. With the rapid growth there has been considerable interest in experimentation in organization, and such units as the 6–4–4 plan have developed more here than elsewhere. The problem of articulation between units, both vertically and horizontally, in this period of growth, as well as the large numbers of migrant workers, have added

---

50. Hollis L. Caswell and Others, *Curriculum Improvement in Public School Systems,* Chap. 14, by G. Robert Koopman (New York: Columbia University, Teachers College, Bureau of Publications, 1950), pp. 422–423. The above description of the Michigan Curriculum Program has drawn heavily on Koopman's chapter.

to the already complicated educational picture. These factors have been so serious that both lay and professional educational leaders have had difficulty developing sound and progressive curriculum programs which will meet the needs not only of the boys and girls of today, but the even larger numbers which will be entering the schools in the immediate years ahead.

At the close of the World War II, professional groups began giving serious attention to improvement of the curriculum, much of which had been neglected during the war years. There was need for some base for state-wide thinking which would give more unity to the expanding educational program without the deadening hand of uniformity. The need was detailed in terms of (1) unity in purpose and action, (2) improvement in educational services on modern lines, (3) similarity of program to facilitate the transfer of pupils, and (4) greater support from a better-informed and understanding public.

The State Superintendent of Public Instruction, in cooperation with his key professional advisory group, the Curriculum Commission, in the fall of 1947 appointed a committee of twenty persons representing all levels and types of public education in California. This committee was charged with the responsibility for developing a "Framework for Public Education in California," which would "be in general rather than in specific terms; yet to be of use to school people in the field it must be definite enough to indicate the purposes, scope and nature of the minimum program."[51] Like many another statement it was to deal with the "why," the "what," and the "when," with some brief attention to the "how," of educational service.

The unique characteristic of this statement is found in the fact that the committee took three years to complete the assignment which involved "the purposes for which schools have been created and maintained, the scope of the services which should be offered, and the principles which should apply to the organization and conduct of these services." Six drafts in all were drawn up and submitted to the professional personnel of the state. During this period *every* major educational group, including both teachers and administrators, devoted considerable time to studying the proposals and making recommendations and changes. One year the lay groups concerned with public education, and particularly the Parent-Teachers Association, gave primary attention to this statement. The fifth draft, a printing of 30,000 copies, was studied by local teachers in the state. The Framework, as it was called, was completed in May, 1950, and is being used at all levels of the state for guidance in the effort to achieve "educational unity without uniformity."

The statement of the framework is divided into sections as follows: (1) the purposes of education in California; (2) the desirable breadth of learning experiences which should be made available in the schools; (3) the funda-

---

51. Roy E. Simpson, *Purpose of the Framework for Public Education in California* 1947 (Sacramento, Calif.: State Department of Education, 1947), p. 1. Mimeographed.

mental concepts that contribute to effective teacher-learning situations; and (4) the principles of organization of the instructional program of the school. A final section describes a number of unresolved problems which confront public education today as a challenge to the thinking of educational leaders.

The specific purposes of education were explored at considerable length, with the committee finally adopting a modification of the very significant set of purposes prepared originally by the Educational Policies Commission in 1938 under the four major headings of: (1) The Objectives of Civic Responsibility; (2) The Objectives of Full Realization of Individual Capacities; (3) The Objectives of Human Relationships; and (4) The Objectives of Economic Efficiency.[52]

The concern of the Committee over the areas of experience which the school must provide is reflected in the scope of the program presented as a guide to adequate curriculum planning:

CALIFORNIA PUBLIC SCHOOLS PROVIDE EXTENSIVE OPPORTUNITIES FOR LEARNING

I. Experiences in using and developing skills in the tools of learning

II. Experiences in solving the problems of group living
    A. Experiences in learning the understandings and skills for effective family living
    B. Experiences in learning to work and play with one's associates
    C. Experiences leading to an understanding of the obligations of responsible American citizenship and to the development of necessary civic skills
    D. Experiences in learning about groups other than those to which an individual belongs

III. Experiences leading to an understanding of one's environment

IV. Experiences in creative expression

V. Experiences in healthful living

VI. Experiences in the area of occupational interests and plans

VII. Experiences in the area of avocational interests

VIII. Concentrated experience in a major area

IX. Experiences especially designed to meet the needs of adults

X. Specialized experiences for exceptional children[53]

Succeeding chapters in this statement illuminate the roles and relationship

52. Educational Policies Commission, *The Purposes of Education in American Democracy* (Washington: National Education Association, 1938), pp. 50, 72, 90, 108.
53. California State Curriculum Commission, *A Framework for Public Education in California* (Sacramento, Calif.: State Department of Education, 1950), pp. 8–18.

of the teacher and the learner, based upon the best thinking in these areas. They describe the best practices in both classrooms and school, for both teacher and administrator.

The concluding chapter deals with "Challenges to Further Action" and raises a number of questions with which California educators will have to deal, but which the Framework Committee could not answer in any detail to the satisfaction of its members or other persons concerned with public education in this state. Among those questions are such challenging ones as the problems involved in

1. Selection and organization of learning experiences
2. Grade level organization
3. Balance of general and special education
4. Comprehensive versus specialized high schools
5. Use of the community in the school program
6. Evaluation and the modern curriculum
7. Articulation of units of the school system
8. Elementary, high school and junior college relationships
9. Patterns of organization
10. Extension of educational opportunity
11. School scheduling of individual students
12. Extension of pupil personnel services
13. Classification and grouping
14. Promotion policies
15. Extension of special classes and services to exceptional children
16. Length of school day and year
17. Teacher load
18. Cooperative development of preservice and in-service teacher education
19. Bridging the gap between research and practice

State of Florida

The Florida Program for the Improvement of Schools was instituted more than a decade ago by a state steering committee of eighteen members under the chairmanship of the State Superintendent of Public Instruction. The committee included local administrators, college deans, and representatives of the Florida Education Association. This group, with the help of two general consultants established subcommittees in fields of special interests with consultants for each of the groups. These subcommittees developed objectives for their special fields, based upon the general objectives of the state program, and produced considerable curriculum materials. No courses of study were prescribed, but units of work, references, and teaching aids were suggested. These materials became guides to individual schools as they developed their courses of study to meet local needs.

During this period the major emphases were upon (1) the improvement of education, including direct instruction and total school activities; and (2) the development of qualified leadership to achieve the first emphasis. With the program closely integrated with the State Department of Education, the services of the Division of Instruction were developed along three lines: (1) activities having state-wide application, such as certification and school accreditation; (2) the general supervisory assistance rendered counties in the development of instruction; and (3) consultative services in special areas. The strength of the curriculum-improvement program was centered under strong state leadership in the field supervisors and consultants, working with and through the state-wide professional conference groups.

The philosophy of this concept of leadership in Florida is well expressed in the following excerpt:

> A basic principle in Florida's program for the improvement of instruction is that continuous effort should be focused on discovering and developing leadership among all groups interested in the improvement of education. The direct supervision of individual schools, classrooms, and teachers is assumed to be a local function. A corollary of this assumption is that the state has the responsibility of bringing about the improvement of local programs through the development of local leadership.
>
> Still a third assumption is that the improvement of leadership cannot be brought about by the exercise of authority but must take place through an educational process. Activities in the program should be so planned that individuals experience those things which they are seeking to learn. The development of in-service programs which meet local needs must come about through active participation of all persons concerned, assisted by trained and informed leaders, working in a democratic manner on problems of concern to all.
>
> The concept of leadership the state staff seeks to demonstrate is shared leadership. All who work together for the improvement of education are at times leaders and at other times followers, depending upon the unique contribution each has to make. State leadership does not assume that it knows all the answers. It doesn't stand out in front and beckon others to follow, but recognizes need for its own development and makes itself part of the problem to be solved.[54]

Under the sponsorship of the State Department of Education and the state universities, production workshops have been held to prepare curriculum materials. The participants are selected by the State Department staff from recommendations by local school leaders, and include teachers as well as administrators. Consultants are provided in the special areas, usually from the state universities.

54. Dora S. Skipper and Sam H. Moorer, "In-Service Education in Florida," *Educational Leadership*, 6:175–176, 1948.

In addition to involving most of the education leaders of the state in this curriculum-improvement program, there has been widespread participation by laymen, who have joined with the professional educators in the Continuing Education Council. This council recently reported that sixteen out of the eighteen state groups represented on this body were noneducational. Through this organization, local areas encourage lay persons to survey, discuss, and interpret their own school needs.

The localization of the curriculum-improvement program is strengthened by the state Minimum Foundation Program which provides for compulsory pre- and post-school planning by the total faculty of every school and school system. The general practice throughout the state is to devote the two weeks prior to the opening of school to planning and the two weeks after the close of school to evaluation. In addition, five regular state-wide conferences are held with the county superintendents, the principals, the classroom teachers, the supervisors, and the Leadership Conference—a training conference for leaders in education. The pattern of work and study of each conference is basically the same:

> 1. A representative committee working with a consultant plans the program of the conference. It selects for study problems which have been previously submitted by the membership of the conference.
> 2. Representative committees are formed by choice of the members to study each problem selected. Sub-committees are formed if desirable.
> 3. Consultants are provided for each committee.
> 4. Time is allocated for committees to study.
> 5. The reports of the committees are submitted to the entire conference for discussion.
> 6. Revisions are made in the reports in light of the discussion and the suggestions.
> 7. The revised reports are mimeographed and distributed to the members of the conference for further study.[55]

Finally, county workshops on curriculum problems are held in increasing numbers with increasing frequency. From this extensive cooperative effort have come numerous publications, bulletins, guides, and other practical curriculum material.

Olson reports that since 1945 two-thirds of the sixty-seven counties in Florida have held at least one workshop.[56] Significant help to these workshops was secured in 1945 when the state legislature provided scholarships to be used by local boards of education for "the professional development of teachers

---

55. Clara M. Olson, in Caswell and others, *Curriculum Improvement*, p. 384.
56. *Ibid.*, pp. 389–91. See also "F.E.A. Reviews its Past," *The Journal of the Florida Education Association,* 25:9, 1948; State Department of Education, *A Progress Report to the People* (Tallahassee, Fla., 1949) ; Florida Citizens Committee, *Education and the Future of Florida* (Tallahassee, Fla.; State Department of Education, 1947).

in service." Scholarships were awarded annually to approximately one-third of the teachers in service.

Another stimulant to workshop activity was the granting of credit by the state universities to participants in this type of curriculum planning. This encouraged teachers to raise their academic standing, while at the same time they assisted in the improvement of the curriculum of their own school.

State of Pennsylvania

The State of Pennsylvania has approached the problem of improving the traditional curriculum through concentrated attention on specific subject fields. One example of state-wide effort is in the field of the sciences, where a state production committee was assisted by representatives from the field of science selected by every county and district superintendent in the commonwealth.

The Production Committee, as it was called, was guided in the development of its objectives by recent reports of national curriculum commissions, such as the committee of the National Society for the Study of Education, in its 1947 *Science Education for American Schools,* when it recommended these criteria:

> First, a statement should be practical for the classroom teacher. Second, it should be psychologically sound. Third, it should be possible of attainment. Fourth, it should be universal. And fifth, it should show the relationship of classroom activity to desired changes in behavior—how the student thinks, feels, and acts.[57]

Based upon these criteria, the committee proposed objectives of the following types: functional information or facts; functional concepts; functional understanding of principles; instrumental skills; problem-solving skills; attitudes, appreciations, and interests.[58]

In the development of a scope-and-sequence pattern for the science program in the secondary schools of Pennsylvania, the committee was guided further by a questionnaire submitted to all the science teachers of the state regarding their needs. The first five needs (in order of frequency), and their percentages, revealed that the teachers wanted:

---

57. National Society for the Study of Education, *Science Education in American Schools* (Forty-sixth Yearbook; Chicago: University of Chicago Press, 1947). Part I.
58. Department of Public Instruction, Commonwealth of Pennsylvania, *Course of Study in Science for Secondary Schools: A Progress Report* (*Bulletin* No. 400; Harrisburg, Pa., 1951).

	Needs	*Per cent*

1. Outline of course content for secondary school science fields — 88
2. Suggested procedures with academic and nonacademic students — 85
3. List of resources—community, speakers, visual aids, etc. — 84
4. Photographic and other illustrative material — 82
5. Suggestions for cooperation with other secondary-school teachers — 76

The Production Committee then produced an extensive report which attempted to articulate the science teaching for the secondary schools within the framework of the traditional science subjects. This report was divided into two sections, one for junior high schools and the other for senior high schools. The unit method was recommended, and the year's work was outlined in the following manner:

SCIENCE IN THE JUNIOR HIGH SCHOOL
General Science

Grade 7

Unit: 1. How does scientific discovery affect our lives?
2. How can I keep healthy?
(and similar units)

Grade 8

Unit: 1. How do we raise and use plants?
2. How do we use the air?
(and similar units)

Grade 9

Unit: 1. How can we control and use the microscopic world?
2. How can I keep my body in good health?
(and similar units)

Science in the Senior High School
Biology

Unit: 1. How do I depend upon my physical surroundings for existence?
2. How do living things obtain food?
(and similar units)

Physical Science

Unit: 1. How can we measure and compare things we buy and use?
2. Why are superstitions disappearing?
3. How do changes in the earth affect my environment?
4. How can we make wise purchases of household machinery?
5. How is electricity of service to me?
6. What should I know about automobiles?
(and similar units)

Educational Policies Commission—
Education for All American Youth

In 1944 toward the close of World War II, the Educational Policies Commission of the National Education Association produced its historic document setting forth the role of secondary education in the years ahead. It not only presented the basic principles but illustrated them with specific programs which might be instituted to implement them. In dramatic fashion the report indicated how a wisely planned program for the improvement, adaptation, and extension of educational services to all youth might be developed by local and state educational authorities. This program high lighted the differences of youth in intelligence, occupational interests, availability of educational services, types of communities, social and economic status, parental and cultural backgrounds, and mental and physical well-being. But it stressed also that youth had a number of important qualities in common, among them being

WHAT ALL AMERICAN YOUTH HAVE IN COMMON

1. All American youth are citizens now; all (or nearly all) will be qualified voters in the future; all require education for civic responsibility and competence.

2. All American youth (or nearly all) are members of family groups now and will become members of other family groups in the future; all require an understanding of family relationships.

3. All American youth are now living in the American culture and all (or nearly all) will continue to do so in the future; all require an understanding of the main elements in that culture.

4. All American youth need to maintain their mental and physical health now and in the future; all require instruction to develop habits of healthful living, understanding of conditions which foster health, and knowledge of ways of preventing disease, avoiding injuries, and using medical services.

5. All American youth will be expected to engage in useful work and will need to work to sustain themselves and others; all therefore require occupational guidance and training and orientation to current economic conditions.

6. All American youth have the capacity to think rationally; all need to develop this capacity, and with it, an appreciation of the significance of truth as arrived at by the rational process.

7. All American youth must make decisions and take actions which involve choices of values; all therefore need insight into ethical values. Particularly do they need to grow in understanding the basic tenets of democracy—that the individual human being is of surpassing worth.[59]

The proposed program was based on the assumption that every youth in

---

59. Educational Policies Commission, *Education for All American Youth* (Washington: National Education Association, 1944), pp. 16–17.

this country should experience a broad and balanced education which would accomplish the following:

1. Equip him to enter an occupation suited to his abilities and offering reasonable opportunity for personal growth and social usefulness
2. Prepare him to assume the full responsibilities of American citizenship
3. Give him a fair chance to exercise his right to the pursuit of happiness
4. Stimulate intellectual curiosity, engender satisfaction in intellectual achievement, and cultivate the ability to think rationally
5. Help him to develop an appreciation of the ethical values which should undergird all life in a democratic society[60]

The commission then proposed a program for a mythical state and a rural and urban community. Since these are described elsewhere in this book, they will not be illustrated here.[61] The National Association of Secondary School Principals issued a shortened and graphic version of this report which, in addition to the communities described in the original report, suggested programs for the junior high school and for a very small rural district.[62]

These national reports as well as the state curriculum movements have done much to improve the secondary school curriculum and have been helpful to local schools in providing the direction for curriculum improvement.

---

60. *Ibid.,* p. 21.
61. See Index.
62. National Association of Secondary School Principals, *Planning for American Youth* (rev. ed.; Washington, 1951).

Chapter Eight

Appraising the School
and the Pupil

THE PRODUCT of any endeavor should be appraised as a part of the process of revising it. The secondary school in America has been in existence for slightly over three hundred years and from time to time has undergone subjective evaluation by public opinion. During the last thirty years the study of the success of the secondary school has been accelerated as we have gained new tools of evaluation and formulated new purposes for the school. Let us examine some of the evidence of recent years pertaining to the success of the teaching of the various subjects and to the progress of the pupils in school.

For this purpose, we will collect the evidence on the following questions:

1. Do youth stay in high school until graduation?
2. Do youth succeed normally in the curriculum, or do they fail to achieve success in the subjects they study?
3. Do youth succeed in college?
4. Do they acquire the attitudes, skills, and information necessary for successful living?
5. Do youth feel that the school is adequately meeting their needs?

In addition to these questions, let us examine the criticisms of adults which are being leveled at the traditional school.

Problem of Elimination

If the school is to succeed, it must first of all keep its pupils attending school. If pupils do not attend school, the fault cannot be laid at the door of the school alone, for the home and modern social conditions themselves play an important part in school attendance. Nevertheless, if youth really feel that the work in school is more important than anything else they can do until they are approximately eighteen years of age, their elimination from school will be numerically much smaller than if they feel otherwise. If school conditions are conducive to the development of pupils in those issues which they regard as crucial, they will make a great effort to remain in school.

Statistical Studies

One of the earliest studies of importance on the problem of elimination was the one made by Thorndike in 1907.[1] In this study Thorndike showed the percentage of elimination in a number of major cities in the United States from

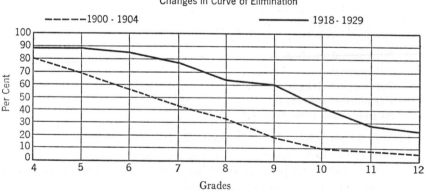

Changes in Curve of Elimination

Based on Thorndike's data for 1900–1904 and that for the same cities 1918–1919, 1923–1924, 1928–1929.

1900 to 1904 in grades four through twelve. Twenty-six years later Kline pointed out the percentages of elimination for the years 1918–1929 in the cities studied by Thorndike in 1907.[2] The following chart shows the percentage

1. E. L. Thorndike, *Elimination of Pupils from School* (Bureau of Education, *Bulletin* No. 4; Washington: Government Printing Office, 1907).
2. Elias J. Kline, "Significant Changes in the Curve of Elimination since 1900," *Journal of Educational Research*, 26:608–616, 1933.

of elimination in these cities for approximately thirty years. By the method of computing elimination used here, 81.7 per cent of those who started school in 1900–1904 were eliminated before or during the ninth grade, while only 39.6 per cent were eliminated up to that point during the period from 1918 to 1929. That is, the greatest elimination in 1900–1904 took place before the pupils reached high school, while from 1918 to 1929 it took place after the ninth grade.

Pushing the analysis into the United States at large, we find these figures of elimination expressed in another way. In 1920 Bonner indicated the elimination as follows:

For every 1,000 children entering the first grade,
   1,000 remained until the fifth grade,
   830 enrolled in grade 6,
   710 enrolled in grade 7,
   634 enrolled in grade 8,
   342 entered high school,
   139 graduated from high school,
   72 entered college,
   23 graduated from college.[3]

These figures were again compiled by Phillips for the years 1929–1930. He gives the following statistics:

For every 1,000 children entering the first grade,
   1,000 completed the fifth grade,
   974 entered grade 6,
   768 entered grade 8,
   610 entered high school,
   260 completed high school,
   160 entered college, \
   50 graduated from college.[4]

In 1926 in 24,590 high schools in the United States, an average freshman high-school class of one hundred had a senior class of 45, in 1938 this figure rose to 60. In 1929, 31.5 per cent of high-school seniors went to college, but in 1938 this figure had fallen to 24.0 per cent.[5]

---

3. H. R. Bonner, *Statistics of State School Systems 1917–1918,* Biennial Survey of Education 1916–18 (Bureau of Education, *Bulletin* No. 11; Washington: Government Printing Office, 1920), p. 155. See also H. R. Bonner, "Waste in Education," *American School Board Journal,* 63:33–35, 124, 1921.

4. F. M. Phillips, "Educational Rank of the States, 1930," *American School Board Journal,* 84:37–39, 1932.

5. "Statistics of Public High Schools, 1937–38," Chap. 5 in *Biennial Survey of Education in the United States (Bulletin* No. 2; U.S. Office of Education; Washington, D.C.: Government Printing Office, 1940), p. 14.

Bell studied 13,528 youth in Maryland, ages 16–24, of whom 10,898 were out of school. Of every 20 of these

> 8 never got beyond grade 8,
> 5 entered high school but did not finish,
> 5 left school after high-school graduation,
> 2 received some education beyond high school.

The median grade completed by the group was nine. He found further that there were twice as many youth staying in school whose families were not on relief as those from relief families; that as families increase in size, the proportion of youth leaving school at grade eight increases accordingly; and that the child of a professional man has twice the chance of going beyond the eighth grade as the child of a man in a managerial position, four times the chance of the child of a skilled laborer, nine times the chance of the child of an unskilled laborer, and twelve times the chance of the child of a farm laborer.[6] These findings might be expected from the various studies on the selective character of the population of the secondary school. Pupils who are left in the secondary school are in the middle and upper economic class, they have higher intelligence quotients as a group than those who leave school, and they have experienced, as a general rule, greater success with the academic subject offerings of the school.[7]

Eckert and Marshall point out that, of the 250,000 or so youth who leave New York State high schools annually, more than half have not completed their high-school course. In New York State, three out of every five high-school pupils leave before graduation.[8] During the year 1936–1937, 20 per cent of the high-school population left school. The typical withdrawing pupil leaves before grade ten, yet little attention is given to practical skills up to that time. The situation becomes acute because the less capable pupil withdraws from school, and, as the authors point out, "the less competent he is to do school tasks the earlier he is released to face adult responsibilities. Those who will be least able to acquire socially useful habits, information and points of view

---

6. Howard M. Bell, *Youth Tell Their Story* (Washington, D.C.: American Council on Education, 1938), pp. 57–58.

7. See especially George S. Counts, *The Selective Character of Secondary Education* (University of Chicago, Educational Monograph; Chicago: University of Chicago Press, 1922). See also the repetition of Counts' study in Grayson N. Kefauver, Victor H. Noll, and C. Elwood Drake, *The Secondary School Population* (National Survey of Secondary Education, U.S. Office of Education, *Bulletin* No. 17, 1932, Monograph No. 4; Washington: Government Printing Office).

8. Ruth Eckert and Thomas A. Marshall, *When Youth Leave School* (Regents' Inquiry, New York State; New York: McGraw-Hill Book Company, Inc., 1938), pp. 40, 48, 67, 177.

without formal instruction are those to whom the school has given least attention."[9]

A very recent national survey by the United States Office of Education reports that even after a half century of effort to make public secondary education the common heritage of all American youth, the statistics show that

For every 100 enrolled in grade 5 in 1938–1939,
    80 enrolled in grade 9 in 1942–1943,
    65 enrolled in grade 10 in 1943–1944,
    53 enrolled in grade 11 in 1944–1945,
    44 enrolled in grade 12 in 1945–1946,[10]
    42 graduated from high school,
    12 entered college,[11]
    5 graduated from college.

A more detailed analysis of these same figures indicate that next to the 20 who drop out before entering the ninth grade, the greatest loss, 15, came at the beginning or during the tenth grade.

Even within the high school itself the problem of elimination from grade to grade continues to be high. In their 1950 report Gaumnitz and Tompkins show that contemporary enrollment ratios for the high schools of the United States in relation to 100 pupils in the ninth grade were 90 pupils in the tenth grade, 75 pupils in the eleventh grade, and 63 pupils in the twelfth grade.

> This would suggest that for the nation as a whole there were ten fewer pupils per one hundred in the second year of high school than in the first; there was a further reduction of fifteen pupils before reaching the third year and twelve more before reaching the fourth. As concerns holdin*r* power, these data therefore suggest an over-all loss of pupils from grade nine to grade twelve, totaling thirty-seven of each one hundred pupils.[12]

All studies reveal that the greatest loss of pupils during the entire half century has been either in grade nine or grade ten. Dillon's research on 1,171 school leavers indicates that 54 per cent left school at the age of sixteen. Of this group 34 per cent left during grade nine and 36 per cent during grade ten.[13] Tompkins' data summarizing the grade levels of greatest loss for nearly

---

9. *Ibid.*, p. 68.
10. Chap. I, "Statistical Summary of Education," *Biennial Survey of Education in the United States, 1945–46* (U.S. Office of Education, Washington: Government Printing Office, 1947), pp. 31–32.
11. Walter H. Gaumnitz and Ellsworth Tompkins, *Holding Power and Size of High Schools* (U.S. Office of Education, Circular No. 322; Washington: Government Printing Office, 1950), p. 1.
12. *Ibid.*, p. 6.
13. Harold J. Dillon, *Early School Leavers* (New York: National Child Labor Committee, 1949), p. 27.

a half century show that prior to the 1937–1945 period, grade nine had the highest percentage of drop-outs, but that recently grade ten, with 16 per cent for 1937–1938 and 13 per cent for 1940–1941, surpasses the previous grade.[14]

A study in California made by Kitch reveals a somewhat similar problem of the high school's holding power. In this state the percentage of change over nearly two decades was very slight.

HOLDING POWER IN CALIFORNIA*

Class Entered Grade 9 in	Percentage of Class Remaining		
	One Year Later Grade 10	Two Years Later Grade 11	Three Years Later Grade 12
1930	92	78	67
1934	96	86	76
1938	98	89	76
1942	91	79	69
1944	100	84	70

* Donald E. Kitch, "Does California Have a Drop-Out Problem?" *California Journal of Secondary Education,* 25:216–217, 1950.

Kitch concludes:

The actual retention rates would be lower than those indicated above if correction were made for the influx of population into the State during the past ten years. The use of any grade prior to the ninth as a base point would also result in lower percentages of retention as would the use of high school graduation rather than fall enrollment as the comparison point for the twelfth grade.

Enough evidence is available from enrollment statistics and from the few studies which have been conducted within the State to indicate that a disturbingly large percentage of California's young people do not choose to take advantage of the full fourteen years of free public education which the people of this State provide. In view of a democratic society's need for educated and competent citizens, it is doubtful that this is a socially desirable situation.

Many cities, concerned over the failure to retain their high-school students, have made extensive studies of the problem. One statistical report by Harold Spears gives the San Francisco picture.

14. Ellsworth Tompkins, "How Can the School Reduce the Number of Early School Leavers?" *Bulletin,* National Association of Secondary School Principals, 35:311–313, 1951.

HOLDING POWER IN SAN FRANCISCO*
Percentage of Class Remaining

Year Grade 9	In Grade 10	In Grade 11	In Grade 12
1934–35	93	75	66
1937–38	94	83	70
1940–41	93	66	52
1943–44	91	73	62
1944–45	91	77	64

* Harold Spears, *Holding Power of San Francisco Public Schools* (San Francisco, Calif.: Office of the Curriculum Coordinator, 1947), pp. 3–5. Mimeographed.

Enrollment trends in the high schools of San Francisco from 1940 to 1947 showed a loss of 19 per cent, although state and national figures showed that the high-school population as a whole was as large if not larger at the later date.

Causes of Elimination

Before the results of these studies on elimination are summarized, another type of elimination study should be mentioned—that which deals with causes as well as with numbers of withdrawals. One of the earliest and still most significant studies was that made in 1911 by Van Denburg, who studied the kinds of pupils who left high school and those who remained. At that time he found that "scarcely more than one pupil in nine of those who enter [New York City high schools] meets satisfactorily the conditions set in advance for the normal pupil" and "certainly not more than two in ten of our original total will ever finish."[15] He found the causes of elimination to be associated with a critical attitude of the pupils toward their work, poor teaching on the part of teachers who were not interested in youth and their problems, and the predominance of college entrance subjects as the major offerings of the secondary school.

Even in 1938 an average of 40,000 pupils a year dropped out of the high schools of New York City. Samler again studied the characteristics of two groups of pupils from New York City high schools from June, 1934, to February, 1936. He selected 4,044 students in all, 2,577 of whom had graduated and 1,387 of whom had dropped out before graduation (80 pupils were

15. Joseph K. Van Denburg, *Causes of the Elimination of Students in Public Secondary Schools of New York City* (Teachers College Contributions to Education, No. 47; New York: Columbia University, Teachers College, Bureau of Publications, 1911), p. 124.

omitted from the final tabulation). All these pupils came from schools offering either academic or commercial courses.[16] He found in both groups that a very large percentage of the pupils had had no assistance in vocational planning while in school; that for 70 per cent of the pupils there was no relationship between their present activities and their vocational plans; and for 70 per cent of them there was no relation between the vocational plans made while in high school and the jobs they were doing. Some of the differences, among many others, between the two groups are indicated as follows:

DIFFERENCES IN TWO GROUPS OF STUDENTS*

	Graduates	Drop-Outs
1. Aptitude (Mean I.Q.)	105.6	96.3
2. Grade averages (% above B −)	72.68%	25.01%
3. Vocational planning while in school	86.25%	91.36%
4. Employment:		
Number holding one job	60.02%	59.15%
Number holding two jobs	21.89%	21.58%
Jobs got through own efforts	17.33%	24.89%
Jobs got through friends	36.25%	38.51%
Average number of jobs held	1.40	1.27
5. Leisure-time activities:		
Reading	27.09%	19.60%
Athletics	30.84%	34.59%
Social activities	13.58%	10.53%
Hobbies	6.44%	10.04%

* Samler, *ibid.*, p. 108.

Bell's study in 1938 of 13,528 youth in Maryland, of whom 10,898 were out of school, showed that of every 25 youth leaving school,

10 left because of economic need,
6 left because of no interest in school or because they were maladjusted in school,
4 left to earn their own money,
3 left because they considered their education completed upon graduation,
2 left because of marriage, poor health, or other reasons.[17]

Studies made a decade later reveal little significant change in the reasons

16. Joseph Samler, "The High School Graduate and Drop-Out," *Journal of Experimental Education*, 7:105–109, 1938.
17. Bell, *Youth Tell Their Story*, p. 66.

given by youth for leaving high school. The study by Dillon in 1949 gives recent important reasons given by 957 youth:

REASONS FOR LEAVING HIGH SCHOOL*

	Frequency	
	No.	*Per cent*
Reasons Relating to School		
Preferred work to school	342	36
Was not interested in school work	104	11
Could not learn and was discouraged	66	7
Was failing and didn't want to repeat grade	55	6
Disliked a certain teacher	47	5
Disliked a certain subject	30	3
Could learn more out of school than in school	16	1
Financial Reasons		
Needed money to buy clothes and to help at home	144	15
Wanted spending money	55	6
Personal Reasons		
Ill health	49	5
Friends had left school	29	3
Parents wanted youth to leave school	20	2

* Harold J. Dillon, *Early School Leavers* (New York: National Child Labor Committee, 1949), Table 24, pp. 50–55.

Dillon points out that there are very definite symptoms of vulnerability to early school leaving, such as

1. Fairly consistent regression in scholarship
2. Frequent grade failures in elementary school
3. High frequency of failure in secondary school
4. Marked regression in attendance from elementary to secondary schools
5. Frequent transfers from one school to another
6. Evidence of a feeling of insecurity or "lack of belonging" in school
7. Marked lack of interest in school work[18]

The Syracuse, New York, Board of Education made a three and one-half year study of its drop-outs from grade seven through grade twelve, beginning in the fall, 1945. An intensive sampling of this group, 194 in number, revealed that 61 per cent of the reasons for leaving school were centered in the following descending order of frequency:

18. Dillon, *ibid.*, pp. 87–88.

1. Dissatisfaction with school
2. Inability to discern the relationship between school subjects and future occupations
3. Overage for grade
4. Inability to get along with teachers
5. Inability to learn
6. Failure of school to offer suitable subjects
7. Lack of sufficient credits for graduation

The remaining 39 per cent of the reasons were personal:

1. Lack of funds
2. Lure of job
3. Family support
4. Illness
5. The feeling of being too poor in comparison with others in the class[19]

A more extended study in New Jersey, covering 524 school leavers, involved home visitation and complete replies to questionnaires. In this investigation, the conclusions were that many of the oral reasons given were not the true reasons. Forty-five per cent of the 1940–1941 drop-outs stated they left school because of lack of interest, while 29 per cent stated they were discouraged. Only 7.8 per cent left school for work. Of the 1945–1946 drop-outs, 43 per cent left because they lacked interest, 21 per cent because of discouragement, and only 11 per cent to go to work.[20]

A summary of the studies of drop-outs made since 1940, including New York, Maryland, Illinois, and Pennsylvania, was undertaken by Nancarrow, who condenses his findings as follows:[21]

1. Size of school has little to do with holding power.
2. In most schools, more boys than girls withdraw.
3. Schools vary in percentage of drop-outs from 5 per cent to 70 per cent.
4. The largest number of withdrawals by percentages is first in the vocational curriculum, then the general curriculum, and finally the college preparatory curriculum.
5. Most studies seem to indicate that the more retardation, the more likely that a drop-out will result.

A summary of the reasons which youth gave for leaving school are

I. Economic reasons (average 53 per cent)
   A. Family needs economic help

---

19. Syracuse Board of Education, *Syracuse Youth Who Did Not Graduate* (Syracuse, N.Y., 1950); p. 2. Mimeographed.

20. Howard W. Brown, "Why They Leave School," *New Jersey Educational Review*, 23:78, 1949.

21. James E. Nancarrow, "Reducing Drop-Outs," *Bulletin*, National Association of Secondary School Principals, 34:183–188, 1950.

B. Needed to work at home
C. Desires to work in order to increase personal funds
D. Lack of pocket money to finance school expenditures

II. Lack of interest in school (average 27 per cent)
A. Not interested—bored
B. Dislike of teacher
C. Disciplinary difficulties
D. Socially maladjusted, so loses interest in extraclass program

III. Maladjustment in school (average 11 per cent)
A. Difficulties in certain subjects
B. Lack of ability to do particular type of school work assigned or selected
C. Retardation—inferiority complex
D. Discouragement on account of school failure
E. Inflexibility of school program

IV. Miscellaneous (average 4 per cent)
A. Lack of proper guidance in vocational choice
B. Mental deficiency
C. Excessive absence, including truancy
D. Social problems

V. Health (average 3 per cent)
A. Ill health
B. Physical defects
C. Illness at home

VI. Marriage (average 3 per cent)

The symptoms of elimination seem to be:

1. Poor attendance
2. Scholarship difficulties
3. Lack of interest
4. "Does not belong" feeling
5. Disciplinary situation

Summary

In a summary of the studies on elimination, the following features appear to be pertinent:

1. During the last forty years in the United States the percentage of elimination from the elementary school has become a minor problem but it is still a major one in the secondary school. Figures for different schools and cities vary widely, but when only from a third to a half of our youth in the United States remain for the duration of the secondary school, we cannot ignore the importance of such wholesale withdrawal. Society has not yet met the conditions whereby the mass of youth of secondary-school age have edu-

cational opportunities suited to their needs, in spite of the claims we make of universal education and the laws we set up to enforce school attendance.

2. No nation in the world has a more democratic educational program than America, but there is still evidence that the more intelligence a youth has and the more money his father makes, the greater will be his chances of remaining throughout high school. The more advanced the classes in school, the higher is the mean intelligence quotient of the group, and the higher is the per capita income of their parents. The higher also in the economic scale are the types of occupations which youth desire and are preparing to fill, so that students in the last two years of the secondary school are largely those who are able to stay in school because their work is not needed by the family or because they are able to deal successfully with the academic curriculum. What Van Denburg said of the New York High Schools in 1911 should be said of the American secondary schools today: "A New York High School is a people's college in its student body and should be in its course of study."

3. The program of the secondary school is inadequate to deal individually with youth. Guidance programs are relatively young, teachers are poorly trained in guidance techniques, and the staffs of most schools are too small. The result is that youth do not receive sufficient counsel on their educational and vocational plans. The schools know best their pupils' intellectual and immediate personal successes; they do not know enough about their home life, their personal and social problems. Neither do educators know enough about individualizing instruction, either in content or in method. Teacher-training institutions, as well as teachers and local school systems, must assume their share of responsibility for these conditions.

4. The school bears little relationship to what youth do when they leave it, except in the case of those who enter college.[22]

5. Most reasons given for elimination reflect upon the inability of the student either to pass the work or to "stick it out," yet writers tend to ignore the great responsibility which the school has to revise its curriculum and to improve the adjustment of its pupils.

6. Pupils who have little success in school tend to leave it. They become discouraged and critical of the subject offerings and the teaching. They tend to look upon high school as a necessary evil for some occupations but tend to avoid it if they can find some other way to satisfy their vocational requirements; they are critical of the worth and purpose of what they are doing. The local community, however, along with the school personnel, must accept responsibility for the elimination of pupils. The availability of jobs for youth, of course, is another factor of importance.

---

22. For a story of what seven communities have done for youth who leave school, see U.S. Department of Labor, *After Teen-Agers Quit School* (*Bulletin* No. 150; Washington: Government Printing Office, 1951).

These conditions cannot be ignored if we are truly interested in making our secondary school universal in both attendance and service. If youth constantly sit in judgment on what they do in high school and if they have unsatisfactory experiences with it, the conditions for their early elimination are right. A mixture of a prejudiced pupil, an improperly trained or uninteresting teacher, and an academic curriculum is too much for a virile teen-age youth. We can never have universal education until we provide the essentials for it. Universal education is not a legal matter; it is an educational, a professional, a community matter, a matter of the organization, operation, and support of a secondary school.

Success in School

Another measure of the success of the school is whether the pupils succeed in the work of the school. Let us look at this in terms of the progress of pupils through school, their promotions, and their failures.

Progress through School

One of the difficulties of using the classification and progress studies of retardation is due to the looseness of the studies themselves and to their great variation in base figures. There has been considerable controversy centering around the age-grade classification schemes, because of the differences of opinion over the ages which should be used as classification bases and over the soundness of classifying pupils as retarded or normal or accelerated on age alone. Since such confusion exists over these studies, the reader should guard against too positive an interpretation of their results.

The *Encyclopedia of Educational Research* reports that most of the studies on school progress indicate that "overageness is a characteristic of from 20 to 40 per cent of the pupil population."[23] Underageness exists in from 3 to 20 per cent of the population, most reports showing around 10 per cent. The *Encyclopaedia* shows that in a recent study of 37 cities in the United States, retardation ran from 21 to 54 per cent, with the median being 38.8, while the acceleration ran from 2 to 30 per cent, the median being 10.25 per cent. In a typical city in the United States in 1922, 52 per cent of the pupils were making normal progress, 38 per cent were retarded, and 10 per cent were accelerated.

In Philadelphia in 1919 it took 9.7 years for the average pupil in Philadelphia schools to complete eight grades.[24] The survey staff commented that

23. *Encyclopedia of Educational Research,* Walter S. Monroe, ed. (American Educational Research Association; New York: The Macmillan Company, 1941), p. 1,055.
24. Pennsylvania State Department of Education, *Report of the Survey of the Public Schools of Philadelphia* (Philadelphia, Pa.: The Public Education and Child Labor Association of Pennsylvania, 1922), Book II, 1921, p. 188.

this condition was then considered normal in comparison with other cities in the United States. In the high schools in Philadelphia at that time, for each 1,000 pupils entering grade nine, only slightly over 500 were regularly advanced to grade ten without some failure. Of these 500, only a few over 300 were regularly advanced to grade eleven, 275 were advanced to grade twelve, and a few over 200 graduated. This is an excellent illustration of a perfect sifting process for the colleges.

One of the most comprehensive summaries of studies was made in 1931 by Cooke,[25] who compiled the figures on progress through school as shown by school surveys from 1908 to 1928 dealing with 2,500,000 pupils. The total figures showed 21 per cent accelerated, 48 per cent normal, and 31 per cent retarded. He commented that a study of the figures during the years analyzed showed that those for normal progress tended to increase, those for retardation decreased steadily, and those for acceleration remained about the same. Part of this, of course, may be accounted for by recent no-failure programs, as well as by improved teaching, guidance, and curriculum reform.

Studies made in Los Angeles, California, in 1936[26] indicate that 4,831 normal children in 31 schools in the city were largely "at age" at the beginning of their school career, yet with each successive grade there was a decreasing proportion of "at age" pupils.

Pupil Retardation

Recent research on retardation is difficult to locate largely because what is done is a product of local schools, and even here flexible promotional practices tend to become more general, thus reducing retardation. In commenting on the recent research in the field of pupil progress, the *Encyclopedia of Educational Research* contrasts the formalized past with the present, stating:

> The early studies of school progress assumed well-defined academic standards for each grade. With the realization that academic training is but one phase of the total development of the child, standards have become more flexible. A general shift in philosophy is shown by the increased number of schools using an ungraded curriculum and promotion according to other bases, such as social maturity.[27]

---

25. D. H. Cooke, "A Study of School Surveys with Regard to Age-Grade Distribution," *Peabody Journal of Education,* 8:259–266, 1931.
26. Zilpha Main and Ellen A. Horn, "Empirically Determined Grade Norms as a Factor in the Educational Maladjustment of the Average Child: The Age-Grade Status of Children in the 90–109 I.Q. Group," *Journal of Educational Research,* 31:161–171, 1936.
27. *Encyclopedia of Educational Research,* ed. Walter S. Monroe (American Educational Research Association; New York: The Macmillan Company, rev. ed., 1950), pp. 1,122–1,123.

Sandin in 1941 is reported to have had difficulty in finding schools which would admit using practices of retardation.[28]

Studies have also been made on the effects of and responsibilities for retardation. Typical are those made by Nifenecker and Campbell,[29] Outland,[30] and Farley.[31] In an unusually careful study of this problem, Nifenecker and Campbell commented pertinently on their findings: "Retardation is not so much a form of pupil maladjustment as it is a measure of the inadequacy of the school's program in meeting the challenge offered by the varying needs of pupils." Outland's study of 3,352 transient boys who registered with the Los Angeles Bureau of the Federal Transient Service, ages sixteen to twenty, indicated that 1,923 of these boys were behind in their school career. Farley found this true of 93 per cent of 422 pupils referred to an attendance officer for truancy in Newark, New Jersey, in 1934.

Sumption and Phillips summarized the research on nonpromotional practices and indicated that retention does not increase a slow rate of learning or assure a mastery of subject matter. It does not increase student morale or tend to facilitate personality adjustment. Retention fails to reduce the variability of achievement found in individual classes and does not increase the grade achievement averages.[32]

Pupil Failures

Failure is only one of the causes of retardation, but it is probably a very important one. One of the ways of discovering its importance is to examine the figures on school failures. Many studies have been made on failures, some of them of very minor and local importance and some of them of value in showing trends in large areas. It is impossible to review more than a very few, but those selected are rather typical of the entire group.

STATISTICAL STUDIES. The National Survey of Secondary Education pointed out that among the 5,290 pupils studied, "between a third and a half

28. A. A. Sandin, "Social and Emotional Adjustments of Regularly Promoted and Non-promoted Pupils." Doctoral Dissertation, Teachers College, 1942. Reported in *Encyclopedia of Educational Research,* rev. ed., pp. 1,123, 1,126.

29. Eugene A. Nifenecker and Harold G. Campbell, *Statistical Reference Data Relating to Problems of Overageness, Educational Retardation, Nonpromotion, 1900–1934* (Bureau of Reference, Research, and Statistics, Publication No. 28; New York: New York City Board of Education, 1937).

30. George Outland, "Acceleration and Retardation among Transient Boys," *School and Society,* 47:413–416, 1938.

31. Eugene S. Farley, "Retarding Repeaters: Sad Effects of Failures upon Pupils," *Nation's Schools,* 18:37–39, 1936.

32. M. R. Sumption and T. A. Phillips, "School Progress," *Encyclopedia of Educational Research,* rev. ed., p. 1,123.

of the boys and between a fourth and a third of the girls reported having experienced repetition [of school subjects] during their school course."[33] In a study of 25 school systems in cities, the rate of failure ran from 4 to 17 per cent, the median being 9.1 per cent.[34] In a study of 304 widely scattered high schools in the United States, it was found that an average of 1 out of every 4 pupils was failing. The rate of failure of work attempted by all pupils was 10.2 per cent.[35] In his study of 6,047 cases of failure in the high schools in 15 Texas cities, Lafferty found that 24 per cent were due to mental deficiencies on the part of pupils and 76 per cent to causes "more essentially the responsibility of the school."[36] Lamson studied a group of gifted children in senior high schools and found that almost one half of this group of gifted children (I.Q. 135–190) received one or more failing marks in secondary school.[37]

In a study in 1930 of almost 58,000 high-school pupils,[38] subject failures ran from 2.8 per cent for the senior students to 8.8 per cent for the sophomores. When subject failures and withdrawals are combined, the percentages ranged from 6.7 per cent for seniors to 16.8 per cent for sophomores. When the various subjects were compared, mathematics, Latin, and modern languages ranged highest with 10.6, 8.9, and 8.0 per cent, respectively. These figures compare reasonably well with those from a recent study made by Farnsworth and Casper of high-school failures in the State of Utah.[39] They found the median percentage of failure in the high schools they studied to be 3.4 and the median withdrawals to be 5.0. The figures for particular schools, however, ranged for failures from 0 to 23 per cent and for withdrawals from 0 to 35.3 per cent. In an analysis of the failures by subjects, the five highest subjects of pupil mortality were commerce (4.7 per cent), agriculture (4.5 per cent), industrial arts (4.2 per cent), English (3.7 per cent), and mathematics (3.7 per cent). These subject failures certainly contradict the trend elsewhere.

These figures for the State of Utah and those for a wide area of the United

---

33. Kefauver, Noll, and Drake, *The Secondary School Population* pp. 34–36.
34. A. O. Heck, *Administration of Pupil Personnel* (Boston: Ginn and Company, 1929).
35. Study made by J. F. Montague, quoted in E. E. Windes, *Trends in the Development of Secondary Education* (U.S. Office of Education, *Bulletin* No. 26; Washington: Government Printing Office, 1927), p. 11.
36. H. M. Lafferty, "High School Failures in Texas," *Texas Outlook,* 21:18–20, 1937.
37. Edna Emma Lamson, *A Study of Young Gifted Children in the Senior High School* (Teachers College Contributions to Education, No. 424; New York: Columbia University, Teachers College, Bureau of Publications, 1930).
38. Department of Secondary School Principals, *Subject Failures by Schools for Semester Ending June, 1929* (Secondary School Studies, *Bulletin* No. 29, Washington, D.C.: National Education Association, 1930), pp. 13–20.
39. Burton K. Farnsworth and Jesse B. Casper, "A Study of Pupil Failure in High School," *School Review,* 49:380–383, 1941.

States should be compared with the statistics on the failures in the Regents' examinations in the State of New York. These figures indicate the percentage of pupils whose examinations were given failing marks in the examinations for the years 1924, 1929, 1933, 1938, and 1948.

FAILURES ON REGENTS' EXAMINATIONS

Subjects	1924*	1929*	1933*	1938*	1948†
English	19.1	14.1	11.0	7.5	12.7
Social studies	19.1	16.7	12.6	8.5	16.0
Mathematics	30.1	29.9	25.7	14.7	18.9
German	22.0	11.8	17.0	12.4	12.4
French	23.4	15.8	11.7	12.2	11.5
Spanish	38.1	20.2	19.3	14.3	10.1
Italian	24.1	24.9	12.9	8.3	16.0
Latin	31.8	27.2	15.7	7.1	17.0
Greek	28.4	10.4	19.0	4.8	..
Science	22.9	15.5	13.8	8.9	17.4
Commercial subjects	20.2	29.8	22.8	19.9	15.2
Art	12.2	26.5	28.8	19.5	16.0
Music	17.0	40.2	19.3	15.3	12.5
Voc., Homemaking, Ag.	..	15.6	8.8	9.5	8.5
All subjects	23.0	21.5	17.3	11.5	15.8

* Herbert G. Espy, *The Public Secondary School* (Boston: Houghton Mifflin Company, 1939), p. 99.
† University of the State of New York, "Statistics for the School Year 1947–48," Forty-fifth Annual Report, Vol. II.

It is obvious that there has been a steady and marked reduction in the percentage of failures on the Regents' examinations, decreasing from one failure out of every four pupils in 1924 to one out of every seven in 1948, although for some reason there has been a sharp rise in failures between 1938 and 1948. The situation is, however, more serious than these figures would indicate; in the first place, the large variations in particular schools are hidden by these mass calculations, and in the second place, many pupils are never allowed to take these Regents' examinations because of failing marks in their own schools. Only the best students in the schools take the examinations.

Contrary to the general opinion that most failures are in the so-called academic subjects, a comprehensive study of the senior high schools in Washington, D.C. revealed that the first ten in percentages of failure were

FAILURES IN SENIOR HIGH SCHOOLS, WASHINGTON, D.C.*

Rank	Subjects	Percentage of Failures
1	Commercial Arithmetic II	33.3
2	Burroughs Calculator	31.4
3	History, Modern (10A)	29.4
4	Consumer Education I	25.8
5	Retailing IV	22.5
6	Geometry, Plane (10A)	18.4
7	French 9A	18.4
8	Printing 12A	18.2
9	Radio II	18.2
10	Forging 10A	17.8

* National Association of Secondary School Principals, *Bulletin,* 30:147, 1946.

In San Francisco, California, studies were made of the failures by departments in all public high schools for the second semester of the 1946–1947 school year. The results are as follows:

FAILURES IN SAN FRANCISCO*

Percentage of Students Failed, Grades 10, 11, 12

Department	Percentage Failed	Department	Percentage Failed
Music	4.3	Social Studies	11.7
Home Economics	6.3	Science	1.9
Art	6.8	Foreign Languages	2.4
Industrial Arts	7.3	English	2.5
Commercial	7.4	Mathematics	3.7

Comparison of Failures in Grade 9 with Failures in Upper Three Grades

Percentage of Failures by Departments

	Music	Home Economics	Art	Industrial Art	Commerce	Social Studies	Science	Foreign Languages	English	Mathematics	All Schools
Grade 9	4.6	3.8	1.5	6.8	6.0	8.2	7.1	16.7	9.4	12.1	9.4
Grades 10, 11, 12	1.9	2.4	2.5	3.7	4.3	6.3	6.8	7.3	7.4	11.7	6.3

* Harold Spears, *Holding Power of San Francisco Public Schools* (San Francisco, Calif.: Office of the Curriculum Coordinator, 1947). Mimeographed.

The last table bears out the fact that elimination from school and ability to make satisfactory grades are closely related. The higher grades are more selective in the abilities of pupils.

Causes of Failure

Farnsworth and Casper asked teachers to suggest the causes of pupil failures.[40] The five causes most frequently mentioned, with the percentage of pupils to which these teachers thought the cause applied, were as follows:

CAUSES OF FAILURE*

Cause	Per Cent
1. Poor attendance	72.3
2. Lack of interest	77.0
3. Improper home conditions	38.0
4. Insufficient study	30.0
5. Dislike of subject	30.0

* Burton K. Farnsworth and Jesse B. Casper, "A Study of Pupil Failure in High School," *School Review,* 49:383, 1941.

It is clear from the reasons indicated that Utah teachers think there is nothing wrong with themselves or the high school; the cause of failure is the fault of the home or the pupil himself. Lack of interest, however, is partially due to the nature of the curriculum and the character of instruction.

Terman pointed out in 1919 that the major cause of the lack of progress of pupils was low mental ability.[41] This, of course, may easily be true; nevertheless it is presumably something about which the pupil can do nothing, and it has become an alibi for the school when it is really no explanation for anything except that the school has failed to adjust its program to the ability of the group it is supposed to serve.

Lafferty examined thirteen studies on the causes of failure and compiled their results.[42] The order of the reasons for pupil failure cited by these studies is as follows:

1. Irregular attendance
2. Poor health

40. "Pupil Failure in High School," *School Review,* 49:383, 1941.
41. Lewis M. Terman, *The Intelligence of School Children* (Boston: Houghton Mifflin Company, 1919).
42. H. M. Lafferty, "A Study of the Reasons for Pupil Failures in Schools," *Educational Administration and Supervision,* 24:360–367, 1938.

3. Poor home conditions
4. Low mentality
5. Lack of interest on part of pupil
6. Poor effort
7. Laziness
8. Poor foundation
9. Teacher inabilities
10. Lack of home study by pupil
11. Dislike of teacher
12. Too many social activities
13. Failure on tests

In the entire list of thirteen, only three are the fault of the school—lack of interest, teacher inabilities, and dislike of teacher—and they rank low in the list. From this list of the causes of failure, one gets the notion that the failing pupil is physically inferior, comes to school intermittently from a poor home, has a slow mind, is shiftless and won't work, never learned much in the past, has a dislike for the teacher and the subjects, and won't study. Such a list is too uncomplimentary to the pupil and tends to exalt the school as a benevolent and tolerant institution.

A comprehensive analysis of reasons for failures in secondary schools is that made by one state director of relations with schools, George E. Carrothers, of Michigan.[43] He finds that the reasons for failure remain approximately the same, over a period of years; but the order of importance changes somewhat. These are the reasons, although not given in order of importance:

1. Heavy load carried by teachers, both in and out of school
2. Lack of interest on the part of the pupil
3. Lack of understanding of pupils on the part of the teacher
4. Indifference and unconcern on the part of the teacher
5. Inability of youth to do the work expected
6. Parental unconcern for the education of boys and girls
7. Community misunderstanding or lack of understanding of what real education consists
8. Inability of educators to measure educational growth and the consequent inability to show the pupil and the public the extent to which growth has been made
9. Spoon feeding in home, school and community
10. Rigidity of school curriculum and school requirements for both pupils and teachers

Our studies are not very helpful in shedding light on the causes of failure. Teachers know too little about home conditions of pupils to stress these conditions as a cause of failure. The general and careless use of the expressions

43. George E. Carrothers, "Why Do High School Pupils Fail?" *Bulletin,* National Association of Secondary School Principals, 30:29, 1946.

"lack of interest," "poor foundation," "laziness," "won't study" is of little help in interpreting the causes of failure; such phrases only confuse the issue. Do they not divert our attention from the study of the techniques of teaching and the effectiveness of individualizing instructional materials? Do they not gloss over the need for studying the pupil from a personal and social standpoint, and imply approval of the curriculum of the school and disapproval of the pupil himself? The intimate personal problems, the home life, and the social and environmental aspects of child life are too important to be ignored. Failure is doubtless an aspect of the home, the pupil, the teacher and the school, and the pupil's health. All these factors contribute to failure and success and must be given the attention they merit.

Summary

From a study of the research on students' progress, classification, and failures, one may conclude the following:

1. There is a large number of withdrawals and failures among secondary-school pupils in the United States today, even though failures have been decreasing steadily during the last forty years. If one believes in universal secondary education, it is obvious that withdrawals and failures are entirely too high.

2. The rate of failure is less in the senior year than in the lower years of the high school. This decrease is due probably to the fact that many of the failing pupils have left school before they reach the senior year.

3. Among different schools, classes, and subjects there is considerable difference in rates of failure and withdrawals.

4. Pupil frustration is being experienced and undesirable attitudes toward teachers and the school are being formed because of failure.

5. The secondary school is not meeting the needs of a large mass of American youth and has not yet adapted its curriculum to the needs of the youth it is set up to serve. It therefore shirks its responsibility by discharging these pupils from school.

6. Success in the secondary school is still defined in terms of the satisfactory completion of subject units, and the chief requirement for graduation from high school is the satisfactory completion of a required number of these units.

Success in College

It has been established repeatedly that no more than 20 per cent of the pupils in high school go to college, and that less than 50 per cent of those who enter colleges in the United States remain to graduate.[44] For years accrediting asso-

---

44. See U.S. Office of Education, *Statistics of State School Systems* (Washington: Government Printing Office, published periodically).

ciations and certain state universities have compiled figures on the scholastic success of high-school pupils in college.[45] These figures vary widely among the different colleges and high schools, running all the way from 0 to 100 per cent success.

College success is very difficult to measure, for many youth go to college for one, two, or three years to secure additional general education or to acquire specific occupational skills or credentials for further vocational training elsewhere. These students cannot be classed as college failures because they fail to remain four years to graduate. Many others attend junior colleges and plan to terminate their education at the end of the two-year courses they pursue. Collegiate success, then, cannot be measured by figures of elimination such as those used as a measure of high-school success.

This point is demonstrated by studies such as the one by Werner,[46] who endeavored to determine the scholastic persistence during a nine-year period of 1,896 students who registered as freshmen in the Teachers College of the University of Nebraska. He discovered that 60.6 per cent of these students stayed in college only four semesters or less, and that only slightly more than 25 per cent of the entire number graduated from the University of Nebraska, while only 3 per cent graduated from other colleges. It is significant that 4.2 per cent of the students earned no hours of credit whatsoever, and 34.4 per cent earned less than thirty semester hours of credit. In other words, one-third of these students left at the end of the first year in college, slightly more than another fourth stayed for two years, and another fourth graduated. The rest dropped out between their second and fourth years. Clearly, persistence for four years is not high. However, those students who remained for two years secured the teaching credentials required by the state and to that extent can be said to have succeeded in their purpose in going to college.

The most significant study on college success is the one made by the Progressive Education Association as a part of the Eight-Year Study.[47] In May, 1932, about three hundred American colleges and universities agreed to a proposal from the Commission on the Relation of School and College of the Progressive Education Association that thirty selected secondary schools should be released by the colleges from the usual program of college entrance requirements to engage in an experimental study. The colleges agreed to accept the

45. See Alvin C. Eurich and Leo F. Cain in *Encyclopedia of Educational Research,* pp. 838–860; Committee on Educational Research, *Studies in Higher Education.* Report of the Committee on Educational Research for the Biennium 1936–1938 (Minneapolis, Minn.: University of Minnesota, 1939).

46. Oscar H. Werner, "Is Scholastic Persistence the Most Reliable Criterion for Evaluating Student Achievement?" *Educational Administration and Supervision,* 25:435–442, 1939.

47. Dean Chamberlin, Enid Straw Chamberlin, Neal E. Drought, and William E. Scott, *Did They Succeed in College?* (New York: Harper & Brothers, 1942).

graduates of these schools for a period of five years without regard to specific subject requirements for entrance.

In order to discover whether these graduates succeeded in college as well as those who entered from conventional schools under standard college entrance requirements, the commission made an intensive study of 1,475 matched pairs of graduates from the experimental and from conventional high schools. Success was measured by the following criteria:

1. Intellectual competence
2. Cultural development; use of leisure time; appreciative and creative aspects
3. Practical competence; common sense and judgment; ordinary manual skills; environmental adaptability
4. Philosophy of life
5. Character traits
6. Emotional balance
7. Social fitness
8. Sensitivity of social problems
9. Physical fitness

A comparison of the 1,475 matched pairs reveals that the graduates of the thirty schools

1. Earned a slightly higher total grade average;
2. Earned higher grade averages in all subject fields except foreign language;
3. Specialized in the same academic fields as did the comparison students;
4. Did not differ from the comparison group in the number of times they were placed on probation;
5. Received slightly more academic honors in each year;
6. Were more often judged to possess a high degree of intellectual curiosity and drive;
7. Were more often judged to be precise, systematic, and objective in their thinking;
8. Were more often judged to have developed clear or well-formulated ideas concerning the meaning of education—especially in the first two years in college;
9. More often demonstrated a high degree of resourcefulness in meeting new situations;
10. Did not differ from the comparison group in ability to plan their time effectively;
11. Had about the same problems of adjustment as the comparison group, but approached their solution with greater effectiveness;
12. Participated somewhat more frequently, and more often enjoyed appreciative experiences, in the arts;
13. Participated more in all organized student groups except religious and "service" activities;
14. Earned in each college year a higher percentage of non-academic honors;

15. Did not differ from comparison group in the quality of adjustment to their contemporaries;
16. Differed only slightly from the comparison group in the kinds of judgments about their schooling;
17. Had a somewhat better orientation toward the choice of a vocation;
18. Demonstrated a more active concern for what was going on in the world.[48]

This study really reveals four things of importance: (1) Students who have superior success in high school, whether it be conventional or experimental, usually succeed in college. (2) There is no pattern of subject preparation for college superior to any other pattern of preparation. (3) Pupils from the experimental schools did a somewhat better job than the comparison group from conventional schools, whether success is judged by college standards, by the students' contemporaries, or by the individual students. (4) When a study was made of the graduates from the "most experimental schools," the results showed that pupils from these schools were strikingly more successful than their partners from conventional schools. In other words, the study revealed that "the more experimental the school, the greater the degree of success [the pupils had] in college."[49]

Vice-President Archibald MacIntosh, of Haverford College, recently made an extensive and critical study of college admissions and the college product. Considerable data on this problem were secured from nearly three hundred colleges and universities, which led to the conclusion that "by far the chief reason for students' leaving college is academic failure," with financial reasons, transfer and health as the three succeeding major reasons.[50] This analysis also reported a survey from the University of Texas which revealed that 44.8 per cent of those freshmen who had ranked in the upper half of their high-school classes graduated from the university, whereas only 16.7 per cent of those ranked in the lower half of their high-school classes graduated. Of all the freshmen who received degrees, 57 per cent came from the upper fourth of their high-school classes.

Beyond the undergraduate level of success or failure, however, the picture is different. An analysis of 40 students at the University of Missouri, in the summer of 1948, gave 138 reasons (with a frequency of more than 340) for failure in college. Only 16 of the 340 were concerned with "lack of proper background and earlier preparation."[51] The vast majority placed responsibility for failure on the student himself.

48. *Ibid.*, pp. 207–208. By permission of the publishers.
49. *Ibid.*, p. 209.
50. Archibald MacIntosh, *Behind the Academic Curtain* (New York: Harper & Brothers, 1948), Chap. 5 and pp. 51–73.
51. A. W. Hurd, "Why Graduate and Professional Students Fail in College Courses," *School Review*, 57:282–285, 1949.

From all studies on college success it is obvious that superior students in high school tend to succeed in college, that many pupils go to college with no clear purpose in mind, and that many go to college who have little or no chance of succeeding. Scholastic success of freshmen entering college, however, is no satisfactory criterion of a successful high school, since more than 75 per cent of high-school pupils never plan to enter college, and clearly the success of high schools cannot be judged by the achievement of the 20 per cent who enter college. The colleges do have a right, however, to expect that the small percentage of high-school students who can succeed in college possess the intellectual and physical qualities they desire.

Successful Living

Studies are legion on the learning of school subjects, but most of them are based on definite experimental situations where the authors are attempting to discover the gains in learning through certain teaching procedures. The studies of large groups of pupils usually have been made by survey commissions, which have pointed out the learning of groups in cities and states in the country. Reference to some of these will suggest the typical pattern of all.

The Regents' Inquiry in the State of New York investigated the work in 62 high schools in 51 communities during the year 1936–1937. On the assumption that "the character of the students who leave the secondary school constitutes a valid measure of the quality of the school's contribution to effective living," Eckert and Marshall indicated the nature of the youth in these communities.[52]

One of the problems to which this group turned its attention was, "What is the social competence of leaving pupils?" It found that only one out of every six pupils who left high school before graduation had the minimum command of reading and arithmetic expected of eighth-grade pupils. Three out of ten leaving before graduation failed in both the reading and the arithmetic tests, while one out of two of those who left at the end of the ninth grade did not pass the reading and arithmetic tests. One out of every fifteen graduates failed to pass the minimum reading and arithmetic tests. One out of ten graduates in the business courses did not attain eighth-grade standards in both reading and arithmetic, and one out of seven in industrial arts and homemaking failed.[53]

Of the withdrawing pupils, 35 to 50 per cent were not recommended by their teachers or principals for job responsibilities, and this was true of from 10 to 15 per cent of the graduates.[54] Pupils who leave school seldom return to it

---

52. Eckert and Marshall, *When Youth Leave School.*
53. *Ibid.,* pp. 88–90.
54. *Ibid.,* pp. 110, 114.

for advice and counsel, except the pupils who enter college, so that when the former leave school they carry their deficiencies with them without further contact with the school. Except in the area of college entrance, where it has established its reputation, the school has not become an effective agency for the improvement of the deficiencies of pupils who have left it.

The study also revealed that teachers think that a "knowledge of the formal duties of citizenship" which pupils possess is more important than having "a sense of personal responsibility or social concern"—a shocking revelation. Yet tests of pupils reveal no reasonable command even in this area. The attitude of teachers is doubtless reflected somewhat in the learning of pupils. There is scant and casual emphasis on the problems of immediate and practical living, and especially is this true for those pupils who withdraw before graduation. Little appreciation of the different goals, abilities, and interests of individual children seems to be held by the teachers, and little is done about it in the secondary schools in the State of New York. The authors report an amazing lack of knowledge about pupils on the part of their teachers and a strong inclination to view them, almost exclusively, in academic terms.

The results of the New York survey are summarized and interpreted by Spaulding,[55] who lists a number of significant findings from the study. Those quoted below give some idea of the competence of the pupils in the secondary schools of the State of New York.

1. Among the boys and girls leaving school every year are a considerable number whom the schools themselves are unwilling to recommend for responsible citizenship.

2. Irrespective of the school's judgment of their readiness for citizenship, the leaving pupils as a group are seriously deficient in their knowledge of the problems, the issues, and the present-day facts with which American citizens should be concerned.

3. The boys and girls who are leaving school are fundamentally conservative in their outlook on social problems.

4. The boys and girls who are on the point of leaving school, whatever they may think about the desirability of certain kinds of actions, are reluctant to assume responsibility for civic cooperation or to commit themselves to action which will involve personal effort or sacrifice.

5. Once he is out of school the ordinary boy or girl does practically nothing to add to his readiness for citizenship, nor does he even keep alive the knowledge of civic affairs or the interest in social problems which he may have had when he finished his schooling.

6. The educational plans of many boys and girls just out of high school are strikingly unrealistic, even if not wholly impossible of fulfillment.

7. Large numbers of even the high school graduates are seriously deficient in the basic tools of learning.

---

55. Francis T. Spaulding, *High School and Life* (New York: McGraw-Hill Book Company, Inc., 1938),

8. Once out of school most boys and girls read almost solely for recreation, chiefly in magazines of mediocre or inferior fiction and in daily newspapers.

9. The radio programs to which these young people prefer to listen are the variety, comedy, and dramatic features and not the educational features or the "quality" musical programs.

10. Despite the fact that movie-going is a habit with them—or possibly because of that fact—few of these boys and girls use much discrimination in choosing the moving pictures which they see.

11. About half the boys and girls who left school are active in some sort of club or organization chiefly recreational in purpose.

12. Large numbers of boys and girls on the point of leaving school have no vocational plans, or they have plans which are quite out of line with their own demonstrated abilities and with opportunities for employment.

13. The high school's opinion of its pupils' vocational competence bears little relation to the actual success of these boys and girls in getting jobs.

14. The boys and girls who succeed in getting jobs are more concerned with the superficial conditions of their work, or with the satisfaction of having any kind of job, than with particular opportunities which their jobs offer.

15. Schools tend to recommend leaving pupils for citizenship or for jobs which have no very definite relationship to the nature of the curricula in which the pupils have been enrolled.

16. The general citizenship and leisure-time activities of pupils who have left school bear no apparent relation to the curricula they have followed.

17. At the time they leave school the ablest pupils possess notably greater information about all sorts of matters than do pupils of lesser intellectual promise; but the ablest pupils are not greatly different from the average in their general social attitudes.

18. More than three-fourths of all the work which boys and girls were taking in New York State high schools in 1937 was academic work or work in music and art, and most of the remainder consisted of training for business.

19. More than half the boys and girls who go through high school choose their course without advice from anyone.

20. Nine-tenths of the academic high schools assume no active concern for their pupils' vocational adjustment when they leave school.

21. Teaching in the high schools everywhere in the state tends to be focused on preparation for the Regents' examinations.

These statements are a severe indictment of secondary education. From the conclusions drawn from the data of the New York survey it is clear that the school is in an academic mold, that it supports a system of examinations which tends to make the whole organization and curriculum static, and that the secondary school is failing to offer youth opportunities for actual experience in activities that will prepare them for normal living in the adult world.

Such conditions are bound to be reflected in the lack of competence of the pupils.

In the survey of St. Louis, Missouri, tests were given to determine the competence of high school pupils.[56] The staff found that twelfth-grade pupils who had taken both general science and biology were not appreciably better in dealing with everyday health problems than were those who had had no science.[57] Twelfth-grade pupils who had had an average of 6.3 courses in social studies were no better able to answer questions on current social-civic problems than were those who had taken only the prescribed minimum of 3 courses. Growth in civic competence seemed to be unrelated to work in school classes. In critical thinking the ability pupils possessed seemed to bear no observable relation to the number of science courses taken. "Instruction in English, in science, and in mathematics no less than in the social studies is based largely, and often almost exclusively, upon textbook recitation."[58] In the ordinary skills these pupils in St. Louis ranked about the same in efficiency as other pupils in the United States. The aims of education in terms of social competence, the assumption of cooperation and responsibility, and the development of critical thinking, as well as the ability to accept and keep a job, seem not to be appreciably developed by the secondary-school programs in either St. Louis or New York State.

In the survey of Pittsburgh, Pennsylvania, the pupils in the high school "did not have much factual information on modern civic affairs" but had "much erroneous information" on such matters. They made low scores on tests of scientific attitudes, and a year or two of study of science in grades nine and ten made no appreciable difference in the scores. There was evidence that pupils free to make their own decisions and run their own school affairs developed a "high degree of sound judgment on what to do in new situations." In formal schools the youth knew what they must do in standard situations but they were poor in making judgments in new and free situations.

In 1936 the Research Division of the National Education Association made a nation-wide survey of the classroom techniques used by teachers of the social sciences and conducted an opinion questionnaire to determine what success these teachers thought they were having with pupils.[59] Approximately 73 per cent of the teachers in the junior and senior high schools thought that giving pupils a knowledge of important facts was an objective of *great im-*

56. Division of Field Studies, *Report of Survey of the Public Schools of St. Louis, Missouri* (New York: Columbia University, Teachers College, Bureau of Publications, 1939).

57. *Ibid.*, p. 44.

58. *Ibid.*, p. 55.

59. Research Division of the National Education Association, *Improving Social Studies Instruction* (Research *Bulletin* XV, No. 5 (Washington: National Education Association, 1937), p. 194.

portance in the teaching of social studies, but only 53 per cent thought they were succeeding "adequately." About 63 per cent thought the "giving of realistic knowledge" was of "great importance," but only 47 per cent were satisfied with the results. About 60 per cent of the teachers thought the "preparation of pupils for promoting cooperation" was of great importance, but only 32 per cent of them thought it was being adequately done. About 53 per cent thought "the training in intellectual processes (skills)" of great importance, but only 37 per cent thought the training was satisfactory. About 73 per cent thought the "training of character" of great importance, but only 29 per cent felt that this goal was being reached. Such a study of what teachers regard as important and their evaluation of their own efficiency is revealing in the light of the figures on pupils' growth and development. Although character development, cooperation, and realistic knowledge rank high as goals in the minds of teachers, they are in general dissatisfied with pupils' achievement of these goals.

Koeninger[60] tested 674 high-school seniors in 10 public high schools in 4 states to determine how consistent they were in their attitudes toward the major social problems of the day. He found only 25 per cent of these seniors consistent in their beliefs. Eckert and Mills[61] found from a study of 500 high-school students that continued instruction in history or the social studies does not tend to change the attitude of students toward international problems.

Kaplan summarizes more recent experimental data on the accomplishments of children in modern or activity programs of education as compared with those being taught by traditional methods:

> Based upon data derived from carefully matched groups of children studied in Houston, Texas; Roslyn, Long Island; Los Angeles; Nashville, Tennessee; and New York City, all investigators concluded that the newer schools with their newer methods achieved results in the basic skills which were as good as or superior to those achieved in the older type schools. It was further found that on the basis of Stanford Achievement Tests, the knowledge of literature, history, civics and geography exhibited by pupils in modern schools similarly equalled or exceeded that of children of like ability in traditional schools. And remember, these results were obtained despite the fact that in the modern school the basic skills are not thought of as merely reading, writing, and arithmetic, but are extended to include study skills, skills in creative thinking, library skills, expressional skills, skills in personal and social relations and many others for which no time was allotted in the traditional schools.[62]

60. Rupert C. Koeninger, "Attitude Consistency of High School Seniors," *School Review*, 44:519–524, 1936.

61. Ruth Eckert and Henry C. Mills, "International Attitudes and Related Academic and Social Factors," *Journal of Educational Sociology*, 9:142–153, 1935.

62. Louis Kaplan, "The Attack on Modern Education," *The Phi Delta Kappan*, 32:225, 1951.

There are at least two disturbing things about the studies on pupil learning: (1) High-school youth are leaving school incompetent to assume their responsibilities either civically or vocationally; and (2) through its emphasis upon a subject-centered curriculum or through its emphasis upon intellectual processes and methodology, the school is doing little to improve the situation.

We have now secured some answers to the questions whether pupils stay in school, whether they fail in the work they pursue, whether they succeed in college, and whether they learn what is necessary for social competence. Let us now look at the fifth question.

The School and the Needs of Youth

One of the difficulties in finding a satisfactory answer to the question whether the school is adequately meeting the needs of youth is the lack of confidence in the source from which it must be secured—youth themselves. One of the strange and interesting things about our behavior is that we as adults feel that youth are not capable of defining their needs and therefore no confidence should be placed in any answers we might get from them. An interesting antidote to this attitude comes from Van Denburg,[63] who comments that "perhaps after all, those unlearned and unabashed children who decide that the high school studies are of no use to them, may be nearer the truth than many of us who are unreasoning servants of tradition and habit." Doubtless a good deal of caution should be exercised in placing too much confidence in the replies to questionnaires sent to youth, but in all probability, for that matter, they are as reliable as those filled out by adults. At any rate, they do reflect some of the attitudes of youth and whether we like these attitudes or not, whether we agree with them, or whether they hurt our pride is of little consequence. The important matter is that these are the attitudes which youth express, and until we are able to improve these points of view we will not teach youth effectively. What do youth, then, think about the secondary school? Only a few of the typical studies can be reviewed.

Opinions of Youth

The New York State survey staff asked youth to describe the things (subjects procedures, problems, activities) about the school which they liked least and those which they liked best.[64] The composite of the picture of least-liked things is a very satisfactory description of the average American high school, while the composite of the things liked best, together with the

---

63. Van Denburg, *Causes of Elimination,* p. 78.
64. Eckert and Marshall, *When Youth Leave School,* pp. 133–135.

interjection of the things they would like to see added, is a very good picture of youth in normal living. Sixteen hundred and forty-one graduates were asked questions. Of them, 75 per cent claimed the school had taken no part in advising them on their high-school curriculum program—an accusation which seems almost inconceivable. What are teachers and counselors and principals doing? Eighty per cent of the young people claimed the school did not advise them on any of their problems. These pupils were almost unanimous in exclaiming that their chief problem now was one of vocational adjustment, yet while they were in school from 65 to 75 per cent of their time was spent on academic subjects which rarely mentioned vocational living. When they were asked what changes they would like to see made in the high school, from 25 to 37 per cent requested more emphasis upon preparation for the work of the world, and 17 per cent of them said everything about the school needed changing. Yet these were pupils who had successfully completed the work of the school. One of the alarming aspects of these replies was that "those students whom the school considers its finest products are just as condemnatory of current [school] programs as less successful pupils."[65] However, when these pupils were asked if they thought they were better off than those who had not been to high school, over 90 per cent of the graduates said they were, while slightly over 80 per cent of the withdrawals answered also in the affirmative. Surely these pupils in New York State are none too satisfied with the high school, even though they do feel they are better off (which to a youth may mean many things unrelated to his high-school education) than those who have not attended high school.

The Maryland youth studied by Bell[66] were also asked their opinion of the secondary school. Did they consider their education to have economic value to them? Forty-eight per cent said it had little or no economic value, 20 per cent said considerable value, and 32 per cent said great value. They were then asked whether they considered their education to have cultural value. Twenty-eight per cent replied it had little or none, 25 per cent said it had considerable, and 47 per cent said it had great cultural value. Half of the youth think secondary education is practically worthless economically, and a third of them think the same of its cultural value. Sixty per cent of the youth said they would leave school immediately if they did not think continued education would improve their vocational chances.

In the extensive study of draftees made by Cunliffe in 1950 in Orange County, California, he asked the 3,936 who were of voting age questions regarding their exercise of the franchise.[67] The replies given were astounding:

---

65. *Ibid.,* p. 118.
66. Bell, *Youth Tell Their Story,* pp. 81, 86.
67. A. J. William Cunliffe, "A Quart of Education," *California Journal of Secondary Education,* 25:477–479, 1950.

Out of 3,936 who were eligible to vote,

  41 per cent had not registered,
  28 per cent registered but had not voted,
  17 per cent voted at the last election,
  14 per cent made no reply.

They were also asked how they spent their free recreational time. The replies were far from satisfactory as the figures will show:

LEISURE-TIME ACTIVITIES

Leisure-Time Activity	Number	Percentage
Loafing	1325	25
Sports	1037	20
Hobby	433	8
Movies	223	4
Cars	209	3
Dancing	145	2

In response to the question whether high school prepared them well for their first job, the 5,376 draftees indicated that 38 per cent felt it had, 27 per cent it definitely had not, and to 34 per cent the question was not applicable. When asked to rate their high-school vocational guidance, 27 per cent said it was good, 29 per cent fair, 9 per cent poor, and to 35 per cent the question was not applicable.

When asked, "What high school subjects were least or most valuable?" the draftees replied:

VALUE OF SCHOOL SUBJECTS

Least Valuable		(First and Second Choice)	Most Valuable	
Percentage	Total	Subject	Total	Percentage
1.5	100	MATHEMATICS	2234	42
7	397	ENGLISH	1880	34
5	275	SHOP	1314	25
7	373	SCIENCE	717	13.5
18	960	SOCIAL SCIENCE	481	10.5
10	549	FOREIGN LANGUAGES		

A recent statistical study of 5,500 high-school seniors in 154 of the 300 high schools in the state of Washington was undertaken by L. J. Elias of the

State College of Washington. This was done by questionnaires to secure youth's attitudes and problems of adjustment. Nearly 110 questions were asked, running the entire gamut of youth's interests, problems, complaints, and ambitions. In the concluding subsumation the total number of personal problems per students were given as follows:

NUMBER OF PERSONAL PROBLEMS PER STUDENT*

Average Total Problems	Boy	Girl	Total
0 to 4	10.3	4.3	7.0
5 to 9	14.6	11.5	12.9
10 to 14	15.5	13.8	14.6
15 to 19	15.8	16.7	16.3
20 to 24	14.2	15.6	15.0
25 to 29	9.4	12.5	11.1
30 to 34	6.3	7.8	7.1
35 and over	11.8	15.4	13.8

* L. J. Elias, *High School Youth Look at Their Problems* (State College of Washington: The College Bookstore, 1949), p. 42.

In seeking information from these Washington youth about how the school might improve its preparatory services, the investigator received these replies:

SUGGESTIONS FOR BETTER PREPARATORY SERVICES*

Things to Do	Boy	Girl	Total
Offer more courses	50.2	46.8	48.3
Give more vocational courses	45.5	42.4	43.8
Teachers could be more friendly	16.8	18.6	17.8
Show interest in what they do after graduation	13.3	7.1	9.9
Provide more guidance and counseling	29.2	29.9	29.6
Tell them what vocation to follow	5.2	3.7	4.4
Give them practical vocational experience	28.8	26.9	27.8
More help with their personal problems	11.2	9.9	10.5
Give them understanding of world problems	11.6	12.8	12.2
School and teachers too strict	4.6	6.3	5.3
No information	12.0	11.1	11.6

* L. J. Elias, *High School Youth Look at Their Problems* (State College of Washington: The College Bookstore, 1949), p. 28.

Answering the question regarding the effectiveness of preparation by the school and teachers, the 5,500 seniors expressed these opinions about whether school and teachers have done their best to prepare students for their next step:

EFFECTIVENESS OF PREPARATION*

	Boy	Girl	Average Total
I do think	73.7	78.9	76.3
I do not think	15.9	13.2	14.4
No information	10.4	7.9	9.3

* L. J. Elias, *High School Youth Look at Their Problems* (State College of Washington: The College Bookstore, 1949), p. 28.

On the very controversial question of their attitude toward class instruction in high school on sex and preparation for successful marriage, these seniors reacted as follows:

PREPARATION FOR SUCCESSFUL MARRIAGE*

	Boy	Girl	Average Total
Very important and helpful	66.3	73.6	70.3
Interesting and useful	20.4	18.7	19.5
Might like such a class	8.8	6.9	7.7
Don't think they would be interested	3.4	2.1	2.7
No interest in such instruction	1.5	1.4	1.4
No information	2.0	.8	1.4

* L. J. Elias, *High School Youth Look at Their Problems* (State College of Washington: The College Bookstore, 1949), p. 29.

Fields carried on a comprehensive study of the opinions of youth regarding their personal and social problems.[68] He also reviewed the chief studies in the area up to that time. Fields asked 818 senior-high-school pupils to rate 152 items on three bases: (1) "Is this a problem with you?" (2) "Should the school deal with it?" (3) "Is the school helping you with it?" The ten

68. Ralph R. Fields, "The Identification of the Interests and Problems of High School Students and Their Implications for Curriculum Development." Doctoral Dissertation, Stanford University, 1940.

statements most frequently rated as personal problems were in the following order:

1. Staying interested in all subjects at all times
2. Knowing the kinds of work in the world and the incomes
3. Knowing the interests and abilities required in each kind of work
4. Expressing self clearly and interestingly
5. Knowing more about own abilities
6. Developing more personal charm
7. Learning to play recreational games
8. Understanding the importance of national problems
9. Getting work experience
10. How to get training for my work

Work, work, work. The cry of youth. Give us something to do and teach us how to do it. Five of these ten items had to do with work—productive work. Such a demand from youth cannot be sloughed off indefinitely. Study after study reveals that youth are crying for work training and work experience followed by a job. Yet studies repeatedly indicate that only a small fraction of the average pupil's time is given over to such preparation, and we adults cry out about youth being lazy and indifferent. Surely these problems raised by youth are intelligent ones earnestly given, and we adults need seriously to analyze the school program we give them.

Fields also asked these youth to indicate the social problems which seemed most pertinent to them. The following rated most frequently in the order below:

1. Keeping out of war (85 per cent of the group total)
2. World peace (83 per cent of the total group)
3. Crime, law enforcement, justice
4. Safety on the highway
5. Causes of war
6. How government can serve the needs of people
7. Public health
8. Raising living standards
9. Size of the Army and Navy
10. Unemployment

Surely no adult can say these are trivial problems. Youth want to look at conditions which exist, they want to delve into the causes and nature of problems, but above all else they want to consider *how* conditions may be improved, just the things which the average teacher and school want to leave to the last five minutes of the period. The "how" is not the stock in trade of the high school, yet if conditions are to be improved, it must be. It does little good to know the number of people killed on the highways and the places where they are killed unless such information is followed by a positive, dynamic, and penetrating study of how to eliminate such slaughter. Youth want to know about the world in which they live and how they can live in it better.

What Youth Desire of School

In an extensive study of more than 2,000 high-school students in several localities, Doane tried to discover the needs of youth.[69] Responses indicated that, first, the greatest concern of the students studied was in the area of vocational choice and placement; and, second, social relationships. These areas of concern were followed by problems of health, philosophy of life, finance, and leisure-time activities. Significantly, religion, government and history, current issues, and problems involving moral standards all received low rankings.

Bell found that 75 per cent of the Maryland youth want sex instruction in high school.[70] Symonds found that youth want help on such problems as the wise expenditure of money, health, personal attractiveness, study habits, personal and moral qualities of behavior, recreation, manners and courtesy, philosophy of life, and family relationships.[71] The youth in St. Louis were asked to indicate the activities in which they would like to engage in school.[72] They replied that they wanted the school to help them with learning how to save and spend money wisely; they wanted to discuss vocational information with people who were already engaged in the occupations of their choice; they wanted to know what high-school graduates did the first year out of school. They wanted to visit the city water-purification plant and a juvenile court, and they wanted to collect clothing for children less fortunate than themselves. They also wanted to discuss the movies.

Another study which gives an indication of what youth think may be pertinent. It shows the judgment of youth on a problem very closely related to the general opinion which youth have of the work of the secondary school. Hart wanted to know what youth thought of teachers and teaching.[73] He invited 10,000 high-school seniors from 66 high schools all over the country to describe the teacher they liked best, the one they liked least, and the "best" teacher they knew. Then he took samplings of 3,725 of these youth and

---

69. Donald C. Doane, *The Needs of Youth* (Teachers College Contributions to Education, No. 848; New York: Columbia University, Teachers College, Bureau of Publications, 1942).

70. Bell, *Youth Tell Their Story*, p. 90.

71. Percival M. Symonds, "Changes in Sex Differences in Problems and Interests of Adolescents with Increasing Age," *Pedagogical Seminary and Journal of Genetic Psychology*, 50:83–89, 1937; "Life Problems and Interests of Adolescents," *School Review*, 44:506–518, 1936.

72. *St. Louis Survey*, p. 49.

73. Frank W. Hart, *Teachers and Teaching; by Ten Thousand High School Seniors* (New York: The Macmillan Company, 1934).

ranked their comments. The teacher these youth liked best had the following characteristics (only the first five are given):

1. He is helpful with schoolwork, explains lessons and assignments clearly and thoroughly and uses examples in teaching.
2. He is cheerful, happy, good-natured, jolly, has a sense of humor, can take a joke.
3. He is human, friendly, companionable, one of us.
4. He is interested in pupils and understands them.
5. He makes work interesting, creates a desire to work, and makes classwork a pleasure.

It is hard to imagine a more comprehensive and excellent list of characteristics of a good teacher for youth. The characteristics of the teacher liked least were as follows (only the first five are given):

1. Too cross, cranky, grouchy, never smiles, nagging, sarcastic, loses temper, "flies off the handle."
2. Not helpful with schoolwork, does not explain lessons and assignments, not clear, work not well planned.
3. He is partial, has pets or favored students and picks on certain students.
4. Superior, aloof, haughty, snooty, overbearing, and does not know you out of class.
5. Mean, unreasonable, hard-boiled, intolerant, ill-mannered, too strict, makes life miserable.

Certainly while the youthful slang may leave something to be desired, the description of the teacher youth do not like is clear and of course elicits immediate approval from everyone. The youth were then asked to say how many of their present teachers belonged in the first group and how many in the second, and they replied that 75 per cent were in the first group and 25 per cent in the second group. If 25 per cent of our teachers answer the description which these youth gave to them, it is time for action on the part of school administrators, even though we can take satisfaction that so large a percentage of our teachers are in the first group. Eighty per cent of these youth said that teachers in the first group were also the best teachers they knew, while only 15 per cent said the teachers in the second group were their best teachers. It is interesting to note the discrimination of youth, however, for 20 per cent of them added other traits to describe other teachers not in either of these two groups which they thought were their "best" teachers.

Long and Farley made a very thorough study of 1,773 students from kindergarten through the twelfth grade to discover what teacher behavior was most disliked by the students.[74] These are the behaviors liked least:

---

74. H. B. Long and Lloyd Farley, "Teacher Behavior Most Disliked by Students." D. Ed. Dissertation, Stanford University, 1949.

TEACHER BEHAVIOR MOST DISLIKED

Behavior Disliked	Number of Students
Poor teaching techniques, including class organization	438
Corporal punishment	255
Creates feeling of insecurity and/or fear	234
Not fair, unjust	185
Failure to arouse pupil interest	145
Partiality—favoritism	95
Disposition	76
Lack of courtesy	50
Lack of rapport	45
Lack of knowledge of subject matter	35
Lack of cooperation	7
Poor personal appearance	3

Among the high-school students, poor teaching techniques ranked first with both boys and girls, with no objection to "corporal punishment" and "personal appearance." Lack of knowledge of subject matter, and the creation of feelings of insecurity ranked second and third with the high-school boys, while unfairness and the creation of feelings of insecurity were similarly ranked by the girls.

It is obvious that youth want the school to help them with more than the acquisition of facts and information. They expect the school to help them form judgments and outline procedures for undertaking the tasks of normal living. As they look at the typical secondary school, they find it wanting in these responsibilities, and when they have a chance to do so, they rate it as failing to complete the job.

Adult Evaluation of the Subject Curriculum

Before we leave this chapter, it may be well to indicate some of the subjective evaluations which adults have given in criticism of the subject curriculum. A hasty overview of some of them is all that can be included here. To counterbalance these, both sides of certain points of view regarding curriculum principles and practices will be reviewed later. If the reader wants to provide himself with antidotes for these criticisms, he need only read Nock's[75]

75. Albert J. Nock, *The Theory of Education in the United States* (New York: Harcourt, Brace and Company, 1932).

criticism of modern education, along with those of Bagley[76] and Hutchins.[77]

Harris contends that "as a creative integrating force at work in reshaping our civilization, the secondary school today seems relatively impotent. It has split its strength into dozens of subjects, each with its own pattern and routine, and it has thus failed to achieve either unity within or a sense of direction and purpose without."[78] Rugg argues that good teaching is made difficult by the array of compartmentalized subjects. The results of such subject division, he says, is a "crazy pattern" which is confusing to pupils and detrimental to their progress because of the lack of relationship among the subject materials themselves.[79] Bode asserts that groups outside the school have used pressure to keep divisions of learning intact and have therefore prevented them from being applied directly to the problems of life.[80] He feels that the unrealistic treatment of ideas in the subject divisions of the school today is definitely responsible for much of the pupils' lack of understanding about the problems of modern life. Sexson makes rather severe charges against the present subjects in the secondary school when he says:

> English as now taught in the American high school is a positive barrier to pupil adjustment. . . . Mathematics is an insurmountable obstacle to many children. . . . Formal and meaningless courses, such as are now character-istic of typewriting, of work in shops and laboratories, and of physical education, are ineffective as learning experiences and thwart any approach to pupil need or interest. General science, when taught as an abstract sam-pling of the fields of science, is non-functional and makes trouble in efforts at pupil adjustment. The present endeavors in such a field as music, wherein all pupils are required to seek self expression in this one medium, with no option, produces a great amount of disturbance and dissatisfaction. . . . The continuing stress upon subject matter to be included, upon scholastic stand-ards to be met, special assignments to cover work missed or not covered by the regular instruction, insistence upon home work, and other pressures tend to defeat the purposes of the school as they relate to individual growth and development.[81]

Hutchins has been more sharply critical than this, for in a Town Hall

---

76. William C. Bagley, *Education and Emergent Man* (New York: Thomas Nelson and Sons, 1934).

77. Robert M. Hutchins, *The Higher Learning in America* (New Haven: Yale University Press, 1936).

78. Pickens E. Harris, *The Curriculum and Cultural Change* (New York: Appleton-Century-Crofts, Inc., 1937).

79. Harold O. Rugg, "The Reconstruction of the American School Curriculum," *The New Era*, 10:81–84, 1929.

80. Boyd H. Bode, "Confusion in Present Day Education," Chap. I in W. H. Kilpatrick, ed., *The Educational Frontier* (New York: Appleton-Century-Crofts, Inc., 1933).

81. John A. Sexson, "A New Type of Secondary School," *Bulletin*, Department of Secondary School Principals, 22:1–11, 1938.

speech in San Francisco he charged that we put youth in school but we do not know what to do to educate them once we have them there. He accuses the educational institutions of saying, "Here we have a period of a young person's life. . . . We don't know what to do with it. . . . Nobody knows what to do with it, so let them spend it the way they choose."[82]

Another severe critic of the college also gives us concern for our school program. Brownell contends the colleges are failing in educating young people, are confused in their objectives, are far away from the realities of human life, and are draining off the vitality of small towns by causing the young people to be educated so that they will not return to the small communities after graduation.[83]

In his complaint against the rigidity of the college-preparatory curriculum commonly found in the high schools across the country, Diederick charges:[84]

> Our system of public secondary schools, therefore, is in the grip of a standard curriculum which is based in the fundamental premise that the pursuit of certain prescribed studies is essential to success in college. It has been proved as completely as anything is ever proved, that this premise is false.

A close student of curriculum improvement, Harold Spears, points out that the subject curriculum is firmly entrenched in the minds of the public, the teacher-training institutions, and the teachers themselves.[85] In a brief but clear manner he indicates the limitations of this pattern: The field of knowledge is broken down into subject fields, organized into innumerable sections on a semester basis with five-hour periods a week; subjects are bodies of content to be mastered; these are arranged in vertical compartments with little relationship one to another; fields are organized by departments for specialization, each with its sequence of subjects; and any change is more readily accepted if it is added to or fits into an already existing subject department.

Alberty, in a recent indictment of the high school, charges that one of the major reasons for lag in curriculum development is the complacency of the secondary-school teachers. He maintains:

> Most teachers are products of the academic tradition which holds that the cultural heritage transmitted in the form of textbooks to be studied and mastered will transfer readily to life situations. They have been taught this

82. Robert M. Hutchins, "One World or None." A lecture delivered at Town Hall, San Francisco, California, November 20, 1951, p. 4. Mimeographed.

83. Baker Brownell, *The College and the Community* (New York: Harper & Brothers, 1952).

84. Paul B. Diederick, "The Abolition of Subject Requirements for Admission to College," *School Review,* 57:366, 1949.

85. For a more detailed analysis see Harold Spears, *The High School for Today* (New York: American Book Company, 1950), pp. 58–61.

in college, and their meager professional training has done little to change their beliefs. All through college they are subjected to logically organized systems of knowledge taught by subject-matter specialists. For the student, academic success was defined as mastery of these materials.

On the whole, the teacher has found that the high school in which he teaches is congenial to the perpetuation of the same values which he learned to cherish in college. When he enters the classroom, he finds a fixed course of study, perhaps prescribing the ground to be covered each semester, and a textbook containing the subject matter to be taught. It is easy to transfer his college experience to this new situation. He cannot be blamed for doing so. Gradually he develops a deep sense of security through teaching the same cut-and-dried materials year after year. The students don't object. The community is satisfied. Why should he change? In such a climate it is easy to be complacent and self-satisfied, and even to build up barriers to prevent change.[86]

Allison Davis' analysis of intelligence tests disclosed that a large proportion of the items in each of the tests "discriminated" between the children from the highest and lowest socio-economic levels. Furthermore, the study reveals that in making the linguistic factor the primary basis for judging mental capacity "the test makers have chosen one of the poorest indicators of basic differences in problem-solving capacity." This linguistic limitation is one example of the fact, according to Davis, that our educational system is based upon a middle-class culture, developed and taught by middle-class teachers, and is slanted toward middle-class values. This restriction is prejudicial toward those who have not achieved this socio-economic level and furthermore does not provide an adequate range and variety of learning experiences of the problem-solving type.

> The present curricula are stereotyped and arbitrary selections from a narrow area of middle-class culture. Academic culture is one of the most conservative and ritualized aspects of human culture. Its formalization, its lack of functional connection with the daily problems of life, has given a bloodless, fossilized character to the classroom which all of us recognize. For over a generation, no basically new type of mental problems have been added to intelligence tests. For untold generations, we have been unable to think of anything to put into the curriculum which will be more helpful in guiding the basic mental development of children than vocabulary-building, reading, spelling, and routine arithmetical memorizing.[87]

> . . . Most of our efforts to revise the curricula of the public schools have been superficial. To make the schools a place where children may learn to analyze facts, to reason from them, to develop insight and inventiveness, we

---

86. Harold Alberty, *Reorganizing the High School Curriculum* (New York: The Macmillan Company, 1947), pp. 13–14.
87. Allison Davis, *Social Class Influences upon Learning,* Inglis Lecture (Cambridge, Mass.: Harvard University Press, 1948), pp. 87–98.

need far more than a systematic method for teaching words or numbers. Those attempts, moreover, which start with sweeping generalizations about reality or community experiences, and other such goals, all start at the wrong end of the learning sequence.

We need to start with simple situations, drawn from the daily life of the pupil. As yet, we do not know what these situations are. We do not know how to use them to guide the drawing of inferences, the processes of reasoning. All we know is that they must be very explicit and short sequences of acts, so that the learner may actually infer the relationship between specific events. The situations must also be chosen from the common life of all the pupils, so that the problems will motivate all social classes. Finally, these curriculum experiences must be intensive, not vague and general; they must be at the molecular level of analysis, so that the child may carry a problem through all the detailed steps to the solution. Yet they will be simple and realistic problems.[88]

Many other criticisms have been made of the subject approach. In the minds of many, the subject approach is unrealistic in that it is based on an organization of material that is unrelated to the use to which the learning is to be put. It sets up the achievement of factual information and knowledge as goals within themselves and evaluates the achievement in the same manner. It leaves to pupils the bringing together of the materials into meaningful patterns. Others have contended that such a composite of unrelated subjects for twelve years of a child's life leaves him frustrated about the things which concern him most and about the institution where he has spent twelve years of his life. No sequence of desirable learning seems to emerge, and teachers are woefully deficient in considering the relationships existing among the subjects they teach. They tend to look at narrow divisions and evaluate pupils in relation to success with their particular divisions of work. They know little about the effect of the materials they teach upon the total development of the child.

Opinion and facts alike substantiate the position that the curriculum of the secondary school is badly in need of careful study. When youth leave school in large numbers before graduation, when they fail of promotion, when they show little significant achievement in the work of the school or in the application of their learnings to life problems, and when they evaluate the work of the secondary school as having doubtful value in their own growth and development, only the conceited or complacent educator can ignore such warnings. Add to these the opinions of adults working with the school, and the barrage of factual information and opinion is enough to shake our confidence in the success of the secondary school.

Surely the secondary school exists as an institution to make learning profitable to youth. If this assumption cannot be accepted, then youth should be turned loose to educate themselves. If learning is therefore to be facilitated,

---

88. *Ibid.*, pp. 99–100.

it must be learning, in the first place, of the type which is related to the needs and problems of youth in the modern world. In the second place, it must be learning which is recognized by youth themselves as having purpose and validity in their own experience. And, in the third place, it must be organized and taught in such a way as to achieve this purpose of relationship and meaning. Finally, it must be taught by those who understand and who are willing to guide and counsel youth. The strength of any program of education depends upon the degree of understanding it creates in the people it serves. Let us, then, turn our attention to an examination of recent attempts to meet these criticisms of secondary education and to discover the changes which are being made in curriculum organization.

Chapter Nine

Theories of Secondary
School Education

CURRICULUM CHANGES are based upon the social pressures of any given time tempered by the educational philosophy and psychology of the period. Research produces evidence of the comparative success of educational methods. Theories of the educational process are made from these components. Little in education is clearly demonstrable; thus the theories of secondary education are gained from rational concepts of man and nature and society and the place of education as a process of inducting the young into a culture. There are several theories of education, basic positions from which certain patterns of curriculum organization follow. An analysis of the basic positions with their implications for curriculum construction is the purpose of this chapter.

If one compares the two extreme positions, he finds curricula all the way from closely organized subject-matter-set-out-to-be-learned to the daily organization of emerging interests in the classroom. One position demands that the materials of instruction be taken from subject matter which has been constant over a period of time and has thus come to be accepted without question; the other position requires the selection of life experiences in the here and now; under one position, knowledge is important for what it does to the human mind, a native quality; under the other, knowledge is important because it is needed to behave intelligently. There are major differences between these extremes. As one moves from one position to another, from the older toward the newer, he finds confusion in some instances, but a mixture of practices in all. Evolution in either man or social institutions takes on this characteristic.

In this chapter we shall draw illustrations of the various positions from the separate subject fields. In later chapters we shall point out the way in which these subject fields restrict, and in some cases make impossible, the attainment of the more liberal position described here. The illustrations used here are given to make clearer the differences among the several positions and are not intended to provide any comprehensive survey of practice, either geographically or in terms of the various fields in the high school.

We may describe the three basic positions as follows:

1. There is the position that the individual is a bundle of faculties who achieves adult status by disciplining these faculties with knowledge acquired under the direction of the school. The school deals chiefly with information and skills. This is sometimes called the "intellectualized subject matter" position.

2. There is the position that the individual is born with intellectual, emotional, and social potentialities which are developed by contacts within a given society. The school guides him in his process of adjustment. This is sometimes called the "functional subject matter" position.

3. There is the position that the individual is a biological organism, a unit with his environment. Experience is the basis of development, and each individual creates for himself a personal way of achieving social and organic unity. The school guides his development and improves his environment. Frequently called the "child-centered" approach, it is better described as the experimentalist position.[1]

Position One: Intellectualized Subject Matter

Man is distinct from other animals in nature. He possesses a mind which is capable of taking on ways of living that make him constantly superior to all the rest of nature. Man's superiority comes from the extent of his knowledge and understanding of the world, from which he gets ideas that are turned into meanings of rationality and goodness. This belief implies faith in an absolutism

---

1. The reader may wish to contrast these positions with the ones suggested by Joseph Justman in his *Theories of Secondary Education in the United States* (New York: Columbia University, Teachers College, Bureau of Publications, 1940). The reader should go to this book for a more complete exposition of the philosophy and psychology behind the positions described here.

of values which transcend human experience and which when sensed serve to regulate and extend progress in human development. Life is continuous with the past, and we build upon this inheritance rather than start with the present. Man accumulates values which he transmits and which must be acquired by each succeeding generation. These values are gained from facts, successful past experience, and ideals which have the stamp of constancy and are therefore greatly dignified. There is the necessity for each man to undergo a certain rigor in conditioning himself to the cumulative values of his race and out of them to build a pattern of acceptable behavior.

The criterion of individuality is the difference in minds, and only those of great power can create values; the others serve as receptors. As one's mind is strong, so are his self-discipline and behavior. Much of this depends upon understanding, and therefore the educational program should be concerned with the transmission of the cultural values—knowledges, values, skills—and the development of the mind. The process is an intellectual one. Knowledge and its extension are foremost.

In this scheme, society is important. While each person is an individual with a "divine spark" moving toward universal greatness, he is a member of a social group. Members of the group may be entirely dependent upon one another for the forging and sustenance of human values. The individual is always the end, and society is a means of achieving individual greatness. Democracy is a collection of capable individuals, and the more intellectually capable the group, the more democratic. As a form of societal living it offers opportunities for individuals to develop according to their capacities. Equality is only a political term; it cannot have biological significance. The school must constantly renew democracy by the education of intellectually endowed youth. It must develop the potentialities of its young, as democracy will rise no higher than the sum total of the ethical and social actions of its constituent members. Education must extend the total number of people who live individual lives that satisfy the criterion of goodness. Liberty is the expression of a disciplined intellect operating with a social consciousness.

The educational process is concerned with directing the individual toward a comprehension and acceptance of the commonly approved manner of living. Education is designed to serve man first and society secondarily, but society supports it because it serves the ends which the majority of those in society approve. Education has two functions: first, to improve the level of living of the masses; second, to develop to its maximum the intellectual capacity of its potential leaders.

Secondary education under this position likewise has two major functions: first, to continue to build upon and intellectualize the accomplishments of the elementary school; second, to differentiate its work on the basis of the abilities of the learner. This function of differentiation has repeatedly appeared in statements of the functions of secondary education. Intellectual ability is the one unchangeable criterion of differentiation. Differentiation means two things. It means, first, variation in method—for the more capable, more abstract material; for the less capable, more concrete material. It means, second, variation in content—for the more capable, more intellectual materials and principles which call for individual reasoning; for the less capable, more indoctrination and emotionalization, and therefore materials which are easier to understand, more definite, and which can be fixed by repetition.

This fundamental position is taken by Mortimer Smith when, in *And Madly Teach*, he maintains that the schools are failing to achieve the real purposes of true education. The purpose he sees is

> To use two terms currently held in great contempt, I think the task of the schools is chiefly intellectual and moral in nature: it must deal with ideas and it must form ideals. In the lower grades the primary task is to impart basic skills and elementary factual background, the three R's; but in the high school—and this is vitally important where the aim is education of the masses, most of whom will never have any further formal education—it is imperative that young people not only be trained in the utilitarian skills of mathematics, practical science, and languages, but that they learn about what we might call the spiritual history of mankind.
>
> The current emphasis on "citizenship training" in the schools is a sound idea only if teachers realize that what some of them contemptuously call the dead past is the chief clue to how we became political animals. I would agree with Sir Richard Livingstone when he says that the two subjects most important in the secondary school are literature and history, "literature, where all the visions of men are recorded; and history, where, behind the confusion of unceasing movement, the human spirit can be discerned weaving, painfully and uncertainly, a coherent design."[2]

The method under the first position is one of dealing with specific items of value, carefully and systematically organized under convenient and accepted subject-matter categories of basic information. Emphasis is upon the intellectual development of meanings. The individual gets these meanings from daily living, but the process can be facilitated and controlled by selecting the proper environment for youth and by controlling it in such a way that youth will learn the things which society approves. There is intellectual growth in dealing with such carefully selected materials, which spreads to other situations. The more meaning there is in the materials chosen for study, the greater is the expected spread. The problem of choosing curriculum materials becomes one of selecting wisely the intellectual materials, and these are not related to time or place; hence, the question of the modernity of the curriculum is pointless.

---

2. Mortimer Smith, *And Madly Teach* (Chicago: Henry Regnery Company, 1949), p. 10.

Illustrations of Position One

THE ST. JOHN'S PROGRAM.   In 1937 St. John's College in Maryland restored the "traditional program of Classics and Liberal Arts unique in American colleges today" which had been in effect in that institution during the latter part of the nineteenth century. The curriculum of this institution has received wide discussion in recent years, largely because of the publicity given to the ideas behind it as expressed by the chairman of the Board of Visitors and Governors of the College, Chancellor Robert Maynard Hutchins of the University of Chicago. His ideas are fundamentally those of position one, with his own personal variations, and St. John's was founded and reorganized upon this basis.

St. John's is a four-year institution, receiving youth at the completion of their sophomore year in high school. The curriculum is divided into four thirty-week sessions. The college catalogue indicates that the subject matter of the curriculum is "man and the world," that the medium used to convey this subject is classical books, that the methods are "the liberal arts," and that the end of the teaching is "insight, understanding, and good intellectual and moral habits which provide the basis for human freedom."

The curriculum is composed of classics to be read by all, beginning with Homer and ending with Veblen, Russell, Freud, and Jung. The first year is devoted largely to the Greeks; the second year is spent on Latin and the Roman and medieval periods; the third year is given over to books originally written in Romance languages and to some books written in English; during the fourth year the student begins his study of German authors, concentrating on the nineteenth and twentieth centuries.

The reward for pursuing this course for four thirty-week sessions is the Bachelor of Arts degree which, St. John's claims, signifies competence in the modern equivalent of the seven liberal arts and sciences—grammar, rhetoric, logic, arithmetic, geometry, music, and astronomy.

The actual teaching is done by five sharply distinguished kinds of teaching techniques—seminar, formal lecture, language tutorial, mathematics tutorial, and laboratory. The outline of the language tutorials will illustrate the nature of the work.

At the meeting of the National Association of Secondary School Principals in Atlantic City in February, 1938, Robert M. Hutchins himself suggested the broad outlines of this program for general education, which he defined as the last two years of high school and the first two years of college:

> I do not hold that general education should be limited to the classics of Greece and Rome. I do not believe that it is possible to insist that all students who should have a general education must study Greek and Latin. I do hold that tradition is important in education—that its primary purpose, indeed,

LANGUAGE TUTORIALS DURING 1949–50

| Assigned Exercises | *Clock-Hours of Classroom Work* | | | |
	First Year (Greek)	*Second Year* (Greek)	*Third Year* (German)	*Fourth Year* (French)
Memorizing Paradigms Selections	60 hours Grammar	24 hours Grammar	40 hours Grammar	30 hours Grammar
Translation and Analysis of Texts	62 hours St. John's Gospel Plato's Meno	80 hours St. Mark's Gospel Epistle to the Galatians First Epistle to the Corinthians, Chapts. I–XIII Aristotle's Metaphysics, Bk. XII Plato's Republic, Bk. VII	64 hours Lessing Herder Schiller Goethe Hoelderlin	70 hours Corneille Racine Moliere LaFontaine Prévost Balzac Stendhal Flaubert Proust Baudelaire Valéry
Formal Logic Treatises	14 hours Logic, translation from Aristotle's Categories and Analytics			9 hours Boole's Laws of Thought
Practice in Analytical Commentary	8 hours Enthymenic analysis of Greek epigrams Translation from selections of Aristotle's Physics	40 hours Plato's Cratylus Euripides' Hippolytus	40 hours Kant	26 hours Pascal Rousseau
Total	144 hours	144 hours	144 hours	135 hours[3]

3. *St. John's College in Annapolis,* catalogue for 1950, p. 48.

is to help the student understand the intellectual tradition in which he lives. I do not see how he can reach this understanding unless he understands the great books of the Western World, beginning with Homer and coming down to our own day. If anybody can suggest a better method of accomplishing the purpose, I shall gladly embrace him and it.

Nor do I hold that the spirit, the philosophy, the technology, or the theology of the Middle Ages is important in general education. I have no desire to return to this period any more than I wish to revert to antiquity. Some books written in the Middle Ages seem to me of some consequence to mankind. Most Ph.D.'s have never heard of them. I should like to have all students read some of them. Moreover, medieval scholars did have one insight—they saw that in order to read books you had to know how to do it. They developed the techniques of grammar, rhetoric, and logic as methods of reading, understanding, and talking about things intelligently and intelligibly. . . . I do say that we must try to do for our own students what the seven liberal arts did for the medieval youth. . . . Most of the great books of the Western World were written for laymen. Many of them were written for very young laymen. Nothing reveals as clearly the indolence and inertia into which we have fallen as the steady decline in the number of these books read by students and the steady elimination of instruction of the disciplines through which they may be understood. All of this has gone on in the sacred name of liberalizing the curriculum. . . . The great works in natural science and the great experiments must be a part and an important part of general education. . . . I suggest, however, that we employ this curriculum for students who can be taught to read and that we continue our efforts to discover methods of teaching the rest of the youthful population how to do it.[4]

This curriculum proposed by Hutchins is clearly a reading program designed to develop intellectual power among youth to meet the problems of the present world. He does not contend that the ideas in these books are ends in themselves but that they are instruments for providing youth with a general education. He believes that the purpose of education is to develop intellectual power and an acquaintance with intellectual tradition. To do this he wants logic, reading, and analysis. These are his methods.

LATIN, SOUTH DAKOTA. In 1934 the State of South Dakota issued a state course of study in Latin which held that the first aim of Latin teaching in the secondary school is the ability to read and understand Latin, an end to be gained from the study of the subject itself. If one achieved this aim he would, they said, gain an increased understanding of the English language and of foreign languages; acquire historical and cultural background and a capacity for literary appreciation; and develop correct mental habits and right attitudes toward social situations. He would also obtain "ennobling incentives"

---

4. Robert M. Hutchins, "The Organization and Subject Matter of General Education," *Proceedings of Twenty-second Annual Meeting* (Department Secondary School Principals, *Bulletin* No. 22; Washington: National Education Association, 1938), 73:6–14.

from a closer acquaintance with some of the great personalities of Roman history—Caesar, Virgil, and Cicero; a feeling of respect for the past and increased capacity for appreciating the present; and "the satisfaction derived from having accomplished well a piece of strenuous intellectual work and consequent effect upon the character."[5] This course of study outlined the work for eight semesters of Latin, as well as suggesting materials for German, French, and Spanish. The course proposed words for work in derivation, the various forms to be taught, the essentials of syntax and Latin readings, some supplementary readings in English, and in the later years some material for metrical reading, with lines to be memorized from Virgil.

SCIENCE, NEW MEXICO. The New Mexico State Board of Education set up tentative guides for high-school teaching in 1946 in the field of science. The goals are formally stated, and then the courses are detailed in outline form. For instance, the following tenth-grade biology course lists three major areas to be studied and the specific topics within the course, some of which are listed below:

I. Characteristics of life
   A. All living matter is protoplasm.
      1. Physical and chemical properties
      2. Functions of protoplasm
   B. All living matter is organized into units of structure and function: cells. Study the function and structure of cells.

II. Struggle to maintain life
   A. The Environment
      1. Composition of air, light, heat, earth
   B. Natural Balance of Nature
      1. Types; causes of disturbance, control of nature
   C. Adaptations: Protoplasmic behavior
      1. Planned and unplanned

III. Classification of life forms
   A. Plant kingdom
   B. Animal kingdom[6]

Position Two: Functional Subject Matter

Man and society are in a constant process of irregular and indeterminable evolution. Each person is born with a nervous system which operates to aid him

5. State of South Dakota, Department of Public Instruction, *Foreign Languages for Secondary Schools* (Course of Study *Bulletin* No. 13; Pierre, S. D., 1934), pp. 30–31.
6. New Mexico State Board of Education, *Science: Tentative Guide for High School Teachers* (*Bulletin* No. 5; Santa Fe, N.M., 1946), pp. 9–23.

in adjusting to life situations, and in the course of adjustment, mind forms. People differ in their adjustive capacity, but each possesses unknown potentialities; and in adjustment, education plays a primary role. In the process of evolution man developed society, which has become one of the ends of human living. He uses society as a storehouse of ideas, in the pursuit of happiness, and as the basis of a means of progress—social evolution. Organically man has changed little; socially he has developed by leaps and bounds. Human values are a product of social adjustment and are not values which are set up outside continuous experience. Man has learned that certain things work better than others, and therefore he places value upon them. These learnings are transmitted to future generations and become major materials of education.

Democracy must make possible a high type of individual adjustment, but it must also provide for constant improvement of the social organism. Man's primary job is one of adjustment, and to achieve this he studies the problems and issues of the present society in which he lives, into which he assimilates the value of the past. Individualism is to be encouraged up to the point that it tends to break down the social unity and the welfare of the larger social group. The measure of democracy is the degree to which *all* individuals in the group are sharing and developing sastifactorily. Mutual helpfulness is a key concept. Individual goodness is measured by sociability and intellectuality. Progress takes place when people face an issue, adjust to it, and then count the gains. Complete individualism is antithetical to democratic living.

There are really two types of inheritance—biological and social—which serve to change the organic nature of individuals. Human behavior, however, is fashioned out of experience, and adaptability is the result of learning, not of natural development. When one learns to control behavior, he has created a mind, and this ability of mind to control behavior is general intelligence.

Man achieves his greatest development through guided learning, the natural way being wasteful. Systematic learning is best, and the conventional school subjects have stood the test of continued human experience. They are logical, systematic, and well organized and therefore should possess great learning values. Science can help in the determination of the materials of instruction by showing how they may be adjusted to the learner and by making analyses of the needs of society.

Education is for everybody and is not to be dispensed in terms of the individual's "native capacity," nor is it to be compartmentalized in terms of emotional, intellectual, or social development. The chief function of education is to improve the adjustment of the individual to the world in which he lives. Education is necessary from the standpoint of society, and its function is to make possible the kind of society which becomes a happy pursuit of living. Democracy must, therefore, maintain a universal school to impart the learning essential for its own perpetuation. Education does not unfold anything; it provides positively those patterns which are necessary for successful living. The curriculum should be determined by an analysis of what society needs today and by a careful study of the continuous adaptations that man has made and history has recorded.

The school subjects, the materials of instruction, are most educative when they are logically organized, when they require sustained intellectual thought, when they are adjusted to the evolving personality of the learner, and when they are well mastered.[7] The materials chosen are not to have practical values; they hold in solution the learnings which are to be absorbed by the learner and distilled or chemically dissolved into adaptable behavior. It makes the process of teaching easier if one can teach the subject material, measure its acquisition, and trust that the process of assimilation into intelligent behavior is automatic. The curriculum (Morrison makes this contention strongly) is common to all; individual differences are not a curriculum matter but a matter of method; hence his emphasis upon the quantity of learning for individuals rather than upon the difference in type. All electives or individualization beyond this have no place in general education, the major function of secondary education. A modification of this position to allow for some differentiation in types of curriculum materials is proposed by Charles H. Judd.

The subjects themselves are not the most important things, but the learnings which they cause. It is exceedingly important that the proper materials be chosen within the subjects and that these be carefully organized and taught in such a way that they will provide the proper learnings. For instance, in teaching mathematics, one should not be concerned with a mastery of the field of mathematics, but with teaching precise thinking and understanding of quantitative relationships. The subject should be organized into compact units, governed by some central concept, well organized around that concept, and comprehended by the learner. The Morrison units form an excellent illustration of this procedure. Morrison further contends that the types of learning differ (he suggests five types—appreciation, science, the practical-arts type, the language-arts type, and the pure practice type).[8] The skillful pursuit of a plan of pretesting, teaching, practicing, and testing is also to be followed.

Judd advocates a less fixed methodological approach. He feels that learning cannot be so carefully organized as Morrison proposes. There is in his point of view the idea of different qualitative aspects in the higher and lower mental processes.[9] Learning, to him, is more an intricate assimilation and reassimilation than a series of single accretions, as Morrison would hold. In both con-

---

7. For the best development of the methods suited to this position see the works of Henry C. Morrison, especially *The Practice of Teaching in the Secondary School* (Chicago: University of Chicago Press, 1931), and *The Curriculum of the Common School* (Chicago: University of Chicago Press, 1940).
8. Morrison, *The Practice of Teaching in the Secondary School.*
9. Charles H. Judd, *Education as Cultivation of the Higher Mental Processes* (New York: The Macmillan Company, 1936).

cepts, however, the development of intellectual independence is the major purpose of secondary education. Education is to be concerned with using the subjects of instruction to get across learnings which will help each individual to adjust himself effectively to his environment. Learning should be carefully organized, and the learner should put forth sustained effort and concentration in order to develop intellectual power to deal with his problems.

Illustrations of Position Two

Educators have claimed for a long time that a knowledge of literature was essential in the building of personal values which were later operative in good citizenship. Literary masterpieces provided the only place where vicarious experiences, universal in their approach and application, might be found: "Through literature one experiences the past, gropes with suffering humanity, shares the hopes and aspirations of all people, experiences the great emotions through which people and nations have lived."[10] The actual content of the literature itself is not the thing to remember, nor is pure knowledge the big value to be derived from the study of the masterpieces, but literature is to contribute definitely toward providing "enjoyment and enrichment of personality," developing "literary sensibilities through guidance of emotional responses and through training of the imagination," establishing "literary standards," developing "insight into the meaning of life through ethical judgments," and developing "a consciousness of changing social responsibilities."

LANGUAGE ARTS, OREGON. In the area of the language arts, which include the "four related skills or activities: listening, speaking, reading, and writing," the high-school program for the State of Oregon is made up of a series of units. Some latitude is permitted in the order and time devoted to each unit, although the recommended subject matter in literature and composition is expected to be covered during the year period. The units in composition, reading skills, and literature have been designed for each grade in such a way that "they are developmental in scope from year to year."

Grade 9

Unit: 1. The spirit of adventure—literature
2. Developing leadership qualities
3. Developing reading habits—reading skills
4. The command of language—grammar usage
5. Planning and writing paragraphs—composition
6. My family, what do we mean to each other—literature
7. My neighbors, how do they work and live—literature
8. What kind of a person do I want to be—literature

---

10. Commonwealth of Pennsylvania, *Literature for Secondary Schools* (Pennsylvania Curriculum Studies, *Bulletin* No. 97; Harrisburg, Pa., 1935), p. 3,

    9. Special kinds of conversation—composition
10. Entertaining others—composition
11. Opinions and discussion—composition
12. Making reports and announcements—composition
13. Writing social letters and postcards—composition
14. Giving explanations and directions—composition
15. American way of life—literature
16. Enjoying my leisure time—literature

Grade 10

Unit: 1. Traditions of sport—literature
2. Language in the making—reading skills
3. Writing the paragraph—composition
4. Reading skills for getting information
5. Vocational interests—composition
6. Language at work—grammar usage
7. Motion picture appreciation
8. Radio appreciation
9. Letter writing, business letters—composition
10. What men live by—literature
11. Spiritual wealth, the beauty of the earth—literature
12. Courage to see it through—literature
13. Everyday problems in conversation—composition
14. Narrative and descriptive writing—composition
15. The realm of fantasy—literature
16. Human affections as seen in literature

Grade 11

Unit: 1. Speeches for special occasions—composition
2. American panorama—literature
3. American ideals—literature
4. The peoples who make America—literature
5. Our roots in the past—literature
6. The business of living—literature
7. Using words with discrimination—composition
8. Style in the sentence—composition
9. Bookways to information—reading skills
10. Preparation for writing longer compositions
11. Straight thinking—composition
12. Patterns for writing—composition
13. Challenges to thinking—composition
14. Bookways to enjoyment—composition

Grade 12

Unit: 1. Writing for print—composition
2. Reading with discernment—composition

3. Growth and development of language
4. This England—literature
5. The English nation—literature
6. The English way of life—literature
7. English men and women—literature
8. Macbeth—literature
9. And Now Abideth—literature
10. From Grave to Gay—literature
11. Writing the research paper—composition
12. Propaganda—composition
13. Formal discussion—composition
14. Transacting business—composition[11]

SCIENCE, LOS ANGELES.   Position two may also be illustrated in the organization of science materials. There are certain significant principles that need to be mastered, attitudes that should be developed, and above all knowledge to be gained of the world in which youth live. After describing briefly the characteristics of the adolescent, the learning process involved in teaching, and the general objectives for general science, the Curriculum Division of Los Angeles City School District points out the concepts to be developed for the general-science course in the junior high school. Among these concepts are those dealing with "Our Living Environment," such as "all plants and animals have the same basic needs"; "Our Bodies," such as "proper health habits will help secure a healthy body"; and "Our Physical World," such as "the earth's surface is constantly changing."

The eighth-grade course in general science in the junior high school is on the general topic of "Understanding Our Environment" with subdivisions under the same headings as the major concepts listed above. These subdivisions include a number of units, one of which must be chosen in each area. The first two units under this topic are

OUR LIVING ENVIRONMENT

Unit I. What living things are found around our homes?

Suggested Problems [only a few of the many are listed here as illustrations]
A. Who are our friends in the garden?
B. How do insects, spiders, reptiles, birds, and amphibians help us?
C. Who are our enemies in the garden?
D. How do insects harm our gardens?
E. How do snails and slugs harm our gardens?
F. How can we choose lawn grasses?
G. How fast do grasses grow?
H. What care should we give a lawn?

---

11. Oregon State Department of Public Instruction, *A Guide to the Program of Studies in the Secondary Schools of Oregon* (Salem, Ore., 1949), pp. 95–107.

Unit II. What living things are found along the seashore?

Suggested Problems

    A. What living things will we find on a rocky beach?

    B. On a sandy beach? In the deep sea?

    C. What kind of food do sea animals eat?

    D. How could you make a living from the sea?[12]

These units are followed by suggested approaches to the topic, suggested teaching and pupil activities, references, and supplementary materials.

MATHEMATICS, OREGON. The curriculum committee on mathematics in the high schools for the State of Oregon in 1949 recommended that the mathematics course be "a continuous integrated program for all students from grades one through nine" with the election of specialized subjects in the succeeding grades so organized "as to provide for a logical sequence and continuous progression." Their program stresses the importance of "functional competence in mathematics for every individual" for effective living, which should "give pupils intellectual equipment to develop quantitative thinking." The high-school offerings beyond ninth-grade arithmetic are outlined in terms of experiences which every student who elects the subject should have.

For example, in algebra the course is expected to "give experiences of sufficient rigor and continuity for subsequent work in mathematics and science," with the "formula . . . used as a basic topic of study." The experiences which the students in algebra should have are

    I. The acquisition of the basic vocabulary

   II. Learning to translate quantitative statements into language of algebra

  III. Interpreting the solution of equations where they have significance and in using rules of equality and transformation

  IV. Solving general verbal problems using as a means of solution the table, graph, formula, and equation

   V. Understanding of carefully considered concepts and principles which should lead to fundamental skills and techniques in:

    A. The four fundamental operations involving positive and negative numbers, algebraic monomials or simple polynomials, and algebraic fractions (mainly monomial denominators)

    B. Special products and factoring such as squaring a binomial, finding the product of the sum and the difference of two terms, factoring a polynomial containing a common monomial term, factoring trinomials of the form $x^2 + bx + c$, and factoring the difference of two squares

    C. Powers and roots, involving laws of exponents and their use, square roots

---

12. Los Angeles City School District, Curriculum Division, *Tentative Outline: Course of Study for General Science, Junior High School* (Publication No. SC–448, Los Angeles, Calif., 1950). Mimeographed.

of positive numbers, and fundamental operations involving radicals of the monomial type

VI. The study of relationships and of dependence
   A. Interpreting tables of related number pairs
   B. Making graphs based on tables of related number pairs and using graphs in the solution of problems
   C. Using formulas as means of expressing relationship or dependence
   D. Equations involving the solution of equations of the first degree in one unknown, fractional equations, equations of the form $ax^2 = b$, and simple radical equations
   E. Using equations in the study of proportion and of variation[13]

MATHEMATICS, FLORIDA. The Florida State Department of Education maintains that

mathematics presents a mode of thinking by which data may be collected and organized, and conclusions drawn. From the unique nature of these conclusions useful interpretations may be made. Normal life today is dependent upon these interpretations. The immense power of mathematics, as a servant of mankind, and as a permanent part of research, is universally recognized . . . it is indispensable in our living.

The sources of mathematical power which enable one to develop more effectively as an individual and as a citizen in this technological age, and which furnishes him with a basis for acceptable contributions to society, are primarily its basic concepts, principles. procedures, and skills. Therefore, the teaching of mathematics should provide for

I. Understanding and appreciation of
   A. The language and vocabulary of mathematics
   B. The basic concepts and principles of mathematics
   C. The quantitative relationships of daily living

II. A degree of mastery which will assist an individual in feeling adequate and secure

III. Competency in basic skills and in the solution of problems

IV. Experiences through which desirable attitudes of social-mindedness and open-mindedness may be encouraged.

V. Experiences through which appreciation and respect for knowledge and good workmanship may be developed

VI. The creation of an impelling desire for continuous mathematical growth

VII. Training that leads "toward the *process* of thinking rather than toward the *product* of thinking." This will include clear, analytical, and critical thinking.

---

13. Oregon State Department of Public Instruction, *A Guide to the Program of Studies*, pp. 109–120.

VIII. Training for transfer of mathematical values to other fields of human relationships

  IX. Training in the selection of that which has significant and enduring values

The bulletin then describes the basic mathematical concepts (some sixty-one in all) to be taught and "thoroughly understood" at different grade levels between the seventh and the twelfth grades on a suggested grade-placement chart. The method provides for checking constantly on such important factors as

1. Spiral learning through repetition of the basic concepts from grade to grade
2. Placing materials where they have most meaning for pupils
3. A horizontal representation of the gradual unfolding of a concept over a period of six years
4. A vertical representation of the basic content, in outline form, for a single grade
5. A means of relating the content material to the basic concepts.

The balance of the bulletin deals with materials of instruction for each of the six grades, and includes concepts, content and teaching suggestions, and teaching references.

Mathematics, in this state program, continues to be an important subject in the secondary curriculum, but its emphasis, although formally centered, is functional throughout. This is particularly true in the junior-high-school grades where, for example, a unit in Arithmetic In Everyday Use suggests to the teacher that she use practical experiences in teaching mathematical concepts through such means as the following:

I. Services of the post office and the bank in handling money

  A. Savings
    1. Services rendered by the savings department of the bank
      a. The steps necessary in the opening of a savings account
      b. Plan to visit a bank in a group or send a committee. Have the pupils make a list of the things they wish to learn. Include such information as rate of interest paid on savings, rate of interest charged on loans.
    2. Bank books—the purpose and use
    3. Use the compound interest table to show how money grows. Explain the meaning of the expression "interest on interest."

This approach would deal with concepts of money, per cent, decimal fractions, time, graphs, denominate numbers, and exact numbers.

In the twelfth grade a similar illustrative approach to problems of money, per cent, and percentage, as well as fractions and mixed numbers, deals with "Consumer Credit," and includes such teaching suggestions as

 I. Discuss the distinction between consumer credit and commercial credit.

II. Installment buying—extension from previous grades

    A. Derive average principal formula for finding rate;

$$r = \frac{24I}{N(F+L)}$$

    in which

    I = amount of interest on charges

    N = number of payments

    F = principal owed the first month of the contract

    L = principal owed the last month of the contract

    B. Use the formula in the solution of problems within the interest and experience of pupils.

    (suggests the process which the students would follow)

III. Loans from finance companies

    (suggests steps used in determining costs)

IV. Comparative study of cost of small loans from banks and finance companies

V. Credit unions

VI. Discuss cost of loans from "loan sharks"—outlaw money lenders.[14]

PHYSICAL EDUCATION, SAN DIEGO.   Proponents of physical education recognize that there is educational value in a sequence of activities "involving basic movements such as running, jumping, throwing, kicking . . . and includes a wide variety of relays, games, rhythms, stunts, tumbling, calisthenics, sports, and other activities." The Physical Education Advisory Committee of San Diego, California, from such a viewpoint, holds that the "outcomes of the physical education program can be expressed in terms of the student's organic development, his neuro-muscular development, and his social and emotional development." In their recent guidebook they have suggested an activity schedule for the year for each grade level. Specific objectives, safety precautions, equipment, instructional content, culminating activities, evaluation techniques, teaching aids, and a bibliography are suggested for each activity. As an illustration, touch football is taught for three or four weeks at all grade levels. The objectives include teaching "the skills of the game, proper attitudes and appreciations, and knowledges and understandings." Instruction starts with the rules of the game accompanying the instruction of skills, and officiating is part of the instructional program. The skills include passing and receiving the ball, running, defensive and offensive tactics, punting, and kicking off. Each year the culminating activity would be a "round-robin tournament within a class," elimination tournament, or an "all-star" game at the end of the season.[15]

---

14. Florida State Department of Education, *Functional Mathematics in the Secondary Schools* (*Bulletin* No. 36, Tallahassee, Fla., 1950), pp. 1–37.

15. San Diego City Schools, *A Guidebook for Boy's Physical Education in the Secondary Schools* (San Diego, Calif., 1951), pp. 1–122.

SOCIAL STUDIES, SAN DIEGO. The Social Studies Steering Committee of the San Diego City Schools, California, after listing the understandings, values, attitudes, appreciations, and skills for each grade in the senior-high-school social studies, outlines the work for each year as follows:

Grade 10—World History

1. What civilizations in the Near East achieved
2. What the Greeks contributed to the beginnings of democratic ideals
3. How Rome organized and ruled the ancient world
4. How the people of Europe met the problems of living during the Middle Ages
5. How the Renaissance brought renewed interest to art, literature, science and religion
6. How nations were formed and later developed into empires
7. What the nations achieved as a result of political and economic revolutions
8. How emphasis is being placed on international cooperation in the world today

Grade 11—United States History

1. How the United States became an independent nation
2. How the United States established a stable government
3. How nationalism unified the people of the United States
4. How sectionalism divided the nation
5. How our present-day political party system evolved
6. How economic changes have influenced the development of the United States
7. How the United States has reached its place in world affairs
8. How the American people are progressing toward equality of opportunity for all

Grade 12—Problems of Citizenship

1. How the people of San Diego cooperate to solve problems of community living
2. How the people of California cooperate to solve state-wide problems
3. How the people of the United States cooperate to solve our national problems
4. How the nations are seeking solutions to world problems
5. How shall I prepare to meet personal economic problems?
6. How shall I prepare for a vocation?
7. How shall I prepare to get along with others?
8. How shall I prepare to meet the problems of home and family life?[16]

Position Three: The Experimentalist Position

There must be supreme respect for every individual, who is different from every other individual. Each person is an end in himself; life cannot be con-

16. San Diego City Schools, *Curriculum Guide, the Secondary Program* (San Diego, Calif., 1950), pp. 203–231.

sidered in the mass. "If a general principle be demanded, the experimentalist says that is good which promotes the happiness and growth of individuals and does not interfere with the happiness and growth of other individuals."[17]

Society is a means of nourishing the individual and in turn is a group of these interacting individuals nourishing one another. Man's chief job is to create conditions which will contribute to his own greatest happiness. Man lives by facing and solving problems. Life is a series of issues, a series of experiments. Man constantly seeks to keep life on a level of equilibrium, and when this balance is disturbed he seeks to restore it. Democracy is a way of life in which the people through the government seek to express their will. If and when the state ceases to represent their desires the people revoke its dictates, and society sets up an alternative way of living.[18] Democracy, however, in its ultimate form is a way which each individual fashions for his own life so that it promotes his own greatest development and happiness and does no harm to others. "Individuality is an achievement," aided by intelligence and social intercourse.

The basis of human development is experience, the personal experience of each individual through which he learns to refashion his own program of activities. Experiences are never common to people. Each individual tests his own wishes against the possibilities of achieving them and adjudges society good or bad in terms of its assistance in helping him to achieve these desires. Progress is the accumulation of these judgments applied to social change. When great social imbalance occurs, there is a frustrating effect upon the individual; society then disturbs him rather than facilitates his adjustment.

> High regard for the individual is probably the most distinctive and pervasive characteristic of democratic living. In democracies, personalities are held to be precious, unique, and not capable of duplication. The optimum development of each individual, irrespective of birth, economic status, race, creed, or color, is to be encouraged and nurtured both because of the enhanced enjoyment of individual living which comes through full development of distinctive qualities and because of contributions which such distinctive qualities make to the common life.[19]

William H. Kilpatrick and others holding principally to this position have

---

17. J. L. Childs, *Education and the Philosophy of Experimentalism* (New York: Appleton-Century-Crofts, Inc., 1931), p. 227.

18. See George S. Counts, *The Prospects of American Democracy* (New York: John Day Company, Inc., 1938), especially Chap. 8.

19. Commission on Secondary School Curriculum, Progressive Education Association, *Science in General Education* (New York: Appleton-Century-Crofts, Inc., 1936), p. 36. By permission of the publisher. See also J. Paul Leonard, "Democratic Basis of Individual Differences" in *Pupils Are People*. A Report of the Committee on Individual Differences, National Council of Teachers of English (New York: Appleton-Century-Crofts, Inc., 1941), Chap. 1; and Educational Policies Commission, *The Purposes of Education in American Democracy* (Washington: National Education Association, 1938).

stressed the fact that our present culture is unbalanced, a condition brought about largely by the unevenness of change in the various social forces. In resources there has been little change in abundance, in organic inheritance there has been no change observable, in institutions there have been few changes, in our methods of distribution changes have been slow, but in our methods of production and processing the changes have been phenomenal. We need urgently to seek balance again, and this means experimental living for society and for individuals. This requires cooperative living rather than again resorting to what we commonly call "rugged individualism."

Cooperative living must not be taken to mean that we must eradicate individuality, for this is a supreme end; but there is a vast difference between the development of individuality and rugged individualism. Democracy as a form of government must continue to provide a satisfactory way of life, or individuals will turn to another form. We must eradicate the present conditions which depress individuals, for the power of a condition in changing a government is greater than the power of an ideal. Vigilance in adhering to the democratic faith and to the methods of peaceful change must be maintained. Democracy is not as good as it should be, but it is not a meek and palliative middle-of-the-road position. It is as dynamic and positive in its concept as any other social or political system. If it should be considered a weak middle position,

> it would become a deceptive haven for the timid and the vacillating, while the bolder spirits would enroll under banners representing positive and challenging philosophies and programs. It [democracy] is another way—unique, radical, revolutionary—the most adventurous way that man has even taken— a way beset with difficulties and demanding the fullest possible development of the powers of the race.[20]

Man is unique, both as a species and as a personality. He is constantly reacting with his environment; it changes him and he changes it. The principal drives of human life are biological, not social. Human behavior is purposive, and the drives to act are the drives to sustain life and to reduce the tensions which arise from an unbalanced environment. Experience is the basis of learning, and man has the power to analyze experience, to associate activities, and from them to predict consequences. Thus he can refashion his life intelligently; he is not a blind creature of circumstances or habit, but is a constantly creating, designing organism. Intelligence is successful adjustment, and personality is the character of the organism at any time.

In his actions man expresses attempts to satisfy needs which are imposed upon him by society and by his organic nature. Needs are created in the process of living. There are no dualisms; there are only fusing positions with

---

20. Counts, *The Prospects of American Democracy*, p. 7. By permission of the publishers.

extending poles of emphases. Children grow gradually into adolescence and then into adulthood, and education must be appropriate to the needs of the maturing individual. Learning is the process of assimilating experience to improve behavior; it is not the process of becoming familiar with subject matter to fortify or intellectualize the mind. Action starts not from artificial motivation but from a disturbance in relation to a need or an unsatisfying condition; it assumes purpose in relation to improved living.

The process of education is not carried on separately from the normal activities of daily life; it is an integral process of guiding living in a selected and an unselected environment. The school is the selected environment whose major purposes are

(1) . . . to incline the individual in the direction of significant experiences, and (2) to help him work his way through these experiences and *all others that he is having,* so that he understands them, sees their import or significance, and can use the meanings distilled from them in the direction of his immediate and future living."[21]

Education cannot exist apart from the total life experience, and whatever is introduced into the school as a part of the curriculum or learning process must be germane to the purposes and needs of the learner himself at the definite stage of his growth and development. It follows then that education is a total community enterprise, drawing upon all individuals and institutions; in fact, it is a process which cannot be carried on within the school alone. The school is not a place where academic subjects are learned for future use or for intellectual development, but a laboratory where experiences are guided, experiences which cut across the total expanse of the child's life. This also gives point to the contention that it is a function of the school to engage actively in improving the nature of the society in which the child lives. It has an obligation to analyze the effects of the environment upon the individual and thus has a stake in the improvement of society. The teacher is not an agent of society to do its bidding, but an evaluator and critic, a student of and consultant on social improvement.

As to the method of doing this, two positions are clear. One is that the teacher must acquaint the individual with the social tensions, pointing out to him the result of these depressing situations upon the development of his own personality, and leaving to the individual the decision about what to do and when to do it. The other position is that the teacher and the school must play a direct role in the reconstruction of society as well as teach the individual to act for himself.

---

21. Joseph Justman, *Theories of Secondary Education in the United States* (Contributions to Education, No. 814; New York: Columbia University, Teachers College, 1940), p. 275.

Social criticism of the group culture must itself become part of the culture. The school must begin the process of the intelligent study and criticism of the culture, for adulthood would be too late to start. . . . We then who have regard for the education of either young or old must, from this angle of conflict within our midst, seek a culture which makes a proper education possible. If we are educators in spirit and in truth we cannot escape this obligation. . . . When we in education see that the social-economic system thwarts and hampers us in the pursuit of our highest ethical and educational aims for those under our care, it becomes our duty to join hands with others to change that system to something better.[22]

Experiences, then, are the substance of education, and the teachers must design the curriculum out of the life and activities of youth and the society in which they live, not only with an eye on present adjustment but also with a view to improving the society which will in turn enrich the personality of the individual. The curriculum will be community-wide, and the personnel of the school will be drawn from as large a number of adults as seems wise. The existing needs of youth at any time and place will be the essential guides to the selection of curriculum materials, and youth themselves will furnish the framework of organization and sequence.[23] The scope of the curriculum will be governed by the nature of the life processes themselves, and the organization of learning experiences will be in terms of units of life experience— problems.[24]

The curriculum should be composed of common situations, to a large extent, from which each individual will draw materials which are to him valuable. This is the desirable process of dealing with individual differences. There is over and above this an area of differentiation depending upon the major interests of individuals. Opinion differs over whether these units of life experiences should be taught and organized around categories representative of the conventional subject fields or around new divisions which are more representative of life itself. The details of this matter will be dealt with later in Chapter 11. Guidance is at the heart of the educational process, and the curriculum is to be as inclusive as life itself.

Illustrations of Position Three

As has been pointed out earlier, the illustrations in this chapter are to be chosen only in terms of reorganizations which have been made without break-

---

22. William H. Kilpatrick, "The Social Philosophy of Progesssive Education," *Progressive Education,* 12:290–293, 1935.
23. See *Reorganizing Secondary Education,* Chap. 4, and Caroline Zachry, *Emotion and Conduct in Adolescence* (New York: Appleton-Century-Crofts, Inc., 1940).
24. See Harold Rugg (ed.), *Democracy and the Curriculum* (New York: Appleton-Century-Crofts, Inc., 1939), especially chapters by Caswell, Hanna, and Leonard.

ing down the barriers existing between the recognized subjects. This method makes it difficult to illustrate position three for several reasons. First, the nature of education under this position dictates that any barriers which do not enhance the organization of learning must be destroyed; since subject lines are ordinarily artificial, they do not belong in this scheme of education. For this reason, the best illustrations of this position are to be found in those situations where subject lines are disregarded. Second, the position is new in practice in the secondary field. Unlimited illustrations can be drawn from the elementary field. Third, the changes made in the subject fields which are in the direction of this position are found more frequently in classroom methods than in curriculum organizations. The illustrations cited here are not true examples of the theory of this third position, then, but are in that general direction only.

SCIENCE, GLENCOE. The teachers in Glencoe, Illinois, have been trying for several years to work out experiences which can be used in the classroom to "provide for continuous self-realization of each individual through opportunities to form those interests, attitudes, and habits which will make for him a pattern of useful living," to make students "aware of economic, social and governmental problems," and to help them "realize and appreciate the vast resources of their own country and to find the true meaning of conservation." In order to carry out these aims, the interests of youth are tapped and their environment is explored. The teachers believe that the "approach taken or the methods used are relatively unimportant, provided the problems raised and the materials used have life meaning and significance for the pupils."

Some of the suggestions made, not as a course of study but as an indication to all teachers of the types of experiences which "seem fruitful and desirable," may help to illustrate the nature of the work of the Glencoe teachers.[25] In science, suggestions like the following are made:

> *Science*—phases of science which children see as affecting their lives offer vital approaches to everyday problems. Children of this age are inventors and discoverers in the making. Their flood of natural curiosity must be kept alive and awake. The phase that is used is of little moment, if only it allows children to raise questions which are real to them and to find answers to their questions. It would be impossible to cover this field in a lifetime of study but the following may hold possibilities:
> 1. The evolution of the clothes we wear, from raw materials to our own garments
> 2. The progress and development in preserving and safeguarding the food we eat
> 3. The growth of preventive medicine from the days of earliest superstitions
> 4. The advance in the control of pests which have made our lives miserable
> 5. A continual opportunity to live in and investigate the out-of-door world

---

25. Glencoe Public Schools, *A Guide for Curriculum Planning* (Glencoe, Ill., 1938).

6. Opportunities to raise their own problems and to experiment with questions that have not yet been answered

The last two years of the elementary school are ordinarily considered to be of the secondary-school period, and hence we can illustrate from it. In Glencoe twelve principles of science have been proposed, around which are grouped activities and sources of help. There is no segregation of these by grade; hence the reader must assume that some of these are dealt with in the seventh and eighth grades, even though many of them are considered in the first six grades. This fact is relatively unimportant, however, as the purpose in citing the materials is to suggest the plan of organization used to implement a philosophy. The twelve principles are

1. All life comes from life and produces its own kind of living organism.
2. Certain elements are essential to the life of an organism.
3. There is great variation in the size, structure, and habits of living things.
4. Nature tends to establish an equilibrium.
5. Some forms of animal life have developed a pattern of socialized living.
6. Environment modifies life; life modifies the environment.
7. The normal functioning of an organism is dependent upon the physical structure and the co-ordination of its various parts.
8. The earth is one of many bodies moving in space.
9. The earth in its slow formation has undergone many changes.
10. The universe is made up of matter which is constantly subject to physical and chemical changes.
11. The sun is the source of all energy. As man has progressed he has utilized many forms of energy.
12. Man has invented many machines. He has utilized various natural forces to power these machines.[26]

An illustration of the definite suggestions under one of these twelve principles may further help to make clear the types of experience.

Principle: Environment modifies life; life modifies the environment

Suggested Experiences	*Sources of Help*
Observing how life has adapted itself to its environment and has been modified by it	Forest preserve Skokie lagoons project
Observing how the environment has been changed because of the activity of living organisms, as growth of dunes, work of beavers, lakes filled in by man, drainage projects	Field Museum Art Institute Rosenwald Museum

26. *Ibid.,* pp. 82–88.

Suggested Experiences	*Sources of Help*
Studying the means by which higher forms of life have adapted themselves to, and learned to control, their environment	Garfield Park Conservatory Bird sanctuary
Home life of different peoples conditioned by the environment	Wild flower sanctuary
Ways in which plants and animals adapt themselves to environment	Truck farm

Observing preparations for seasonal changes:
   migrations   clothing
   food   shelter
	Department stores

SCIENCE, OHIO STATE UNIVERSITY SCHOOL. An illustration from the science program in the high school of the Ohio State University may further illustrate some of the points in this position. The reader will recognize places where the program represents some compromise of positions.[27] Basic to this curriculum are the ideas that "the school should be the finest possible illustration of democratic living," which is founded upon "respect for human personality," and that the optimum value is the "development of the individual." This concept implies physical development conducive to normal growth, and mental development to plan one's own work and life activities with due consideration for consequences upon others. It implies that human personality evolves "living and working together for common purposes and ends," and that the test of every social and political institution is "the effect which it has upon the individuals who are touched by it." The school attempts to provide for both common and specialized individual needs and recognizes the reciprocal relationship between the individual and the society in which he lives. To achieve these goals the curricular experiences "evolve from continuous student-faculty planning in the light of these significant needs, interests, and problems of young children."

Grades 7, 8, 9: Science experiences are handled in classes other than ones devoted to science.

Grade 10: Devoted to study of the natural environment in terms of the materials or natural resources of the world, especially the United States, their location, abundance, and the means by which they are prepared for use. The main topics dealt with were coal, petroleum, metals, waterways, farm land, lumber, limestone, and similar building materials.

Grade 11: The work was organized around three large study units: (1) the

---

27. A Description of the Curricular Experiences of the University School of the Ohio State University for the School Year of 1939–40: *The Upper School—Grades Seven to Twelve Inclusive*. Mimeographed (Columbus, Ohio: Ohio State University School, 1940).

nature of life, (2) the nature of heredity, (3) a study of human behavior. The first was largely a study of plant life in relation to human existence, the second a study of mechanics, theories of inheritance with use of state marriage laws, choosing a mate, Nazi claims regarding Aryans. The third unit was strongly psychological in content and was based upon questions regarding human behavior which the students gathered themselves. It was aimed at building up self-control in the individual to overcome the feeling among many of the pupils that in the world today one individual could do little.

Grade 12:   There were two groups working on science in this grade. One group spent the year studying matters of human biology and then in a smaller group working upon problems in chemistry or in astronomy. The work was organized around such problems as: What food is necessary for good health? How should one eat to get a sufficient supply of vitamins and calories? There was nothing novel about the work in chemistry or astronomy, it being a reversion to organized subject content in the fields. The other group spent a year specializing in an organized course in chemistry.

MATHEMATICS, OHIO STATE UNIVERSITY SCHOOL.   One additional illustration may be taken from this school in the field of mathematics in the seventh grade. The work for this year is described by the teacher, Mr. Ramseyer, as follows:

At the beginning of the school year the teaching staff for the seventh grade agreed that an attempt should be made to develop a more intimate relationship between mathematics and the other activities which the pupils experience. With this in mind the mathematics teacher was given the privilege of attending the core to determine in what ways a mutual working relationship might be accomplished. An attempt was made to discover (1) what mathematics would aid in the solution of the larger problem of the core, (2) in this study, what interests of mathematical character were aroused, and (3) what needs of the seventh grade students could well be served through experiences largely mathematical in character and hence serving as a basis for the origin of activities in the mathematics laboratory.

In answer to the first query it was found:

As the pupils were attempting to make their room more livable it became necessary to carry out such activities as the following:

1. Measure the dimensions of the room and the furnishings therein.
2. Make a scale drawing and by means of it plan the spacing and arranging of furnishings.
3. Determine the amount and cost of draperies.
4. Plan the construction of a bookcase, measuring to a degree of accuracy sufficient to obtain a good fit.

In connection with a study of diets it became necessary to

1. Develop skill in handling per cents, decimals, and metric units of measure.
2. Develop skill in the handling of balances and in changing the units of measure from one denomination to another.
3. Collect data and keep accurate records of it.
4. Organize data in some intelligent symbolism for use in solving problems and reporting progress in experiments. (In this case it was the building of graphs to show the trend of weight changes brought about in rats through the feeding of different diets.)

In connection with a class party the following mathematical activities were used as aids:

1. Determining the amount of food needed in feeding forty people.
2. Determining the cost of each item of food as well as the total cost. Food prices were compared to determine the most economical ways of buying.
3. Division of the cost among the pupils.
4. Keeping accurate records and paying the bills.

Problems of mathematical character which were raised through core experiences but taken to the mathematics laboratory (in a special period) for special consideration included:

1. Difference in precision in measurement when used for different purposes.
2. Why the scientist uses the metric system of measurement instead of the English system.
3. How measurement systems originate.
4. The development of skill in the handling of fractions, per cents, decimals, metric units of measure.
5. How to measure very tiny objects, even those which cannot be seen with the naked eye.
6. How to measure very large amounts even to those distances which cannot be traversed.
7. Study of time, the units of measure involved, the origin of these units, time belts, and time schedules.
8. Study of electrical units of measure.

Those needs of the students which could well be served through experiences largely mathematical in nature included:

1. Study of individual differences of human characters by application of units of measurement.
2. Study of trends in school citizen problems such as tardiness, attendance, etc.
3. Study and record of personal allowances.
4. Study and record of time available and an attempt to budget it to the best personal use.
5. Personal satisfaction through improvement in skills thought to be important.

This school is making an attempt to reorganize its materials of instruction for youth around the basic concepts of position three. Progress is not complete, of course, and there are characteristics which break over into other ideas, but basic changes are being made which are very definitely in harmony with this position.

MATHEMATICS, REPORT OF MEEK AND ZECHIEL.   An interesting contrast to the ordinary mathematics course may be found in the work of a class reported by Meek and Zechiel.[28] This teaching was based upon the assumption that the belief

> that a unit of work is functional because it deals with an adult activity or with possibly a future activity of the student is a false one. Many units in mathematics, such as banking, are taught in order to teach percentage, interest, investments, savings, and the like. This is reversing the proper order. To be functional an immediate purpose must be served, not a remote, unrecognized and unaccepted purpose. In other words functional teaching is purposeful teaching in such situations that skill or concept is learned for an immediate purpose and then used immediately.

On the basis of this belief a unit on insurance was taught in the seventh grade. The question arose whether youth their age might use insurance, since otherwise insurance was an adult problem to them. The discussion centered upon lost books because many of the pupils had been compelled by their parents to pay for their lost books out of their weekly allowance. It was obvious that the price of a sizable book from a weekly allowance left little for anything else for several weeks. The group decided to organize an insurance company of its own to insure its books. Agents were consulted to see how an insurance company works, what insurance costs, how claims are adjusted, how payments are made by policyholders and by the company, how policies are made, and so on. Officers were appointed for the company, premiums were calculated, claims were made, and when a book was lost, the rest of the school was brought into the picture by the use of the established offices in the search for it. As money accumulated, the problems of money and banking and investment appeared, and the postal savings was finally decided upon as a place to put the money. When one of the pupils moved out of town, the problem of refunding premiums arose.

The members of this group stayed together for three years and continued for that length of time their project of insuring their books. This is another indication of values to be arrived at through some continuity in a program. Adequate learning will never be secured by a series of separately taught, organized, and administered units or unrelated learning experience.

THE CORE CURRICULUM, MIDWOOD SCHOOL, NEW YORK.   In 1944, a com-

---

28. Ruth A. Meek and A. N. Zechiel, "Functional Mathematics Teaching," *Educational Research Bulletin*, 19:479–482, 1940.

mittee appointed by the Association of First Assistants of New York City requested the high-school division to chose carefully the faculty of one of the new high schools with a view to making it an experimental school. The initial experiment was a core curriculum offered to a small group, carefully controlled. The experiment was limited to the ninth year, since the number of qualified teachers was limited. Furthermore, it was the concensus of opinion that the ninth year was the most impressionable period in the pupil's secondary-school life.

Under this experimental program, the pupil remains in the experience curriculum for one year with the same teacher. The class meets with this one teacher for four periods, plus a home room period each day. The block is divided into two long double-period sessions. Between these two sessions and the end of the day, the pupils mix with the rest of the school and attend health education, music, and a fourth major, in either mathematics or language. The "experience" period takes the place of the traditional English, social studies, general science, and art.[29]

The objectives of this program are

1. To develop effective work habits and skills
2. To develop effective methods of thinking
3. To assist the pupil in personal and social adjustment
4. To develop social attitudes in a sense of social responsibility
5. To widen interest, expression, and appreciation
6. To acquire fundamental knowledges and understandings

In class organization and activity, units are selected through careful pupil-teacher planning according to the criteria that have been previously agreed upon. Suggestions are made by both pupils and teachers. As a group nears the end of the old unit, the class begins to think ahead about what to do next. A time is set when they can make their suggestions. These are listed and the students are told to think about and talk over the suggestions with others in the school and at home. Small groups meet to share thinking. The advantages, possibilities, and disadvantages are thoroughly discussed. The chairman of each group presents his case to the class at the proper time, followed by voting and a majority decision on the next unit.

There is extensive preplanning by the teacher, a great deal of committee work, and cooperative decisions are made in a planning committee consisting of teacher and pupils. Subject matter from the four basic fields, as well as from other areas, are found in each unit. Typical units are: orientation to school; physical and mental health; personal relationship; the world at work; and leisure time.

---

29. Elsbeth Krober, "The Experience Curriculum at Midwood," *High Points*, 30:16–26, 1948.

The evaluation of this experience curriculum has been conducted by the Bureau of Reference, Research and Statistics of the New York City Schools, under the leadership of Dr. J. Wayne Wrightstone. Under his direction, each pupil in the experience curriculum was matched with a pupil who was learning under the regular curriculum of the school to evaluate "growth in certain knowledges, in skills and attitudes, and in the powers of critical thinking." Standard tests in English, social studies, mathematics, and civic beliefs were used.

The conclusions, based upon the findings under Wrightstone, showed that the experimental group gained more than those in the ordinary ninth-grade curriculum, with the largest gain being shown in the social studies. In addition, commendable gains were found in the academic skills, powers of thinking, and civic attitudes. Other gains were disclosed in the areas of student interests, appreciations, and personal and social adjustment.

COMBINATION COURSES, NORTHWESTERN HIGH SCHOOL, DETROIT. Under the Michigan Curriculum Study, a three-period fusion of social studies, English and fundamental skills for the tenth grade was developed at Northwestern High School in Detroit, Michigan. Two periods were devoted to the instructional part of the Effective Learning Program, while one was reserved for occupational planning with the counselor.

The scope of the program is described by the Effective Learning Committee as follows:

> The content of the Effective Learning Program should result from pupil-teacher planning, and as we develop more skills in working with the community from pupil-teacher-community planning.
>
> The skills to be used in the program are those necessary for the development of more effective citizens.
>
> . . . These groups will surely want to refer to the data gathered by means of the community survey; to the evaluation framework based on criteria for democratic living and characteristics of child growth and development; to the problems of school living; to the problems of the local and larger communities; to the needs and interests of the pupils; or to any other sources which will be an aid in determining the problem to be worked on by the pupils.
>
> When interests and needs of pupils in each group are determined, undoubtedly we shall find that not all groups will work on the same problems. Since it is the skills and techniques of solving social problems which are of greatest concern, the criteria for the selection of problems will be based on interest and needs of the individuals, the school and/or the community.

The program, problem-centered, requires only two problems for all groups: orientation to school, and setting of citizenship goals. Under the listing of areas of needs it is recommended that the following problems be included sometime during the school year:

1. Health needs—nutrition and rest
2. Social needs—recreation, cultural heritage
3. Economic needs—budgeting, consumer education
4. Emotional needs—understanding of behavior

Skills of learning, according to the committee, are the "skills necessary in democratic living" which are stressed in the Effective Learning Program. These are: thinking, listening, reading, speaking, writing, discussion, evaluation, library use, and use of sources of information.

The evaluation of pupil growth is based on the extent to which the pupils indicate achievement in the following:

1. Development of a loyalty to democracy and an understanding of democracy
2. Ability to plan and discuss with the group
3. Skills of solving social problems and participating in the activities of the group
4. Skills in reading, speaking, listening and writing to the limit of his capacity
5. Growth in democratic practices
6. Evidences of social adjustment in his group
7. Evidence of growth in personal adjustment[30]

A Fusion of Positions

There are distinct differences in the three positions just outlined. Position one represents the extreme of tradition, and position three the extreme of experimentalism, while position two is a modification of position one. Probably the basic changes being made in secondary education today represent a fusion of positions two and three. An understanding of some of these more generally accepted beliefs may help to give the reader a better orientation to modern curriculum practices.

Much stress is being laid on the influence of society in the education of youth. If youth are to be educated to improve their living they must find in society a hospitable attitude toward social betterment. The school cannot even teach youth to practice good living in a community ridden by poverty, disease, and prejudice, or a home weighted down with lethargic and ignorant parents. The social environment must be conducive to good living or else society breaks down the teachings of the school. Society itself has a definite value as does the individual, even though the major purpose of society is to improve the lives of the individuals which comprise it.

---

30. San Diego City Schools, Department of Research, *Recent Developments in General Education* (San Diego, Calif., 1949), pp. 67–69. Mimeographed.

Man thus loses some of his personal liberties to the group—this corporate society which is judged by the same general criterion of values as are individuals. Societies are effective, as are individuals, when what they do contributes to their own development and to that of those in the group. The majority opinion determines group practices except in cases where science has shown a different way; in that case opinion should not even be consulted. This method of operation is the way society works—the democratic way. Democracy involves the acceptance of the principle that all members of society have equal rights and an equal voice in the determination of societal policies.

People are different in many ways, and democratic society needs these differences; therefore, society must support ways and means (the school for one) to develop and utilize these differences. All shall be educated to their maximum development, and out of this practice will emerge satisfactory leadership. All must *work together* collectively to develop the resources of the country and to pool their best thinking for the type of institutions and the policies which shall be operative in society.

Man has needs which he tries to satisfy. They grow out of the nature of his organism (physical needs) and out of society (societal needs imposed by the group). The former are the only innate ones and can probably be rather definitely determined by scientific diagnosis; the latter grow out of the operation of experience and are very subjective and elusive in character. They are largely judgment needs. The individual must know the world about him, the particular society and the physical environment into which he is born. Education must take its beginning cue from this primary need and give attention to physical, emotional, and intellectual training, which is worthless, however, unless it eventuates into acceptable forms of behavior. Experiencing is probably the best way to learn to behave—"we learn to do by doing"—and as we do, we enhance our differences. Capacities, which are somewhat differently distributed among men, are revealed in the course of behaving. The curriculum should, then, be composed of activities which approximate or which are life patterns of social experience.

The school is a social institution—a state investment—to aid the state in integrating the young into the pattern of social living. It is not an agent of revolution or a laboratory of reform; it should not set out to cure social ills directly. The school can sponsor no program which society itself does not accept; it cannot be conservative, behind society; it must constantly reinterpret and reformulate its program and goals; it must analyze society and become a member of the group constantly working to improve living conditions. To do this, education must deal with citizenship, vocational competence, consumer problems, leisure, work, adult status, and other problems. How and when this shall be done is a matter of variation and will be guided by opinion, factual information, scientific proof, and emerging social conditions.

Illustrations of a Composite Position

There are many types of organization which may be used to illustrate the major tenets of this fused position. Some teachers would organize materials strictly around social or personal problems either in particular subject fields or without reference to subjects. Others would draw up a framework of social activities in which people engage, and build their materials of instruction around them. There are those who would organize materials around centers of interest, planned by the teacher and checked with the child. Illustrations of some of these types of organization will serve as examples of different procedures.

SCOPE AND SEQUENCE PATTERNS, WISCONSIN. The Wisconsin Cooperative Education Planning Program suggests the following grade-level themes in their social-studies scope and sequence development:

Kindergarten: Getting acquainted with school living
Grades 1–3:   Home, neighborhood, community
Grade 4:   How kinds of communities developed—Wisconsin, world
Grades 5–7:   Understanding our world neighbors—American and world geography and history
Grade 8:   Community problems *or* building and maintaining our country—United States history
Grades 9–10:   The world and its people—a two-year combined course in world history and world geography *or* geographical world patterns and community problems in grade 9 and world history in grade 10
Grade 11:   America's industrial growth and her place in the family of nations—United States history
Grade 12:   Knowing ourselves and understanding human relationships—problems course[31]

I. James Quillen has suggested a sequence for twelve years of social studies in the school system as follows:

SEQUENCE FOR A SOCIAL STUDIES PROGRAM IN THE PUBLIC SCHOOLS

Kindergarten and
  Grade 1:   Home and school   ⎫
Grade 2:   Neighborhood   ⎬
Grade 3:   Larger community   ⎬ Ways of living
Grade 4:   State   ⎬
Grade 5:   Nation   ⎬
Grade 6:   World   ⎭

---

31. Wisconsin State Department of Public Instruction, *Scope and Sequence of the Social Studies Program* (Wisconsin Cooperative Education Planning Program, *Bulletin* No. 14; Madison, Wis., 1947), pp. 14–52.

THE INTEGRATIVE THEME FOR LEARNING

Helping Children and Youth Develop Understanding and Behavior

SEQUENCE OF

THE ELEMENTARY SCHOOL:

Helping Children Understand and Improve Their Participation in Human Groups and Their Control over the Environment through Comparison and Contrast of Cultures Using Mechanical Power and Machines with Cultures Using Human Energy and Simple Tools.

Carrying On the Human Activities in the Child's Contemporary Immediate Environment		Comparing Means of Carrying On Human Activities in Contrasting Communities (Geographic, Pioneering and ADJUSTMENT)		Carrying On Human Activities in Our Contemporary World Community (Technological CONTROL)	
Kdg. and Grade 1	Grade 2	Grade 3	Grade 4	Grade 5	Grade 6
Home and School Life	Neighborhood and Community	Simple Communities without Machinery	Story of Our Community (Local Hist.)	Men's Needs and Earth's Resources	Modern Production and Distribution

POSSIBLE

Living in Our Homes Living in Our School Living in a Farm Home Living in a City Home Schools in a City and Country Etc.	Neighborhood Workers Who Protect Us Neighborhood Workers Who Help Us Communicate Neighborhood Workers Who Help Us Travel Neighborhood Workers Who Feed and Clothe Us Etc.	How People in a South Sea Island Village Live How People in an Indian Pueblo Live How People in Rural Mexico Live Etc.	How Our Ancestors Lived in This New Community How Our Schools Have Grown How Our Community Changes Its Ways of Communicating and Traveling Etc.	What Goods and Services Do We Moderns Need? Where Are the Earth's Resources Located and Are There Sufficient Resources to Satisfy Our Needs?	How Do Moderns Extract, Gather and/or Grow the Earth's Resources and Produce the Goods and Services Needed within a World System of Production? How Do Moderns Distribute Finished Goods and Services on a World-Wide Scale?

BASIC HUMAN

a. Protecting and conserving
b. Producing
c. Distributing
d. Consuming
e. Transporting

*Prepared by Paul R. Hanna,

EXPERIENCES IN GENERAL EDUCATION*

Essential for Survival and Progress in Our World Community

GRADE EMPHASES

THE SECONDARY SCHOOL:

Helping Youth Build Understanding and Behavior Essential to Participate in the Elimination of Cultural Lag in Democratic Social, Economic, and Political Behavior and Institutions, and Values, of Our Contemporary World Community.

Developing the Concept of Cultural Change in Carrying Out Human Activities, and the Role of Democracy in Controlling Change			Participating Effectively in Improving Human Relations thru Strengthening, Modifying, or Creating Social, Economic, and Political Arrangements and Values in:				
Grade 7	Grade 8	Grade 9	Grade 10	Grade 11	Grade 12	Grade 13	Grade 14
Story of Pre-Scientific Man	Story of Scientific Man	Nature of Democracy	The Local Community and State	The Region and Nation	The World Community	?	?

TEACHING UNITS

| How Did Ancient Man Live? The Story of Man's Slow Development from Pre-History to the Beginning of the Industrial Revolution. | How Does Modern Man Live? The Story of Rapid and Uneven Development of Man and His Institutions from Beginning of Industrial Revolution to the Present. | How Is Democracy Suited to the Social Needs of Modern Man? The Story of the Slow Development of Democracy and the Imperative Need for Its Acceptance by the World Today. | How Can We Improve All Human Activities in Our Community and State by Changes in Our Institutional Controls and in Strengthening Our Values? | How Can We Improve All Human Activities in Our Region and Nation by Changes in Our Institutional Controls and by Strengthening Our Values? | How Can We Improve All Human Activities in Our World Community by Changes in Our Institutional Controls and by Strengthening Our Values? | Survey Courses in {Social Sciences, Natural Sciences, Humanities} | |

ACTIVITIES (Scope)

f. Communicating
g. Expressing aesthetic and religious impulses
h. Providing recreation
i. Providing education
j. Organizing and governing

Stanford University.

Grade 7:	Orientation and process studies of modern industry	Emphasis on 1. How institutions help individuals to meet needs
Grade 8:	Building of the nation	2. Responsibility of individual citizens to make institutions work effectively
Grade 9:	Civics—local, state, nation and world	3. Enriching experiences in art, music, literature
		4. Orientation to home, school, community, and future vocational possibilities
		Emphasis on
Grade 10:	World civilization	1. Contemporary problems
Grade 11:	American democracy in its world setting	2. Understanding contemporary world situation
		3. Appreciation of the values of American democracy
Grade 12:	Problems of youth in the world today—the road ahead	4. Transition from high school to adult responsibilities[32]

One of the most complete illustrations of the use of the scope and sequence pattern is the one proposed by Paul R. Hanna for the elementary and secondary schools. The chart suggests the integrative themes for what he calls "general education," by which he means the basic common learning experiences for all pupils. This chart has some similar grade emphases to the one proposed by Quillen but it differs in other emphases, illustrating the differences in proposals even within a common plan.

SOCIAL STUDIES, FORT WORTH. In Fort Worth, Texas, curriculum committees in social studies declared themselves to favor the principle of selecting the critical social and personal problems which youth are facing, of organizing them effectively into "units," and of working them out with youth so as to help the learners "to become increasingly effective in solving the problems with which they are and will be confronted." The committees chose the following units:

Grade 9: 1. Installment payments
2. Orientation to school
3. Safety
4. Physical activity and health
5. Family harmony
6. Analysis of personality
7. Need for recreation
8. The importance of religion

32. A statement prepared especially for this book. Unpublished and contained in a letter to the author, November 18, 1951.

    9. Democracy and the citizen
   10. Current problems
   11. A survey of occupations
   12. Social security
   13. Learning how to learn
   14. Control of infection
   15. Health of the skin, hair, and nails
   16. Home and friends
   17. Developing socially
   18. Recreational conduct
   19. Control of traffic
   20. Crime and its prevention
   21. Current problems
   22. The selection of a vocation

Grade 10: 1. Advertising
    2. Available colleges
    3. Clothing versus health
    4. Health versus fads and fallacies
    5. Wise spending
    6. Physical improvement
    7. Recreation in the home
    8. Peaceful settlement for international differences
    9. Our city government
   10. Current problems
   11. Securing employment
   12. Consumer education
   13. Other educational opportunities
   14. Cleanliness
   15. Care of the injured
   16. Homes which are convenient and attractive
   17. Mental development
   18. Recreation in our city
   19. An awareness of the beautiful
   20. Law and the citizen
   21. Current problems
   22. A survey of occupations

Grade 11: 1. Personal credit
    2. Propaganda
    3. Stimulants and narcotics
    4. Professional health service
    5. Selection of home furnishings
    6. Understanding others
    7. Where to go and what to do
    8. Nature of happiness
    9. Better inter-racial relationships
   10. Current problems

11. Holding a job
12. Investments in insurance, stocks, and bonds
13. Developing special abilities
14. Care of the sick
15. Mental and emotional health
16. Selection of a home
17. Self-analysis
18. The relation of recreational activities to civilization
19. The economic and social well-being of the worker
20. Ethics in business and government
21. Current problems
22. The selection of a vocation[33]

These units, proposed for the last three years of the secondary schools of Fort Worth, represent a departure from the traditional grouping of social studies material. They deal with problems directly related to the life activities of youth but which heretofore have been considered outside the area of the social studies.

MATHEMATICS. According to Betz, three principal approaches have been tried or suggested in American secondary schools in their attempts to provide functioning types of mathematical training for *all* American youth:

> The *first* is anchored on the popular doctrine that "life situations" should be the primary basis of all curricula. But since mathematics is a *system* of ideas and processes, whereas life situations are incurably *unsystematic,* this approach has failed completely wherever it has been tried. It has always resulted merely in a chaotic "mathematics without mathematics" and it has ignored fundamental aspects of the problem we are considering.
>
> The *second* approach hopes to find dependable answers in the recommendations of authoritative committees and in the techniques of curriculum workshops and laboratories. However, the thousands of mathematical syllabi now crowding the shelves of our curriclum morgues have merely dramatized a hopeless confusion of objectives. And even the reports of *national* committees have regularly been attacked by leading educators as mere reflections of unsupported private opinion.
>
> There remains a *third* approach, often explored partially, but never with anything like scientific completeness or thoroughness. It is that of making a really dependable, full-length study of the role of mathematics in the modern world, from both a practical and a cultural standpoint. . . .
>
> It is believed that only on the basis of such objective findings will it be possible to obtain a convincing and enduring foundation for the mathematical curricula of the modern school. It will then be our major task to build a two-track program or even a three-track program, for the divergent

---

33. Fort Worth Public Schools, *Social Studies: A Tentative Course of Study in Personal and Social Problems for Grades Nine, Ten, and Eleven* (3 separate bulletins, one for each grade, Curriculum *Bulletins,* Nos. 115, 116, and 117; Fort Worth, Tex., 1940).

needs of those seeking an immediate life preparation and of those who aim at foundational studies in our colleges and universities.[34]

An illustration of how the functional type of mathematical organization gets into the classroom may be drawn from a recent textbook organized upon the principle of dealing with social problems.[35] A unit called *Providing for Economic Security* deals with the following materials.

The unit begins with the home of Mr. and Mrs. Johnston, a family of five living on an income of $225 a month which Mr. Johnston makes as an accountant. Mrs. Johnston sees in the evening newpaper some graphs on unemployment. This leads to a study of percentages in fluctuation of employment, the family budget, and then into the item of savings. Compound-interest tables are studied, securities in bonds, accrued interest, bond quotations, purchasing bonds, bond yields and maturity, stock investments, income from stocks, stock exchange, buying and selling stocks and bonds, comparison of the two as investments, insurance of all kinds, social security—individual and social.

This material is social in character and is a long step from the meaningless problems of "When do two trains pass?" However, it is doubtful whether these problems are actually on the experience level of youth themselves. In general, they deal with adult matters and meet only one aspect of the major tenets in this position—that the materials of instruction shall be contemporary and prepare youth for problems which they are likely to face.

Implications of a Composite Position

The last position described in this chapter gives us leads which we want to follow in the remaining chapters of this book, leads to organization around social problems, functional areas of living, and needs; leads to the problem method through the use of units and emphasis upon learning by experience; leads to group planning, to new functions of education, to common learnings, and to differentiated education. The basic tenets of this position also draw attention away from the subjects themselves as the centers of organization and direct it to searching for new frameworks which will unify instructional materials around social goals and purposes. The first step, however, in this direction has been the movement to seek to establish relationships among the various subjects.

34. William Betz, "Mathematics for the Million, or for the Few?" *The Mathematics Teacher,* 44:20–21, 1951.
35. Harl R. Douglass and Lucien B. Kinney, *Everyday Mathematics* (New York: Henry Holt and Company, 1940).

Chapter Ten

Reorganizing the

Subject Curriculum

THE GENERAL PLAN of curriculum reorganization has centered around taking the conventional school subjects and making specific changes in the content. A few things are usually dropped, some are added, and in many instances new wordings or forms of organization are substituted. These changes, however, do not grow from a change in philosophy of education or of curriculum materials, but are in general a mechanical process for subject reform. These forms of change usually fall into three classes:

1. Organization centering around topics, generalizations, concepts, or principles (topical type)

2. Organization based upon cultures of people or of periods of time (cultural type)

3. Organization based upon problems, personal and social, which are of importance to the learner and which require him to make a choice (problems type)

Illustrations of each of these types in recent curriculum practice will make clearer their nature and meaning.

The Topical Type

In this type there is selected from the basic field to be studied a list of important principles, or concepts, or generalizations, or understandings, to be grasped, proved, or learned. Around these are then grouped content or activities or even some types of problems. One of the early workers in this type of organization was Morrison, who developed and expanded his ideas several times.[1] In the type of organization which he advocated he says there is "pre-eminently intellectual discipline, but not mental discipline."[2] The divisions of subject matter which he suggested are to him basic understandings which the pupil learns and by so doing increases his intelligence. To most of us they are only topics, however. When we organize a course around the conventional classification of verbs, pronouns, conjunctions, and clauses, as he suggested in English, or around such things as subtraction and multiplication and addition of integers and fractions in mathematics, or around the conventional topics of heat, light, sound, and magnetism in science, most of us will be willing to admit that we have used the topical plan of organization.

Morrison made definite suggestions of materials for study, which when put together comprise the complete outline of the course. He expected the teacher to follow his outline exactly, as it represented the logical organization and the desired one about which all pupils in the common school should have some *understanding*. These *understandings* sound like mental discipline.

Illustrations of the Topical Type

MATHEMATICS, NATIONAL COUNCIL OF TEACHERS OF MATHEMATICS. The joint Commission of the Mathematical Association of America and the National Council of Teachers of Mathematics outlined in their 1940 yearbook two plans for the teaching of mathematics in the secondary school. They divided the whole subject of secondary-school mathematics into seven fields: (1) the field of number and of computation; (2) the field of geometric form and of space perception; (3) the field of graphic representation; (4) the field of elementary analysis; (5) the field of logical thinking; (6) the field of relational thinking; (7) the field of symbolic representation and thinking. They further divided each of these seven fields into the following categories: (1) basic concepts, principles, and terms; (2) fundamental processes; (3) fundamental relations; (4) skills and techniques; and (5) application.[3]

---

1. See especially H. C. Morrison, *The Practice of Teaching in the Secondary School* (rev. ed.; Chicago: University of Chicago Press, 1931).
2. H. C. Morrison, *The Curriculum of the Common School* (Chicago: University of Chicago Press, 1940), p. 62.
3. *The Place of Mathematics in Secondary Education* (Fifteenth Yearbook of the National Council of Teachers of Mathematics; New York: Columbia University, Teachers College, Bureau of Publications, 1940), p. 61.

The field of algebra is illustrative of how the materials in each of these courses might be organized.

ALGEBRA

I. Basic concepts
  A. The acquisition of the basic vocabulary
  B. Developing the ability to explain clearly the meaning of key concepts, such as exponent, positive, negative, ratio, proportion

II. Fundamental skills and techniques
  (These should be based on an understanding of carefully considered *concepts* and *principles*. Work with polynomials should be restricted to very simple cases.)
  A. The four fundamental operations, involving
     1. Positive and negative numbers
     2. Algebraic fractions, mainly with monomial denominators
  B. Special products and factoring, as follows:
     1. Squaring a binomial
     2. Finding the product of the sum and the difference of two terms
     3. Factoring a polynomial the terms of which contain a common monomial factor
     4. (Optional) Factoring trinomials of the form $2x + bx + c$
     5. Factoring the difference of two squares
  C. By formulas
     1. Formulas as means of expressing relationship or dependence
     2. Making formulas based on verbal statements; on geometric figures; on tables
     3. Evaluating a formula
     4. Transforming a formula (only simple cases)
  D. By equations
     1. Equations as means of expressing quantitative relationships
     2. Solving equations of the first degree in one unknown
     3. Solving pairs of equations of the first degree
     4. Solving fractional equations
     5. Solving equations of the $ax^2 = b$
     6. Solving simple radical equations
     7. Using equations in the study of proportion and variation
     8. Using equations in the solution of problems stated in verbal form

· · ·

V. Using algebra in life situations and in problem-solving
  A. Learning to translate quantitative statements into the language of algebra
  B. Learning to make generalizations suggested by the techniques and principles of algebra, particularly with relation to the precise way in which definitely related, changing quantities will influence each other under given conditions
  C. Solving general verbal problems, using as a means of solution the table, the graph, the formula, the equation

D. Applying the techniques of algebra in problem situations arising in business, in the shop, in science, in everyday life

E. Interpreting the solutions of equations, including negative values, where they have significance[4]

MATHEMATICS, BROCKTON. Another illustration in mathematics can be drawn from a recent course of study in Brockton, Massachusetts, for grade nine. This course suggests to the teacher the aims to be achieved and the content of the unit in terms of topics to be studied.

MATHEMATICS

Grade 9

I. Aims:

A. To insure that the pupil maintains such basic skills and understandings as he may have previously acquired

B. To make up for any deficiencies in the basic skills which tests administered early in the year may have brought to light

C. To develop in the pupil a realization that mathematics is understandable and to make it possible for him to understand fully all that he has shown himself able to do as well as all that he must now learn to do

D. To help the pupil gain the desired understanding through the unification of many different topics under a few general principles, thereby reducing the number of seemingly different things which he will need to remember, etc.

II. Unit One: Remedial and refresher work in fundamentals

A. Content

B. A screening test on the four fundamental processes with integers, common and decimal fractions, and mixed numbers to locate areas of weakness

C. Such additional tests for the group and for individuals as may be necessary to isolate special deficiencies, including tests on the basic addition and multiplication facts

D. Remedial practice as shown to be needed

E. The nature of our number system with its base ten

F. The meaning of the fundamental process

G. Addition and subtraction as inverse operations

H. Multiplication as abbreviated addition

I. Division as abbreviated subtraction and the inverse of multiplication

J. Operations upon and with zero

K. The composition of numbers

    1. Numbers as sums or as products

    2. Factors including the recognition of multiples of 2, 3, 4, 5, 6, 9, 10

    3. Prime numbers

    4. Finding prime factors and cp. pm. factors (G.C.D.)

    5. Finding common multiples (L.C.M.)

---

4. *Ibid.*, pp. 89–90.

L. Abstract, concrete, denominate numbers
M. Common fractions
  1. The concept of a fraction as a denominate number
  2. The concept of a fraction as an indicated quotient
  3. Two methods of multiplying a fraction by an integer
  4. Two methods of dividing a fraction by an integer
  5. Two ways of changing the form but not the value of a fraction
  6. Addition and subtraction of fractions as of denominate numbers
  7. The meaning and method of multiplying fractions
  8. The meaning and method of dividing by a fraction
N. Mixed numbers and complex fractions
  1. Interchanging improper fractions and mixed numbers
  2. Fundamental processes with mixed numbers
  3. Complex fractions and divisions of mixed numbers simplified by multiplying both numerator and denominator by the L.C.D. of the component fractions
O. Decimal fractions
  1. The relation between the decimal and the common fraction systems and interchange of notations
  2. Reading and writing numbers in the decimal system

III. Unit Two: The formula
  A. Aims
    1. To understand the uses of formulas in solving problems
    2. To be able to write formulas to express rules already learned in arithmetic
    3. To be able to write formulas to express verbal statements of quantitative relationships
    4. To be able to evaluate simple formulas
  B. Content
    1. Reviewing and strengthening the concept that a formula is a short way of writing a rule of mathematical relationship
    2. Extending the knowledge of symbols and abbreviations commonly used

IV. Unit Three: The simple equation
  A. Content
    1. Meaning of terms: digit, numeral, literal number
    2. Literal number as a substitute for an unknown quantity
    3. Expressing the four processes with literal numbers, including the use of coefficient
    4. The equation

V. Unit Four: Ratio and proportion
  A. Content
    1. Ratio
    2. Proportion

VI. Unit Five: Percentage and interest
    A. Content (continued)
        1. Percentage problems viewed as product problems
        2. Uses of percent in business situations
        3. The solution of problems
        4. Solving as equations for any unknown

VII. Unit Six: Graphic representation
    A. Content
        1. Definition of graph
        2. Importance of stating the scale, types of graph: bar, line, circle, pictograph
        3. Reading graphs

VIII. Unit Seven: Measurement and informal geometry
    A. Content
        1. The nature of measurement
        2. Introduction to the metric system of linear measure and appreciation of its advantages

IX. Unit Eight: Indirect measurement
    A. Content
        1. Development of the concept of the term "similar" from its common usage to the geometric definition
        2. Discovery of the conditions which make triangles similar
        3. Applying the definition of similar triangles to indirect measurement[5]

SCIENCE, PROGRESSIVE EDUCATION ASSOCIATION. The Committee of the Progressive Education Association on the Function of Science in General Education likewise presented the basic concept of adolescent needs and proceeded to show how science could contribute to them. It followed this with a suggested organization of materials, and here its goal was to develop *understanding of principles, concepts,* and *generalizations.* An example from its suggestions for the study of the country's economic resources will illustrate the general technique and principle of organization proposed by the committee. It will be noted that the opening list of major generalizations is followed by other generalizations under these major ones, which in turn are followed by suggested pupil activities.

I. Major generalizations
    A. Men are influenced by their environment in their use of energy and materials.
    B. Natural energy is controlled and used for the purpose of economic life.
    C. The production of the great variety of goods now used depends upon the availability, creation, utilization, and control of a wide variety of materials.

5. Brockton Public Schools, *Course of Study in Mathematics, Grades VII–IX* (Brockton, Mass., 1947), pp. 27–45.

D. Application of the sciences increases control over energy and materials.
E. Social and economic conditions depend in part upon the distribution, use, and control of energy and materials.
F. Conservation of exhaustible natural resources is a social responsibility.

II. Tentative list of generalizations bearing on IA
   A. Geographical surroundings affect man's material needs and occupations, his racial characteristics, and his cultural forms.
      1. Since soil, weather, and living things are important for the subsistence and health of human beings, men have always tried to control or adjust to these factors of the environment.
      2. Differences in the quality and quantity of the production of various peoples are due in part to differences in the resources of their lands.
      3. Temperate regions with variable climate are those in which agriculture, stock raising, manufacturing, and other economic activities may be carried on most vigorously.
      4. Large bodies of water are a service to man as a source of rain, regulators of temperature, an aid to health, a source of food, and an aid to travel and transportation.
      5. The agriculture of the future may depend more largely upon crops from trees and vines, because of their greater yield and adaptability to soils not fitted for grains.
   B. The sun is the source of practically all the energy that men use.

III. Illustrations of possible student activities
   A. Study the soil and climate of (a) the Sahara Desert, (b) the Arctic or Antarctic, (c) the tropics, (d) the local community. Relate what you find out to the plants and animals available in each area. Relate soil, climate, plants, and animals to the food eaten in each place, the building materials, textiles, tools, etc., in common use. Can you see any relation between soil and climate and these elements of the civilization of the inhabitants?
   B. In what ways does water constitute a limiting influence upon a civilization?
   C. What environmental factors influence the cultural patterns of a people?
   D. Look up in an economic geography or atlas the density of population (in persons per square mile) in various parts of the United States and account for the differences in terms of soil and climate.
   E. Make a map showing the location of the great steel mills in the United States, and indicate the reasons for their geographic position. Do the same for the main centers in this particular area.
   F. Study the three most important local industries to determine the reasons why they developed in this particular area.
   G. Why have many textile plants migrated from the North to the South?
   H. Examine a world map showing the areas devoted to the cultivation of sugar beets, and find out what factors of soil and climate account for their location.

I. Why are the wheat growing locations generally located between latitudes 30° and 60°?

J. Explain how the small but natural fertility of New England soil is derived from the granite rock which composes its hills and mountains.

K. Compare the health statistics for people living in the city with those living in the country. Which group has the higher mortality rates, sickness rates? Which has more health regulations? For which have more health provisions been made? Why? What differences do you see in the respective physical environments?

L. Compare the health statistics for people living in the slums with people living in the suburbs. In your opinion, how much of the difference, if any, is due to the physical environment?

M. Compare the stature of a large number of students whose parents are immigrants with the stature of their parents. Look up the results of similar studies. Find out how the stature of recent Harvard students compares with that of their parents. How do you explain these facts?[6]

SCIENCE, LOS ANGELES AND SAN JOSE. Two more illustrations in the field of science will show the use of this method in two California cities—one for Los Angeles for life science in the senior high school, the other for San Jose showing the basic concepts to be gained in science in the senior high school.

LIFE SCIENCE

Senior High School

I. Orientation
   A. Life science in our world today
      1. Scope and biological science
      2. Vocations and hobbies
   B. Methods of science
      1. Experimentation, observation, and conclusion
      2. Keeping records

II. Characteristics of living things
   A. Activities of living things
   B. Composition
      1. Biological significance of
         a. Elements
         b. Compounds
         c. Chemical and physical changes
      2. Unit structures
         a. Cells and tissues
         b. Organs and organisms

---

6. Committee of the Progressive Education Association on the Function of Science in General Education, *Science in General Education* (New York: Appleton-Century-Crofts, Inc., 1938), pp. 258–291. By permission of the publishers.

C. Elimination of waste
   1. Skin
   2. Kidneys
D. Behavior
   1. Nervous systems
   2. Reflexes and habits
   3. Special senses
      a. Sight
      b. Hearing
      c. Feeling
      d. Taste and smell
   4. Endocrine glands
   5. Mental health
E. Continuing the species
   1. Simple types of reproduction
   2. More complex types of reproduction
      a. Plants
      b. Animals
      c. Development of the plant and animal embryo
      d. Building wholesome attitudes

III. Basic life processes of living things
  A. Nutrition
     1. Food getting
        a. Sources—plant and animal
        b. Balanced diet for optimum health
     2. Digestion
        a. Mechanical—teeth and peristalsis
        b. Chemical—enzymes
        c. Absorption
        d. Hygiene of digestion

IV. Conservation of health
  A. Cause and prevention of disease
  B. Drugs and patent medicines
  C. Community health
     1. Federal, state, and local health agencies
     2. Food and water supply
     3. Sewage and garbage disposal
     4. Health organizations
        a. Red Cross
        b. Tuberculosis associations, etc.[7]

---

7. Los Angeles City Schools, *Life Science* (Publication No. 441; Los Angeles, Calif., 1947), p. 15.

SPECIFIC CONCEPTS FOR SENIOR HIGH SCHOOL LIFE SCIENCE

I. Characteristics of growth in plants and animals
   A. Every living thing starts its existence as a single cell.
   B. Single-celled plants and animals are self-sufficient.
   C. Higher forms of plants and animals are more complex, having special-
      ized groups of cells which function as organs.
   D. Cell division is responsible for growth in plants and animals.
   E. The pattern of individual growth differs because of heredity.
   F. Individual growth differs at various age levels.

II. Characteristics of higher forms of life are
   A. Their fewer offspring
   B. Their need of greater protection before birth
   C. Their longer dependency
   D. Their highly specialized reproductive process
   E. Their complex nature—each individual is the product of his experi-
      ences, his training, and his germ plasm.

III. Each individual has a responsibility for the health of himself and his
     species.
   A. The body systems and their functioning
   B. The food and oxygen needs of the body metabolism
   C. Preventive measures to protect human health

IV. Each individual has a responsibility for the mental health of himself and
    others through his contributions to satisfactory social adjustments.
   A. Humans have characteristic behavior at various age levels.
   B. Knowledge of characteristic group behavior helps individuals make
      normal adjustment to age mates.[8]

SOCIAL STUDIES, NEW JERSEY.   Material of interest to a larger number of
youth and more liberal plans of organizing materials under this same general
approach are to be found in the field of the social studies. The following outline of content on The Industrial Revolution by W. Harry Snyder of Mont-
clair, New Jersey, will illustrate another method of organization:

THE INDUSTRIAL REVOLUTION

General Problem: How has the Industrial Revolution influenced the conditions
under which we live?

I. Could we get along without machines?
   A. How would we build our houses, churches, schools, and places of
      business?
   B. In what way would we prepare our foods, grind our grain, and slice
      our meats?

8. San Jose Unified School District, *Life Science Program* (San Jose, Calif.: Department
of Instruction, 1950), pp. 11–14. Mimeographed.

C. How would we weave our cloth and sew our clothing?

D. Would we be able to travel from one place to another, communicate with one another and transport our freight?

E. Could we light, heat, and clean our dwellings?

II. Was there ever a time when men did not have machines?

A. By what means did the Egyptians build their pyramids?

B. With what power did the Romans propel their boats across the sea to attack Carthage?

C. How did the feudal knights construct their armor and shields?

D. With what did the peasants on the English manors sew the seeds and cut the harvests?

III. Why did men first invent and use machinery in England about the middle of the eighteenth century?

A. Did England possess better natural advantages for industry than other nations?

B. To what extent had England's commerce been hampered by medieval laws?

C. How had England developed colonies to supply raw materials and serve as markets for surplus manufactured goods?

D. How had Englishmen stored up idle capital for investment in industrial enterprises?

E. Did England's textile industry lend itself especially to the use of machinery?

F. To what extent did England possess those natural resources—iron and coal—which proved so essential in making machinery?

G. How did the stability of the English government compare with that of the nations on the continent?

IV. What were the first mechanical developments to be made?

A. In the spinning and weaving of textiles?

B. For the production of power?

C. For the manufacture of iron and steel?

D. In coal mining?

E. For improving transportation?

V. Did the change to mechanical production have much influence on the life of the people who lived during the century following 1750?

A. Why did it cause the people to leave the country and congregate in towns and cities?

B. Why did it force the women and children to work in the factories?

C. How did it lead to long working days and unhealthful living conditions?

D. Why did the new class of capitalists obtain the position of influence in British politics which had formerly been held by the land owners?

E. Why did the backward section north of the Trent rapidly become a busy hive of industry?

VI. How has governmental legislation improved those conditions created by the Industrial Revolution?
  A. What has been the effect of child labor laws?
  B. What have been the advantages of compulsory compensation in case of injury to a workman?
  C. What have been the best provisions of more recent "factory" laws?

VII. What new conditions have resulted from the spread of the Industrial Revolution throughout the world?
  A. How many new opportunities have been brought to the peasants of France, Germany, and Russia?
  B. How have the common people been encouraged to fight for freedom from the oppressive rules of absolute monarchs?
  C. In what ways has its spread helped to break up the large feudal estates into small privately owned farms?
  D. How has it aided the development of nationalism?

VIII. To what extent has the spread of the Industrial Revolution to the United States had an effect upon you?
  A. How has it kept prices lower?
  B. Have transportation and communication been made easier and more rapid?
  C. Has your choice of an occupation been widened?
  D. Have articles that you use become more standardized and free from imperfections?
  E. Has it given you more time for recreation and travel?[9]

Study of this method of organization will reveal that the fields of social science—civics, economics, sociology, politics, and history—are really woven together to develop the desired understanding of the Industrial Revolution. The material is set up in the form of questions which provide the basis for study by pupils, questions which are within their age of development and conceivably within their level of interest. The unit starts with some present interest or time to give it a setting in the present and to get the pupils to seize the study of the unit quickly. It proposes to give purpose to historical material by posing a present time value and then going back to develop the meanings. There is also the use of contrast in periods with and without machinery. The material offers opportunities for discussion, for differences of opinion, and for the formation of social attitudes. The questions lend themselves to the use of many references and modern materials, as well as to visits to slums and factories. It is possible, however, to perform the work of the unit entirely by the use of restricted reading materials if the teacher desires to do so. The material is designed to establish in a comprehensive manner certain understandings of the growth of industry in our civilization and to lead the pupil

---

9. Used by permission of W. Harry Snyder.

to form certain intellectual attitudes about what he might do when at some later time he would have a chance to act on certain questions. No immediate action at all is necessary on this unit, nor is there really a place for any. The unit requires almost entirely an intellectual process. Social-studies teachers can reorganize their material in this fashion without reference to the work in other subject areas.

PERSONAL LIVING, LOS ANGELES.   Another variation of this general type of problem is one found in the area of personal living. For illustration we might go to the Los Angeles, California, course in Senior Problems in Family Relationships and Personality Development for a unit on *Learning about Ourselves*.[10] This unit is divided into three parts: Part 1—Nature of the Individual; Part 2—Bases of Personality, Heredity, and Environment; Part 3—Development of Personality. This unit then deals with the physical, mental, and emotional aspects of the individual; with individual differences; with heredity, including how we inherit, what we do and do not inherit, the truth about prenatal influence and birthmarks and marriage between cousins, the meaning and importance of eugenics and the environment. The part dealing with personality discusses basic desires, emotional growth and maturity, the psychology of habit, and common emotional problems growing out of anger, fear, and jealousy. It deals also with introversion and extroversion, inferiority and superiority, and other personality difficulties. All this is material for the general study of the subject.

Evaluation of Topical Plan

In all these illustrations of the building of curriculum materials around generalizations, concepts, understandings, or principles, the basic pattern of thinking is the same, whether the materials are said to contribute to general education, to belong in the common school, or to be required of all pupils. The pattern is an intellectual one, and its success is dependent upon the youth's ability to organize concepts or principles in his mind. The purpose of curriculum content is to enable the learner to develop either a knowledge or an understanding of a principle, or to acquire a concept which will provide intellectual discipline. The content itself has a logic about it, and that logic dictates the nature of the organization; it is material which has organization within a field of thought or an area of activity. It takes its cue not from the nature of the individual problem but from the nature of the field. It depends upon "application" to life situations for its transfer to immediate need. It deals with an intellectual problem, not one which frustrates the youth, either emotionally or objectively. The problem is a question or a group of questions thrown into

10. Los Angeles City Schools, *Senior Problems* (Publication No. 336; Los Angeles, Calif., 1940).

a larger one which the adult poses. The answer is known and the youth is put on the search of it. He can be successful in his pursuit only if he follows the pattern for the solution. The real purpose of the teaching is to develop the higher mental processes of man and to inform him of the nature of science, culture, art, and mathematics. If he sufficiently understands these disciplines and can intelligently apply his knowledge to his immediate personal and social problems, he will be able to live with more intelligence than if he did not possess this understanding.

This is obviously a program for the more intelligent of men. It has less to offer to the mass of people. It is geared to understanding rather than to experience. It is focused on a motive from without the experience of the individual rather than on one from within him. It is orderly, scholarly, academic, and satisfying to the teacher, the college professor, and the intellectual student, if the teacher is the least bit careful to provide sufficiently interesting motivation. It is founded on reason and omits the emotional content of experience. It has a place, to be sure, but it can never be the sole type of education offered to the masses of youth in our secondary schools. It is concerned not with people but with ideas and principles. It is traditional education made more interesting.

The Cultural Type

The second type of organization uses world cultures as a base of organization and stems from the idea that to understand the world in which we live and the forces which are controlling it, many of them having their roots in the past, it is necessary to understand the unity of man's living. To develop this understanding some people suggest having parallel classes running in history, literature and art; others suggest having the materials of civilization organized around certain cultural groupings or accomplishments. The cultural approach ensures the inclusion of the art, music, politics, sociological mores and laws, the history and economics of the people. When these are bound together in a unity there results an effective and rather natural integration or correlation (the word to be used will depend upon the individual talking).

Illustrations of the Cultural Type

ORIENTAL CULTURE, LINCOLN SCHOOL, NEW YORK. An illustration of this approach is the organization used in the Lincoln School of Teachers College in 1939.[11] This unit was really the work of an entire year and is not compara-

---

11. Frances Gertrude Sweeney, Emily Fanning Barry, and Alice E. Schoelkopf, *Western Youth Meets Eastern Culture* (New York: Columbia University, Teachers College, Bureau of Publications, 1932).

ble as a unit to the others we have been discussing. It included a complete canvass of the Orient for several centuries, for the pupils "toured" the Orient without regard to time. They looked into the social problems, the living conditions, the musical compositions, the creative products, and the literary contributions; and, as they surveyed these fields, they constantly drew for comparisons upon their knowledge of their own culture in New York City.

CULTURAL PLAN, HORACE MANN SCHOOL, NEW YORK.   Another illustration of the organization of materials around cultures is represented by the Horace Mann School, Teachers College, Columbia University, where a three-year coordinated program in the junior high school was planned to help youth understand the progress of man throughout the ages. The first year was devoted to a study of the early people in Greece and in the Nile and the Euphrates valleys, the second year to a study of life in the Middle Ages and the Renaissance, and the third year to a study of the Modern Age. In each year the use and invention of tools were stressed, as well as transportation, communication, history, worship, art, literature, music, and other forms of aesthetic expression.[12]

In the senior high school period, Horace Mann School[13] centered its study upon American civilization and culture in grade ten, while the work of the eleventh year was designed to give an understanding of modern cultures. The four selected for study—modern England, modern France, Oriental culture (Pacific area), and modern Russia—were studied as a unit and embodied material from social studies, literature, art, music, science, and household arts. These were organized around four large units dealing with these four cultures.

SOCIAL STUDIES, OREGON.   One of the modern types of cultural organization where a fusion of several subject fields has been effected can be illustrated by a world-culture unit from Oregon.

This is the alternative program for ninth- and tenth-grade social studies whereby the work in orientation, Northwest resources, world geography and civilizations, and world history is combined in a two-year sequence extending through grades nine and ten. Since an adequate treatment of geography and present-day civilizations cannot be accomplished without some knowledge of the historical background, this plan of fusing the two subjects into a two-year course is offered. Some schools staffed by competent instructors may wish to adopt this plan. It should be understood that students who elect this course would be expected to complete the two years' work. Adoption of this plan would ulimately lead to a four-year sequence in social studies and would be required of all graduates.

---

12. Orielle Murphy and Alice M. Torrey, "Introducing High School Students to a Study of Man through the Ages," *Teachers College Record*, 38:324–336, 1937.

13. Mary Harden, Margy G. Marshall, and Willis C. Armstrong, "Introducing High School Students to Modern Cultures Other Than Their Own," *Teachers College Record*, 36:675–687, 1935.

The following are two plans for combining the work in geography and history into a world-culture course:

World Culture

A two-year combined program using geography of the world and story of nations

(This course might include the following objectives.)

I. Understandings of
   A. The geographical setting of each of the main world cultures
   B. The important forces and influences that have shaped the modern world
   C. The important contributions made by various peoples to the development of modern civilization
   D. Nature furnishes direction but does not determine the culture and progress of man
   E. Culture patterns and contemporary actions are the result of the interweaving of history and environment and character, manifested by individuals
   F. There is an underlying unity in the world, reflected through many influences

II. Appreciation of
   A. The contributions of other cultures to the development of our own culture and to world civilization in general
   B. The extent to which all parts of the world have become interdependent and the necessity for institutions of world cooperation to be truly functional
   C. The aesthetic and spiritual values of life

III. Skills in
   A. The mechanics of learning, such as acquiring facility in locating and selecting information and materials
   B. The use of the scientific method

IV. Attitudes of
   A. Personal responsibility, intellectual curiosity, and honesty in searching for truth
   B. Civic-mindedness—respect for law and order
   C. World-mindedness—interest in and responsibility for general welfare of mankind

Story of Nations	Geography of the World
The story of early men	Man and mother earth
1. The earth before the time of man	1. Progress of mankind
2. The earth became the home of man	2. The earth in space

3. Mankind at the dawn of civilization

The Egyptians built a great civilization on the banks of the Nile.
1. The fertile valley of the Nile.

2. The Egyptians built a foundation for greatness.
3. A mighty empire rose and fell.
4. Egyptian life reflects a remarkable culture.

3. The atmosphere about us

4. The face of the earth
5. How the earth provides for man's needs (Unit I, 3–4 weeks)

Africa—the lost frontier of the nations

1. North Africa—farm lands and deserts
2. Egypt—the seat of ancient civilization
3. Anglo-Egyptian Sudan
4. Ethiopia—Haile Selassie's Empire (Unit II, 1–2 weeks)
5. British East Africa
6. Madagascar
7. British South Africa—a land of gold and diamonds
8. Portuguese Africa
9. West Africa—a terminus of trans-Atlantic air lines
10. Gold Coast
11. Belgian Congo
12. Liberia[14]

WORLD CITIZENSHIP, LOS ANGELES COUNTY. Another rather interesting version of the general cultural approach is to be found in the Los Angeles County unit on world citizenship. Only brief illustrations, sufficient to give the general idea of the approach to the unit, are cited.

TEACHING WORLD CITIZENSHIP

The committee viewpoint:

From the narrowest loyalty of the tribe to the broadest ideal of human brotherhood, mankind's concept of social unity has grown like all its culture from its circumstances, geographic, social, and economic, and from its ability to master them. Today, in a world shrunken to neighborhood size, men are assuming the responsibilities and duties of a new kind of citizenship of which some had long dreamed but for which the world had not yet been ready.

The public schools have a new duty:

Ratification of the United Nations Charter, as reinforced by the introduction of the atomic bomb, has placed upon the public schools of the United States the obligation to provide youth with information, generalizations, and attitudes appropriate to the performance of their expanded civic responsibilities. The schools will need no persuasion to agree with General Eisenhower that "the kind of

---

14. Oregon State Department of Education, *A Guide to the Program of Studies in the Secondary Schools of Oregon* (Salem, Ore., 1949).

peace we have will depend largely on the kind of education we have in the immediate years ahead."

While there is little doubt that much that is taught in the schools will be modified toward an expanded use and understanding of world art, literature, and other "cultural" materials, it is in the social studies that the need is most immediate and can be most squarely met.

Teachers to avoid their former errors:

But the Committee believes that social studies teachers must not, in their postwar concern for world understanding and cooperation, make again the mistake of assuming that communication is synonymous with understanding. Teachers may well set up a few "don'ts" to guide them in avoiding some of the commoner errors of prewar "education for world friendship." Care should be taken not to over-emphasize:

1. *"Fancy-dress" internationalism.* Stress upon the picturesque and primitive, while bringing out the variety among cultures, has often led to obscuring the contrasts within individual cultures as well as the conflicts between cultures.

2. *Uncritical "good will."* The "good will" approach, sponsored by interested agencies, has sometimes tended to promote "appreciation" at the expense of understanding. Not all that a friendly nation is doing may be worthy of praise; much that needs to be done, it may not be doing. In this regard, teachers should examine free materials carefully for possible distortion.

3. *Utopianism.* The views of organizations and individuals advocating the surrender of national sovereignty should be presented as utopian, as directive, rather than immediately practical. Otherwise there is danger of the student's relegating the whole area of world citizenship to the realm of the unlikely.

4. *Technicalities of organization.* Above all, teachers must beware of reducing the study of world citizenship to the memorization of a maze of technicalities. Textbooks may be expected to appear soon with accounts of all the political developments in internationalism since the time of the Greeks, culminating in a 200-page treatment of the organization of the United Nations under the Charter.

What should be emphasized in education for world citizenship:

Every community in the United States now has home again a hundred men who know what the rest of the world looks like and how it behaves. There is sure to be an emphasis in their conversation, as there has been in their letters, upon the ways in which other cultures differ from ours. "Friendship" is all very well, they may say and are saying, but do you know how the Indians, the Chinese, the Burmese, the islanders actually live?

In short, their experience has given servicemen a viewpoint based upon rock-bottom realism. National thinking, self-conscious and critical in the best sense, must be built upon that realism. If an awareness of the power for good that lies in joint action on battlefield and in laboratory is to be kept alive and extended to the promotion of world peace and world welfare under the United Nations Charter, then education for world citizenship must build upon the new realism.

The new realism, the Committee feels sure, will be tolerant neither of sentimentality nor of distortion.

In the following pages, the material that is suggested for use in teaching world citizenship has been worked out to emphasize (1) the difference in cultural levels among peoples of the world as well as the growth among them of common cultural concerns, (2) the need for joint action to improve the common world welfare as well as to preserve peace, (3) the joint action now going on in various areas of inter-dependence, and (4) the individual responsibility of the world citizen to act in terms of his knowledge and beliefs. Each of the five "strands" in world citizenship is outlined with suggested information, generalizations, and attitudes that may be taught.

WORLD CITIZENSHIP

Unit One. Culture: The interaction of peoples in the world of common culture

I. Objectives: What are we trying to do?
   A. Generalizations: What do we need to know?
      1. That peoples differ one from another largely as their cultures differ
      2. That culture, as it includes the total way of life of a people, determines to a great extent how an individual behaves and what he believes
      3. That cultures do change, through the actions of man and the impingements of forces beyond or outside his local culture
      4. That as cultures change, man's ways of behaving and believing change
      5. That we are concerned not only with the conflicts between local cultures but with the growth of the world culture that defines our role as world neighbors, world workers, and world citizens

   B. Behaviors: How do we need to act?

II. Introductory activities: How shall we start our study?

III. Information: What do we need to understand?
    A. The nature of culture
       1. The components of culture
       2. The effects of culture on individual and group
       3. Causes of conflict between local cultures
    B. The developing world culture
       1. World-wide advance of the common man
       2. Communication and world culture

IV. Developmental activities: How can we realize our objectives through use of the information we study?
    1. A museum field trip would offer an opportunity for students to observe and compare artifacts that represent differing cultural levels. Planning the trip in terms of a limited number of key subjects, such as farm implements, foot-wear, and storage vessels, would increase the likelihood of the note taking and subsequent class discussion's having maximum value.
    2. Making a tour of "foreign" sections of community or district, or visiting

shops and restaurants of differing nationalities, might provide concrete evidence of the cultural differences studied in class.

3. Preparation of bulletin board displays, with student drawings and writing, collected around changing themes, might serve to inspire further illustration of some of the concepts under study.

4. Students may conduct school or community surveys on attitudes dealing with culture concepts.

V. Concluding activities: How should we summarize and evaluate our study?
1. A "test" film might be presented to the class as subject for written analysis in terms of the generalizations drawn from the study of interesting cultures. One of the films suggested under introductory activities may be used for this purpose.
2. Survey results might be summarized for school or community newspapers.
3. Programs in the form of panel discussions, individual speakers, or playlet might be presented in assembly, before other classes, or in the community.[15]

Evaluation of Cultural Type

The cultural approach represents several positions in the curriculum movement. One is the attempt to give the pupils a thorough orientation to the life of a country, a race, or an ethnic group. A second is an attempt to fuse or integrate several subject disciplines around some specific goals of education, pulling from geography and history and economics and sociology those topics which can be related to a particular set of aims. Many variations of these two major positions exist.

Basically, this approach represents an attempt to restore some relatedness to the previously divided subject fields. However, as in the topical plan, there is still missing the fundamental approach to learning through problems of significance to youth. The approach is one of rearranging subject matter to exploit an adult concept. There is not a "forked-road situation" which would naturally enlist the youth's interest; there is no fundamental problem to which he at the teen age can give himself. However, within this approach does lie the seeds for relating subject matter previously structionalized by traditional disciplines and of bringing these within the sphere of pupil need and within the range of his experience.

The Problems Type

This type will be illustrated by reference to both social and personal problems. Under the concept of a social problem developed here the material must be

15. Los Angeles County Schools, *World Citizenship* (Social Studies Curriculum monograph SS–55; Los Angeles, Calif., 1946), pp. 1–10.

organized around a statement which provides opportunity for collecting data, analyzing it, organizing and interpreting it, drawing conclusions and applying them.[16] For instance, "How did the people in England live in the sixteenth century?" does not fit our definition of a problem. Neither would the problem "How does St. Louis today provide recreation for its children in school?" But "How can we improve our record of safety in the state?" would be a problem satisfying the required conditions.

Illustrations of Social Problems

INFLUENCING PUBLIC OPINION, SANTA MARIA.   An illustration of this type of organization may be drawn from curriculum work done in Santa Maria, California.

The unit opens with an introduction giving the purpose for teaching it, the basic objectives to be attained, and its relation to other units. The suggested materials are then organized under headings, and under these are suggested areas for appropriate study and activities.

INFLUENCING PUBLIC OPINION

I. What aspects of our thinking are influenced by others?
  A. In the community
    1. Drives: Boy scouts, infantile paralysis, Red Cross
    2. School: School games, ticket sales, elections, rallies
    3. Newspaper: Stories, editorials, advertising
    4. Church: Teaching of gospel, socials, youth groups
    5. Leading citizens: Mayor, police, businessmen, "town boss," social leaders
  B. Social
    1. Public health: Tuberculosis, infantile paralysis, clinics, quarantine
    2. Child labor: Arguments for and against the amendment, books such as *Cry of the Children* by Browning and *Oliver Twist* by Dickens
    3. Labor organization: Strikes such as Pullman in 1892, steel in 1877, Pinkerton detectives, IWW as Wobblies, agitators, Communists, CIO, AF of L
    4. Public school: Arguments for and against free public education, the life of Horace Mann, Booker T. Washington, opinions of Jefferson and others
    5. Ideological conflicts: Plato's *Republic,* Plutarch's *Lives,* Declaration of Independence, Constitution, Bill of Rights, Magna Charta, democracy and its competitors

---

16. For a very valuable study of the problem, see Lavone Hanna, Edward Krugg, and I. James Quillen, *The Problems Approach* (Stanford Social Studies Investigation, *Bulletin* No. 10; Stanford University, Calif., 1940). Mimeographed. Also I. James Quillen and Lavone A. Hanna, *Education for Social Competence* (Chicago: Scott, Foresman and Company, 1948.)

C. Political
    1. Campaigns: Slogans such as "Tippecanoe and Tyler too" of 1840, "Win with Old Hickory" of 1824, "Full Dinner Pail" of 1900; platforms such as "help the farmer," "help business," "help labor," "help children," conventions, radio broadcasting, candidates fishing
    2. Public figures: "Cactus Jack" Garner, "Rough and Ready" Theodore Roosevelt, "Silent Cal" Coolidge
    3. Party favoritism: "If we win, you'll get . . . ," job preferences for leaders and workers

D. Industrial
    1. Railroads: Built up by advertising in Europe and the United States for people to occupy free land in the West, railroad strikes and labor unrest, travel advertising
    2. Eulogizing self-made man: Millionaires such as Carnegie, Vanderbilt, Rockefeller, Astor; Horatio Alger series, Beer's *Mauve Decade,* Hendrick's *Life of Carnegie,* Sullivan's *Our Times* (Vols. I and II)
    3. America, the land of equal opportunity: Barefoot boy to president, melting pot, log cabin to White House
    4. Child Labor: *Oliver Twist* by Dickens, *Cry of the Children* by Browning, child labor amendment struggles
    5. Machinery: Monsters or saviors, *R.U.R.* by Carel Capek, *Adding Machine* by Rice, cause of unemployment
    6. Advertising: Main reliance of big business, a big business for big business, mainspring of mass consumption
    7. Labor versus capital: Strikes of 1877, 1892, 1936, rise of IWW and CIO, *Life of Samuel Gompers* by Harvey, Reds, agitators, Wobblies, shorter working hours and more pay, wages and hour legislation

E. War
    1. Revolutionary War: "Common Sense" pamphlets by Paine, ballad "Battle of the Kegs," "Yankee Doodle," the Declaration of Independence
    2. Civil War: *Uncle Tom's Cabin, John Brown's Body, God's Angry Man, Conciliation* by Burke, rebels, Yankees, slavery, *Webster's Reply to Hayne*
    3. Spanish-American War: Yellow journalism, "Remember the Maine," Millis' *The Martial Spirit*
    4. World War I: Liberty Loan posters, plays such as *Journey's End,* cartoon, songs
    5. World War II: Propaganda battle, America First Committee, Committee to Defend America by Aiding Great Britain

Suggested Pupil Activities

What are some examples of groups influencing the thinking of others?

Examine and discuss pamphlets of the Revolutionary War period (Paine's pamphlets) for evidences of attempts to influence public opinion.

Tell of ballads, and sing songs which were written during the early Revolutionary period to influence people, such as *The Battle of the Kegs* and *Yankee Doodle.*

Dramatize the signing of the Declaration of Independence or the making of the Constitution to show how groups work together to influence others; bring out the purposes for action taken, and show the conflicting interests of various groups and the part general welfare played in resolving them.

Read books which are highly emotionalized in order to see the attempts to influence others. Keep a record of emotional personal experiences while reading such books as *Uncle Tom's Cabin, Oliver Twist,* or poems like *Cry of the Children* or *Man with the Hoe.*

Discuss Revolutionary and Civil War heroes such as Washington, Lincoln, Douglas, and Lee, from the standpoint of prestige, to see how they influenced others during their time, and how their memories are used for influencing others today.

Consider attempts to influence people during the first World War by observing and analyzing the appeals used in posters of the Liberty Loan Drive.

Have the music teacher or some student present several songs of World War popularity so students may notice the emotional effect of these songs.

Present or read plays such as *Journey's End* or *What Price Glory* to show appeals for peace made to the people after the war.

Observe and analyze attempts made by the student body to sell tickets and annuals, or elect school or class officers.

Make scrapbooks of illustrations taken from newspapers and magazines which show the use of advertising to influence people.

Make a display of photographs of near-by billboards to show how they attempt to influence people.

Report on advertising heard over the radio and offer examples of the various means by which this channel of communication is used by advertisers to influence people.

Collect from newspapers and magazine articles, pictures, cartoons on the recent war which attempt to influence public opinion, centering these around the countries involved.

Illustrate the use of slogans, platforms, and qualifications of candidates to influence people during political campaigns and during elections.

Gather evidence of attempts to influence public opinion and analyze these for possible general devices or methods used to influence people.

Compare an English author's and an American author's accounts of the Revolutionary War and the War of 1812.

Report on Hamilton's writings about the Constitution in the *Federalist.*

Compare advertisements in women's magazines which show fashions of different periods. Notice changes in fashions and changes in appeals made by advertisers.

Collect posters and advertisements used in recent community drives, such as Red Cross, infantile paralysis, community chest; notice the appeals made.

Collect news stories, editorials, advertisements from local papers which deal with some current local problem. Notice the appeals made and the points of view taken.

Gather statements made by leading citizens of the community which were reported in local papers. Observe for evidences of attempts to influence others.

Study the labor movements and appeals made by these groups to the people during the last 100 years, the last 50 years, the last 10 years.

Read the life stories of some educator such as Horace Mann or Booker T. Washington. Show the odds and opinions against which the struggle was made to bring us free education.

Summarize the basic points of several ideologies as expressed in such books as Plato's *Republic,* Plutarch's *Lives,* and such documents as the Declaration of Independence, the Constitution, the Bill of Rights, and the Magna Charta. Show how these appealed to the people.

Make a collection of slogans used in the various political campaigns. Present these to the class for an analysis of what they possibly meant.

Collect information about presidential candidates. List those personal qualities of each which were used to "sell" the candidate to the people.

Post appeals or names given to candidates, such as "Silent Cal" Coolidge, "Rough and Ready" Theodore Roosevelt, and show the auras built around each.

List the platforms and planks used by parties in presidential campaigns and show the appeals used.

Collect information about the rise of big business. Notice various appeals they have made to the public for support.

Read the biographies of such men as Carnegie, Vanderbilt, Rockefeller, Astor, and others to "see how they do it."[17]

HUMAN RELATIONS IN ECONOMIC LIFE, LOS ANGELES.   Los Angeles city and county have jointly prepared a teaching unit on Human Relations in American Economic Life. Its purpose is to develop

> a clearer understanding and appreciation of 1) the basic economic life of our country, 2) the interrelations of our modern industrial, business and agricultural world, 3) the many economic problems which confront the worker, the employer, the public, and government, and 4) the importance of good human relations which are fundamental to the solution of all problems.

The unit is designed to give the teacher assistance in giving the background, interpreting and clarifying the problems, analyzing suggestions and solutions, and in "pointing the way to human relations in labor and management." Only the suggested objectives for each "lesson" are cited here.

HUMAN RELATIONS IN AMERICAN ECONOMIC LIFE

Specific Objectives

LESSON I. All economic factors are interdependent.

A. Ability to analyze the economic problems of family life in relation to the community situation

---

17. Santa Barbara County, *Curriculum Guide for Teachers in Secondary Schools* (Santa Barbara County, Calif.: Schauer Printing Company, 1941), IV, 83–130.

B. Understanding of
    1. Ways in which our economic needs are met
    2. The factors which make up our economic life
C. Attitude of citizen cooperation

LESSON II. Employees need to know their role in American economic life.
    A. Ability to define clearly the terms "worker" and "employee"
    B. Understanding of
        1. The importance of security to all workers
        2. The importance of all jobs
        3. Ways in which wages are determined
    C. Attitude of appreciation of the importance of common human needs

LESSON III. The individual conduct of the employee is an important link in the chain of economic production.
    A. Ability to identify traits from which good attitudes are developed
    B. Understanding that the attitude of the worker is important in employee-employer situations
    C. Attitude of
        1. Cooperative work habits
        2. Constructive criticism
        3. Respect for company property and trade ethics

LESSON IV. The manager's responsibility is wider than his own personal goals.
    A. Ability to identify the risks and responsibilities of management
    B. Understanding of management's responsibility to his supporters
    C. Understanding of ways in which profits are determined
    D. Attitude that management, like the worker, is entitled to a just return for his efforts

LESSON V. Many of the manager's needs are comparable to those of the worker.
    A. Ability to discuss intelligently and unemotionally the advantages and disadvantages of being a manager
    B. Understanding of the employer's needs
    C. Attitude of being willing as a worker to contribute to the future development of the enterprise

LESSON VI. The individual conduct of the employer is an important factor in the chain of economic production.
    A. Ability to recognize and accept scientific methods in placing employees and adjusting problems
    B. Understanding that an employer's problems are affected by changing conditions
    C. Attitude of being willing to contribute to good human relations
        1. Employers have special interests in good relations with employees
        2. Employees have special interests in good relations with employers

LESSON VII. Efforts of workers and managers to achieve their goals have assumed many different forms.

A. Ability to see the logical and meaningful development of labor and industrial organization

B. Understanding of the development of labor organization in relation to the evolution of our industrial growth

C. Attitude that the formation of labor organizations is an effort to restore the natural balance of human relationships disturbed by the unprecedented growth of business

LESSON VIII. A variety of methods have been developed to secure industrial peace.

A. Ability to apply peaceful methods of settling disputes to a variety of situations

B. Understanding of the procedures in use today for bringing about agreement

C. Attitude of accepting the fact that the public is vitally concerned with peaceful settlement of labor-manager problems

LESSON IX. Public welfare is protected by government participation.

A. Understanding the major provisions and objectives of past and present labor legislation

B. Understanding the need for government regulation in addition to other means of settlement

C. Attitude of accepting the fact that progress is being made in solving problems of human relations in economic life

LESSON X. Human relations chiefly emphasized today

A. Ability to locate and use current information to form opinions

B. Understanding of
1. The need for personal responsibility in working toward improvement
2. The effect of our progress on the other countries of the world

C. Attitude of willingness to grow in understanding and knowledge[18]

Illustrations of Personal Problems

The personal problem must be of immediate importance to the individual or group, or both, and must set up the Dewey "forked-road situation." It must make a difference to the youth, it must carry about it an element of emotional disturbance, and it must require the pupil to make a choice which affects him. It possesses the same characteristics as the second type of organization described, but deals with a problem of personal growth.

A sampling of illustrations will serve to give the general nature of this type of organization. Throughout the country are various types of units on orientation. Some of these are taught in the seventh grade, as the pupil enters the

---

18. *Human Relations in American Economic Life: A Teaching Unit* (A Joint Publication of the Los Angeles County Schools, Secondary Curriculum Monograph M–71, and Los Angeles City Schools, Curriculum Division Publication No. SC–428; Los Angeles, Calif., 1949).

junior high school, and others are taught at the beginning of the tenth grade as the pupil enters the senior high school.

SENIOR GOALS, SAN FRANCISCO, CALIFORNIA.

SENIOR GOALS

The emphasis throughout the secondary school curriculum has been the development of self-dependence. To bridge the gap between self-dependence in a school situation to self-dependence in actual life situations, Senior Goals has become a part of each graduating senior's program. Because living in a modern world is becoming more complex, youth must be trained from childhood to know how to apply the principles of American democracy in the home, on the job, and in the community.

Senior Goals is a group of experiences concerned with the pupil's adjustment to life after leaving high school. The purpose of this course is to make our high school seniors aware of their responsibilities in living the fullest life possible in a democratic society.

What are the desired end results of this new group of experiences?

I. Transition: The high school senior realizes that he is about to enter a new phase of life and feels the necessity of preparing himself for this transition.

II. Adjustment: The maturing adolescent recognizes that he is going to have to make adjustments. He is willing to develop behavior patterns which will lead to personal and family happiness, and satisfying and useful community and civic participation.

III. Growth in responsibility
    A. Personally
        1. He becomes the finest person it is possible for him to become.
        2. He practices the principles underlying successful family living.
    B. Socially
        1. He lives and works cooperatively with others.
        2. He makes his best contribution to society.
    C. Economically
        1. He uses resources wisely.
        2. He earns a living in work for which he is suited and prepared.
    D. Civically
        1. He acts upon an understanding of and loyalty to our American ideals.
        2. He achieves skill with processes of group action.
        3. He accepts individual responsibility for civic improvement.

IV. Self-evaluation: He continually evaluates himself to take stock of his development and progress toward these ends and plans for improvement.

This course proposes to help boys and girls think seriously about worthwhile goals in life and the ways and means of achieving them. Since good human relations are basic to our democratic way of life, it stresses the importance of individual personality, the process of group responsibility and cooperation, and the contribution of reflective thinking.

It provides for group problem-solving in three basic areas:

      1. Understanding of yourself and your family
      2. Understanding of yourself and personal economics
      3. Understanding of yourself and your job

I. Understanding of yourself and your family: Desired end results
   A. The student understands why people do the things they do.
   B. He distinguishes between self-interest and self-centeredness.
   C. He knows that continuous growth is possible.
   D. He recognizes that his own well-being depends upon his working toward the well-being of groups to which he belongs.
   E. He solves personal and social problems by getting facts and facing reality.
   F. He knows the important things to consider in anticipation of establishing a home and family.
   G. He realizes that marriage is a matter to be worked at with all the intelligence and devotion anyone can muster.
   H. He appraises his personal development and human relationships in the light of his developing sense of values.

II. Understanding yourself and your job: Desired end results
   A. The student is familiar with the opportunities for employment and advancement in the Bay Area.
   B. He recognizes the practical necessity of choosing his vocation in terms of physical fitness, his interests and desires, his abilities, and his need for further training.
   C. He makes an analysis of the traits, qualities, temperament and attitudes he possesses for his chosen vocation.
   D. He knows how to look for and apply for a job.
   E. He keeps his job by giving good service to his employer and advances in his work by accepting responsibilities to his job.
   F. He realizes that human relationships become more and more important to his vocational success as well as to his enjoyment of the cultural values of life.
   G. He appraises his behavior and his vocational goals with his developing sense of values.

III. Understanding yourself and personal economics: Desired end results
   A. The student understands his role as a consumer in the American way of life.
   B. He has a deep sense of responsibility for the social effect of his consumer activities.
   C. He sets standards for living toward which he is willing to work.
   D. He knows how to get facts and relies intelligently on those who are experts.
   E. He improves all his techniques of buymanship.
   F. He uses and cares properly for the things he owns.

G. He plans for the long-term money management problems through savings, insuring against risks, and investments.
H. He appraises his buying habits and purchases with his developing sense of values.[19]

The actual materials of the course are not cited here but only the directional purposes which are designed to aid the teacher in the selection of appropriate instructional materials.

SENIOR PROBLEMS, LOS ANGELES.   In the city of Los Angeles seniors take a course entitled Senior Problems designed to assist them with immediate problems of importance to them. A brief outline of the units will reveal the nature of the course.

SENIOR PROBLEMS

UNIT I. Understanding yourself in relation to others
A. Our drives
B. Individual differences
C. Reactions to conflict
D. Steps toward straight thinking
E. Development of specific character values
F. Good relations with others
G. Habit formation
H. Experiments in personality adjustment
I. Aid in formulating a philosophy of life

UNIT II. You and your family
A. Approach to marriage
B. Home and family

UNIT III. Personal and family finance
A. Planning your spending—budgeting
B. Using credit
C. Using bank services
D. Investing your savings
E. Selecting insurance policies
F. Paying taxes
G. Appreciating agencies, regulations, authorizations for the common good
H. Facing problem of employment of the wife or homemaker
I. Taking inventory

UNIT IV. You and your job
A. Discovering occupational interest
B. Determining probable ability and aptitude in the field of the student's interest area
C. Obtaining occupational information

19. San Francisco Unified School District, *Senior Goals* (Secondary Schools; San Francisco, Calif., 1951), pp. 21–24.

D. Tentatively selecting area of work for further study
E. Planning a training program
F. Studying how to get the right job and hold it
G. Making out a post-high school vocational plan card after personal confer-
   ence in which all of the above data have been considered[20]

EFFECTIVE LIVING, FLORIDA. The Florida State Department of Education
has suggested units based upon problems of concern to youth. The following
one consists largely of material related to certain physical characteristics about
which all youth are concerned. Problems suggested for the teacher are stated
in the form of questions.

EFFECTIVE LIVING

Problems and Content

I. Your goals
   A. What do you really want in life?
   B. How can studying yourself help you attain these things?
   C. If you want to make the most of yourself, in what ways will you need
      to grow and develop?

II. Personal inventory
   A. What does the term "inventory" mean?
   B. What are the purposes of an inventory?
   C. In this "business of living," what should a personal inventory include?
   D. How can you make such an inventory?
   E. Why should you take such an inventory?
   F. How can a periodic health examination be of value to you?
   G. What does a health examination usually include?
   H. What other tests may be provided which will help you determine your
      physical condition?
   I. If the health examination is made by the school physician, what follow-
      up procedures will he use?
   J. How can you cooperate with the physician and nurses?
   K. What are the dangers of self-diagnosis and self-treatment?
   L. What type of training is required before a medical school feels that a
      doctor can practice medicine?
   M. What are some of the specialists you should know and what specialty
      does the name indicate?
   N. What should you consider in choosing your doctor?
   O. How would you obtain information about physicians in a city to which
      you were moving?

III. The teeth behind your smile
   A. What do the teeth behind your smile reveal about you?
   B. What are the advantages to you of a clean mouth and sound teeth?

---

20. Los Angeles Schools, *Senior Problems* (Publication No. 410, revised; Los Angeles,
Calif., 1949), pp. 11–17.

    C. What is the condition of your teeth and gums?

    D. What changes have occurred in your teeth since birth?

    E. What principally has affected the condition your teeth are in today?

    F. What has happened when a tooth becomes carious and aches?

    G. What comparatively recent experiments have given us new information in regard to reducing dental caries?

    H. What can you do at your age to take care of your teeth to make them last as long as possible?

    I. What care should a child be given to help him develop sound and beautiful teeth?

    J. What should a person look for in selecting a dentist?

IV. Skin, hair, nails

    A. What has the greatest appeal to members of opposite sex in regard to skin, hair, nails?

    B. What general ways of living are especially reflected in the skin?

    C. How is the skin constructed and what are its functions?

    D. What are people trying to do with cosmetics and beauty treatments of all kinds?

    E. What are some common skin problems and what can be done about them?

    F. How can hair be kept glossy and healthy?

    G. What are some special problems in keeping hair attractive?

    H. How can superfluous hair be removed?

    I. What care should the hand and nails receive?

V. Your body lineup

    A. What are the advantages of good posture to you?

    B. What are some causes of bad posture?

    C. What are some common abnormal spinal curvatures?

    D. What should one strive for in posture?

    E. What are correct positions for?

VI. Feet

    A. How does the normal foot look?

    B. What are some common foot troubles?

    C. What may be some effects of foot trouble?

    D. What are some indications of weak or flattened arches?

    E. What are the causes of foot trouble?

    F. What are the characteristics of a hygienic shoe?

    G. How can one correct foot troubles?

    H. What care should feet and shoes receive?

VII. Nutrition for you

    A. What are signs of good nutrition?

    B. What is the difference in hollow hunger and hidden hunger?

C. How can you tell whether or not you have hidden hunger?

D. What is malnutrition?

E. Where does malnutrition begin?

F. What does the body do with food?

G. What determines how much food a person needs?

H. What practical plan can one follow for selecting a well balanced diet daily?

I. What can one do to preserve mineral and vitamin values of food?

J. How can you get the most value out of your food dollar?

K. Your weight

VIII. Your voice

A. How do you convey your ideas to others?

B. What does your voice reveal about you?

C. What are the physical factors entering into production of the human voice?

D. How does the larynx function in producing sound?

E. What are the resonant chambers and how do they affect voice?

F. How do voices vary?

G. What can you do to take care of and improve your voice?

IX. Your vision and hearing

A. What symptoms or signs indicate the need for a vision test or eye examination?

B. How is the eye constructed and how does it work?

C. What are common visual defects?

D. What precautions should you take if you wear glasses?

E. Whom should you consult about your eyes?

F. What care should you take of your eyes?

G. What are some indications of hearing loss?

H. How may impaired hearing affect an individual?

I. What are the major causes of hearing loss other than congenital deafness?

J. What measures should you take to protect your ears?

X. Exercise, fatigue, rest

A. What values have you received from the exercise which you have been taking?

B. What determines the type of exercise an individual takes?

C. What are dangers of overactivity?

D. What signs indicate overactivity?

E. What is difference in exercise and recreation?

F. What conditions may produce a feeling of fatigue?

G. What are the effects of fatigue?

H. Why is sleep so valuable to an individual?

I. How does constant loss of sleep affect an individual?

J. What conditions promote sleep?

K. What may aid one in going to sleep, if one is wakeful?[21]

Improving the Curriculum through Subject Unity

Several stages of development can be followed by groups who wish to change their curriculum, yet do not wish to abolish subject matter lines. All the proposals suggested in this chapter can be adopted within fields of existing studies, if intelligent cooperation is practiced among established departments. To do this, however, it is obviously necessary to cease justifying existing subjects or subject organizations as such, bargaining for the retention of subject offerings, quarreling over proportionate amounts of time in the school program, scheduling rigidly the time for each subject division, requiring an equal amount of work from all pupils, and maintaining the attitude that the other fellow will do the changing. Any inflexibility will tend to block any change, whether it be within or beyond subject lines. The spirit of experimentalism and flexibility and generosity must prevail first and last equally among all.

If basic changes are to be made in the patterns of organization, numerous studies should be made by teachers. There need not be any set order to these studies, but the life of the community—its resources, its mores and customs, its social and economic conditions and problems, and its educational facilities —should be analyzed. If education is to be a local affair, as most men contend, it must be seated in the life of the community and as far as possible be indigenous to its culture. This must be true for as many subject materials in the curriculum as possible, and applies with primary force to the social studies, science, art, speech, music, industrial arts, homemaking, and the area of personal problems. Such an analysis can be made by a well-planned community survey, following any of the many excellent patterns which have been developed.

There must also be an analysis of the problems which youth in the community think they face. Whether the teacher thinks a certain situation is a problem or not is of no import so long as the youth himself genuinely feels that the matter is a problem to him. The study of the problems of youth can be made by several techniques, and many must be used, for no one singly is sufficient. Parents should be consulted about the problems which youth talk about and face with their parents. Guidance workers and teacher counselors should report on problems which youth bring to them. Every teacher can keep a record of topics which have interested pupils, of questions and problems which seem to be of greatest importance to them. Youth themselves can be consulted,

---

21. Florida State Department of Education, *Health Education* (Secondary Schools, *Bulletin* No. 4–B; Tallahassee, Fla.: 1950), pp. 41–72.

and they must not be left out of the picture. From all these sources and from people in the community who work with youth—recreational leaders, boy- and girl-scout directors and troop leaders, church workers—help can be secured in finally drawing up a list of pertinent problems of youth.

Canvass should then be made of the pertinent social problems which are of significance to the community and about which youth should be able to form some intelligent opinions. These problems must be ones with which the young people are acquainted and should offer some immediate opportunities for observation or actual experience. They need to be the most pertinent problems facing democracy today and should be added to the list of materials for use.

Once such collections are made, the question then arises how to organize and teach them. Here is a need for teachers to sit down and review the significant literature of the last ten years on the problems of growth and development and the concepts of curriculum organization. To introduce this item as a study program before any work is done on the curriculum, such as has just been suggested, is to do with teachers what one should not do with youth. Now a need exists; the material must be organized. At this stage, then, through reading and discussion teachers should make ample canvass of the pertinent literature treating psychological growth and learning techniques, that of the past ten years particularly. As such study proceeds, present practice in the school should constantly be examined for illustrations. Is what we are doing an illustration of a disappearing practice? Is it without present psychological justification? What is suggested as a substitute? The subject fields, principles, concepts, and skills should all be adequately discussed.

At the same time committees of teachers should study and analyze the methods other groups use in organizing curriculum materials. Any attempt to imitate another program uncritically will be an indication of weakness on the part of the staff and will defeat the purpose of the study. Not that imitation of good practice is wrong, nor that one should not use the good work of others, but the person who adopts another's work without having gone through a thorough process of making it his own is acting contrary to the principles of growth.

The staff is now ready to experiment with suggested reorganizations of materials. Many suggestions and types should be tried out, for only through this method will the opinions and feelings of individual teachers be satisfied. It is more necessary to please them and give them a feeling of having made worthy contributions than it is to have the final curriculum uniform. Uniformity will come later as a product of continued experience rather than earlier as a result of voting or compulsion. It is better to try first to organize as far as possible by the problems approach; then for definite purposes and levels of development other types of organization should be suggested. Of course, criteria to guide decisions must be made and faithfully followed; otherwise, favorite blocks of subject matter will be found hidden in the finished product.

Constant vigilance must be practiced by the leaders to see that each decision conforms to the criteria that have been adopted. If they are adopted prior to the making of decisions they will be of greater service than if they are decided in the heat of controversy.

The cooperation of the school administrator is very important. He must be more than willing to change anything possible to allow for greater flexibility in the organization of the program. Because of their own reluctance to disturb their pet schedule, many administrators retard the programs which they have urged teachers to adopt. Practically anything can be scheduled within reason, and unless principals are ready to assume this attitude they might as well give up the idea of curriculum change. A rigid schedule is by all odds the least defensible reason for retarding curriculum change.

Two things should be watched in this process of curriculum reorganization. First, make all relationships among subject fields genuine ones in terms of the problems chosen. Do not be guilty of making unsupportable correlations. In the second place, changes in classroom methodology will be required to accompany changed curriculum organization. The problems type of organization, for instance, simply cannot be carried out in the traditional recitation method of classroom procedure. Such a method of organization should be accompanied by experimentation in teaching procedures. Discussion, wide reading, excursions, out-of-school activities, construction projects, community participation, use of visual materials, and many other types of activities need to be introduced. Along with these changes in teaching methods should come a different relationship between pupils and teacher. The teacher is no longer the only authority to answer the questions. When the school deals with materials to which only teachers know the answers, there is quite naturally the development of an authoritarian attitude among teachers. The stage is set for it, the program demands it. But when problems are introduced to which teachers do not have final answers, a different attitude of working together prevails. Unless teachers are willing to say unashamedly that they do not know and are willing to try new paths of working with pupils, the curriculum will never move beyond the stage of the topical type of organization. But teachers do not like to tell pupils that they do not know the answers. It gives them a feeling of insecurity. This attitude of uncertainty, so uncomfortable and seemingly unbecoming to many teachers, is a major cause of curriculum conservatism. Every attempt possible should be made to retain a high degree of teacher security in dealing with new materials and methods. Teachers frequently feel, and justifiably so, that their efficiency is impaired and their "face" is lost when they are placed in a position where they are not facile with answers. But teachers are obligated to improve their teaching. They *cannot* fall back on tenure or complacent ignorance and be truly professional. Obviously, if the criterion of a teacher's success is competent scholarship in his field, then teachers will not move beyond the areas in which they have demonstrated competence. But if growth through the resolution of confusion and the learning of new and different ways of doing things are the criteria of success, then the teachers will develop a different attitude. Here again the administrator is the key to the situation.

These suggestions for reorganization can be carried out by any ordinary faculty of teachers and principles working together intelligently and consistently. They can be accomplished without the destruction of subject lines, but they do call for the lessening of sharp distinctions between different divisions of given fields. They call further for cooperation between departments and for a willingness to break down those barriers which make greater unity difficult or impossible.

Chapter Eleven

Recent Curriculum

Concepts

T HE GREATEST CURRICULUM unrest in this country probably came during the third decade of the twentieth century. Following World War I people were ready to break the mold of tradition somewhat; they were a little tired of the centralized control which they had experienced during the war; they were questioning the form and content of the social experience to which they were accustomed; they were anxious to try something different. The whole pent-up enthusiasm for change which had been checked during the war was ready to spring into action. It went into action locally, however, and national groups—educational or social—were not able to direct it. During the latter part of the decade, prosperity began to return, and conservatism again took over. The reaction to change swung back apace and liberals were somewhat less popular than they had been five years before. But at the close of the decade, and concurrent with the onset of our greatest depression, these same liberals were blessed with a most attentive audience. People were beginning to believe that things could not be patched up or repaired by the same social adhesives which they had used; they were more willing to experiment with

306

fundamental changes. This attitude continued until the darkest days of the depression; by that time nearly anything that approached common sense could get a hearing.

For nearly three hundred years in this country the basis for organizing and selecting curriculum content had remained unchanged and practically unchallenged except by a few "visionaries" and idealists. The subject framework— a grouping of content around a segment of a field of learning—was the form of curriculum organization. To be sure, the Herbartians as a group asked for more and greater relationships, and many local workers in education were seeing other ways of organizing content, but, on the whole, national committees and leaders in education saw nothing about the subject organization to cause them to propose changes. However, with the advent of the scientific movement in education, the growing heterogeneity of the population of the secondary school, the Dewey theory of living and learning, and the increase in invention, knowledge, and social change, something had to be done with the curriculum. But just following a confusing war and a more confusing peace, educators were bewildered by the deep-reaching implications of a philosophy they did not understand and the whirl of a social change they could not control. So they began individually and collectively to reform, reorganize, and reshape the curriculum. The result was a riot of activity with a mass of confusing ideas and terms—correlation, integration, coordination, fusion, common learnings, and others—all attempts to establish some sensible relationship among a staggering number of discrete subject fields.

Discoveries in the Nature of Individual Development

Education cannot deal only with social aims; it must, if it expects to achieve them, give heed to the nature of individual development. For the first twenty-five years of the twentieth century, American psychology was burdened with mechanistic explanations of human behavior. The method of minute analysis, so common to industrial and technical processes, was applied to an organism capable of unlimited and uncontrollable variables. Mechanistic science holds true only for controllable factors; it cannot completely explain human behavior. However, out of the attempt of psychologists to draw inferences for human behavior (a complicated pattern) from careful experimentation with a simple environment (rats in a maze) have come great gains in the techniques for studying human behavior. Hypotheses have been formulated which are being used to guide the extension of psychological investigations in the complex human organism.

These psychological findings have great significance for the teacher and the curriculum worker. Bell has summarized their implications in the following manner.

1. General psychology has shifted its emphasis from the study solely of mental life, or of specific behavior to the study of human personality, the total quality or pattern of an individual's behavior.

2. The psycho-biologist and physiologist, the clinical psychologist, the social psychologist and anthropologist, even the psychiatrist are bringing their data and tentative conclusions to bear on this same problem. All of them are seeing individual behavior as a manifestation of a dynamic give-and take between the individual and his fellows in society. It is the fruit of his social and inner experience.

3. Educational psychologists, when they are asked to assess the value of their findings in terms of their worth for education, become social psychologists. They see the school as one of the social forces which affect personality. Insisting on the social nature of personality, and defining the function of the school in personality terms, they are logically driven to see the major personality task of the school as a social task. In the interests of the personality development of its pupils, the school becomes concerned with every aspect of community life which affects the child.

4. This conception of the school as a force in molding personality means that psychologists are bringing their data to bear on educational objectives as well as on educational methods and processes. They are concerned with the kinds of experiences which make up the curriculum. The clinical psychologists, out of their study of maladjusted behavior-problem children, are particularly insistent on this. They see clearly that adjustment is a two-way matter—not solely the adjustment of the individual to his environment and group, but often the adjustment of intolerable social situations to the individual.

5. The first curriculum emphasis growing out of this kind of thinking is one upon *orientation*—an emphasis upon the necessity of leading children to understand their relation to society. This means at all levels of the school inclusion of social experiences that will result in understanding self and society, and the relationship of the two. The Gestalt psychologist insists that this is the fundamental problem of all life, the relationship of the whole to the part, freedom of the individual under subordination to the group. The "social frontier" thinker deals with the same problem in immediate socio-economic terms. He asks: How can the individual be other than maladjusted to a society which is run by static, social, political, and economic conceptions? Society is not a static system; it is not in unchanging equilibrium. It is rather a fluid energy system subject to the laws of dynamics, constantly in process of adjustment and change. Can not this change be controlled in the interests of the individuals who make up the system?

6. Turning to a second major phase, namely, *psychological processes underlying school activities,* I would emphasize first *maturation*. It is being recognized as particularly stupid to ask children to perform beyond the level of their bodily development in the attempted learning of skills, or beyond the level of their insight in the attempted learning of mental-intellectual concepts or processes. Studies of what children do at specific maturation levels give us clues as to what they can do at those levels, though

unfortunately our knowledge is all too scanty here. Our next major psychological contribution to education may be on the implementation of the principle of "pacing" based on a definite knowledge of maturation.

7. A second emphasis that is coming increasingly into psychological prominence is that of *interest* and *motivation*. All studies of learning emphasize its *purposiveness*. Certain psychologists make all organismic activity purposeful, explaining it as an attempt to move from a state of disturbance to a state of equilibrium. Watson and Spence state that the major lines of tension in such an organism are such as to further movement

From	*Toward*
Situations involving pain, physical injury, deprivation	Situations involving improved health, well-being, euphoria
Situations involving thwarting, defeat	Situations bringing mastery, successful completion
Situations involving scorn, contempt, disapproval	Situations bringing approval, recognition, appreciation
Situations involving worry, anxiety, fear	Situations offering security
Situations involving boresome, monotonous repetitions	Situations offering new and stimulating experiences

8. Observers of activity motivated by purpose are pointing out that experience is of most value to the individual when within the activity itself there is meaning in terms of the pupil's own purposes and goals. It must not only be couched in terms that he understands, but it must have the quality of *reality* for him. (This is not to deny the reality of imaginative experience.) In addition it must have the quality of *novelty*.

9. Many psychologists, too, are pointing out that *successful* experience is of far more value to the individual than is failure, which is primarily a personality depressant.

10. The experience should be of such a nature that it helps in the process of *integration* in the individual. It should have a quality of *centrality*, helping him to see things in their relationships, and to focalize his energies, abilities, and understandings in meeting new situations. This probably means more problem-project work and more teaching of one subject through others.

11. Closely allied to this is the problem of transfer of training, transposition, and the development of the generalizing powers of the individual. The process of transfer probably resides both in the individual and in the recurring situations he meets. Both as a problem and as a fact it cannot be ignored by the curriculum maker.

12. The third general aspect I should mention is *methodological cues derived from psychology for the curriculum worker*. Dr. Raymond Wheeler would list the following:

1. Units selected should be successively expanding, differentiating units within the grasp of the student—going from the gross outlines of whole concepts (or body movements) to differentiated wholes whose parts

are seen in relationship to each other and to the whole. (A difficult cue to follow.)

2. Examples and problems must illustrate principles. Students must build up a conception of the world and of society as an ordered integrated whole.

3. Subjects shall be taught through each other, or in correlation.

4. We shall move from the general to the particular rather than from the particular to the general.

5. The program shall be based on individual activity and on individual attention, interest centered.

6. Some form of the unit-project method seems to lend itself best to the working out of our principles.

7. There shall be chronological, sequential unification of the entire experience pattern set up as a curriculum.

8. Lessened use of failure, of grades and other extrinsic rewarding devices, less teaching and more pupil activity.

13. Drill, i.e. repetition of the same learning experience, has been vastly overemphasized. Refinement of skills or differentiation of concepts out of broad categories of ideation comes about with individually motivated practice in which consecutively new relationships, new values, or new techniques are mastered.

14. The departmentalized system of teaching is under fire from a number of quarters as being fractionating, not integrating, for the individual.

15. New developments relative to human nature as a derived function of the environment are changing the deterministic educational practices based on conceptions of the biologically limited inherited nature of the individual. All growth is basically due to the interaction of both factors in the whole—heredity and environment—the individual in his setting—through a long series of experiences.[1]

Philosophical Concepts

The second factor affecting the curriculum is a series of vitalizing philosophical conceptions. Most of these are not new but are being reemphasized and re-stated. Since these also have been developed in detail in other places in this book, they will only be summarized here.[2]

---

1. Reginald Bell, *Some Implications of Modern Psychological Developments for the School*. Statement prepared for the author.

2. The following sources are especially helpful for getting the significant philosophical points of view: Joseph Justman, *Theories of Secondary Education in the United States* (New York: Columbia University, Teachers College, Bureau of Publications, 1940); Norman Woelfel, *Molders of the American Mind* (New York: Columbia University Press, 1934); John Dewey, *Experience and Education* (New York: The Macmillan

William H. Kilpatrick summarizes some of these philosophical principles, as far as they relate to ethical practice, as follows:

1. Each person is to be treated always as *end* and never merely as *means*. In this ethical respect all men are to stand equal.

2. Conversely, each person is under moral obligation so to act as, negatively, not to hurt the good life of others and, positively, to foster the good life for all.

3. The more honestly and carefully study is carried on by different individuals and groups, the more likely will they be to reach like results.

4. The free play of intelligence stands as our final resource to tell us what to do—intelligence playing freely upon experience in any and all of its content, including the use of intelligence itself.

5. We know no absolute principles; that is none which stand properly above criticism or which may not conceivably be modified, perhaps in intent, perhaps in application, as new conditions arise.

6. From all the foregoing, democracy follows as the effort to run society on the combined basis of the good life and ethics, as these are managed cooperatively by the members themselves.[3]

The Experimentalist Position

To these we might add the three dominant conceptions of the experimentalist outlook: "(1) the conception that ideas mean only their consequences in experience; (2) the conception that experience, at least of the kind we are interested in, is essentially social in origin and predominantly social in purpose; and (3) the conception that we find out what to expect in life by studying experimentally the uniformities within experience."[4]

The experimentalist position in education is essentially a statement of the nature of the good life. This concept gives dynamics to education, for it becomes goals or purposes to be achieved through education. Justman characterizes the essential concepts regarding the good life somewhat as follows:

1. The good life of man is to be defined in terms of a flexible, adaptable method of living rather than in terms of fixed adherence to fixed goals.

2. The good life is essentially individual.

3. The good life is in acting and behaving, not in contemplating.

Company, 1938); John S. Brubacher, *Modern Philosophies of Education* (New York: McGraw-Hill Book Company, Inc., 1939); National Society for the Study of Education, *Philosophies of Education* (Forty-first Yearbook; Chicago: University of Chicago Press, 1942), Part I; John L. Childs, *Education and Morals* (New York: Appleton-Century-Crofts, Inc., 1950).

3. *Philosophies of Education,* Part I, pp. 3–4. Chap. 2 succinctly summarizes the experimentalist point of view.

4. *Ibid.,* p. 44.

4. Learning to live the good life is learning to deal properly with experience.

5. Experiences are within a social culture.

6. Good living needs to receive systematic guidance in experiencing.

7. The job of the school is to produce intentionally an environment in which experiences would be more truly educative than they otherwise would be.

8. Method is an intrinsic part of the experiencing process.

9. Education is a part of the natural experiencing process, not something different from, apart from, or even in addition to.

10. The transmission of culture is a means of enabling the individual to deal more intelligently with his own experience.

11. Education takes in the total of all human experience, in and out of school.

12. Education is an enterprise of the total society, not one between teachers and children in a school.

13. The conditions prevailing in society are of utmost concern to education, and in order to improve the good life of children the social conditions of society at large which prevent it must be changed. This is a function of education— of the school and of other elements in society working together.[5]

14. The new materials of education are experiences, and the personal and social needs of all adolescents must be met in the secondary school.[6]

The social, psychological, and philosophical dynamics have forced education to reconsider its premises and practices. They have forced the school to take in all youth, to canvass carefully their needs as a basis of reorganization, to use modern problems and the problem method, to become a democratic sociological unit, to make instruction out of experience, and to vary it according to the differences in purposes and powers of individuals. No less emphasis can be placed upon continuity, and the scope of activities must be widened, but the bases for defining the scope and sequence of learning experiences must transcend and even differ in kind from those used under the concept of traditional education. Greater social knowledge and competence are required of teachers, and the administrator needs to become a social engineer. Guidance will take its place as an integral part of proper learning, and teachers will find cooperation more necessary than ever before. In terms of these dynamics the wholeness of the curriculum and the instructional process will become a problem of the utmost importance. Subject divisions will break down and new orientations will arise.

---

5. This position is opposed by those moderns who believe the job of the school is to orient the child to the world in which he lives, to point out its depression zones, and to send the youth into the world to work out his own problems democratically.

6. See Justman, *Theories of Secondary Education*, pp. 273ff.

Utilizing Philosophy in Curriculum Development

For the past twenty years local schools and state systems have been promoting curriculum development and have issued bulletins to guide teachers. These bulletins have contained statements of philosophy; or, to put it more accurately, they have contained statements of points of view on a wide array of issues.

Typical of these statements is the one prepared by the State of Minnesota, which defines the official position of the state as follows:

1. The school as an institution of our social order has been organized to promote and perpetuate the fundamental aims, purposes, principles, and objectives of our democratic society.
2. The task of education in our society is to provide the environment which will enable the pupil through experience to acquire not only knowledge and information but also the attitudes, ideals, understandings, appreciations, and skills necessary for participation in a democratic society.
3. The curriculum consists of all of the experiences of whatever nature the child has under the guidance of the school and it is the function of the school curriculum to suggest the types of experiences we desire pupils to have in order to facilitate the learnings we believe best to equip youth for successful, happy adjustment in a democratic society.
4. We believe that the primary function of the public school is conceived to be one of general education; namely "an education capable at once of taking on many different forms and yet of representing in all of its forms the common knowledge and the common values on which a free society depends."
5. Although it is true that general education is the primary function of the public school, we also believe that education for adaptability is essential. Vocational and personal-interest courses fulfill definite needs for many pupils, especially those who do not go to college, and should become a part of the curriculum.
6. One great problem in education is the reconciliation of the necessity for common belief based on heritage and the equally obvious necessity for new and independent insights leading to change. In making this reconciliation we do not believe that education can be wholly devoted either to tradition and heritage, with their feeling of commitment to allegiance, or to experiment and pragmatism, with their tone of curiosity and their readiness to change; but we do believe that education must at the same time uphold both tradition and experiment—the ideal and the means, bringing about, like our culture itself, change within commitment.
7. We believe that in a democratic society the basic element is the individual and by the same token the individual pupil is the basic element in

the school. We, however, recognize the dual nature of our responsibility to serve both the individual and society and the fact that the two purposes are mutually interlocking and interdependent rather than antagonistic. We, therefore, believe that the best possible education program will so influence the growth of each individual that he will be able to achieve personal happiness and self-realization within the culture and accepted patterns of our society through his own and cooperative purposeful activity in the interest of all.

8. In directing the growth of the child we recognize the fact that the school is only one of a number of forces that influence. . . . Nevertheless, we believe that the school has the major responsibility for the education of the child and is obligated to coordinate and use as much as possible the varied educative forces that bear on him, to the end that the optimum outcome in desirable thoughts, feelings, and action shall be realized.

9. One of our basic concepts is the desire to secure the equalization of educational opportunity for all the children of all the people regardless of race, color, creed, or economic social status.

10. We believe that the hope of the American school system, indeed of our society, is precisely that it can pursue two goals simultaneously—to give scope to the ability group and to raise the average group—while at the same time, despite their different interests, helping both achieve from their education some common and binding understanding of the society which they will possess in common.

11. We believe that education in a democracy must deal with dynamic changing conditions rather than with static unchanging ones and, therefore, the problem of philosophical and curricular revision is of necessity a continuous one.

12. We believe the teacher needs a personal philosophy of education and living, rooted in the best of the past and nourished by the conditions of modern society. The development of this personal philosophy will help the teacher not merely to teach school but to define values and to establish goals for the better of education. The best ideas for improving education, and thereby life itself, must be projected upward and onward as ideals. Thus will American public education help to bring to pass the great American dream of perpetuating and improving democracy.[7]

Toward Greater Unity

Correlation and Integration

One of the first terms to become current was "correlation." To many it meant the initial step toward greater unity in the several subject fields of

7. Minnesota Department of Education, *A Guide for Better Instruction in Minnesota Schools* (Curriculum *Bulletin* No. 1; St. Paul, Minn., 1946), pp. 17–21.

instruction. It probably first implied nothing more than cooperation between departments, such as English and social studies or science and mathematics, which had always existed in well-taught classrooms. From there, the term came to suggest definite administrative rearrangements so as to make possible a closer synthesis. Attempts were made to teach the history of the westward movement at the time that the literature of the pioneer was being studied, and to teach Shakespearean England simultaneously with Shakespeare's plays. From this, the term came to include attempts to select some culture for study and at the time of study to examine the history—political, social, and economic —geography, art, and literature of the people. Later on, broad topics or units were chosen, and materials were selected with reference to their relationship to the major principles or generalizations. As the movement went from departmental cooperation to interdepartmental reorganization, it invoked more and more change in administration and curriculum organization, together with more and more criticism from conservatives.

To most curriculum workers correlation meant a movement to bring relationships into focus between the several departments of the school, such as history, English, and mathematics. But in the report of the National Council of Teachers of English on correlation, one of the most extensive reports on this subject in the field, the term "correlated curriculum" was used to describe certain major attempts to "effect some educational synthesis." In speaking of these attempts the report said they "have been variously called correlation, fusion, and integration." In this particular report, the term "correlation" was used

> . . . because it has had the greatest currency and may thus suggest to more people the idea of making clear to students the relation between the various subjects of instruction and their place in the total scheme of life. The present report is so arranged as to pass from the most conservative sort of merely incidental correlation through the correlation and fusion of subject matter to the more radical forms of complete integration.[8]

The multiple use of the term "correlation" is confusing until one realizes that the committee used it as a generic term to cover all types of synthesis. The report further stated the six forms of "correlating the materials of English instruction" as follows:

> 1. Correlation of English with other fields through incidental references and isolated projects
> 2. An English course based on correlation with other subjects, but not

---

8. Committee on Correlation of the National Council of Teachers of English, Ruth Mary Weeks, chairman, *A Correlated Curriculum* (New York: Appleton-Century-Crofts, Inc., 1936), p. 5. The excerpts here reprinted from this report are used by permission of the publisher.

implying the modification of courses in any other field or the cooperation of other subject teachers

3. The fusion of English with one other subject
4. The fusion of groups of subjects
5. A curriculum based on the integration of all educational subjects
6. A curriculum transcending subject matter divisions[9]

However, when the committee spoke of a "correlated curriculum," it meant what others have meant when they used the term "integrated curriculum":

> An integrated curriculum as conceived in this report is a curriculum integrated in world pattern, in subject pattern, in experience pattern, and in the psychological growth pattern of the individual being taught. It can be integrated in world pattern and subject pattern by the administrative framers of the curriculum. It can be truly integrated in experience pattern and in the psychological growth pattern of the individual being taught only by a teacher who can adjust materials to the group before him by enlisting their cooperation in setting goals and shaping activities for their attainment. A curriculum so planned and executed will deal with life, with the subject matter of instruction, with experience, and with the child himself as wholes.[10]

This plethora of words, coming from a group of English teachers, fails to provide any sharp differences in meaning. Later on in the report the committee said that "correlation means . . . recasting the whole educational program in the mold of a central purpose, so that not only the parts but the whole will have a meaning, a meaning which will tie part to part by a recognizable bond."[11]

Hopkins defined the correlated curriculum as "an attempt to bring vertical and horizontal unity into isolated subject matter" and indicated that such unity is obtained in three different ways:

> The first is a synthesis of subject matters from various subjects in one field into a larger whole, such as the correlation of history and geography, or economics and government, or history, geography and government into social sciences or social studies. Reading, writing, spelling, language and grammar may be correlated into a larger unit known as language arts. This type is frequently called *fusion*. The second type is the synthesis of one subject with another not in its own field, such as the correlation of English with history, or science with English. The third type is the synthesis of the subject matter of any subject with the life activities of children outside the activities of the school. This means unification of history with present problems of family relationships; the unification of mathematics with buying the necessities of life more wisely; the unification of art with personal appearance; or some other aspects of daily living. Types

9. *Ibid.,* pp. 5–6.
10. *Ibid.,* p. 4.
11. *Ibid.,* p. 10.

two and three are frequently called *integration,* since they deal with relationships outside of a particular subject.[12]

In general, we may say that the term "correlation" usually describes attempts to find points of contact between different fields, while the term "integration," as far as its application to the curriculum organization is concerned, is used to describe any plan which endeavors to establish new threads of relationships, by cutting across subject lines, usually by establishing new groupings, subject areas, or problems. Occasionally it is applied to the meanings inherent in the relationship between in-school and out-of-school experiences. Both terms, however, are used loosely, and to establish their meanings in particular situations one will have to examine the curriculum under each term.

Fusion

"Fusion" is the third term most generally used to describe the attempt to bring about greater relationships among the subjects of the curriculum. Hatch says fusion "looks forward to the end resultant. The ultimate product may be composed, to be sure, of various elements from history, geography, and civics, but it will all be so welded or fused that distinctive lines are gone."[13] He implies that this fusion is to be around the pupils' attempts to find the meaning of life. Pupils are to try to understand the nature of society by studying problems dealing with the growth and development of civilization. There is an indirect approach to behavior by establishing an understanding of the nature and problems of the culture, as well as a direct approach to action through the organization of the class around the socialized recitation technique. The combination of these produces an intelligent and understanding citizen. Hatch says he does not want a new synthesis of materials, but a "fusion," by which he means really the blending of the materials of the social studies together into one course, to contribute to "the main stream," as he calls it. He does not want to abolish subject lines but only "subject viewpoint."

Many other curriculum workers reorganize the curriculum in various ways and call it fusion. Some prepare a series of units on such things as *Municipal Organization and Growth, Organized Labor and Its Problems, The Changing Standards of Living, Recreation;* and because these cut across many fields and include a collection of related materials—related around the unit topic—they are said to be fused. Others have organized what they term "social living units" which deal with community life, vocational information, and critical social problems. In fact, the recipe for these types of "fused" organizations

---

12. L. Thomas Hopkins, *Interaction: The Democratic Process* (Boston: D. C. Heath and Company, 1941), p. 55.
13. R. W. Hatch and DeForest Stull, "A Unit Fusion Course in the Social Studies for the Junior High School," *Historical Outlook,* 17:371–374, 1926.

might read thus: Take some minimum amount of social facts in the separate social science courses, add some local conditions, some topics from current literature, some suggestions for improving social practice, put in some activities which range out into the community, enlarge a bit to care for individual differences, cut into a series of units, and serve in the grades desired.

The most complete study on fusion was made by Howard Wilson, who undertook to determine the meaning, history, theory, and nature of fusion. After a careful analysis of a large number of courses and writings, he suggested that the "fusion platform" could be expressed in the following terms:

> 1. Only such material as has direct value in developing in pupils intelligent understanding and tolerant, cooperative appreciations fitting them to engage in the activities of the life of the time shall be taught.
> 2. Selected subject matter in the social studies must be organized in units of experience, psychologically appealing and learnable, and corresponding as closely as possible to life situations.
> 3. Traditional subject boundaries shall be ignored in the construction of the social-science curriculum; subject fields not only fail to achieve the purposes of education but interfere with the selection and organization of a curriculum which will achieve these purposes. The current problem rather than the subject fact is the heart of a functional unit.[14]

After Wilson had thus analyzed the materials of fusion and formulated this platform he proceeded to show that these were really not characteristics of fusion. Whether it was originally an error to design the straw man which he set up to knock down or whether it was an apologia for his later presentation of "subject values" may be an academic question. However, this very careful and scholarly report does point up again the need for an analysis of the fields of fusion, correlation, and integration. It has been nearly twenty years since Wilson prepared his study and one cannot today attack the work of an author in terms of his point of view at that time unless he has persisted in holding it, and Wilson has changed his position markedly.

After Wilson presented his preliminary review of this study to the National Council for the Social Studies, Professor Edgar C. Bye followed with a vigorous attack on Wilson's conclusions.[15] Bye attacked Wilson first for saying that the theory of fusion is no better than the theory of subject groupings, for the same cultural influences have been at work on the fusion as on the subject workers and have in reality produced about the same thing. Bye countered with the suggestion that there was some virtue in the idea of *organization* behind the fusion movement which Wilson did not recognize, and that at least the fusion plan of organization was a more "hospitable medium for the cultiva-

14. Howard Wilson, *The Fusion of Social Studies in Junior High Schools* (Harvard Studies in Education, No. 21; Cambridge, Mass.: Harvard University Press, 1933), pp. 180–181. By permission of the publishers.
15. Edgar C. Bye, "Fusion or Confusion?" *Historical Outlook*, 24:264–267, 1933.

tion of functional bacteria" than was the subject organization. All he contended was that the units in the fused course were *more likely* to be functional than those in the subject courses. The "fusion people" believe that fusion will be promoted by fusion and use units as a medium of doing it. Bye agreed that both groups are interested in functionality and in some unit groupings, which, in the face of the evidence, seems entirely reasonable.

Bye then pointed out the essential difference in the use of the term "fusion" by Rugg and by Hatch. Hatch, he contended, does not want the abolition of subject lines but the blending of several courses in social science into one. On the other hand, Rugg totally disregards the argument over subject lines and ruthlessly builds his organization without regard to subject distinctions. Bye contended that Hatch invented the term "fusion" and that it should be applied only to the type of organization which he uses. He thus pointed up two groups of people, one represented by the Rugg viewpoint, which he called "unificationists"; the other represented by the Hatch viewpoint, which he called "fusionists." The fusionists are blenders who are not so ambitious as the unificationists, who want to find a "new strand" of orientation.

Appraising These Approaches

The movement to bring into greater unity the subjects of the curriculum is a significant one and is a step forward in planning an educational program for youth. It signifies a recognition of the extreme extent to which curriculum workers and teachers have gone in separating the subject fields and of the need for changing the trend. It represents also a belief in the natural unity of many materials which should be retained rather than divided. This unity is especially necessary for the beginner in any area of study. The movement acknowledges the psychological principles of securing mass impressions and large overviews of patterns before details are discovered, and, although it pays tribute to order and organization, to the logic of separate disciplines, at the same time it recognizes that functional subject matter needs to be selected in terms of the nature and abilities of the learner. In all probability this emphasis upon subject reorganization would have been the prevailing principle of curriculum reorganization had it not been for John Dewey and his philosophy of experimentalism, coupled with modern investigations into the organic nature of experience. A pragmatic philosophy and a psychology of organic unity held up to the light some of the shortcomings of the juggling of subject matter, and led into the Dewey problem-type materials.

In the majority of these approaches the starting point of learning and the bases for the selection of subject matter have not changed. They are still within the area of organized knowledge; they emerge not from the immediate nature of the culture and the developmental level of the learner, but rather from the body of cultural experience deemed important achievements of men.

In the second place, these approaches rely upon intellectual development as the basic means of changing human experience. Human advancement comes, it is held, from a knowledge of the growth and development of civilization, of the way things work, of the status of human living. The school seeks to explain the past to the present; it does not primarily seek to study the problems that lie ahead. In the third place, those who hold this position expect to improve human behavior, to be sure, but to do it through knowledge of what is good and what is "fundamental," a word so bandied about now that it has become entirely a qualitative word and therefore meaningless in a general sense. By this technique, behavior is changed indirectly by teaching the individual what is the proper thing to do in general, finding some situations which can be used for illustration, and trusting that he will perform intelligently in whatever future situations he meets. This attitude is contrary to the belief that direct teaching is necessary for competent handling of modern issues. These issues are different enough in kind from those of past human history that what we learn from historical experience is too general to be effective unless accompanied by direct analysis of the changed aspects of present experience. The blood and thunder of daily living, the problems of immediate experience, the issues of life must form an important part of the "teething" content for youth.

Scope and Sequence

Elsewhere in this book[16] reference has been made to the importance of sequence in curriculum development. The use of two common nouns—scope and sequence—to designate a particular plan may be confusing, but the meaning is easily understood. The scope simply refers to an attempt to define those continuing and universal activities of men which are common to all people.

The most extensive listing of the activities common to mankind was made by Frederick and Farquear in connection with the Mississippi State Curriculum Program.[17] They examined social literature to discover the different analyses which had been made of the recurring activities of living, and reported on thirty-eight classifications. Many more, of course, have been listed since this study was made, but none of them depart essentially from this listing. Beginning with Herbert Spencer's five classifications—(1) life and health, (2) earning a living, (3) family rearing, (4) citizenship, (5) leisure—and going on through those proposed by Clark Wissler, George Counts, Franklin Bobbitt, the Lynds, John Dewey, Edward L. Thorndike, W. W. Charters, and by state curriculum programs, they arrived at a set of nine which were by far

---

16. See Chap. 5, pp. 128–130 and Chap. 14, pp. 432–434.

17. O. I. Frederick and Lucile J. Farquear, "Areas of Human Activity," *Journal of Educational Research,* 30:672–679, 1937. For other methods of determining the scope of the curriculum, see Hollis L. Caswell and Doak Campbell, *Curriculum Development* (New York: American Book Company, 1935), pp. 141–189.

the most frequent ones suggested in all these lists. They are, for all practical purposes, as good as any other list, for it is not the exact wording which is important, but the procedure and understanding involved in their use. This list of nine which they discovered to be most common were as follows:

1. Protecting life and health
   Medical science, life, health, conservation, mental health, safety, protection against disease, accidents, fears
2. Getting a living
   Vocations, maintenance, production, distribution, consumption, economy, labor, occupation, industry, unemployment, work, capital wealth, income
3. Making a home
   Parental responsibilities, practical activities, domestic, family, childhood and youth, biological heritage, personal and household regimen, child rearing, private property, conservation of property, sex, marriage, courtship and love, eugenics, housing, food, clothing, "we consumers," parent education, position of women
4. Expressing religious impulses
   Morality, religious organization, the church, religious practices, philosophy of life
5. Satisfying the desire for beauty
   Culture, fine arts, mythology, aesthetics, literature, language arts, charm and good manners
6. Securing education
   Mental efficiency, culture, self-improvement, childhood and youth, the school, the press, cinema, the radio, integration of the individual, intellectual vision, how to study, reflective thinking and capacity for work, prevailing ideals, "folkways," and "mores"
7. Cooperating in social and civic action
   International relations, social relationships, citizenship, justice, crime and punishment, government, social and public welfare work, taxation, law, ameliorative institutions, social attitudes, the community, democracy, farm relief, social protection, war, conservation of property, extension of freedom, the constitutions, legislation, population, people, social intercommunication
8. Engaging in recreation
   Leisure, enjoyable bodily and mental activity
9. Improving material conditions
   Communication and transportation, physical heritage, invention, exploration, discoveries, technological development, science, material traits, scientific knowledge, conservation of material resources, nature, men and machines, power, steel, mastery of material circumstances, expanding the sources of science, adventure and risk, plants and animals, climate, natural wealth, standards of living[18]

---

18. For the more complete report of this study, see *Areas of Human Activity and Problems of Life.* Report of a research committee in the curriculum laboratory at the University of Mississippi (Oxford, Miss., 1936). 42 pp. Mimeographed.

The term "sequence" has been used to represent the headings for the vertical placement of materials by school year to assure developmental continuity of learning experiences, to prevent needless overlapping, and to provide guidance to different teachers of the several grades in a school system. This procedure of setting up an orderly and overriding framework to guide the selection of units and instructional materials represents a recent form of curriculum planning.

In utilizing the scope-and-sequence pattern several considerations need to be observed. The following are pertinent:

1. The development of a pattern of sequential areas is necessary because of the departmentalized teaching in the secondary school, the lack of understanding on the part of the teacher concerning the problems of a rapidly changing civilization, and the poor guidance and evaluation systems current in the secondary school. To say that a single teacher working for a year with a group an hour or so a day can develop the desirable sequence of learning experiences for the group, and that all teachers who follow her with the same group can do the same is to be more theoretical than practical. It is nothing but wishful thinking.

2. The desirable pattern of learning experiences needs to be mapped by cooperative planning on the part of all the teachers, each bringing his training and experience to bear upon the problem and each taking some part in the additional research necessary to build an adequate pattern. It should be built by both the elementary and the secondary school teachers together and should cover the whole range of these school years.

3. The framework of scope and sequence should be general enough to permit flexibility of teacher-pupil planning, but at the same time it should be specific enough to help guide the teacher in selecting and rejecting problems which may arise to claim the time of the pupils. It should be planned also to avoid duplication of work and provide for a totality of experience.

4. The pattern should be rooted in the nature of the culture in which it exists and should vary somewhat from community to community. However, this local community variation has been overplayed. It must also be adjusted to the maturation of the pupils for whom it is intended. It cannot ignore the extent or the nature of the pupils' experiences and abilities.

5. The pattern must be built by the teachers using it; it cannot be imported and be helpful, understood, or utilized properly.

6. The scope and sequence taken together should provide for a complete pattern of cumulative development in each boy and girl in those common social problems which all in a democracy will face. It does not undertake to provide for the *whole* of the educational program; it provides only for the *core* experiences or for the problems which are common to all members of the group. Special interest areas need to supplement these core experiences, and abundant variation needs to be made within the class in the study of any problem designated by the scope and sequence.

Before the teacher builds a pattern of sequential development he must have in mind the actual processes man has followed in developing his culture and the way in which these are comprehended by children and youth. He must understand that life has always been a struggle to provide the necessities to satisfy human needs, that this process has been long and slow, and that man has relied heavily upon chance and superstition. Recently man has discovered that science has given him new tools, a new way of thinking about his problems, and new controls over natural phenomena. Thus there has resulted new economic and production systems, but these require new social controls and new institutional practices. Man's institutions have not kept pace with his technological advances, and the result is frustration in the use of the controls of science. Man's next job is to pioneer in the social fields as he has in the scientific fields, so that he may utilize these gains over the physical world. To meet his needs adequately through the use of the new tools, man must engage in cooperative efforts and reorganize his mores and institutional living.

Once the understanding of the necessity for these broad goals is achieved, the teacher is then ready to select experiences which will teach cultural achievements and problems and develop in youth an attitude which will cause them to want to tackle the job of social pioneering. This selection will also be guided by the knowledge that the learning of children is conditioned by the environment in which they live, and that they comprehend these basic understandings not by simply reading about them but by experiencing them in the community in which they live. From this they learn to extend their thinking into other times and places and to see the relationships existing between their own community and the rest of the world which so vitally affects their own lives. From these actual community experiences they learn to generalize to other lands and peoples and to the issues in problems which are world wide or national in scope. Youth should finally come to see the organic relationship of communities, of peoples in different communities, and of the institutions, the political ideology, and the natural resources by which men live.

Illustrations of Scope and Sequence Patterns

SANTA BARBARA. One of the best illustrations of a sequence designed upon the basic ideas just reviewed is to be found in Santa Barbara, California, where over a period of years the teachers have been at work building and using a pattern of scope and sequence to guide their instructional experiences. This scope and sequence provides for eight items of the scope and a sequential statement for nearly all grades in the school. In two instances two grades are covered under a single statement.

A variation of the plan is illustrated in the scope-and-sequence pattern from Santa Barbara County, California, where for the most part the sequential statements apply to two grades. The same basic understandings and principles, however, are used in the preparation of both statements.

SANTA BARBARA, CALIFORNIA[19]

Scope

Developing and conserving personal resources
Developing and conserving other than personal resources
Producing, distributing, and consuming goods and services
Communicating
Transporting
Recreating and playing
Expressing and satisfying spiritual and aesthetic needs
Organizing and governing

Sequence

First Year (Kindergarten)	Second Year (Grade 1)	Third Year (Grade 2)	Fourth Year (Grade 3)
Growth in effective living through *self-adjustment within the immediate environment*		Growth in effective living through *adjusting to the community*	Growth in effective living by further adjusting to the community through the development of insights into the manner in which the *natural and controlled environment* is contributing to life *in our community*

Fifth Year (Grade 4)	Sixth Year (Grade 5)	Seventh Year (Grade 6)
Growth in effective living by further adjusting to the community through developing insights into the manner in which the *present culture-groups* are adjusting to life *in our community*	Growth in effective living through developing insights into the manner in which *present as compared with former culture groups* carry on the basic functions of human living in *Santa Barbara* and *California*	Growth in effective living through problem-centered experiences directed toward understanding how *modern technics* are being utilized in carrying out the basic functions of human living in the *United States*

Eighth Year (Grade 7)	Ninth Year (Grade 8)	Tenth Year (Grade 9)
Growth in effective living through problem-centered experiences directed toward understanding the interdependence of individuals in our school, our community, the regions of our nation, and in the countries of our American neighbors	Growth in effective living through problem-centered experiences directed toward understanding how man's courage, knowledge, discoveries, and inventions have affected his way of living.	Growth in effective living through problem-centered experiences directed toward understanding and appreciating the individual's privileges and responsibilities as an American citizen

Eleventh Year (Grade 10)	Twelfth Year (Grade 11)	Thirteenth Year On (Grades 12 and On)
Growth in effective living through problem-centered experiences directed toward happy, effective, personal, spiritual, social, recreational, and vocational living in the home, school, and community	Growth in effective living through problem-centered experiences directed toward achieving the highest possible quality of experiences through striving for social, political, and economic democracy in local, state, and national setting for peace and cooperation on the international scene	

19. Santa Barbara City Schools, *Developmental Curriculum* (*Bulletin* No. 1, Revision No. 1; Santa Barbara, Calif., 1941), pp. 22–24.

SANTA BARBARA COUNTY, CALIFORNIA[20]

Scope

Developing and conserving human resources
Developing, conserving, and intelligently utilizing nonhuman resources
Producing, distributing, and consuming goods and services
Communicating
Transporting
Recreating and playing
Expressing and satisfying spiritual and aesthetic needs
Organizing and governing
Providing for education

Sequence

Kindergarten Grades 1, 2, 3	Grades 4, 5	Grades 6, 7, 8
Guiding the growth of children toward living more effectively in their immediate and expanding environment (home, school, neighborhood and community) through participation in activities involved in carrying out the basic functions of human living	Guiding the growth of children toward living more effectively in a changing world and understanding it through investigating man's relationship to his physical environment, comparing and contrasting our increasing control of the environment with the simpler adjustment techniques utilized by people of simpler cultures	Guiding the growth of children toward gaining increasing effectiveness in carrying out the basic functions of human living through developing the ability and desire to react to the total environment according to a pattern which is based upon (1) an adequate understanding and appreciation of scientific principles and methods involved; (2) an understanding of the resulting increased possibilities of control, and (3) an understanding of resulting rapidity of change

Integrating Theme for Grades 9, 10	Integrating Theme for Grades 11, 12	Integrating Theme for Grades 13, 14
Planning with respect to educational, vocational, personal, and social goals and gaining in understanding of the relationship between the problems of the individual and those of the school, community, state, and nation	Developing in understanding of the ways man has met and is meeting his major problems with emphasis upon the solutions now proposed and upon the historical foundations of present problems	Developing in understanding of democratic ideals and their implications for social organizations

20. Santa Barbara County, *Curriculum Guide for Teachers in Secondary Schools* (Santa Barbara, Calif.: Schauer Printing Company, 1941), iv, 38–39.

STATE OF CALIFORNIA. Over a three year period (1945–1948) the California State Curriculum Commission, in cooperation with the State Department of Education, members of special social-studies committees of several professional organizations, and individual school people worked on a proposed Social Studies Framework. The "framework" concept was not a course of study, but a "guide in the development of an educational program in a specific situation."

Certain broad areas of subject matter in the social studies were designated for attention at certain grade levels, leaving the development of the program to the varying needs and interests of the local school districts.

The commission defined social studies as those studies "that provide understandings of the physical environment and its effects upon man's ways of living, of the basic needs of man and the activities in which he engages to meet his needs, and of the institutions man has developed to perpetuate his way of life."[21] The social studies are recognized as the principal part of the total school program in achieving the major goal of education, namely, the development of the highest quality of citizenship.

In organizing the studies program, the commission held that "the scope of the social studies is as broad as the range of human experience." They include all of the social processes in which man engages to satisfy his basic human needs, such as

1. The protection and conservation of human and natural resources
2. The production of goods and services
3. The distribution of goods and services
4. The consumption of goods and services
5. The transportation of goods and services
6. Communication
7. The expression of esthetic and religious impulses
8. The provision for education
9. The provision for recreation
10. The provision for government[22]

The sequence of learnings in the social-studies field is recognized as involving many aspects. It is impossible, the commission states, "for a child during the years of his elementary school life to master all the facts and concepts involved in the cultural heritage." The school's responsibility, therefore, is to help children select, with intelligent guidance, what they need within rather broadly defined areas. The logic in the selection of the subject matter is provided as children's needs and interests are satisfied. The framework sequence begins with institutions and activities close to their experience, such as home, school and neighborhood, extending gradually to include other cultures of the world in their present and historical relations. The complete framework is as follows:

I. Grades 1 to 8
   A. Primary grades: It is assumed that the social studies program of the primary grades will provide experiences leading to a social understanding

21. State Curriculum Commission, *The Social Studies Program for the Public Schools of California* (*Bulletin* XVII; Sacramento, Calif.: State Department of Education, 1948), p. 3.
22. *Ibid.*, p. 8.

of home, school, and community life, and such problems as how man obtains food, clothing, and shelter, appropriate to the maturity of primary children.

B. Grade 4: California and Mexico
    1. Early California
    2. Contemporaneous Mexican life

C. Grade 5: The United States
    1. Colonization and settlement
    2. Geographic studies, including the physical features, natural resources, and conservation needs of our country
    3. American period in California with emphasis on geographic environment

D. Grade 6: The Western Hemisphere and Pacific Area, with emphasis on the functions of transportation and communication as integrating factors
    1. Emphasis on discovery, and colonization and settlement
    2. Consideration of chief geographic features, economic resources, and occupations of people
    3. Transportation, emphasizing a better understanding of economic and geographic relationships
    4. Communication, emphasizing a better understanding of cultural relationships

E. Grade 7: The Eastern Hemisphere—the cultures and their contributions to our civilization
    1. A study of the geographic, economic, and cultural factors underlying the life of selected peoples in Asia, Europe, and Africa

F. Grade 8: United States History, Geography, and Civics
    1. Development of the United States with emphasis on large movements, social, political, and economic
    2. Regional geography
    3. The people of our nation
    4. American ideals, beliefs, and conceptions as expressed in great American documents
    5. Rights, privileges, and responsibilities of citizens

II. Grades 9 to 12

A. Grade 9: The World of Industry
    1. The development of industrial civilization
    2. Impact of science upon industry and living
    3. Individual in relationship to the world of industry
    4. Education as a means of orienting the individual to the world of work

B. Grade 10: Emphasizing the nature and development of world interrelationships and organization by such means as tracing the origin of democratic ideals and institutions, together with the growth of organizations which threaten democratic ideals

C. Grade 11: United States history and civics

D. Grade 12: Problems of citizenship[23]

23. *Ibid.*, pp. 10–11.

Social Class and Education

In recent years study has been given to socio-economic factors which affect the curriculum, such as the class structure of society and the economic pressures upon youth. These are important in any consideration of the curriculum and are fundamental factors that must be considered as curriculum changes are being made. A brief examination of their implications is pertinent.

American society is divided into social classes, and this stratification is reflected in the schools of the country. Members of society assume places in the class hierarchy according to such factors as income, occupation, place and length of residence, family connections, and clique membership. Furthermore, wealth is distributed unevenly according to class membership.

The schools are involved in this class structure. Teachers are conscious of the status of their pupils, and many are influenced in their reactions by the social position of the young people in their classrooms. Membership in clubs, participation in programs, responsibilities in class are affected by both the teacher's and the pupil's attitude toward social class.

Social Class and School Attendance

The influence of economic status upon continuance in high school and college has been studied by several investigators. Counts found in 1922 that the ratio between the percentages of children from the top and bottom income groups who were graduated from high school, using equal numbers in grade nine as the bases, was about five to one.[24] When this study was repeated a decade later, there was no evidence of any marked improvement.[25] A few years afterward, Bell's significant study, *Youth Tell Their Story,* revealed that the odds were eight to one in favor of the well-to-do student compared with the lower economic group youth.[26]

The selectivity of the conventional high school is shown by Warner, Havighurst, and Loeb in *Who Shall Be Educated.* In a five-year study of the graduates of "Old City High School," most of the upper-class students attended college, although they formed only 7 per cent of the total graduating class. Of the upper-middle group (28 per cent of the total) 69 per cent went on to college, whereas of the lower-middle class, (23 per cent of the graduates) only 16 per cent continued to college. "Stated another way, of all those who go on to

---

24. George S. Counts, *The Selective Character of American Secondary Education* (Chicago: University of Chicago Press, 1922), p. 38.

25. Grayson N. Kefauver and others, *The Secondary School Population* (U.S. Office of Education; Washington: Government Printing Office, 1933), pp. 11–15.

26. H. M. Bell, *Youth Tell Their Story* (American Youth Commission; Washington: American Council on Education, 1938), p. 140.

college, the upper-class students constitute 14 per cent, and there are no lower-class students during this period who go on to college."[27]

The facts quoted earlier regarding the holding power of the high school bear out the truth that on the secondary-school level educational opportunity is far from being equally available to all. Various studies have shown that socio-economic factors are important elements in determining the retention of students in high school and college. The Pennsylvania study in the mid-thirties of 910 pupils with intelligence quotients of 110 or above, who logically might be considered good high-school and college material, revealed that of the upper socio-economic group, 93 per cent graduated from high school and 57 per cent attended college, while of the lower socio-economic group, 72 per cent graduated from high school and 13 per cent entered college.[28] A similar study by Goetsch of 1,023 able students who graduated from Milwaukee high schools, 1937–1938, with intelligence quotients of 117 or above, revealed the following relation of parental income to full-time college attendance:

INCOME AND COLLEGE ATTENDANCE*

Parental Income	Per Cent in College Full-Time
$8,000 plus	100.0
5,000–7,999	92.0
3,000–4,999	72.9
2,000–2,999	44.4
1,500–1,999	28.9
1,000–1,499	25.5
500– 999	26.8
Under $500	20.4

* Helen B. Goetsch, *Parental Income and College Opportunities* (Teachers College Contributions to Education, No. 795; New York: Columbia University, Teachers College, Bureau of Publications, 1940).

Social Class and Intelligence Quotients

Allison Davis reports that most "standard" intelligence tests reveal that children eight to fourteen years of age from lower-class groups have an average I.Q. of from 8 to 23 points beneath that of the higher occupational groups.[29]

27. W. Lloyd Warner, Robert J. Havighurst, and Martin B. Loeb, *Who Shall Be Educated?* (New York: Harper & Brothers, 1944), p. 60.
28. Harlan Upedegraff, *Inventory of Youth in Pennsylvania* (American Youth Commission; Washington: American Council on Education, 1936). Mimeographed.
29. Allison Davis, "Socio-Economic Influences upon Children's Learning," *Understand-*

Likewise, according to present tests, rural children on the average are less intelligent than urban children; southern white children are less intelligent than northern white children, and so on. Evidence now shows that the problems used in the tests consist of material far more frequently met in the urban middle-class culture. Recent research, in testing 5,000 pupils during the past five years under a grant from the General Education Board of the Rockefeller Foundation, indicates that socio-economic factors influence the school's diagnosis of a child's intelligence. The ten most widely used standard tests of intelligence reveal the higher socio-economic groups to be superior, but this superiority is found to be associated with the kinds of questions asked, the type of vocabulary used, and the greater training and motivation of these groups with regard to these tests.

Economic Pressures on Pupils

The economic pressures upon youth are important, particularly on those from homes in the lower income brackets, the effects of which have been described in an earlier chapter. The need for money and the lack of what money can buy, have been significant factors in the failure of many young people to remain in high school. Nearly every drop-out study in recent years has given this factor as one of the chief reasons for leaving school.

Despite the trend toward providing free textbooks and transportation, as well as some federal aid to the school lunch program, for a large number of students the cost of attending high school is often too great to permit the young people to pursue their work satisfactorily. Hence a substantial percentage of youth, both boys and girls, decide to leave school.

One conspicuous type of financial pressure upon high-school youth is the direct charges made by the school itself, either through state legislation or by local regulation. Two studies of this problem in one state give some indication of what and where these costs are. North Carolina in 1941 made a study of fees charged in 69 city-run high schools, both large and small. A follow-up study of 45 of these schools was made in 1950.[30]

In 1941 all 69 high schools charged some kind of a fee. There were 23 different kinds of fees charged at that time. In 1950, in the 45 high schools restudied, each one of these schools had one or more fees and there were *46 different kinds of fees.* The percentage of schools charging the several different fees was *greater* in 1950 than in 1941, with the exception of rental on textbooks. The rental percentage dropped from 93 per cent to 87 per cent in

---

ing the Child, 20:14, 1951. See the complete report by Kenneth Eells and others in *Intelligence and Cultural Differences* (Chicago: University of Chicago Press, 1951).

30. William E. Rosenstengal, "School Fees Increase," *High School Journal,* 33:177–179, 1950.

the high schools studied. However, several new fees appeared in the 1950 study, such as fees for woodworking, driver education, mechanical drawing, machine shop, and audio-visual education. Two of the schools charged an examination fee and three schools charged an assembly fee. The amounts charged for each fee in 1941 ranged from a low of 10 cents for publications to a high of $24.00 for band. In 1950 the same low figure held, but the high was $36.00 for band.

To these direct charges are added the indirect or hidden charges which fall upon all students if they are to remain active participants in the life of their high school. Some of these may be incorporated in the direct charges mentioned above (such as the band), but others are related to the extraclass and social activities of the school. The most definite and comprehensive study of this problem is the one being made under the auspices of the Illinois Secondary School Curriculum Program, in which Harold Hand has developed a procedure for securing the facts on hidden tuition costs within a local school. Pilot studies made recently in certain Illinois cities reveal that, excluding food, clothing, shelter and transportation, the typical high-school costs per student are $125.00 per year. These have been typically shown to range upward from freshmen $95.00, sophomores $117.00, juniors $134.00, and seniors $155.00. Hand strongly "suspects" that the cost factor may be the cause in restricting participation in extraclass activities and reducing the holding power of the high school.[31]

Social Class and Extracurricular Activities

David Wright's study of participation in extraclass activities by students from different economic groups reveal that in forty-one comparisons, including all the student activities in a four-year high school of 1,450 students,

> In seven of the activities the youth from the lower income brackets were completely frozen-out. In eighteen others, their participation was sixty per cent or more below reasonable expectation. In thirty-two of the forty-one activities their participation ranged from twenty to 100 per cent below expectation. In only six of the forty-one activities were the more economically underprivileged youth found to have a representation equal in magnitude to that of their relative number in the total population of the school. In short, the two topmost socio-economic groups had about thirty-five per cent more representation or participation than would have been the case

---

31. See Harold C. Hand, *How to Conduct the Hidden Tuition Costs Study* (Circular A, No. 51, Illinois Secondary School Curriculum Program, *Bulletin* No. 4; Springfield, Ill.: Office of Superintendent of Public Instruction, 1949). See also Harold C. Hand, *Principal Findings of the 1947–49 Basic Studies of the Illinois Secondary School Curriculum Program* (Circular Series A No. 51, ISSCP *Bulletin* No. 2; Springfield, Ill.: Office of Superintendent of Public Instruction).

had they been represented in proportion to their relative number in the total population.[32]

A recent study of the relationship of socio-economic status and participation in the extraclass activities of the secondary school was undertaken by thirteen schools under the Illinois Secondary School Curriculum Program. In this particular study, each pupil was questioned as to sex, age, grade, location of home, school marks, socio-economic status, and the extent of extraclass participation. According to Hand's report, the "only factor that was found to make a difference was the socio-economic status of the pupil's family."

In this investigation, the extraclass activities of the school were divided into three categories: "primary group" (team membership, play cast, club membership, and so forth); "secondary group" (attending games, seeing school play, getting the yearbook, and so forth); and "leadership" activities (captains of teams, presidents of groups, chairmanships of committees, and so forth.) The pupils were divided into three socio-economic groups, and the relative number of each who fell into the three categories was recorded. In each of these three categories, where the normal ratio of proportionate participation would be 1 to 1, the ratio differences based upon the socio-economic status of the family were consistently high, favoring the upper groups always. In the "primary group" (belonging to) activities, the ratio went from 1.1 to 1 at the top to 6.5 to 1; in the "secondary group (going to) activities, the ratio was 1.1 to 1 at the top and 3.1 to 1 at the bottom family-income groups; and in "leadership" activities, the top ratio was 1.4 to 1 for the upper group and 6.5 to 1 for the lowest group. Hand raises the pertinent question: "Is it possible that the unhappy experiences mirrored in these ratios bear some casual relationship to the findings that 72% of all the pupils who withdrew from school came from the lower income families?"[33]

Dillon's thorough study of 1,360 early school leavers included an examination of school records to determine whether the early leaver was one who did or did not participate in extraclass school activities. This area was considered important because many of the activities under the direction of the school "help to develop interests of both vocational and avocational nature and contribute to the student's social development." Dillon found that for 562 individuals, or approximately 40 per cent of the total group, there was nothing in the school records to show whether they had or had not participated. From data on 798 of the individuals studied, it was discovered that 586, or 73 per cent, had not participated in any extraclass activities; 190 or 25 per cent

---

32. Quoted in Harold C. Hand, *General Education in the American High School* (Chicago: Scott, Foresman and Company, 1942), p. 21.
33. Harold C. Hand, "For Whom Are High Schools Designed?" *Educational Leadership*, 6:364–365, 1949.

had participated in one or two; while 22 or 2 per cent had participated in two or more.[34]

Social Class and Social Goals

Allison Davis maintains that most of our teachers come out of and are trained for a middle-class culture. With 70 per cent of the elementary children coming from the lower socio-economic groups, there is a wide gap between the teacher and these pupils. "This vast store of ability in these millions of children . . . is largely wasted because their teachers do not understand the basic cultural habits of the working groups." The lower socio-economic group of pupils, on the other hand, do not understand and cannot learn the teachers' culture. We have then, in the public school of our country, a cultural conflict, or a "cultural divide." The teachers are trying to change the culture of more than half the children in America, yet they do not understand the behavior and goals of these masses of youngsters whom they wish to stimulate to learn.

Furthermore, as Ralph W. Tyler pointed out in the centennial observance of the founding of the American Association for the Advancement of Science, "American schools and colleges place primary emphasis on memorization of textbook content" and "the requirements of school are largely those of a verbal sort." Davis holds that with such a curriculum it is impossible to teach children how to think, or how to learn to solve real-life problems.

> The daily effort to teach these uninteresting, memorized materials to children is an experience which would drive most people to the verge of a nervous breakdown—which is where most conscientious teachers seem most of the time. But it is clear that any other group of human beings, faced with the same task, would be just as anxious and "worried" as teachers.
>
> When, in addition, the children who have to be taught these lifeless, rote-learned materials are from the lower socio-economic groups, whose habits and culture the teacher does not understand, the teaching process involves at least a 50 per cent waste of the children's abilities and of the teachers' efforts.[35]

The studies by Davis and others of the influence of middle-class culture upon teacher training, teacher attitude, and curriculum values is strengthened by the extensive work of the Kluckholns in their analysis of the conflicts of power in our modern culture. They point out the wide differences between the middle and lower socio-economic groups, particularly in family life and in the

---

34. Harold J. Dillon, *Early School Leavers* (New York: National Child Labor Committee, 1949), p. 44.

35. Allison Davis, "Socio-Economic Influences upon Children's Learning," *Understanding The Child,* 20:11, 1951.

wide divergencies of aspirations and expectations on the part of the parents for their children. They have outlined in a fashion helpful to the teacher the expectations which middle- and lower-class children experience. They list these expectations as follows:

I. Middle class expectations

    A. The child is encouraged to save pennies and coins, to have a bank account. He accumulates and is expected to take care of his possessions. He is urged to have systematic hobbies.

    B. Many specific patterns for specific goals relating to "good" standing in the community:

        1. Early tabu on the manifestation of sexual interests is maintained. The child hears little or no talk about sexual activities of his parents. The need for "sexual education" is verbally recognized.

        2. Emphasis on washing hands, regular bowel movements, wearing clean clothes, keeping his room in order, eating neatly, etc.

        3. Patterns relating to emotional control:

            a. Control of aggression: The child is prohibited from hitting other children, except in self-defense, especially younger ones. He is told to "stand up for himself" and to "be brave" when hurt. Aggression is canalized into verbal expression.

            b. The child is taught to control his temper.

            c. Achievement is important but the child is expected to restrain expressions of overt pride.

        4. Conformance to the rules of the game is expected. The child is told to pay attention to the approval of others.

        5. The child receives careful training in table manners; he learns the proper forms of all sorts of letters, greetings, gifts, expressions of apology, sympathy, etc.

        6. The child is not permitted to associate with "undesirable" playmates. He is told not to speak to strangers. There are specific patterns of acceptance for desirable playmates, such as having the child over to the house, giving parties, and exchanging birthday gifts. There are also patterns for "joining" organizations.

        7. Respect for the policeman is instilled. Obedience to parental authority, to school rules, and to organizational rules is expected.

    C. Patterns which stress ownership of property: the child is taught to say "this is mine—this is yours." These patterns relate to property, school work, and other types of achievement.

    D. Interest in school grades is inculcated. Stress is put on homework, and it is supervised by the parents. Opportunities are provided for attending dancing school, art classes, and for having hobbies, etc.

    E. Patterns for "good marriage" are the same as those found under sex tabus and proper companions.

    F. The child is taught to respect his parents as the main authorities. No great respect for grandparents is required. There is discrimination among relatives because of concern for family status.

    G. Patterns relating to recreation:

1. There are specific patterns for individual and organized sports and games. The training is supervised and there are rules.
2. Parents take the children on trips.
3. Supervision of commercial recreation: The child is told what movies he may and may not see and is warned against going to beer parlors, night clubs, and cabarets.

II. Lower class expectations

A. Stress is put on getting a job, and getting one early. The child learns early responsibility in financial matters.
B. Patterns relating to "good" standing in the local neighborhood:
1. A child is left to collect companions "on his own." Autonomy at an early age is encouraged.
2. In their gangs children encourage each other to fight. There is little or no tabu on the expression of overt aggression in the family situation.
3. Relatively speaking there are few tabus in the sexual sphere.
4. The attitude of "do it, and try not to get caught" is prevalent. Fear of, rather than respect for, policeman and other authorities is emphasized.
C. The parents take no daily interest in the education of children. If the child "skips" school, he frequently is not punished by the parents. Little attention is paid to the child's homework, and there is little supervision of home-study. There is little realistic planning for long-term education or efforts to relate education to practical goals.
D. There is general recognition of the relatives in the extended line with more attention placed on the maternal relatives. The child lives with relatives for extensive periods. Children take care of siblings and share in household responsibilities. (Here also there are ethnic variations.)
E. Children are allowed to spend money on recreation as they please when they have the money. The recreation of the children is not highly supervised by the parents.[36]

Implications of Social Class Structure

Some would contend that the factors of class structure were unimportant, but quite the contrary is correct. Their significance is constantly being recognized for the following reasons:

1. Effective citizenship in a democratic society is posited upon universal education. However, if our schools, through neglect of the importance of hidden school costs, of economic conditions at home, and of social acceptance in group activities, lose a large number of pupils through elimination, we will leave a large segment of our population ill equipped for civic responsibilities.

2. These same economic and social factors if neglected will produce mal-

---

36. Clyde Kluckhohn and Florence R. Kluckhohn, "American Culture: Generalized Orientations and Class Patterns," in Lyman Bryson, Louis Finkelstein, and R. M. MacIver (eds.), *Conflicts of Power in Modern Culture* (New York: Harper & Brothers, 1947), pp. 123–127.

adjustments, misbehavior, lowered character, and curtailed participation in school activities.

3. Our school program is largely verbal and thus unsuited to a large portion of our youth. When this "upper-class" program is required of all pupils the result is an enormous waste in the learning process. There is a constant struggle in the school where a "middle class" teacher teaches "middle-class culture" and "upper-class" content to "lower-class" children.

4. Standard tests used to classify and group students have been found to favor the youth from higher occupations groups. This superiority is due primarily to a cultural bias in the make-up of the tests which deal largely with materials with which the "superior" group has had experience. The tests then which in the past have tended to indicate that the average I.Q. of children from lower economic groups was substantially lower than the average of the higher groups lose some of their validity in the light of this significant cultural bias. Grouping and instructional materials based upon these tests thus become unsuitable for certain youth.

5. Friends and judgments are being made upon class structural criteria by the time of the eighth grade, and the pupils in the junior high schools have already reached definite ideas on this matter. This requires the teacher to provide adequately the extracurricular life of the school and to overcome undesirable class attitudes to build social solidarity.

6. Prejudices and generalizations play a large part in learning, and the curriculum must seek to deal with those which are formed from class consciousness.

7. Effective teaching of children of various cultural levels is impossible unless the teacher knows the cultural environment from which the pupil comes, for this determines his values, his vocabulary, his previous experience, his morals, his goals and motivation, his former behavioral patterns, and similar factors so important to learning.

8. If we are to select and organize instructional materials for all social classes, we must teach analysis, reasoning, and collection of facts, and we must develop insights through a variety of experiences and cease laying such great stress upon formal verbalized skill in reading, vocabulary building, and arithmetical processes.

Cultural Change and Education

Probably the most significant item of all is the factor of cultural change itself of which we are all more cognizant daily. Cultures of other people are better known to us than ever before, and as America becomes more world conscious the future of the world becomes more and more confusing and unknown to us. According to Margaret Mead, we as parents, teachers, and citizens are rearing "unknown children for an unknown world." We cannot meet their needs upon the basis of our past experience with similar needs.

> American children are growing up within the most rapidly changing culture of which we have any record in the world, within a culture where for several generations each generation's experience has differed sharply from the last, and in which the experience of the youngest child in a large family will be extraordinarily different from that of the first born. Mothers cannot look back to the experience of their mothers, nor even to that of their older sisters; young husbands and fathers have no guides to the behavior which they are assuming today. So long standing and rapid have been these processes of change that expectation of change and anxiety about change have been built into our character as a people. Our homes have become launching platforms from which our children set out on uncharted seas, and we have become correspondingly more anxious that they should be perfectly equipped before they go. . . . Without the help of tradition, or with a religious tradition faced by unprecedented conditions of conflict and doubt, we have come to rely more and more upon the new sciences of child development, and the studies of the world around us, on nutrition and pediatrics, on new forms of teaching and therapy. . . .
>
> We have given our children an incomparable heritage of independence, willingness to go out into new places among new people, willingness to stand on their own feet and answer for their own deeds. Now because the task ahead of them is even more exacting than any task which Americans have yet faced, we must use the knowledge which the new sciences of human behavior have given us, to create the conditions of the strength that will be needed, to give protection against loneliness, new sources within the self, new capacities for moving into that future which is the only earthly future to which a democracy can commit itself, a future in which only the general direction of the next step is clear, in which men have the faith to say, although the night is dark, and they are far from home,
>
> > "I do not ask to see
> > The distant scene
> > One step enough for me."[37]

37. Margaret Mead, "The Impact of Culture on Personality Development in the United States Today," *Understanding the Child*, 20:17–18, 1951.

Chapter Twelve

Recent Projects in
Curriculum Improvement

I N RECENT YEARS significant progress has been made in cooperative group work and in the enlistment of community groups in curriculum enterprises, as well as in knowledge of the processes of group action. "Group dynamics" has come to mean a study of the factors which influence group behavior, and the terms "intergroup" and "intercultural" education have come into general use. Study of these fields is significant for the curriculum worker, not only for securing group cooperation on professional problems but for understanding group structure and patterns of motivation. If we understand what provokes individual behavior in groups, we may find the key to greater domestic and international harmony, and this is certainly a remote if not an immediate goal of education.

Intergroup Education

During the period of World War II there was real concern over intergroup education and over what could be done about intolerance and discrimination.

The war years accentuated a number of existing problems, due in part to the rapid migration of racial and economic groups because of employment opportunities and demands, housing shortages, and transportation difficulties. To these domestic problems were added many international ones, such as the shrinkage of the world through the development of transportation and communication facilities, and the new role of world leadership which the United States had assumed.

Project of the American Council on Education

Certain educators and laymen became concerned with problems of individual and intergroup relations as they affected democratic living. They believed that many of these problems were present among children and youth, and the schools could and should deal with them. Financed by a grant from the National Council of Christians and Jews, but conducted by the American Council on Education, the project was begun in 1944 and ran for a period of nearly four years—January, 1945, through August, 1948.[1] The project involved eighteen school systems, mainly urban, in fourteen states, and in all parts of the country except the South. The aim of the limited staff was to "assist in every possible way such relevent projects as the schools might themselves devise in the light of their particular needs." Early in the project it was discovered that schools concerned with these problems tended to emphasize tensions which were national (and frequently remote) in scope, and to neglect the less dramatic but more immediate problems of local origin, such as those which arise in classroom, corridors, school activities, and community living. Furthermore, it was discovered that problems of group relationships are found in every community, even if its population is homogenous. Acute provincialism might mark one community, while racial cleavage might be most evident in another. The problems are ever present, and skills and techniques need to be developed at the proper age and level in an attempt to reach solutions.

The program of this project was developed along certain lines which permitted

1. Planning for a continuous emphasis in the schools from kindergarten to twelfth grade

2. Preparing young children for better understanding and more adequate orientation toward race, religion, and economic status

3. Teaching children in terms of their own life experiences

4. Focusing attention on behavior itself

5. Using local intergroup problems as training grounds for analyzing and attacking these problems

---

1. For a full description of this project see Hilda Taba, Elizabeth Hall Brady, and John T. Robinson, *Intergroup Education in Public Schools* (Washington: American Council on Education, 1952).

The four main aspects of growth which the cooperating schools emphasized as goals in the development of a sound program were

1. There are certain facts, ideas, and concepts basic to intelligent understanding of group relations. People need to know facts about human beings and groups and their functioning in society.

2. Living in a multigroup world requires feelings, values, and attitudes that add up to a comprehensive and cosmopolitan cultural sensitivity.

3. Human relations require ability to think objectively and rationally about people, about the problems of their relationships and about cultures.

4. It is necessary to develop certain skills in order to get along with individuals and to work successfully in groups.

The plan of work dealt with three aspects of education, the instructional program, group activities in school, and those in community relations. Working from the specific to the general, the project concerned itself with studies based upon the four aspects of growth enumerated above and placed its primary emphasis upon reshaping existing curricula and courses to serve the objectives of intergroup education.

Four basic areas were established in which intergroup education could be most effectively developed, areas which impinged most directly upon the lives of children and youth and in which the school curriculum could provide some insights and direction:

1. *Family patterns,* which provide the clearest reflections of cultural backgrounds and which concern all young people, were used by many teachers to teach concepts of intergroup education. At various grade levels the family is a frequent center of study, and work in this area dealt with family similarities and differences, the psychological and cultural facts, the mores and roles.

2. *Community life,* appearing in many grades and in several forms, provided another wide range of continuity of study. Local history, vocational opportunities, and social problems were the concern of students at different grade levels. In this area they gained clearer insights into the ways our multigroup communities work and live. The understanding of other types and aspects of community living by urban and rural children and by minority or underprivileged youth grew out of this emphasis. The breaching of the characteristic segmentation of city life was another objective achieved, resulting from the recognition of the interdependence of modern living. Stereotyped and prejudiced attitudes were exposed and modified through school studies and practical experiences, such as field trips and surveys.

3. *American culture* usually was studied within the framework of the conventional courses in American history and literature. History provided insights into the immigrant background of our nation, past and present, and the socio-economic struggle of all newcomers to get ahead. Both subjects afforded an opportunity for perspective on the cultural problems which have gradually developed over a period of time. Democracy was studied realistically in terms

of human rights and responsibilities. The effect of rejection and acceptance and of discrimination and prejudice was explored in the study of standards for democratic conduct. Special areas of culture, particularly racial and religious differences, were studied explicitly. The study of the American people themselves was the most frequent project—their multicultural background, differences, experiences, opportunities and limitations, attitudes and adjustments, weaknesses and strengths, and the divisive and unifying characteristics of our great nation.

4. *Interpersonal relations* was the last area of concentration, where understanding of behavior and methods of solving conflicts were stressed, as well as analysis of relations in situations involving cleavage, social distance, or misunderstanding. The range of content included school life, work experiences, and leadership, as well as general problems of rejection and belonging. These problems were studied mainly in courses which dealt with orientation, general education, group guidance, and personality development. Schools concerned with this area studied problems of exclusion of newcomers, cleavage of racial, ethnic, or economic elements, participation by all students in school activities and especially in school government, social activities, and general human relationships.

Los Angeles County Project

Another project in this field was launched in 1949 by three school systems in Los Angeles County. A year later twenty-one schools were involved.[2]

The purpose of this project was to discover just what the concept of democracy means in everyday living: "What understandings, what knowledges and skills must people have in order to live democratically as individuals, as group members, as citizens of America and of the world?"

The participants entered the program on a voluntary basis to consider the age-old problem of human relations from a problem-solving approach. There are no prescribed courses to be taken or programs to be followed. It is not intended to be a "mass education movement," but an attempt to provide consultant service, printed materials, audio-visual aids, and other resources for those who wish to make use of them in terms of their local problems.

Another characteristic of this study in curriculum improvement is that action-research techniques are used. Research findings are made available to all, with an emphasis upon using them rather than upon merely knowing what they are. Promising practices coming from a single classroom, a school, or a district are shared with others for further experimentation and evaluation.

In the second year of the project certain major fields of study have evolved.

---

2. The Project Staff, "Cooperative Project in Human Relations," *Educational Leadership,* 8:170–175, 1950.

One of the first is in the area of human development—"growing up." Recognizing that children grow up in a conflicting environment, the project seeks to discover some of the understandings in this field which are needed by teachers. "Community living" is another area in which teachers are encouraged to study and participate with members of either neighborhood or community-wide groups. "Intergroup education and learning experiences" is a third major area of emphasis in the present study, and a fourth is in the whole field of "group relations and skills." This last seeks to deal with the causes of the feelings of frustration, inadequacy, and insecurity.

The area of intergroup study is relatively new and promises to have impact upon the instructional process. Certainly, improved processes of group action will result and from them will come better methods of working with youth and adults.

Business, Industry, and Education

Another force in our society which has concerned itself with the educational program and which influences curriculum development has been that of business and industry. Over a long period a gap has been developing between education and business, with the former becoming increasingly suspicious of business because it feared the danger of exploitation, while the latter questioned education because of its so called "liberal" leanings and increasing costs. This atmosphere of mutual distrust was quite prevalent in the 1920's and 1930's and again around 1950. Recently there have been intelligent efforts to reconcile the two groups, and to discover how both education and business might understand each other better and mutually benefit from close cooperation.

In contrast to the earlier period, which was characterized by efforts at propaganda and distortion of viewpoint on both sides, there is developing a different attitude on the part of both. This is due in part to the recognition by business of the necessity for education and to the realization that criticism and attack do not achieve understanding and confidence, and to the recognition by educators that men of business and industry, products of the public schools, were interested in their welfare and success and that the schools could not exist without public support. Efforts have been made by a number of groups, both educational and economic, to bridge the gaps which had separated the two.

United States Chamber of Commerce

One of the most significant and encouraging moves was that taken by the United States Chamber of Commerce, which many educators had considered a severe critic of public education. After a very thorough study, the Committee on Education of this organization produced a report in 1944–1945 entitled *Education: An Investment in People* which documented the high correlation between the standards of living of a community and the character of its educational program.[3] This report showed convincingly that cities which had better schools also had all the other attributes of a high-level community— better business, better homes, better health, better government.

National Association of Manufacturers

Another organization representing business and industry is the National Association of Manufacturers, which in the past has been considered by many to be frankly unfriendly to the public schools. It is true that there has been a definite gap between this organization and educators in terms of understanding of purposes and services. Lately, this body has sought to work with the schools through an improved public-relations program to make for greater understanding between education and management. One of its efforts, illustrating the present position of the National Association of Manufacturers, is the publication of pamphlets describing the opportunities and challenge to youth of leadership in industry, under such headings as *Your Future Is What You Make It, The Free Enterprise System,* and *Your Opportunity in Management.*[4] The Congress of American Industry of the National Association of Manufacturers in December, 1948, called for support and expansion of the elementary- and secondary-school system, local in character, with reasonable and suitable diversity in the curriculum. And on October 30, 1951, the board of directors called upon the members of the National Association of Manufacturers to support public and private schools, colleges, and universities by helping to secure adequate state support and by contributing financial support.

A third major approach by industry, in an effort to reach education with its message, is through its generous supply of printed materials for use in the classroom.

Specific Businesses

As in the case of the National Association of Manufacturers so even more in the case of many specific businesses, a large amount of money has been spent on all types of "educational" materials—books, pamphlets, films and filmstrips, and periodicals—which have in the main been supplied free of charge to teachers and schools. An extensive survey by an independent organization to determine whether these materials are meeting the needs of education reveals

---

3. U.S. Chamber of Commerce, *Education: An Investment in People* (Washington, U.S. Chamber of Commerce, 1945).
4. National Association of Manufacturers, 14 West 49 Street, New York, New York.

that more than 90 per cent of teachers and administrators queried use the materials in their classes, and nearly 100 per cent requested more curricular materials and "especially more cooperative projects—plant tours, exhibits, vocational guidance, and similar activities." The educators asked for *good* materials which tell what industry contributes to everyday life; what kinds of jobs are made possible by industry; what industry labor relations involve; and similar information. The conclusions of this study, which has definite curriculum influence, include such recommendations as: "materials should be prepared to fit school curricula"; "the community-centered school encourages cooperation"; and with these recommendations goes the suggestion that "business should help boys and girls to learn about local industries, their products and their services"; "business and industry should make the most of the present opportunities for greater cooperation with the schools"; and "industry and business should support educators in developing improved techniques in the schools."[5]

The cooperative attitude of one large corporation toward the public schools is reported by the Chairman of the Board, Standard Oil Company of New Jersey. The board of directors adopted a statement regarding their employees and their responsibility toward the public schools. This is significant action and probably the first time it has ever happened. The statement is as follows:

> The importance of our public school system to the growth, prosperity, peace, and security of our country can scarcely be overestimated at any time. Its significance is never more apparent than in times of emergency. At times like these the relationship between freedom and a literate and educated population is thrown into clear focus.
>
> American business enterprise is aware of its great debt to the public school system of this country, because that system is essential to the survival and growth of business.
>
> The right and duty of the individual to support our public school system is clear. One such duty is, of course, that of paying taxes. But it seems to us clear that the obligation of each of us as an individual runs beyond mere payment of taxes.
>
> Over the years many Jersey Standard employees have participated actively in their local school programs. The company would like to see more of its people take an active interest in the problems and opportunities facing the public schools in their own communities. Obviously, the conditions affecting the individual's ability to participate in school activities will vary, but our company encourages its employees, as good American citizens, to undertake this important work.[6]

---

5. John W. Hill, *Study of Education-Industry Cooperation* (New York: Hill and Knowlton, Inc., 1951).

6. Frank W. Abrams, *The Stake of Business in Public School Education* (New York: National Citizens Commission for the Public Schools, 1951), p. 11.

Still another approach to curriculum modification is adopted by a specific type of business or industry; materials are prepared for classroom use to provide information and understanding of one of the major economic needs of youth and adults. An outstanding example of this is in the field of life insurance, where the National Better Business Bureau in cooperation with the National Association of Secondary School Principals has produced a unit on this subject for use in senior high schools.[7] This publication is intended to be objective and factual, and seeks only to give the facts and problems involved in life insurance.

One of the foremost leaders in this field is the Metropolitan Life Insurance Company, which has a staff in its New York City office devoted to assisting the schools with pamphlets, films, consultant service, and conferences on health education. Several million copies of their publications have been distributed and these have been prepared under the direction of an advisory committee of professional educators. They have also undertaken school research studies on such things as school absenteeism and health and the training of teachers in health information.[8]

Business-Education Day

A specific attempt to improve the relationships between teachers and business leaders is the very recent idea called "Business-Education Day." This movement originated with Carl M. Horn, at Michigan State College, where he brought together many leaders of business and education in an effort to set up local programs for cooperative understanding. The United States Chamber of Commerce gave support to the idea, and it has been adopted widely throughout the country. In essence this program consists of the teachers in a local community devoting a day to acquainting themselves with the various local businesses and industries, usually through a tour of the plant and luncheon with the executives as hosts, to be followed by discussion sessions on problems and activities of specific companies as well as on the general meaning of the free enterprise system.[9] Although the survey reported above revealed that only one in twenty teachers participated in such a program, recent periodical articles indicate an increase in this type of activity across the country. A second step in this same area is a reciprocal program which the schools have inaugurated. Here the reverse program is followed, and business

7. Consumer Education Study, *Buying Insurance* (Washington: National Association of Secondary School Principals, 1946).

8. School Health Bureau, Health and Welfare Division, Metropolitan Life Insurance Co., New York, New York.

9. For a detailed description and analysis of a typical program see Ivor F. Callaway, *Business-Education Day: A Cooperative Community Project* (San Francisco, Calif.: San Francisco Unified School District, 1950). Mimeographed.

leaders are invited into the schools for a day to see education in action. This part of the cooperative program has not been developed as much as has the first, where industry has taken the initiative.

Consumer Education Study

The National Association of Secondary School Principals in 1942 set up the Consumer Education Study. This undertaking was conducted by professional educators selected for their experience and ability to find out what education of consumers should be, what facts they should know, what habits they should develop, and later to prepare materials for use in high schools.

The study was financed by the National Better Business Bureau through special contributions from some of its members. In addition, the bureau assisted the staff of the study in reaching authoritative sources of information. Under the direction of Thomas H. Briggs, a staff of experts prepared materials and unit texts on various topics connected with the consumer field. Most of the unit texts were over one hundred pages in length and were addressed directly to the students, but with abundant suggestions for the teacher. The titles of these books indicate the content to be presented. Among them are: *Learning to Use Advertising, Using Standards and Labels, The Consumer and the Law, Managing Your Money,* and *Using Consumer Credit.*

The origin and method of these units are quite new and have considerable attraction for the average high school student. Dealing with problems of immediate or near-future concern they have an appeal to students as well as to teachers as they seek to meet the needs of youth. The approach is in line with the new emphasis on life-adjustment education as part of the program of general education.

Joint Council on Economic Education

The School of Education of New York University, concerned over the need for interpreting the economic structure of American society to the youth of our schools, secured a grant from the Committee for Economic Development to undertake a Workshop in Economic Education in the summer of 1948. During a three-week period, this workshop sought to give schoolmen from thirty-three city school systems a basic understanding of the structure and functional operation of the American economic system. Out of this gathering came the Interim Committee which organized and incorporated the Joint Council on Economic Education.

The council has invited affiliations from interested organizations and includes such groups as the National Association of Secondary School Principals and the Association for Supervision and Curriculum Development. It seeks to reach the educational leaders and other interested adults. It does not publish or distribute materials for pupil use, leaving this to the professional organizations and commercial publishers. Its purpose is to help build economic literacy primarily among secondary-school teachers.

Among its various activities now under way are workshops, both regional and state, services to regional councils, cooperation with professional organizations, research and materials development, and consultant services to interested groups.

Curriculum Units

Through these several channels, as well as others, business and industry in America are taking a more active and effective approach to education than they have in the past. The response to these more professional approaches will have a definite influence upon the development of the curriculum in many schools and districts.

Various industrial groups are seeking, as in the Business-Education Day program, to assist their own members to understand better the teacher and the school in their aim of fitting students "for a life of community usefulness." In addition to considering the general problems confronting education today, these industrial programs seek to build upon the "community-school" concept and urge their members to "join forces in developing materials and methods for classroom aid." These include plant study trips and discussions to fit the teacher's subject; making company personnel available for classroom discussions; providing materials which show the connection between the classroom and the working world; and joint sessions in which "education and community seek continual improvement of the curriculum." Company staff members are urged to become acquainted with the teachers and their schools, and to become familiar with the specific needs in the special subject fields in which their business might make an educational contribution. One industrial publication suggests that "a company should appoint a person from the management level to supervise long-range programs among industry, school and community." This results in a "modern grasp of education on the part of the company; its objectives and its possibilities for contributing to better living" and finally "the satisfaction of knowing that you are helping prepare the young people of your schools for a place in the world."[10]

LOS ANGELES COUNTY AND CITY. One promising approach to a better understanding of certain phases of American economic life has been found in the preparation of a very substantial teaching unit by the combined curriculum staffs of Los Angeles City and Los Angeles County. The primary purpose of the unit was to develop a clearer understanding and appreciation of

10. American Iron and Steel Institute, *Partners in Community Enterprise* (350 Fifth Avenue, New York, New York, 1951).

1. The basic economic life of our country
2. The interrelations of our modern industrial, business, and agricultural world
3. The many economic problems which confront the worker, the employer, the public, and government
4. The importance of good human relations which are fundamental to the solution of all problems

The content of the unit is arranged in problem form and deals with many of the crucial problems relating to economic life, and particularly to management-labor relationships. With a strong emphasis on human relations as basic to any solution, a brief outline of the unit will reveal the type of problems considered:

HUMAN RELATIONS IN AMERICAN ECONOMIC LIFE—A TEACHING UNIT

Problem I. How do economic conditions affect all of us? What can we do about them?

Lesson 1. All economic factors are interdependent.

Problem II. How do we make our best contributions to American economic life as *employees?*

Lesson 2. Employees need to know their role in American economic life.

Lesson 3. The individual conduct of the employee is an important link in the chain of economic production.

Problem III. How can we make our best contribution to American economic life as *employers?*

Lesson 4. The manager's responsibility is wider than his own personal goals.

Lesson 5. Many of the manager's needs are comparable to those of the worker.

Lesson 6. The individual conduct of the employer is an important factor in the chain of economic production.

Problem IV. What have been the methods of solving problems in human relations in our economic life?

Lesson 7. Efforts of workers and managers to achieve their goals have assumed many different forms.

Lesson 8. A variety of methods have been developed to secure industrial peace.

Lesson 9. Public welfare is protected by government participation.

Problem V. How can we continue to improve human relations in our economic life?

Lesson 10. Human relations are chiefly emphasized today.

The Appendix includes:

Are your prejudices showing?
Implications of economic life for the family
Implications for vocational education[11]

---

11. *Human Relations in American Economic Life: A Teaching Unit* (A joint publication

Citizenship Education

William H. Kilpatrick maintains that the great need of our country is adequate citizens. He claims that the elementary school has a distinct advantage over the secondary school in the teaching of citizenship because the "activity program" permits purposeful activities in life areas instead of the older process of teaching separate school subjects. This means "not less regard for the Three R's, but actually more use of them with their better learning." In contrast to the elementary teacher, the secondary teacher, even though interested in citizenship education, "cannot easily take his class out of the school into the community; the schedule does not allow it." This time-table, departmentalized and specialized, is a handicap to the secondary school. Furthermore, many secondary teachers are "primarily concerned with subject matter," while citizenship education is "no special concern of most of the teachers." He emphasizes the contrast between the two levels:

> The secondary school is set up on the basis of (1) learning from books the formulated thoughts of others, largely by memory, (2) with the work divided logically into separate subjects, (3) with a program which practically ties the teacher to the classroom or at least to the school. The elementary school is set up to permit integrated education for all-around character; the secondary school is set up to deny this.[12]

One of the more promising areas of curriculum study is in the field of citizenship education. Although the general objective of citizenship has been a primary one from early colonial days, our schools have frequently neglected or limited it to the actual practices within the school.

Illustrations of Citizenship Education

Recently, more specific attention has been given to this very important area, with several projects in citizenship education being undertaken by leaders in this field.[13] In each case there is a direct focus upon the all-essential need for better citizenship training in our educational programs, with extensive exploration in a number of the more fertile areas for its improvement.

---

of the Los Angeles County Schools, Secondary Curriculum Monograph M–71, and the Los Angeles City Schools, Curriculum Division Publication No. SC–428; Los Angeles, Calif.: 1949). Mimeographed. Specific objectives for this unique unit are listed above in Chap. 10, pp. 293–295.

12. William H. Kilpatrick, "Better Education for Citizenship," *Educational Forum,* 15 (May, 1951), 419.

13. For a complete survey of current projects in citizenship education see the *Phi Delta Kappan,* Vol. 33, December, 1951, devoted to education for citizenship, from which much of this section is drawn.

TEACHERS COLLEGE, COLUMBIA UNIVERSITY, NEW YORK. The premise upon which the project at Teachers College was undertaken was that "if we are to preserve democracy as a system of government, ways must be found to reach realistically and meaningfully the principles underlying our democratic political system." This project, therefore, is concerned with the large numbers of citizens who fail to accept their responsibilities in our democratic society because of apathy, lack of understanding, or lack of "know-how" regarding the vital role that each must assume in the decision making.

The Carnegie Corporation recognized this situation and consequently made a substantial grant to Teachers College to establish the Citizenship Education Project and to finance its operation from September, 1949, to July, 1953.

The project provides resources and services to assist collaborating schools to improve their citizenship-education programs. It seeks to identify, develop, and test resources and through its services make these resources available to professional and lay leaders. The actual steps in improving local programs are taken individually and independently by the teachers of the collaborating schools.

The leaders of the project seek to concentrate attention on the heart of citizenship, namely, "the degree and quality of influence exercised by the people over their leaders and over policy formation." To implement this approach, "Premises" were prepared, based upon our great national documents, to enable youth better to grasp the core values in our democracy. In addition, there has been developed a "Materials Card File" which contains full bibliographical data and annotations of books, pamphlets, films, and recordings, to provide teachers and pupils with a rich source of pertinent materials, plus "Laboratory Practices," which are descriptions of activities in which students can engage to gain actual experience in citizenship practices.

The Citizenship Education Project started slowly, with eight pilot schools. Recent reports indicate that it now has nearly 150 schools, with many more being added.[14] It is also extending its services through study councils, state departments of education, and colleges. Staff assistance is provided these groups for special workshops on this subject.

CAMBRIDGE, MASSACHUSETTS. The project in Cambridge is committed to the preparation of materials which will aid teachers in "clearer thinking, larger understanding, and firm faith in democracy." Its point of view is based largely on the major objectives of civic education set forth by its codirector John J. Mahoney:

> 1. An adequate understanding of the democratic way of life and our representative system of government; and a wholehearted allegiance to both

---

14. For a detailed report on progress for the first two years see a report on the Citizenship Education Project, *Improving Citizenship Education* (New York: Columbia University, Teachers College, Bureau of Publications, 1952).

2. An appreciation of the rights, protections, duties, and responsibilities which political democracy ensures and exacts

3. A keen interest in things political

4. A determination to try always to vote intelligently, and to form thoughtful judgments about political issues and problems

5. An honest effort to help elect a larger number of superior political leaders

6. An understanding of the place of law in our lives and the will to oppose delinquency in its observance

7. A deep desire to increase intergroup understanding, respect, and good will

8. A grasp of the understandings and attitudes needed by citizens to make the American scheme of competitive enterprise work with maximum efficiency in our democratic society

9. An understanding of the major features of the present international situation and an attitude of hope toward cooperation under peace and freedom

10. The will to translate into civic behavior the basic teachings of religion[15]

The primary project undertaken by this group is the preparation of pamphlets of substantial size and content on topics pertinent to civic education. The pamphlet form was adopted instead of textbooks to supplement and enrich existing courses in civics, rather than to prepare materials which would require new courses in our schools. Thirty-one pamphlets are projected, with at least eight already prepared. These include such titles as: *The Isms—and You: How Fascism and Communism Threaten Our Democracy; They Made a Nation; How the Founding Fathers Went about Their Task; It Has Been Done: Case Studies of Political Improvement in Local Situations; Who Says So? Senior High School Students Learn about "Public Opinion"; What Is Capitalism? Issues and Problems to Be Faced and Solved.*

Parent and Citizen Participation in Curriculum Planning

In recent years the schools have become increasingly more conscious of the parents' role in the education of their children. Due in part to the larger numbers of pupils with the resultant problems of housing limitations and teacher shortage, to the greater sense of social responsibility, and to attacks upon the public schools, parents have rapidly entered into the life and problems of their local schools. Beyond the conventional parent-teacher

---

15. Henry W. Holmes, "The Civic Education Project of Cambridge," *Phi Delta Kappan,* 33:170 (December, 1951), adapted from the original list in John J. Mahoney, *For Us the Living: An Approach to Civic Education* (New York: Harper and Brothers, 1945), Chap. 13, pp. 265–273.

organizations, which long have served education well, parent groups have begun to concern themselves with problems of their schools in such major areas as buildings, finances, and curriculum.

Roles of Parents and Citizens

There are at least three points of view regarding the role of the parent in home-school relationships. The first is a traditional one, frequently referred to as the "hands-off" position, in which the school received from the home the raw product, then fashioned it, and finally delivered it back as finished as possible to be sent on for distribution. This assembly-line concept continues to prevail in some communities and maintains the wide gap between home and school. Many of the problems existing today in our school-community relationships stem from the lack of contact and understanding which such a policy creates. Under these circumstances, if the curriculum is improved at all, the process is strictly professional, by educators only, with little or no concern about the participation and interest of the "stockholders," namely, the parents and citizens of the community.

A second point of view can be characterized as that of school "publicity" through messages sent home by pupils, newsletters, articles in the school and community newspapers, parents' nights at school, and similar devices. In this manner the school seeks to "inform" the parents of it program. This approach is more positive than the first, but much of its purpose is to reduce or prevent criticism by the parents or the public and to create a general favorable community feeling within which a more modern curriculum can be developed.

The third, more recent and effective, is the concept of parent-school "partnership." This involves the home and school working cooperatively with other community agencies on planning and carrying out a more effective educational program for their children and youth. Under such a plan parents share with teachers and administrators in curriculum discussion, the school budget, auxiliary school services, and policies and procedures affecting the health and welfare of the pupils. An analysis of several earlier studies of this type of cooperation in different communities leads Bess Goody-koontz, Associate Commissioner of Education, United States Office of Education, to conclude that "parents know, in general, what they want schools to do for their children; they have an idea as to whether the schools are effectively carrying out functions they consider desirable; and they have some concept of what their own educational responsibilities are."[16]

The latest development in this area of "partnership" grows out of the

---

16. Bess Goodykoontz, "Parents Know What They Want for Their Children," *Educational Leadership,* 7:286–291, 1950.

third position. This is the rapid organization of citizens' committees for improving educational services in local communities. Led by the lay organization known as the National Citizens Commission for the Public Schools, under the chairmanship of Roy E. Larsen, this movement has had two goals: "(1) to help Americans realize how important our public schools are to our expanding democracy; and (2) to arouse in each community the intelligence and will to improve our public schools."

The latest report by this national organization indicates that it is now helping more than 1,500 local groups to meet their school needs. Although the primary problem for many communities today is in the financial and housing areas, for many others the cooperative effort is being made in the curriculum and instructional fields.[17]

Community Surveys

Many illustrations could be given of surveys of community opinion of school practices. Some have been published in popular national magazines. They all indicate that the parents by and large are pleased with the work of the public schools and are critical only of details and of failure with individual pupils.

PARENTS POLL, PALO ALTO. Typical of such community studies is the one in Palo Alto, California, an upper-level economic community. The work was begun in 1948 under the auspices of an Educational Council with the help of forty-nine civic organizations, a membership of three hundred, an executive committee of twelve, and between fifty and seventy-five citizens, representing a broad cross-section of the city, actively participating in committee work. In 1951 an extensive effort was made to obtain parent opinion on what they wanted the public schools to do for their children. This was secured through a questionnaire sent to every family which had a child in school. It contained twenty-five statements which gave the respondents an opportunity to indicate the degree of agreement, uncertainty, or disagreement with the curriculum and instructional program of the schools. The replies from nearly three thousand parents are significant, and will have a definite bearing upon the curriculum development in that community.[18]

THE QUESTIONS ANSWERED IN PALO ALTO POLL

Here is how 2,703 Palo Alto parents responded to 25 questions pertaining

---

17. See a detailed description of how citizens committees are functioning in such cities as Manchester, Vermont; Eugene, Oregon; Fairfield, Connecticut; and others, in *The School Executive*, 71:81–90, 1952.

18. Palo Alto School District, *What Do the People of Palo Alto Want from the Schools?* (Palo Alto, Calif., 1951). Mimeographed. Also summarized in the San Francisco *Chronicle,* April 29, 1951.

to school aims. The figures in parentheses following each question show, in order, percentages of "yes," "undecided" and "no."

1. *The basic task:* Has the task of the school been fulfilled if a child has mastered reading, writing, spelling, and arithmetic, and has learned how to study? (28–4–68)

2. *Learning to interpret:* In addition to learning and reciting assigned lessons, should pupils be taught how to secure and interpret facts? (98–1–1)

3. *Studying all sides:* Should a student be taught to get information on all sides of a controversial question before forming his opinion? (98–1–1)

4. *Group activity:* In school should everyone learn through experience how to share effectively in group planning and action? (96–2–2)

5. *Finishing assignments:* Should pupils be required to finish assignments or other work which they have started? (94–3–3)

6. *Tolerance:* Should all pupils be taught to recognize and respect the rights of other races and religions? (98–1–1)

7. *Social responsibility:* Should the schools develop in every pupil a strong sense of responsibility for the welfare of the school, the community, State and Nation? (98–1–1)

8. *Habit of obedience:* Should schools instill the habit of prompt, cheerful obedience in all pupils? (88–4–8)

9. *Training for social situations:* Should the school teach every pupil to know how to act appropriately in social situations? (78–8–16)

10. *Hygiene:* Should hygiene and cleanliness be taught in the schools? (92–3–5)

11. *Morality:* Is the teaching of morality a responsibility of the schools? (54–12–34)

12. *Civil liberties:* Should the school lead every pupil to understand and to prize for himself and all others the rights of freedom of press, freedom of religion and other civil liberties guaranteed in our Constitution? (96–1–3)

13. *Arts and crafts:* Should elementary, junior and senior high schools give all pupils experience in working with the hands in such activities as drawing, painting, clay modeling, weaving, wood and metal work, ceramics, etc.? (86–6–8)

14. *Tests for guidance:* Should the school make fullest use of aptitude and achievement tests for teaching and guidance? (87–7–6)

15. *Counseling staff:* Should the school provide an adequate staff of counselors able to help pupils with personal as well as school problems? (78–10–12)

16. *Purpose of education:* Should the school lead each student to think clearly about the purpose of his own education? (94–3–3)

17. *Extra curricular privileges:* Should pupils be permitted to participate in planned extra-curricular activities, such as athletic games, school plays and clubs, even though they may not be doing satisfactory work in their classroom studies? (49–11–40)

18. *Literacy standards for diploma:* Should a student receive a high school

diploma until he has learned to read well and to express himself clearly in speech and writing? (19–10–71)

19. *Vocational training:* Should every student be prepared to earn a living by the time he graduates from high school? (45–12–43)

20. *Concern for non-college students:* Should the high school be just as much concerned with the students who are not going to college as with those who are? (97–1–2)

21. *Vocational guidance:* Is the school responsible for helping students choose a vocation? (69–10–21)

22. *Job placement:* Should schools help students find jobs for which they are suited after they are through school? (43–18–39)

23. *Preparation for adult activities:* Should the school emphasize preparation for adult activities, such as family life, recreation, community improvement, etc.? (74–12–14)

24. *Sex instruction:* Should appropriate sex instruction be given to all pupils in elementary, junior and senior high schools? (70–11–19)

25. *World affairs:* Should the school develop in every student an intelligent interest in world affairs? (96–2–2)

CITIZENS' POLL, SAN DIEGO. Another type of sampling to get citizen opinion on school problems is that used by Denver, Colorado, and San Diego, California. In each case, where there had been community criticism and attack upon the school program, the district employed an independent survey organization to secure a cross section of the opinions and attitudes of the adults in their respective communities. In the San Diego poll, the questioners sought to obtain the degree of satisfaction or dissatisfaction with the local school program on such controversial issues as "teaching the three R's," "homework," "teaching of American history," and "character education."[19]

The fifteen hundred respondents scientifically sampled represented an accurate cross section of the city. The degree of approval or disapproval manifested by this poll will have a definite bearing on the type of curriculum development undertaken in this city.

The conclusions from this survey revealed that: (1) San Diegans are firmly in favor of public education and rather than wanting to see some activities cut, most citizens probably would like to see an even greater extension of activities. (2) The citizens overwhelmingly approve many of the special activities that are outside the traditional schooling. (3) The San Diegans indicated their willingness to approve an additional bond issue to relieve overcrowded conditions. (4) Great ignorance was revealed over the instructional program and the curriculum. In answering the key ques-

19. The Phillips-Ramsey Company, *What San Diegans Think of the Public Schools,* Mimeographed Report to the Board of Education, San Diego City Schools, September, 1951. A similar survey by an independent concern was undertaken in 1950 by the Denver Public Schools, entitled *Denver Looks at Its Schools,* by Research Services, Inc., Colorado, 1950.

tion, "Taking everything into consideration, would you say that you are satisfied, only fairly well satisfied, or not very satisfied with the public school system of San Diego?" Thirty-five per cent said they were satisfied; thirty-six per cent said they were fairly well satisfied; and ten per cent said they were not satisfied, and nineteen per cent didn't know!

The Community School

The movement toward what is known as the "community school" has evolved largely out of the elementary school program, and its functional curriculum now is quite generally accepted. To a lesser degree, the secondary school has followed through an occasional class contact with the life of the community and through total curriculum effort the pattern of the elementary school.

The community-school idea is based upon the concept of the school as a social institution helping students to learn to *live in* rather than to *learn about living* in their community and state. The movement is not highly organized nor is it promoted by any national group. But the idea is soundly based upon three developments in educational thinking: first, the newer understandings regarding the learning process; second, the recognition of how the real needs and interests of children are to be met; and third, the demands of society for training and experience in preparing for adulthood in a modern society.

This movement has been an important factor in the development of the general education program which seeks to deal with the broader aspects of living on the part of every youth rather than the narrower vocational needs of individual students. As the community-school idea developed it has taken two trends: one is the attempt to bring the resources of the community into the program of the school; the other and more significant is the effort to take the school out into the community. Certain states have pioneered in this emphasis, supplying guidance and direction to the local communities and their schools. Outstanding in this is the State of Michigan, whch has focused its program upon local development. Since 1938 the community-school movement has been an integral part of the Michigan Curriculum Program. Florida, likewise, has made this movement an essential part of the Florida Program for the Improvement of Schools. This state, working cooperatively with a number of major lay organizations interested in education (such as the American Legion Auxiliary, the American Federation of Labor, the Florida Medical Association, and the Young Mens Christian Association), has produced materials which aid local communities and schools in working together on problems pertinent to children and youth.

The modern school is concerned about the use of the three major types of resources in every community: (1) physical resources, (2) human resources, and (3) social organizations. Upon these resources the cultural, economic, and political life of every community is built. The good community school will utilize all of them in planning its program to improve the quality of living in the community.

Some schools have progressed much further than others in this movement. It is well then to have some criterion to use to compare success in a given community with the goals of the idea as most intelligently conceived. Several have been prepared and the following one is typical of the better statements.

SIXTEEN CHARACTERISTICS OF THE COMMUNITY SCHOOL

1. The community school seeks to operate continuously as an important unit in the family of agencies serving the common purpose of improving community living.
2. The community school shares with citizens continuing responsibility for the identification of community needs and the development of subsequent action programs to meet these needs.
3. The community school begins its responsibility for better living with the immediate school environment.
4. The curriculum of the community school is sufficiently comprehensive and flexible to facilitate the realization of its purpose.
5. The community school program is dynamic, constantly changing to meet emerging community needs.
6. The community school makes full use of all community resources for learning experiences.
7. The community school develops and uses distinctive types of teaching materials.
8. The community school shares with other agencies the responsibility for providing opportunities for appropriate learning experiences for all members of the community.
9. The community school recognizes improvement in social and community relations behavior as an indication of individual growth and development.
10. The community school develops continuous evaluation in terms of the quality of living for pupils, teachers, and administrators; for the total school program; and for the community.
11. The pupil personnel services of the community school are cooperatively developed in relation to community needs.
12. The community school secures staff personnel properly prepared to contribute to the distinctive objectives of the school, facilitates effective work and continues professional growth by members of the staff, and maintains only those personnel policies which are consistent with the school's purposes.
13. The community school maintains democratic pupil-teacher-administrator relationships.
14. The community school creates, and operates in, a situation where there

is high expectancy of what good schools can do to improve community living.

15. The community school buildings, equipment, and grounds are so designed, constructed, and used as to make it possible to provide for children, youth and adults those experiences in the community living which are not adequately provided by agencies other than the school.

16. The community school budget is the financial plan for translating into reality the educational program which the school board, staff members, students, and other citizens have agreed upon as desirable for their community.[20]

COMMUNITY STUDY PROGRAM, BALTIMORE.   A three-year program in a city school system to enable its teachers to use better the community resources was undertaken by the City of Baltimore. In this metropolitan community, nearly all the teachers lived in the middle-class residential areas, northeast and northwest Baltimore, while more than half of the children attended schools in the older eastern and southern sections. Many of the teachers knew little or nothing about their city, aside from their own homes and the schools in which they taught. Many did not know that even in 1949 more than 200,000 Baltimoreans lived in substandard housing; that 25,000 dwelling units lacked private inside toilets, and that 30,000 units had no private baths. In addition, the children in the blighted areas were the very ones who lacked any recreational facilities and who attended schools which were sometimes a hundred years old.

In an effort to acquaint the teachers with community needs and problems, 800 teachers enrolled in the Baltimore Community Study In-Service Workshop. The program has three objectives:

1. *Child acculturation:* understanding the environmental and cultural influences that affect the child in his relation to the school and to learning

2. *Curriculum revision:* working with students, community leaders, parents and others to bring about learning that has meaning and purpose in terms of the child's developmental tasks and his societal needs

3. *Community action:* working with community agencies for the improvement of the child's environment and toward social progress

Over a three-year period these objectives have been attained through four progressive levels of community study, each of increasing complexity and significant returns: (1) understanding the community, (2) using the community's resources, (3) contributing to the community, and (4) working with community agencies toward common goals. During the first year of the study, major attention was given to the first two levels; the second year, attention

---

20. *Second Report of the 1948 National Conference of Professors of Educational Administration* (New York: Columbia University, Teachers College, Bureau of Publications, 1949), pp. 7–9.

focused on the third level; and, the last year was concentrated on the fourth level. At the outset, teachers were given the option of joining individual school groups which paid particular attention to the needs and problems within their school and its immediate environs, or joining a larger city-wide group (usually with a number of sections) which concentrated on understanding the city and its larger problems.

The second year saw similar choices being offered, to work either in school groups to consider problems on the use of neighborhood resources and school contributions to the area, or to work with larger city-wide interest groups in terms of housing, recreation, government, human relations, social welfare, city planning, historical resources, and health on a city-wide basis. Each one of these city-wide interest groups had from eight to thirty members, and included a resource person who was a specialist in that particular field. From this level of study came several contributions. One group working on housing produced a booklet on *Tenant and Landlord Responsibilities,* which contained so much valuable material that the City of Baltimore plans to publish it. Recreational and neighborhood studies have produced tangible results in improved services. Two high schools have developed a civic participation project in which seniors in their modern-problems courses spend part of the school day and some time after school performing civic and voluntary work for agencies such as the Red Cross, District Health Center, and the Baltimore Safety Council.

Finally, in the third year, with participants remaining with their school or city-wide interest groups, major attention was given to working with community agencies in improving individual and group living. The organization relationships of these groups were integrative rather than divisive, with the school and other agencies united in their approach to each problem. Emphasis was upon the importance of the individual citizen and his responsibility, with the institution providing full support and assistance. Out of this effort came such significant groups as school-community councils. One such council persuaded a group of landlords in a slum area to surrender their back-yard properties for a playground which was equipped by the local Kiwanis Club, staffed by the recreation department, and directed by the school. Another council worked on problems of housing, in cooperation with the health department, sanitation bureau, police department, and other agencies. This latter was broadcast over NBC by the Twentieth Century Fund, on a program entitled "Crusade in Baltimore."

Probably the greatest values have come out of the school groups dealing with problems within their immediate community. Improvements have been made in school facilities, grounds, and classrooms. Curriculum changes have accompanied these improvements. City-wide groups have seen the larger problems and the necessity for close community cooperation.[21]

----

21. Harry Bard, "Baltimore's Community Study Program," *Educational Leadership,* 8:399–405, 1951.

A HIGH SCHOOL PROGRAM, EAST HAMPTON, CONNECTICUT. One small six-year high school in the average community of East Hampton, Connecticut, sought to improve itself through a pupil-and-community-centered program based on sound educational procedures. The faculty of sixteen teachers was the first to be concerned over the needs of the 350 pupils in the school. They felt that the conventional college preparatory program was serving only a portion of the students and that many of the major needs of all youth were not being met.

In analyzing its students, the drop-out rate was found to be high; discipline was a problem; the daily schedule was rigid and crowded; while "sixty per cent of the pupils were not receiving the type of education needed!" The staff quickly determined that any improvement should be the concern of those involved, and called upon the parents and pupils to cooperate in building a new philosophy and a set of workable objectives. Some of the problems which led to this cooperative effort were

1. The subject and activities load of pupils should be increased without increasing the length of the school day.
2. A wider selection of program offerings should be provided without increasing the staff.
3. The school's program should utilize all the community's resources—the homes, the stores, the factories, community organizations, the fields, the woodlands, the lake and the hills.
4. The secondary school should be an active rather than a passive center of community life.
5. Pupils should be led to a desire to understand and to share responsibilities within the community.

For a period of two years the staff discussed with pupils, parents, and community leaders the philosophy, objectives, and program of the high school. Obviously, as work progressed it became clear that the students had good ideas and that they should be included in the discussion. The method used to get student participation was direct. The principal spent one period each day with one of the English classes, starting with the seniors, and working through to the seventh grade. Discussions on this important subject took considerable time, frequently lasting ten to fifteen class periods. Following these class meetings, assemblies, PTA meetings, Board of Education discussions, and a number of other community forums were held.

The staff then felt impelled to develop their course outline in consonance with the school's philosophy and objectives as these had evolved during the preceding two years. The four basic ideas which a faculty committee suggested as a foundation were

1. Certain common objectives must pervade all teaching.
2. Additional specific objectives must become the special burden of each subject.

3. There must be cooperation, not competition, among the subjects.

4. Children, not subjects, are developed and taught.

Each teacher then undertook to prepare course outlines for his subject fields to provide (1) for the common objectives outlined for all teaching, and (2) for those essential skills and appreciations to be derived from the specific subject.

As the cooperative thinking developed, all groups—pupils, parents, teachers, townspeople, and the Board of Education—agreed that significant changes meant major modification of the program or plan of the school. Among some of the areas affected were the weakness of study hall, the need for time for field trips and community services, the brevity of the class period (forty-five minutes), and the limited program of most of the pupils. With the main purpose to increase substantially the number and variety of educational experiences, the schedule was revised to provide for six one-hour periods a day, five of which would be devoted to regular subjects and the sixth to free electives and activities. Out of this came the unique proposal for a five-period day in a five-day week, each subject class meeting four times weekly. This modification increased the total class time devoted to each subject, since five forty-five-minute periods totaled only two hundred twenty-five minutes per week, while four one- hour periods provided two hundred forty minutes weekly. This left free a fifth hour (which came to be called X-period) for each of four days, and cleared one hour (later called Z-period) for extraclass activities on the fifth day.

Probably the most revolutionary, yet the most sensible, possibility that developed at this stage was the square scheduling (five-period day, five-day week), which permitted the turning of the horizontal schedule to a vertical position, thus allowing the pursuance of one subject all day. Only after full consideration of this radical suggestion by all concerned—Board of Education, parents, pupils, reporters, and townspeople—was the idea approved.[22]

A COMMUNITY SERVICE PROGRAM, STEPHENSON, MICHIGAN. The community of Stephenson, Michigan, working through its Board of Education, accepted the challenge to discover newer techniques of community improvement. The experimental program came to be known as the Community School Service Program, and was assisted financially by the Kellogg Foundation.

After securing the cooperation of the public in the village and surrounding community, the Board of Education organized a Community Coordinating Council, with the Superintendent of Schools as the executive secretary.

Objectives for cooperative improvement of the community were accepted,

---

22. Grace S. Wright, Walter H. Gaumnitz, and Everett A. McDonald, Jr., *Education Unlimited: A Community High School in Action* (U.S. Office of Education, *Bulletin* 1951, No. 5; Washington: Government Printing Office, 1951).

and seven problem-study committees were organized, namely, Education, Healthful Living, Community Service, Trade and Industry, Religious Life, Farm and Land Use, and Home and Family Living. Any community problem could be directed to one of these committees for consideration. Membership on the committee was purely voluntary and not limited in numbers. Approximately 175 citizens participated in the work of these committees, meeting monthly to consider problems. The Michigan Department of Public Instruction assisted by supplying consultant services and by offering opportunities for the members of the community to participate (1) trips outside the community to study other communities, (2) state conferences and workshops in leadership training, (3) scholarships to institutions of higher learning to study community problems, and (4) scientific surveys to discover community needs and problems. Up to March, 1950, some fifty projects of minor and major importance have been completed. The curriculum was influenced in several ways, and the changes have been accepted by the general public. The influence of the Community School Service Program has been significant, both upon teachers and pupils. Some of the generalizations which leaders of the program make are

1. No set pattern of organization will fit every community. The organization must come from the people and be designed to serve their interests.
2. The school is one of the major social agencies within the community and should play a major role in a community school service program. The job of the school administrator changes from that of a business manager sitting behind a desk to that of a social worker and consultant on community problems working with the people of the community. The building and its facilities should be open to the public when not in use for educational purposes.
3. Parents will gladly participate in revisions of the school program if given the opportunity.
4. The community has greater respect for the school that uses the natural and human resources of the community in its educational program.
5. The state department of public instruction should motivate communities to action. State and federal agencies are in a position to render invaluable services to any community by giving technical advice and consultative service.[23]

COMMUNITY PLANNING, BRADFORD, PENNSYLVANIA. The interest of a few leading citizens in a typical American city was the forerunner of a plan which enabled senior students to take an active, adult interest in problems of the community. In the city of Bradford, Pennsylvania, the members of the City

---

23. Joseph B. Gucky and Herbert Corey, "A Community Organizes to Help Itself," *Educational Leadership*, 7:388–392, 1950.

Planning Commission suggested to the Superintendent of Schools the need for a long-term planning program for that city. The Superintendent consulted with the faculty and students of the high school, and out of this group came the proposal that the major project of the senior social-studies classes be the needs and problems of Bradford. This plan envisioned a study of the needs of the community over a period of years by these classes: the needs to be analyzed scientifically and adequately; the recommendations to be submitted to the proper bodies; and an over-all program of community improvement to be undertaken. Some adults at first questioned the "ability" of high-school students to make careful study of city planning, which is a difficult task for trained engineers. Others wondered what practical value would come from this undertaking.

It was agreed, however, that there are two essentials which a city must have before improving itself—*ideas* as to what can be done, and *public opinion* to carry out these ideas. It was further agreed that although high-school students could not make a complete blueprint of a new city plan, they did have many valuable suggestions; many of them will influence others in a position to affect change; and a large proportion of them will be young adult citizens in the community when these changes are being effected. Consequently, the classes in Problems of Democracy, beginning in 1946, undertook a major community project of study, devoting several weeks to one of these areas: streets; streams and bridges; zoning; parks and playgrounds; housing; transportation and safety; parking; and civic buildings. In addition to the class gathering data, other classes cooperated in the preparation of the materials. The mechanical-drawing classes made maps and charts, while the art class began the building of a relief model which will record the progress of the studies over a period of several years. Specifically, the record of class studies during the past few years show that the first class made a general survey of conditions, listed some of the major problems, interviewed the citizens. Their first report *It Pays to Plan* was an intelligent presentation of the importance of planning in meeting Bradford's needs. The next class made a survey of all land within the city limits, noting its use. This was the basis for a land-use map of the city, made by the drawing classes. The third class studied zoning, endeavoring to determine what can be done in a small "boom" town in allocating land for certain purposes. The 1949 class prepared information and maps on proposed street changes, and the use of land for industries, business, and residence.

The values obviously are not alone in the immediate experiences which these students have in collecting data and making suggestions. The greater values in the school-community project lie in the point of view and sense of shared interest and responsibility which should carry over into adult life of the participants. Dealing with real-life problems in their own community,

Bradford seniors should have a permanent attitude toward community improvement that should pay dividends in the near future.[24]

Many other illustrations are available in the literature which could be used to illustrate the idea that the modern American high school can become a valuable community-wide institution, where youth and their parents plan and work and learn together. Through such cooperation the community calls upon the school to use its resources to improve community living, and the youth of the community learn by actual experience how to analyze and solve community problems. Everyone profits by such a program, and the curriculum of the school becomes learning experiences vital to all youth in school. This effort of school-community cooperation is one of the most important developments in curriculum reconstruction.

---

24. The Class of 1946, *It Pays to Plan* (Bradford, Pa.: Bradford Senior High School.) Mimeographed. Also, Nellie B. Moore and Joseph E. Walker (instructors), *It Pays to Plan: A Manual of City Planning for Bradford Senior High School* (Bradford, Pa.: Bradford Senior High School, 1949). Mimeographed.

Chapter Thirteen

General Education

for All Youth

WITHIN THE PAST DECADE the American Youth Commission of the American Council on Education was the forerunner of many studies which concentrated attention on the needs of youth and the attempts to solve their problems. Their work in publications and conferences during the late 1930's and the early 1940's pointed up the serious plight of the young people who had come out of the depression period. Through their books, such as *Youth Tells Their Story, How Fare American Youth,* and several others, leaders in education and allied fields became increasingly conscious of the responsibilities of society for youth, so long neglected.

With the onset of the World War II, "forgotten youth" became "fighting youth," and this same society called upon our young people to fight for and work to save democracy. The acute economic and social problems of just a few years past were soon forgotten as everyone became absorbed in war activities. Much of the data from this prewar period were set aside, and the solutions to the problems so clearly outlined were deferred until a later day.

National Youth Studies

Certain of our educational leaders, however, continued to be concerned with youth needs and with the failure of the secondary schools to meet them.

National Education Association

One influential group under the leadership of the Educational Policies Commission of the National Education Association, who earlier had produced such significant documents as *The Purposes of Education in American Democracy* (1938) and *Learning the Ways of Democracy* (1940), set out to plan the ideal secondary school for democratic America in the postwar period. Near the close of the war years they issued the challenging book, *Education for All American Youth*,[1] which described two hypothetical communities, Farmville and American City. The organization, financing, and curricula of the schools in these communities were described in complete detail.

National Association of Secondary School Principals

At the same time, in an effort to state simply and clearly that which was detailed in *Education for All American Youth,* the National Association of Secondary School Principals graphically summarized this publication in a booklet entitled *Planning for American Youth.* This publication outlined in sixty-four pages the proposed programs for Farmville and American City, using effective illustrations, charts, and diagrams to high light the significant points. In addition it included the seventh and eighth grades as part of the secondary school as well as the thirteenth and fourteenth grades of the junior college, thus spanning an eight-year secondary school program. A revised edition, published in 1951, included a third area, Frost County, and suggested for each area a modern curriculum organization designed to meet both general and special needs of its youth in relation to the type of community in which they live.[2]

University Committees

Paralleling in time the work of the Educational Policies Commission was a unique undertaking by twelve members of the faculty of Harvard University

---

1. Educational Policies Commission, *Education for All American Youth* (Washington: National Education Association, 1944).
2. National Association of Secondary School Principals, *Planning for American Youth* (rev. ed.; Washington, 1951). See also "The Imperative Needs of Youth of Secondary School Age," *Bulletin,* National Association of Secondary School Principals, Vol. 31, March, 1947.

to study general education for Harvard College. One section of the report gave brief attention to the secondary school. Their publication in 1944, *General Education in a Free Society*,[3] created considerable discussion, particularly when compared with the proposals contained in *Education for All American Youth*. After reviewing the needs of youth in the secondary schools, the Harvard committee proposed the subject areas for the secondary schools and related them to specialized areas. The proposals were definitely subject centered and far less carefully prepared and less significant than the proposals for Harvard College.

Following the Harvard report many colleges and universities gave attention to their general education programs for the lower-division students, and many junior colleges pursued such studies. Columbia College and Chicago University had antedated Harvard in analysis of their lower-division program but had used a different base for establishing their curricula. Probably the most significant junior-college study was the one over a two-year period in California. Since our purpose here is to study the secondary curriculum, the college programs will not be reviewed; however, they have a significant bearing upon the programs in the secondary schools.

John Dewey Society

A significant contribution to the improvement of the curriculum in the secondary school was the report, after a three-year study, by eight members of the John Dewey Society, in their stimulating book *The American High School*, published in 1946.[4] This report posed several major questions involving not only the high school itself but society at large. Like the earlier studies listed above, this report dealt with the needs of youth, defined at this point as developmental tasks. The proposal is that the common needs of youth be met through a core program unified under one teacher, which would include the "common learnings" in such areas as oral and written expression, citizenship, and other aspects of general education.

United States Office of Education

In the years immediately following World War II the vocational educational leaders in cooperation with the United States Office of Education were giving increased attention to the needs of youth of all types and abilities. A series of conferences were stimulated by a dramatic resolution prepared originally by a dean of vocational education, Dr. Charles A. Prosser. It called

---

3. The Harvard Committee, *General Education in a Free Society* (Cambridge, Mass.: Harvard University Press, 1945).

4. Hollis L. Caswell (ed.) and others, *The American High School* (Eighth Yearbook of the John Dewey Society; New York: Harper & Brothers, 1946).

upon educational administrators and others to work with vocational-education leaders in developing a curriculum which would meet the needs not only of the comparatively small percentage of students who are college-bound or training for the skilled trades, but for the "neglected 60 per cent" of youth who do not fit into either of these two categories. This movement was soon called "Life Adjustment Education."

In 1948 a National Commission on Life Adjustment for Every Youth was appointed by the United States Commissioner of Education, with representation from all the major professional organizations concerned with secondary education. At one of its early work conferences the commission developed the following concept:

> Life adjustment education is designed to equip all American youth to live democratically with satisfaction to themselves and profit to society as home members, workers, and citizens. It is concerned especially with a sizable proportion of youth of high school age (both in school and out) whose objectives are less well served by our schools than the objectives of preparation for either a skilled occupation or higher education.

Several national conferences have followed, together with a number of state-wide organizations which sought to give emphasis to the point of view developed by the National Commission. Its chief value to date has been to stress the meeting of the common needs of *all* American youth of secondary-school age. The Office of Education has also promoted state and local conferences and has stimulated a number of secondary schools to pursue studies of their pupils and to unify those subjects which are designed to meet the needs which all youth have in common. To make clear the ideas in the program a number of documents have been published.[5]

Studies of Purposes and Practices

Prior to 1940 the changes in high-school curricula had been very slow and nearly all changes made were in the reorganization of topics within special subject fields. Willing has summarized the trends that took place in the secondary school between 1890 and 1940 as follows:

> Great as may be the changes that are now taking place in American secondary education, they are not of the nature of violent upheavals or radical

---

5. See particularly U.S. Office of Education, *Life Adjustment for Every Youth* (Washington: Government Printing Office, 1948) ; Harl R. Douglass (ed.) and others, *Education for Life Adjustment* (New York: The Ronald Press Company, 1950) ; Howard A. Cummings and others, *Developing Life Adjustment Education in a Local School* (U.S. Office of Education, Circular No. 253, rev. ed.; Washington: Government Printing Office, 1951).

alterations of direction. Development has been accelerated of late but not to the degree that the present is no longer connected with the past. The selective and narrowly functioning high school of 1890 has merely grown into the universal and comprehensive high school of today. There have been no fresh starts. . . . No specific change occurred universally. A reading of the National Survey of Secondary Education will convince anyone that almost every feature of the high school program and practice prevalent in 1890 still remained in some high schools in 1930. Other sources are available to show that the greater part of the changes that marked advance did not so much as cause a ripple in the placid traditionalism of thousands of small high schools. All that one may safely assert about changes in the period is that this and that appeared in a good many schools and had such general professional approval that they bade fair to become more and more common throughout the country.[6]

Following the first shock of the depression, the influx of all youth into our secondary schools during this period, the tragic revelation of their needs and the inadequacy of the high-school program to meet these needs, all coupled with the threat of a national competitive educational program in the C.C.C. and the N.Y.A., leaders in the field of secondary education began to give serious attention to the fundamental purposes and the implementing program for our American high schools. A series of national studies as well as a few local surveys pointed up the problems and the needs to be met if the high schools of this country were to serve youth in terms of their real needs. Beginning with the late 1930's and on down to the present we have witnessed an impressive and challenging list of recommended purposes and practices for a functional secondary-school program.

National Association of Secondary School Principals

The Committee on the Orientation of Secondary Education, in 1937 under the chairmanship of Thomas H. Briggs, proposed ten basic functions of secondary education and suggested how these might be implemented.[7] These functions were the first to be presented since the Cardinal Principles of 1918 and were discussed enthusiastically by school administrators and teachers across the country. This was followed by the work of an implementation committee to secure consideration and discussion of the functions.

National Education Association

Following closely on the Brigg's report came the Educational Policies Commission in 1938 with their report on *The Purposes of Education in Ameri-*

---

6. Matthew H. Willing in *General Education in the American High School* (Chicago: Scott, Foresman and Company, 1942), pp. 41, 66.
7. Thomas H. Briggs and others, "Functions of Secondary Education," *Bulletin*, National Association of Secondary School Principals, Vol. 21, January, 1937.

can Democracy which set forth the concept of education in these terms:

> The general end of education at the present time is the fullest possible development of the individual within the framework of our present industrialized democratic society. The attainment of this end is to be observed in the individual behavior or conduct. The term education implies the existence of some person other than the learner, a person, moreover, who is interested in the outcome to encourage one type of conduct rather than another.[8]

The objectives which this report presented, and which today are accepted rather generally as the basic purposes of education, are: (1) the objectives of self-realization, (2) the objectives of human relationship, (3) the objectives of economic efficiency, and (4) the objectives of civic responsibility.[9] The forward-looking position taken in these objectives is even more significant when the commission proposes the practices consonant with these purposes:

> While the primary contribution of the school is its long-range educative service to society, the immediate measures available for direct action need not be disregarded. A school which makes a careful, scientific study of the handicaps and assets of each learner, to the end that he may be properly guided, has taken the first step to the attainment of its objectives. A school which helps parents in their homes to do a better job of educating their own children will have less to correct. A school which links its efforts to those of other like, motivated agencies makes all such efforts more effective. A school where teachers maintain close contact with the homes of the children and participate in community activities can more readily offset adverse out-of-school forces. A school which is a center of wholesome recreation and education for an entire neighborhood is already doing much to offset undesirable influences. A school which can arrange to be open on Saturdays and Sundays, in the late afternoons and evenings, as a community center, is not only grasping a direct educational opportunity but is making all of its "regular" work more effective by reducing the effectiveness of opposing forces.[10]

Regents' Inquiry

Paralleling these national studies was the New York Regents' study of the effectiveness of secondary education in that state. Known as the Regents' Inquiry, the facts regarding the glaring deficiencies and lacks in meeting youth needs in New York State secondary schools served only to emphasize the seriousness of the situation as described by the American Youth Commission. Among the eleven books issued in this study, the most pertinent at this point are *High School and Life, Education for Citizenship, When Youth Leave*

8. Educational Policies Commission, *The Purposes of Education in American Democracy* (Washington: National Education Association, 1938), p. 41.
9. *Ibid.*, p. 47.
10. *Ibid.*, pp. 132–133.

School, and *Education for Work.* The implications of this study had national repercussions and served as a challenge for curriculum improvement along the lines of practical education to meet life needs, citizenship, and vocational training.

Trends in Course Changes, 1940–1950

But the secondary school changed slowly. Studies have been cited previously to show changes in the secondary school prior to 1940. One can catch an idea of what changes have actually taken place from 1940 to 1950 by examining the data collected by Graves from eighty-three high schools in forty-two states. He asked these schools to indicate what courses had been added and what had been dropped between 1940 and 1950. Although one cannot tell much from a title, nevertheless certain trends are observable. He summarizes the results of his analysis as follows:

1. The additions to the curriculum in the field of social studies reflect an emphasis upon human relations, the world picture, and contemporary problems.
2. In mathematics, most of the courses added have been of a general or practical nature.
3. Specialized courses have been added in the language arts. Most of these are of a functional nature.
4. A dropping out of foreign language courses is indicated. Eleven high schools have dropped Latin during the ten-year period studied.
5. The trend in science is not clear. The number of courses added or dropped is small.
6. An increase in both general and specialized arts courses is noted.
7. Vocational education courses are being added to the curriculum in great number.
8. There is a continued interest in family life education. None of the courses added is the traditional foods or clothing course. They deal with the realistic aspects of family life. Few courses are being dropped.
9. A few courses in the fundamentals are being added. Twenty-one additional programs of driver education are noted. Six high schools are adding courses in health or health education.[11]

Holding Power of the School

Continued concern over drop-outs has also been troubling secondary-school leaders. Approximately the same number of pupils attended the last four years of high school in 1949 as in 1934. Some gain had been made in retention, how-

---

11. Albert D. Graves, "Ten Years of Change in Secondary Education," *Bulletin,* National Association Secondary School Principals, 35:62–68, 1951.

ever, for in 1934 there graduated from high schools 333 of every 1,000 pupils who had been in the fifth grade in 1926–1927. In 1948 there graduated 480 of every 1,000 pupils in the fifth grade in 1940–1941.[12] While gains had been made, there were still more pupils failing to complete high school than there were graduating.

Continued dissatisfaction with the effectiveness of the present-day high-school program and its inabilty to retain the interest and attendance of many youth led the superintendents of the metropolitan cities of this country to ask the United States Commissioner of Education to call a conference on this problem. This was held in Chicago in January, 1950, and included forty representatives from school systems from cities of more than 200,000 population. Giving primary attention to the holding power of the high school and what can be done about it, the conference came up with several specific recommendations, among which is this significant list:

1. The primary purpose of the secondary school is to continue the general education of all youth.
2. The secondary school has the responsibility for providing education so that each student's program shall be balanced in terms of general and special education in line with his individual needs and abilities.
3. Learning experiences should be provided in many different forms (within the school and out) so that progress is possible in terms of each individual's needs, abilities, and interests. Such experiences should be provided in other ways than by adding to the number of courses.
4. Curriculum planning and the development of teaching procedures in each school should be based on understanding and knowledge of the community in which the pupils live.
5. Teachers and administrators should be encouraged to be always alert to the necessity for curriculum modification in terms of the changing needs of pupils and community.
6. School organization and curriculum practices should discourage rather than encourage social stratification.
7. The emphasis in teaching and learning should be on effective community living and adjustment rather than on the contents of books.
8. Increased opportunity should be provided for school experiences which require "doing" and the demonstration of performance in real life situations.
9. Standards of achievement should be in terms of behavior and individual ability to learn rather than in terms of the mastery of subject matter.
10. Evaluation of student progress should be made on the basis of modified behavior, and teachers should seek meaningful ways of reporting student progress.

12. Taken from the *Biennial Survey of the United States 1946–1948* (U.S. Office of Education; Washington: Government Printing Office).

11. With individual achievement the basis of progress and evaluation, students will be able to progress from grade to grade with a minimum of repetition and failure.

12. More instructional materials must be adapted to the ability and maturity of students using them.

13. The relationship between teacher and student is particularly important. Each student needs to feel that at least one teacher knows him well, and is interested in him as an individual. Teachers should be selected for their ability to make a contribution to students rather than solely on the basis of their competency in a subject field.

14. Administrative procedures should be devised so that data and information on individuals and groups are made available to teachers, so that they can be used in individualizing instruction.

15. Opportunities should be provided pupils for the realistic consideration of vocational interests and for the special education required in advancing them.

16. Specialized vocational training should be deferred as long as possible so that it may come just prior to the student's leaving or graduating from school and actual employment.

17. The general education which is needed by all students as citizens, homemakers, and workers should begin sufficiently early in the secondary school so that it will reach all students before compulsory attendance laws permit them to leave.

18. Curriculum planning should be done by teachers and other school workers who are responsible for implementing and carrying out plans.

19. Curriculum planning and teaching procedures should be based on the increasing quantity of research on how children learn.

20. Increased attention should be directed to inform parents as well as students of what the schools are attempting to do.[13]

Several other factors have been significant in changing the secondary school curriculum the last ten years. Some of them have been previously developed, such as changes in the concept of the defensible basis for planning the curriculum—i.e. a curriculum based on student needs, and changes in the basic theories of learning.

Meeting the Needs of Youth

One of the most significant changes, however, has been a return to the more fundamental purposes of American secondary education. The free public high school was born out of a desire to extend the general education program of

---

13. Work Conference on Life Adjustment Education, *Why Do Boys and Girls Drop Out of School and What Can We Do about It?* U.S. Office of Education (Circular No. 269; Washington: Government Printing Office, 1950).

the elementary school to all youth, but the idea was lost in a resurgence of classical education for a few youth who wanted to prepare for college. The development of free men became a conscious goal, and this goal was broken into definable and achievable characteristics. Individual needs for effective citizenship, parenthood, and economic efficiency became impossible to achieve through the continued use of meaningless subjects. In addition to individual success, society had needs which could be met only through well-educated citizens. Statements of needs such as the following were important factors in changing the curriculum.

I. The ten imperative needs of youth

All youth have certain educational needs in common. All parents can agree that the school should meet these needs, which become the modern goals of education.

1. All youth need to develop saleable skills and those understandings and attitudes that make the worker an intelligent and productive participant in economic life. To this end, most youth need supervised work experience as well as education in the skills and knowledge of their occupations.

2. All youth need to develop and maintain good health and physical fitness and mental health.

3. All youth need to understand the rights and duties of the citizen of a democratic society, and to be diligent and competent in the performance of their obligations as members of the community and citizens of the state and nation, and to have an understanding of the nations and peoples of the world.

4. All youth need to understand the significance of the family for the individual and society and the conditions conducive to successful family life.

5. All youth need to know how to purchase and use goods and services intelligently, understanding both the values received by the consumer and the economic consequence of their acts.

6. All youth need to understand the methods of science, the influence of science on human life, and the main scientific facts concerning the nature of the world and of man.

7. All youth need opportunities to develop their capacities to appreciate beauty, in literature, art, music, and nature.

8. All youth need to be able to use their leisure time well and to budget it wisely, balancing activities that yield satisfactions to the individual with those that are socially useful.

9. All youth need to develop respect for other persons, to grow in their insight into ethical values and principles, to be able to live and work co-operatively with others, and to grow in the moral and spiritual values of life.

10. All youth need to grow in their ability to think rationally, to express their thoughts clearly, and to read and listen with understanding.

II. The imperative needs of society

Modern society in the United States also has certain problems which all citizens must face, deal with, and endeavor to solve. Youth should learn to understand and to deal effectively with them.

1. Society needs to be organized and governed so that differences will be respected and peace and political stability shall prevail among all nations.
2. Society needs a free economic system which supplies the basic needs of people without interruption.
3. Society needs to develop a condition which facilitates co-operation among labor, government, farmers, and industry; which promotes free discussion of differences; and which enables groups to reach agreements for co-operative planning and action.
4. Society needs to make it possible for organized business and labor to share the benefits of production on terms reached by bargaining among themselves.
5. Society needs to provide opportunities for individuals to work continuously at living wages and enjoy security after they have passed their productive period in life.
6. Society needs to develop loyalty to the principles of democracy, to protect individual freedom of thought and expression, to assure justice to all its citizens, and to develop independent people free from harmful propaganda and uniformity.
7. Society needs to make it possible for people of all races, colors, and creeds to be respected, with equal opportunities for work, legal protection, and education.
8. Society needs a strong popular government to protect the welfare of all its citizens from illegal practices or irresponsible groups.
9. Society needs to protect and replenish its natural resources so that they may not be wasted or exhausted.
10. Society needs to preserve the basic social institutions of home and family and church and school so that fundamental social, moral, and spiritual values may be learned, cherished, and perpetuated.

It is the responsibility of the school to meet the individual needs of youth and to make them competent to deal effectively with the common problems of society.[14]

There is indeed then a definite trend toward planning a unified curriculum to meet the needs of youth and of society. McGrath has characterized this movement as follows:

1. It is that which prepares the young man for the common life of his time and kind.

---

14. Both statements are taken from National Association of Secondary School Principals *Planning for American Youth*, rev. ed., 1951. See also their "Imperative Needs of Youth of Secondary School Age," *Bulletin*, Vol. 31, March, 1947.

2. It is not concerned with the esoteric and highly specialized knowledge of the scholar.
3. The salient feature of this movement is a revolt against specialism.
4. Another characteristic of the movement is its reaction against over-emphasis of vocationalism.
5. The reaction against specialism and vocationalism is accompanied by an effort to integrate the subject matter or related disciplines.
6. To increase further the scope of education and to combat specialism, a large proportion of the total program is being prescribed.
7. Exponents of this movement believe that education should be more closely related to the vital needs and problems of human beings.
8. Those interested in this movement seek an improvement in the teaching of the general student.[15]

Finally, the movement toward unification has been helped by experimentation with longer periods in classes, by cooperative teaching, and by a single teacher remaining with a given group of pupils for longer than a single class period or even a single year. In addition, experimentation with various approaches to curriculum construction have shown that orderly changes can actively be made. The "task basis" of organization, whereby specific developmental tasks of pupils at the time they face them are studied in school; the "pupil need" basis, where needs of pupils are analyzed, isolated, and studied; the "social needs" approach, where certain major social problems of common concern are organized and studied; and the "community resource" approach, where problems and activities within the community form the base of curriculum planning—all these depart from the subject-discipline organization and are forerunners of unified curriculum approaches. No one of these is sufficient to develop a complete and well-balanced program of secondary education, but when put together they provide experiences which can point the way to sounder approaches.

Before we describe the most significant experiments of the last few years, we should first give some attention to an understanding of the philosophy and terminology behind these innovations.

Basic Concepts of General Education

Probably the most carefully prepared exposition of the basic theory of general education is found in the Harvard report. The line of reasoning the report follows, runs like this:

1. Our American culture predicates certain traits of mind and ways of looking at man and the world.

---

15. Earl J. McGrath, "The General Education Movement," *Journal of General Education,* 1:3–8, 1946.

2. These traits embrace heritage and change.
3. A successful democracy demands that these traits and outlooks be shared as far as possible among all the people.
4. There exist great differences of opportunity, gifts, and interests among people.
5. General education should be adapted to different ages, abilities, and outlooks so as to appeal deeply to each, yet remain in goal and essential teaching the same for all.[16]

General education, then, is designed to develop the traits and understandings that men must have in common to sustain a democracy, despite the differences among individuals. The basic job of educators is to prepare an educational program to satisfy the needs of the great mass of average citizens (not alone the gifted), upon whom our great democracy rests and who are most susceptible to regimentation. Democracy requires all of them to exercise intelligence and independent judgment, and the great job of the school is to provide for them the education which will make them competent free citizens able to determine wisely the government policy for all people. Significantly, the report points out that it is not merely courses we need but a broad school program. With respect to courses, however, which are important, the Harvard report says:

> They must not be simply watered down versions of more complex courses but authentic and fresh vehicles of the spheres of general education—the world, man's social life, the realm of imagination and ideal—designed to implant the power of thought and expression, the sense of reliance and value. They must avoid the extremes either of talking down to students or of dazing them with abstractions. They must make increasing use of what appeals directly to the senses and clothes ideas with warmth—movies, singing, plays—yet never to the neglect of reading and discussion. . . . Further still the whole life of the school must be such as to embody these higher ends.[17]

General education essentially consists of those higher levels of democratic life which are common to all citizens and of all the experiences and understandings required to achieve these ends.

Briggs holds that general education has at least three distinct meanings, all of which combined should determine its purpose and processes:

1. General education concerns that development which is desirable, even necessary, for every normal individual.
2. General education must produce the well-rounded individual.
3. General education must integrate every youth with his environing society.

---

16. The Harvard Committee, *General Education in a Free Society*, summarized from p. 93.
17. *Ibid.*, p. 95.

However, educators pay considerable lip service to these ideas, but the practice is lacking. Briggs points out:

> It is assumed that everyone approves in principle a program that will seek the three objectives here presented: to give an education that is desirable for the effectiveness and happiness of every individual, to give whatever is necessary to help every individual become a well-rounded person, and to integrate every individual into the social and political group with which he must live harmoniously. Approval of these objectives carries with it also approval of compulsory attendance at school—even with financial aid, if necessary—until these ends are reasonably achieved. Required attendance on courses not maximally profitable to an individual, however, is a theft of the precious nonrenewable opportunity of youth; required attendance on courses that do not make a maximum return to the investing community is malfeasance in the trust imposed on school authorities. This trust cannot be justified unless education attempts more seriously than it has ever done before to produce citizens actively effective in our democracy.[18]

B. Lamar Johnson has done effective work in planning and discussing the program of general education, especially for the thirteenth and fourteenth years, commonly considered the terminal years of secondary education. He says general education is general in at least the following three respects:

> First, *general education is intended for everyone*—not merely for the select few who become scholars or who enter the professions. No longer will preparation for college entrance dominate the curriculum of the high school which is committed to the objectives of general education. The program of such a school will be planned to meet the varied needs of all young people of the community which it serves.
>
> Second, *general education is concerned with the total personality*—not merely with the intellect but with emotions, habits, attitudes. General education regards the student as a single unified being rather than a compartment of knowledge, one of feelings, and another of beliefs. This means that specific general-education programs must be defined in terms of what the learner is or does rather than in terms of course content or a body of knowledge.
>
> Third, *general education is concerned primarily with the individual's non-specialized activities.* It consists of preparation for efficient living, no matter what one's vocation. This does not at all imply a lack of concern for vocational training. Since two of the responsibilities of every person are a contribution to society and the earning of his own living, general education should include the choosing of a vocation in relation to both one's own aptitudes and interests and to the needs of society.[19]

18. Thomas H. Briggs, "The Role of General Education," *Bulletin,* National Association of Secondary School Principals, 32 (March, 1948), 90–100.
19. B. Lamar Johnson, "General Education: What It Is and Why," in *General Education in the American High School* (Chicago: Scott, Foresman and Company, 1942), Introduction, p. xii.

General education, therefore, seeks to meet the general needs of youth in a democratic society. It endeavors to cut across subject-matter lines and draws on material from all sources which will assist youth in becoming responsible citizens. It should not be confused with required courses. Quillen points out that "it is not general education because it is required; but it is required because its purpose is to help boys and girls develop into competent, intelligent citizens by meeting needs which are real and meaningful to them."[20]

Common Learnings

If general education calls for possession of competencies that are common to intelligent citizens, then there are certain experiences, problems, skills, understandings that youth should have in common. This has led curriculum workers to study the heritage, the social issues, the needs of youth and society to determine these common learnings. Herrick has proposed a set of characteristics of these common learnings as follows:

1. The Common Learnings program is a "thread of experience" that runs through all or part of the curriculum and is not confined to one particular course or area. Safety education is an illustration, where various aspects of safe living and practice are found in many phases of the school program—the various subject fields, the recreational program, the traffic situation.
2. Common Learnings' activities are based upon the needs of the immediate society in which the student lives. It is concerned with the school as well as the civic community of which he is a part. In this connection, housing is a problem which concerns most youth, and affects them at a number of key points in their lives. It is part of different portions of the school program.
3. Common Learnings use information, facts, and other data as means to an end—improved living. These facts deal primarily with the present situation. The historical past is drawn upon to interpret the present and to plan for the future. Birth rate, vital statistics, and bank clearings all are important in terms of the life of the community and its improvement.
4. Common Learnings stress skills, attitudes, understandings, and appreciations in the many aspects to which they are related. The use of these characteristics in an intelligent manner provides solutions to the problems which arise. Family living is a concern of all, and, in the various problems which confront youth, all of these aspects are present and must be used.
5. Common Learnings give particular attention to the developmental tasks of youth, as he seeks to grow in his relationships to his age mates, his

---

20. I. James Quillen and Lavone A. Hanna, *Education for Social Competence* (Chicago: Scott, Foresman and Company, 1948), p. 96.

parents and family, his vocation, and his values. In extraclass activities, the orientation program, and the guidance areas, these tasks are highly involved.

6. Common Learnings are so essential to everyone that they must be experienced as often as necessary. Based upon the maturity of the learner, this repetition is valuable at each stage. Citizenship education is a primary responsibility of the school, and, in terms of the learner's development, there are repeated and expanded experiences which are most essential at every grade level.

7. Common Learnings frequently involve cooperative planning by teachers from different subject areas, usually with one teacher having primary responsibility for a group of students. There is extensive cutting across subject lines to make for more effective and more economical learning, with emphasis on the functional aspects of each learning experience. The subject areas usually involved are those in the fields of English and social studies, with science, mathematics, and some of the arts frequently included.

8. Common Learnings usually use the unit method of teaching, with the units selected according to the needs of the class. In the selection of topics and the development of units on these topics, there is frequently teacher-teacher planning, and usually extensive teacher-learner planning.

9. Common learnings are more effective when there is more than one period daily devoted to this program. The extended period provides the opportunity for more activity, participation, research and conferences on the problems involved. In the program where materials are drawn from a number of areas, the experiences tend to cover much of the subject matter usually included under separate subject offerings. Problems that relate to the community illustrate this point—drawing from most of the conventional fields, social studies, science, mathematics, communication, and arts.

10. Common Learnings make their greatest contribution when the problem-solving technique is used in classroom method. This involves maximum participation by the learners in terms best suited to their needs. In personality development, for example, the questions and problems of youth are best met by this method.

11. Common Learnings tend to include services from the nonsubject areas, such as the guidance, extraclass, student government, and leadership fields. These frequently are incorporated as a definite part of the program, or may be drawn on incidentally as the need arises.

12. Common Learnings encourage the development of school-community relationships. Much of the activity within the common learnings program tends to take the school out into the community and to bring the community into the school. For example, in the consideration of vocations, there is a rich opportunity to involve the community in this vital problem through visits to various businesses and to bring representatives of different occupations into the school.

13. Common Learnings use a variety of methods in the development of the program and utilize a wide range of teaching aids. Committee work, discussions, panels, reports, excursions and field trips are some of the methods frequently used. In aids, beyond the conventional textbooks, there are surveys, resource persons, audio-visual aids, and work experiences as typical of the newer devices used.[21]

Core Courses

Core courses have been used in many school systems to carry the common learnings fashioned under the philosophy of general education. These courses cut across subject fields, they extend over several periods, and they are organized around the objectives of general education. They are usually developed cooperatively by a group of staff members, they emphasize problem solving, they follow the personal and social needs of youth, and they are intimately tied into the guidance and extracurricular program of the school.

Sometimes the terms "core courses" and "common-learnings courses" are used interchangeably. One of the most widely distributed descriptions of the courses comes from the report of the Educational Policies Commission—*Education for All American Youth*. The report gives the following explanations of these courses:

> It means that this course consists of learning experiences which *everyone* needs to have, regardless of what occupation he may expect to follow or where he may happen to live. . . .
>
> "Common Learnings" . . . extends through the three years of high school and the two years of community institute. It meets for two periods daily, in grades ten, eleven and twelve, and for one period daily in grades thirteen and fourteen. It is required of all students. . . .
>
> Here is a course designed to provide most of the learning experiences which, it is believed, all young people should have in common in order to live happily and usefully during the years of youth and to grow into the full responsibilities of adult life. It is not intended to provide education in vocational skills and knowledges; in mathematics, the sciences, foreign languages, or other subjects required for vocational purposes or for advanced study; or in a vocational and intellectual field which students may elect because of personal interest.

Briefly stated, the distinctive purposes of the course in common learnings are to help all youth to grow in six areas:

1. Civic understanding and competence
2. Understanding of the operation of the economic system and of the human relations involved therein

---

21. Modification of Theral T. Herrick, "Common Learnings: The What, Why, and How," *Clearing House*, 23:529–533, 1949.

3. Family relationships
4. Intelligent action as consumers
5. Appreciation of beauty
6. Proficiency in the use of language

To these should be added certain other purposes, which are not distinctive of this course alone, but which are looked upon as common aims for every course and teacher in the American city schools. Chief among these are the purposes to help youth grow:

1. In ability to think rationally and in respect for truth arrived at by rational processes
2. In respect for other persons and ability to work cooperatively with others
3. In insight into ethical values and principles
4. In ability to use their time efficiently and to budget it wisely
5. In ability to plan their own affairs, as individuals and as groups, and to carry out their plans efficiently.[22]

Illustrations of General Education

DANIEL WEBSTER HIGH SCHOOL, TULSA, OKLAHOMA.   The Daniel Webster High School has developed a general-education program in which English, social studies, and science are separate courses with all subject matter correlated through the problem approach. Although each subject operates as a separate course, they are blocked together in the pupil's schedule so that his three subject classes follow each other in the block sequence. The English, social studies and science teachers within each block have a common planning period each day to organize their material around a broad problem. Through this preparation period the general-education teachers have been able to unify their purposes and provide for informal correlation between the subject areas.

The block teachers organize their material around problems; for instance, when the ninth-grade pupils enter the building in the fall they have an orientation unit. Each department makes its specific contribution. In this particular problem the science teacher spends the time with such things as the construction and mechanical features of the building, for example, the heating plant; the English teacher uses the time to teach the flag salute, the school creed, the school song; while the social-studies teacher works on such things as the school traditions and the purposes of education in America. At times during the year the block teachers work in parallel units rather than integrated units. Through the block arrangement, considerable group guidance is carried on as well.

DENVER.   The general-education program in the Denver high schools grew

22. Educational Policies Commission, *Education for All American Youth*, pp. 248–252.

from workshops of teachers in all fields. General objectives, a framework, and specific outlines resulted. Members of all departments teach in the program, and general education is required all four years for five hours a week. Guidance is an integral part of the courses, and teachers tend to remain with the same pupils for four years. The outline of these courses is as follows:

OUTLINE OF GENERAL EDUCATION, 1950–1951

I. 9B—General education
   A. Orientation to the building, the personnel, and the rules
   B. School citizenship and the school organization
   C. How to get the most out of high school
      1. How to study
      2. Library information and skills
      3. Planning a four-year program
   D. Vocational orientation
   E. Personality development
   F. Contributory units (certain contributory units which are considered essential are shifted within half grades so that all pupils receive the instruction).
      1. World geography
      2. Graphic language
      3. Math fundamentals
      4. Choral music

II. 9A—General education
   A. History and government of Denver and Colorado
   B. Contributory units
      1. Math fundamentals
      2. Graphic language
      3. Choral music
      4. Science

III. 10B—General education
   A. Citizenship—school, city, state, nation, world
   B. Contributions of past ages to modern civilization
   C. Orientation (for pupils new to the school)
   D. Library information and skill (if not studied in 9B)
   E. Contributory units
      1. Personal health
      2. Vocational analysis
      3. Auto driving
      4. World geography
      5. Medieval cultures

IV. 10A—General education
   A. The world of work
      1. Surveying fields of work

2. Investigation of specific vocations
3. Basic economics
B. Replanning the high-school program
C. Library information and skill (if not given in 9B and 10B)
D. Wise use of leisure time
E. Contributory units same as for 10B

V. 11B and 11A—General education

A. American history
B. Contributory units
   1. 11B
      a. World problems
      b. American problems
   2. 11A
      a. World problems
      b. Word study

VI. 12B and 12A—General education

A. Student evaluation of school program up to the present based upon the Ten Educational Needs of All American Youth
   1. To develop saleable skills
   2. To maintain good health and physical fitness
   3. To understand the rights and duties of the citizen
   4. To understand the significance of the family
   5. To purchase and use goods and services intelligently
   6. To understand the influence of science on human life
   7. To appreciate beauty in art, etc.
   8. To use leisure time wisely
   9. To develop the ability to live and work successfully
   10. To think rationally, to express thoughts clearly, and to read and listen with understanding
B. Development of a plan for living in a democracy and a code of ethics through
   1. Study of basic problems of human living
      a. Dating
      b. Family relationships
      c. Marriage
      d. Personal and family finance
         (1) Everyday law
         (2) Program of insurance
         (3) Installment buying
         (4) Buying
      e. Consumer education
      f. Religious values
      g. Strategy of job finding

VII. 12B—Physical education includes: Senior boys' problems and Senior girls' problems, each 2 days per week.[23]

ILLINOIS SECONDARY SCHOOL CURRICULUM PROGRAM. The basic purpose of the Illinois Secondary School Curriculum Program is to assist local school groups to make their curricula functional in terms of real-life values for all the children of all the people. The philosophy is positively "grassroots," based on the belief that only the local lay and professional citizens and the local students can achieve effectively any change in the high-school curriculum. The permissive character of the ISSCP makes the program distinctive; any high school may participate or not, as it sees fit. Despite the voluntary aspect, a large number of the secondary schools of the state are actively sharing in various phases of the program.[24]

Some of the significant activities projected by the ISSCP include an attempt to coordinate the activities of all persons and groups, on both a state-wide and local level, that are concerned with improving the secondary-school curriculum.

A unique cooperative endeavor is the close relationship of the ISSCP to the Life Adjustment Program developed on the national level. The joint activities are carried on under the following purpose: to coordinate on a state-wide level and on a local-school level all the persons who are, or who should be, interested in the high-school curriculum. The several studies which are reported below have been cooperatively sponsored by the two major bodies, the ISSCP and the ILAEP (Illinois Life Adjustment Education Program).[25]

At the local levels, groups similar to the state-wide steering committee have been established, under the latter's sponsorship. Local studies basic to curriculum development have been made available through these committees for wider dissemination. Workshops of several types have been sponsored: for example, 600 school administrators have attended one or more three-day workshops; 6,200 administrators and teachers have attended one of 23 county meetings. Many workshops have been conducted by each of the state teachers' colleges and by certain of the universities. Experimental curriculum projects are supported by the ISSCP, with consultant and other services being supplied free of charge by the colleges and universities. The publications have been of two types: (1) findings of studies and (2) general guides for investigation of

---

23. Sam R. Hill, "How Adequate Are Today's Secondary Schools?" *Bulletin,* National Association Secondary School Principals, 34:156–158, 1950.

24. Harold C. Hand, *How the Illinois Secondary School Curriculum Program Basic Studies Can Help You Improve Your High School* (Illinois Secondary School Curriculum Program, Circular Series A, No. 51, *Bulletin* No. 13; Springfield, Ill.: State Department of Public Instruction, May, 1951). See also above, Chap. 7, pp. 174–175.

25. Charles W. Sanford, *The Illinois Secondary School Curriculum Program—The Illinois Life Adjustment Education Program* (Springfield, Ill.: State Department of Public Instruction, 1950). Mimeographed.

the needs of local schools with suggestions as to how these schools may improve their curriculum services.

Most outstanding are the 5 studies which have been conducted in 178 Illinois high schools, as follows:

1. The *Holding Power Study,* 79 schools cooperating, which was concerned with the drop-outs of the high schools in Illinois
2. Participation in *Extracurricular Activities Study,* which involved 13 high schools on a selected-sample basis
3. The *Hidden Tuition Costs Study,* in which 79 schools participated
4. The *Guidance Study,* 93 schools cooperating, which undertook to determine the problems of pupils and the adequacy of the guidance services
5. The *Follow-Up Study,* conducted in 95 schools, to determine the real-life problems encountered by former pupils, how well they were meeting them, and how well the schools had assisted them in meeting these same problems

The most recent series of studies, *The Local Area Consensus Studies,* is an effort to secure from the public, the teachers, and the students their judgments on the best possible program the local community can understand, accept, and support. In particular, the concern of this study centers in the need for unity on the part of the teachers who are vitally concerned in any curriculum change. The faculty of a local school, therefore, must:

1. Consider together the purposes of each of the subject or service areas of the school;
2. Consider together which of the accepted purposes of each subject or service area are and which are not currently being embodied in the program of the school; and
3. Consider together what can and should be done to implement those of the accepted purposes in each subject or service area which are currently being neglected.[26]

These studies so far have indicated the need for greater concern over the fact that the present program is highly departmentalized in most high schools and the real-life needs of youth will probably have to be met through improvement of the subject pattern. With this in mind, further projects are under way which seek:

1. To stimulate the local school to consider in some detail *what it should be doing* in each subject or service area to meet the particularized needs of youth which are sensibly related to each subject or service area
2. To stimulate the local school to bring to light, in the same particularized detail, *what it is now doing* in this regard in each subject or service area

---

26. Harold C. Hand, *Prospectus of the Local Area Consensus Studies* (Illinois Secondary School Curriculum Program, Circular Series A., No. 51, *Bulletin* No. 15; Springfield, Ill., State Department of Public Instruction, 1951), p. 8.

3. To stimulate the local school to consider, in the same particularized detail, *what in addition it can do, or what it thinks it should be doing* in each subject or service area; to make and to put into operation plans for doing what can now be done; and to spot and describe the limiting factors so that plans for remediation may be gotten under way

4. To stimulate the state-wide development through ISSCP–ILAEP of ways and means for overcoming or removing commonly encountered limiting factors

EVANSVILLE, INDIANA. The general-education program in Evansville is organized under six categories.

I. Guidance and treatment

A. The health program begins in the kindergarten and continues through the twelfth year with periodic health examinations, nurse-teacher service in each school, dental clinics, classroom instruction, and school programs and projects.

B. A cumulative record beginning with kindergarten is used for guidance and adjustment of each pupil during his school experience.

C. A testing program provides the information and understanding needed for curriculum planning and course selection, vocational and college guidance, and personal adjustment.

II. Fact-finding studies to determine needs of youth and changes which should be made in the high school program

A. Student reaction to the social-hygiene program in the health and safety course on the eleventh-year level

B. Follow-up study of high-school graduates

C. Studies made under direction of the Curriculum Commission
1. Student attitudes and practices
2. Leisure-time activities
3. Vocational information and attitudes of Evansville school children

III. Lay participation

A. A Lay Advisory Committee cooperates with the Curriculum Commission in improving the school program.

B. In developing a cooperative work-experience program and utilizing vocational resources, lay industrial, commercial, and civic groups have been organized and called in as advisory and participating groups.

IV. Administrative reorganization and activity better to meet the needs of youth

A. A Curriculum Commission representative of every department and grade level is functioning to direct evaluation and improvement of the public schools' curriculum.

B. In-service training of teachers is being encouraged through
1. Local faculty meeting programs

2. The Evansville Center for Advanced Study.[27] The Evansville Public Schools, Evansville College, Purdue University, and Indiana University cooperate in extension classes and workshops in guidance and family-life education.

V. Curriculum changes in reorganizing the school better to meet youth needs
   A. The ninth year is receiving special emphasis as an orientation and exploratory year to understand the pupil and help him understand himself, plan, and adjust successfully to school life.
   B. An integrated family-life education program is being developed, kindergarten through twelfth grade.
   C. Student-government programs provide for democratic participation and civic training.

VI. Evaluation procedures
   A. Extensive testing program to evaluate the outcomes of instruction
   B. Cooperation with Indiana University consultants on testing programs

For over twenty years, the Evansville public-school system has been moving progressively into a program to provide for the imperative needs of all the youth of the community. Certain of the elements considered essential in general education have long been an integral part of the educational program of that city.

Life Adjustment Education

In the spring of 1945, when the Division of Vocational Education of the United States Office of Education held a conference in Washington, D.C., to plan a vocational education program for the years ahead, Dr. Charles A. Prosser made a dramatic appeal in his resolution for the improvement in high school offerings to meet the real needs of what he called the "60 per cent" of students now being neglected in favor of the 20 per cent preparing for the skilled trades and the 20 per cent who are college-bound. The following year, five regional conferences were held under the combined auspices of the Divisions of Secondary and Vocational Education of the United States Office of Education. The consensus of opinion in this series of conferences was

1. Secondary education today is failing to provide adequately and properly for the life adjustment of perhaps a major fraction of the persons of secondary school age.
2. Public opinion can be created to support the movement to provide appropriate life adjustment education for these youth.
3. The solution is to be found in the provision of educational experiences based on the diverse individual needs of youth of secondary school age.
4. A broadened viewpoint and a genuine desire to serve all youth is needed

27. L. T. Buck, *Evansville's Approach to Meeting the Imperative Needs of All Youth* (Evansville, Ind., 1950). Mimeographed.

on the part of teachers and of those who plan the curricula of teacher-training institutions.

5. Local resources must be utilized in every community to a degree as yet achieved only in a few places.

6. Functional experiences in the areas of practical arts, home and family life, health and physical fitness, and civic competence are basic in any program designed to meet the needs of youth today.

7. A supervised program of work experience is a "must" for the youth with whom the resolution is concerned.

8. One of the principal barriers to the achievement of the ideals of the resolution is the multiplicity of small, understaffed, and underfinanced school districts in this nation.

9. An intimate, comprehensive, and continuous program of guidance and pupil personnel services must constitute the basis on which any efforts to provide life adjustment education must rest.[28]

A year later, at a national conference held on this topic in Chicago in May, 1947, the Prosser Resolution, as it had come to be called, was restated, with the percentages eliminated because of the wide variations of such figures in different communities. However, it called for a "suitable educational program" to meet the needs of all youth of high-school age. The same group identified a number of obstacles to goals of life-adjustment education as it was conceived. Among these are: (1) Many state departments are not effectively organized to provide the necessary leadership. (2) Too large a number of small high-school districts are incapable of offering an adequate program. (3) High schools are dominated by college preparatory courses. (4) The prestige of academic offerings restrains change; and (5) other factors limit the programs, such as the Carnegie unit, inadequate finances, excessive teacher load, inferior teacher training, inadequate use of community resources, and the conservative attitude of portions of our society.

A Nation-wide Program

Finally, each of the nine national education organizations concerned with secondary education submitted names to the United States Commissioner of Education for membership on a National Commission for Life Adjustment Education for every youth, whose purpose was "to promote, in every manner possible, ways, means and devices for improving the life adjustment education of secondary school youth."[29] The commission met in Washington, in October, 1948, and developed the following concept:

---

28. Quoted by Harl H. Douglass in *Education for Life Adjustment* (New York: The Ronald Press Company, 1950), pp. 4–5.

29. National Commission for Life Adjustment Education, *Life Adjustment Education for Every Youth* (U.S. Office of Education; Washington: Government Printing Office, 1948), p. 40.

Life adjustment education is designed to equip all American youth to live democratically with satisfaction to themselves and profit to society as home members, workers, and citizens. It is concerned especially with a sizable proportion of youth of high school age (both in school and out) whose objectives are less well served by our schools than the objectives of preparation for either a skilled occupation or higher education.

The National Commission described life-adjustment education in its Introduction:

It is concerned with ethical and moral living and with physical, mental and emotional health.

It recognizes the importance of fundamental skills since citizens in a democracy must be able to compute, to read, to write, to listen, and to speak effectively. It emphasizes skills as tools for further achievements.

It is concerned with the present problems of youth as well as with their preparation for future living.

It is for all American youth and offers them learning experiences appropriate to their capacities.

It recognizes the importance of personal satisfactions and achievement for each individual within the limits of his abilities.

It respects the dignity of work and recognizes the educational values of responsible work experience in the life of the community.

It provides both general and specialized education, but, even in the former, common goals are to be attained through differentiation both as to subject matter and experience.

It has many patterns. For a school, a class, or a pupil, it is an individual matter. The same pattern should not be adopted in one community merely because it was effective in another. It must make sense in each community in terms of the goals which are set and the resources which are available.

It emphasizes deferred as well as immediate values. For each individual it keeps an open road and stimulates the maximum achievement of which he is capable.

It recognizes that many events of importance happened a long time ago but holds that the real significance of these events is in their bearing upon life today.

It emphasizes active and creative achievements as well as adjustment to existing conditions; it places a high premium upon learning to make wise choices, since the very concept of American democracy demands the appropriate revising of aims and the means of attaining them.

It is education fashioned to achieve desired outcomes in terms of character and behavior. It is not education which follows convention for its own sake or holds any aspect of the school as an end in itself rather than a means to an end.

Above all, it recognizes the inherent dignity of the human personality.[30]

The commission also set up certain guiding principles which should be used

30. *Ibid.*, pp. 4–5.

by those states and communities concerned with life-adjustment education. A school seeking to meet the needs of all youth will observe these:

1. Respects individual worth and personality
2. Enrolls and retains all youth
3. Required courses and course content to be concerned with problems of living
4. Emphasis upon direct experience
5. Planning, organization, operation, and administration to be democratic
6. Records and data to be used constructively
7. Evaluation to be for desirable changes in pupil behavior

This commission, working without special funds, has sought to stimulate and encourage a wide range of experiments, studies and practices, in secondary-school curriculum improvement on both state and local levels. In some states, where curriculum development was well under way, life-adjustment responsibilities were incorporated in their already established program. Typical was the cooperation with the Illinois Secondary School Curriculum Program. In other states, state committees on life-adjustment education have been set up, such as in Colorado and West Virginia. In still others, such as Washington and Kansas, special committees have been appointed to investigate particular problems relating to life-adjustment education.

State and Local Programs

The attempt to move from the general and theoretical aspects of the life-adjustment education program to the specific and practical is now the concern of many leaders in the field. Most efforts have been centered in local schools.

STATE OF TEXAS.   In the state of Texas, a survey was made of the life-adjustment education program in 169 secondary schools in the state. Using an extensive check list, the data collected showed "a definite and vigorous development of one or more aspects of life adjustment education in approximately seventy-five" of these secondary schools and a developing awareness of the desirability and feasibility of such an emphasis in the others. A majority of these schools recognized the problem of increasing the school's holding power through this type of program. The survey revealed that many changes in methods of instruction, school administration, guidance, the home room, the student council, and student activities were being effected by this new emphasis upon a functional secondary-school program. Some thirteen fields of study, including art, business, health, homemaking and practical arts, music, and the more formal academic subjects, all were influenced in many of the schools by this new approach.[31]

---

31. Texas Study of Secondary Education, *Self-Appraisal Checklists: Life Adjustment Education in the Secondary Schools* (Austin, Tex.: University of Texas, 1950) ; John W. McFarland, "Life Adjustment Education in Texas Secondary Schools," *Bulletin,* National Association of Secondary School Principals, 36:97–105, 1952.

SENIOR HIGH SCHOOL, BILLINGS, MONTANA.   A unique attempt to develop a life-adjustment program parallel to the subject curriculum was begun in the fall of 1948 at the Senior High School, Billings, Montana. To graduate from high school each student has to meet the following prerequisites:

I. Fulfillment of purposes

    A. He must fulfill his purposes, which means working out an individual goal and arranging subjects, time schedule, and activities appropriately, demonstrating growth in planning, in evaluating, in knowledge, in maturity, in health knowledge and practice, and in recognizing and solving his personal problems.

    B. He must fulfill the purposes of the community through growth in service as well as growth in character.

II. Four requirements

    A. Subject matter: the conventional 61 units, which are part of every traditional high school.

    B. Attendance: a minimum of two and a half years in senior high school or the equivalent time in other schools. The record must be consistent with the standards the student has set to meet his goal and must be satisfactory to the deans and counselors.

    C. Achievement: demonstrating achievement of high quality in some phases of life, such as a high scholarship record, a successful athletic record, or any school activity. It may be in service to parents at home, or in community leadership. The counselor and the student share in the evaluation of the activity record.

    D. Activities: students must earn a total of 200 points in activities and special projects outside the classroom. There is provision for loss of points through antisocial conduct. Positive points can be achieved in the following required and elective areas:

        1. School and life planning (required). Worked out with counselor, 20 to 50 points. Includes a six-page form entitled *School and Life Planning* which is filled out and filed with the counselor as guide.

        2. Growth toward maturity (required). 20 to 50 points. Based upon another six-page form entitled *Growth Toward Maturity* which is developed with the counselor.

        3. Scholastic achievement (elective). 20 to 50 points. Based not upon arbitrary grades but on how well the individual student measures up to his possibilities.

        4. Learning to work (elective). 20 to 50 points. Another counseling relationship to assist student to learn how to work and work well.

        5. Service to the school (elective). 5 to 50 points. All types of service opportunities are offered to students who wish to make a positive contribution to the school community.

        6. Other elective areas: safety in general and auto safety in particular; free reading; home study; understanding and appreciating a free

society; helping plan school curricula and objectives; boy-girl relationships; preparation for marriage; and activity points.[32]

.Although the point system would seem to be directed toward an artificial
a'nd extrinsic type of motivation, the counseling basis as well as the variety of
υpportunities would appear to provide for a close relationship of subject class
and extraclass experiences in a wide range of youth needs. The purpose is:
"To provide opportunity and to encourage growth in personally satisfying and
socially acceptable patterns of behavior and to develop a sense of values that
contribute to individual happiness and the social good."

BYERS JUNIOR HIGH SCHOOL, DENVER. The general-education program of
the Byers Junior High School, Denver, Colorado, is centered in a period
devoted to special emphasis on the vital interests and needs of boys and
girls and includes considerable group and individual guidance. In setting up
the units which would attack the problems confronting pupils, a faculty committee decided that if the program was to represent the interests and meet
the needs of boys and girls, two other groups should be consulted, the students and the parents. To accomplish this a student subcommittee, consisting of a boy and girl from each of the half grades 7B to 9A, inclusive, was
organized. This committee set out to make a systematic study of the real
problems of adolescents in order to make the general-education program more
meaningful for the students and more unified for the teachers.

At the outset, each general-education class submitted to the student committee a report of the unit it was currently studying. The committee, working
cooperatively with a teacher and a representative from the central office,
reviewed these units and added other subjects which were not included in the
original list. This revised list was then classified according to the areas of
interests, based upon the ten Imperative Needs of Youth, as outlined in
Education for All American Youth. Each life-experience area was considered
by the committee. Pupils were asked to indicate problems in each area, and
these problems were combined under common headings to form units. In
cooperation with the teacher committee, a tentative list of forty-four units
was prepared (with brief summaries of each) for submission to the pupils of
the school. Typical topics included family problems, understanding other races
and religions, prejudice, making our world organizations succeed, success at
Byers, making Denver a better place in which to live, getting the most for
your money, living in an air age, leisure time, sports, appreciation of fine arts.

These topics were presented to the student body in the form of a questionnaire. The presentation involved three assemblies, one for each grade, at
which time the students on the committee reviewed their work, why they
had done it, how the school was sincerely interested in this program, how the

---

32. J. G. Ragsdale, *Life Adjustment Curriculum* (Billings, Mont.: Senior High School,
1950), pp. 1–12.

questionnaire was to be filled out, what use was to be made of the results, and how a topic could be developed. The questionnaires were answered in the general-education classes, and the student council tabulated the results.

Teachers who felt insecure in developing units of study were released for brief periods to obtain instruction in unit development. Faculty meetings were devoted to consideration of these methods. A sampling of parents was undertaken, using the same questionnaire as that used by the students. When pupil, faculty, and parent results were assembled the differences were not wide.

Based upon the results of the questionnaire, the units desired were listed according to grade. A committee of teachers reviewed the topics and the grade placement, which were found to be adequate in all areas. The top five preferences for each grade were taken by the student committee and given appealing titles, such as "Getting ready for high school and college" (the first choice in the upper grades); "Making money for yourself at junior high school age"; and "Boy-girl friendships."

These units formed the basis for study in the general-education period at Byers Junior High School. Small cooperative committees of teachers worked on the preplanning of these units. Student committees cooperated also in helping to set up and develop the units. A materials committee assisted the classes in the selection and securing of supplementary materials. The units developed in this way seemed to have several advantages, according to the reports:

1. They are based on the expressed interests and concerns of the boys and girls studying them.
2. The units retain the spontaneity that is often lost when they are worked out by one group, put in cold print, and then followed methodically by others.
3. The units are developed systematically, first by pre-planning by the teacher or a group of teachers, then by pupil-teacher discussions within the group, and then by using techniques for its development by the nature of the unit.
4. Each pupil has an active part in the development of the unit and in the techniques used in arriving at conclusions.
5. The units that are considered to be satisfactorily worked out by the teachers are filed in a central office and are available to other teachers for suggestion and inspiration.[33]

Significance of the General Education Movement

The recent progress made in developing programs of general education are especially significant for several reasons. First, they recognize the need for

33. Ruth Irene Hoffman, "Students Help Plan a Life Adjustment Program," *Educational Leadership*, 7:393–397, 1950.

common skills, attitudes, behaviors, and understandings among all youth in a democratic society. Second, they are centered in the social and personal needs of youth. Third, they are related to goals deemed desirable rather than to subject disciplines. Fourth, they are orderly and carefully planned, worthy in themselves, and pupils recognize their significance for their own living and education. Fifth, they give a truly significant purpose to universal secondary education and relate to its proper place the development of special interests and aptitudes for college entrance, occupational competence, and personal development. These programs really represent the first significant fundamental change in the curriculum of secondary education the past fifty years.

Much work needs to be done to secure appropriate criteria to use to select the common learnings. There are gaps and overlappings, and now that definite gains are being made in general-education programs in colleges, attention needs to be paid to developing appropriate and orderly sequences in general education from grades seven through fourteen. Once this is done and the goals are sharpened, our secondary schools will make a significant contribution to the lives of boys and girls and to the supporting society.

Chapter Fourteen

Developing
Core Courses

I N THE PREVIOUS CHAPTER the basic concepts and principles of general education, common learnings, and life adjustment have been explored. These basic areas of the curriculum, designed for all pupils and organized in a unified fashion, have been instrumental in the organization of core courses as a desirable way to achieve the purposes of common learnings or general education. Other terms which have been used to refer to the idea of a core are "basic courses," "foundation courses," "social-living classes," "integrated courses," and "unifying courses." There probably is no really good name to express the idea which ought to be uppermost in the idea of a core course.

It has been mentioned earlier that the scope and sequence is one design which gives direction to the selection of the problem to be developed in the core class. This framework of scope and sequence is a design for achieving the central purpose of the school—the development in understanding and practice of the behaviors required for effective citizenship in a democratic society. The core, then, as we are using the term, refers to that part of the curriculum which takes as its major job the development of personal and social responsibility and competency needed by all youth to serve the needs of a democratic society. This area would encompass the personal problems which all youth in the high school are facing, some of which may be treated in groups and some through contact with individuals through a carefully prepared guidance program. The area would also include those dominant social problems which are impinging upon the life of all youth in some way.

There is one important point that needs to be understood clearly in this concept. Experiences are not common, but problems are. It is necessary, therefore, that each child as he works through these dominant social problems identify himself with those aspects which give meaningful direction to his own experience and goals. The problem of employment, for instance, is of concern to all of us. Whether we be born with or without the traditional silver spoon to nurse, we must all be socially concerned about the employment of people, for to a large extent it determines the character of the larger social scene. Some are concerned about immediate personal employment, some about employment after additional years of schooling, some about its effect on the present standard of living in their home, and some about the larger social problem of economic employment in a social order. Here is a common problem, but each youth identifies himself with a different aspect of it according to his goals and interests. Core courses properly developed will give youth an opportunity to see the significance of each problem as a social issue, and will at the same time enable them to find opportunities for answering some of the crucial issues in their own personal development.

Characteristics of the Core

The first characteristic of the core phase of the curriculum is that it utilizes the problems of personal and social development common to all youth. A second characteristic is that it develops these problems without reference to the traditional subject-matter fields. In the early development of core work, attempts were made to apply the idea to large social problems; then the science teacher and the English teacher and the social-studies teacher were asked what they had to contribute to the solution of the problem. Frequently, they returned to their classes to do what they could with the problem in their own fields. This scheme not only led to trouble in organizing and scheduling the school program, but it was based upon an unsound premise: it led each teacher again to place his subject interest uppermost and to try to build it up in relation to a problem previously agreed upon.

Contrary to this practice is the more desirable one of having all teachers in the school work together to determine the crucial social and personal problems youth are facing in their community. This project should include a study of the literature on modern social problems, a study of the crucial social issues in the immediate community, a study of the problems of the youth themselves, and a canvass of the opinions of youth as to the issues they consider important. From these various sources will come enough material to determine the common social and personal problems for consideration. The next step should be the building of units on these problems. A large number of teachers with different experiences, backgrounds, and training should participate in this work. The point of approach is not "What can my subject contribute?" but rather "What is needed to develop the desired understandings and skills?" This should be answered without respect to subject lines. Instead of trying to put as much into the unit as possible or trying to select a modern issue and then beginning it by going back to ancient times to develop the problem (the academic approach), the teachers concerned should face the problem squarely, ask what is needed to understand and solve it, and then decide upon the absolute minimum of materials necessary to do the job. There is such an abundance of materials available today for the secondary-school curriculum that we will have to begin immediately to eliminate rather than to add to existing organizations of courses.

A third characteristic of the core is that it encourages the use of the problem-solving technique to attack problems. These core issues are problems, not topics of subject matter. They require a wide variety of techniques and materials for their development. The use of visual aids, excursions into the community, some work experience, reading, demonstrations, and some construction are also essential if they are to be solved adequately. The greatest revolution we need in the secondary curriculum, after that in the selection of new materials, is the use of new and improved methods of work and study.[1]

---

1. For help here, see H. H. Giles, *Teacher-Pupil Planning* (New York: Harper & Brothers, 1941); H. H. Giles, S. P. McCutcheon, and A. N. Zechiel, *Exploring the Curriculum* (New York: Harper & Brothers, 1942); *Thirty Schools Tell Their Story* (New York: Harper & Brothers, 1942); Educational Policies Commission, *Learning the Ways of Democracy* (Washington: National Education Association, 1940); R. O. Billett, *Fundamentals of Secondary School Teaching* (Boston: Houghton Mifflin Company, 1940), Chap. 19; For other illustrations of newer school practices, see North Central Association Committee, *General Education in the American High School* (Chicago: Scott, Foresman and Company, 1942), especially Chaps. 3, 7–9. The most complete investigation on the core curriculum is Gordon N. Mackenzie, "A Critical Evaluation of Certain Current Theories and Practices in Respect to the Organization and Content of the Secondary School Curriculum," Ph.D. Dissertation, Stanford University, 1941. See also J. Paul Leonard, "Some Reflections on the Secondary Core Curriculum," *Curriculum Journal*, 10:250–252, 1939; Roland C. Faunce and Nelson L. Bossing, *Developing the Core Curriculum* (New York: Prentice-Hall, Inc., 1951). Harold Alberty, *Reorganizing the High School Curriculum* (New York: The Macmillan Company, 1948), Chaps. 6 and 7. For the most complete bibliography on the core curriculum, see Grace S. Wright, *The Core in Secondary Schools: A Bibliography* (U.S. Office of Education, Circular No. 323; Washington: Government Printing Office, 1950). A recent brief but significant summary of core practices can be found in Grace S. Wright, *Core Curriculum in Public High Schools*

A fourth characteristic of the core program is its provision for individual and group guidance. The traditional secondary school is organized to make it easy for teachers to be ignorant of their pupils. It is set up on the belief that an intimate knowledge of the child is unimportant. Teachers have large numbers of pupils in classes once a day for a semester or a year, and during that time they are supposed to teach them the subject matter of the course. They have little or no time for knowing them or for studying their total development. At the beginning of the guidance movement, there grew up a system of office guidance where a specially trained person was to find out as much as he could about the pupils and, from a central office, "guide them." This movement is typified by a sign in the principal's office in one of the large Eastern high schools which reads, "All pupils desiring guidance go to Room 263 after school." This kind of guidance system is little better than none. It probably is injurious not only because it harms the guidance movement, but because it actually does harm to the youngster by permitting the guidance officer to advise him after even less contact than the teacher has. The guidance person in such an office knows the pupil on paper; the teacher knows him as a student in his subject; but nobody really knows him.

The core program places the function of guidance in the forefront. The class should be organized so that the teacher will have ample time for studying the pupil with the aid of all the information he can secure from office records and specialists in the school services. He feels that part of the so-called class time, which traditionally has been considered time only for recitation or for "telling the pupil," is to be used for the kind of teaching which proceeds from individual and group counseling. The ideal organization is probably the one where the same teacher stays with the pupils in the seventh and eighth grades one full half day, tapering this off in the ninth and tenth grades probably to one period less, and in the last two years to one period a day for two years. This gives the teacher time enough to become really acquainted with the pupils and is a far more successful arrangement than the one provided in the idea and basic setup of the old home room. Such a school organization does away with the need for the heavy emphasis upon extraclass organizations and minute divisions of the day into small time periods.

A fifth and final characteristic might be mentioned. The core program provides for a scheme of organizing around the core the majority of the teachers of the school in relation to a dominant central purpose—that of developing social competence—and of building the rest of the school program around

(U.S. Office of Education, *Bulletin* No. 5; Washington: Government Printing Office, 1950). Harold Alberty and others, *Preparing Core Teachers for the Secondary Schools* (Columbus, Ohio: Ohio State University, College of Education, 1949). Mimeographed. Harold Alberty and others, *Utilizing Subject Fields in High School Core Program Development* (Columbus, Ohio: Ohio State University, College of Education, 1950). Mimeographed.

individual interests and purposes supplementing the core work. At present the high school is so finely divided into small groupings and departments and curricula that there is no obvious centralizing force in the school. There is no major purpose around which the offerings of the school radiate. Each teacher goes about his job of teaching his subject and serving his time. With the traditional school program we can never really educate adolescent boys and girls to work in a complicated social order today.

Advantages of the Core Program

In dealing with the advantages of the core program the Social Studies Investigation Workshop group at Stanford University proposed the following advantages of the core organization over the conventional program:

1. It cuts across subject matter boundaries and draws upon materials from all fields for the solution of problems.

2. It leaves the elective portion of the curriculum free to focus upon the special needs and interests of boys and girls.

3. It emphasizes the necessity for teachers to work cooperatively in planning the educational experiences of students.

4. It especially emphasizes the importance of pupil-teacher planning because of its focus upon the personal-social needs of pupils.

5. It offers greater flexibility in organization, procedure, content, and materials.

6. It provides for a larger block of time to be set aside for the consideration of problems.

7. It affords greater opportunity for more effective guidance because of the emphasis upon the child and his needs and because of the longer contact which core teachers have with the students in their classes.

8. It emphasizes the development of the whole personality of the child and is as much concerned with the development of desirable personality characteristics such as attitudes, interests, critical thinking, social sensitivity, as with the acquisition of skills and information.

Selecting Core Problems

Some bases are necessary for selecting core problems. A group of Denver teachers proposed the following criteria for the inclusion of problems in a core curriculum. These overlap to an extent the five criteria suggested, but they offer a good summary and extension of this same general position. They recommend including only those units, activities, or problem areas which have the following characteristics:

1. They are common to large groups of pupils, if not all.

2. They are persistent or recurring in human experience, or are related

to or illustrative of such problems (for example, a bond issue for the construction of a local sewage disposal plant may illustrate the persistent problem of sanitation).

3. They are not likely to be handled well by any of the traditional subjects (as family relationships).

4. They require, or would profit from, cooperative planning, teaching and learning.

5. They call for exploration in several areas of experience (as health in biology, recreation, the home, sex, care of children, public health, health hazards in industry, the consumer, safety, etc.).

6. They require orientation in a wide range of relationships and implications for their significance to become apparent (for example, the corporation—as related to mass production, advertising, absentee ownership, labor problems, propaganda, war, imperialism, pressure groups, etc.).

7. They require consideration of various points of view in addition to factual data (as race relations).

8. They require larger blocks of time than conventional periods (as community study and participation).

9. They call for relatively continuous experiences rather than a unit course (for example, the arts are not strictly "problems" but kinds of experience which should be included in the core curriculum).

10. They extend the application of such objectives as techniques of thinking, work habits, study skills, social sensitivity, creativeness, etc., over a wider range of experience than the traditional subjects.

11. They require a minimum of specialized laboratory equipment.

12. They do not require extended drill in specific skills (as taking three months off for drill in typing or percentage or cabinet making).

13. They do not require sudden extension or drastic modifications of present levels of work habits and study skills (as a sudden shift from lesson learning to complete responsibility).[2]

Status and Practice of the Core Curriculum

Although the concept of a curriculum based upon the demands of a society and the needs of youth has been steadily gaining acceptance in theory by the educational leaders of this country, actual practice lags far behind. The only national survey, made in 1949 by the United States Office of Education, gives some indications of trends and developments.

Extent of Adoption

As in earlier days, core courses are found under different headings, such as "common learnings," "general education," "unified studies," "basic course,"

2. H. H. Giles, S. P. McCutcheon, and A. N. Zechiel, *Exploring the Curriculum* (New York: Harper & Brothers, 1942), pp. 49–50.

"integrated course," or just "core." Only 3.5 per cent of the 24,000 secondary schools in the nation have adopted the core program as defined by the survey, namely those courses which "involve the combination of two or more class periods from subjects that would ordinarily be taught separately." Ten states reported no such programs. Seven states—California, Maryland, Michigan, Minnesota, Missouri, New York, and Pennsylvania—have 62 per cent of the total core offerings. Maryland had a large proportion of core courses, two-thirds of the schools in that state having adopted the core curriculum.

In actual practice the core curriculum today is a junior-high-school development, junior high schools having 86 per cent of all core offerings. Thirty-six per cent of all core offerings are in the seventh grade, 30 per cent in the eighth, and 20 per cent in the ninth, with the senior-high-school grades (10–12) having only 14 per cent.

Combination of Subjects

Out of 1,119 core courses reported, the combination of subjects was predominately English and social studies—813 courses or 73 per cent of the total. In the few three-period combinations science was included in seventy-five schools, mathematics in forty-six, and science and mathematics in twenty-nine. Core programs which are unifications of subjects other than English and social studies comprise but 8.1 per cent of the total.

Sixty-eight per cent of the core classes meet ten periods per week, while the three-period combination was reported by 16.4 per cent of the total number. Nearly half of the core courses meeting for more than ten periods a week were two-subject combinations.[3]

Illustrations of Core Programs

In order to illustrate what core programs actually look like, a number are chosen for illustration. These are offered without comment, as their organization will be obvious to the reader from this analysis of what the core is and from the previous descriptions of the nature of the methods of selecting problems for consideration in core programs.

OTTAWA HILLS, OHIO. An example of the simple type of core program, which is found frequently in secondary schools, is that at Ottawa Hills, Ohio. This core course consists of a fusion of English and social studies taught as a double period by one teacher. On the college transcripts, the core courses become a unit of English and a unit of history or social studies for each academic year. In reality the course is more than simply a combination of two subjects. It is a "central integrating course," correlating English, music,

---

3. Wright, *Core Curriculum in Public High Schools.*

history, art, communications, government, and modern problems. It gives special attention to the basic skills, to skill and power in oral and written communication and civic education, to sensitivity to human values, and to knowledge of the strategic role which our nation has played in the past as well as its leadership position today.[4]

GARRETT COUNTY, MARYLAND.   In a three-week workshop in August, 1949, the public schools of Garrett County set out "to organize a curricular structure for grades 7–12 based on needs of adolescent pupils that will enable them to solve their problems in a way that is consistent with our accepted philosophy and purposes of secondary education." In this study, three types of needs were identified: expressed or felt needs, needs predicted by adults or societal needs, and needs related to human development. Using the needs disclosed under these three categories, seventeen problem areas were agreed upon and allocated to the different grades, as follows:

Grade 7: School living
Health and safety
Transporation
Communicating ideas

Grade 10: Intercultural relations
Living in one world
Leisure and recreation
Communicating ideas

Grade 8: Knowing Garrett County
Natural environment
Leisure and recreation

Grade 11: American heritage
Personal development
Establishing beliefs

Grade 9: Making a living
Establishing beliefs
Consumer problems
Personal development
American heritage

Grade 12: Family living
Role of education
Making a living
Health and safety
Consumer problems
Technology of living[5]

FLOODWOOD, MINNESOTA.   The common observation is made, when discussing curriculum development, that it is the larger secondary school which is able to improve its program because of finances, size and quality of staff, facilities, and community support. It is significant that several interesting and challenging descriptions have come from the smaller secondary schools. One such place is Floodwood, Minnesota, with a total enrollment of 450 students in the twelve grades, divided into two educational segments of six years each. This is a small town, in a rural setting, largely a lumbering community. The philosophy of the school is based on the objective "to develop effective citizens in a democracy," with the program built around community needs. The staff

---

4. Francis W. Brown, "Living and Learning in a Modern High School," *North Central Association Quarterly*, 33:323–333, 1949.
5. Garrett County, Maryland Public Schools, *Cooperating, Organizing, Reasoning, Experiencing with Garrett County Youth* (General Bulletin of the High School Workshop, August, 1949). Mimeographed.

believes that "community resources and community problems should form the core of learning activities of the school." This pattern of approach was followed in developing the curriculum for a community-centered school:

1. A complete community survey was made to determine the life and background of the people, their desires and needs. This study is being continually revised, and the process of revision is carried on with parent, pupil and teacher cooperation.
2. A serious attempt was made to study the child, to know him not only as a pupil within the school, but as a person in the home and community. This entailed frequent home visits and parent conferences.
3. Developed democratic procedures in all school relationships, between parents, teachers, administrators, school board, and students.
4. Established a habit of group action in solving community and school problems. In this they used parent-pupil-teacher planning in the development of the experience learning units.
5. Modern evaluation procedures and techniques were used insofar as they were applicable to the local needs.
6. Time was provided for faculty conferences and planning. This necessitated occasional shortened days to permit ample faculty consideration of the program, and involved time before and after the school year for concentrated efforts on curriculum problems.
7. Community and school committees were established to work together on common problems. Typical of these were the agricultural council, health, recreation and homemaking council, and a conservation council.[6]

The core program in the high school is called "general education," which appears to have more community acceptance than the term "core curriculum." On the senior-high-school level "G.E.," as it is nicknamed, takes three hours daily and includes most of the basic learning experiences which all youth should have. Within this program are the community services and much of the guidance activities. The balance of the day is devoted to special interests and college preparatory subjects, for the 15 per cent going on to higher education. Special vocational offerings are provided, such as agriculture, mechanical, home-economic, and commercial subjects. These, too, are outside the general-education program.

SANTA BARBARA COUNTY

SUGGESTED PROBLEMS TO SERVE AS ORGANIZING CENTERS FOR CORE SOURCE
UNITS FOR GRADES 9–12

Santa Barbara County, California

1. Preventing accidents
2. Promoting international understanding

---

6. L. E. Harris, "Developing a Community School in Floodwood," *North Central Association Quarterly*, 33:334–338, 1949.

3. Building a happy home life
4. Planning my education
5. Securing mental and physical health
6. Making our water supply serve human needs
7. Regional planning for the use of our resources
8. Spending your money wisely
9. Understanding the business world
10. Controlling ideas through communication
11. Our changing population
12. Understanding labor problems
13. Planning your vocation
14. Using leisure time
15. Making democracy work
16. Governing our local community
17. Organizing and controlling
18. Democracy versus communism and fascism
19. Becoming acquainted with our school
20. Social security
21. Understanding our farm problems
22. Housing the nation
23. Using arts in public life
24. Religion
25. Preventing crime
26. Securing justice
27. Taxation as group purchasing
28. Providing for public education
29. Making machines serve mankind[7]

LINCOLN SCHOOL, NEW YORK.   A core course conducted by the science and English teachers at Lincoln School for the tenth grade dealt with problems of human living as they concerned youth at mid-adolescence. The emphasis here was to help these boys and girls understand their own growth and development in a meaningful social perspective.[8]

At the outset, there was considerable class discussion of the differences among members of the class, leading to a consideration of stages of human development. At this point, each student "placed" himself on a time line. At first, this line was short; but gradually it lengthened as the student broadened his ideas, going back first to birth, then to conception, next to ancestors, and finally to the long line of beings that lived before man emerged. Likewise, the student was encouraged to think forward to maturity, old age, and finally death as an inevitable part of the life cycle.

During this period, the English teacher read aloud Arnold Gesell's *Biography*

7. Santa Barbara, County Secondary Committee, *Bulletin* No. 172, May, 1942.
8. See Anita Duncan Laton and Samuel Ralph Powers, *New Directions in Science Teaching* (New York: McGraw-Hill Book Company, Inc., 1949), pp. 72–75.

of a Wolf Child, discussing in detail the steps in this "child's" growth and development. In general, study followed the various stages in the life span. Interest was greatest in the study of young children, which included visits to the baby ward of a hospital under guidance of the school nurse, and the viewing and discussing of a number of Gesell's films from the Yale Institute for Child Study. They read a wide variety of articles and books, technical and popular, in every pertinent scientific field. In the laboratory a number of simple experiments were performed, chiefly physiological and psychological. A continuing responsibility for each student during the year was the preparation of an autobiography, with stresses being laid on the reliability of the sources consulted and on the comparison of his development with what had been revealed in the study of children in general.

The following outline will give some indication of the extensiveness of the autobiography and its relationship to the study for the year:

SUGGESTIONS FOR WRITING "MY AUTOBIOGRAPHY"

I. Gathering your personal data (sources of data)
   A. Your father and mother, brothers and sisters
   B. Your family doctor, records of birth, early and later attendance
   C. Diaries kept by yourself or your parents
   D. Picture records (arrange in chronological order if possible)
   E. Teachers and their records
   F. School records—health, attendance, etc.
   G. Other records available to you

II. Evaluating and interpreting data
   A. School nurse, school psychologist, counselor
   B. Books on psychology, child development, biology, and anthropology
   C. Class discussions, readings, laboratory work, motion pictures
   D. Observation of younger members in the family
   E. Observation of children of different ages, in hospitals, in elementary school, on the street, in parks, etc.

III. Preparing your outline or questionnaire for gathering data (a first draft designed to develop techniques for obtaining significant data)
   A. Physical development. Outline or questionnaire should include at least the following:
      1. Early body movements—use of hands and legs
      2. Eye movements, movements of head
      3. Changing position—to back from stomach, etc.
      4. Reflexes—withdrawing, sneezing, coughing, etc.
      5. Feeding responses—drinking, eating, swallowing, etc.
      6. Sitting, standing, crawling, walking
      7. Sleeping, resting
   B. Mental development—learning
      1. Manipulation

2. Language
3. Reading
4. Play
5. Number
6. Responses to form, color, size, etc.
7. Likes and dislikes with respect to foods, objects, sleeping arrangements, etc.

C. Personal-social development
 1. Likes and dislikes with respect to people
 2. Table manners
 3. Dressing, care of self
 4. Play with others
 5. Communication
 6. Learning social customs

APOPKA, FLORIDA. The junior-high-school teachers in Apopka, Florida, were concerned over the difficult adjustments the average seventh-grade student had to make in the transition from the elementary school to their institution. The many teacher contacts as well as the usual hour class created a problem which did not meet the needs of the pupils and frequently caused difficulty for both teacher and students. Four years ago the seventh grade went on a core program, with one teacher for all subject matter other than art, music, and physical education. Results indicated a much higher achievement at all aptitude levels, with fewer disciplinary problems, and a better adjusted eighth-grade student.

Going one step beyond this, the school now has both seventh and eighth grades functioning as a six-teacher block, three acting as seventh-grade sponsors and three as eighth-grade sponsors. Operating on what is called a "partner type" of teaching program, the sponsors have their own groups during the morning period except for an hour when the grade is in physical education. During this physical education period for one grade, the sponsoring teachers meet for a planning period. Required subject matter is covered during this morning period, including stress on reading and spelling techniques.

In the afternoon, the sections switch: the seventh-grade teacher has eighth-grade pupils for a two-hour block, while the eighth-grade teacher takes over the seventh-grade pupils for the same length of time. In this period, through careful teacher selection, the students are permitted a choice of areas from industrial arts, home economics, and general science. The longer periods enable the students to experience a more diversified program and permit the teacher an opportunity to know the students better. Citizenship training becomes a more natural process, with group and committee work supplementing the guidance interests of the teacher.[9]

---

9. Adapted from Essie Oliver, "Curriculum Experiment in Junior High School," *Nations Schools*, 49:46–48, 1952.

UNIVERSITY HIGH SCHOOL, MORGANTOWN, WEST VIRGINIA.   In their experimentation with "core" work at the University Demonstration High School (grades 7–10), teachers who have worked for several years together in the area are basically agreed upon at least four considerations regarding those they teach:

1. The individual student transcends systems of education or prescribed courses of study in any subject-matter field.

2. For all their apparently human similarities, students are individually different and this fact must receive primary consideration if they are to be taught.

3. These individual differences necessarily call for departures from many established practices in their education.

4. The purpose of their education is ultimately the release of their individual potentialities in the interest of their personal and group development.

Objectives have been set up for the core groups, which are as follows:

To study with our pupils ways in which we may come to understand more significantly one's attitude toward oneself, toward others. To realize more significantly our reactions to nature, and to life generally. Some more specific aims are

I. Orientation to immediate environment
   A. Helping the student to find his place in his own age group
   B. Helping the student to realize his position in the school organization
   C. Helping him to a better understanding of his part in the life of his family
   D. Helping him to know where he belongs in his community
   E. An encouragement of opportunities for better understanding of human relationships—at home (the family) and at school (boy and girl relationships. Special groups such as committees, etc.)
II. The development of a sense of values in appreciation of the inherent worth of all groups in the scheme of things (labor, capital, all occupations, races, nationalities, and cultures)
   A. An understanding of the interdependency of various industries in Monongalia County
      1. Coal production
      2. Glass manufacturing
      3. Other industries and businesses
III. An awareness of the beauty and worth of our local "natural" environment; that is, the appreciation for those aspects which are peculiar to Monongalia County
   A. Animal life in the county—the deer, the bear, the squirrel, etc.
   B. A study of the conditions which make this life possible within our locality
   C. A knowledge of protective laws for this life

D. Encouragement of expression of experiences with this aspect of nature; that is, individual experiences
E. A knowledge of trees within the county, and what they furnish as to utility and beauty
  1. Trees on our own school grounds
  2. Trees in our communities
  3. Trees on the university campus

General group discussions are conducted around such topics as the following:

1. Good group behavior in assembly
2. The proper way to celebrate Halloween
3. The cost of food and clothing
4. Coming to school by bus
5. What it costs to attend high school
6. What is meant by freedom with responsibility
7. The need to know how to guide oneself in his work
8. Proper use of one's time

Certain units have been developed to achieve the goals of the program. The following are illustrative:

1. *Who Am I?*—a unit designed to teach youth their places in American community life
2. *Food and Human Destiny*—a unit planned by pupils and teachers to give an idea of the importance of food in all countries and in critical war periods
3. *Into the World of Men and Women Whose Labors Make My Own Life More Significant*—a unit to teach the occupations that are important in a community

This course is set up on a two-hour-period basis, and the teachers feel this arrangement has the following advantages:

1. It provides good opportunities and more time for "seeing a job through" without interruption of a bell.
2. It provides for the development of a steadiness of purpose.
3. It is an advantage in that it offers a better opportunity for pupil-teacher planning and the utilization of time toward the accomplishment of purposes.
4. It provides more time for the field trip and social activity which are often the basis or outcome of our work.[10]

WELLS HIGH SCHOOL, CHICAGO.   Located in a large metropolitan city, with no special advantages in terms of facilities and equipment and serving a less-favored socio-economic school population, Wells High School in Chicago has attempted over a period of years to develop a basic educational program

10. Anna Brochick, "Core Studies: A Concept," *Bulletin,* National Association Secondary School Principals, 33:203–208, 1950.

geared to meet the needs of *all* of its 2,200 students. The philosophy upon which the curriculum is based is found in the following principles:

1. The curriculum consists of successful democratic living.
2. Pupils learn the curriculum by carrying out the activities of successful living under teacher guidance.
3. Democratic living is divided, for purposes of learning, into major divisions or functions . . . The major divisions used at present are thus stated:
   Advancing physical welfare
   Building democratic relationships
   Developing economic competence
   Enjoying wholesome leisure
   Meeting work responsibilities
   Satisfying religious and esthetic needs
   Thinking, and communicating ideas
4. These major divisions of living are in turn analyzed and subdivided into significant problems, units, and activities for classroom learning.
5. The planning and carry-out of units of learning are done by teachers working cooperatively, first with pupils, and then with parents and community members.
6. The performance of the activities of successful living in school, home, and community is both the *method* and the *test* of learning. The subject fields, with their information and skills, are used as means for performing the activities intelligently and effectively.
7. The general-education, or core, division of the curriculum consists of the activities necessary for *all* as worthy members of our democratic order. The subject fields contributing to this curriculum are social studies, English, science, physical education, art, and music. These are supplemented by homeroom, guidance, and auditorium activities.
8. Special education, or the elective divisions of the curriculum, deals with smaller, personal spheres of living. Such subjects as algebra, shorthand, Latin, and chemistry make up this part of the curriculum.
9. Reorganization deals chiefly with general education. The core curriculum, the main vehicle of general education, is the concern of all pupils and teachers.

The faculty members of Wells High School have worked together on their curriculum improvement program; they function through six course-departmental committees to plan the grade-level and other phases of the school program. These groups enlist pupils, parents, and lay citizens to work with them. The chairmen of these grade-level committees make up a central, all-school committee for coordinating the work. The principal serves as consultant to the grade-level committees and as chairman of the coordinating committee. These groups meet during and after the school day, with their findings mimeographed as "unit leads" for core-curriculum classes to use as they cooperatively build their units of learning.

The framework of the core curriculum in this high school has a broad base on the ninth- and tenth-grade levels, with provision for only one elective outside the core. It tapers off in the eleventh and twelfth grades to permit more electives in the specialized or vocational (including college-preparatory) fields. Although the learning fields of the core program retain the traditional labels, the content and methods have been greatly modified in accordance with three main principles:

1. The *broadening* principle has been applied to replace academic content with activities of high-grade daily living.
2. The *integrating* principle has been used to form broad learning fields by drawing important elements from related subjects.
3. The *learn-by-living* principle insures that the activities are lived, rather than merely studied academically. All units of learning involve performance of important activities of living in school, home, and community, under the guidance of teachers, parents, and key citizens.

The core program in Wells High School occupies more than half of the student's class time. Through wise guidance, the sequence necessary for graduation, college entrance, and business employability is provided outside this program.

According to the principal, Paul R. Pierce, the core program is carried on in this manner:

> In the core-curriculum classrooms, the pupils are taken into partnership with teachers respecting the nature and purposes, as well as the content, of the curriculum. While no set pattern is followed, a way often used is for teacher and class to examine, before beginning a new unit of learning, the main purposes of education—why so much effort and money are expended in high school work. It is remarkable how effectively pupils, with understanding guidance, think this out. At first a pupil will say "to get a better job." Another will offer, "to get along better with others," and still others, "to have better health," "to spend time better," and "to talk and write better." When led to attempt a generalization on these specifics, they eventually arrive at such a conclusion as, "We go to school to live better."
>
> The teacher may next lead the pupils to consider the main purposes of the learning field in which the class is working. In English, with what phase of the better life does it deal? Through patient guidance of discussion, they arrive at "communication" as a main purpose. By recalling units carried out in English during past semesters and discussing what important things ought still to be done, the pupils, with the teacher's easy guidance, approach the unit that ought next to be done by the class. Sometimes such an overview includes the work of the entire term.
>
> Once the class arrives at the particular unit to be done, it considers the *nature* of the enterprise, the reasons *why* it should be done, and the *way* it should be done—the "what," the "why," and the "how." This process may take days or even weeks, but it is absolutely necessary to intelligent

learning. In the work stage of the unit, small groups and individuals engage in various activities which utilize the varied ways of learning, such as observing, dramatizing, constructing, discussing, viewing, in addition to reading and writing. They find it necessary to stop from time to time to take stock of the progress of the unit as a whole and the contribution of their own activities to that progress. The pupils culminate the unit, under teacher guidance, by synthesizing the findings of the various groups, and by carrying out these learnings in their daily living in school, home, and community.

The unit enterprises thus cooperatively carried out consist of direct aspects of the pupils' daily living. Examples in science are "Making Home-life Healthful," "Growing a Garden," "Becoming Young Men and Women," and "Basing Our Buying on Science"; in social studies, "Sharing in Wells Government," "Saving and Using Money Effectively," "Living and Working Together," "Planning Our Careers"; in English, "Using the Radio Effectively," "Detecting the Channels of Propaganda," "Exploring the World through Books," and "Living Courteously in the School"; in art, "Enriching the Home through Art"; and in music, "Being an Intelligent Consumer of Music."

In addition to these large cooperative units of living and learning, the core class also carries on a series of "current" or "on-going" life activities. The 9A semester in social studies, for example, has as cooperative enterprises "Sharing in Wells Government," "Living and Working Together," and "Increasing Our Employability," as current living activities. ... The cooperative unit becomes a current living activity at higher grade-levels and with increasingly mature treatment. Just as in actual living, many enterprises are carried on concurrently in class.

To insure that the activities of living that are intensively studied and planned in the classroom are put into practice in everyday living, a current-activity sheet with spaces for anecdotal records is used. On this, four scheduled activities, and/or more free-choice activities, are accounted for by the pupil each month. There are spaces on the sheet for the verifying signatures and comments of parents, teacher sponsors, and workers in community agencies, in their role as the teachers' guidance assistants. The anecdotal record of completed activities is evaluated by the teacher, credited toward the pupil's classwork and grade, and filed in the pupil's class folder.[11]

The school places great emphasis on relating the school work to community living. The high-school community provides a wide area for developing pupil activities through each pupil's devoting a period a day of service to the school. Under the guidance of the core teacher, these services are designed to provide wholesome experiences in living and learning. Parents likewise are involved through a unique organization called the Parent-Teacher-Student Association. In addition, the services of key citizens are drawn on to relate the students

11. Paul R. Pierce, "Shaping the Curriculum of Youth," *North Central Association Quarterly,* 33:339–344, 1949.

to the wider opportunities of community participation in the problems and the organizations of their area. Furthermore, special projects are undertaken at each core level that involve *all* the students in some aspect of community living, such as surveying local governmental machinery, studying labor organizations and activities, or a social affair.

In an effort to guide pupils in democratic action, the student government provides for participation by the students in home-room, council, and service projects. Every student has an opportunity not only to feel that he belongs to the school, but that he serves the school and the community, and in so doing takes his place as a leader and follower in a democratic community.

NEW YORK CITY HIGH SCHOOLS. The high schools of New York City, in an effort to deal with the students who were slow learners, have experimented with a number of programs (called XG—Experimental General) for those who did not take the Regents' examinations required for the regular diploma. Fifteen high schools started with two classes each, working with the slowest learners on the assumption that (1) the most retarded children were getting the least out of school and were most likely to fail and become discipline problems and drop-outs; (2) what could be done with these could be done with others; and (3) the schools were liable if they did not meet the real needs of these slower youth.

Although each high school was permitted to develop its program as it saw fit, the most satisfactory program was developed as follows:

> *Ninth Year:* Each class has, as a group, a two-period core (usually, but not necessarily, consisting of English and social studies) taught by a teacher who also acts as guidance counselor. In addition, the class studies general science and mathematics. For the "minor" subjects, members of the class are scattered among other classes. Science and mathematics are sometimes taught in combination, sometimes separately. The teachers of XG pupils are programmed so that they can meet together every day to report what each is doing, make plans and discuss the problems of individual pupils.
>
> *Tenth Year:* Each group has a two-period core of English and social studies, a period of general science or biology and one or two periods of vocational or prevocational work—commercial studies, home economics and home nursing, industrial arts, art or music. In the vocational and prevocational work, and in art and music, pupils are programmed in classes with non-XG pupils.
>
> *Eleventh and Twelfth Years:* The program has not yet (1951), except in a few schools, reached the eleventh and twelfth years. The plan for these years is to continue the core in social studies and English with pupils who are programmed with non-XG pupils in vocational and other elective classes.[12]

___
12. Reprinted by permission of the Board of Education of the City of New York from "Suggestions to Teachers of Experimental Core Classes," *Curriculum Bulletin*, 1950–51 Series, No. 2, p. 2.

The objectives of the XG program are identical with those of all education: to make better human beings and more effective citizens of the boys and girls of New York City. The term "core" in the XG program means a class (1) which meets two or more hours per day with a teacher acting as guidance counselor for the group, and (2) which deals with problems that are selected by teachers and pupils cooperatively and that cut across traditional subject-matter lines.

The specific objectives in this experimental program are

1. To learn pupils' backgrounds, abilities, interests and problems and to win pupils' confidence

2. To help pupils understand their own abilities, strengths and weaknesses, face their own problems, make realistic plans, and accept responsibility for their own actions

3. To help pupils to work together, and understand and get along with others

4. To look for and act upon opportunities to help pupils develop standards of judgment and standards of ethical conduct

5. To develop useful skills

6. To improve pupils' ability to listen and to communicate orally and in writing

7. To help pupils integrate the experiences they are having elsewhere in the school and outside the school with what they are learning in the class

8. To teach as much as possible of the subject matter commonly taught in the subjects that are combined in the core[13]

The teachers who have been working in this program believe that it has these definite advantages:

1. Teachers are able to know pupils better, since each teacher works with fewer pupils and is with them a longer period each day.

2. Teachers feel free to take up problems which are of immediate interest to pupils and which cross subject lines.

3. Pupils get better acquainted with the teacher and feel free to consult him.

4. The work crystallizes around a smaller number of problems than in the usual curriculum; this simplification is better suited to the pupils' powers of comprehension and concentration.

5. There is a saving in time: teachers agree that more work can be covered in a double period than in two separate periods; besides, there is less duplication of topics.[14]

AMERICAN CITY, FARMVILLE, AND HOPE VALLEY. Nowhere in educational literature has the core or common learnings course been more fully explored

---

13. *Ibid.,* pp. 4–5.
14. *Ibid.,* pp. 5–6.

than in the description of the programs in American City, Farmville, and Hope Valley, hypothetical communities created by the Educational Policies Commission.[15] In American City this course is one of five major areas into which the program of the secondary school is divided, the other four being vocational preparation, individual interests, personal interests, and health and physical fitness.

The basic purpose of the course in common learnings was to organize effectively learning experiences which all boys and girls should have in common. The criterion for selecting these experiences was found in the statement of ten imperative educational needs of youth. Instead of meeting these needs by a series of separate courses in citizenship, science, literature, English, consumer economics, family life, and the arts, a single basic course was planned which would be continuous throughout the entire secondary school period, supplemented by special courses in certain fields. This arrangement had the advantage of tying the learnings closely to the imperative needs of youth, to problems as they are found in life outside the school, and to problems in their entirety without the restrictions of subject matter lines.

The basic course in common learnings was planned to meet the following specific objectives of the school:

1. To help all youth grow in knowledge of their nation and the world of nations; in understanding of the rights and duties of citizens of the American democracy; and in diligent and competent performance of their obligations as members of the community and as citizens of the state and nation.

2. To help all youth grow in the knowledge of the operations of the economic system and in understanding of the human relations and problems in economic activities, particularly of the relations between management and employees.

3. To help all youth grow in understanding of personal relations within the family, of the conditions which make for successful family life, and of the importance of the family in society.

4. To help all youth grow in the ability to purchase and use goods and services intelligently, with accurate knowledge of values received by the consumer and with understanding of the economic consequences of one's acts.

5. To help all youth grow in appreciation and enjoyment of beauty in literature, art, music, and nature.

6. To help all youth grow in ability to listen and read with understanding and to communicate their thoughts with precision and clarity.[16]

---

15. See descriptions in Educational Policies Commission, *Education for All American Youth* (Washington: National Education Association, 1944), Chap. 4, and National Association of Secondary School Principals, *Planning for American Youth* (rev. ed., Washington: National Education Association, 1951), pp. 46–48.

16. Educational Policies Commission, *Education for All American Youth,* p. 249.

The following description of the common-learnings courses will indicate their nature and organization.

> The course [in American City] was to be three periods daily from grades 7 through 10; two periods daily in grades 11 and 12, and one period daily in grades 13 and 14. The Board of Education approved this plan, and unified courses in Common Learnings were established.
>
> The learnings in the unified courses at present consist of learning experiences which everyone needs to have, regardless of what occupation he follows or where he happens to live. These courses are designed to meet three of the *Imperative Needs of Youth:*
>
> 1. Their need to grow in understanding and in competent performance of their obligations as members of the community, state, and nation.
> 2. Their need to grow in the skills, knowledge of social and ethical principles involved in their relations with other people, particularly in family life.
> 3. Their need to grow in the understanding of democratic principles, in their application of the scientific method, and in their acceptance of the values basic to our civilization.
>
> The general purposes of the courses are planned in advance, but the teachers have latitude to plan details of the courses and to determine the order of teaching problems. Pupils also assist in planning the details of the courses.
>
> At the present time, in the three years of the lower secondary school, pupils become acquainted with themselves and with the school and its offerings. They learn about the way people serve their community, the way they are fed, and the way goods are distributed. They study the history and development of the community and state; become acquainted with the basic principles of American democracy embodied in the Bible, the Declaration of Independence, in the Constitution, and the way they are practiced by our great leaders and presented in our best literature. They investigate the ways in which science has changed the world, and develop the essential skills in reading, expression, study habits, and mathematics. In all skill development, attention is centered on developing the reason and purpose and basic thought involved. Pupils learn language and grammar, for instance, by learning to give effective expression to their own thoughts. This approach, rather than the grammar approach, is accepted practice by all teachers. All skills, outside of short practice periods, are taught in relationship to their use.
>
> In grade ten, pupils learn to feel at home in the senior secondary school. They study the use of their time effectively; take tests on speed of reading, understanding of what is read, basic abilities in mathematics, English, and study habits, and study ways to improve these. They study American City at work—how people live—by visits, reading, motion pictures, talks, discussions; check up on their own qualifications for different occupations; fit together these learnings into an economic system and then try to see how the system works.

Later, certain other problems are studied—family life, labor unions and management, sanitation and community health, consumer spending, and personal problems.

Certain studies are made of life in American City, such as the voluntary service organizations and what they do for youth, recreation in American City, and planning in residential neighborhoods. All of these combine instruction in understanding and improvement in the basic skills of analysis, study expression, and the scientific method applied to social problems.

In grade eleven, emphasis is placed upon education for civic competence, civic leadership, community improvements, housing projects, welfare services, problems of group living, employment situations, and the process of city planning. The connections between these problems in the city and the nation are examined.

The roots of these problems in our national history are studied. Interdependence between city and rural communities and between city, state, and the nation are stressed. Literature and history provide sources for these ideas, supplemented by a continuation of visits and the use of much visual material. Teachers try to make certain that all youth reach an understanding of the development of our nation as a democracy and as a country with a definite culture.

In grade twelve, youth study the problems of the nation in a world setting. Usually about three domestic and three international problems are singled out for study. Such problems as the maintenance of our domestic economy on a high level of production and employment (our domestic problem number one) and the problem of international organization for peaceful living (our international problem number one) are examples. In both of these problems, international interdependence is stressed. American foreign policy and its background, and the problems and lives of other peoples which affect our foreign policy are examined. Literature and art of our own and other nations are studied.

In grade twelve, personal problems again arise, and the teachers return to them, especially those involving family living in which the responsibilities of homemakers are stressed. In this grade comes the very popular unit on *Friendship, Courtship, and Marriage.*

In all these unified courses, study and work experience are combined; skills are taught as needed; and guidance is carried on by the teachers of Common Learnings classes, acting as counselors to the youth in their classes.

Each unified class is in charge of one teacher who is assisted by other teachers as needed. All teachers meet together weekly to plan their work.

The unified class is the local unit of the school government, electing representatives to the school council.

At the present time, science and health are not combined in the courses of Common Learnings, except that the basic social problems of community health and the social changes wrought by science are included. American City teachers of Common Learnings are not yet ready to teach effectively materials in the fields of science and health, but they feel that the basic

The Curriculum in American City Is Divided into Five Major Areas.[18]

The pupils in American City are at present working with
a curriculum which contains the following major areas:

Personal interests - grades 7, 8, 9
Individual interests - grades 10-14
Vocational preparation - grades 10-14
Common learnings - grades 7-14
Health and physical fitness - grades 7-14

Periods per day	GRADES							
	Early Secondary School			Advanced Secondary School or Community Institute				
	7	8	9	10	11	12	13	14
1	Personal Interests. Exploration of personal abilities and individual interests; discovery of interests in art, music, science, languages, sports, crafts, home and family problems, and leisure activities.			*Individual interests. Election by the pupil under guidance of teacher in fields of avocational, cultural, or intellectual interest.				
2				Vocational Preparation. Includes the study of sciences, mathematics, social studies, literature, and foreign languages, in preparation for advanced study in Community Institute, college and universities, as well as education for industrial, commercial, homemaking service and other occupations, leading to employment, apprenticeship or homemaking at end of grade 12, 13, or 14, and work experience.				
3								
4	Common Learnings. A continuous course in Social Living to foster growth in personal living and in civic competence. Guidance							
5								
6	Health and Physical Fitness. Includes games, sports, and other activities to promote physical fitness, together with the study of individual and community health.							

*Broken line indicates flexibility of scheduling for youth who need to spend more time in either of these areas, depending upon their occupational or future education plans.

[18] Ibid., p. 48.

understandings in these fields should eventually become a part of the courses in Common Learnings. They are, therefore, studying this problem, hoping to move in this direction as fast as their own command of these fields will permit.[17]

The year's schedule at Farmville allows adequate time for occupational, civic, and personal development.[19]

All of the activities, courses, and projects of Farmville Secondary School must be fitted into a school schedule for the year. During the first four years, the program is organized under three curriculum areas. The number of hours which are devoted to each of these areas varies, but, in general, the following divisions are used:

Curriculum Areas

		Grades		
	7	8	9	10
I. Developing as a citizen— Principles and practices of local and national government; school government—nature and management; people and agencies in the community serving youth; dependence on many workers for clothes, food, shelter; consumer education; social traditions of environment; organic and inorganic world; skills in study, scientific method, expression, numerical relationships; American culture and biographies of leaders.	500	500	400	400
II. Building health and physical strength— Physical and emotional changes of organism during adolescence; sex instruction; relations with opposite sex; health habits of cleanliness; food, body care, disease; games and sportsmanship; development of physical strength.	300	300	300	200
III. Exploring personal interests and abilities— Analysis of interests and aptitudes; acquaintance with nature, tools, and mediums of expression in music, art, dancing, sports, crafts; acquaintance with different languages as mediums of expression, and with wide areas of interests and leisure activities.	400	400	500	600
Note that materials in science, English, mathematics, etc., are taught in all three areas. Total	1200	1200	1200	1200

During the last four years of the secondary school, three areas are used, differing somewhat from those in the first four years. In general, the follow-

---

17. National Association of Secondary School Principals, *Planning for American Youth,* rev. ed., pp. 45–46.
19. *Ibid.,* p. 32.

ing amounts of time are devoted to each area during these four grades of the program. For those students who are planning to leave school at end of grade 12, the time in Areas I and II is increased and decreased in Area III.

Curriculum Areas

		Grades			
		11	12	13	14
I.	Preparing for an occupation— Occupational study, self-analysis, job preparation for agricultural, mechanical, commercial, and homemaking occupations; work in science, mathematics, social studies, and English when preparatory to advance study in college; productive work experience.	300	400	600	600
II.	Developing civic competence— Community studies and civic projects; historical study of development of democracy; ideals and principles of democracy; community work; current political, economic, and social problems and historical backgrounds; civic projects; consumer education.	300	200	200	200
III.	Developing interests and aptitudes through elective subjects— Family life, health, mental hygiene; physical education, leisure and recreational interests; music, art, literature, science, and understanding of cultural heritage.	400	400	200	200
	Elective studies or individual projects in English, mathematics, history, science, languages, and remedial instruction, if needed.	200	200	200	200
	Total	1200	1200	1200	1200

The general requirements are appropriate for youth in Hope Valley. The school schedule in Hope Valley cannot be as extensive and diversified as in Farmville. After careful study, Frost County teachers concluded that certain features would be necessary to provide a well-balanced program. They are as follows:

I. Centers of interest should be areas rather than subjects, and the following were chosen and required of all pupils:
  A. Area 1
    1. Home and Community Life
    2. American Institutions and Ideals
    3. American Social Problems
    4. Basic Communication
    5. Literature
  B. Area 2
    6. Personal Development and Health
    7. Arts and Crafts
    8. Recreational Skills

    C. In Area 3, one general course in farm-home management to be pursued for two years is required for girls, and two general courses are required for boys, as follows:

      9. Farm Production

      10. Farm Marketing

II. Several basic courses may be taught with as many as two grade levels in one group since no one course is really dependent upon the other.

III. The basic ten centers of interest are discussion courses primarily, supplemented by laboratories where needed and by community work experience.

IV. Special supporting subjects are taught which will meet the special abilities or interests of the youth; such as repair of farm machinery, special talent in art and music, general mathematics, farm accounting. These are rotated in scheduling from year to year.

V. Special courses for those leaving Hope Valley for work or further study are offered by individual study and correspondence. Such subjects as languages, mathematics, business, history, and literature are offered in this way.

VI. Recreation, assemblies, clubs, athletics, band, choral groups and hobbies as well as student councils, are important aspects of education. Therefore, in order to provide for these activities in this rural area, no regular classes are held Tuesday and Thursday afternoons, this time being used for these activities and for faculty conferences, counseling, and conferences with parents.

VII. By basic courses, rotation, correspondence, and constant study of the needs of pupils, the program of education in Hope Valley goes far in providing opportunities equal to those in Farmville.[20]

Developing Special Interest Areas

In addition to the core organization of the school, the program should provide ample opportunity for youth to develop their special interests and abilities in terms of their goals. These areas will refer to their vocational goals, their own intellectual development, and their personal hobbies or fancies.

The secondary school must provide opportunities for youth to achieve vocational success. Whether they plan to enter college to prepare for a professional career or whether they plan to enter the skilled labor market, youth should have the opportunity to develop competency in the work needed to achieve their goals. Enough variation in the vocational program of the school should be arranged to care for a large variety of needs, and this program,

20. *Ibid.*, p. 35.

like the core program, should be constantly reorganized in terms of technological changes in our society. The program should also be made up of problematic materials. If a particular youth desires to enter college, he should develop the necessary abilities to use the English language and achieve the study habits required of him in the vocational career he chooses. The additional specific requirements for college are just as vocational for those going to college as shop courses are for those planning to enter certain trades. The college entrance requirements can be met in the secondary school by those who will enter college without all pupils having to take them for high-school graduation. Research has shown repeatedly that a specific subject pattern for college entrance produces no better qualified student than any one of a dozen patterns. There is little justification for colleges to require any specific set of subjects for admission to college, but there is no justification for requiring *all* high-school pupils to take a given set of subjects dictated by the colleges. The biggest danger is that college entrance subjects tend to become the only "respected" subjects and are likely thereby to attract pupils who can never succeed with them.

For the advanced intellectual development of "superior" pupils courses can be organized which will appeal to them. The historical method, the scientific method applied to higher branches of science or mathematics, the logical method applied to the humanities may be pursued by certain pupils with profit if the interest and ability are present to carry the study through to completion. This again needs to be highly selective and must not be allowed to become the standard program for those for whom it is not suited.

For the development of hobbies and recreational and leisure interests the school has a marked responsibility. Youth in the years ahead will have great amounts of leisure, for with our modern technology the hours of labor are becoming constantly shorter. The experience of idle youth during the depression indicates that the school must carry with other agencies the responsibility of helping them to plan and utilize their leisure intelligently. Youth must be able to plan their own recreation independently and without the necessity of someone else's constant prodding and planning. They must also be taught to prefer the activities in which they participate as a member, not those in which they can passively and lazily be entertained by others.[21]

When these programs of special interests for youth are possible, three kinds of opportunities may be offered. One is the especially organized course which may be developed by the teacher in terms of the intellectual concepts inherent in the fields in which youth are especially interested. A second is in terms of general laboratories where youth may find abundant materials and

---

21. One of the most interesting recent expressions in this field is from the pen of Dorothy Canfield Fisher in *Youth and the Future,* a report of the American Youth Commission (Washington: American Council on Education, 1942). See the last chapter in the book.

equipment and a capable and sympathetic teacher who will help them with those interests which they may wish to develop. These are especially appropriate for building leisure-time interests. The third is the field of work experience, where youth may participate under guidance in the actual work in which they are interested. This work may be related or not to vocational interest. If these offerings are possible, youth will have ample opportunities to develop their personalities and individual interests which will make life more worth while and profitable to them.

Leadership in Developing the Core Program

Core courses, like any improved program, don't just happen. They are brought about by careful planning, resulting from vision and adherence to a point of view. Several factors are important in bringing about these changes.

Leadership is necessary if the curriculum is to be improved. If the chief administrator is uninterested or inactive, not much progress will be made either by teacher or by members of the administrative staff. Few changes are made in a school where the chief administrator has little concern.

Leadership must also be shared with others in the system—directors, supervisors, and teachers. Leadership is best exemplified in the search for talent and the release of opportunities for talent to function. The result is shared leadership.

Much devolves upon the core teacher, her education and experience, her philosophy, her ability to work with others, and her ingenuity in group planning. Let us review briefly each of these important factors in the development of the core program.[22]

The Administrator as a Leader

In improving human relations in and around the school, the responsibility of the administrator is paramount. He must come to understand teachers, both as professional workers and as people. In the same way, he must understand community adults and learners as people. In the concept of shared leadership, where participants have a dual role of leader and follower, the administrator must have insight into the "teacher culture," as Prall calls it,[23] and recognize the unique characteristics of teacher relationships. The first characteristic of this relationship is a strength that grows out of a similarity of interest and purpose, the very real desire to see a better school. Yet within

22. For a good treatise of the whole problem of group planning for core courses, see Donald Berger, "Planning in the Core Class," *Educational Leadership*, 8:208–214, 1951.
23. Charles E. Prall with C. Leslie Cushman, *Teacher Education in Service* (Washington: American Council on Education, 1944), p. 277.

this common desire there is independence and dependence, there is cooperation and frustration. Another factor to be considered by the leader is the lack of information and consistency on the part of the school staff on matters of economics, politics, and current social problems. Another characteristic of teacher culture is the "peculiar remoteness from the stream of community life. . . . The community and the teachers themselves have operated on the assumption that here was a group apart, a state of affairs that has caused dismay among those who desire to hasten the arrival of realistic community education."[24]

Effective leadership in curriculum improvement demands recognition of these characteristics of the teacher culture. The administrator must study his teachers in many ways, placing them in the most promising working situation, where their potentialities can best be realized. In addition, he can influence the experiences of teachers through finding new adventures in the school system. It is a delicate role, one of peer relationships, which requires tact and judgment. The administrator must also look to the community, utilizing lay citizens' skills and services, to the end that the school program may be more functional.

The concept of shared leadership, which is all-essential in effective curriculum improvement, is defined by one state curriculum guide:

> The effective administrator is he who challenges teachers and parents to develop into leaders by inspiring and leading them to participate in planning, executing, and evaluating activities within a school. Furthermore, the effective administrator is one who is himself continually inspired and guided into participating as one of the group, by leadership which emerges from teachers, parents, and students.[25]

Hanna points out that the role of status leader is as follows:

> Status leadership helps groups and group members to
> 1. Discover group goals sufficiently vital that they will call forth a maximum of cooperative effort
> 2. Set up a system of values enabling the group to define, select, or choose the needs and interests of first priority
> 3. Instill in others a desire to "belong" and to take active part in group action
> 4. Discover their skills, competencies, interests, and abilities so that each, while taking part in group processes, may gain the maximum security which results from each having a part to play and a contribution to make
> 5. Develop good human relationships and satisfactory personal interactions

24. Alice Miel, *Changing the Curriculum: A Social Process* (New York: Appleton-Century-Crofts, Inc., 1946), pp. 157–171.

25. Michigan Department of Public Instruction, *Planning and Working Together* (*Bulletin* No. 337; Lansing, Mich., 1945), p. 154.

so that a cooperative, permissive atmosphere characterizes group functioning[26]

TECHNIQUES OF LEADERSHIP. If the administrator is to be effective and successful he needs to arrive at some techniques of work which he uses to establish good working relations. The following procedures suggested by Wiles will be helpful to the administrator:

1. Establish a permissive atmosphere in which mistakes in judgment are not punished.
2. Accept opposing points of view as a contribution to group growth.
3. Bring the staff into the process of identifying the problems on which the group should be working.
4. Share determination of goals and method of operation.
5. Work for responsibility to the group rather than to the supervisor.
6. Encourage committee work where teachers and supervisors work together as equal members of a team.
7. Recognize that planning sessions are responsibility-assuming situations.
8. Provide opportunity to volunteer to assume preferred types of responsibility.
9. Agree on deadline for fulfillment of responsibility.
10. Share necessary authority to carry out responsibility.
11. Refrain from temptation to grab control when a staff member makes a mistake.
12. Keep channels of communication open by which teachers can make suggestions for improvement to the staff and by which persons requiring help in carrying out an assignment can make their needs known.
13. Encourage the staff to recognize the exceptional contribution of members to the group and the program.
14. Share all praise and recognition.
15. Seek equality of load within the staff.
16. Ask no greater load of any staff member than the supervisor assumes.
17. Take a firm stand against teachers' assuming too many responsibilities.
18. Assume that the staff member is going to accept responsibility.
19. Emphasize that persons learn through mistakes.
20. State belief that there is no one best method of teaching.
21. Decrease city-wide or school-wide regulations to the absolute minimum.
22. Never insist that the supervisor's ideas about teaching are the correct ones.
23. Ask as frequently for proof why a new method should not be tried as for reasons why it should.
24. Encourage teachers to develop distinctive classrooms which reflect the work and activities of their classes.

---

26. Lavone Hanna and others, *Group Processes in Supervision* (*Bulletin,* Association for Supervision and Curriculum Development; Washington: National Education Association, 1948), p. 59. For a fine treatise on leadership see Ordway Tead, *The Art of Administration* (New York: McGraw-Hill Book Company, Inc., 1951).

25. Recognize persons who are trying new procedures.
26. Be sure that the same persons are not always being given recognition.
27. Establish a petty-cash fund for the purchase of expendable materials whose use has not been foreseen.
28. Provide a socialization program which will increase teachers' self-assurance and social skills.
29. Provide in-service training experience in self-expression in a variety of media.
30. Help teachers develop techniques for evaluating a variety of types of pupil growth.[27]

The Core Teacher

The key to the success of the core curriculum lies with the classroom teacher. Her interest, abilities, understandings, training, and experience are important factors in effective core teaching. It has long been recognized that this type of teaching demands an able if not a superior teacher. Alberty and a group of graduate students at Ohio State University have defined the competencies essential to successful core teaching as follows:

The core teacher should

1. Know the contributions of the leaders in the field of general education and how to utilize these contributions in developing and improving the core program
2. Be able to interpret present day events and movements as they relate to the learning activities of the core
3. Understand the processes of growth and maturation in children and adolescents for the purposes of identifying common basic needs and interests in various levels of development
4. Be able to develop learning units in broad problem areas with the purposes of improving human relations
5. Know how to utilize and direct the various types of student activities (e.g. student councils, assemblies, publications, social clubs, parties, and sports) and relate them to the common learnings part of the school program
6. Be able to evaluate programs of leading schools with an emphasis on core curriculum and understand their contribution for the improvement of education
7. Be able to draw upon major fields of knowledge (the humanities, social studies, science and art) in helping youth to meet their common needs and solve their problems
8. Understand the nature and significance of controversial issues in terms

---

27. Kimball Wiles, *Supervision for Better Schools* (New York: Prentice-Hall, Inc., 1950), pp. 82–84.

of the major fields of knowledge and develop suitable techniques for dealing with them in the core class

9. Know how to utilize guidance and counseling techniques in relating the activities of the core to the total development of the adolescent
10. Know how to utilize the resources of the community (e.g. institutions, organizations, agencies, and personnel) in solving the common problems dealt with in the core
11. Be able to utilize the occupational opportunities of the immediate and wider community for providing general vocational orientation for the adolescent
12. Have an ability to utilize techniques of cooperative planning and to work with colleagues in coordinating all the learning activities of the core group
13. Know how to set up problem areas based on common problems, needs, and interests and how to utilize them in evaluating learning activities
14. Be able to build resource units related to broad problem areas and to utilize them in planning learning units with pupils[28]

Faunce and Bossing have looked at the teacher from the standpoint of functions to be performed. They suggest the following:

1. *The teacher as participant.* As the most mature member of the group the core teacher operates as a member of the group, participates and suggests as do other members of the group. When a course of action is decided upon, he accepts responsibility along with other members of the group. He helps others to develop their own assignments in their approach to a problem.

2. *The teacher as friend and counselor.* With the longer period of time each day and the reduced number of different students contacted, the teacher has time to study and know each individual member of his group. The teacher has an increasing amount of information in file and on hand to use in this relationship. He visits with the students, the parents, and in the homes. He shares with his students many extra-class activities, such as picnics, sports, and social affairs. Discipline in this relationship is transferred to the group, and the core teacher serves in a friendly, non-directive counseling role.

3. *Expediter.* In addition to being a mature participant and counselor, the core teacher expedites group plans and projects. Knowing resources which are available he helps direct students to these sources. He makes contacts with resource persons, and acts as a liason with the school administration and the community.

4. *Technician.* Skilled in the functioning of the group process, he understands the principles of group planning and group activity. As a student of

---

28. Harold Alberty and others, *Preparing Core Teachers for the Secondary Schools* (Columbus, Ohio: Department of Education, College of Education, Ohio State University, 1949), pp. 31–33. Mimeographed. Also see Harold Alberty, "Core Teachers for Secondary Schools: A Study," *Educational Leadership,* 3:97–101, 1949.

adolescent psychology he knows much about growth and development, and uses this knowledge to develop the best in each member of the group.[29]

Group Planning

An influential development which has affected curriculum improvement in a constructive manner is the emphasis upon democratic group planning and action. Believing that cooperation among the members of groups is necessary in all societies, but particularly essential in democracies, certain key organizations have given special attention to this approach. The Association for Supervision and Curriculum Development, and its predecessor, the Department of Supervision and Curriculum Development, of the National Education Association, have laid particular stress on this important process. In both yearbooks and periodicals, group process is stressed as essential to effective democratic planning and action. The basic principles, arrived at deductively, which guide this procedure are given by Corey:

1. The goals must be such that group activity will expedite their attainment.
2. Work is undertaken that is relevant to the goals the group wants to achieve.
3. Activities in cooperative group work are in sequence: (a) clarification of goals or purposes, (b) consideration of means for the attainment of these goals, (c) action in terms of the means decided upon, and (d) appraisal or evaluation of consequences.
4. There is free interplay of minds during all stages of the cooperative activity.
5. A consensus of opinion is striven for.
6. Cooperative projects tend to grow out of an existing group structure.
7. Specific cooperative work projects usually lead to other projects.[30]

Pupil-Teacher Planning

Cooperative learning is an important factor in better teaching and an essential factor in developing the social skills demanded by a democratic community. Cooperation is "the combined action of individuals or groups toward the achievement of a common purpose." The unity of purpose actively accepted by the individual students within a class is a motivating force which frequently extends beyond the walls of the classroom to the principal, other teachers and

---

29. Roland C. Faunce and Nelson L. Bossing, *Developing the Core Curriculum* (New York: Prentice-Hall, Inc., 1951), pp. 161–167.
30. Stephen M. Corey in *Group Planning in Education* (1945 Yearbook, Department of Supervision and Curriculum Development; Washington: National Education Association, 1945), pp. 130–138.

students, and even out into the community. There is no place in this picture for antagonistic rivalry or bitter competition. The basis is mutual respect, confidence, and understanding of the individual and the group in terms of direction and participation.

> Cooperative learning means cooperative goal setting, cooperative planning of experiences, and cooperative evaluation of progress toward goals. The teacher carefully thinks about the skills, attitudes, appreciations, and undertakings that he feels are important objectives in a democratic way of life. Before he meets his group for the first time, he studies all sources of information and help available to him. . . . But he does not come to the classroom with his goals crystallized; his goals for the group must not be *frozen* before he discovers what goals the pupils have for themselves. Indeed, goals should be changing constantly as individuals and groups change and grow. . . .
>
> A teacher who knows how to plan effectively with pupils leaves no room for constant, aimless floundering around. Planning together the experiences of a class means setting up a working pattern together, one that is accepted by the group. The experiences that pupils need to have, individually and in common, in order to grow and develop, determine what is to be done day by day and week by week.[31]

One of the problems the teacher of core courses has is the selection of appropriate problems for study. Cooperative planning is essential here, and teachers and pupils both need to help select the problems. The following criteria will be helpful to teachers and pupils alike in making these choices.

1. Is the problem important to this specific group of young people at this particular time?
2. Does it provide opportunity for some intelligent social participation of young people—that is, does it have leads for something they might *do* about a problem?
3. Does it have many related problems so that provision can be made for the interests and needs of those young people who do not find satisfying possibilities in the specific problem chosen by the class?
4. Does it lend itself to a variety of learning activities, such as taking field trips; making interviews; seeing moving pictures; making maps, charts, posters, or pictographs; listening to speakers; participating in panel or forum discussions; or writing a dramatic skit for stage or radio?
5. Does it call for information that is readily available?
6. Is it capable of development at the present level of comprehension of the pupils in the class or group?
7. Does it involve considerable research and use of imagination so that there is provision for growing interests and everyone has something to do?

---

31. *Toward Better Teaching* (Forty-ninth Yearbook, Association for Supervision and Curriculum Development; Washington: National Education Association, 1949), pp. 50–51.

8. Does the problem provide a central idea that is illuminated by all of the activities carried on?
9. Does it provide for experiences which give young people the opportunity to develop behavior characteristics significant for individuals living in a democratic society—characteristics such as clear thinking, social sensitivity, appreciations and creativeness, a disposition to participate with others in the solution of common problems, and respect for personality?[32]

Moving into a Unified Program

The disturbing question to the majority of teachers is "How can we move from our traditional program into the unified program?" This is a legitimate question to ask the curriculum director, and one to which he should give careful study. Let us see if we can point out some procedures which will be helpful.

There are probably three ways this can be done, the effectiveness of each depending upon the character of the school personnel and the temper of the community. The first way is to withdraw from the classroom a group of the most capable teachers and give them time and materials and direction while they prepare a new course of study for all teachers in the system to use. This method may get an excellent paper document, but the chances are that it will pile up so much teacher rebellion that the "central office gang" cannot break it down. Therefore, as a single method or as a method of getting a new course written which is to be followed by a "selling campaign," we should abandon it. It has failed too many times to warrant further serious consideration. And it has failed because it is not educational and it is not democratic.

A second plan is to organize the entire school and the community to study the needs for changing the school system or the school curriculum. This stimulates all teachers to think about improving their own methods and materials and about the larger social and psychological needs to which their teaching relates. It stimulates the community to think about the larger issues of education, rather than only about the teaching of the three R's. It requires the participation of all members of the school system in a program of discussion concerning educational reorganization. This is what we might call an all-out attempt to revise the school program.

The third plan is to begin gradually to make certain changes, either by working with one or a few special subject fields or by having a few teachers work together to reform their own classes or groups of classes. This might be called the step-at-a-time approach and may be applied either to subjects or

---

32. Prudence Bostwick and Chandos Reid, *A Functional High School Program* (New York: Hinds, Hayden & Eldredge, Inc., 1947), pp. 27–28.

to teachers, and either to the ones most in need of change or to those most easy to change. Plans two and three can be used singly or together.

The All-out Approach

In the all-out approach the leadership should come from the top of the administrative ladder—the superintendent. In this approach he alone will be the most likely to suffer if the plan fails, but he is also in the best position to acquire fame if the program succeeds. The program must have his cooperation and leadership, not merely his verbal support and the financial backing of the school system; he must work as he expects his colleagues to work on the program. He must also receive the cooperation of his principals, supervisors, the curriculum director, and any other office specialists he employs.

Careful planning is necessary to the success of this approach. Such planning could start with an over-all educational commission in the community made up of representatives from the elementary and secondary teachers and principals, from the supervisors and other professional workers, and from the community. The Educational Policies Commission recommended for one community a commission made up of the following members: the directors of research, instruction, and curriculum, of guidance and personnel, and of vocational education; one teacher and one principal from each of the elementary-high-school, junior-high-school, and senior-high-school levels; the chairman of a community vocational advisory committee; the chairman of a citizens' advisory committee; a full-time executive secretary; and the superintendent himself as chairman.[33] The vocational-advisory committee would be a community committee made up of representatives of management and labor to advise on the vocational program in the school; the citizens' advisory committee would be made up of representatives of every important community organization.

The educational commission should be responsible for formulating basic policies to guide the study of the reorganization program and should be the clearinghouse for all important ideas. Into its deliberations should pour the reports of all committees and the suggestions of all informal committees. It should issue plans for organization, study, and analysis of existing programs, reports for study and discussion by groups of teachers and citizens, reports to the press, and final approval of basic policies and definite changes. This commission is not a superior body of brains to supply ideas and make assignments to a group of working teachers; it is a representative body established to secure order in accomplishing a difficult and important community task.

In conjunction with this commission there should be organized a number of committees to study and discuss various problems and phases of the program —the character of the offerings in each subject area or in each course now

---

33. See Educational Policies Commission, *Education for All American Youth*, p. 206.

being offered; vocational persistency of the youth in the community to determine to what extent the high school is serving their vocational needs; the changes in the character of the commercial, agricultural, and industrial world in the past decade with special reference to the local community; failures, teaching methods, the availability of materials, the community resources available. But there would be two important committees appointed which would work directly under the educational commission and would represent the entire school system: the committee on philosophy and aims, and the committee on scope and sequence.

The committee on philosophy and aims would be responsible for suggesting the basic goals which the schools in the local community should strive to achieve. It should point out modern conditions in the community and in the world, changes in the understanding we have of how children learn and develop, changes in the philosophy of education and of democracy; and out of these basic concepts there should grow a conception of the place of the school in the community. Preliminary reports of this committee should be discussed by every teachers' group in town, in every building, in every subject, and in every grade. The committee personnel should represent all levels of development and broad areas of study in the school system. Its report should also be discussed by groups of citizens in the community under the direction of the leaders of citizens' organizations. This discussion should be given ample range and time, and out of it should come a revised statement of philosophy and aims which, when discussed again, should be further amended and approved and then referred to the educational commission for final approval as the basic policy of the school system and the major document upon which the reorganized school program should be built.

The second and equally important committee is responsible for building a statement of the scope of the school curriculum from the kindergarten through the topmost year of the local system. When this is done it is best to keep the elementary school unified, that is, it should not be broken up into any subject divisions. In the secondary-school periods there should be four areas, or some comparable division: (1) basic, core, or common-learning area (an extension of the elementary-school purpose of developing competent citizens); (2) individual or special interests; (3) health and physical fitness; and (4) vocational preparation, beginning about the eleventh year in the secondary school.

The first and basic area will require a statement of scope and of sequential learnings running consecutively from the kindergarten through the last year of the school system, covering the unified program in the elementary school and the core or common-learning program in the secondary school. This is the basic sequence for citizenship. The committee which is to prepare this statement should be appointed by the superintendent and should represent all levels of the school system. This committee should make an intensive study of the character of society and of the nature of individual development. It should do this without reference to subject boundaries, as has been illustrated earlier in this chapter. It should prepare a preliminary report which should be referred to all teacher groups in the school, all levels, and all subjects, for such a program should be understood by all teachers, since it determines the organization of curricular materials and will affect every teacher's subject and program. Universal agreement should not be expected, but every effort should be made to secure general understanding and at least a majority acceptance.

Opinion may differ on whether the report of the scope-and-sequence committee should be given the same kind of discussion by citizens in the community as the report of the committee on aims and philosophy. Some believe that the community should have everything presented to it; others feel that the community should understand the basic policies and goals and should leave to professional educators the responsibility for working out the procedures, materials, and methods. This last position appears reasonable and is comparable to policies followed in other professional areas. There is little help an average citizen may give to the technical study of the character of individual development or even to the study of the sociological and cultural development of society. Therefore, it seems wise to suggest that, because of its technical nature, the report of this committee should not be passed upon by the community as was suggested for the report of the committee on aims and goals. It should, however, be reviewed again and again by the teachers and by the educational commission; when approved it should become the basis for the selection of instructional materials for the elementary schools and for the common-learning area for the secondary school.

For each of the other three areas—special interests, health and physical fitness, and vocational preparation—a program must also be developed. This should be built after the curriculum in common learnings has been approved, not before, and should be arranged so that it dovetails into the core program. The division into these four areas does not imply necessarily that the school program will be sharply divided into these areas with heads of departments and special teachers, as now exists in the different subject fields, although this procedure could become a first step in the process of reorganization in a given community if it appeared necessary. Care should be exercised, however, not to set up an organization which would have to be abolished in a short period or which would prevent the corodination of all programs.

The sequence for the program of health and physical fitness should run from the first to the last years of school and should take account of all factors of physical growth. The sequence for the program in vocational education should start with vocational guidance and orientation in the early years of the secondary school and should continue through the last year of the school system, being adapted to suit the various occupations for which training is offered in the school. The program for special or individual interests need not have the sequential aspect of the others herein described, but it needs to be planned in terms of enriched experiences for children and youth in both the elementary and the secondary schools and in such a way that definite arrangements are made for children and youth to participate in these offerings according to individual need and patterns of growth and development.

If this plan of curriculum reorganization is followed, progress will be made faster than if the work is done piecemeal. The plan has the advantages of being important, of being supported by leaders in the school system and by citizens in the community, of taking into its compass all teachers in the school system, and of launching an all-out attack on the problem. Experimentation can be carried on with new suggestions as they emerge, and many committees can be organized to work during the time the basic committees are functioning. Once these basic reports are completed, committees should be appointed in the several areas to suggest instructional materials, procedures, and supplies needed for effective instruction. These suggestions should be accompanied by a description of methods of evaluating the success of the instruction. Ample experimentation in these new techniques should follow, and each teacher should feel a definite responsibility to contribute to the work of the committees. Out of this combined activity would be likely to come new outlines, resource units, and other teaching aids for a new curriculum program in the community.

The Step-at-a-Time Approach

The third method of moving from the traditional to the unified curriculum is to take a step at a time by encouraging individual teachers or groups of teachers to experiment with new procedures. There may be, for instance, teachers in English and social studies who want to work together to unify their teaching in these two areas. They may start a modified core program by coalescing their separate subjects into a unified program for a part of the school day. They may work out a sequential arrangement of the major ideas they wish to establish and may enrich both their teaching methods and their subject materials.

Another plan might provide that certain problems courses be introduced as a major social-science sequence, into which might be placed the entire scope of materials needed to study the problems successfully. Science, literature, history, economics might all be drawn upon for material to solve the problems. Several teachers might work together, for instance, to prepare large units on such things as family living, industrial and labor relations, housing, or minority groups in America. These attempts to reorient the curriculum around major problems and issues are to be commended, as they represent an approach to the problem of breaking down barriers between separate subjects.

They are only a first step, however, and should be watched to see that they do not become the end of the reorganization program. They may even become a substitute course—one in modern problems, but they may soon fall into the difficulties from which they sought to escape. There is also the danger that this area of reorganization will be completely unrelated to the areas not touched. Continuity for the total offerings of the entire school must be planned, and it is endangered when basic changes are made in different subject fields or by groups of teachers without reference to a basic pattern. There is also the danger that traditional teachers who oppose curriculum changes will sabotage or criticize the new programs or the new teachers, simply because they either do not believe in the changes or dislike the attention being given to the experimental teachers. Extreme care has to be exercised when any teacher is singled out or set apart from the group.

Moving from one type of curriculum to another requires much re-education of the total school staff. This calls for diplomatic handling of all personnel, watching to see that criticisms and suggestions are considered fairly and honestly, and making sure that places are made for all teachers. Feelings of insecurity result from assignments which require knowledge that teachers do not possess. Ample time must be given for learning to take place; opportunities must be provided for free discussion and for viewing all sides of the issues. Honest differences must be treated fairly, but the will of the majority here, as in other areas of democracy, should prevail. Teachers need to recognize this and accept it, as they must accept their responsibility for improving the procedures and materials of their profession, even though the wishes of each individual cannot be entirely satisfied.

Chapter Fifteen

Organizing and Using

Units of Work

O NCE THE CURRICULUM is planned and the teacher has accepted the place of the objectives and needs of youth and society, and the philosophy of individual differences and the wholeness of learning, it becomes necessary to organize the curriculum into parts or units small enough to be handled day by day in the classroom. A unit then is no more than a division of work organized around a set of related objectives, a problem or a principle which has significance for the pupil, the school, and society.

The traditional subject unit was organized around a subject topic or a textual chapter, taught and then tested. The modern unit is organized around an idea to be acquired and is planned with reference to the experiences most desirable for a pupil, the content most appropriate, and the evaluation most fitting. The most acceptable concept of a unit today is that it is a carefully considered body of related activities of significance to the pupil and so planned as to develop insight, skill, understanding, and control of some important aspect of human experience. Before these ideas are developed, it might be well to look at the conflicting ideas regarding units.

Different Meanings of the Term "Unit"

Division of Subject Matter

Morrison uses the term "unit" to mean "a comprehensive and significant aspect of the environment, of an organized science, of an art, or of conduct, which being learned results in adaptation in personality."[1] Several years ago Wilson indicated that the term "unit" was used to mean "a body of subject matter, every item of which is related to a central core of thought. The central core of thought is a unifying agency and the distinctive mark of a unit; it is an interpretation of the subject matter clustered about it. The unit idea, or central core of thought, is a generalization, comprehensible through the data grouped about it, and the data themselves acquire full meaning only when they are in direct focus on the generalization."[2] This concept is the same as the one Charles and Frank McMurry expressed in their early work with the project.[3]

These definitions of the term "unit" are dealing with the same concept—a division of subject matter—and such an organization may be termed the intellectualized subject approach. The central unifying thought is some principle, or generalization, or basic understanding. In order to facilitate the learning of these abstractions, some central unifying thread is pulled out and the rest of the related materials are grouped around it. The purpose of the unit is to develop understanding rather than memorization and to portray unity and relationship in materials which otherwise may appear only successive in character. This was a step forward, to be sure, in the organization of learning, for it was an honest attempt to bring meaning and understanding into a school program which had been chiefly notable for its lack of unity and relatedness. Idea followed idea in rapid order, but all attempts to form a comprehensive picture of the serial learnings were the responsibility of the pupil.[4]

Fusion of Child Interest and Educational Aim

The Lincoln School group used the term "unit" to mean "a series of worthwhile experiences bound together around some central theme of child in-

1. Henry C. Morrison, *The Practice of Teaching in the Secondary School* (rev. ed.; Chicago: University of Chicago Press, 1931), pp. 24–25.
2. Howard E. Wilson, "The Unit in the Social Studies," *Junior-Senior High School Clearing House*, 9:30, 1934.
3. Charles A. McMurry and Frank M. McMurry, *The Method of Recitation* (New York: Macmillan Company, 1903), pp. 10–11.
4. For a good contrast of these points of view, see Roy O. Billet, *Fundamentals of Secondary School Teaching* (Boston: Houghton Mifflin Company, 1940), Chap. 16.

terest."[5] The group working on the Virginia curriculum program defined units of work as "a series of related activities engaged in by children in order to realize a dominating purpose or interest which is compatible with the aims of education."[6] Others have used the term "unit" to indicate the organization of activities which have social and personal meaning (problems of social import if you will), which are within the range of experience and understanding of the pupil, and which are compatible with the aims of education.[7]

The chief characteristic of this type of thinking regarding the unit is that there is an attempt to relate the experience of the child to experiences which are of importance to adults. In the Lincoln School it led to extensive units of work running sometimes throughout an entire year; while in Virginia and in other places dealing with social problems it led to shorter units organized around problems considered important by adults but which could definitely be connected with the interest or experience level of pupils. This type of unit organization is a very marked improvement over the first type and brings the curriculum much closer to the learner. This use of the term "unit" reveals a desire to unify materials around both the interests of the learner and the demands of knowledge. It achieves fusion by finding the source of unity both from within and from without the learner.

The Experience Unit

Recent workers in the curriculum field have used the term "unit" still differently. They wish to unify the materials of the unit entirely, or as much as possible, around the experiences, the needs, and the purposes of the learner. Caswell and Campbell point out that a unit of this type is based on "a series of activities engaged in to achieve an end or outcome which the learner considers worth-while and wishes to achieve."[8] In Alabama the "experience unit . . . has its primary point of orientation in the experience of the learner. . . . Needs, purposes, and interests are considered essential elements in determining whether a series of activities or body of content has real unity. . . . Consquently the units of the experience type find their sources of unity in the learner and their primary points of reference in the experience of the learner."[9] The Mississippi program is based on the point of view that

5. Katherine L. Keelor and Mayme Sweet, *Indian Life and the Dutch Colonial Settlement* (New York: Columbia University, Teachers College, Bureau of Publications, 1931), p. 1.
6. Virginia State Board of Education, *Tentative Course of Study for the Core Curriculum of Virginia Secondary Schools* (Richmond, Va., 1934), p. 281.
7. See Joseph Justman, *Theories of Secondary Education in the United States* (New York: Columbia University, Teachers College, Bureau of Publications, 1940), pp. 339–366.
8. Hollis L. Caswell and Doak S. Campbell, *Curriculum Development* (New York: American Book Company, 1935), p. 421.
9. Alabama State Board of Education, *Procedures in Large Unit Teaching* (*Bulletin* No. 9; Montgomery, Ala., 1937), pp. 14–15.

a unit "evolves from the experiences which children find necessary to the accomplishment of some purpose which is to them real. It is significant to the extent to which the achievement of the purposes of the pupils contributes to their progressively enlarging understanding of the problems of living in a democratic society."[10]

This third type of unit, commonly called the experience unit, grows out of the fundamental belief that the centralizing and organizing point of the unit must be within the learner himself. He must have a need accompanied by a purpose, or the learning becomes imposed and to that extent ineffective. Life itself is a series of experiences, each appropriate to the maturation of the individual, and education must originate in the problems and needs which the individual faces. It goes beyond the idea of child interest, as the immediate interest of a child may not be the same as the basic need he has. The need rather than the interest, accompanied by a purpose, gives the unit a social environment as well as the environment of individual organism. Such a concept provides a basis, then, for studying the wholeness of the individual as a reacting personality within a social setting and gives point to the determination of the scope of the unit within the framework of the complete set of conditions surrounding the need. Without this concept, one experiences danger in dealing with transitory interests or with subject matter rather distantly related to the central purpose.

There is a danger in the experience unit that the criteria for selecting the content of the experience may get away from the teacher into the hands of the learner entirely and thus become a wandering mass of satellite activities. This leads to unorganized and pointless multiplicity of activities and as such may produce as much unrelatedness as the formal subject-matter unit. In addition it may lead to disorganized thinking, lack of continuity and proper individual development, and weakness in basic skills and understandings. We can hold no brief for such a process of organizing instruction if it leads to loose or ineffectual learning. On the other hand, there may be danger that the unit, once started around the needs and purposes of the learner, may lead off quickly from these pupil orientations into teacher orientations, and the desire or knowledge of the teacher may become the basic content of the unit. This, too, is as dangerous to the basic concept described as where the process centers entirely in the pupil. Either extreme is unsatisfactory. If purpose and pupil needs are to be the focal point in the organization of the unit, they must remain so throughout the entirety of the experience. This calls for teacher guidance and teacher planning.

Units organized without planning and guidance in advance are likely to be very spotty in their relation to the total sequence of the development of

---

10. Mississippi State Board of Education, *Curriculum Reorganization in the Secondary School, Grades 7–12* (*Bulletin* No. 7; Jackson, Miss., 1939), p. 71.

individuals. Our puplic schools are too much organized upon a basis of individual teachers working alone or with a text. They are too little the result of organized planning and cooperative thinking regarding the continuity of experiences throughout the entire school period. The unit based upon experience must not be taken to mean a unit springing up spontaneously and entirely out of the immediate classroom situation. While a few units may legitimately do this, such a policy of operation leads to both overlapping and to untouched areas of pupil development. Defenses for this hit-or-miss plan are postulated on a belief in a situation which does not exist—a continuity of development through common teacher understanding or the power of the individual child from the first grade through the twelfth to give guidance to his own experimental development. The concept of the experience unit has nothing in it to warrant lack of cooperative planning in advance of the actual classroom experience nor does it favor lack of continuity, both vertical and horizontal. Connections between experiences and between individual experiences and the environment must be planned carefully, or relatedness does not occur. Relationship is no more an automatic function of the experience unit than of the subject-matter unit. No one has better expressed this idea than Dewey when he said:

> An experience has pattern and structure, because it is not just doing and undergoing in alternation, but consists of them in relationship. To put one's hand in the fire that consumes it is not necessarily to have an experience. The action and its consequences must be joined in perception. This relationship is what gives meaning; to grasp it is the objective of all intelligence. The scope and content of the relations measure the significant content of an experience. A child's experience may be intense, but, because of lack of background from past experience, relations between undergoing and doing are slightly grasped, and the experience does not have great depth or breadth. No one ever arrives at such maturity that he perceives all the connections that are involved. There was once written (by Mr. Hinton) a romance called "The Unlearner." It portrayed the whole endless duration of life after death as a living over of the incidents that happened in a short life on earth, in continued discovery of the relationships involved among them.[11]

The modern experience unit differs in many respects from the former subject-centered unit. Units prepared by teachers and faculty committees fall into two categories—subject-matter units and life-problem units. Subject-matter units are developed primarily for subject mastery with faith that such activated material, by being taught in a better manner, will provide information for life situations. Life-problem units, on the other hand, are focused directly upon life, using content from many sources as a tool—how to avoid

---

11. John Dewey, *Art as Experience* (New York: G. P. Putnam's Sons, 1934), p. 44. By permission of the publishers.

delinquency, how to choose a career, what to eat, how to grow up, how to enjoy good literature, how to improve the community, what our state has done for freedom, how to take care of money, how to spend money. These are problems of significance in pupil's lives. Every school subject contains essential functional values of this type. There is great need for such functional subject mastery for life adjustment and for the preservation of American freedom.

An experience unit permits practice of the desirable behaviors needed for personal, social, and vocational competence. In addition to the conventional skills, students need equally the skills of planning, organizing, discussing, analyzing, interviewing, outlining, generalizing, applying, and evaluating. Here there is actual practice of "the ability to live successfully with others; the ability to think, plan, and work together for the common good." At the same time, group work makes possible provision for differences in pupil abilities and for occupational intentions.

A good experience unit, then, has several characteristics which may be briefly summarized as follows:

1. It is a series of activities planned by both teacher and pupils around some need of the pupil. The pupil accepts the pursuance of these activities as being necessary to satisfy his needs. This is the *binding force* of the unit.

2. The activities grow out of a problematical situation and are designed to require thought and research in their solution. This is the basic *method* of the unit.

3. The unit possesses a wholeness within itself in that it provides for the knowledge and skills—regardless of any preconceived notion of subject fields —attitudes, and appreciations necessary to face the problem, and pupils gain the relatedness of an experience from this wholeness. Units are long enough in time and broad enough in extent to solve the problem. This is the *scope* of the unit.

4. Collectively, a series of experience units forms a pattern of growth and development in the life of the child, skillfully adjusted to individual differences, common enough to provide basic social understanding, and sequential enough to avoid duplication and promote continuity. This series is referred to as the *sequence* of units.

Experience units, then, provide opportunity for more and closer relationships in the materials of instruction, for pupil-teacher planning, for emphasis upon social and individual needs, for relating all the factors in learning— drills, research activities, reading, discussion, expression—into a composite whole with a dominating purpose. They provide for the development of social cohesion, for individual growth and development, and for improved relationships in the classroom and in the entire school. They are based on the stuff of life itself.

Values of Unit Instruction

Some communities have, in their curriculum literature, indicated to teachers the values of the experience-unit plan of instruction. Recently, the Minnesota State Department of Education listed the values of the unit of instruction. This list is typical of those in most curriculum literature.

1. The unit of experience begins with the needs and interests of the children.
2. Interests can be created by teachers through arranging an environment out of which will grow the purpose and enthusiasm for the work to be undertaken.
3. Problems are set up and solved by the pupils and the teacher.
4. Pupil planning and replanning takes place under teacher guidance.
5. Units cut across subject-matter lines, thereby providing for integration.
6. Units provide for many firsthand experiences.
7. Lifelike situations in which the child may organize, evaluate, build, experiment, interview, read, share, dramatize, and express his ideas in various media are important parts of the unit.
8. The unit centers in the present, using the past for the purpose of interpreting existing conditions, and stimulates an interest in future living.
9. Individual differences are represented by helping each child develop according to his capacities and potentialities.
10. The children, under teacher guidance, constantly evaluate attainment and methods of work.
11. Many opportunities are provided for developing skills in meaningful situations.
12. Drill becomes functional, as needs for drill arise in the unit.
13. The unit contributes definitely to the development of study skills.
14. Subject matter is used in solving problems, thereby giving meaning to factual material.
15. Units develop about an understanding and appreciation of the child's environment.
16. Desirable social habits are developed as the children work on committees and in groups.
17. Critical thinking is stimulated.[12]

Organizing, Reporting, Evaluating Units

Many forms have been suggested for expressing units. The Pennsylvania State Department of Public Instruction suggested the following form, growing out of a study of a large number of school systems:

---

12. Minnesota State Department of Education, *A Guide for Better Instruction in Minnesota Schools* (St. Paul, Minn., 1946), pp. 120–121.

I. Preliminary teacher planning

    A. How did the problem originate?

    B. How was (will) the unit be introduced?

    C. How were (will) the purposes and concerns of students be enlisted?

    D. What central life objectives and contributing objectives should be (or were) organized? What cooperative group planning was (will be) used?

    E. What pupil experiences, content, sources, and measurement may be (were) planned?

II. Orientation (by the class)

    A. What considerations and appropriate facts should be (were) presented in an overview?

    B. What techniques will (were) used in providing motivation and orientation? (field trips, library work, visual aids, etc.)

    C. What objectives actually were established through teacher-pupil planning?

III. Learning period

    A. What committees were (will be) set up? How were members chosen?

    B. What individual or group learning activities were (will be) engaged?

    C. What community contacts were (will be) utilized?

IV. Culminating activity

    What form did (possibly, will) this "fixing" activity assume? (Individual or group reports, dramatizations, demonstrations, models, graphs, exhibits, charts, debates, panel discussions, mock trials, etc.)

V. Evaluation

    A. What evaluative criteria were (will be) used?

    B. Did students develop the life master inherent in the central objective?

    C. Were desirable behaviors of social competence enhanced?

    D. Was achievement worth while from the standpoint of content?

    E. How much time was used?

    F. What need for drill or formal instruction is indicated?

    G. What further study may follow or grow out of this unit?

VI. Bibliography and listed material with publishers, etc.[13]

The merits of a unit may be estimated on the basis of commonly accepted criteria of what makes a good unit of learning. To what extent does the unit accomplish the following:

    1. Represent a persistent life problem

    2. Meet the needs of students at their particular age level

    3. Clearly set out aims or objectives, so both the teacher and students can understand them and work together cooperatively for their realization

---

13. Pennsylvania Department of Public Instruction, *Curriculum Improvement by a Secondary School Faculty* (*Bulletin* No. 243; Harrisburg, Pa., 1950), pp. 102–104.

4. Provide for student participation by offering the opportunity to help plan, originate, and direct the phases of the unit which are to be worked out "on the spot" in the classroom
5. Reproduce life situations and make use of activities, experiences, and materials which are found in the experience of the learner and in the life of the community
6. Show clear and definite organization so that the work can proceed efficiently without the teacher's constant direction
7. Make provision for individual differences
8. Provide for the inductive method; proceed from concrete to abstract, from simple to complex, from particular to general
9. Have complete and exact reference material
10. Show coherence in the various phases—presentation, objectives, activities, materials, evaluation
11. Provide various opportunities for evaluation, including self-evaluation by the pupils
12. Enable the student to learn the type of behavior—thinking, feeling, acting—which constitutes the central objective

Illustrations of Units

A series of units is presented in order to make clearer the differences as they actually exist in the organization of classroom materials when based upon the principles just outlined for the various kinds of units. These units run all the way from the subject-matter unit through progressive stages to the experience unit. From the descriptions of the characteristics of each type of unit, the reader can recognize the various types and can at the same time make his own judgment as to those which most nearly accord with the educational point of view he holds to be sound.

HISTORY, NORTH CAROLINA.   In the North Carolina curriculum program the materials of instruction were organized into subject-matter units. The course was given a title, centers of interest (not to the pupil, however; really a perversion of the term) were set up, and the course was broken into units. Under each unit were suggested "concepts to be developed," "aspects to be emphasized," and "suggested activities." In a course in North Carolina history the following "centers of interest" were suggested:

Unit I.   North Carolina as the white man found her
Unit II.   Permanent settlers in North Carolina
Unit III.   Early North Carolina government (1663–1776)
Unit IV.   North Carolina during the Revolutionary War
Unit V.   Life in North Carolina from 1790 to 1860
Unit VI.   North Carolina blighted by the Civil War
Unit VII. North Carolina's return to prosperity since 1900

For illustration, Unit III is outlined:

Concepts to Be Developed	*Aspects to Be Emphasized*	*Suggested Activities*
Life in North Carolina under proprietors and under a king	How a country is ruled by a king or queen How North Carolina came to have proprietary government and the effect on the people How representatives were chosen by the people to help make the laws. Effects Why proprietors sold land, collected rent and taxes. Results Why the English King reclaimed Carolina and how he ruled. Effect Why North Carolina fought for her king Effect of sectional disputes over allegiance Why North Carolina took steps toward independence. Period of Stress Final results	Dramatize colonial life under the proprietary government Study "Trade Laws" of this era List England's advantages in getting Carolina away from the proprietors Summary: Construct a "time line" (1663–1729) locating leading events of whole period Debate: North Carolina government under the king versus proprietors Reports on Transylvania Watauga settlements Make scrapbooks of local history (Moore's Creek bridge, Hillsboro) Summarize entire period[14]

MATHEMATICS, BROCKTON, MASSACHUSETTS. In Brockton, Massachusetts, a course of study in mathematics for the junior high school was divided into units. The following units were listed for grade eight:

1. Refresher Unit (5 weeks)
2. Relationships between Numbers (5 weeks)
3. Percents and Their Applications (9 weeks)
4. Interest and Banking (6 weeks)
5. Ratio and Proportion (2 weeks)
6. Measurement (7 weeks)
7. Square Root (2 weeks)

The unit on Percents and Their Applications offers a good illustration of all the units used in this course of study. Both these units from North Carolina and Brockton are purely subject-matter units.

---

14. North Carolina State Department of Education, *A Study in Curriculum Problems of the North Carolina Public Schools* (Raleigh, N.C., 1935), pp. 209–212.

UNIT III: PERCENTS AND THEIR APPLICATIONS

I. Aim

A. To review the meaning of percentage through common and decimal fractions

B. To review finding percentage and rate

C. To teach finding the number when a percent of it is known

D. To teach finding percents of increase and decrease

E. To teach finding percents of profit and loss

F. To review and extend teaching the various applications of percentage to life situations

II. Content

A. Percent and its applications

1. Changing decimals and common fractions to percents and the inverse process

2. Percents larger than 100% and less than 1%

3. Percent of a number

4. What percent one number is of another number

5. Amount and rate of commission

6. Amount and rate of discount

7. Finding the number when a percent of it is known

8. Percents of increase and decrease

9. Net price when successive discounts are allowed

10. Percents of profit and loss, overhead and margin

B. Insurance

1. Purpose

2. Common terms: policy, face of policy, policyholder, premium, beneficiary

3. General types of policies

4. Determining rates

5. Benefits of annuities and social security

C. Taxation

1. Purpose

2. Common terms: tax budget, assessed value, tax rate

3. Determining tax rate from amount of tax budget and assessed value

4. Determining amount of tax budget from tax rate and assessed value

5. Determining assessed value from tax rate and amount of tax budget

6. Source of federal government receipts: internal revenue and customs

III. Vocabulary

percentage	taxes	policy
base	real estate	face of policy
rate	personal property	policyholder
commission	budget	premium
discount	assessed valuation	beneficiary

increase and decrease	assessors	annuity
list price or marked price	tax rate	income tax
net price or proceeds	net cost	customs or duties
successive discounts	gross cost	import and export
profit and loss	net gain or profit	tarriff
overhead	gross gain or margin	net income
social security	insurance	specific duty
		ad valorem

IV. Related Activities

    A. Collect copies of advertisements using percents.

    B. Collect newspaper clippings of major league baseball standings.

    C. Collect clipping showing batting averages of National and American League players.

    D. Obtain for discussion a copy of the tax budget for the city of Brockton.

    E. Collect various kinds of insurance policies.

V. Bibliography

    Clark, Otis, Hatton, Schorling, *Modern School Arithmetic,* pp. 58–88, 201–235, World Book Company, Boston, Massachusetts, 1938

    Degroat and Young, *New Standard Arithmetic,* pp. 323–352, 407–431, 437–464, Iroquois Publishing Company, Syracuse, N.Y., 1945

    Edgerton and Carpenter, *Second Course in the New Mathematics,* pp. 79, 244–249, 292–297, 337, 349–353, Allyn and Bacon, Boston, Massachusetts, 1944

    Hayes, Gibson, Bodly, Watson, *Modern Practical Arithmetic,* pp. 24–83, 194–195, 248–251, D. C. Heath and Company, Boston, Massachusetts, 1926[15]

KANSAS, SCIENCE. In Kansas, units were suggested which were planned around social problems and which unified the materials of the various fields of instruction. These units also attempted to combine the interests of pupils with learning content which was considered to be socially significant. The following unit from grade eight was to occupy a total time of three weeks.

A STUDY OF BACTERIAL DISEASES—PRACTICE OF PREVENTIVE MEDICINE

I. *Suggestions to the teacher*

As a graduate of the rural schools of Kansas, the author is conscious of the fact that conditions for putting this unit into operation vary in the different communities of the state and are often not as conducive to its best use as one might like. Herein, however, lies the basis for the statement that there is a

---

15. Brockton Public Schools, *Course of Study in Mathematics,* Grades VII to IX (Brockton, Mass., 1947), pp. 17–18.

great need for information of this character among the youth of rural districts as well as among the older population. The results to be derived from the inclusion of this unit in the course of study obviously will depend to a very large degree upon the interest, initiative, sympathy and good judgment of the teacher.

More material is contained in the various parts of the unit than most instructors will be able to use, but this provides a greater variety from which the teacher can select what seems best suited to her group, materials, community conditions, etc. At the same time, there is afforded a greater variety of suggestions, as well as an allowance for some materials which the teacher for various reasons may not be able to secure.

The author's experience with pupils of the seventh- and eighth-grade levels leads him to believe that they like to learn new ideas and are especially interested in matters which pertain to their own well-being and the welfare of their associates. They are usually anxious to know even more than we can give them concerning disease, and are especially apt to put a great deal of dependence in what the teacher says and does along these lines. They also like to do things for themselves. Because of these facts it is very important that the teacher be prepared to give them the truth or suggest an easily accessible and authentic source of the desired information about disease, disease germs and their activities. The various reading materials listed in this unit are authentic, and most of it is free or inexpensive. An effort should be made to have some of these periodicals on hand before taking up any of the study.

If funds cannot be provided in your school to purchase the needed materials, contact the chairman of your local Christmas seal sale committee. Some of these have a small fund which can be spent for such purposes. If not able to obtain funds from this source, ask your county superintendent about it as some of them took part in the Christmas seal sale last year under the "Nebraska plan," which gave them a small fund to use for health purposes. Another suggestion is that some type of community program be arranged and part of the receipts from it be used to purchase some of the books suggested in the bibliography. In many communities there are clubs of various types which could easily be interested in helping to provide a small fund for such purposes when the members are convinced of the teacher's *real* interest in the welfare of their children and the community. The Kansas Tuberculosis and Health Association, Topeka, Kansas, is a good source of material for health teaching, especially that pertaining to tuberculosis, and these publications are free. The secretary of the State Board of Health, Topeka, Kansas, is always glad of an opportunity to be of service in providing whatever information or materials he may have at his disposal on the topics of disease and disease control, and a teacher should feel no hesitancy about seeking such cooperation.

II. *Objectives*

A. To learn something of the cause, source, general means of spread, and the chief methods of controlling some of the more common communicable diseases

B. To show the pupil that most of what is known today concerning infectious diseases is the result of carefully planned and executed scientific research and subsequent discovery

C. To acquaint the child with several of the world's outstanding leaders (Health Heroes) in the quest for truth about disease

D. To help the student to understand that improvement in the health of any community depends to a very large degree on the knowledge and cooperative activities of each and every citizen

E. To establish in the child's mind the idea that his own ability to resist infection is determined in a large measure by how he lives and cares for himself from day to day—that an "ounce of prevention is worth pounds of cure"

F. To give the child some idea of the enormous cost of communicable diseases in terms of time lost from school and work, unhappiness, suffering, physical disabilities, deaths, medical and hospital care, as well as money

G. To create a wholesome and intelligent attitude toward health departments and due respect for their regulations and a willingness to cooperate with health officers whenever the occasion arises

H. To call the child's attention to the fact that modern knowledge of most of the communicable diseases, combined with modern laboratory equipment and methods, makes accurate diagnosis the rule rather than the exception, and that guessing is no longer necessary

I. To point out some of the unsolved present-day problems of communicable diseases and to create an interest in the same

J. To attempt to supplant with truth whatever prejudice and superstition may exist in the child's mind with respect to infectious diseases

III. *Generalizations*

> NOTE: Select and develop from the following list those best suited to the conditions existing in your school.

A. Disease germs are living creatures, growing best at body temperature, in the absence of light, and requiring plenty of moisture and proper food.

B. Infectious disease represents a struggle going on within the body.

C. Human beings can protect themselves against disease-producing organisms by:

1. Keeping the body strong by good daily health habits
2. Avoiding unnecessary contact with those who are infected
3. Preventing germs entering the body with food, drinks, dirty fingers and playthings, public drinking cups, open wounds, etc.
4. Eliminating dangerous insects, rodents, and other animals
5. The use of proper means of immunization
6. Destruction or proper disposal of human excreta

D. Whenever modern man focuses any considerable proportion of his attention and efforts on the solution of a problem of human welfare, improvement or complete elimination of the problem can be expected, and vice versa.

E. The control of communicable diseases helps to make growth more perfect, decay less rapid, life more vigorous and enjoyable.

F. Neglect and indifference toward the infectious diseases make for loss of time, energy, life, money, and happiness in living.

G. Infectious disease is not a punishment for sin, but is an inevitable result of failure to pay attention to one or more immediate health problems such as:

1. Improper care of one's body with respect to cleanliness, clothing, food, drink, irregular habits of waste elimination, rest, fatigue, worry, lack of fresh air and sunshine, etc.
2. Failure to control insects and other biological carriers of disease (flies, mosquitoes, ticks, lice, fleas, rabid dogs, and others)
3. Lack of early and rigid enforcement of isolation and other health regulations
4. Indifference, opposition, or neglect to take advantage of such safe and effective measures as toxoid immunization to diphtheria, vaccination for smallpox and the typhoid fevers antitoxin administration for the prevention of diphtheria, scarlet fever and lockjaw, and the Pasteur treatment for rabies

H. Intelligent cooperation of all concerned is a keynote to the successful control of communicable disease in any community, be it large or small.

I. Much of the progress of modern civilization can be directly attributed to man's mastery of infectious diseases.

IV. *Suggested approaches*

A. Read and discuss chapters 16–19 of *Health Habits,* Book II, or similar chapters from some of the other books given in the list of reference books.

B. Approach by studying and assigning class reports on the infectious diseases most common in your community, placing the emphasis on sources, causes, means of spread and methods of control as given in the various books and pamphlets mentioned in this unit.

C. Discuss some of the outstanding discoveries bearing on communicable diseases and point out some of the interesting characteristics of the "Health Hero" who made the discovery. For this purpose, the Health Hero series, and especially the book *Microbe Hunters* will be found extremely interesting, e.g., Pasteur's work with sheep and anthrax, or Leeuwenhoek and his homemade microscope, etc.

D. A very interesting approach is to relate the work of the Yellow Fever Commission to the building of the Panama Canal, since completion of this project was not possible until yellow fever and malaria were placed under control. (See work of Walter Reed.)

E. Secure a copy of Laws, Rules and Regulation of the Kansas Board of Health from the secretary of the board at Topeka, and study some of the laws relating to the infectious diseases common in your community. Point out the reason for the various parts of each regulation and, where it is difficult to see what the reason is, have the pupils make a study of the disease and see if they cannot discover the basis for this part of the law. Such laws are supposed to be based on what we know about the life requirements of disease germs and how they are spread from one to another person.

F. From the following table (taken from U.S. Public Health Report, Oct. 19, 1934) pick out the diseases which seem most important and then begin a careful study of the sources, causes, incubation periods, means of spread, and methods of controlling infections.

[A table showing causes of death and number of deaths from all diseases in the United States was then given but is not reproduced here.]

V. *Suggested activities*

A. Study the following table made by the United States Public Health Service. Make another table and list the diseases in the order of their importance according to which caused the most absences.

[Here follows a table of diseases and disorders and school days lost per 1,000 pupils per school year.]

B. Try to find out how the list in Activity A compares with a list of the causes of absence from your school.

C. Read to find out something about the care and treatment of the sick during ancient times; medieval times.

D. Read to learn about the sanitary measures of the early Greeks and Romans.

E. Read from encyclopedias and health books about the "Black Plague" or some similar plague.

F. Read to learn something about our Health Heroes—Louis Pasteur, Joseph Lister, Robert Koch, Florence Nightingale, Edward Jenner, Abrise Paré, Michael Servetus, William Harvey, and others.

G. Read to learn something of witchcraft as a remedy for illness as practiced in the early colonies, medicine men, voodooism, etc.

H. Read to learn something about the following diseases and how these have been conquered or controlled by man: malaria fever, malta fever, smallpox, typhoid fever, yellow fever, spotted fever, sleeping sickness, bubonic plague, scarlet fever, measles, whooping cough, and others.

I. Read to find out something about the diseases that are caused in other ways than from germs, such as diabetes, heart disease, etc.

J. Read to find out how diseases carried by germs are checked today—quarantine, vaccination, immunization, sterilizing equipment, etc.

K. Read to find out how people in certain industries have become ill by working with certain materials; for example, in the match-making industry; what steps have been taken to prevent such illness?

L. Read to find out something about diseases caused from parasites, hookworm, etc.

M. Read to learn about tuberculosis and what methods are being used to combat this disease.

N. Read to learn about infantile paralysis and the Warm Springs Foundation established by President Franklin D. Roosevelt.

O. Collect articles from newspapers and magazines on unusual feats in surgery.

P. Read to find out about Colonel Gorgas and his work of stamping out yellow fever in Cuba and in the Panama Canal Zone. Also read about the work of Sir Ronald Ross and Dr. Walter Reed and their connection with the control of yellow fever.

Q. Read to find out how Edward Jenner enabled us to conquer smallpox.

R. Find out some other germ diseases not shown in the chart under Activity A, and learn the causes and means of spreading each one of them.

S. Find out from your available reading materials why diphtheria is becoming less common and is killing fewer people than it did one generation ago.

T. Prepare a report on what pupils of the school can do to keep the school buildings and grounds clean and more healthful.

U. Examine a school well or cistern and decide on the things that should be done to keep the water from receiving the overflow from the near-by ground when it rains, or the water which is spilled on the curb. If a cistern is used, try to find out why the pipe from the roof should not be connected with the cistern all the time, but only after the roof is well washed, and also why the wall of the cistern should not have any cracks in it.

V. Talk to the other students at various opening exercise periods on:

1. Why they should not do the following:

   a. Wash hands, feet, or anything else under the pump spout

   b. Allow their hands to touch the water when dipping a cup of water from a bucket or other container

   c. Use other person's cups, combs, handkerchiefs, and towels, especially those of people outside their immediate family

2. Why they should do the following:

   a. Cover the nose and mouth with a handkerchief when sneezing

   b. Wash hands before handling food and keep fingers, pencils and various other objects out of the mouth. (This includes moistening the finger or thumb before turning a page.)

W. Find out who your local county health officer is and write him an invitation to talk to your school about his work. If he can't accept try to secure a good medical doctor who may be nearer.

X. Prepare for him a list of the things you are doing in your school and community to help control the infectious diseases.

Y. Point out to him some improvements that you think could be made in your school and ask his advice on these suggestions.

VI. *Expressional activities*

A. From chart under Informational Activity A, make a list of the diseases caused by germs and another list of those not caused by germs.

B. Make a list of the above mentioned germ diseases which may be spread by secretions from the mouth and nose, and state for each of them some things children and adults can do to prevent these infections.

C. Give oral or written reports on important Health Heroes.

D. Write an essay about insects that spread disease and how each may be controlled.

E. Make a scrapbook from newspaper and magazine articles about infectious diseases.

F. Choose partners in your class and debate the following topics:

1. "Pasteur has done more for humanity than any other of the Health Heroes (Koch, Jenner, Reed, Trudeau, Nightingale)."

2. "It is easier, cheaper and more gratifying to prevent disease than to cure it."

3. "Bacteria do more harm than good."

4. "Disease germs are more dangerous than swords."

G. Write a story about what each person can do from day to day to keep his body healthy and resistant to disease germs.

H. Write a letter to a good friend telling him or her what you think are the most important things you have learned from your study of the infectious diseases.

I. Tabulate the number of children in your school who have been immunized to diphtheria and smallpox. Do the same for all the preschool children in your district. From this data figure the percent of all children in the district who are immune to diphtheria. To smallpox.

J. Write to the secretary of the Kansas State Board of Health for a free copy of a Chart of the Infectious Diseases for use in schools.

K. Prepare a poster exhibit made by cutting from colored and advertising sections of papers and magazines pictures dealing with any phase of the disease problem.

L. Arrange a spelling match using only words that you have encountered in the study of this unit, especially the new terms.

M. Arrange a contest to see which member of the class can give the meaning of the most new terms used in your study of disease.

N. If possible visit some good city water plant, milk pasteurizing plant, large bakery, sewage-disposal plant, Board of Health laboratory for disease diagnosis or some private physician's office.

O. Compare the number of deaths given in the table shown in item F of the list of "Suggested Approaches" with the causes of absences from school as presented in the table in VA above. Repeat VIA and VIB above, using this table.

P. List the diseases that are increasing each year and try to find out why such is the case.

Q. Make a list of health rules intended to help prevent infectious diseases in your home and school.

R. Make another list for use in your community.

S. Write an item for some newspaper about disease germs, intended to explain what they are, where they are found, what they need for growth, how they pass from one person to another, and some of the methods of controlling them.

T. Draw in your scrapbook as many different kinds of disease germs as you find pictured in books and magazines. Label each one properly.

VII. *Individual reports*

NOTE: In addition to the more general reading material in the various books and publications listed elsewhere, we are giving under each of the topics listed below, one or more specific references which contain very valuable as well as interesting and condensed material for the report. They can all be secured either free or for a few cents to cover the cost of publication. Most of them are written especially for children of seventh-

or eighth-grade levels, and so an effort should be made to secure and use as many of them as possible.

A. The great white plague: "You Should Know about Tuberculosis." Kansas Tuberculosis and Health Association, 824 Kansas Avenue, Topeka

B. How smallpox was conquered

C. Pasteur—the great discoverer and master of disease

D. The scientific discoveries of Robert Koch

E. Walter Reed and the conquest of yellow fever

F. Some facts about hydrophobia

G. Whooping cough—its nature and prevention

H. The nature of some unseen friends and enemies

I. Health through the ages

J. What a common cold may be

K. Florence Nightingale the heroine

L. Tuberculosis and the Saranac Lake experiment

VIII. *Some present-day problems*

A. Conclusive proof of the exact nature of the germs which cause measles, smallpox, mumps, influenza, typhus, Rocky Mountain spotted fever, colds, sleeping sickness, and numerous other infectious diseases is yet to be produced.

B. At the present time there is no certain and practical means of immunizing persons before exposure to many of the infectious diseases, such as measles, whooping cough, mumps, colds, influenza, Rocky Mountain spotted fever, typhus, rheumatic fever and others.

C. Likewise there is known no certain cure of the diseases listed in B above, as well as many others, once they are contracted.

D. Another problem of great importance is that of insuring that all cases of infectious diseases are diagnosed very early, at which time there is a much greater hope for cure. This is also the time when isolation has its greatest value in preventing further spread of the disease.

E. One of the big problems of today is that of giving everyone the truth about the common diseases in order to enable him to act intelligently with respect to the source, means of spread, control measures, and the need of proper medical care and treatment. Superstition and prejudice in such matters always lead to disaster, sooner or later.

IX. *Culminating activities*

NOTE: It is expected that the teacher will select for use from this list those which are best adapted to the conditions in the school and the community. A list of this character is, at best, only suggestive, and its effectiveness is determined in a large measure by the interest, sympathy, knowledge, initiative, and good judgment of the teacher.

A. If the number of seventh- and eighth-grade pupils is sufficiently large, organize the group into a county health unit having a county health officer, county nurse, county sanitary inspector, and county rural school inspector, and encourage them to function in these capacities in the school.

B. Make a constructive study of the school water supply on the basis of adequacy of supply, possibilities for pollution from toilets, school grounds, curb washings, neighboring farmyards, etc. Have the group prepare a report embodying the findings, along with a list of recommendations for improving the situation. By exercising tact and good judgment such finding may be communicated to the school board, which in many cases will welcome the suggestions and do their utmost to improve the conditions. This will, in many cases, lead directly or indirectly to improvement of the private family water supplies of the community.

C. Make a similar study of facilities for washing and for the serving of water in the school, remembering that drinking utensils and the like which are used in common are always potential means of spreading infections from one person to another. Also that there is little or nothing to be gained by requiring individual cups and at the same time permitting all these to be dipped into a common bucket or other container of water. Some type of closed container equipped with a faucet should be provided.

D. Put into operation a campaign to eliminate flies, mosquitoes, and rats. In doing this make a study of the conditions about the school building and grounds which are conducive to the existence of insects and rodents, particularly flies, mosquitoes and rats. Here attention should be directed to the fact that flies always live upon and rear their young in nearly every type of waste to which they can gain access, including human waste; that mosquitoes are reared in standing water; and that rats will not remain where there are no places to hide and no food to eat. Flies, particularly, are very unclean, even if they were not a possible means of spreading infections.

E. If possible, arrange for a talk and demonstration by the local county health officer on what he is trying to do to prevent the spread of disease in your county. Suggest that he bring a microscope and some slides of disease germs to show your group. It would be well to suggest that he show some samples of vaccines, antitoxins and the like, or you might prefer that he explain some of the common health regulations and suggest to the pupils how he would like to have them cooperate with his office. In case you are not able to arrange for such a meeting with the county health officer, try to make a similar arrangement with a good local physician. If you can arrange for such a meeting with someone who has a microscope, but no slides of disease germs, the author of this health unit would be glad to loan several slides for the purpose upon request.

F. Discuss with your school board the feasibility of arranging with the county health officer, or other proper person, for toxoid immunization of all children in the community whose parents are willing. There is no more certain means of preventing diphtheria than this, and it is neither harmful nor expensive. The State Board of Health will furnish the needed toxoid free.

G. Determine the number of absences from your school on account of disease for the period of one month, or longer, and have the pupils figure the cost of such to the school district, supposing that each day's absence costs fifty cents per pupil absent. This, of course, does not take into account all phases of the cost of disease, such as the cost of medical care, the loss from not being able to do good work just before and immediately after being absent, etc.

H. Have the students arrange and present a program for the whole school in which some of the phases of the problem of infectious diseases in your com-

munity are represented with reports, poster exhibitions, newspaper and magazine clippings, etc. This might also be given very effectively as a part of an
evening community meeting.

I. Arrange with the secretary of the Kansas State Board of Health to carry
out a "nine-point" child program. He will supply you with the needed information and the pins used as rewards to all children who fulfill the requirements.
This alone constitutes a noteworthy achievement.

[The unit also contains suggestions for evaluating it and suggestions for
books, journals, pamphlets, and miscellaneous materials and their sources.][16]

Several things should be noted about this unit from Kansas on bacterial
diseases. In the first place, it is a unified body of suggestions for the teacher to
use in planning the actual classroom experiences on this problem, and it
starts with suggestions to the teacher for using the unit. In the second place,
it is not a set of specific activities which are to be imposed upon the class;
rather it is a rich source of organized problems, activities, and suggestions for
dealing with the problem. In the third place, objectives are definitely established and the unit is organized to achieve them. Even here the teacher is to
choose those which are appropriate to her class. Fourth, there is a great
variety of activities outlined, different enough in kind and scope to permit
individual choices for the different pupils in the class. Thus these activities
are for the class as a whole and for individual reports; moreover, they unify
the study at the end into culminating activities. In the fifth place, the unit
relates past and present, as well as affording opportunity for dealing with
unsolved problems. The subject matter is drawn both from written sources
and from community experience. Units of this character are of great aid to
teachers, but they must be used as sources of ideas, not as mimeographed
outlines of materials and activities to be handed to the pupils.

LOS ANGELES, SCIENCE.   Another interesting unit in science can be illustrated from the junior-high-school course in general science in Los Angeles.
This is a sample unit on the general theme of Understanding Our Environment
and uses the experiences and everyday life of the pupil as a basis for extending
learning in these areas.

WHAT LIVING THINGS ARE FOUND AROUND OUR HOMES?

I. *Suggested problems*

A. Who are our friends in the garden? How do insects, spiders, reptiles,
birds, and amphibians help us?

B. Who are our enemies in the garden? How do insects harm our gardens?
How do snails and slugs harm our gardens? Why is the black widow spider
an enemy? Why are gophers, moles, mice, and rats our enemies?

---

16. Kansas State Department of Education, *Unit Program in Social Studies* (Topeka
Kan., 1936), pp. 469–482.

C. What should we know about flowers for the garden? How do plants grow? What care do plants need? How can we reproduce plants? What plants should we select for our gardens?

D. How can we choose lawn grasses? How fast do grasses grow? What care should we give a lawn?

E. What shrubs will be useful and beautiful around our homes? What should we know about the size and rate of growth of shrubs? What care should we give the shrubs in our gardens?

F. Why did the planters choose certain kinds of street trees? What should we know about the appearance and growth habits of street trees? What kinds of street trees are most commonly used?

II. *Teacher orientation*

This area begins with the plants and animals to be found in the immediate vicinity of the pupil. Since some pupils will be unable to travel often to the shore or the mountains, we must help them be aware of the interesting neighbors with whom they may easily get acquainted and through whom they will learn much that pertains to all forms of life wherever it occurs.

In order to introduce this unit, a class may be made aware of the living things in the school yard or in the home yard. The room should have stimulating pictures and living material well arranged to please and attract. Questions used as titles of the displays help to start ideas. "Do you recognize this?" "What does this plant do for man?" "Where could you find me?" and the like.

III. *Suggested approach*

A. Bring in specimens for an exhibit.

B. Take class on exploration tour with an assignment such as the following:

1. Find identical twins (2 leaves, 2 plants, etc.).
2. Find five new things never noticed before.
3. List all things you think interesting, and describe to the class. Have the class choose several places to visit in order to decide a starting point for study. (In the fall of the year insects, leaves, bare branches, etc., offer possibilities for study. The teacher should make note of all possible points of interest on a scouting trip taken before the class goes out, and thus be able to maneuver the class in the direction for discovering challenging spots.)
4. Upon return from the trip arrange for a free discussion of findings, and a display of collections made.

C. Class questions should arise which will help the teacher and the class plan the method of approach. Some ways of evoking questions are:

1. Listen and make note of free conversation—seize upon leading ideas even though they may have been imperfectly or incompletely expressed. By rephrasing or by leading questions, help the pupil express the idea toward which he is groping.
2. Have enough materials in the room, pictures on the bulletin board or other visual aids to arouse curiosity and result in questions.
3. List pupils' questions on the board and lead the class to see that some

method of classifying questions may be found which will help them approach the work in some logical order.

4. Lead the class to see that some possible avenues of approach might be:
   a. Individual research in library
   b. Committee projects
   c. Class reading in texts
   d. Finding information from experts at home or elsewhere
   e. Planning and doing experiments
5. Cooperatively set up with the help of the class the standards of work and achievement which should be reached. Have this recorded so that it may be referred to at times of evaluation.

Suggested Problems	*Materials and References*
WHO ARE OUR FRIENDS IN THE GARDEN ?	*Texts*
How do insects, spiders, reptiles, birds, and amphibians help us ?	Parker, INSECT SOCIETIES ——, INSECTS AND THEIR WAYS Clark, Fitzpatrick and Smith, SCIENCE ON THE MARCH, Book 2 Phillips and Wright, PLANTS AND ANIMALS, Book 3 Powers, Neumer and Bradley, OUR WORLD CHANGES

Insects:
  Bees
  Ladybird Beetle
	Beauchamp, Williams and Blough, DISCOVERING OUR WORLD, Book 2
	
	Library References
	(See Reference List)

Lacewing Flies
Wasps
Dragon Flies and Samsel Flies
Tiger Beetles
Ant Lion
  (Doodle Bug)
	Audio-Visual Materials
	Charts: Coleoptera—G8 Bee—G3
	  Wasps and Bumblebees—G9.1
	Exhibits: General Insects
	  Butterflies of California
	  Beneficial Insects
	Films:
	  HONEY BEE—Fsd. 595.7-9
	Filmstrips:
	  Butterflies—THE GROWING UP OF THE MONARCH BUTTERFLY, S-3.1
	  Butterflies—THE LIFE OF THE SWALLOWTAIL BUTTERFLY, S-3.2
	  Insects—HOW INSECTS GET FOOD, S-6.1
	  Insects—HOW INSECTS GROW UP, S-6.2

Suggested Teacher Activities	*Suggested Pupil Activities*

Suggested Teacher Activities

Display insect material.

Set up demonstration beehive.

Help pupils make cages for insects collected.

Provide reference materials.

Locate and introduce to students new source material.

Provide assistance to pupils in their research.

Help pupils plan activities.

Check with pupils on skills being practiced such as: oral and written, expression, accurate observation, and objective thinking.

Evaluate progress of pupils by teacher-pupil evaluation.

Test skills and knowledge acquired by pupils.

Suggested Pupil Activities

Collect insects from garden or backyard.

Try to find the eggs or larval stages of insects. Watch them develop in the classroom.

Identify insects collected.

Make lists of insects collected with notations about their feeding habits, and how they benefit man.

Watch ladybirds eat aphids by placing an aphid infested leaf in a petri dish with several ladybird beetles.

Give reports of research committees on life histories of various insects, food habits—Smyrna fig and its wasp, clover and its bumblebee, etc.

Keep some insects alive in cages for demonstration of their habits as: feeding, stages in metamorphosis, etc.

Provide proper food for insects in cages.

Collect flowers showing modification in flower shape and petal markings for insect pollenation.

Read and discuss reference material.

Carry on self-evaluation of knowledge accumulated, and skills practiced.

As a culminating activity, set up an exhibit displaying various beneficial insects, and the ways in which they benefit man.

Suggested Problems

WHAT SHOULD WE KNOW ABOUT FLOWERS FOR THE GARDEN

How do plants grow?

What care do plants need?

How can we reproduce plants?

What plants should we select for our gardens?

Growth habits determine their selection for the garden.

    Work of roots, stems, and leaves

Materials and References

Texts

Clark, Fitzpatrick and Smith, SCIENCE ON THE MARCH, Book 3

Phillips and Wright, PLANTS AND ANIMALS

Parker Series:

FLOWERS, FRUITS, SEEDS

SEEDS AND SEED TRAVELS

TREES

PLANT FACTORIES

PLANT AND ANIMAL PARTNERSHIP

ADAPTATIONS TO ENVIRONMENT

Size
Length of life—annuals and perennials
Plants that are easy to care for and
free from diseases are desirable.

Ease and speed of reproduction
  Seed
  Cuttings
  Bulbs and rhizomes
Appearance
  Color
  Size and shape
  Fragrance
  Period of bloom
  Use as cut flowers
Selection
  Recognition of some common kinds.

Powers, Neuner and Bradley,
  OUR WORLD CHANGES
Corwin, JUNIOR HIGH SCHOOL SCIENCE
Beauchamp, Williams and Blough,
  DISCOVERING OUR WORLD, Book 2

Audio-Visual Materials
  Charts: The Root—G-50
    Stems—G-20
    Green Leaf (Section)—G-53
  Films: SENSITIVITY OF PLANTS—
    Fsd 589-1
    ROOTS OF PLANTS—Fsd 581.3-1
    PLANT GROWTH—Fsd 581-1-1
    LEAVES—Fsd 581.4-1
    THE GIFT OF GREEN—Fsd 581.1-2
Catalogs from seed companies

Suggested Teacher Activities
Show pictures of home with and
  without flowers.

Suggest a visit to admire some attractive or well-kept yard nearby, or
  take the class on a "field trip" to
  see an attractively landscaped garden.
Display cross sections of stems and
  branches, pointing out how stems
  grow and perform their work.

Lead discussion of material read.
Introduce vocabulary words such as,
  photosynthesis
  osmosis
  venation
  annual
  perennial
Suggest sources of information for
  individual or group research.[17]

Suggested Pupil Activities
Pupils study yards near their homes.
Look for examples of desirable and
  unattractive planting.
Read and discuss pp. 11–28, Phillips
  and Wright, PLANTS AND ANIMALS.
Perform experiment on osmosis, pp.
  104–107, SCIENCE ON THE MARCH.
Read pp. 158–160 and perform indicated experiment. Bring in and examine different types of roots.
Compare leaves as to size, shape, venation, and arrangement on stem.
Plant some seeds in pots or trays and
  watch their growth in different
  parts of the room, comparing needs
  as to light, water, etc.
Make cuttings of geraniums or other
  easily rooted plants.
Examine bulbs—cut some in half to
  see their structure.
Plant some bulbs and rhizomes.

PERSONAL AND SOCIAL PROBLEMS, PASADENA. In Pasadena, California, some very interesting work has been done in developing units on Personal and Social Problems. One of these units devoted to school problems offers a good illustration of how they have been developed.

---

17. Los Angeles City School District, Curriculum Division, *Outline Course of Study for General Science* (Publication No. SC–448; Los Angeles, Calif., 1950), pp. 32–39.

SCHOOL PROBLEMS

Problems, Adult-Stated	*Problems, Youth-Stated*

A. HOW CAN WE HELP YOUNG PEOPLE TO SEE THAT THERE IS A CLOSE RELATION BETWEEN THE DECISIONS THEY MAKE AS TO WORK AND PLAY AND THEIR CONCERN ABOUT SUCCESS IN SCHOOL LIFE?

1. Being late for school worries me.
2. I worry about grades.
3. Misplacing my locker key is my greatest bother.
4. Teachers who do not speak plainly worry me.
5. It worries me when my teacher gets angry at me, moves my seat, or puts my name on the board.
6. I worry about failing in school studies.
7. I do not like to see bad grades on my work.
8. "Knowing school work" worries me.
9. My teachers "pick" on me all the the time.
10. We haven't enough time between classes.
11. I worry about tests.
12. We should have a longer lunch period.

* * * * *

B. HOW CAN WE HELP YOUTH TO DEVELOP A FEELING OF SECURITY IN ALL THEIR SCHOOL WORK?

1. How can I overcome an urge to "sass" my teachers or someone I do not like?
2. When friends are angry at me I am unhappy.
3. I want to be popular and well-liked. I am between the "top two or three" and the "secondary group" in my class and so I am left out of the "top things" because I am in between.
4. I am an "A" student in almost all of my classes. I have a brother who is almost eighteen and he is a "D" student. Sometimes I hate to take my report card home because I know that it hurts him when I do. My parents want him to go to college and his life-long dream has been to go to Stanford, but, unfortunately, with his low grades, he could never make it.

Problem-Solving Activities   *Notes*

1. Have a group discussion on "The Basic Aims of Education in the Pasadena City Schools," pages 7–9, *The Pasadena Junior High Schools,* Secondary Curriculum Publication No. 9.

2. Keep a time check during study period for a day or two on students who feel that they have too much home work. Follow with a consultation as to how wisely time is spent at school.

3. Interview teachers of ninth grade subjects to discover how much time the homework assignments will require. Make a time budget for next year on this basis.

4. Help students to set up some standard of values and arrive, at least tentatively, at some decision as to what they want from school.

5. Keep a record of time spent on various activities for a week such as: school, home duties, homework, movies, outside games, etc. Have class discussion on some typical time records.

6. Make a time budget for a week of work and play.

                    *   *   *   *   *

1. The instructor should refer to the students' personnel folders to get all the information possible concerning the personality of each student in class. This information will form the basis for the cooperative arranging and assigning of class and other activities designed to help the students to recognize and correct their weaknesses and to use their strong qualities to the best advantage for themselves and others. Frequent personal conferences should be held.

Problem-Solving Activities

2. Have class or group discussion on "Wise Decisions."

3. Make lists of the resources of the public schools of Pasadena that are available to students and their parents. These lists may be combined, then discussed in detail.

4. Make a list of services which, so far as you know, the schools do not provide, but which, in your opinion, they should render to the public.

5. Make a list of services now provided by the public schools which in your opinion are not adequate, and give reasons for the inadequacy.

6. Keep a scrapbook or bulletin board section containing news, favorable or unfavorable, on public education. Check carefully to see whether the news items may have some propaganda slant.

7. Have students write themes on "What Relation Exists between Education and Standard of Living?"

8. Have students report on what Washington, Jefferson, Madison thought about free public education.

9. Arrange for the maladjusted child to work on many committees and occasionally act as the leader.

10. Name some of the recreational opportunities for a student who is interested in athletic games, in music, in journalism, in conversation, in nature, in making collections, in social activities.

11. The instructor might find it very helpful to make a Sociogram of the class. It can be used as the basis for individual conferences and in the organization of group activities. Instructions on how to

make a sociogram and suggestions
on how to use it may be found in
"How to Construct a Sociogram,"
Teachers College, Columbia University.

12. Give timid and self-conscious students much practice in reporting
with groups rather than singly
until they feel more confident.

13. Invite a member or panel of the
library-craft class to discuss the
services of the school library.

14. Have a committee visit the home
of a shut-in student (with the
school doctor's approval) and report on the kind and quality of
educational experience which is
available.

15. Have students compare our present-day schools with colonial
schools.

16. How are the seriously handicapped
children in Pasadena given a
change to get an education? Have
a committee interview the Director of Child Welfare and/or visit
the schools with him. Source materials: Secondary Curriculum
Publication No. 9, pages 40–44.

17. Introduce the students in the class
who are new to the school and
read their programs to the class.
Ask for students who have the
same programs to act as hosts and
hostesses until the new students
come to feel thoroughly at home.

18. Invite members of the Student
Council to talk to the class about
new school regulations, if any, and
to answer questions about existing
rules.

19. Organize programs and parties in
which maladjusted students share
responsibilities.

20. Give a test to see what school
regulations and other information

Problem-Solving Activities

about the schools need to be reviewed. Use the school handbook, if any, and the Secondary Curriculum Publication No. 9, and No. 10 as source material.

21. Prepare and cooperatively produce the script for a radio or movie program on "Democracy in the _____ (your own) Junior High School."

* * * * *

1. Make a list of the distractions which interfere with your studying. Prepare a plan for overcoming each and discuss your plan at home and in your classes at school.
2. Ask the entire class to read "Improving Your Study Habits" in Aker and Aker, *You and Your Government,* pp. 749–750. Encourage the class to put these principles into practice for a week and report on results.
3. Have students rate themselves as "good," "fair," or "unsatisfactory" on the following abilities:
   a. Ability to use an index
   b. Ability to use a dictionary
   c. Ability to use a table of contents
   d. Ability to use the library and files
   e. Ability to use keys, tables, graphs, etc.
   f. Ability to use an encyclopedia
   g. Ability to use the Readers' Guide
   h. Ability to use dictionaries of biography and history
   i. Ability to use an atlas
   j. Ability to use various yearbooks
   k. Knowledge of the organization and operation of the library
4. Discuss these activities.

* * * * *

Problems, Adult-Stated	*Problems, Youth-Stated*

C. HOW CAN WE HELP YOUNG PEOPLE TO IMPROVE THEIR LEARNING TECHNIQUES AND TO ACHIEVE TO THE BEST OF THEIR ABILITIES?

1. I am very self-conscious in class, so giving oral reports is a strain.
2. Getting my lesson on time is a cause of worry.
3. How can I learn to concentrate on my work and not daydream and look out the window?
4. Before and while I am reciting I think I am not sure of it.
5. It is annoying to have a teacher give you something to do in a few minutes, then start talking and take up the time.
6. It is hard for me to concentrate on my homework. We live in an apartment and I have to study in a room where others congregate.
7. I worry a lot about my grades. When tests come along, I am nervous and cannot do my best.
8. I am too lazy or don't try to do homework. I am the same in school.
9. I do not have a suitable place to study at home.
10. Homework gets me down.
11. My attention is so easily distracted that I miss part of my work and sometimes my grade suffers.

* * * * *

D. IN WHAT WAYS MAY WE SECURE THE MOST ACTIVE COOPERATION OF PARENTS IN A UNITED APPROACH AT HOME AND SCHOOL TO FACILITATE THE MOST EFFECTIVE GROWTH AND ADJUSTMENT OF EIGHTH-GRADE STUDENTS?

1. How can I practice a half hour each on piano and ballet when I have so much homework?
2. A friend of mine has an inferiority complex because her mother and father are always telling her that she will never amount to anything. She does not get perfect grades in school, but I think she does very well. Her parents tell her that she is a lazy good-for-nothing just because they expect their daughter to be a genius. How could this situation be corrected so that they may be a happy family again?

Problems, Youth-Stated

3. I can't find time to do homework. When I arrive home from school I work around the house until six o'clock. After dinner I practice music until eight o'clock. I go to bed at eight-thirty because I have to get up at five-thirty to go on my paper route. Half an hour is not enough time to do all my homework.

4. Homework bothers me a lot. There are four in our family and we live in three rooms.

5. I have tried desperately to get good grades. Now my parents tell me that I should not go to college. Why try for grades now?

6. Why do parents force children to continue to take piano lessons when they know they do not have the ability to make good? One's loyalty becomes strained after five years of wasted effort. Besides it is a waste of money.

7. Should there be any difference of opinion between a father and mother about their children?

8. I must practice my music for long periods of time, usually right after school, so I do not have much time for homework. Our family does a lot of church work which takes up most week nights. That is another reason why I cannot get all of my homework done.

9. I live in a busy, noisy store. Our home is rented. How can I do my home study?

10. My mother gives me no encouragement in my home study.

11. I have been absent very much and am worried about my work and grades.

12. I worry about getting to school on time after my paper route; and I worry about my complaint record.

Problems, Adult-Stated

Problems, Youth-Stated

13. If a person seems always to have to go some place which is really necessary, how can school work get done?

14. How can I study when a little spoiled "kid" is bothering me and my parents favor him because he is little?

15. How can I study when my sister is always coming into my room to listen to the radio?

16. How can I finish my homework and be in bed by 10:30 since I must catch the school bus at 8:00?

17. How can I get my homework done, deliver papers in the morning, do odd jobs in the afternoon, and go to bed at 7:30 so that I can get up at 5:00?

18. How can I do my homework when there are too many people living in the house and it is too noisy?

19. How can I do homework with a paper route and going out four nights a week?

20. My parents take no interest in my homework or school affairs.

21. I have a paper route which takes a long time. I have to go to the store every day after which comes supper. My bedtime is nine o'clock. That doesn't leave much time for homework. As a result I do not get very good grades.

· · ·

Problem-Solving Activities

Notes

1. Make a list of all known recreational facilities for young people in Pasadena and neighboring territory. Discuss good and bad points of each.

2. Refer to a copy of the "Junior High School Growth Report Form." Discuss the meaning of the Growth Report, especially in terms of how

Problem-Solving Activities

it relates to the evaluation of the achievements of eighth grade students. Encourage students to bring questions from home, and assist students in providing the answers to the question from parents.

3. Ask parents and students jointly to check on time actually spent on home study.

4. Consult with students and parents as to whether they feel that the schools are providing the information necessary to justify requesting the students, with parents' approval, to accept the final responsibility for making out their programs, meeting graduation requirements, meeting requirements of their major, etc.

5. Describe the place in your home where you study regularly. List the conditions that are favorable to studying and those that are not satisfactory. Ask the members for suggestions on how to change the unsatisfactory conditions.

6. Post on the bulletin board clippings from the city newspaper containing news of any kind concerning your school.[18]

CALIFORNIA TEACHERS ASSOCIATION. One of the most interesting teaching units on the subject of the school is that found in a published volume of eighty pages of the California Teachers Association. It has a wide number of activities from which the teacher may choose, much resource data, very interesting and effective charts and graphs, suggested culminating activities, and an extensive bibliography. It is designed to achieve the following three main areas of motivations:

I. Are the successful men and women of our day just lucky, or have they been helped by some special agency?

A. Identify successful personalities in local areas or situations.

18. Pasadena City Schools, *Personal and Social Problems of Eighth Grade Students in Pasadena* (Secondary Curriculum Publication No. 18; Pasadena, Calif., 1949–1950), pp. 1–11.

B. Get lists of successful Americans in all fields.

C. If you could get into the shoes of any man in the United States—
Whose? Why?

D. Is school the stepping stone to all occupations and professions?

E. Is the length of time to be spent in school for all these people the same?

II. How would you like the kind of job that offered these advantages?

A. Variety, rather than the monotony of most jobs

B. Salaries improving all the time

C. Many fields of service and many levels in each field

D. Prestige as a professional educator

E. Great contributions to public welfare

III. Do educational opportunities and high standards of living go hand in hand?

A. Countries with great resources but little education—low standards

B. Countries with few resources but good opportunities for education—
high standards (United States Chamber of Commerce charts)

C. Countries with little education have little demand for the world's
business.

D. Charts show these relationships

E. Education as a factor in vocational success[19]

Outline of Unit

I. History and growth

A. A brief history of the modern high school

B. Great teachers
1. Horace Mann
2. Woodrow T. Wilson
3. Booker T. Washington
4. John Dewey
5. Charles W. Eliot

C. Types of schools
1. General educational facilities
2. Special educational facilities

II. Contributions of education to society

A. Personal
1. Need for fundamental processes
2. Health and safety
3. Job opportunities
4. Leisure-time activities

B. Community and State
1. Standards of living
2. Vocational training

---

19. Emery Stoops and others, *The Contribution of Education to American Democracy*
(California Teachers Association, Southern Section, Los Angeles, Calif., 1946), p. 4.

3. Society and culture
4. Civic growth

C. National and international
1. Comparison of national education with national prosperity
2. Contributions to representative government
3. Contributions to national security
4. Peace through education

III. Opportunity in education

A. Social advantages
1. Professional status or prestige

B. Cultural advantages
1. Associations with people of similar educational background
2. Opportunity for cultural avocations
3. Opportunity to mold cuture of the future

C. Personal advantages
1. Activities which may be related to salaries in teaching
a. In your community
b. In your state
c. In other states
d. Federal aid
e. Upward trend in salaries
f. Trends toward salary schedules
g. Retirement
h. Opportunities to advance
2. Activities which may be related to working conditions
a. Pleasant surroundings
b. Freedom from occupational diseases and hazards
c. Security of income
d. Freedom from dictatorial supervision
e. Cultural and professional growth through leaves of absence
f. "Working with youth keeps one in touch with the youthful outlook"
g. Professional organizations work for teacher betterment

D. Training required for teaching
1. How much training?
2. Reasons for raising the requirements
3. What will future requirements be?
4. Where is additional training obtained?
5. Comparison of requirements[20]

ALABAMA, SCIENCE.   For a final illustration, of the experience-unit type, one is selected from a junior high school in Alabama. This unit is reported by the teacher, Edna Collins, and represents a clear-cut report of the nature and scope of the unit.

---

20. *Ibid.*, pp. 17–18.

CONTROLLING SOIL EROSION

An Experience Unit

Reported by Edna Collins, Teacher

A group of twenty-seven junior high school pupils were discussing laws recently passed, and bills pending before the Alabama legislature. Their interest was keen. Several of the bills had a direct bearing on their lives. They knew the need for increased revenue for relief and education. Some of them lived in the homes of teachers who had been meagerly and irregularly paid. The proposed sales tax might be the way out here. They were concerned, too, about the new laws governing the licensing of automobile drivers, laws that delayed that coveted experience two or more years for them.

The question, "Are there any bills before our national legislature that will affect us as citizens in this community as directly as the local bills?" provoked a lively discussion. Our attention became centered on the Omnibus Flood Control Bill. That there was a national need great enough to justify the expenditure of the stipulated three hundred twenty millions of dollars was soon apparent. None of us could forget the tragic disaster wrought by the floods of last March. Newspaper and magazine articles, and informal talks with two of our teachers who had been in one of the flooded areas made us appreciate more fully the extent of the loss of life and property, and the degree of suffering brought on by such a catastrophe. Further discussion revealed the fact that Alabama had suffered floods from the Cahaba, Alabama, and Warrior rivers, that even our own immediate vicinity had not escaped, two creeks having overflowed, a regular occurence with one of them.

"Have we always had floods?" "Had any part of our country escaped them?" Parents, neighbors, friends, and books were consulted. The answers to these questions were shown on a graph and a map. The results presented a new problem. "In view of the frequency and prevalency of floods, what has been done about them?" Two of the boys volunteered to interview a man whose small farm is flooded annually. Others found out about the great dams being constructed throughout the country—about levees, retaining walls, and spillways; their kinds, sizes, uses, and costs. This last item caused one alert youngster to raise this question "If it costs that much to control floods, wouldn't it be better to find out what causes floods and control the causes?"

At this point we realized we needed the help of our science teacher. With him we discussed floods—what they are, what causes them, their advantages and disadvantages, and control methods. We experimented with soil and water. We made a field trip to see stratification, and to find the types of soil in our locality. The science teacher outlined for us the activities of the Tennessee Valley Authority, particularly those at Norris. His account of the damage done by erosion, and the great need for controlling it, opened our eyes to a local situation. We realized for the first time that erosion was a spectre in our own midst. Again we made a field trip, this time to note the extent of the erosion taking place in our school yard and immediate neighborhood. We returned to our classroom acutely aware of the need for immediate control. We were set for action.

The M.E.C.P.—Montevallo Erosion Control Project—was established. Volunteers built sign posts bearing the letters neatly painted in red, and later placed them on the sites selected for control and experimentation. We collected pertinent material from many sources—encyclopedias, yearbooks, magazines and newspaper articles, free and inexpensive literature from the Departments of Agriculture and the Interior. We read widely and freely. We plied our science teacher with questions concerning details of the control carried on by the TVA. As they were found, principles and methods of control were earnestly and carefully discussed.

As a result of this study five committees were formed, each member of the group selecting the committee on which he would serve. One group established a Weather Bureau. The children worked in the laboratory, spending every possible moment there, returning daily to work after school. There they built and collected equipment with which they constructed four weather stations. Each consisted of two thermometers, a barometer, a wind gauge, and a rain gauge. A mercury barometer and a wet and dry bulb thermometer, also made by the youngsters, were kept in the laboratory. Readings from these and the weather stations were taken twice daily and recorded on a chart made for the purpose.

Another group made erosion traps to measure the amount of erosion taking place in different places. There were placed in each location, a denuded hillside, a grass covered hill, a cultivated field, and a wooded area. The amount of soil in each trap was measured each day, and an average taken for each group. By this method we were able to find out how erosion is influenced by the types of coverage, and the degree of land slope.

A reforestation group was organized. This group spent the most of its time in the fields studying the local types of vegetation—grasses, shrubs, and trees. Some planting was done, and recommendations for future plantings were made on the basis of root systems, usefulness apart from soil anchorage, and rate of growth.

Muscle and brawn, as well as ability to think clearly, played a big part in the activities of the dam builders. They selected two large gullies and a roadside ditch for the scenes of their labors. They prepared a permit form which they had signed by the proper authorities, granting them the privilege of building on public property. In the gullies they constructed three types of dams—log, plank, and brush—using boards discarded by workmen, finding logs and brush in nearby woods. The ditch, because of its location, needed greater beauty. A concrete dam was designed for it. What planning was needed here! Careful study with heads bent over the plans, discussions of the best proportions for a concrete mixture, estimation of the amount of material needed, perusal of price lists, computation of cost, arranging to have the materials delivered. Tools and a mixing box were borrowed from a contractor who was working nearby.

Excitement ran high the day we were ready to place the form and pour the concrete. Our Weather Bureau discouraged us, predicting unfavorable weather, but a lack of time forced us to go ahead anyway. The job was completed at the end of the school day on Friday. Wearily the tools were returned. An hour later the rain fell in torrents. The builders, alert to every need, were soon back on the job and had the dam covered. During the entire weekend the rain fell, our hardest, longest precipitation. Individuals and groups made trips to see the dams, and came back elated, rejoicing because they were holding. Quantities of good soil were being caught.

Because mosquito control is a necessary accompaniment of dam building, and because apart from dams our town had its share of these disease carrying pests, another group made a survey to locate the places where mosquitoes were breeding. They read widely about mosquitoes, learning to identify the disease carrying variety and something of their life cycle, and finding out modes of extermination. They collected the necessary materials. Then, armed with test jars, rubbers, oil, and sprays, they went to the places previously located, spelling doom for the mosquitoes. These trips were repeated, the test jar bearing mute evidence of success.

During the weeks that these activities were in full swing the midwest was suffering its worst drought. Our reading and our own experiments convinced us that water, caught by dams and stored in reservoirs, and water held in the ground by proper coverage would do much to prevent such a catastrophe. Articles about dust storms, together with the stories told by one of our teachers who lived through such storms in the great "Dust Bowl," and by another who had lived in a section where great quantities of the dust had been deposited, made us further aware of the need for coverage and wind breaks. We were amazed by our own ignorance of and blindness to a problem of such great importance. Were others, the great rank and file, just as blind? We realized that this was a battle to be fought, not only by our government, but by every individual, particularly the farmers. How could we warn people? How could we disseminate our information?

The way opened unexpectedly. The owner of the local newspaper offered us as much space as we could use. After two days of thinking in terms of headlines, news, and editorials, of writing, changing, and writing again, the copy went to the press. The results were highly satisfactory.

As we evaluated our work we had only one regret—the shortness of time. Our experience and our dependence on the weather called for more time, and the amount of work to be done in our community would have been enough to keep us busy for many months longer.[21]

---

21. Alabama State Board of Education, *Procedures in Large Unit Teaching,* pp. 64–70.

Chapter Sixteen

Developing

Resource Units

I N THE SECONDARY SCHOOL the selection of units of work depends upon several factors which must be considered before the teacher makes a decision. In the first place it is necessary that the teacher have a point of view regarding the needs of the youth with whom she is dealing. These needs must be studied in the light of the previous growth and development of the pupils, their economic and social backgrounds, their abilities, attitudes, and interests, their levels of maturity, and their vocational choices. The precise nature of these needs can be learned by reference to cumulative records kept by previous teachers, by contacts with parents, by knowledge of other children of similar ages and experiences, and by reports of any tests or studies of these youth.

In the second place, it is necessary that the teacher have a fundamental social philosophy of the place and function of instruction in the secondary school in the world of today. Much of the effectiveness of the selection of teaching materials depends upon the social understandings of the teacher. If the school is to participate with other social institutions in improving the democratic way of life, the teachers in the secondary school must understand the issues of modern living and be able to make them clear and meaningful to youth.

A third consideration is the community in which the youth live. Community resources, problems, deficiencies, and opportunities for extending the experiences of youth are all vital factors in the development of an educational program. Community surveys can supply much of this information. Reports from institutions and services in the community likewise offer available materials. Intimate knowledge of the community itself, its people, its institutions, and its resources, is one of the basic qualifications for successful teaching. It stands to reason, also, that teachers should not plan units of work without regard to the availability of books, magazines, films, pictures, reports, excursions, and any other valuable classroom aids which bear upon the subject.

A fourth factor is some basic framework itself. If each teacher is free to determine each unit without reference to the work of her colleagues, there is likely to be either duplication or gaps in development. A general framework of reference which is suggestive to all teachers and which grows out of group consideration is an invaluable aid in guiding the selection of units of experience. This framework itself must be determined by reference to youth's needs and to social problems. The framework should be built upon basic life activities and the aims of education. When such a pattern, is constructed cooperatively, it serves as a guide for continuity in pupil development.

Initial Teacher Planning

There are two stages in the planning process: one involves the work of the teacher in making herself as competent as possible; the other involves building on the pupils' purpose and their ability to plan. Much planning can be done by the teacher before she ever meets the pupils. Care must be exercised, however, that this initial planning is kept within the framework of the experiences and needs of youth and that it is not transferred as the teacher's work to become the exact plan of the pupils. If the teacher plans entirely for the pupils, we are likely to be back again to units of work logically organized but ill adapted to pupil growth and development. We are also likely to be guilty of depriving pupils of the opportunity of learning to plan their own work.

Nature and Purposes of Resource Units

One of the most effective ways of teacher planning in recent years has been by the use of resource units. These units have been variously defined.

Lavone Hanna describes a resource unit as a "reservoir from which teachers can draw suggestions and materials for making a teaching unit or for preparing for student-teacher planning."[1]

The Commission on the Secondary School Curriculum of the Progressive Education Association has defined the resource unit as "a preliminary exploration of a broad problem or topic to discover its teaching possibilities . . . A source unit usually contains some analysis of the problem or topic under consideration to show its relationship to common and recurrent problems of children and of our society. It may include lists of pupil needs and interests which may give rise to the study of this problem, and lists of desirable changes in pupil behavior which may be effected by this study. The heart of a source unit is usually a list of possible activities and experiences to meet these needs and interests and bring about these changes of behavior. There may also be a bibliography of helpful materials and suggestions for evaluation."[2]

The National Council of Social Studies defines a resource unit as "rich resources from which the individual teacher can extract procedures which will help him teach most effectively."[3]

Essentially, then, a resource unit is a comprehensive analysis and organization of the objectives, problems, activities, and materials which form a unit in a sequence of plans for achieving the purposes of education. It is made by teachers and is a form of preplanning designed to guide them in their selection of instructional problems and materials. Out of resource units an actual teaching unit may be built. A resource unit may be made by one teacher or by a group of teachers.

The purposes of resource units may be listed as follows:

1. To furnish suggestions for materials, methods, activities, teaching aids, and evaluative procedures for building a learning unit
2. To provide a means of helping the teacher to organize materials so that he can depart from the traditional use of the textbook as a guide in curriculum development
3. To provide suggestions for the teacher for translating an educational philosophy into practice
4. To serve as a guide in helping the teacher to include in the learning unit certain important values basic to education in a democracy
5. To sensitize the teacher to all of the significant problems and issues that have a bearing on an area of living

1. James A. Michener and Harold M. Long, *The Unit in the Social Studies* (Harvard Graduate School of Education, 1940), p. 108; I. James Quillen, *Using a Resource Unit* (National Association of Secondary School Principals or National Council for the Social Studies, Washington, 1942), p. 30; I. James Quillen and Lavone A. Hanna, *Education for Social Competency* (Chicago: Scott, Foresman & Co., 1948), p. 186.
2. Progressive Education Association Commission on the Secondary School Curriculum, Committee on the Function of the Social Studies in General Education, *Social Studies in General Education* (New York: Appleton-Century-Crofts, Inc., 1940), Chap. 12.
3. John H. Haefner and others, *Housing America: A Source Unit for the Social Studies* (National Council for Social Studies, *Bulletin* No. 14; Washington, 1940), p. 11.

6. To utilize the personnel resources of the school appropriate to the cooperative pre-planning of a particular unit
7. To conserve the time of the teacher
8. To make it possible to have teaching materials available when needed[4]

All these definitions of the resource unit imply several characteristics: (1) it is prepared by teachers for the use of teachers; (2) it is not to be handed to pupils to become a plan for the study of the unit; (3) it is to be organized around a central problem; (4) it contains more materials than any one teacher can use; (5) it contains suggestions for aims, activities, bibliography, and other types of classroom materials. When resource units are built and used in this fashion they become very important aids for teachers who are reorganizing their programs of instruction.

After one examines a large number of resource units, he begins to see the characteristics which they have in common. Many of the resource units begin by general orientation statements regarding the philosophy of education, or the nature of the curriculum program of the particular community. Some of them define the concept of student needs and list needs that may be met; others suggest ideas for teachers to use in motivating learning and in selecting the appropriate topics for discussion in the classroom. Some will also give the relation between the particular resource unit and the general sequence or framework of the curriculum organization. But, generally, there are certain specific characteristics that most units have in common. They can be summarized as follows:

1. The unit begins with a statement of the objectives, goals, or purposes to be achieved by following the unit organization or outline.
2. The units usually contain an introduction which orients the teacher to the basic concepts or principles involved in the unit, and relates them to previous units.
3. Usually a large number of problems, issues, basic concepts, generalizations, or skills involved in the unit are listed so that the teacher may select the specific ones she desires to use.
4. A large number of group activities which the teacher may use with the students are suggested. These are usually very definite and specific, and are so numerous that the teacher would, by virtue of their number, be forced to choose rather than to follow them all.
5. Definite suggestions are made for procedures, methods, or plans of attack, and may be used to initiate the unit, to proceed with certain problems or issues, and to culminate the unit into a well-rounded learning experience.
6. Large numbers of reference materials, many of which are usually an-

---

4. Harold Alberty, *Reorganizing the High School Curriculum* (New York: The Macmillan Company, 1949), p. 272.

notated, are suggested. These reference materials are in the forms of books, pamphlets, slide films, records, radio programs, magazine articles, and other kinds of audio-visual materials. Usually community resources are also listed in terms of people, institutions, or important places, which may be visited.

7. Ways and means of evaluating the learning outcomes of the unit are usually suggested, and in some units specific tests and forms of testing are given.

8. In many units suggestions are given for related materials to be used with students with a special interest or special abilities.

Sometimes the difference between a resource unit and a teaching unit is not clearly understood. The difference lies chiefly in the fact that the resource unit is made for the teacher rather than for direct student use. It contains more suggestions than can be used by any one teacher and it contains a large number of materials which are suggestive to the teacher rather than prescriptive. Instead of giving a few possibilities or a minimum of suggestions for activities, it usually provides a large number, so that the teacher may choose those most appropriate for her purpose or her class. It is not organized as a direct teaching guide for the student which he may take and pursue. It is extensive and suggestive and flexible, and encourages the teacher to make whatever adaptations are necessary to meet the individual needs and interests of her own class.

Forms of Resource Units

Different people and groups have set up a variety of forms around which units might be built. In a resource unit entitled *Housing America,* the following eleven items are developed in a unit totaling eighty pages.

1. The basic understanding to be developed
2. Suggested objectives for the unit
3. The scope of the unit
4. Motivating the unit
5. Pretest
6. The facts in the case
7. Some housing terms
8. Suggestions for daily procedures
9. Further activities
10. Sources of information
11. Suggestions for evaluation[5]

The National Association of Secondary School Principals and the National

---

5. Haefner and others, *Housing America,* p. 11.

Council for the Social Studies have jointly issued over twenty-five resource units on various social problems. In their manual for teachers they indicate the various parts of a resource unit as follows:

1. Analysis of the problem
2. Statement of significance
3. Statement of anticipated outcomes
4. Suggested problems and questions
5. Suggested activities
6. Evaluation
7. Bibliography[6]

One of the unique and important features of this series of units on Problems in American Life is the fact that the basic textual material of the unit was prepared by social scientists, while the teaching aids and suggestions were prepared by teachers and curriculum workers. Thus the units combine scholarship in the social sciences and professional competence in instructional practices.

Quillen and Hanna have suggested the following form for resource units:

I. Title.

II. Analysis of the area: an extended analysis of the area covered by the unit including basic background information for the teacher.

III. The statement of significance.
    A. The social significance of the area covered by the unit
    B. Its relation to student needs
    C. Its contribution to the development of effective citizens and the achievement of democratic values
    D. The placement of content and experiences from the area in the program of study

IV. Statement of anticipated outcomes: this part contains a statement of specific objectives defined in terms of behaviors.

V. Suggested problems and questions: this defines the content of the area covered by the resource unit. More problems and questions are included than can be used in any one teaching unit.

VI. Suggested activities: the heart of the resource unit—these should be varied, extensive, and directed toward the collection of information on the problems and questions and the achievement of the objectives formulated for the unit. These should be selected carefully and organized so as to be most helpful to teachers in the following several ways:
    A. According to activity types
    B. According to objectives

---

6. Quillen, *Using a Resource Unit*, pp. 12–15.

C. According to problems and questions

D. According to the steps in teaching a unit

VII. Suggested evaluation techniques and instruments: unlike the teaching unit, the resource unit contains a section on evaluation based directly on the statement of objectives.

VIII. Bibliography: lists of materials divided for pupil and teacher use according to types include not only reading materials but also audio-visual aids and environmental resources.[7]

A second outline suggested by Alberty is as follows:

I. Philosophy: a statement consistent with the philosophy of the school.

II. Objectives of the resource unit: should be consistent with the philosophy of the school or that which is adopted by the makers of the resourse unit.

III. Scope: determined by two factors:

A. The nature of the unit itself

B. The possible uses to which the unit will be put

IV. Using a resource unit: should contain suggestions to the teachers who are to use it concerning the possible ways the material might function in developing the various steps of the learning unit. The following suggestions are based upon the conception of the learning unit as involving three interrelated phases—initiatory activities, developmental activities, and culminating activities.

V. Suggested types of activities for students:

A. Planning of units of learning cooperatively in selection, development, methods and procedures, and evaluations

B. Selecting appropriate audio-visual material

C. Utilizing the community resources

D. Working jointly with other classes to carry out worth-while projects

E. Using creative and constructive activities

VI. Evaluation: a continual process of the entire teaching-learning program. Some suggested techniques include:

A. Paper and pencil tests and instruments

B. Anecdotal records of student behavior

C. Student records, diaries, and other records of self-appraisal

D. An analysis of jobs and projects undertaken by students

E. School records

F. An analysis of written and oral work

G. Reports and observations by parents

---

7. I. James Quillen and Lavone Hanna, *Education for Social Competency* (Chicago: Scott, Foresman & Company, 1948), pp. 186–189.

VII. Teaching materials and aids: comprehensive lists of available materials such as

    A. Books, pamphlets, and periodicals

    B. Films, slides, pictures, recordings, etc.[8]

Illustrations of Resource Units

YOU AND YOUR FAMILY, LOS ANGELES. In Los Angeles, California in the senior year there is a Senior Problems course. One of those problems is devoted to Family Life Education, and one of the units in this course is called You and Your Family.[9] The unit which has been developed on this subject starts off with giving the general point of view of the course in Family Life Education, and then follows with a statement on the relationship of this resource unit to the general outline for the course in Senior Problems. Specifically in the unit on You and Your Family, the material begins with a statement of objectives of the unit. They are stated as follows:

1. To understand the function of the modern home in democratic society and to appreciate its values
2. To establish sound, wholesome, boy-girl relationships
3. To achieve the maturity necessary to accept the responsibilities of marriage
4. To establish a sound basis for the selection of a life partner
5. To understand the factors that contribute to the establishment of happy homes

The second feature of the unit is headed Initiatory Procedures. These are given to assist the teacher in helping to establish interests among the pupils. Such procedures as the following are suggested:

1. Spend at least an entire period in talking over the purpose of the unit, the need for it, and its carry-over value into adult life. Rapport with the class is a vital part of the teacher's successful presentation of the unit.
2. Survey by means of unsigned statements what the class hopes will be taken up in the course. Collect and tabulate these to use as a basis for the development of the specific content of the unit with the class.
3. Discuss the bibliography and encourage students to suggest additional material. Post a copy of the bibliography, or better still, give each student a copy if your school provides facilities for mimeographing.

The general unit then is divided into three areas: (1) changing pattern of family life, (2) approach to marriage, (3) home and family. Under each of these three areas are suggestions for content and procedures. Then, for the

---

8. Alberty, *Reorganizing the High School Curriculum*, pp. 276–286.

9. Los Angeles City Schools, *You and Your Family:* A Resource Unit for Senior Problems (Publication No. SC–432; Los Angeles, Calif., 1949).

entire unit there are suggested references for the pupils, another set for the teachers for their background, and then a series of suggestions for tests which can be bought or which can be made by the teacher to use in evaluating the outcomes of the unit. Some illustrations of the content and procedures will suggest the general body of the unit. Under content we find the following in Area I.

I. Changing pattern of family life
   A. Functions of the modern home in a democratic society
      1. What is the importance of the home?
         a. Insures care and protection of offspring
         b. Provides feeling of emotional and physical security
         c. Provides a center for love and protection
         d. Provides training in living cooperatively and creatively with other people
         e. Establishes basic patterns of thinking and behaving
         f. Passes on the heritage of the race
      2. What does the family give to the individual?
         a. Hereditary potentials
         b. Opportunity to fulfill special roles successfully
         c. Protection
         d. Satisfaction of affectional needs
         e. Character training
         f. Encouragement and opportunity to become one's finest self
         g. Security—the feeling of belongingness
      3. What are the earmarks of the democratic family?
         a. Father and mother share equally in basic leadership
         b. Decisions are reached by joint discussion of all members
         c. Cooperative planning of household management
         d. Share of responsibility for the work of the home
         e. Joint goals

Opposite this suggested content is a list of procedures:

1. Discuss the basic needs of individuals. Have the class make a chart showing the kind of affection typical of each age. What people are involved in each stage of development? Encourage students to give concrete examples to illustrate points.
2. Have the class list ten factors that contribute most to the establishment of an ideal home.
3. Compile a list of unsigned student questions in the area of home and family living. Organize results in problem area for group work.
4. Suggestive charts for selected students to make:
   Working of Mendel's law
   Graphic illustration of chromosomes and genes
5. Compare the advantages received by a child reared in an institution and a child who is given love and affection in a home. Cite articles, fiction, and personal knowledge to bring out points.

6. Assignment: Clip current news articles which illustrate family friction. Paste this on notebook paper, analyze the basic problem in the light of democratic family relations.

The remaining part of the unit is done in the same general fashion except that the procedures vary from time to time. Some of the procedures are suggested under panel discussions; some under certain small group discussions; some under general student activities; some under basic problems for analysis; and some on suggested papers to write.

APPRECIATING DEMOCRACY, LOS ANGELES COUNTY.   In Los Angeles County a curriculum monograph has been developed entitled *Appreciating Democracy* which suggests a sequence of materials recommended for use in eleventh- or twelfth-grade social-studies classes.[10]

This bulletin is really a large resource unit organized under several headings. It starts out by suggesting a number of introductory activities. There are five of these as follows:

1. Considering the news
2. Considering the theories and practices of certain forms of government
3. Considering the races and nationalities contributing largely to life in the United States
4. Considering the development of important democratic concepts
5. Evaluating student participation in school government

Under each of these five is contained information on possible problems, suggested activities, and materials to use in the classroom. Then, following these suggested introductory activities, are three main sequences as follows:

1. United States democracy and the individual
2. Democracy and the economic system of the United States
3. United States democracy and the world

Under each of those three, information is also given on possible problems, suggested activities, and materials.

At the beginning of the unit, several pages are devoted to assisting the teacher to understand the use and meaning of this resource unit. Since this is controversial material, suggestions are also given to the teacher on how to handle controversial material fairly. These suggestions are followed with directions on measuring the success of the sequence, maintaining the timeliness of the material, and evaluating the success of the unit. A few brief quotations from the unit will give an idea of its general nature. Under the main sequence, United States Democracy and the Individual, appears first the statement of objectives. These objectives are as follows:

---

10. Los Angeles County Office of Education, Division of Secondary Schools, *Appreciating Democracy* (Los Angeles, Calif., 1949).

1. To see that under the democratic system great emphasis is placed upon the individual
2. To know what rights the individual possesses, by what documents they are guaranteed, and in what respect they are limited
3. To become acquainted with the agencies and institutions through which rights are safeguarded and extended
4. To be aware of the responsibilities which the individual should assume because he has these rights
5. To know what problems concerning individual rights are of special interest today

Following this comes a section headed Information on Possible Problems, and under this heading are such materials as the following:

I. In what ways does democracy recognize the importance of the individual?
   A. By declaring that government rests on the consent of the people (Declaration of Independence)
      1. Provisions for amending Constitution (Article V)
      2. Provisions for impeachment of officers (Constitution, Article I, Section 3)
      3. Provisions for initiative, referendum, recall (See state constitutions, statutes of local government)
   B. By forbidding titles of nobility thus strengthening the doctrine of the equality of man (Constitution, Article I, Section 9)
   C. By guaranteeing specific rights to the individual
      1. Civil or personal rights
         a. Freedom of religion, Bill of Rights, Article I
         b. Freedom of speech and press, now extending to all forms of communication, radio, movies, so that it is sometimes called "freedom of expression"
         c. Freedom of Assembly implying the right to membership in organizations
         d. Right to bear arms
         e. Right of personal security as indicated by protections from search and seizure and from quartering
         f. Right of affairs, speedy public trial with provisions for specific protections
         g. Right to due process of law
         h. Freedom from Involuntary Servitude
         i. Right of equal protection of the laws in any state

The unit also goes on to outline what are called "political rights" and "economic rights."

Then, under the heading What Are the Responsibilities of the Individual in a Democracy, we find the following:

I. Be informed so that he will
   A. Exercise his vote wisely: only 55% to 70% of those registered vote even in national elections
   B. Disobey no law through ignorance
   C. Speak judiciously in matters of current debate

II. Use his rights in accordance with the spirit as well as letter of the law so that there will not need to be further legal limitations created to protect people from the less scrupulous among themselves

III. Take part in government when his talents are needed

IV. Be interested in good government so that mismanagement and dishonesty may be reduced to a minimum

V. Relate the cost of the services of government and be willing to pay in taxes for the kind of government he expects to see maintained

Then, under the general heading What Problems in the Fields of Personal Rights Are Being Much Discussed Today, we find the following:

I. A more equitable maintenance of rights for minority groups as indicated by proposals to secure these rights
   A. To maintain the right to safety and security
      1. Laws to deal with lynchings
      2. More equitable treatment by police in courts of justice, and of prisoners whose labor may be used
   B. To maintain the rights of citizenship
      1. Outlawing devices such as the white primary and the poll tax which restrict the right to vote
      2. Altering the inferior status of the Negro in the armed services as an infringement of the right to bear arms
   C. To maintain economic rights
      1. Establishing non-discriminatory policies on hiring, wage scales, opportunities for advancement
      2. Eliminating unequal educational opportunities
      3. Eliminating discriminations in housing

II. Extensions of Social Security
   A. To reach more people
   B. To include more services

III. Improvement of educational opportunities particularly in low income states: Federal supports for schools

IV. Improvement of the nation's health

V. Revision of the electoral system

Following these questions and topics is a suggested vocabulary of words and phrases that may be used generally in the discussion of the problems and issues. Then comes a list of suggested activities. These activities deal with such things as gathering information individually or in groups, presenting material as individually or in groups, utilizing the material by developing procedures to use in school, in the community, or in the home. A number of activities are suggested. Then there is a list of materials made up first of books which are carefully annotated, films likewise annotated, recordings, and transcriptions. All in all, the unit contains a wealth of material for a teacher to use in developing a unit on this subject.

SENIOR GOALS, SAN FRANCISCO. In San Francisco, California, a course in Senior Goals has been prepared containing three resource units.[11] These units are the product of a curriculum committee of teachers from the San Francisco high schools working with the consultants in the central office responsible for curriculum building and coordination and with a consultant from San Francisco State College. The resource unit contains first a general introduction which outlines for the teacher the basic ideas involved. This is followed by a statement on student interest and needs. Then comes a statement on how to use the resource units that are developed. Following this is a statement on cooperative planning by students and teachers looking for the utilization of the resource unit material in the classroom situations. Then comes a list of the objectives of Senior Goals. The units state definitely that the basic objectives of the course are to enable the student to make the transition from high school to another phase of life, to become a maturing and adjusted adolescent, to grow in responsibility, personally, socially, economically, and civically, and to learn to evaluate himself. It provides for group problem solving in three basic areas: (1) understanding of yourself and your family, (2) understanding of yourself and personal economics, and (3) understanding of yourself and your job. Following the listing of these three are definite, specific, desired end results for each of them stated in the form of the kinds of behavior that the student is expected to follow if he has achieved these end results.

An illustration under the heading Understanding Yourself and Personal Economics will indicate the pattern used.

DESIRED END RESULTS

1. The student understands his role as a consumer in the American way of life.
2. He has a deep sense of responsibility for the social effect of his consumer activities.
3. He sets standards for living toward which he is willing to work.
4. He knows how to get facts and relies intelligently on those who are experts.

---

11. San Francisco Unified School District, Secondary Schools, *Senior Goals,* Preliminary Report (San Francisco. Calif., 1951).

5. He improves all his techniques of buymanship.
6. He uses and cares properly for the things that he owns.
7. He plans for long-term money management problems through savings, insuring against risk, and investments.
8. He appraises his buying habits and purchases with his developing sense of values.

Under each of these three group problems, a teacher can find very helpful material. First is listed some suggested ideas as to the relation of the basic problem and the life of boys and girls.

Then come certain suggested group activities. For instance, under the problem Understanding Yourself and Your Family are suggested such things as these:

I. Buzz sessions may be used as a valuable aid in giving students an opportunity to compare their thinking with others. The students may group themselves in units of four or five and discuss the emotional behavior of the people in the following cases:
   A. Mary, 15, has an ungovernable temper. Hardly a day goes by in which she doesn't fly into a rage to her own unhappiness and her parents discomfort.
   B. Mrs. White, 28, can't bear any criticism from her husband without bursting into tears.
   C. Sarah Lou, 23, is so reserved that everyone who meets her is repelled by her coldness.
   D. Barry, 17, a student with high grades is missing a great deal because he is shy.
      Each group, after thinking through the possible causes for behavior, may decide what advice should be given to each person. Following reports of chairmen, class discussion may lead to the effect of health, environment, economic background, age, drives, appearance, social adjustment, ability, and ethical values on the development of personality.

II. Committees may report on the lives of Lincoln, Theodore Roosevelt, Alec Templeton, Helen Keller, Franklin Roosevelt, Glenn Cunningham, Thomas Edison, Jim Thorpe, or any other person that the class may wish to suggest. Each group may indicate the handicaps that have been overcome. These may be followed by group discussion on the value of recognizing strength and weaknesses, and learning how to work with them for personal adjustment and success.

III. Select a situation in which emotional maturity or immaturity is clearly evident in the person involved. Perhaps the rain has suddenly interrupted a picnic; perhaps a father has lost his job; perhaps the last good tire has gone flat. Choose rules for social dramas portraying the ways various person of differing levels of emotional maturity might act. Change roles and show how the person might learn to act in such a situation.

IV. Prepare a social drama of two people in a private conversation when a third person joins them. Try out different ways of meeting the situation and see which is most effective.

V. List various psychological drives on the board and ask students to select some emotions that might contribute to them. Let each student select one emotion he has felt and analyse his understanding of it to be handed in to the teacher unsigned and discussed by the group. Discuss ways each of these drives may contribute to a fuller and more complete life, and how each may cause frustration and discontent.

VI. Have two people in the class describe the personality of one of its members. Each student may write the name of the person he thinks they are describing. This may be repeated for four or five students in order to demonstrate the individuality of personality and the common traits that are recognized in a mature person.

VII. One panel of students may present their ideas on a well-adjusted personality considering the following qualities:
   A. Ability to face others, self, and problems
   B. Freedom from unnecessary worries, tears, and anxieties
   C. Genuine interest in others of both sexes
   D. Value of understanding and practicing tolerance
   E. Utilization of abilities for others as well as self
   F. Maintenance of a sense of proportion and balance
   G. Many and varied activities
   H. A well-developed sense of humor
   I. A justifiable standard of morals and conduct to live by

VIII. Arrange for showing of the film *The Feeling of Rejection*. Have a panel discuss the pertinent points raised by the film on what makes us feel left out.

Following these suggestions for group activities is a list of individual activities of which the following are typical:

1. Give a standard personality test such as the Science Research Associates' Interest Inventory, or the California Test of Personality. Each member may develop his own tests or equate his own strength or weakness to use in planning his individual program for improvement.
2. Collect a number of cartoons that illustrate types of personality. Better yet, draw original cartoons to illustrate different temperaments. Arrange your Bulletin Board for display.
3. Write a short story on someone in your school whom you think is especially well-adjusted.
4. List common fears. Let each student write a short story about how he would overcome something that he is afraid of. Write a story to tell how he plans to overcome a fear which he has.
5. Each pupil might call on five people and find their answers to the

questions: "How do you feel about failures?" "What possible values might they have?" Then have a summary of this presented to the class.

Following a large listing of activities of this kind for each of the basic problem is a bibliography for understanding the problem, divided into materials for the pupils and those for the teachers. Pamphlets and library books are listed organized according to specific headings that may be helpful for the students. Films are then listed and annotated.

A unit of this kind is a well-suggested outline to the teacher so that she may be able to select quickly those basic questions, activities, topics, and materials which have been carefully chosen because they have bearing upon the basic objectives of the resource unit. From these materials and suggestions, she then organizes her own teaching outline.

APPRECIATING OUR NEIGHBORS, PHILADELPHIA.   One additional unit will suffice to show the characteristics of good resource units. This one comes from the Philadelphia public schools and contains a wealth of materials from which teachers may select to use in planning and organizing actual teaching units designed to focus learning upon the problems of adolescent growth and life in American society. The unit is designed to show how racial experience, current written source material, and the past experience of the learner may be correlated in providing experiences for the development of social competence.

HOW CAN WE LEARN TO APPRECIATE OUR NEIGHBORS

A Resource Unit

I. Why and what? An overview

Most teachers in this country are kindly, tolerant people, who accept their friends, acquaintances, and pupils at their face value; who recognize ability no matter what kind of person possesses it; and who realize that we shall never have a truly democratic society in which to live, until all people believe that everyone should possess equal economic, political, and religious freedom. Unfortunately, this is not true of a great many citizens of this country. Every alert individual realizes that, in spite of great progress, prejudice and discrimination still exist.

The schools of the country have done much to promote better intercultural relations among pupils and parents. However, many of our children come from homes where bigotry and intolerance still prevail. Many of them truly believe that: "Members of the white race are more intelligent than those of the black." . . . "Catholics are not patriotic." . . . "All Japanese-Americans are disloyal to the United States." . . . "All Jews are rich." . . . "All Italians have quick tempers."

Of course not many people believe all these pernicious stereotypes, but nearly everyone has at least one pet prejudice which he jealously guards against all scientific, ethical, or logical consideration.

This raises several important questions: (1) Should the schools do something about this problem? (2) What can they do? (3) How can they attack it? These are the questions with which we shall deal in this resource unit.

Should the school do something about the problem? The answer seems obvious. Our schools exist to give the children experience in democratic living and to prepare them for the responsibilities of adult citizenship in America. Democracy cannot exist in an atmosphere of hate, distrust, envy, and fear. The promise of democracy is lost unless a progressive solution is worked out for all people. All forces of good should develop an attack on the problem; therefore, we believe that there is nothing more worthy of inclusion in the curriculums of our schools. No two schools can use the same program, because no two schools have the same problems confronting them. In a great many schools there exist tensions which should receive prompt treatment; in others, where the school population is more homogeneous, the problem must be considered from a different point of view. Each school will have to decide on its own methods, materials, and means of cooperation with community agencies interested in the same problems. Also, we must point out that an educational program must not only make contact with those in school; it must make contact in many ways with those adults in the school community who can by word and deed contribute richly to or destroy all that the school is striving to do.

Knowledge, unless translated into action, exists as excess mental baggage. Planning assembly programs that use all children who have contributions to make is a demonstration of democracy in action. Inviting outstanding members of racial and nationality groups to the school, thereby developing an appreciation of their contributions, is important. Relating issues of school tensions to community problems of a similar nature can serve to give a broader understanding of what is involved. Recognizing ability in any field—social, intellectual, artistic, or mechanical—may lead to appreciation of people who, on the surface, appear to be different.

In order to use this or any other intercultural unit successfully, it must be developed in a favorable atmosphere. This condition will exist only if the principal, teachers, and all members of the staff having any contact with the children, actively contribute to the program.

This resource unit can only make a little scratch on a tremendously large surface. We shall attempt to develop suggestions for three approaches to the problem of intercultural relations. They are

1. Scientific or by proof
2. Cultural
3. Religious

Each approach will be presented separately for purposes of clarity and organization; but it will be obvious that various combinations can be made in the approach. It is entirely possible that none of the three will be specific enough for a given situation in a given classroom or school. In that case, perhaps, the learning activities, bibliography, or evaluation techniques will prove helpful.

II. Part Two: Learning activities

A. Introductory
  1. Discuss meaning of the word "prejudice."
    a. Derivation of word
    b. Difference between relatively harmless and harmful prejudices

2. Make a survey of prejudices existing in the class or observed by its members.
3. Study how prejudices have affected families.
4. Collect news items proving the existence of prejudice in the world today.
5. Discuss reasons for the existence of prejudice.
6. Make a map of the community or city, showing where different nationality groups have settled. Discuss reasons for the distribution.
7. Discuss the result of prejudice and discrimination on the victim, on the aggressor, and on society as a whole.
8. Read and discuss the pamphlet *Probing Our Prejudices* by Hortense Powdermaker.

B. Let the facts speak (the use of scientific method to examine prejudice).

The ways of thinking scientifically are powerful weapons to use against the forces of intolerance and misunderstanding. Science recognizes the common origin of races and does not assume that there are pure races or that there are unique racial characteristics. Racial blood differences, we know, do not exist. Hair and skin differences do exist, but do not in any way indicate inferiority or superority.

Correct thinking, when it is developed, can prevent the fixation of many fallacies. Generalizing with too little data, confusing fact and assumption, and applying conclusions to unrelated data are common mistakes which lead straight to undesirable thinking about races, religions, and nationalities that happen to be different from our own. The whole concept of differences needs clarification among our youngsters. It must be made clear that a difference in appearance or manner, custom, speech, or dress is not a sign of a better or poorer human being.

The evil that can come about as a result of distorting facts about race, religion, and nationality must be apparent to all people today. It seems to us that even children can be led to understand this. We hope that this resource unit will help the teacher to make the study of this unit interesting. Even if only a little better understanding and action result, the effort and experience will be well rewarded.

1. Present the familiar situation, "If there were a ladder standing against a building, would you walk under it?" Discuss superstition involved. Make a list of other superstitions that little children know. Attempt to arrive at an understanding of the origin of a superstition.
2. Choose one or two superstitions like the one about placing a horsehair in water and try it out as scientific experiment. From the results, draw the obvious conclusions and make as detailed a comparison as possible between superstition and fact.
3. Discuss the reasons various people have for holding on to superstitions.
4. Read a pamphlet on the fight against germs to get an understanding of the way in which a scientist works to combat superstition. Reports, oral or written, would be appropriate.
5. With the background of some of the learning activities already given, write and discuss how to go about proving or disproving the following statements:

a. All Orientals are sneaky.

b. Mexicans are dirty.

c. All Scottish people are stingy.

Distant groups were purposely selected for this first try at developing a scientific way of judging people. Collecting data from reliable sources, checking all facts, stating conclusions that are in harmony with the facts—these things should be done carefully without formalizing the intellectual process that is here involved. The common fault of generalizing on meager information should be constantly exposed as the loose talk of the intolerant and the prejudiced.

6. Read appropriate portions of *Races of Mankind,* by Ruth Benedict and Gene Weltfish, to get an elementary understanding of the meanings of race, religion, and nationality.

7. Make reports on the following topics:
   a. How did Hitler use false ideas about race?
   b. What are the main races of mankind?
   c. Why are many ideas of Catholicism, Protestantism, and Judaism alike? (Use *One God,* by Florence Mary Fitch.)
   d. Why are there so many different nationality groups in our United States?

8. Make drawings of racial types. Emphasize the fact that large variations exist among the members of any one race.

9. Mark, on a world outline map, the places of national origin of the parents of the children in the school. Graphs could also be made.

10. Test the accuracy of understanding of race, religion, and nationality by asking for the racial identification of each of the following:

a. Chinese	*h.* Buddhist	*o.* Scottish
b. Negro	*i.* Porto Rican	*p.* Caucasian
c. Jew	*j.* Englishman	*q.* Arabian
d. Turk	*k.* Mongoloid	*r.* Japanese
e. American	*l.* Catholic	*s.* Christian
f. Hindu	*m.* Mexican	*t.* French
g. Spaniard	*n.* Mohammedan	

11. Trace the development of the idea of the master race from about 1930 to the present. Relate the investigation to the war that is now over.

12. Pose two questions for discussion:
    a. Does our Constitution allow the grouping of people as superior or inferior? Locate and read the portions of the Constitution that prohibit this.
    b. Are there Americans who prove, by what they say and do, that they think other Americans are inferior? Discuss experiences.

13. Collect and post under the following bulletin-board headings (*a*) *This Is America* and (*b*) *This Is Democracy,* pictures that show cooperation or true American behavior. Pictorial magazines and newspapers can be used for this. Discuss the pictures and relate what they show concerning the guarantees of the Constitution of the United States.

14. List the common prejudices that pupils know about cultural groups in the neighborhood. Plan how to get at the facts to prove or disprove a given stereotype. Personal investigation, reading, invited outside speakers, invited teachers who belong to the cultural group in questions, and films are suggested as learning activities. It is important to draw definite conclusions in written or oral form, or in the form of posters, graphs, or scrapbooks.

15. Discuss what is meant when a person is described as "being different." Point out the fact that "different" doesn't mean superior or inferior.

C. Let the record speak (the use of cultural differences as a means of developing intercultural understanding).

Your class is a community. In many ways it reflects the problems that concern our city, State, and nation. Tensions often exist both within and among cultural groups; bad feeling may be above or below the surface; pupils may or may not be friendly toward each other. There are good and bad leaders; some children follow blindly, others show some independence of action. Intelligence is endowed variously—this, too, in the classroom as in larger communities, leaves its mark on the intercultural attitudes that young people acquire. Some have enough money, others must learn to compensate for the lack of it. It's a tremendous complex of differences. The teacher is faced with the task of resolving some of them.

Further complications set in when racial, religious, and national minorities are part of the composite scene. It's a difficult job to develop democratic behavior in the daily personal and group relationships in the school and in the outside community. Yet, this job must receive attention; otherwise, the school can be charged with closing its eyes to an urgent fundamental need. Rights and responsibilities must be clearly taught and understood. Sympathy, friendliness, and patience must temper the relations of teachers and pupils. An appreciation of the contributions of different cultural groups must be developed through learning activities that are interesting and concrete enough to influence the behavior of youngsters.

Perhaps the following suggestions can help to make young people regard each other as worthwhile human beings so that America will keep moving toward its ideals of humanity and justice.

1. Make a survey of the major cultural groups represented in this country, considering when and why they came here, and where they settled.

2. On an outline map of the United States, locate and mark concentrations of different groups. Use maps of your town for the same purpose.

3. Make graphs showing:
   a. Numbers of immigrants to this country over periods of several years
   b. Numbers of immigrants from different countries of the world
   c. Number and origin of foreign-born citizens living in this country at present
   d. Composition of class according to national background

4. Study immigration tides in relation to the demand for labor when America's basic industries were being developed. For example:

  a. Importation of Negro slaves from Africa to work in the cotton fields of the South

  b. Use of Chinese coolie labor to help build the Western railroads

  c. Slavic immigration to the Allegheny Valley in Pennsylvania to work in the iron and coal mines, and in the steel mills

5. Prepare a program of songs and dances from different cultural groups. Use native costumes if they can be obtained.

6. Compare words which are nearly the same in English as they are in a foreign language.

7. Listen to recordings of music written by members of groups being studied.

8. Listen to and compare recordings of folk music of groups being studied.

9. Visit art museums to see famous works of art of the native country of each of the groups under consideration.

10. Look at paintings done by Americans of various racial or national origins.

11. Make a study of the handicrafts typical of certain groups. For example, the needlework of the Italian women, the pottery of the Pennsylvania Dutch.

12. Find the sources of some popular American dishes such as goulash, corn bread, spaghetti.

13. Make designs that are similar in motif to those that have distinct national character. Apply these designs to handkerchiefs, clothing, curtains, ceramics, and tablecloths.

14. Invite speakers from various intercultural organizations to tell of the contributions of their groups to American life.

15. Prepare an exhibit of arts and handicrafts typical of various national and racial groups.

16. Read and discuss poems and folk tales of other countries.

17. Discuss the effects of improved transportation and communication on bringing people together.

18. Discuss the effect of the war on intercultural understanding.

19. Let children make scrapbooks entitled

  a. Famous People of My Race

  b. People Like Me

20. Find out the racial and/or national background of famous Americans living today.

21. Discuss motion pictures having authentic cultural material. If possible see some outstanding examples of this type of picture.

22. Have children ask parents and grandparents to tell them about the life they led in other countries and their reasons for coming to the United States.

23. Collect and compare folk tales that have been told to the children by the adults in their families. These may also be compared with stories that children have read.

24. Write and produce a pageant which will illustrate the contributions that immigrants have made to the United States.

25. Arrange a folk festival which will illustrate folk songs and dances of groups represented in class, school, or neighborhood.
26. Visit a Folk Festival, if it is held during the time the class is working on this topic.
27. Relate economic status to causes of prejudice. Children are prejudiced early by quality of dress, amount of spending money received, and kinds of homes their classmates live in. Adults very readily classify occupations on a scale of desirability. It is important that children come to realize that all honest work makes necessary contributions to society.
28. Have pupils correspond with children in other lands. (Use facilities of Junior Red Cross.)
29. Paint a frieze that will show the Americanization of an immigrant. This should cover at least two generations.
30. Study the biographies of outstanding representatives of the cultural groups under consideration.
31. Visit community agencies, churches, stores, markets, restaurants, intercultural agencies which serve the different groups in the city.
32. Use bulletin boards or scrapbooks that have as their theme:
    a. Who's Who?
    b. Hall of Fame
    c. Do You Know?
33. Use any current radio programs which are pertinent to the problem.
34. Study the achievements of members of different groups in the following fields:
    a. Scientific research
        (1) Medicine
        (2) Agriculture
        (3) Industry
        (4) Chemistry
        (5) Communication
        (6) Transportation
    b. The arts
        (1) Music—classical and modern
        (2) Literature
        (3) Painting
        (4) Sculpture
        (5) Architecture
        (6) Interior decorations—furniture, rugs, wall paper, draperies, lamps, pictures, and other decorative articles
        (7) Theater—playwriting, acting, stage designing, lighting
        (8) The dance
        (9) Radio and motion pictures
        (10) Industrial arts—textiles, metals, ceramics, plastics
        (11) Commercial art
    c. Government
        (1) Local

(2) State

(3) National

D. Let religion speak.

Children are aware of religious differences. It's a fact that even the very young may have strong religious prejudices. These are often expressed in name-calling, formation of cliques and gangs, and fighting. Yet close examination of the spirit of various religions will reveal many elements that should promote rather than destroy unity.

This part of the unit presents a few learning activities that might be used to stimulate thought about some of the important similarities of Protestantism, Catholicism, and Judaism. No more than that is intended.

It's a job to be done delicately and with sensitivity. It's a job that adult groups are attempting today. We in the schools may have a part in helping to form desirable interreligious attitudes.

1. Make a list of the religious groups found in the neighborhood.

2. Discuss various definitions of religion.

3. Discuss standards of right and wrong as taught in every religion. Emphasize the fact that all Jews, Catholics, and Protestants worship the same God and base their principles on the same Ten Commandments.

4. Some children may wish to read and discuss *One God* by Florence Mary Fitch.

5. Make a collection of newspaper and magazine articles which tell of incidents that demonstrate the fact that members of one religious group can work with and help those of another. There are many such stories being printed, especially those relating to the armed forces.

6. Invite a priest, a minister, and a rabbi to visit the class to talk to the children and answer their questions.

7. Visit a Jewish Synagogue, a Catholic Church, and a Protestant Church. Arrange, in each case, to have the rabbi, priest, or minister present to show the children around, and answer their questions.

8. Write and produce plays demonstrating religious living together. Plan assembly programs or pageants to celebrate Jewish and Christian festivals which occur at approximately the same time of year.

9. Study biographies of some outstanding religious leaders and their contributions to American life.

10. Examine prayers and hymns used by members of different faiths for points of similarity.

11. Discuss the fact that many of the early settlers came to this country for religious freedom. Visit old churches.

12. Examine newspapers and magazines for examples of religious tolerance and intolerance in modern times.

13. Discuss the effects of intolerance on life in America.

14. Collect and display pictures of the interior of churches and synagogues, of various religious services and of symbols used by different religious groups.

15. Collect copies of and discuss some of the great paintings inspired by religion to see how religion has influenced art.
16. Study pictures of famous stained-glass windows found in some of the great churches of the world to find the influence of common beliefs in religion.
17. Have children make designs of stained-glass windows using religious symbols.
18. Listen to recordings of religious music by famous choruses, and discuss the emotions which these engender. Include Negro spirituals.
19. Read and analyze poems which present ethical standards that are expressed by many religions.
20. Study poems based on religious legends.
21. Study poems, stories, war correspondents' reports, letters, and messages from the battle fronts which express religious sentiments.
22. Point out that no one can be a good Catholic, a good Protestant, or a good Jew if he does not practice "charity for all and malice toward none."

III. Part Three: Evaluation—are we getting any results?

It is the belief of the writers that teachers should assume a responsibility for doing work on this vital spot in social relations. This resource unit is offered as a possible help. We realize that many people have successfully worked out their own techniques and materials. For others who recognize a need for doing constructive work on intercultural education, perhaps what we suggest will be helpful.

It is extremely difficult to find out how children change their attitudes and behavior toward people of other races, nationalities, and religions. Testing is usually complex and often unrelated to the heart of the problem—the emotionally charged reactions that compel people to cling to their prejudices.

Teachers will know—from the numerous and varied interactions among pupils, spoken and unspoken, change in facial expression, friendships and enmities that are acquired—just how deep or superficial are the misunderstandings that exist in the classroom. This is the evaluation that goes on continuously; naturally the evaluator, the teacher, will interpret with varying degrees of accuracy.

A teacher should feel it necessary to know if he is getting anywhere with work that has been stimulated by suggestions taken from the resource unit. The informal, observational kind of appraisal has already been recognized as important. The writers have organized other materials that can be used for evaluation. There will follow listings of situations, right and wrong concepts, and forms of prejudice that may be used as (1) a basis for discussion, (2) a means of securing individual or group written reactions, (3) a stimulation for research.

A. True or false test
1. The Constitution of the United States can help you find your rights as a citizen.

2. Everything in the Constitution of the United States is carried out by all Americans.
3. Nobody pays much attention to the Constitution because it was written long ago.
4. A man whose parents were born in the United States has more rights than a foreign-born citizen.
5. Our democracy is perfect.
6. Our democracy is becoming better.
7. All religions are entirely different.
8. Many people are friendly towards people who belong to different religious or racial groups.
9. Different kinds of people should live in separate parts of the city.
10. A master race would help to give us good leaders.
11. Only the English have helped to build up this country.
12. History should tell about outstanding leaders only.
13. All people who come from the same country behave in the same way.
14. You can judge a person from the things you hear about him.
15. Once you have formed your opinion about a person you should never change it.
16. One way of checking on facts about any group of people is to use good reference books.
17. Another way of checking on facts about a group of people is to take the word of someone you like.
18. Protestants, Catholics, and Jews worship the same God.
19. If enough people believe a rumor, then it must be true.
20. Poor home conditions keep people from making the best of themselves.
21. All people who come from poor homes never get very far in life.
22. The real cause of prejudice is fear.
23. Good health and brightness in school go together.
24. Different races have different kinds of blood.
25. If you believe in a thing for a long time, it must be true.
26. A superstition is a fact but no one can prove this.
27. The main races of mankind are Aryan and Jewish.
28. You can easily judge a race of people from the actions of ten people who belong to that race.
29. Some people have no prejudices.
30. All prejudices are harmful.

NOTE: More than one answer is possible for some of the items included above. Differences in reactions may serve as a basis for worthwhile discussion.

B. Test on emotional reaction

How would you feel?

a. Glad; *b.* Sorry; *c.* Angry; *d.* No feeling at all

IF?

1. You found out that three girls in your room were spreading a false rumor about another girl.

2. Someone called you a name that showed a lack of respect for your religion.
3. Someone called a stranger a name that showed a lack of respect for his religion.
4. The boys in your class refused to vote for a Jewish boy for class president.
5. A classmate was having a party and had invited everyone in the class except a Negro girl.
6. Your classmates made fun of a new pupil who had a strange way of talking.
7. Your class was made up of members of six national and three religious groups, and they got along very well.
8. Your class would not make friends with a new pupil whose nationality was different from that of any other pupil in the room.
9. You over heard a conversation in which a man said, "All foreigners should be sent back to the country they came from."
10. You found out that a group of boys were going to gang up on one boy because he had just moved into the neighborhood.
11. Everybody lived according to the ideas that were written in the Constitution of the United States.
12. All people were treated fairly and squarely.
13. The people who believed in a superior race decided that their idea of a superior race was all wrong.
14. America became a model of equality.
15. You helped to clear up a misunderstanding between two friends of yours.

NOTE: Here, too, opinions will vary, and there are no absolute answers to many questions.

C. Test on tolerance

What would you do?

a. Nothing; b. Get the facts; c. Agree; d. Disagree; e. Try to prevent trouble; f. Call the police; g. Fight; h. Ask for teacher's help.

IF?

1. A boy you knew said that Jews did not believe in the same God as Christians.
2. A group of your friends said things about a classmate that you knew were not true.
3. You argued with a friend and neither one of you was convinced.
4. You picked up a circular and on it were printed terrible things against one group of Americans.
5. Your friend was prejudiced against foreign-born Americans.
6. Many people you knew refused to make friends with you because your religion was different from theirs.
7. Someone said, "Hitler was right!"
8. You realized you had a harmful prejudice and you wanted to get rid of it.

9. You had a prejudice against certain foods.
10. Someone you liked was ridiculed by most of your class because she spoke with a foreign accent.

NOTE: Here, too, take advantage of the diversity of reaction to increase understanding.

SUPPOSE?

1. Four candidates, competing for the office of council president, are presented to the school. One candidate is Jewish; three are Italian. If a pupil votes for the Jewish candidate it should be only because:
   a. The candidate is Jewish.
   b. The candidate seems to be the one best qualified.
   c. The Jewish students in the school are in the majority.
   d. You want to give the Jewish candidate a "break."

2. A group of people sitting in a trolley, and belonging to one nationality group, annoy the rest of the people by loud talking and laughing. Would you:
   a. Think to yourself that all people of that nationality group are the same?
   b. Try to forget what the group is doing?
   c. Try to think about other people in that national group who are well behaved?

3. Trouble, outside the school, has developed between two racial groups. Would you:
   a. Take sides immediately?
   b. Take sides after you find the facts?
   c. Keep out of the thing altogether?
   d. Try to get the two groups together, with the help of the school?

4. A friend whom you always considered fair-minded suddenly shows by his words and actions that he has a strong prejudice against a racial group.
   Would you:
   a. Pay no attention to his prejudice because of your friendship?
   b. Try to find out what has caused the prejudice?
   c. Try to soften the prejudice?
   d. Give up your friendship immediately?
   e. Give up your friendship if the prejudice lasts?
   f. Try to acquaint your friend with good people and good deeds in the racial group for which he has his prejudice.
   g. Accept your friend's prejudice and adopt it as your own?[12]

NOTE: Use the sample situations as an illustration of a technique you can employ for the purposes of discussion or for written reactions.

---

12. Pennsylvania State Department of Public Instruction, *Curriculum Improvement by a Secondary School Faculty* (*Bulletin* No. 243; Harrisburg, Pa., 1950), pp. 134–144.

Chapter Seventeen

Developing

Classroom Units

WE HAVE STRESSED the fact that the resource unit is the teacher's homework in the sense that she, and usually a group of teachers working with her, prepare the resource unit in advance of the time it is to be taught. These units may be prepared a summer in advance or sometime during the year, and they may even be designed to serve for a few years, with major changes and modifications in bibliographical materials and teaching aids as evaluation of the unit shows changes necessary and as new materials become available.

The resource unit is built for the study of certain fundamental social and personal problems which have been discovered to be pertinent to needs of youth in the community. The decision as to the nature of the resource unit is a matter of basic curriculum planning and construction; the unit should be appropriate to the underlying philosophy of the curriculum program of a particular school. After the outline of the resource unit has been made and all the material has been secured for its construction, the teacher is ready to take the material and shape it to meet the needs which she has with a particular class.

The resource unit serves two basic purposes: first, it offers a wide and varied storehouse of suggested classroom techniques and content to be used in actual situations; second, it indicates the broad areas necessary to adequate understanding of the purposes of the unit. From these, individual teachers in classes may develop specific teaching units according to their interests and needs.

The teaching units may develop different centers of interest, degrees of difficulty, and points appropriate to a particular class, but they should all aim at the same objectives. Each teacher may use the same resource unit, while each develops for her particular class a different teaching unit. The teaching unit essentially grows out of her judgment of the needs, interests, and abilities of a particular group of pupils as they approach a basic problem which has been determined as having value for all pupils at a given age and time. Each one of these teaching units is an actual plan prepared from the resource unit for use day by day in the classroom. It may be planned by teachers, but it is preferable to have it planned by both students and teachers. The teacher may use the resource unit as a guide for discussing certain ideas with her pupils and for calling attention to certain activities and materials supplemented by the suggestions offered by the pupils.

Resource units differ from teaching units in that resource units are prepared for use by teachers and not by pupils. They cover a broad area rather than a specific topic or problem. They contain more material than can be used with any one class. They offer various possibilities for achieving the same objectives, and they are so organized that they possess possibilities for developing several teaching units. Furthermore, the material suggested in the resource unit provides varying degrees of difficulty and it contains suggestions which may apply to many classes.

The teaching unit, on the other hand, is organized around one central problem, issue, idea or topic. All the materials of the resource unit that bear directly upon this problem or topic, together with the activities which may be appropriate for the individuals in the class, constitute the principal aspects of the teaching unit. A resource unit in only an outline of possibility. The teaching unit is a definite blue print for studying a problem in a class. In the resource unit a large number of activities may be suggested. In the teaching unit a definite selection has to be made of which ones to use. In the resource unit dozens of films, recordings, books, magazines, and pamphlets may be suggested as possibilities. In the teaching unit these are narrowed down to the exact few which may be useful or available to the particular teacher. In the resource unit a number of objectives similar in character but specifically related to the broad problem or topic are outlined. In a teaching unit these goals are usually narrowed to a few which are attainable by a particular class and are supported by principles, activities, problems, and materials which are needed to attain these goals and which can be evaluated after the unit has been taught. Both the resource unit and the teaching unit are organized materials. They represent preplanning at its best.

Planning a Teaching Unit

Planning a teaching unit involves knowledge of the content of the area to be studied, knowledge of the general curriculum program of the school, an understanding of the abilities and interests of the students who have been in class, a knowledge of the resource materials in school and community that are available for use by the pupils, and insight on the part of the teacher of the potential goals that may be achieved within a reasonable time with a given class as a result of well-organized and well-planned instruction.

A teaching unit usually includes

1. A statement of specific objectives in terms of behavioral changes desired in pupils

2. A topical outline or a list of questions phrased in terms of student language which may be used to select the content to be utilized

3. A specific list of activities and projects which should be useful or helpful for all of the pupils in the class

4. Those activities which would be especially valuable for particular individuals with different interests in a given class

5. References which provide the information needed. These should be specified in very definite terms so that the pupil will not be required to read dozens of pages in order to find a few particular ideas.

6. Suggestions for evaluation should be included in the teaching unit. These will be useful and necessary each step of the way.

In order to develop a teaching unit a teacher should follow certain definite steps:

1. She should familiarize herself with the materials in the resource unit by reading the introduction, checking objectives she hopes to develop, checking generalizations that she thinks can be accomplished by her pupils, reading carefully and selecting the materials she thinks are most likely to meet the needs and interests of all her pupils and those which would be helpful in stimulating additional interests and in caring for specific individual differences, and studying suggestions for evaluation.

2. She should read the books and pamphlets listed in the bibliography that are available in the library or may be made available in the classroom or in the community. These should be carefully checked for paging, illustrations, type of content, difficulty of wording, specific relationship to topics, and many other items that determine whether the actual reference material can be economically, intelligently, and effectively utilized.

3. She should be familiar with all community resources that may be

utilized in the unit. Some definite planning will have to be made for the utilization of individuals or institutions within a community. She should also examine and study the various visual aids, preview films, records, slides, and any other type of visual material which she can select to use in the unit.

Finally, from these she builds up a careful outline of those things most appropriate to her own individual class. This, then, is her homework in the second stage. It is the stage where she takes the general over-all material that she and others have prepared and builds it into a program for her own situation. Once these basic selections are made, she will then need to give consideration to the way in which the problem may be approached by the students.[1]

Cooperative Planning by Pupils and Teachers

In recent years, much stress has been given to the fact that teachers and pupils together should plan what finally goes into the teaching units in the classroom. There are several reasons for this, the most significant ones being

1. Such a process teaches pupils the principles, meaning, and procedures of cooperative group planning which is so necessary in modern life.

2. The utilization of such a procedure will ensure that the pupils in the class become naturally interested in studying the problem because they have participated in planning it.

3. The teacher is more likely to find that the problems, activities, and topics selected for study will be more closely in harmony with the interests and capacities of the students if they have a part in determining them than if the teacher determines them alone.

4. Individual differences will be more readily met because pupils with all shades of differences will participate in selecting the activities.

5. By the process of pupil and teacher planning ideas grow beyond what either the teacher or the group would be likely to consider alone, and thus the teaching unit is enriched.

If appropriate and well-ordered planning is to result from the teacher and pupils working together, certain principles will need to prevail. Stephen Corey suggested the following principles of cooperative group work:

1. The goals must be such that group activity will expedite their attainment. Many satisfactions can be achieved. Much worthy and educative work can be done in a highly individualistic manner. A great number of the

---

1. For further suggestions for preliminary planning see Ruth G. Strickland, *How to Build a Unit of Work* (U.S. Office of Education *Bulletin* No. 5; Washington: Government Printing Office, 1946), pp. 1–2.

cynical comments about democratic activity result because teachers and others demonstrate their devotion to group planning by voting on everything. The only rational justification of cooperative group activities is a pragmatic one. It must lead to greater satisfactions to members of the group than any feasible alternative procedure. In the long run, children or teachers, when on their own, will continue to engage in cooperative group planning and action if they have learned that it gets them more of what they want, broadly defined, faster, and more smoothly.

2. Work is undertaken that is relevant to the goals that the group wants to achieve.

The important thing in this connection is that the members of the group accept or appreciate or want to attain the goals suggested. This appreciation must be genuine . . . the standards of achievement that count and that actually motivate cooperative group work are the standards accepted by the members of the group.

3. Activities in cooperative group work are in sequence: (*a*) clarification of goals or purposes, (*b*) consideration of means for the attainment of these goals, (*c*) action in terms of the means decided upon, and (*d*) appraisals or evaluations of consequences.

Pedagogically the soundest procedure is for these steps to emerge from evaluation of a number of projects. The only value in any analysis of procedural sequences is that attention to *each* often assures more successful work. It is obvious, of course, that each of the four steps is not taken seriatim and cleaned up before the next is approached. Goal clarification, for example, frequently goes on throughout the group activity.

4. There is a free interplay of mind during all stages of the cooperative activity.

This free interplay of minds is more than mere talk. It is pertinent talk. To engage in such discussions calls for much practice. Exchanging views in a fashion actually to communicate them is hard work. Most children and adults are unaccustomed to discussions that are relevant to a project, that are neither *ad hominem* nor repetitious and that lead to action.

5. A consensus of opinion is striven for.

The necessity for having a cooperatively working group eventually of one mind in all essentials (except in a discussion group) has many implications. In the first place, it means that progress will be slower than some members of the group desire. The second implication is that, while a group allocation of responsibility to individuals or committees is in the interest of efficiency, the entire group, in order to be kept of one mind, must not only be apprised constantly of what is going on, but must know that it can affect what is going on. In other words, the responsibility cannot only be assigned, but it can be withdrawn.

6. Cooperative projects tend to grow out of an existing group structure.

In schools the conventional class or room arrangement imposes a rigidity of organization that almost precludes the spontaneous forming of groups to undertake cooperative work with much intellectual content, or in which teachers are resources and hence apt to know what goes on and be able to report it. This condition in schools is somewhat analogous to American society in general. The interest should be in achieving some common goal that can be reached more readily by cooperative attack. Advantages are gained if the members of the group can feel no guilt when, after the project is completed, the group dissolves. The fact that new projects grow out of old ones may keep such groups intact longer than was originally contemplated.

7. Specific cooperative work projects usually lead to other projects.

Experience is continuous and all new interests grow out of preceding ones. Work that represents an assignment is of a different order. An assignment is a circumscribed activity. It is a request to perform certain acts and by implication to quit. It is often an indication of a degree of coercion with respect to group definition when all members of an original group decide to work together again upon a subsequent activity.[2]

It is obvious, therefore, that pupils and teachers can gain much by planning units together. Some teachers do this by taking a resource unit, developing from it an outline of a teaching unit, mimeographing it, and presenting it to the pupils. As soon as the pupils have it in hand, the teacher discusses it and asks them for suggestions or additions, for changes and for any alterations that should be made before the unit is begun. This however is a very doubtful way of enlisting any real genuine enthusiasm on the part of pupils in actually planning a unit. The more successful teacher will probably be the more clever one—that is the one who has a thorough understanding and command of the teaching unit, but who does not reveal her hand on what she has planned until she has thoroughly introduced the idea to the pupils and then has genuinely enlisted their cooperation in group planning as the unit progresses. There is little reason for a teacher to ask a particular group of pupils if they would like to study a given topic. Many times the answer is "no," and many times pupils will not propose any topics to study that will fit directly into the generally planned curriculum of the school. Pupils must, of necessity, accept the basic purposes of any educational experience, but they do not need of their own volition to create and initiate these purposes for them to be valid and acceptable to them. Therefore it devolves upon the teacher to plan the introduction of the unit into the classroom and, on the basis of these initial plans, to establish sufficiently a proper rapport and understanding with the pupils so that throughout the study of the unit constant pupil participation and continued planning will result.

---

2. Department of Supervision and Curriculum Development, *Group Planning in Education* (1945 Yearbook; Washington: National Education Association, 1945), Chap. 6, by Stephen M. Corey, pp. 131–138.

Initiating the Unit

Suppose the teacher has developed the resource unit, which we illustrated in the previous chapter, "How Can We Learn to Appreciate Our Neighbors." It is assumed that the pupils are interested in this general problem, or that the problem is of crucial importance in the community, otherwise the resource unit should not have been built. The teacher may then go into the classroom to explore the problem with the pupils. She is anxious to know the extent to which the pupils sense the nature and meaning of the problem. She can start this exploration in a number of different ways. Recent events in the community, for instance, such as an outbreak of racial or religious intolerance, an inflammatory speech or newspaper article may provide a starting point; or she may plan definite experiences to initiate the unit such as the showing of a film, the telling of a story, the introduction of certain superstitions, or even a tea party with a group of children from foreign countries or from different cultures represented in the community. At any rate, the ingenious teacher will find a way to initiate a discussion of the problem.

Once the discussion is started, the teacher has the job of working with the pupils to outline the problem, discuss work to be done, determine areas to be explored, choose references, decide upon trips, choose individual, group, or total-class projects, and of planning the schedule of the activities. This is no time for the teacher to pull out her teaching unit and hand it to the pupils. She may refer to it now and then, but the organization and selection of the material for the problem should be a responsibility of the group working cooperatively to select and plan those materials centering around the basic ideas agreed upon after the unit has been properly initiated and accepted by all members of the group as an important area of study. This will undoubtedly take some time—two or three days—but it is worth all of that time. It really saves time later on. More than that, it teaches pupils how to organize and plan their own work. This is an important skill for them to learn.

This planning period, however, is not restricted to two or three days. The unit should be planned carefully, but it should also be changed as work on it progresses, so that during the entire time of study there may likewise be a continuous period of planning. Such questions as the following should constantly be asked: What are the problems in this area? What should we know and do? What materials and people should we consult? What will each of us do? What behaviors are desired after the study of the problem? How do we evaluate the results of our work? How should we present the results? In the process of examining these questions, the teacher can teach planning, group cooperation, selection of important and unimportant items, outlining and sharing of ideas—all significant outcomes of education.

When the teacher gets the work under way, making sure that the total group sees clearly the purposes it will get from the study, and when each individual has proposed his own additional purposes, the teacher must endeavor to select a sufficient variety of activities, have on hand a large number of resources, constantly keep the group and the individual proceeding together, and continuously plan and replan for success with each individual, as well as with the total group. Discussion reports, visual aids, trips, interviews, reading, instruction, and other types of activities suited both to the development of the desired goals and to the abilities of individuals, should be constantly supplied and evaluated.

Culminating the Unit

After the material outlined in the unit has been studied, it is frequently wise to have culminating or summarizing activities. Students can draw their conclusions and try to put them into action, or they may make some reports which will be of interest to the class or to individuals within the community. Some of the reports might even be given to the entire school. This last procedure is not necessary; however, it is valuable to summarize what has been gained within a class. A feeling of accomplishment and satisfaction should be felt by the whole class. They should relate their experiences to what they have already learned, studied, or observed in and out of school.

Many times group projects, such as student-made movies, plays, radio skits, or quiz programs, reflect an understanding by the students of the problems considered, and their growth in the skills necessary for organization and presentation is easily detected. Exhibits may be used as concrete proofs of definite participation. Written work often gives the pupils a chance to demonstrate individual interests and competencies, to select pertinent material, to suggest solutions to problems, and to demonstrate developments over preceding periods in basic skills and principles of organization. In using the problem approach, generalizations may be presented by the use of discussion groups or panel discussions or even by use of socio-dramas. Tests which show the pupils' individual grasp of the problems and their ability to express themselves clearly and correctly are also valuable. Self-appraisal by means of graphs, charts, or short papers may make the student more aware of his own growth. Direct action sometimes may be attained through community projects such as clean-up campaigns, surveys of immediate needs in housing or recreation facilities, or participation in community agencies. All these kinds of activities give the teacher and the group an opportunity to summarize and relate to the whole the details, individual projects, and committee work in which they have participated.

Evaluating the Unit

As the unit is being taught, the teacher should constantly evaluate its success in terms of selection, content, methods, and materials used. She should, of course, evaluate it primarily in terms of the effect it has upon achieving the ends or purposes of education for which it was taught in the first place. One of the better lists of criteria for judging the value of units and the activities in them was prepared by the teachers of the Denver, Colorado, public schools. These criteria will illustrate the need and means of evaluating a unit of work from the standpoint of a teacher's subjective analysis.

JUDGING THE PROMISE OR THE RESULTS OF A TEACHING UNIT

Denver Public Schools

Directions: This list of questions is to help teachers and pupils in judging the value of units of activity. Use the upper words in the parentheses if the unit is proposed for future use and the lower words if the unit has just been completed. Notice carefully this answer key:

Answer Key

1 means to a minimum degree or not at all
2 means to a small degree
3 means to a moderate degree
4 means to a large degree
5 means to a maximum or the largest possible degree

Read each question carefully; decide which of the above numbers will, in your judgment, indicate the correct answer and then circle that number on your answer sheet. Watch that the answer you circle is numbered the same as the question you are answering.

A. *How well is the unit likely to meet important needs of the pupils?* (*or, how well did it meet such needs?*)

1. (Does) (Did) the unit have its origin in an important need experienced by the pupils?

2. (Do) (Did) the pupils believe that the purpose of the unit of activity (is) (was) worth while?

3. (Will) (Did) the unit reproduce actual life situations as far as possible?

4. (Will) (Did) the unit provide abundant opportunity for projects or activities based upon individual interests and needs?

5. Have the pupils cooperated with each other and with the teacher in selecting and planning the unit?

6. $\dfrac{\text{(Does)}}{\text{(Did)}}$ each pupil have opportunity to enjoy success in one or more activities of the unit?

7. $\dfrac{\text{(Is)}}{\text{(Was)}}$ the unit of such interest that the pupils $\dfrac{\text{(are likely to go)}}{\text{(went)}}$ through with it successfully?

B. *How well is the unit likely to fit into the past experiences and present activities of the class and its members? (or, how well did it fit in?)*

8. Have the members of the class had a similar activity on an *easier* level in a previous school grade?

9. To what extent $\dfrac{\text{(is)}}{\text{(was)}}$ the unit a useful extension or development of interesting activities in previous grades?

10. To what extent $\dfrac{\text{(have)}}{\text{(had)}}$ the out-of-school experiences of the pupils prepared them to take advantage of the experience of the unit?

11. $\dfrac{\text{(Will)}}{\text{(Did)}}$ the pupils have the knowledge, skills, and other abilities needed to carry on the activities successfully or $\dfrac{\text{(can)}}{\text{(did)}}$ they master them in reasonable time?

12. $\dfrac{\text{(Will)}}{\text{(Did)}}$ this unit provide for consistent growth toward the accepted goals of education?

13. $\dfrac{\text{(Will)}}{\text{(Did)}}$ the activities tie in with and give more meaning to other units?

14. $\dfrac{\text{(Will)}}{\text{(Did)}}$ the activities help pupils to be more successful in important out-of-school activities in which they $\dfrac{\text{(are)}}{\text{(were)}}$ engaged?

C. *How richly* $\dfrac{\textit{(will)}}{\textit{(did)}}$ *the unit provide for the values of democratic living?*

15. $\dfrac{\text{(Will the pupils)}}{\text{(Did the pupils)}}$ share in planning, carrying on, and evaluating the unit?

16. How much opportunity $\dfrac{\text{(will)}}{\text{(did)}}$ the unit provide for intelligent pupil self-direction?

17. $\dfrac{\text{(Will)}}{\text{(Did)}}$ the unit give experience in scientific thinking?

18. $\dfrac{\text{(Will)}}{\text{(Did)}}$ the unit promote development of attitudes and abilities, important in working democratically with others?

19. $\dfrac{\text{(Will)}}{\text{(Did)}}$ the unit encourage creative thinking and activity?

20. To what extent $\frac{(will)}{(did)}$ the pupils recognize the major purpose of the unit in all of its activities?

21. $\frac{(Will)}{(Did)}$ the unit contribute to the understanding of the institutions and values of our democratic society?

D. *What resources of curriculum materials, of leadership, and of community contacts* $\frac{(are)}{(were)}$ *available?*

22. $\frac{(Are)}{(Were)}$ the textbook, library, and other reading materials sufficient and well suited?

23. How sufficient $\frac{(are)}{(were)}$ visual aids such as charts, maps, pictures, lantern slides, motion pictures, and the like?

24. How well $\frac{(will)}{(did)}$ the unit use current periodicals and newspapers, and other materials as they occur in life?

25. $\frac{(Can)}{(Did)}$ the available staff (teachers and others whose assistance $\frac{(can\ be)}{(was)}$ secured), give adequate direction for the effective development of the unit?

26. $\frac{(Will\ there\ be)}{(Were\ there)}$ sufficient time and assistance for gathering, evaluating, and experimenting with materials?

27. To what extent $\frac{(will)}{(did)}$ the unit enable pupils to use the community for illustrative materials and learning experiences?

28. $\frac{(Does)}{(Did)}$ the unit provide opportunity for a variety of activities other than reading, writing, and talking?

E. *To what extent* $\frac{(is)}{(was)}$ *evaluation of the results of the activity practicable?*

29. $\frac{(Will)}{(Did)}$ the unit offer opportunity for frequent cooperative evaluation of success and for reorganization of activities in the light of evaluation?

30. $\frac{(Can\ evaluations\ be)}{(Were\ evaluations)}$ made of each pupil's acquisition of working tools and methods of procedure?

31. $\frac{(Can\ evaluations\ be)}{(Were\ evaluations)}$ made of each pupil's social adaptability?

32. $\frac{(Can\ evaluations\ be)}{(Were\ evaluations)}$ made of each pupil's growth in social understandings and in ability and disposition to carry social responsibility?

33. $\dfrac{\text{(Will)}}{\text{(Did)}}$ the unit offer opportunity to evaluate both individual and group success?

34. $\dfrac{\text{(Can evaluations be)}}{\text{(Was evaluation)}}$ interpreted by both teacher and pupils in relation to all-around development of personality?

35. $\dfrac{\text{(Can evaluations be)}}{\text{(Were evaluations)}}$ easily reported to parents, colleges, or others who may have a right to know?[3]

Suggestions have been made for judging the success of a unit from the standpoint of a teacher's subjective analysis. For the work of each unit, the teachers and students should be so oriented that the unit may end with a critical analysis of the entire procedure, activities, and outcomes. Some of the following questions would be helpful in this analysis.

FOR THE GROUP

1. How has the unit increased the students' ability to adjust to personal, family, and community relations?
2. Has language growth contributed to awareness, understanding, and appreciation of world conditions?
3. Have the students worked effectively in groups?
4. Have they helped in planning and developing the work of the unit?
5. What use have they made of community resources?
6. Do they evaluate their own group work?

FOR THE INDIVIDUAL

1. Has the student increased his ability to listen carefully and critically?
2. Has he increased his reading speed and comprehension?
3. What has he learned from both intensive and extensive reading?
4. Is he reading for pleasure?
5. Does he recognize the beauty and meaning of what he has read, heard, and seen?
6. Has he gained in ability to speak with poise and confidence?
7. Has the work of this unit helped him to find something to write and speak about and to express his thoughts in a fluent, acceptably correct style?
8. Has his efficiency increased in the use of library and audio-visual aid material?
9. Has he offered all that he could in planning and accomplishing the class work?
10. Does he evaluate his own growth?

FOR THE TEACHER

1. What has been the attitude of the class toward the unit?

---

3. Mimeographed outline from Denver, Colorado, Public Schools.

2. Has it held the interest of the group?
3. Has it aided in developing the particular standard set for the grade in speaking and listening, reading and understanding, appreciation, writing, and music?
4. Has it helped to disclose and correct individual weaknesses in the use of the communicative skills?
5. Have we seen any definite changes in the attitude and behavior in the class as individuals and in groups?
6. Have we observed increased freedom in student-problem solving?
7. Does the individual student show growth in adjusting to class and life situations?
8. Have you seen any evidence of improvement in performance?[4]

Reporting on the Unit

After each unit has been taught the teacher should make a report on it for his own future guidance and for use by the whole school in continuing to build the curriculum program of the school. This report, which should be attached to the source unit and filed for future use, may be written in several different ways. One way to save time and yet be quite complete is to check the actual teaching unit against the source unit. The items listed below should be taken into consideration, along with the accompanying suggestions.

1. Prepare a short statement on the nature of the pupils using the unit, including such items as their grade and maturity, major interests, vocational plans, general and special abilities.
2. Check the objectives of the unit you feel you actually achieved and add others not originally in the source unit.
3. Describe how you initiated the unit and how successful you were. Tell the situation out of which the problem arose, what the pupils proposed to do, the plan of work followed, and the division of work the pupils actually carried out.
4. Describe the various teaching procedures you used and comment on their success. Add others you want to try next time.
5. Tell how you closed the unit.
6. Check the bibliography, visual aids, sources you actually used, and evaluate them. Add others not previously listed.
7. Indicate nature, address, purpose, and evaluation of excursions, trips and interviews made.
8. Check the activities you actually carried out against those previously listed in the source unit.

---

4. San Francisco Unified School District, *Senior Goals* (San Francisco, Calif., 1951), pp. 16–17. Mimeographed.

9. Evaluate the weakness and strength of the unit, the appropriateness and setup of the unit, suggestions for improvement.

A description of a unit taught in a high school in Pennsylvania may serve further to illustrate how a unit once taught may be reported. Such reports may have great value in making plans for teaching aspects of it from year to year.

UNEMPLOYMENT AND FUTURE EMPLOYMENT

Report of a Completed Experience Unit in Problems of Democracy

I. Approach

The students decided that they wanted to do a unit of study like a previous one on crime. Several topics were offered by the pupils and put on the board. The topic chosen by the majority was Unemployment and Future Employment.

II. Objectives

A. To understand the reasons for unemployment
B. To find remedies for unemployment
C. To contact various agencies and arrange for speakers to address the class
D. To obtain films on unemployment and the possibilities of future employment
E. To arrange field trips to various industries
F. To find out facts about all types of employment, such as salary, sex, future, and other information
G. The students at the end of the unit will give their ideas concerning the strength and weaknesses of the "Teacher and Pupil Planning Method."

III. Skills (students)

A. To learn how to cooperate and work with one another
B. To learn how to look up reference material and tabulate it
C. To learn how to read charts, diagrams, and graphs
D. To find out by field trips what is needed to keep industry going in our township as well as in the State
E. To find out by direct observation on field trips why an education is extremely necessary
F. To get over the fear of meeting strangers by interviewing them
G. To learn how to contact agencies and obtain data
H. To learn how to find the strengths and weaknesses of films

IV. Procedure

A. The student chairman on the project took her place in front of the desk to arrange the groups.
B. The students and teachers decided to divide the class into *three* groups, each group taking two objectives.
C. Each student decided, by secret ballot vote, what group he preferred.

D. The student chairman then appointed two pupils to help arrange the names and the respective groups.

E. We found that we had a majority of students in two of the groups and a small minority in one. The chairman then appealed to the students for some of them to leave the majority groups and go to the minority one so as to make the groups more nearly equal in number. After a little discussion in the class, the chairman secured a fair division into groups.

F. Each subgroup selected its chairman.

G. The student chairman took the names of each group and recorded them in the unit notebook.

H. The instructor told the groups to hold discussions and formulate their plans while he took the chairmen aside for a conference on procedure.

I. The instructor and the chairmen developed various procedures for the chairmen to follow.

J. The groups decided by popular vote to give a report to the class every three days.

K. A summarization would be given by each group.

L. At the end of the unit a test would be given to each group.

M. The chairman of each group would evaluate the work of his group for the instructor in a way cooperatively developed.

V. Activities

A. Speakers

B. Oral and written reports

C. Films

D. Interviews in and out of school

E. Field trips

F. Agencies contacted for material

G. Cartoons and pictures

H. Charts, diagrams, and graphs

I. Library research for material

VI. Weaknesses (evaluated by students)

A. Some people do more work than others. (60 per cent voted)

B. The method creates some loafers as chairman shows favoritism in certain respects. (85 per cent voted)

C. Committees were not evenly selected according to intelligence.

D. Lack of library reference material. (100 per cent voted)

E. Room too small for groups as each group had a tendency to get noisy. (100 per cent voted)

F. Teachers don't get enough opportunity for making contact with individual students. (50 per cent voted)

G. Each room should have an ample supply of dictionaries and a good library shelf. (100 per cent voted)

H. One group finished before the others; the teacher had to keep them busy. (100 per cent voted)

VII. Strengths (evaluated by students)

    A. This method is intended to take care of the interest of each student. (90 per cent voted)

    B. Speaker from outside the school gave up-to-date interpretations of unemployment. (100 per cent voted)

    C. Students learn more by working together. (90 per cent voted)

    D. Students got others' points of view. (100 per cent voted)

    E. Students remember content longer than they would by textbook study. (100 per cent voted)

    F. More interesting. (100 per cent voted)

    G. We learned what type of work we are suited for from our Agency Committee because they received actual data reports from various field agencies. Such materials are not obtainable from the textbook; the teacher may be asked to obtain them for the class. (100 per cent voted)

    H. We had a variety of angles and ways to approach the subject. (100 per cent voted)

    I. Movies made the subject more interesting and we saw the facts shown to us on the screen. (100 per cent voted)

    J. Field trip to James Lees and Sons was very educational. (100 per cent voted)

    K. It's easier. (100 per cent voted)

    L. No homework. We like the subject better this way. (100 per cent voted)

    M. We learned through actual experience. (90 per cent voted)

VIII. Outcomes (evaluated by teacher)

    A. The groups worked very well in most instances. They attained as a whole very good results for their objectives.

    B. The chairman followed instructions in most cases, but they seemed to be afraid to keep certain individuals busy as they should have done. The teacher stepped in several times and straightened out difficulties in various groups.

    C. The teacher is enabled to keep moving from one group to another.

    D. The groups in selecting their chairmen seemed to base their choice on popularity rather than ability.

IX. How to avoid main difficulties (evaluated by teacher)

    A. Students getting finished sooner than expected

        1. Have plans in addition to your original one to offset this difficulty.

        2. If the student or students are exceptional, have them help the slow groups.

        3. Put the brighter students on material which you have found too difficult for the average student.

    B. Loafing

        1. A daily check is made by chairmen and the teacher.

        2. Keep visiting the groups frequently so as to keep them on the alert.

3. If the student is dissatisfied with his group, find another one for him or find special work to keep him busy.

C. Different group projects being attained by all
1. Have each group summarize its material.
2. Have each group mimeograph or ditto its material.
3. Have each student receive a copy of everything that has been done in the class.

D. Oral reports
1. Make sure that the main topics of the report are received by all students. This could be done by ditto or mimeograph.
2. Teacher could teach as a drill method the proper procedure in taking notes. This is good training for life outside the school.

E. Lack of material
1. This seems to be one of the main difficulties in certain units of study.
2. Outside material must be secured by the groups and the teacher. The library doesn't always have enough material available.
3. Teacher must have the problem of materials in mind before the unit is set up and make preparations to meet this difficulty.

F. Library facilities
1. Check facilities of library in advance.
2. Make arrangements to have material brought into the classroom.

G. Films
1. If the films don't arrive as scheduled, you will have to show them when they do. Provide a space in your planning to facilitate this.
2. Try to avoid too many free films as they are too much in demand and very seldom arrive as scheduled.

H. Individual differences
1. If you find a child who you may think can't get along with a certain group, put him in another one.
2. Give him special work to do.
   a. Oral report
   b. Writing for material

I. Students' irresponsiveness to groups
1. If you find a certain few that don't want to work in a group but would rather work by two's, let them work by themselves if you can't guide them into a group.

J. Evaluation (by chairmen)
1. Have certain criteria developed for evaluation so that each chairman will have standards by which to judge his group.
2. Make sure he understands it.

K. Overflow of students in one particular group project
1. Try to appeal to individuals to go into the smaller groups.
2. You might take them to one side and explain how they could help in the other groups.[5]

---

5. This unit has been taken from Pennsylvania State Department of Public Instruction, *Curriculum Improvement by a Secondary School Faculty* (*Bulletin* No. 243; Harrisburg, Pa., 1950).

Developing Units in the Core Program

A good deal has been said in this book about core classes, and teachers need much help in developing units within these classes. The junior-high-school teachers in Elizabeth, New Jersey, have been working for several years on this problem and their experience can be helpful to others. The basic problem they attacked was "How can the core curriculum be taught?" Committees from the schools sought answers to such questions as these: If the core program attempts to handle problems selected by students, how does the teacher avoid the chaotic pursuit of transient interests of an indiscriminating group of adolescents? How does a teacher learn enough about each child so that he can realistically develop a program meaningful and suitable to every individual within the framework of the group activity? How can a teacher possibly be presumed to know enough about various fields of learning to dare face a high school class as an expert on everything from Latin syntax to cyclonic disturbances? How can a teacher possibly get the time to prepare for and do this more demanding kind of teaching?

Accepting the basic principle of flexibility in developing a core curriculum adapted to the local needs of the individual schools, the Elizabeth study produced a workable procedure for core-curriculum structure rather than the usual preparation of specific units. The result was agreement upon a number of problem areas, the over-all objectives for the core program, objectives for each problem area, kinds of skill experiences, objectives in skill learnings, and an extended list of possible resources and activities. These are published in sequential order for use by other groups developing core-curriculum programs.[6]

Early in the study, "knowing the child" was stressed as basic to a functional core-curriculum program, considering such vital questions as: Who are the children in your class? What kinds of homes do they come from? What kinds of individuals are they? What about their achievements; their adjustments to the school, the community, and their peers? What are their tensions, their preparations for working together, their attitudes, their hopes, the principles by which they live? The subject matter as taught in the core curriculum stems from the problems with which children are concerned. Any adequate solution depends upon the extent to which the teacher "knows the child." Several ways are suggested through problem leads, such as school records, health facts, and citizenship; anecdotal records; others' opinions; the family; autobiographies, hobbies; and tests.

Furthermore, the selection of problems raises these questions: How does the teacher operate in the classroom to discover student interests and needs? Some of these needs are revealed as the teacher comes to know the pupils; others have to be sought out; others arise from general discussion, frequently

6. Leon Ovsiew, *Making the Core Work* (Metropolitan School Study Council; New York: Columbia University, Teachers College, Bureau of Publications, 1951).

around the common problems of students. Certain of these common-problem areas are revealed from studies of pupils' adjustment to school, from homework, current events, the unexpected interest, interests which arise out of other classes, or from outside activities. The rapport which the teacher establishes with her students is an all-important factor in getting at the problems facing boys and girls. In addition, the planned problem, a more systematic and formal procedure, under the careful guidance of the teacher as class leader helps the class in the process of problem selection.

In determining whether a problem fits into the school's total curriculum plan, the following procedure is recommended in the construction of a set of standards for the choice of a problem:

1. Individual preparation of a set of standards to govern the selection of problems for class study can be made.
2. Together with this preparation, arguments and evidence should be formulated by students to defend their suggestions.
3. Suggestions from each individual are transcribed on the blackboard by the class secretary.
4. The list must now be reduced to workable proportions—an exercise in group planning. The teacher should take a firm lead in this final phase.
5. The list of standards can be printed on cards, written in notebooks, or written on a poster for the bulletin board.[7]

An example of such a set of standards was formulated by one of the core classes in Elizabeth:

1. Each person in the class should have an opportunity to suggest what he wants to select as the problem to be studied.
2. The problem to be studied should be about people and how they live in the world; ideas which are important and valuable for everyone.
3. The problem to be studied should call for a variety of kinds of things to be done.
4. The problem which is selected for study should be agreed upon by a substantial majority of the class.
5. Each person who participates in the study of the problem is responsible for understanding the contributions of everyone else.
6. Each person in the class should have the opportunity to help plan the work which is necessary for studying the problem.[8]

Integrated with the total school program, the core program becomes a unifying force for the pupil's learning experience. The core teacher utilizes the resource people of the school and community, such as the students' own abilities and interests, the art and music teachers, parents and other adults from outside the school. Adequate time is provided the core teachers in pre-

---

7. *Ibid.,* pp. 18–19.
8. *Ibid.,* p. 19.

planning the use of these resources. The resources have value not only for the skills but for the subject matter as well, all set in a functional context as part of the common learnings. In addition, the classroom atmosphere is improved through cooperative effort toward a common purpose. Group cooperation is taught through these basic conditions:

1. Each child is respected as a person and has equal rights in the class-room group.
2. There must be abiding faith in the validity and importance of group cooperation.
3. The classroom temper must be stimulating.
4. The classroom atmosphere must be permissive.
5. Motivation should be intrinsically rather than externally inspired.[9]

Group discussion, therefore, becomes an essential part of the social procedure of the core class. Good intraclass relationships come from adequate group activity based largely upon intelligent and competent discussion activities. Discussion behavior must be learned just as any other skill pattern is learned. Some of the factors which are essential in satisfactory group discussion are: an interest motive; rules agreed upon; adequate background and preparation; the framework, frequently through committee organization; and reporting techniques.

With the aforementioned steps well established, the core-curriculum method can be used as a most effective device in the production of well-adjusted personalities—children who are beginning to develop and to solve problems rather than be frustrated by them. The problem-solving method operates in this logical fashion:

1. Student suggestions for problem studies are phrased with precision, in order to define the problem in the most clear-cut terms.
2. To discover the solution to these problems, work will need to be done since no one has answers immediately available.
3. After a solution is discovered, some action or decision must result.
4. The nature of the action or decision must be defined in the clearest possible terms so that the purpose of the study is clear for each student.
5. The next step is to begin to plot the work which will need to be done. This is a cooperative venture.
6. Once the work has been planned, the class must be grouped for the job.
7. Handling these groupings involves many teacher skills.
8. In possession of all the information the class may reasonably be expected to gather materials to meet the defined objectives.
9. The teacher must be free to work with each group as needed.
10. After information has been gathered and organized into usable form, each group must report to the class.[10]

---

9. *Ibid.*, pp. 31–33.
10. *Ibid.*, pp. 41–46.

Chapter Eighteen

Evaluating
Pupil Learning

EVER SINCE SCHOOLS have been organized some attempts have been made to determine how much pupils learn. However, the prevailing sentiment prior to 1900 was that learning was largely intangible and could be measured only by the individual teacher in a class. Once he made an estimate of how much his pupils learned he then expressed it in a numerical or letter grade which was recorded and used for many purposes, mostly administrative in character.

About 1910 work started on the development of standardized tests of intelligence and subject achievement and were probably applied for the first time on any large scale in the New York City survey of 1911–1913. World War I gave impetus to the movement, and soon after 1920 large batteries of such tests became generally published and widely used. Norms were developed and pupil scores were compared throughout the nation. After 1930 new tests were devised in the less tangible areas of human characteristics and accomplishments, and evaluative criteria appeared for high schools and colleges to be used largely by the accrediting associations. Then following 1940 much refinement was done, and measurement merged into broad programs of evaluation for use in national studies and in evaluating total school systems. Today we have the advantage of the previous work in measurement and evaluation, largely coming from the field of psychology, and we can apply it to a concept of evaluation concerned chiefly with determining the extent to which the school has accomplished pupils' achievement in certain behavioral goals which have been set as the objectives of the school.

Meaning and Significance of Evaluation

Evaluation is an essential aspect of any successful curriculum program. It is not alone concerned with pupil learning but with every aspect of the school program. A successful evaluation program will be concerned with the following:

1. The extent to which the objectives of the school are clearly related to the needs of the pupils and the community.
2. The extent to which the school is organized so as to promote effective learning.
3. The presence of instructional equipment and supplies required for maximum learning.
4. The quality of the administrative and teaching staff required for effective instruction and supervision.
5. The degree of interest and participation of lay citizens and the regulation given to such cooperation.
6. The morale and growth potentials present and operating for faculty and pupils.
7. The provision of resources for proper guidance and for pupil learning through group activities of a nonclassroom character.
8. The degree of democracy required to develop an effective laboratory in democratic living.

Whenever, therefore, we consider the evaluation of pupil learning, we must likewise consider the evaluation of the school, for the success of the pupil depends upon how it is organized and operated.

Evaluation is the process of appraising behavioral changes and the relation of certain conditions to them. It focuses attention upon (1) the individual and his accomplishments, (2) the group and the interactions between the individual and the group, and (3) the total environment in which the pupil lives. It seeks to determine the relationships between pupil behavior and environmental conditions and between achievement and goals. It is descriptive as well as quantitative. It involves teachers, parents, pupils, and the community. And, finally, it is definite enough to be objective and yet comprehensive enough to cover those aspects which lend themselves only to subjective appraisal. All in all, it is an intelligent and critical appraisement of the pupil and what affects him.

Many writers in the field have suggested certain principles of evaluation, but one of the better lists comes from a group of teachers and the administrative staff of a local community, the Oak Ridge Schools of Oak Ridge, Tennessee. As a result of study and discussion, they developed the following list of principles of evaluation to use as a guide for their evaluation study:

1. Evaluation is a constant process of the consideration of the degree to which the results and by-products of the education program reached the stated and implied objectives of the program.
2. Evaluation is concerned with more than end products; it must be seen as a continuing process. Therefore, it is concerned both with means and ends.
3. All who are concerned in any experience will inevitably make judgments upon it; therefore, it is a part of the responsibility of the schools to provide such information and such leadership that the community's evaluations shall be intelligent. This means that evaluation should be cooperative. It includes administrators, teachers, pupils and parents, and any others who are concerned with the schools.
4. Evaluation should start out as a means of discovering group and individual growth rather than of determining merely whether children possess or do not possess certain abilities.
5. Evaluation should determine how well the school provides conditions of growth and the experiences which make learning economical and effective.
6. Children learn more effectively when they take part in evaluation. The objective should be self-direction and self-evaluation.
7. Evaluation is concerned with all aspects of the school curriculum—administration, buildings, grounds, equipment, finances, community relationships, and so forth.
8. A long-range evaluation program should be planned so that no one year would involve the school in a complete study of every aspect of its work. Time should be budgeted so that specific items of the program will be evaluated.
9. Research studies should be carried on in the schools when they contribute to the best interests of pupils and the schools, to the professional improvement of the teachers, and to the development of a better program in the schools.
10. The collection of data and the keeping of records in the school have no value in themselves. Only as records aid in evaluating the true functions and the true objectives of the schools do they attain value.
11. Any evaluation program should be subject to revision. It must be responsive to changes in the curriculum and to conditions outside the school which affect children. It should be flexible so that it can be modified in accordance with advances in the techniques of evaluation.[1]

---

1. R. H. Ostrander, "Evaluation in the Oak Ridge Schools," *Educational Leadership,* 8:87–88, 1950.

Evaluation Activities

Reference has been made to the fact that early work in evaluation consisted simply of individual teacher appraisals of learning and later of standardized tests of achievement or aptitude. The modern scope of evaluation activities goes far beyond these limited instruments and consists of a wide range of activities and instruments. A composite list could be given but the scope can be quite adequately illustrated, and at the same time the idea can be made realistic by presenting the list of activities which was actually used by the high school of Wayne, Michigan, in making appraisals of pupils. They listed the following:

1. Course content examinations: written, oral, check lists, multiple choice
2. Informal observation: appearance; general attitudes and reactions; participation in class discussions; study habits; associations with other children—acceptances, rejections, social adaptability, acts of aggression, withdrawing tendencies, nervous habits; physical weaknesses; satisfactions; dissatisfactions; attitudes toward parents, brothers, sisters, home
3. Teacher, self, and peer evaluation registering opinions on the basis of leadership qualities, degree of participation, type of discussion, changed behavior, conduct, respect for others, willingness to listen, personal growth, change in personality, open-mindedness
4. Sociograms (group adjustment)
5. Group evaluation about group feeling, self-discipline, discussion technique, planning, making choices, attitudes
6. Problem census: Mooney Check List, California Test of Personality, autobiographies, discussions, etc.
7. Growth in reading: reading tests (Traxler Reading Test), maturation of intelligence (MA Test), screening special aptitudes
8. Personal interviews and conferences with students, teachers, counselors, administration
9. Participation in activities
10. Anecdotal records
11. Parent conference and parent evaluation
12. Opinions about attitude toward peers, school, teachers, family, money, morals, opposite sex, sex, nutrition, movies, radio, race, reading, religion, class procedures, etc.
13. Interest check lists: Kuder Test; California Personality Test
14. Cumulative records: data on family health, work, etc.; classroom; counselors; administration; official office records
15. Attendance: school in general, particular activities
16. Case studies
17. Informal contacts with students
18. Aptitude Tests (USES Battery)

19. Miscellaneous: time budget, follow-up data, socio-drama, panel discussions, group thinking, drop-out data, etc.[2]

The extent and character of the instruments and activities used will depend upon the purposes to be achieved through the evaluation. While this Wayne High School list does not include all the types of instruments or activities available, it enumerates more than most schools use. It also gives some idea of the extensive character of evaluation compared with the simple measurement of achievement.

Steps in Developing an Evaluation Program

In building an evaluation program for a school, certain steps should be followed. These may be listed thus:
1. Prepare a list of objectives appropriate to the philosophy of the school.
2. Justify the objectives psychologically and sociologically.
3. State the aims in terms of pupil behavior.
4. Organize the objectives into simple and logical classifications.
5. Select the objectives which are practical and suited to the learning experiences.
6. Determine the situations in which the extent of the desired behavior will be revealed.
7. Build or secure and apply appropriate instruments to the situations selected for study.

Setting the Goals

The first steps in an evaluation program are also the first steps in a curriculum program: namely, to set up the goals that are desired. The statement of aims provides the basis for the selection of content and for the evaluation of learning experiences. In the statement of these aims, attention must be paid to the philosophy of the school. In the past many programs have been well padded with aims, but frequently they have had little relationship to any fundamental philosophy or to any practical reality in the classroom. Fundamentally, the aims must match the needs of the pupil and the needs of society with the possibilities of the school. Only those aims which are appropriate for the school and can be attained by the pupils should be stated. The teacher is more likely to make effective statements if he knows his pupils, their purposes, desires, interests, and backgrounds, and if he knows well the community in which the pupil lives. His knowledge of community life, of course, must

---

2. From an unpublished report from Wayne High School, Wayne, Michigan, and quoted in Roland C. Faunce and Nelson Bossing, *Developing the Core Curriculum* (New York: Prentice-Hall, Inc., 1951), pp. 270–271.

extend beyond his own town, but he should be an expert on local affairs and well informed on state and national problems. If he also knows enough about how learning takes place to evaluate the possibility of attaining certain goals in an economical way, he will have the requisites needed to state the aims of education.

Justifying the Aims

After these aims have been stated it is good practice to attempt to justify them both sociologically and psychologically. Under this scrutiny there may be some which should be thrown out. The key question is "Can pupils be stirred to accept these aims as their own?" The aims, in so far as possible, should arise from group planning on the part of the teacher and the pupils. In this case, many of the aims will be accepted naturally by the pupils because they had a part in setting them. But, as has been pointed out before in this book, if pupils do not or cannot propose aims appropriate to the functions of the school, they should be led to accept as desirable those aims proposed by the teacher. This is dangerous doctrine if carried too far, as it gets us back to traditional practice, but a wise teacher will see the necessity for the statement without feeling the need for relying upon traditional procedure.

If pupils do not accept the aims established, they then become aims only of the teacher, and the extent of learning is seriously jeopardized at the start. For the sake of evaluation as well as for learning, it is worth while to spend enough time at the start to get pupils to accept the aims as their own. If the aims are accepted by the pupils as their own and thus furnish the drive to the actions necessary to achieve them, they are then psychologically justified. This justification must also verify the feasibility of the aim; that is, whether it is possible to achieve it and do so within a reasonable length of time. Assume, for instance, that a teacher proposes to develop honesty or mental powers through the teaching of mathematics. Here the question of possibility enters, for modern studies have thrown serious doubt upon the existence of such general traits, and further doubt upon the possibility of their being developed by any one subject even if they do exist. This aim, then, is not verified psychologically.

Aims which have psychological justification may not be worth seeking and therefore may not be justified sociologically. Why is the aim important? What social significance does it have? Does it contribute more to the group than other aims would in a similar length of time? In answering these questions, one cannot resort to the demands of the course of study or of tradition, or of community pressure groups, or even of the principal or superintendent. The criterion should be the extent to which the aim promotes the general welfare of the group or the social competence of the individual.

For illustration of psychological and sociological justification, let us take four aims: (1) teaching pupils to multiply by two digits, (2) learning how the state government is organized, (3) learning how to sail paper airplanes out of the window, (4) learning how to make the city more beautiful.

The first aim cannot be criticized as being undesirable, but it states an aim of the teacher rather than a goal of the pupil. It may well be a by-product which the pupil secures while engaging in some activity where such skill is required, but it does not represent in its present form a common purpose which the teacher and the class will usually share. It is better for the teacher to use it as a check list of the breadth of her own teaching than as a statement of a goal which is accepted by the pupil.

The second aim, learning how the state government is organized, has psychological appeal to only a limited group. It, too, may be accomplished as a by-product of some larger aim, such as understanding how legislation can be enacted to reduce taxes or how government jobs are secured through civil service. To normal children, the aim as stated does not have much appeal and hence not much psychological justification, except for those pupils who have through other experiences come up against this proposition and recognize the goal as being necessary.

The third aim, learning how to sail paper airplanes out of the window, is psychologically sound for the majority of children. It poses an interesting problem, a definite goal which is recognizable, and one which is generally achievable with a measure of satisfaction in the end. If child interest were the only criterion, this goal would rank high. Such a goal, however, seldom results in a social contribution, and its achievement is usually disrupting to the organized school life of the group. It is probably neutral and harmless at its best, and disrupting at its worst. It sounds like some of the aims of the extreme moderns who are anxious to get results through too easily accepted goals and through child interest alone. Thus it is not sociologically justified.

The last aim, learning to make the city more beautiful, is characteristic of a number of aims in modern education. It may not have instantaneous appeal to children, like learning to sail the airplane; nevertheless, it makes much better sense to them than an aim of "learning the names of the presidents of the United States." Pupils can, with some skill on the part of the teacher, be easily led to accept this aim as a major one for themselves as well as for the teacher. It is psychologically sound, for it calls for much activity and a variety of experiences, and it is attainable and recognizable in its completion. It offers many opportunities for securing a variety of by-products which have been indicated as being the outcome of larger aims rather than as immediate goals. From the social standpoint, the aim is justified since it contributes to group welfare, it develops individual social competence, it represents a responsibility which needs to be accepted by youth, and it involves opportunities for cooperation of social groups.

Stating Aims Behaviorally

The next step—to state the aims in terms of pupil behavior—is necessary if the teacher is to prepare definite criteria for determining the extent to which the aims have been achieved. The process implies answering two questions: (1) What do pupils do who have achieved growth in this objective? (2) How does their behavior differ from those who have not achieved such growth?

This step is especially important when we list such aims as development in social effectiveness, in group cooperation, or in the ability to think critically. These aims must then be reduced to behavioral terms. Such descriptions as the following are illustrative of practice in line with this requirement. They are appropriate for a teacher in science who wants to determine whether his pupils are growing in their interests in science.

1. He develops a hobby which requires the use of science experiences.
2. He joins a science club.
3. He subscribes to science magazines.
4. He sets up a science laboratory at home.
5. He asks to be allowed to spend extra time in the science laboratories at school.
6. He reads widely in science without assignments.
7. He brings materials to class for analysis and study.

Classifying the Aims

The aims should now be organized into simple and logical classifications so that proper evaluative instruments may be selected. Some of the aims will extend through many activities and over long periods of time; some will be school-wide, some community-wide. Others will concern only a specific class or unit of work. Some will deal with skills, some with attitudes and appreciations, some with generalizations. The purpose of classifying these is to devise some form of organization which will make them easily handled. The evaluation staff of the Progressive Education Association's Eight-Year Study used a classification as follows:

1. Functional information, including vocabulary
2. Reflective thinking
3. Attitudes
4. Interests
5. Appreciations
6. Work habits and study skills
7. Social and personal adjustment
8. Social sensitivity

J. Wayne Wrightstone has suggested four general headings:

1. Intellectual factors

2. Dynamic factors (beliefs and attitudes)
3. Social performance factors
4. Physiological factors

There is no necessity for following any specific classification that has been used. The teacher can prepare one of his own, but organization of the aims into some classification as to nature and extent of solution will be helpful in building evaluative instruments.

Selecting Objectives

The next procedure is to select the objectives which are practical and are suited to the learning experiences. Some objectives, such as reading ability, need not be evaluated with every unit. Some are especially developed by the unit, and some are purely incidental to the content investigated. Some are so long term that any extended attempt to measure their results from a single unit would end only in disappointment. It is not possible to include all objectives, since time will not permit. Rather than do a poor job of evaluating many aims, the teacher will be well advised to select those most consistent with the nature of the unit and concentrate on them. Some forms of behavior are almost apparent and require no formal evaluation, while others present so difficult a problem of collecting evidence that the result hardly justifies the effort. Many skills are determined in reference to larger outcomes and need not be measured specifically. The choice of objectives for investigation should be a conscious one, based on the nature of the objectives attainable from the unit and upon the ability of the evaluator to determine the extent of their presence in an economical way.

Selecting Situations and Instruments

The teacher is now ready to determine the situations in which the extent of the desired behavior will be revealed. Often the ordinary situations of the classroom will afford just the opportunities needed for observation. The idea of the formal examination, where selected days had to be set aside in which students were to write their answers to questions, need not carry over into the evaluation program to any extended degree. The range of means of evaluation is so great that many types of situations are desired. The interest of a pupil in science, for instance, can be determined day by day as the pupil brings in materials, reads extensively, and carries on research beyond class requirements. The problem simply becomes one of recognizing these activities in relation to goals and of recording them properly.

Special or planned situations need to be set up where pupils will have special opportunities to demonstrate their ability and the extent to which they have achieved certain goals. Careful observation of the extent to which a pupil can plan an experiment, set it up, draw conclusions, and make generalizations will reveal weaknesses which need to be discovered. Action in social situations will come about daily, but many actions will have no occasion for experience unless specific situations are planned. And the conventional written test will reveal strengths and weaknesses which otherwise may be overlooked in daily situations. Both types of situations are necessary to successful evaluation.

Using Evaluation Instruments

The final step is to build and apply the appropriate instruments to evaluate the goals in the situations selected for study. Many types of instruments are available to the modern teacher. He need no longer rely only on essay tests or on standard published tests. He need not rely on tests prepared by others, nor need he confine his instruments to those which yield comparative scores over the country or to those which are purely objective.

The instruments or techniques chosen must be appropriate to the objectives stated. Using an achievement test just because the scores are objective and specific and can be compared with those of other pupils throughout the United States is quite indefensible. The modern evaluation instruments are professional tools and should be selected with the same care which a factory superintendent uses to select machines to produce a certain product. A lathe is a fine machine tool but it is no good for stamping automobile bodies. Many types of instruments can be used, such as

1. Stenographic reports of behavior or activities
2. Sound recordings of activities
3. Pupil products or reports
4. Anecdotal records
5. Check lists of various kinds
6. Time samplings and controlled observation of pupil behavior
7. Pupil diaries
8. Self-rating scales
9. Questionnaires
10. Scales of judgment of pupils or teachers
11. Interviews
12. Tests of achievement, aptitude, attitudes, personality, and interests

Organizing the Staff for Evaluation

If evaluation is to be done effectively, plans must be made to utilize the entire staff most effectively. An analysis of this problem was made by a group in Michigan for the Michigan Study of the Secondary School Curriculum. They list the following possible patterns of organization:

1. *Evaluation solely by individual teachers.* In this pattern, which is a very common one, no systematic provision is made for cooperative approach to evaluation. Whatever activity is carried on is done by each teacher working individually without regular consultation with other staff members.

2. *Evaluation through executive action.* In this pattern the evaluation activity is usually initiated and carried out directly by the administration with little or no consultation with the staff. Frequently this pattern includes the calling in of outside experts who make a survey and usually submit a report to the superintendent and board of education. Sometimes the survey is carried on by a committee from within the system, but appointed by the administration without necessarily any consultation with the staff as a whole. Too often accreditation procedures utilize this type of evaluation activity.

3. *Department committees.* Usually these are committees appointed from among the staff along subject matter lines. In this pattern the English committee studies the problems of the English curriculum; the mathematics committee studies the problems of mathematics, etc. There is little opportunity for intercommunication among departments or among those teaching in different subject fields.

4. *Organization around general curriculum problems.* In this type of organization there may be a health committee or a committee on intercultural education, or a guidance committee, or a committee organized around any other fundamental curriculum problem without regard to subject matter lines. Such a general problem committee is likely to be responsible for formulating general, over-all purposes in its selected area of work. It has the task of evaluating the effectiveness of the school with respect to its assigned area, and of proposing program improvement in both a vertical and horizontal sense, crossing the various grade levels and departments as the need may be. Since it is sometimes difficult to make such a general committee continuously and directly responsible to those who may have to carry out its recommendations, many schools are organizing a different kind of implementation committee on a grade level basis.

5. *Grade level committees.* In this pattern all the teachers in a given grade meet to consider any common problems and to develop programs in harmony with the total faculty policies developed by more general committees and adopted by the faculty. The grade level committees are therefore often implementation groups consisting of teachers who have the same youngsters during the day. It is important that channels of communication be kept open between one grade level committee and the others so that a continuous program of general education can be developed vertically as well as by grade levels. The grade level committee serves its most valuable function in the junior and senior high school where departmental organization prevails. In the elementary school which has self-contained classrooms it has been found helpful to organize such committees across several grade levels, thus producing an early elementary group, a later elementary group, etc.

6. *Teacher teams.* Another kind of curriculum committee consists of a team of teachers, either in the same grade level or cutting across grades, but with the same assignment. For example, the teachers in the building may form a core curriculum team, which is somewhat different from the department committee mentioned earlier. Another type of team is that in which teachers who have the same group of students organize and meet periodically. Still another example is the informal teacher team which develops in a summer workshop or conference and continues to work together on the problem which initially brought them together.

7. *Building committees.* In our larger school systems two basic trends are evident in organization for curriculum study and evaluation. In the one, primary emphasis is placed on system-wide curriculum committees which may or may not contain representatives from all the different school buildings in the system. In the other pattern there may be system-wide committees but these are usually in addition to building committees which deal primarily with the offerings of the individual school. In either case, it is important that communication be maintained between committee groups and the constituents whom they represent.[3]

All or certain combinations of these patterns can be used by local schools, but it is important that the following conditions be present:

1. Communication must be maintained among individual teachers, committee members, and the entire school staff.
2. Both building faculty meetings and city-wide meetings should be maintained in order that all teachers and staff may be informed on the general purposes, procedures, and results.
3. Ample provision must be made for sufficient expert consultant service to ensure that the evaluation is done skillfully, since the average teacher is not trained in the detailed techniques of interpretation and of instrument construction.
4. Ample time must be provided by the school system for study, application, and analysis of evaluative activities. Evaluation is more than leisure-time activities.

Evaluative Criteria and Specific Programs

Illustrations of Evaluative Criteria

STATE OF MARYLAND. A number of evaluative criteria have been developed by local or state groups and by commissions representing national organizations. The State Department of Education of Maryland prepared a bulletin

3. Ruth Boot, Roland C. Faunce, Russell Isbister, and Leon S. Waskin, *Organization of School Staff for Evaluation* (Michigan State Board of Education, Education Series, Leaflet No. 1; Lansing, Mich., 1950).

giving criteria for evaluating the state's public-school program. The criteria were prepared to be useful in evaluating (1) the teaching and learning conditions in relation to objectives, (2) the results of the program in educating children, (3) the motives underlying behavior and behavior itself, and (4) the educational process and product.

The bulletin is organized around the following seven threads:

1. Developing democratic beliefs, values, and practices
2. Developing ethical, moral, and spiritual values
3. Learning to adjust to life situations
4. Using wisely human, natural, and material resources
5. Developing sound habits of thinking
6. Appreciating and responding to the beautiful
7. Acquiring competence in the tools of learning

Under each of these seven threads are listed several criteria with a large number of specific statements under each criterion. Following these are statements of desirable individual behavior and group action. An illustration from thread four will serve to show how the threads are organized and the help the criteria will be to local schools. The statements are listed under only one criterion for illustration.

THREAD FOUR

Utilizing Wisely Human, Natural, and Material Resources

I. Criteria

    A. Criterion one—The school utilizes wisely the human resources of the school and the community for the mutual benefit of the individual and his social group. [Twenty-four statements are listed under this criterion.]

    B. Criterion two—The school program promotes the wise use of the natural resources of the community, state, and nation. [Twenty-two statements appear under this criterion.]

    C. Criterion three—The material resources at the disposal of the citizens in the community are widely utilized.

        1. The school stresses consumer education as an integral part of the curriculum.

        2. The school's facilities are wisely used by planning boards, legislative bodies, and other groups to stimulate action at the local and state level.

        3. The school encourages pupils to locate and submit new sources of learning materials.

        4. The school provides opportunities for pupils to evaluate cooperative projects; e.g. yearbooks, school papers, and other similar projects involving school and pupil funds.

        5. The school emphasizes the use of school materials and facilities.

        6. The program teaches the pupil to use effectively inexpensive and adaptable local materials and resources.

7. The school shops produce handmade materials and equipment for class and home use.
8. The school and community library facilities help pupils and patrons to develop wide use of materials and resources.

II. Resulting desirable individual behavior and group action
   A. Fulfilling the individual and community requirements of wise consumership in an intricate industrial society
   B. Acquiring an individual and group attitude of respect for public property
   C. Setting up an effective individual and community program which assures maximum protection of life and property
   D. Coordinating the work of the various service organizations, the governmental agencies, and industrial groups which seek to end such hazards as fire, accidents, and crime
   E. Recognizing that common courtesy and consideration of other people are essential elements in conserving life and prosperity
   F. Using wisely mass media of communication to help conserve our resources[4]

NATIONAL ASSOCIATION OF SECONDARY SCHOOL PRINCIPALS. A second major set of evaluative criteria for secondary schools was prepared for the National Association of Secondary School Principals in connection with the Ten Imperative Needs of Youth set forth in their *Planning for American Youth*. For each of the ten needs a series of statements was prepared, and the school was to check the extent to which it was achieving these needs. Five degrees of success were possible running from very superior to very inferior, and a space was also available to check the statement if it did not apply to the particular situation. An illustration taken from Imperative Need Number Seven will serve to illustrate how all needs were developed.

Imperative Need Number 7: All youth need opportunities to develop their capacities to appreciate beauty in literature, art, music, and nature.
   1. The school offers courses, particularly in art and music, in which the discovery of special aptitudes is a chief objective.
   2. Emphasis is upon what might be called "consumer" activities, including the avocational, rather than upon vocational competence in these fields.
   3. As aptitudes are discovered, they are encouraged by means of opportunity for exhibition of work to classes and other groupings of students, as well as to the public.
   4. Many opportunities are provided for large numbers of pupils to participate in displaying their varying levels of aptitude in these areas.

---

4. Second Annual Maryland Educational Conference, *Some Suggested Criteria for Evaluating Maryland's Public School Program* (State Department of Education, Baltimore, Maryland, Volume 30, Number 1, July, 1949).

5. The program in these areas is planned under the principle that *enjoyment* of the current "sample" experience promotes habitual recourse to the area in which the experience occurs.
6. The school staff also recognizes that the outcome which improves taste is the *understanding* of the experience.
7. The school uses the drama as an introduction to full appreciation of literature.
8. Characters and situations in literature are given life by comparison with local and prominent persons in current affairs.
9. The school enlists community support in developing art projects which are of both a practical and an appreciative nature.
10. Many opportunities are provided for all pupils to participate to some degree in musical activities.
11. Through field trips, hikes, etc., the school provides opportunities for pupils to ascertain the beauties of immediately surrounding territories.
12. The school uses students' current preferences as starting points for the development of higher levels of appreciation.
13. The school is committed to the practice of teaching students to appreciate beauty when and where the opportunity arises.
14. The school building lives up to its responsibilities as the setting in which the teaching staff labors to cultivate appreciation of beauty.
15. Any courses which may be offered in these areas are accorded the status of diploma credit.
16. In all these fields the school is guided in its choice of materials by student reaction to the materials.
17. Where interest and enthusiasm warrant further opportunity than can be provided in regular class activities, extracurricular activities are used to supplement classroom work.
18. The school takes pains to see that students are kept aware of community activities in these areas.
19. The school makes use of many devices to evaluate the growth of the capacity of its students to appreciate beauty in literature, art, music, and nature.
20. The school does not allow hindering forces in the community to discourage it in its efforts to meet the aesthetic needs of its students.[5]

COOPERATIVE STUDY OF SECONDARY SCHOOL STANDARDS. A third set of criteria which has influenced secondary education was the self-study and self-improvement instruments called *Evaluative Criteria,* first published in 1940 and revised in 1950 after experimentation with a large number of secondary schools. These criteria have been developed for all phases of the secondary school and are intended to be used by local schools to evaluate the extent to

5. Will French and William L. Ransom, *Evaluating the Curriculum for Provision for the Imperative Needs of Youth.* Reprint from *Bulletin,* National Association of Secondary School Principals, Vol. 32, No. 154, April, 1948.

which they have achieved certain goals. One of the more controversial aspects of the criteria were their quantitative emphasis combined with so called "thermometers" which purported to indicate the degree of success.[6]

Illustrations of Evaluation Programs

COLORADO STATE COLLEGE OF EDUCATION. The staff at Colorado State College of Education has studied and experimented with reporting practices for nearly two decades. The final outcome, recently reported, set up their objectives in behavioral terms, with specific pupil behaviors listed under general headings, as follows:

I. He directs his individual activities effectively.
   A. He begins work promptly.
   B. He makes good use of his time.
   C. He requires a minimum of supervision.
   D. He does more than the least that will be accepted.
   E. He meets his responsibilities promptly.

II. He follows plans and directions.
   A. He listens to and reads directions carefully.
   B. He follows and completes plans and directions that have been set up.

III. He gets along well with others.
   A. He is considerate of the rights and wishes of others.
   B. He is courteous and tolerant.
   C. He controls his temper.
   D. He conforms to reasonable social standards.

IV. He takes an active part in group living.
   A. He participates in group planning.
   B. He volunteers his services.
   C. He does his share in group activities.

V. He speaks correctly and effectively.
   A. He speaks clearly.
   B. He adjusts his voice to the size of the group.
   C. He uses an adequate vocabulary to express himself interestingly.
   D. He speaks with ease and confidence.
   E. He uses correct grammatical forms.

---

6. Cooperative Study of Secondary School Standards, *Evaluative Criteria* (rev. ed.; Washington: American Council on Education, 1950). See also Carl G. F. Franzen, "An Analysis of the Reactions of Schools Evaluated by the Evaluative Criteria of the Cooperative Study of Secondary School Standards," *Bulletin,* National Association of Secondary School Principals, 32:23–47, 1948; R. D. Matthews, "The Evaluative Criteria—1950 Edition," *Bulletin,* National Association of Secondary School Principals, 35:226–229, 1951.

VI. He takes good care of personal and school materials and equipment.

    A. He shows respect for property.

    B. He does not waste or damage materials or equipment.

    C. He returns things when they are due.

    D. He reports breakage and loss.

VII. He observes attendance regulations.

    A. He is regular and prompt in attendance except for approved causes.

    B. When possible he arranges in advance for absence.

    C. He takes the initiative in making up work missed.

    D. He makes proper use of the school health service.

    [Semi-general objectives, involving two or more but not all the teachers, courses, and activities, were also set up]

VIII. He reads with ease and understanding.

    A. He selects important ideas.

    B. He understands and evaluates what he reads.

    C. He reads with reasonable speed.

IX. He expresses himself correctly and effectively in writing.

    A. He expresses ideas clearly.

    B. He uses correct grammatical forms.

    C. He punctuates correctly.

    D. He spells correctly.

    E. He writes legibly.

X. He utilizes available sources of learning materials.

    A. He selects and uses appropriate sources of information.

    B. He uses the library and library tools effectively.

    C. He effectively engages in interview and observation.

XI. He uses the problem-solving method.

    A. He recognizes problems.

    B. He states problems clearly.

    C. He collects and records appropriate information.

    D. He arrives at sound conclusions.

XII. He uses the basic skills in mathematics.

    A. He uses accurately the simple fundamental combinations.

    B. He computes with reasonable speed.

    C. He uses fractions and per cents correctly.

    D. He selects correct processes.

Specific objectives of different uses or courses are also listed, one of which is illustrative, in music:

    1. He reads music at sight, with accuracy as to tone, rhythm, and interpretation.

    2. He sings or plays with good tone quality.

3. Into group discussions he brings music information based on reading and listening.
4. He works consistently for the purpose of developing better performance.
5. He asks for help when he needs it to improve his performance.
6. He listens to radio music programs and attends musical shows and concerts.
7. He participates in community music activities.
8. He chooses suitable music for his own performance.[7]

EVALUATING A UNIT OF WORK. In evaluating a unit of work, the teacher wants to know to what extent the unit was responsible for development toward the objectives which he listed for it. He then wants to use the instruments most nearly suited to making this determination. A group of teachers from Santa Maria, California, presented a unit of work on Making Our Water Supply Serve Human Needs. The teachers also prepared an analysis of the evaluation program needed to accompany this unit. It will serve here as an illustration of how a group of teachers set out to evaluate a unit.

These evaluation techniques are developed in terms of this particular unit, Making Our Water Supply Serve Human Needs, but they may be adapted to any unit. In most instances only excerpts of tests are included.[8]

I. *Cooperation and Social Effectiveness*—Growth in these attitudes is evidenced by
  A. Disposition to project oneself appreciatively into the lives, motives, and problems of other people in the group by
    1. Looking behind events to discover the underlying conflicts and problems in social life
    2. Cooperative participation in oral discussions in class
    3. Considering problems as solvable—not accepting them as unanswerble or inescapable
    4. Considering the effect of one's personal action on others
    5. Viewing difficulties of the individual or group as symptoms of need for general social adjustment
    6. Feeling personal concern and responsibility for social problems
  B. The ability to
    1. Perceive and identify problems
    2. See the relationship between specific human problems and general social conditions
    3. Judge the consequences of social events, plans, and actions
    4. Project theoretical or actual solutions to social problems

7. William L. Wrinkle, *Improving Marking and Reporting Practices* (New York: Rinehart & Company, Inc., 1947), pp. 100–102.
8. Santa Barbara County, *Curriculum Guide for Teachers in Secondary Schools* (Santa Barbara, Calif.: Schauer Printing Studio, 1941), pp. 64–74.

EVALUATION OF STUDENT ACHIEVEMENT

College High School of Colorado State College of Education at Greeley

Student							Date of This Report			, 195 ___
	1	2	3	4	5	6	2½	5	10	15
			Secondary School Year				Regular Periods Each Week			
Course or Activity	6	8	12	12	36					
			Weeks Enrolled							

GENERAL OBJECTIVES: The evaluation of the student's achievement of the twelve general objectives which follow is made in terms of what normally might be expected of students of similar age and school placement. O—OUTSTANDING. S—SATISFACTORY. N—NEEDS TO MAKE IMPROVEMENT. U—UNSATISFACTORY. X—INSUFFICIENT EVIDENCE OR DOES NOT APPLY. SPECIFIC BEHAVIORS ESPECIALLY RESPONSIBLE FOR O, N, OR U EVALUATIONS ARE CHECKED. SPECIFIC COMMENTS PARTICULARLY WITH REFERENCE TO O, N, AND U EVALUATIONS ARE WRITTEN ON THE OPPOSITE SIDE OF THIS SHEET.

___ 1. HE DIRECTS HIS INDIVIDUAL ACTIVITIES EFFECTIVELY ( ) begins work promptly ( ) makes good use of time ( ) requires minimum of supervision ( ) does more than the least that will be accepted ( ) meets responsibilities promptly

___ 2. HE FOLLOWS PLANS AND DIRECTIONS ( ) listens to and reads directions carefully ( ) follows and completes plans and directions which have been set up

___ 3. HE GETS ALONG WELL WITH OTHERS ( ) is considerate of rights and wishes of others ( ) is courteous and tolerant ( ) controls his temper ( ) conforms to reasonable social standards

___ 4. HE TAKES AN ACTIVE PART IN GROUP LIVING ( ) participates in group planning ( ) volunteers his services ( ) does his share in group activities

___ 5. HE SPEAKS CORRECTLY AND EFFECTIVELY ( ) speaks clearly ( ) adjusts his voice to the size of the group ( ) uses adequate vocabulary to express himself interestingly ( ) speaks with ease and confidence ( ) uses correct grammatical forms

___ 7. HE OBSERVES ATTENDANCE REGULATIONS ( ) is regular and prompt in attendance except for approved cause ( ) arranges in advance for absence when possible ( ) takes initiative in making up work missed ( ) makes proper use of school health service

___ 8. HE READS WITH EASE AND UNDERSTANDING ( ) selects important ideas ( ) understands and evaluates what he reads ( ) reads with reasonable speed

___ 9. HE EXPRESSES HIMSELF CORRECTLY AND EFFECTIVELY IN WRITING ( ) expresses ideas clearly ( ) uses correct grammatical forms ( ) punctuates correctly ( ) spells correctly ( ) writes legibly

___ 10. HE UTILIZES AVAILABLE SOURCES OF LEARNING MATERIALS ( ) selects and uses appropriate sources of information ( ) uses library and library tools effectively ( ) effectively engages in interview and observation

___ 11. HE USES THE PROBLEM SOLVING METHOD ( ) recognizes problems ( ) states problems clearly ( ) collects and records appropriate information ( ) arrives at sound conclusions

540

— 6. HE TAKES GOOD CARE OF PERSONAL AND SCHOOL MATERIALS AND EQUIPMENT ( ) shows respect for property ( ) does not waste or damage materials or equipment ( ) returns things when due ( ) reports breakage and loss

—12. HE USES THE BASIC SKILLS IN MATHEMATICS ( ) uses accurately the simple fundamental combinations ( ) computes with reasonable speed ( ) uses fractions and per cents correctly ( ) selects correct processes

SPECIFIC OBJECTIVES: The specific objectives of each course and activity have been discussed with the student and used in classroom instruction and evaluation activities.

HIS ACHIEVEMENT OF THE SPECIFIC OBJECTIVES OF THIS COURSE OR ACTIVITY HAS BEEN:

☐ better than ☐ consistent with ☐ poorer than what reasonably might have been expected of him in terms of his background and ability

☐ Such that full credit is not recommended on administrative records.

☐ Such that he cannot be recommended for admission to college courses or training programs to which this course is prerequisite.

Such as to justify encouraging him to enroll in _____

not to enroll in _____

_____
Supervising teacher

This section is for record purposes and is to be detached before the report is issued to the student or his parents.

	OUTSTANDING	ABOVE AVERAGE	AVERAGE	BELOW AVERAGE	VERY POOR*
ACTUAL ACHIEVEMENT:	☐	☐	☐	☐	☐
EXPECTED ACHIEVEMENT:	☐	☐	☐	☐	☐

*Adjusted credit recommendation (in full year courses only): ⅓ ½ ⅔ regular credit should be allowed.

541

5. Apply scientific techniques to formulate and undertake social action, within the limits of one's capacity

The first test is a rating scale designed to test cooperation and social effectiveness during work on Sources.

To what extent did you participate in the construction of such activities as:	I did not help	I helped	I was in charge
a. Leak-proof box for checking runoff			
b. Apparatus to measure soil absorption			
c. Apparatus to measure evaporation			
d. Apparatus to observe effect of cover crop and care of cover crop			
e. Geological cross section of the local area			

Following is a scoring scale designed to evaluate cooperation in initiating the unit.

To what extent did you help in planning the unit:	Your own opinion	What I think others think of me	Opinion of student group	Opinion of teacher
a. Suggested questions and problems for study				
b. Participated in group planning				
c. Displayed a willingness to participate in class activities				
d. Gave fair consideration to the ideas and suggestions of others				
e. Attempted to direct the activities of yourself and others in a purposeful manner				
f. Cooperated with others to make the fullest use of facilities and materials				

The following are scoring scales designed to test cooperation and social effectiveness while studying the section Man's Dependence on the Water Supply, and Conservation of the Water Supply.

Place check marks in the space after the groups in which you think your PERSONAL welfare is involved:

a. Private homeowners

b. Farmers

c. Sportsmen

d. Commercial fishermen along Santa Barbara County coast

e. Oil companies

f. Dairymen

g. City Council

h. Central Valley Water Project

i. County Sanitation Board

j. Students in school

To what extent do you feel concern about your part in securing:	No Concern	Some Concern	Great Concern
a. Cheap water for irrigation			
b. Adequate sanitary disposal			
c. A program to prevent intrusion of salt water at the mouth of the Santa Maria River			
d. Good leadership in county water conservation			
e. The mineral content of domestic water			
f. Water level in Santa Barbara County			

The test below is designed for use in planning excursions, such as A Trip to a Soil Conservation Project.

Check the following which you heard explained:
_____broad base terrace
_____basin listing
_____border listing
_____etc.

Place a check in the square which represents your (pupil, student, committee, teacher) opinion:

a. Punctuality at times on the trip
b. Staying with group
c. Courtesy to others
d. Paying attention to discussion and observation
e. Encouraging other students in good conduct

For free writing evaluation have the students write a paragraph reaction to each of the following:

Our Water Conservation District is being promoted by large landowners, and for their benefit only.

In what ways is the water conservation problem in Santa Barbara County important to each of the following: private homeowners, farmers, sportsmen, oil companies, dairymen, city government, county sanitation board, and students in school?

Finish the following topic sentences and write the paragraphs they introduce. Be certain to include your reasons for your opinions:

a. If my farm were situated in the area needed for the water conservation dam, I would _____

b. Since my farm is not threatened by flood or soil loss, I _____

II. *Scientific Attitude*—In order to facilitate the evaluation of this attitude, the following analysis of behavior which would indicate its presence is suggested.

A scientific attitude would be indicated by:

A. Ability to recognize problems.

B. A tendency to analyze problems.

C. A tendency to seek, assemble, organize, interpret, and evaluate data before reaching tentative conclusions.

D. A tendency to draw only those conclusions that relate to the data at hand.

E. A tendency to use newly understood principles wherever they apply.

F. A tendency to modify one's behavior in accordance with the conclusions reached in the study of a problem.

G. A tendency to revise conclusions in the light of new data.

The above analysis is made to facilitate evaluation, but development of the scientific attitude should be regarded as an integrated process.

Teacher judgment based upon observations is probably the best way to evaluate the scientific attitude. The three methods suggested here for accumulating and recording teachers' judgments are: (1) scales and check charts on which teachers may record their judgments; (2) the accumulation of all sorts of raw data; and (3) the accumulation of anecdotal records. Since these last two are self-explanatory, no illustrations of them are included. The following examples will illustrate the first test mentioned. They are directly related to the items of the above analysis of the scientific attitude.

To what extent did this pupil recognize problems relating to this unit? (Check the column which represents your observation of each of the following.)	Suggests Problems	Expands Problems	Discusses Problems	No Recognition
Within the school				
In the home situation				
In the community				
Elsewhere				

What tendency to analyze problems does this pupil show:	Seldom	Frequently	Nearly Always
Does he tend to attack a problem persistently?			
Does he tend to attack a problem systematically?			
Does he select all of the relevant factors?			
Does he relate his problem to previous experience?			

Teachers should not attempt to find ready-made pencil and paper tests for the evaluation of the scientific attitude in this unit. They should develop tests that apply directly to the experiences of the pupils. Existing tests may serve to provide ideas as to how they may be made.

To evaluate the tendency to use newly understood principles wherever they apply, the following test of superstitions, unfounded beliefs, and false advertising is suggested.

Before the following statements place "Yes," "No," or "?"

_____1. Running surface water purifies itself.

_____2. Everyone should be permitted to drill water wells on his own land.

_____3. Chlorination of water assures destruction of typhoid germs.

_____4. A forked stick can be used successfully to locate underground water.

_____5. Bottled drinking water has greater health-giving qualities than tap water.

III. *Self-Respect*—Anecdotal records and pupil diaries will probably serve best to record evidences of self-respect on the part of individual pupils. Following is an example of an anecdotal record containing such evidence.

George was asked to give his report a day earlier than it was scheduled, being told that it would be satisfactory even if it were not quite complete. He demurred, saying that he was not willing to give it in its present state of incompleteness, but that he would do so if it was the best arrangement that could be made for the whole class. He stated that he preferred to have his work completed to the best of his ability before reporting on it. This is typical.

This test applies to pupils' behavior during the time devoted to this unit. Have them compare their ratings with those of others in the class who have rated them on the same items.

	Too Much	Enough	Not Enough
a. Did I respect the opinions of others?			
b. Did I respect my own abilities?			
c. Did I respect my own conclusions?			
d. Did I depend on others?			
e. Did I participate in class?			
f. Was I critical?			
g. Did I care for my personal appearance?			
h. Was I painstaking about my work?			
i. Did I respect authority?			
j. Was I interested in others?			
k. Was I concerned about my own development?			
l. Did I have confidence in myself—Socially?			
In classwork?			
m. Did I have emotional control?			
n. Did I face reality?			

IV. *Creativeness*—It is felt that growth in creativeness has two main aspects: growth in ability to meet life situations in ways that are new to the individual, and increased desire on the part of the individual for creative expression. The essence of creative action lies in problem solving. Creative efforts come from the application of imaginative thought to a perplexing or disturbing situation; e.g., the need for water in a given community may lead to the construction of a dam or an irrigation ditch, or the formation of a dry farming project. The projection of creative thought to concrete form is the final development of creative activity, and may be expressed either in construction activities or in the development of individual or group insight and understandings.

Obviously, the solution of certain problems demands the invention or discovery of new methods, techniques, and conceptions. Still other problems may be solved by the application of concepts or methods unique to the individual but not new to the teacher or to society. Creative expression will vary with each individual and with each unit studied. Some units will offer little opportunity for construction activities, but may be rich in activities involving reports, visual aids, and interpreting real life situations.

The following list of questions may be found helpful in analyzing pupil behavior for evidences of growth in creativeness:

A. Is the problem solved in a way new to the individual?
B. Did the pupil originate the method of solution?
C. Did the pupil plan his own procedures?
D. Does the pupil seek and see problems for original solution?
E. Does the pupil set his own standards?
F. Is the pupil's participation the result of his own volition?
G. Is there discernible improvement in breadth of concept and in technique of problem solving?
H. Is there improvement in the technique of expression?
I. Is creative thought carried over into some concrete form of action?

Skills

A diary may be kept for each student by the teacher, recording student growth and experiences in such usual speech situations as participating in group discussion, conferences, reporting, or in such special speech situations as making an announcement of participation in a program.

Various ways of evaluating skill in the use of reference materials are suggested:

A. Give an assignment which requires students to use the Reader's Guide.
B. Devise a series of topics and references, and have the pupils match them, to test familiarity with standard references.
C. Observe student while using the dictionary. If some are slow at this it is possible they do not know the alphabet.

D. Have each pupil use the card catalog to find pamphlets or books which would give information on a specific topic.

Members of a class may check the growth of fellow students on a chart which has been worked out by the class. A suggested form follows:

Name of Student_____Name of Rater_____

Date_____Subject and Type_____

Speech Qualities	Rating (1 is the highest rating; 3 is the lowest)			Comment
	1	2	3	
a. Voice pleasing and appropriate				
b. Sufficient mastery of subject				
c. Enunciation distinct and clear				
d. Language free from grammatical errors				
e. Manner suggesting ease				
f. Forceful in use of words				
g. Evidence of quick thinking at time of speaking				
h. Original and apt phrases				
Additional Comment:				

Evaluation as Part of the Curriculum Program

An evaluation program is a definite and integral part of a curriculum program. Space does not permit us here to propose all the problems and the types of instruments which can be used to evaluate learning in a modern school.[9] But it should be clear to any teacher that the cycle of effective learning which starts with a fundamental philosophy of education and goes on through the establishment of aims and the selection of appropriate content and methods is not complete without the evaluation of the extent to which the pupil has developed the competencies desired and the school has succeeded in reaching its objectives. Ample use must be made of the wide variety of instruments available to suit the broad range of objectives to be met. The teacher is central in the evaluation program, for the day is past when an

9. For a very excellent, practical, and illustrative guide for the classroom teacher, see *Evaluating Pupil Progress* (Bureau of Education Research, California State Department of Education, *Bulletin* No. 6; Sacramento, Calif., 1952).

individual from the outside can come in and look over the boys and girls, give them tests, and come out with an objective story about the success of the school. The day is also past when the modern school can be measured adequately by the success of a few of its graduates in college or by the results made by pupils on subject-matter tests. Since the objectives of education are as broad as life itself, they require a program of evaluation equally comprehensive and versatile.

Chapter Nineteen

What of the
Future?

THERE ARE approximately twenty million youth in the United States between the ages of twelve and twenty, and eighteen million of these are in school. Eleven and one-half million of these youth live in cities, four and one-half million live in rural-suburban areas, and four million live on farms. These figures indicate the mass nature of our secondary-education program. An increasing number, now approximately two and one-half million youth, are attending colleges.

The nature of secondary education has been debated by many people. There are those who, like Jefferson, advocate that education above the elementary grades be confined to those youth who have demonstrated high intellectual ability. Some have criticized the schools for failing to give adequate attention to the superior youth; others believe that there should be no failures in high school and that secondary education should assist each child to develop his potentialities without reference to arbitrary standards.

The secondary school has had a phenomenal social problem in recent years, the problem of taking youth of all degrees of interest and of varying abilities,

motivations, and backgrounds and offering each of them through group instruction a program which would make competent citizens of them all. That
the high school has succeeded as well as it has is a high tribute to teachers
and administrators. Recent years have made this task even more difficult
because of: (1) increased pressure from communties for the realization of
ever higher expectations from secondary education; (2) greater criticism of
secondary education from parents for what they consider failure on the part
of the school with their own children; (3) pressure from communities where
schools try to modernize their program to prepare youth for citizenship
through a study of modern problems; (4) criticism of the increasing cost of
education and requests for elimination of costly laboratory and field-service
courses; (5) increased attendance of youth with limited academic ability;
(6) great difficulty of group instruction in large classes with wide heterogeneity
of abilities and motivations; (7) increased pressure from colleges on the
high-school curriculum, resulting from the increased number of youth attending college; (8) many pressures upon youth resulting from confusing values,
television, automobiles, and all the lures for excitement thrown around them;
and (9) the confusion and uncertainty of youth resulting from the demand
for military service which prevents them from making plans for college, jobs,
and marriage.

Those people who work with youth realize how sensitive they are to public
confusion. They represent, in accelerated pace, the uncertainty of our adult
society. But universal secondary education is here to stay, and it will inevitably result in still greater costs in public taxes. Youth will not be able
to achieve any great uniformity in educational accomplishment, and the
school cannot fulfill its function by setting arbitrary standards of achievement,
which result in excessive failures. Thus the job of the secondary-school teacher
and administrator in the years ahead is one for courageous souls, one which
will require knowledge of youth and society, a philosophy geared to youth
needs, the ability to work with community leaders for support, and skill in
explaining to parents, in convincing language the layman can understand, the
reasons for the secondary program.

If the secondary school is to remain universal and be sensitive to existing
social, political, and economic conditions, then the directions in which the
school is to go in the foreseeable years ahead need to be set forth. This can
best be done by the professional staff and leading laymen in the individual
community, but the following suggestions may prove helpful in stimulating
the process of local improvement. In these suggestions, it is assumed, as earlier
in the book, that secondary education includes grades seven to fourteen,
roughly ages twelve to twenty.

1. We must interpret to parents and citizens in the United States the basic
   purposes and advantages of a system of universal secondary education.
   Educators have been so busy providing classrooms, teachers, and

textbooks that they have spent too little time discussing the great goals of universal secondary education—the goals of unity among men, of equal opportunity for all, of understanding of differences in abilities and interests and beliefs and vocational choices, and of no class distinction. Once these are understood, many of the petty criticisms of the high school will disappear. We need as wide an understanding of the place of universal secondary education as we can get, and educators need to review the philosophy of democratic education again and again.

2. Secondary education needs to be built upon a well-conceived and well-understood philosophy of unifying knowledge, emotion, and action around the commonly accepted principles of our society.

Too much of our secondary curriculum represents a collection of unrelated or poorly related courses, each based upon a purpose of its own, but without a central unity of understanding of our culture. Two units of English, one of mathematics, a laboratory science, history, government, and a shop course make neither an educated man nor a good citizen. We need to select our content by reference to a fundamental philosophy of the needs of our youth to face the issues in our society. If the teachers can't do this, we can't rely upon youth to do it by an elective system.

We need also to face the reality of an overemphasis upon knowledge, discipline, formal instruction, and transfer. Some of our courses are based upon disproved psychology and an unwarranted faith in facts. The content of secondary education differs too little from that of colleges, and much of it fails to elicit sufficient attention from youth to change their behavior. A bold new orientation is required, orientation around youth, their needs and motivations, and around the dynamic problems of our times. Unless we are willing to free the secondary curriculum of the demands of colleges for the teaching of academic subjects, we will defeat the purpose of universal secondary education.

3. The upper years of secondary education, grades thirteen and fourteen, need to be made available through widespread community colleges.

More and more of our young people desire to continue their education beyond high school, but they do not wish to continue through a four-year college. Many, however, go to a four-year college, pursue academic work for which they are not suited, and drop out during the first two years. Community colleges offering extended general education and vocational education for many semiprofessional fields will extend education appropriate to a large number of youth at a cost to themselves and the state below that required for their attendance at four-year institutions.

The community college is in its infancy, and the years ahead will see its expansion, but it should be organized as a community college with a broad program, not as the regular lower division of the standard four-year college and university.

4. Educators working within the system of group instruction and universal education must discover ways and means to accelerate the quality of education for gifted youth, while providing a balanced education for the retarded and physically handicapped.

We have not yet found the way in secondary education to educate properly all levels of our youth. Youth differ greatly, and education cannot be the same for all. We have planned the difficulty of our curriculum for the middle 50 per cent, but the character of our courses is more suited to the interests of the upper 40 per cent. We can no longer let our alibi of its being undemocratic prevent us from doing whatever is necessary to improve the education of our gifted youth; nor can we let any pseudo criticism of careful attention to specific learning prevent us from caring for those with handicaps. One of the great unsolved problems is to teach all youth the great purposes and goals of democracy by methods and materials most appropriate to their talents and motivations.

5. Vocational education needs to be appropriately geared to the nature of industrial processes and planned for those occupations which require extended study beyond what can be learned quickly on the job. It needs also to be advanced into the upper years of the secondary-school years.

Educators need to study carefully the nature of the requirements of modern business and industry and to plan vocational education in terms of clusters of industrial processes requiring common skills. Education for specific firms or for those things which can be learned quickly on the job need not be duplicated in school. Special emphasis should be placed upon those qualities needed for good personal relations, for acting as members of groups, and for developing satisfactory work habits. Business and industry are likewise placing more emphasis upon an extended general education as better equipment for many jobs than education in special skills. Furthermore, vocational education is being concentrated more in the community colleges, leaving the secondary schools free to build personality, character, and citizenship. This trend needs acceptance and encouragement. The high school should discontinue its programs of vocational education.

6. Systems of guidance need to be developed so that youth are guided into appropriate learning situations and personal stability and security are increased.

Youth need help in seeing clearly their place in the world, in choosing properly the fields of study most suited to their abilities and likelihood of success, and in directing the course of their own lives as independent citizens and responsible individuals. The confusion in social values and the increase in pressures upon young people for military service and delayed entrance into marriage and careers are disturbing greatly the confidence of youth in themselves and in society. Adequate systems of guidance can aid these young people to discover ways and means to solve their problems independently and with success. The only security these young people need is confidence and faith, securely fixed and founded upon knowledge, skill, and hope. Secondary teachers and administrators can and must devise ways and means to achieve these goals and organize them to meet the needs for guidance.

7. We must find ways and means of teaching to all youth fundamental values by which they can live.

Our society will never be stronger than the individual morality of our people. Each person needs to develop for himself a system of values by which he lives, and the home, the church, and the schools are partners in this enterprise. Guarantees of freedom of person, religion, and speech are meaningless unless each citizen shapes his own life by values which he understands and in which he believes firmly enough to guide his behavior by them. Respect for each other, freedom from prejudice, belief in the worth of each individual, self-respect, self-discipline—all of these are beyond the role of legislation.

Our principles of ethical behavior are undergoing change, and the actions of public citizens are in many instances inconsistent with our traditional concepts of honesty and integrity. War has cheapened human life; lack of close acquaintance with others in city life has increased callousness to former concepts of virtues and duties; these and the loss of faith in authority have all contributed to despair, cynicism, and loss of hope. Such a loss is not conducive to faith and to the acceptance of basic values. Crime and legal violations are increasing, especially among youth. Getting caught is more of a disgrace than performing an illegal act. Self-discipline is the basis of law in a democratic society, and our codes are no stronger than the will of our people to observe them without constant supervision and policing. A valuable corollary endangered by democracy is a respect for excellence.

The secondary school of the future must find some way to join hands with the home and the church to teach youth the basic values of our society. It must be done without relinquishing education to either of these social institutions, for to do so would destroy the stake society has in universal education for citizenship in a democracy. Moral and spiritual values can be taught without involvement with religious creeds which separate adults. Youth must believe in something and believe in it deeply enough to live by it. To date, the secondary school has done an unsatisfactory job with this responsibility.

The problem is made more difficult by the diversities in our society, a characteristic fundamental to democracy, but one which nevertheless increases the complications of teaching. We need not attempt to establish definite and unassailable truths; we need rather to realize that values are conditioned by time and place and motives. But neither should we go to the other extreme and give no secure basis for action. Such teaching is sheer opportunism and leads to spiritual nomadism. The problem is to reconcile the "absolutes" with the "changing values" and establish some norms for regulating behavior. To indoctrinate for absolutes beyond the reach of change leads to sterility in the process of rational decision. To teach that all norms are illusory leads to cynicism and insecurity. Finding the "middle ground" in this area is one of the unsolved problems in secondary education and one which we can't neglect much longer.

8. The universal secondary school will fail in its primary function unless it discovers the process by which more vital and active citizenship responsibilities will be accepted by all our youth.

Democracy depends upon well-informed and active citizens. An unthinking citizenry or one dependent upon authority for solutions to problems will be easy prey for unscrupulous politicians or demagogues. Unthinking citizens will yield their rights to those who promise most; they will assume that security and prosperity can be gained without individual enterprise; they will sell their freedoms and birthrights by being easily deluded; they will, through carelessness and neglect, permit the unfit to assume the positions of power; and finally they will be unable and unwilling to face the issues of life and solve them for themselves. They will forget that freedoms and the right to independence are dearly bought by constant vigilance.

Knowledge is not enough. The school needs to discover those appeals which incited our forefathers to fight for freedom. The emotions of youth must be aroused toward our democratic rights, duties, and responsibilities. They must be made to feel that democracy is a trust in their keeping and, like an investment, it must be worked to remain vital or even intact.

In this respect we need to sharpen the differences between the goals of a totalitarian nation like Russia and a republic like the United States. Youth need to understand that the facade of communism serves to confuse us and the other nations of the world. They need to feel the tactics of propaganda and to understand its insidious influence to the extent that they can recognize it, know that it is unreliable, and refuse to be confused by it to where they are willing to adopt communistic methods to secure certain conformity in our democratic society. They will also need to come to terms with the fact that conformity and uniformity are more basic to authoritarian government than to democracy.

In order to protect the rights to which they are entitled, they will need to be so conscious of their own responsibilities that they will work in the community to retain our way of life and will acquaint themselves with the issues before us and will without fail vote at all elections. Our small voting percentage is a disgrace to our attempts to teach citizenship. The school will need to be more effective in helping youth to identify issues, to think deeply and constructively about them, and to be active in the protection of civil rights. The tendency that some people have to want to protect the rights of the conformist but to deny rights to the individualist is fatal to democracy. Once the security of individual rights is broken, the chain is weakened and eventually becomes so rusted it is useless.

9. If democracy is to be strong, the universal secondary school must be a laboratory for the elimination of prejudice.

Prejudice or any system of social classification based upon race or religion or color is a luxury democracy cannot afford. The body politic that supports it will find it to be malignant. Most of the prejudice found among youth is learned from the adults with whom they associate. Discrimination embodied in laws, agreements, and in accepted regulations of private or public enterprises, sets the tone for prejudice among our youth. Prejudice is generally an emotional condition which is little affected by knowledge. What is known to be true may have little effect upon the way we act. Tolerance is not enough; the action must be a positive one of recognition of the fact that differences build strength.

If the school is to assist in eliminating discrimination, at least two avenues are open to it. One is to build the intellectual rationale behind nondiscrimination so that youth, when accused of being spineless or ignorant because they refuse to act upon prejudice, will have the essential defenses of the mind to support their position and thus gain courage and strength. The other avenue is that of creating within the secondary school a situation where discrimination does not exist and by this process to demonstrate the fallacies in thinking about differences as well as the values that can be gained by freedom. Once youth have lived with those who are racially or culturally different, the ogre of difference will diminish in size and the reality of a society with no discriminations will become an acceptable and sensible practice. The universal secondary school should face this problem squarely. There is plenty of experience upon which it can draw.

10. Effective education is greatly influenced by the use of methods appropriate to different purposes and to individuals with differing abilities and interests.

The traditional secondary school has relied upon a uniformity of methods based upon written and oral communication and reading. Success in the average high-school subject is dependent upon a good memory and good reading ability. Answering questions, writing assignments, and listening to teachers constitute the favored methods in school. We have not yet learned how to emotionalize learning, except in some instances to produce a dislike for it, or to use the laboratory or group processes or problem-solving procedures or the synthetic methods in achieving the goals of education. Methods are not vital enough, not varied enough, not effective enough, not related closely enough to the objectives of the school. Proper motivating factors are absent, and the work of the school is not challenging. The pupil feels no loss when an absence or holiday occurs.

When they are not achieving as much as they might, pupils in secondary schools cannot generally be said to be working to capacity. Ineffective methods, too much factual teaching, and unsatisfactory curriculum choices can be responsible for this condition. Ways will have to be found to secure more learning, better understanding, and emotionalized behavior in approximately the same time now devoted to secondary education. The present neglect of those of superior abilities should be increasingly deplored by the community. Better teaching can and should result from more careful planning and experimentation. A methodology profitable to only a few cannot serve a universal system of compulsory education. If society forces a youth to attend school, he has a right to expect a program and methods appropriate to the goals he can achieve. Our modern society has stressed action, and learning to *act* properly requires methods different from those used to develop contemplation or accuracy in reproducing events. We have tried to build character and values and competence in activity largely by methods used for traditional academic competence.

11. Knowledge of the world and its people is one of the fundamentals of a modern secondary education.

The secondary curriculum has been crowded to the point where the development of an understanding of the character and problems of the people of other lands has been left largely to chance. But until the end of World War II there seemed little need to teach these matters to any but those going to college. If foreign policy is made by the man on the street and if America is to lead the world, then world affairs are everybody's affairs, and the teaching of them in the secondary school becomes imperative. Yet an understanding of other people cannot be acquired by reading widely in the history and diplomacy of the chief nations. Adequate knowledge cannot be gained within a reasonable time by this method, and the motivation of youth is insufficient for them to retain interest enough to complete such a program. Many of our youth in recent years have been transported to many parts of the world by the military forces they have served. Our American schools are filled with youth from foreign lands. The upper years of secondary education provide excellent opportunities for discovering the basic essentials of the culture of the chief ruling nations, if only educators can select, organize, and teach these essentials and can combine the intellectual content with the experience of youth. At present the means for doing this economically and effectively do not exist, but they must be found within the near future.

12. Youth need to be brought face to face with the unsolved problems of a democracy and be taught to attack them with vigor, understanding, courage, and the skills of rational analysis.

The future security of democracy at home and abroad depends upon the degree to which youth can face the unsolved problems, both domestic and international. The United States really is inexperienced in international affairs, especially when these affairs cover the entire globe. Our knowledge of geography, culture, and philosophy, and of the motives of men of all races is far too meager for us to solve the problems we now face. The United Nations, all forms of international organization, economic assistance to underdeveloped countries—these are new ventures for our country. Selling the democratic way of life to people excited and influenced by communism is a major undertaking. We have not yet found the way to peace and yet we are convinced that it is hardly possible for anyone to profit from another world war. These problems are fundamentally philosophical and political in character.

Within our own country we have many unsolved procedural problems. The majority of them have an economic base—labor-management relations, governmental control of enterprise, taxes and international trade, government provision for welfare services, subsidies. These are only a few of the many problems we all face. Yet our schools have during the secondary years failed almost entirely to develop any understanding of the economic character of our society. Occasionally, a dull course in conventional economics is added to the curriculum as a senior elective or an economic problem is given meager treatment in a senior-problems course. Both are inadequate.

And, finally, our democratic philosophy needs continuous review. The protection of basic constitutional freedoms without being hospitable to the enemy; the areas of life which should be governed by the local communities, the state, and the federal government; the passion for security in contrast to freedom of enterprise; government protection against exploitation and devastating uncertainty; government support of prices and production—all these are problems which need careful thought, thought governed by principle, by philosophy, by rational analysis. They cannot be solved by political slogans.

13. Those charged with teaching and administering our secondary schools will need to increase greatly their skill in evaluating the success of the enterprise.

We have taken much for granted in our secondary program—knowledge produces understanding; information leads to intelligent action; knowledge of grammar produces skill in expression; skill in foreign languages creates skill in the mother tongue; study of certain subjects develops a quality of reasoning; and skill in solving problems in science will affect the methods we use to solve social problems. Research and careful observation have shown that these assumptions are just not true. Yet we have faithfully adhered to them in our selection of content and methods in the secondary schools. The result is poor learning, drop-outs, failures, resentment, and despair. The public has a right to have some evidence of the success of the school program if they are to be asked for continuous support. Those working in the secondary school need to discover ways and means to evaluate the success of different experiences with different methods and content. They need to be able to show evidence of adolescent growth through guidance service, and they need to show the relative effectiveness of instruction. Some teachers are not successful, and there is no reason why the desirable practice of protecting teachers through tenure from unscrupulous attacks should be extended to cover the incompetent or the sluggard. Educators should develop means of evaluating the success of their enterprise and they should not be surprised when the public requires it.

14. The leaders of youth need to build a climate of faith in the future with the skills of cooperative action.

Youth cannot be challenged unless they have faith and hope. Courage does not exist where there is despair over the outcome. Many of our youth feel that the great explorations are over, peace and continued prosperity are visionary, and war is inevitable. Some of our adults are so committed to the theory of cyclic pressure that they pass on to youth a belief that history repeats itself, that war is inevitable, that business prosperity and depression come in unavoidable cycles, that every nation rises, prospers, and decays. The inevitable question from such a belief is "What can one man do?" And the general answer is "Nothing. You are a passing element in history." Once this is believed, youth either become cynical, commit suicide, or eat, drink, and make merry. Such an attitude never built a nation nor made it strong or great.

Opportunities for explorations in science and industry and human relations are greater than ever before. Opportunities to prevent the recurrence of war and depression and unemployment are ever present.

The call for leadership is loud, the places for competence and insight are multiple. We need, therefore, to create in our youth the feeling that the United States and the world are alive with opportunities of all kinds, that individual initiative and competence is as valuable as ever, and that even though cooperation is more needed than ever before, this does not deter the creative, the ambitious, the competent, the secure youth from succeeding. In a sense Horatio Alger still lives.

These then are some of the problems and opportunities facing those working in secondary education. The secondary school, standing between the elementary school and the college and serving a group of youth compelled by law to attend it, is an institution beset with problems and pressures. Until men of courage and ability face the needs of youth squarely, youth will continue to receive inadequate service. The future secondary school, if it meets the call of youth and society, will be harmonious with the destiny of a democratic society and millions of freedom-loving youth.

Index

Index

A

F

G

M

O